Lecture Notes in Computer Science 9175

Commenced Publication in 1973
Founding and Former Series Editors:
Gerhard Goos, Juris Hartmanis, and Jan van Leeuwen

More information about this series at http://www.springer.com/series/7409

Margherita Antona · Constantine Stephanidis (Eds.)

Universal Access in Human-Computer Interaction

Access to Today's Technologies

9th International Conference, UAHCI 2015
Held as Part of HCI International 2015
Los Angeles, CA, USA, August 2–7, 2015
Proceedings, Part I

 Springer

Editors

Margherita Antona
Foundation for Research and Technology –
 Hellas (FORTH)
Heraklion, Crete
Greece

Constantine Stephanidis
University of Crete
Heraklion, Crete
Greece

and

Foundation for Research and Technology –
 Hellas (FORTH)
Heraklion, Crete
Greece

ISSN 0302-9743   ISSN 1611-3349 (electronic)
Lecture Notes in Computer Science
ISBN 978-3-319-20677-6   ISBN 978-3-319-20678-3 (eBook)
DOI 10.1007/978-3-319-20678-3

Library of Congress Control Number: 2015942613

LNCS Sublibrary: SL3 – Information Systems and Applications, incl. Internet/Web, and HCI

Printed on acid-free paper

Springer International Publishing AG Switzerland is part of Springer Science+Business Media
(www.springer.com)

Foreword

The 17th International Conference on Human-Computer Interaction, HCI International 2015, was held in Los Angeles, CA, USA, during 2–7 August 2015. The event incorporated the 15 conferences/thematic areas listed on the following page.

A total of 4843 individuals from academia, research institutes, industry, and governmental agencies from 73 countries submitted contributions, and 1462 papers and 246 posters have been included in the proceedings. These papers address the latest research and development efforts and highlight the human aspects of design and use of computing systems. The papers thoroughly cover the entire field of Human-Computer Interaction, addressing major advances in knowledge and effective use of computers in a variety of application areas. The volumes constituting the full 28-volume set of the conference proceedings are listed on pages VII and VIII.

I would like to thank the Program Board Chairs and the members of the Program Boards of all thematic areas and affiliated conferences for their contribution to the highest scientific quality and the overall success of the HCI International 2015 conference.

This conference could not have been possible without the continuous and unwavering support and advice of the founder, Conference General Chair Emeritus and Conference Scientific Advisor, Prof. Gavriel Salvendy. For their outstanding efforts, I would like to express my appreciation to the Communications Chair and Editor of HCI International News, Dr. Abbas Moallem, and the Student Volunteer Chair, Prof. Kim-Phuong L. Vu. Finally, for their dedicated contribution towards the smooth organization of HCI International 2015, I would like to express my gratitude to Maria Pitsoulaki and George Paparoulis, General Chair Assistants.

May 2015

Constantine Stephanidis
General Chair, HCI International 2015

HCI International 2015 Thematic Areas and Affiliated Conferences

Thematic areas:

- Human-Computer Interaction (HCI 2015)
- Human Interface and the Management of Information (HIMI 2015)

Affiliated conferences:

- 12th International Conference on Engineering Psychology and Cognitive Ergonomics (EPCE 2015)
- 9th International Conference on Universal Access in Human-Computer Interaction (UAHCI 2015)
- 7th International Conference on Virtual, Augmented and Mixed Reality (VAMR 2015)
- 7th International Conference on Cross-Cultural Design (CCD 2015)
- 7th International Conference on Social Computing and Social Media (SCSM 2015)
- 9th International Conference on Augmented Cognition (AC 2015)
- 6th International Conference on Digital Human Modeling and Applications in Health, Safety, Ergonomics and Risk Management (DHM 2015)
- 4th International Conference on Design, User Experience and Usability (DUXU 2015)
- 3rd International Conference on Distributed, Ambient and Pervasive Interactions (DAPI 2015)
- 3rd International Conference on Human Aspects of Information Security, Privacy and Trust (HAS 2015)
- 2nd International Conference on HCI in Business (HCIB 2015)
- 2nd International Conference on Learning and Collaboration Technologies (LCT 2015)
- 1st International Conference on Human Aspects of IT for the Aged Population (ITAP 2015)

Conference Proceedings Volumes Full List

1. LNCS 9169, Human-Computer Interaction: Design and Evaluation (Part I), edited by Masaaki Kurosu
2. LNCS 9170, Human-Computer Interaction: Interaction Technologies (Part II), edited by Masaaki Kurosu
3. LNCS 9171, Human-Computer Interaction: Users and Contexts (Part III), edited by Masaaki Kurosu
4. LNCS 9172, Human Interface and the Management of Information: Information and Knowledge Design (Part I), edited by Sakae Yamamoto
5. LNCS 9173, Human Interface and the Management of Information: Information and Knowledge in Context (Part II), edited by Sakae Yamamoto
6. LNAI 9174, Engineering Psychology and Cognitive Ergonomics, edited by Don Harris
7. LNCS 9175, Universal Access in Human-Computer Interaction: Access to Today's Technologies (Part I), edited by Margherita Antona and Constantine Stephanidis
8. LNCS 9176, Universal Access in Human-Computer Interaction: Access to Interaction (Part II), edited by Margherita Antona and Constantine Stephanidis
9. LNCS 9177, Universal Access in Human-Computer Interaction: Access to Learning, Health and Well-Being (Part III), edited by Margherita Antona and Constantine Stephanidis
10. LNCS 9178, Universal Access in Human-Computer Interaction: Access to the Human Environment and Culture (Part IV), edited by Margherita Antona and Constantine Stephanidis
11. LNCS 9179, Virtual, Augmented and Mixed Reality, edited by Randall Shumaker and Stephanie Lackey
12. LNCS 9180, Cross-Cultural Design: Methods, Practice and Impact (Part I), edited by P.L. Patrick Rau
13. LNCS 9181, Cross-Cultural Design: Applications in Mobile Interaction, Education, Health, Transport and Cultural Heritage (Part II), edited by P.L. Patrick Rau
14. LNCS 9182, Social Computing and Social Media, edited by Gabriele Meiselwitz
15. LNAI 9183, Foundations of Augmented Cognition, edited by Dylan D. Schmorrow and Cali M. Fidopiastis
16. LNCS 9184, Digital Human Modeling and Applications in Health, Safety, Ergonomics and Risk Management: Human Modeling (Part I), edited by Vincent G. Duffy
17. LNCS 9185, Digital Human Modeling and Applications in Health, Safety, Ergonomics and Risk Management: Ergonomics and Health (Part II), edited by Vincent G. Duffy
18. LNCS 9186, Design, User Experience, and Usability: Design Discourse (Part I), edited by Aaron Marcus
19. LNCS 9187, Design, User Experience, and Usability: Users and Interactions (Part II), edited by Aaron Marcus
20. LNCS 9188, Design, User Experience, and Usability: Interactive Experience Design (Part III), edited by Aaron Marcus

Universal Access in Human-Computer Interaction

Program Board Chairs: Margherita Antona, Greece, and Constantine Stephanidis, Greece

- Gisela Susanne Bahr, USA
- João Barroso, Portugal
- Jennifer Romano Bergstrom, USA
- Margrit Betke, USA
- Rodrigo Bonacin, Brazil
- Anthony Brooks, Denmark
- Christian Bühler, Germany
- Stefan Carmien, Spain
- Carlos Duarte, Portugal
- Pier Luigi Emiliani, Italy
- Qin Gao, P.R. China
- Andrina Granić, Croatia
- Josette F. Jones, USA
- Simeon Keates, UK
- Georgios Kouroupetroglou, Greece
- Patrick Langdon, UK
- Barbara Leporini, Italy
- Tania Lima, Brazil
- Troy McDaniel, USA
- Ana Isabel Paraguay, Brazil
- Helen Petrie, UK
- Michael Pieper, Germany
- Enrico Pontelli, USA
- Jaime Sánchez, Chile
- Vagner Santana, Brazil
- Anthony Savidis, Greece
- Hirotada Ueda, Japan
- Gerhard Weber, Germany
- Fong-Gong Wu, Taiwan

The full list with the Program Board Chairs and the members of the Program Boards of all thematic areas and affiliated conferences is available online at:

http://www.hci.international/2015/

HCI International 2016

The 18th International Conference on Human-Computer Interaction, HCI International 2016, will be held jointly with the affiliated conferences in Toronto, Canada, at the Westin Harbour Castle Hotel, 17–22 July 2016. It will cover a broad spectrum of themes related to Human-Computer Interaction, including theoretical issues, methods, tools, processes, and case studies in HCI design, as well as novel interaction techniques, interfaces, and applications. The proceedings will be published by Springer. More information will be available on the conference website: http://2016.hci.international/.

General Chair
Prof. Constantine Stephanidis
University of Crete and ICS-FORTH
Heraklion, Crete, Greece
Email: general_chair@hcii2016.org

http://2016.hci.international/

Contents – Part I

Universal Access to the Web

Universal Access to Mobile Interaction

Universal Access to Information, Communication and Media

Design and Evaluation Methods and Tools for Universal Access

Elderly Speech-Gaze Interaction

State of the Art and Challenges for Interaction Design

Cengiz Acartürk[1(✉)], João Freitas[2], Mehmetcal Fal[1], and Miguel Sales Dias[2,3]

[1] Informatics Institute, Middle East Technical University, Ankara, Turkey
{acarturk,mehmetcan.fal}@metu.edu.tr
[2] Microsoft Language Development Center, Lisbon, Portugal
{t-joaof,miguel.dias}@microsoft.com
[3] Instituto Universitário de Lisboa (ISCTE-IUL), ISTAR-IUL, Lisbon, Portugal

Abstract. Elderly people face problems when using current forms of Human-Computer Interaction (HCI). Developing novel and natural methods of interaction would facilitate resolving some of those issues. We propose that HCI can be improved by combining communication modalities, in particular, speech and gaze, in various ways. This study presents *elderly speech-gaze interaction* as a novel method in HCI, a review of literature for its potential of use, and discusses possible domains of application for further empirical investigations.

Keywords: Multimodal · Gaze · Eye tracking · Speech · Elderly · Interaction

1 Introduction

A significant advance in human history was the invention of reading: The invention that the visual system could be employed for representing speech. The research in the past several decades has shown that human visual system is active in speech communication in various other ways, such as lip reading and silent speech (thus leading to the term *audio-visual speech*). Human Computer Interaction (HCI) has a broader potential to employ these modalities than it seems at a first glance. One example is the improvement of Automatic Speech Recognition (ASR) by modeling contextual gaze behavior during interaction. We propose that further improvement of HCI can be achieved by designing interfaces for elderly speech and elderly gaze. In the following section, we present a review of these two research fields to provide an interdisciplinary HCI background for *elderly speech-gaze interaction*.

2 Impact of Aging in Communication and Interaction

Elderly individuals have developed resistance to conventional forms of HCI, like the keyboard and mouse, therefore making it necessary to test new natural forms of interaction such as speech, silent speech, touch, gestures, body and head movements, gaze and emotions [1, 2]. In addition, elderly people often have difficulties with motor skills

© Springer International Publishing Switzerland 2015
M. Antona and C. Stephanidis (Eds.): UAHCI 2015, Part I, LNCS 9175, pp. 3–12, 2015.
DOI: 10.1007/978-3-319-20678-3_1

due to health problems such as arthritis. Therefore, small and difficult-to-handle equipment such as smartphones, may not be easily adopted. It is also known that due to aging, the sensory systems, such as vision become less accurate, therefore difficulties in perception of details or important information in graphical interfaces may arise. On the other hand, current mainstream interfaces, most notably in the mobility area, are rarely designed by taking into account those difficulties that elderly users may face. As a response to those challenges, several devices have been specifically designed or adapted for seniors in the telecommunications market (e.g. Snapfon Ez One, Samsung Jitterbug, ZTC SP45 Senior, etc.).

The broadening of the age-group coverage in user interfaces is necessary given that the population is ageing rapidly in many countries throughout the world, notably, in Europe and Japan. The European Commission estimates that by 2050 the elderly population in the EU (European Union) will be around 29 % of the population. Accordingly, it is hastily becoming necessary to create solutions that allow overcoming age-related difficulties in HCI.

Elderly people who are connected to the world through the internet are less likely to become depressed and have greater probability of becoming socially integrated [3]. Therefore, the internet and user interfaces that allow access to the internet are means for people who want to remain socially active and integrated. In the recent state of technology, however, technological and interaction barriers still do not allow seniors to take a full advantage of the available services and content [1, 4, 5] despite that elderly population is the one that has been more rapidly going online [6].

Several research initiatives and supporting frameworks, have been paving the way to close this gap, with Ambient Assisted Living (AAL) solutions for home and mobility scenarios that have been positively evaluated with elderly populations [1]. We conceive speech systems as a potential complementary solution for HCI usable by elderly speakers, a group of users which has been found to prefer speech interfaces in the mentioned scenarios [1, 7], but also facing limitations in their use due to the inability of these systems to accurately model this population group.

2.1 Elderly Speech

The research literature on elderly speech characteristics does not provide a consistent, general picture. The major source of the divergence is that aging increases the difference between biological age and chronological age, whereas biological aging can also be influenced by factors such as abuse or overuse of the vocal folds, smoking, alcohol consumption, psychological stress/tension, or frequent loud/shouted speech production without vocal training [8, 9]. Accordingly, it may be difficult to determine an exact age limit for *elderly* speech. A usual assumption is that the ages between 60 and 70 are the minimum for the elderly age group [10]. Putting aside the difficulties in the operational definition of elderly age range, there exist specific levels of characterization that make explicit the differences between elderly speech and teenagers or adults speech, such as the acoustic phonetic level [11]. With increasing age there is a deprivation of chest voice, general changes in frequencies, in the voice quality and the timbres. Changes in the heights of vowel formant frequencies particularly occur in older men, not only for biological reasons, but also because of social changes. Moreover, a slower speech-rate, greater use of pauses, elimination of articles and possessive pronouns, and lower volume of speech are detectable [11–13].

Although being a stable characteristic when compared with the awareness and emotional state of a speaker, human age influences the acoustic signal and the performance of an ASR (Automatic Speech Recognition) engine, as several parameters of the speech wave form are modified, such as fundamental frequency, first and second formants [14], jitter, shimmer and harmonic noise ratio [15]. Those differences between elderly and other user population influence the performance of human-computer interfaces based on speech [16, 17]. This is because the majority of the methods employed for ASR are data-driven. Most techniques (such as Hidden-Markov Models or Deep Neural Networks) model the problem by establishing a generalization that allows inferring recognition results of unseen data. However, different speech patterns such as the ones seen in elderly and children, which are not often used to train such models, cause a decrease in performance of such data-driven systems. The typical strategy to improve ASR performance under these cases is to collect speech data from elderly speakers in the specific domain of the target application and train elderly-only or adapted acoustic models [18–20]. Recent initiatives from the research community that have followed this strategy, specifically for European Portuguese, French, Polish and Hungarian, that targeted speech data collection and acoustic modelling towards the improvement of elderly speech technologies in these language, can be found in the literature [4, 21, 22].

In summary, conventional ASR interfaces do not handle well elderly speech in the recent state of technology. The ASR systems, if trained with young adults' speech, perform significantly worse when used by the elderly population, due to the various mentioned factors as stated above, as well as in the relevant research literature [10]. A solution is to train the systems with elderly speech. However, considerable cost and effort are required for these collections [22]. A complementary solution is to employ modalities other than speech to support ASR. In the present study, we propose that gaze offers this potential to support elderly ASR. The following section presents a brief review of gaze characteristics in elder adults. We believe that this provides the necessary background for using gaze to support elderly speech interfaces.

2.2 Elderly Gaze

Elderly population exhibits different gaze-behavior characteristics than both younger adults and children in some respects. Compared to research on gaze characteristics of younger adults and children, much less research has been conducted for elderly. In this section, our goal is to present an overview of elderly gaze, in comparison to gaze in both younger adults and children where applicable.

A general finding is the loss of inhibitory processing capacity by aging [23], as measured by the so-called antisaccade task. The antisaccade task has been conceived as a measure of general inhibitory control, specifically the control over gaze behavior. In this task, the participant is asked to suppress the reflexive saccade at a visual target that suddenly appears at the periphery of the acute visual field by performing a saccade to the opposite direction of (i.e., by looking away) of the visual target. In particular, the saccadic reaction time (the time to onset of the eye movement) has been shown to be negatively influenced by age. It has been also shown that elderly participants exhibit longer duration saccades compared to both younger adults and children [24]. This loss in top-down inhibition in elderly may also be observed in patients diagnosed with certain neurological and/or psychiatric disorders [25]. The antisaccade task has also been conceived as an index of cognitive processes, in particular working memory [26], thus as a potential indicator of earlier stages of cognitive decline.

On the other hand, the research literature on aging has revealed that higher-level cognitive abilities are less influenced by aging compared to sensory abilities. For instance, it has been shown that visuospatial memory is not heavily influenced by aging [23]. Similarly, elderly exhibit similar characteristics to younger adults in visual search for targets that are defined by a conjunction of features (in contrast to children, who exhibit slower performance in this task). The major difference between elderly and younger adults is that the elderly have difficulty in moving attention from one item to another [27]. This difference is usually attributed to elderly participants' difficulty in locating peripheral targets rather than a difference in the attentional system between elderly and younger adults [28]. The difficulty in locating peripheral targets is due to a more general finding about the shrinkage in the *useful field of view* (UFoV, the area from which useful information can be extracted) by age [29].

The challenges that elderly people face in reading processes also seem to be related to the shrinkage in the useful field of view (UFoV). Reading comprises both *foveal processing* (for acute visual processing in recognition of letters and words) and *parafoveal processing* (for detecting spaces between words, paragraphs, as well as a few characters to the right of fixation) [30–33]. The previous research on elderly reading shows that elderly readers have a smaller visual span than younger readers [34]. Masking the *foveal* region by means of gaze-contingent eye trackers (thus asking the participants to read *parafoveally*) results in a higher difficulty in elderly readers compared to younger ones [35]. Moreover, a more symmetric visual span is observed in elderly readers. The span in younger adults is asymmetric towards the right or left of fixation, depending on the writing direction. In cultures with left-to-right writing, the span extends to the right of the region, and vice versa for the right-to-left writing cultures. In both cases, the challenge for elderly readers is *parafoveal* processing.

In the studies that present more complex stimuli than the stimuli of the antisaccade task, such as a traffic scene image, the findings address a broader range of eye movement parameters. For instance, in a driving simulation study, the results revealed that elderly participants had more frequent fixations with shorter saccadic amplitudes compared to younger participants. In terms of the scene viewing characteristics, elderly participants spent more time on local regions where younger participants more evenly distributed their gaze throughout the scene [36, 37], accompanied by decreases in elderly drivers' peripheral detection [38]. A similar "tunnel effect (or perceptual narrowing)" phenomenon is observed in elderly drivers in simulated driving context with increased complexity, such as passing maneuvers [39].

These findings suggest that gaze-based interfaces can be used as an interaction method for the elderly. The decrease in inhibitory control of eye movement and the shrinkage in useful field of view (UFoV) by age indicate that a gaze-aware (i.e., gaze-contingent) interaction has the potential to facilitate visual search and browsing by elderly by providing explicit instructions (e.g., attention attractors) towards the periphery of the visual scene (such as, arrows and other graphical cues that show the direction of the relevant region of interest on the screen).

Finally, there are further aspects of eye movement characteristics that we have not touched upon in the above review. One is pupil size and dilation, which may be employed for detecting emotional states of the participants, as well as cognitive processing difficulties. The general finding is that a smaller maximum dilation velocity characterizes elderly gaze. Moreover, the resting pupil diameter is smaller in elderly compared to younger adults [40]. Recent studies reveal that pupil size is also influenced by processing difficulties in word recognition and response selection in elderly people with hearing loss [41]. Given that elderly users exhibit different emotional patterns, such as the tendency to favor positive stimuli over negative stimuli [42], elderly dilation may require a different interpretation than younger adults, as a measure of users' emotional state. Further research is necessary to reveal the potential of these gaze behavior characteristics in HCI. In the following section, we focus on specific methods of multimodal interaction, which aim at improving elderly speech recognition by gaze.

3   Combining Eye-Gaze Information with Speech

Speech communication is usually a multimodal process in the sense that multiple sources of information are used by humans and affect the way we interpret and issue speech messages. For example, evidence that speech perception employs both hearing and visual senses has been shown by McGurk [43] in 1976. In literature we also find studies that show the use of contextual information such as head and full body movements, gesture, emotions, facial expressions prosody and gaze in human-human speech communication [44–46]. In this analysis we focus our attention in the advantages and disadvantages of the combined use of eye-gaze information along with speech for HCI, since the current literature suggests that a combined application of ASR and gaze information can be used to improve multimodal HCI.

In 2008, Cooke and Russell [47] used the gaze information to change model probabilities of a given word based on the visual focus. In this study the authors assumed a relation between eye movements and the communicative intent. Later studies from the same authors towards noise robust ASR, suggest a relationship between gaze and speech in noisy environments, a "gaze-Lombard effect" [48]. Also in 2008, Prasov and Chai [49] examined the relation between eye-gaze and domain modeling, in a framework that combined speech and eye-gaze for reference resolution. Their conclusions show that eye-gaze information can be used to compensate the lack of domain modeling for reference resolution.

Other authors of multimodal HCI have suggested that the use of gaze information in web-browsing scenarios might provide substantial improvements [50]. This was later verified by Slaney et al. [51]. Slaney et al. reported improvements in ASR performance when accomplishing common browsing tasks such as making a dinner reservation, online shopping and purchasing shoes, and reading online news. The authors used eye-gaze as contextual information in order to constrain the ASR language model. In terms of the results, improvements of 25 % and 10 % word-error rate (WER) were achieved over a generic and scenario-specific language models. A similar study was conducted by Hakkani-Tür et al. [46] where a conversational web system was developed for interpreting user intentions based on speech and eye-gaze. In this study improvements were also reported not only in predicting the user intention but also in resolving ambiguity, a common technical problem in dialog systems.

Gaze information has also been found to be useful for spoken message dictation scenarios [52–54]. In these studies gaze information has been used as a secondary modality to help choosing between recognition hypotheses in a text entry interface. Additionally, gaze is also used to support correction of speech recognition errors. In the adopted interface model gaze partially replaces the use of the mouse in navigation functions, such as zooming through the presented recognition hypotheses, and for selecting the correct word.

Recent studies also reveal that estimation of eye gaze based on facial pose can have a positive impact in ASR [55]. Other related studies include the analysis of tonal and segmental information, in languages such as Mandarin Chinese, [56], the study of perceptual learning application in speech perception [57], the analysis of the interpolation of lexical, eye gaze and pointing models, which was performed in order to understand aspects of situated dialogues [58], and an in-car multimodal system, which uses information from geo-location, speech, and dialog history, alongside gaze information (estimated from face direction) to interact with the driver [59].

4   Discussion and Conclusion

The studies reviewed in the present paper reveal that eye-gaze information has the potential to significantly increase performance of ASR when combined with speech. However, it is not clear if this fact is applicable to persons of all age groups such as children and elderly.

Analyzing the modalities (speech and gaze) in isolation, and starting by speech, the literature findings suggest that current speech interfaces suffer from its generic modeling approach, not specifically targeted for adult users. Taking into account speech for different age patterns, would resolve this issue but with high cost and effort. As for the literature on eye-gaze information, the studies suggest that it is possible to collect gaze data from all age groups. There is also a fast paced evolution of eye-tracking devices. The cost of desktop-mounted eye tracking sensors has significantly decreased in the past few years, approximately by one hundredth. Although these eye trackers are not appropriate for testing saccade metrics that require high accuracy, they exhibit acceptable performance for spatial precision and accuracy, thus for fixation detection [60]. Therefore it seems plausible to consider its use for real-world scenarios. However, more studies are necessary to have a better understanding of the impact of aging problems upon interaction through eye tracking.

The studies also suggest advantages in the combined used of these modalities. For example, they can be collected in a non-invasive and non-obtrusive manner (not considering mounted/wearable eye trackers) and allow for a natural interaction with the computer or device. Thus, we believe that elderly could eventually benefit from a multimodal interface based on the analyzed modalities. However, empirical investigations are needed to understand whether a multimodal approach using eye tracking and speech recognition would in fact introduce benefits in HCI with elderly users. Recent research on eye movements and aging reveal that laboratory studies only partly resemble the studies in the real world [61]. Therefore field studies are necessary for testing the settings that are proposed in the present study. In particular, usability studies of multimodal HCI scenarios based on speech and gaze gain relevance and can provide useful feedback about the application of this sort of setups in real environments.

Future work will focus on conducting experimental investigations of the proposed speech-gaze interfaces. This includes exploring novel scenarios such as: (1) the use of gaze combined with speech in mobile scenarios (e.g. interaction with a tablet), which take advantage of new technological solutions in terms of eye tracking; (2) to assess the usability of such multimodal interfaces with users from different age groups, particularly elderly users; (3) to extend the number of HCI tasks which benefit from the combined use of speech and gaze, such as access to online content or interaction with assistive technologies; (4) to understand which of these scenarios can be tackled with an ubiquitous and affordable solution.

Acknowledgment. This work was partially funded by Marie Curie Actions IRIS (ref. 610986, FP7-PEOPLE-2013-IAPP) and METU Scientific Research Project scheme BAP–08-11-2012-121 Investigation of Cognitive Processes in Multimodal Communication.

References

1. Dias, M.S., Pires, C.G., Pinto, F.M., Teixeira, V.D., Freitas, J.: Multimodal user interfaces to improve social integration of elderly and mobility impaired. Stud. Heal. Technol. Informatics. **177**, 14–25 (2012)
2. Phang, C.W., Sutanto, J., Kankanhalli, A., Li, Y., Tan, B.C.Y., Teo, H.-H.: Senior citizens' acceptance of information systems: a study in the context of e-government services. IEEE Trans. Eng. Manag. **53**, 555–569 (2006)
3. Cisek, E., Triche, K.: Depression and social support among older adult computer users. In: 113th Annual Convention of the American Psychological Association (2005)
4. Oliveira, C., Albuquerque, L., Hämäläinen, A., Pinto, F.M., Dias, M.S., Júdice, A., Freitas, J., Pires, C., Teixeira, V., Calado, A., Braga, D., Teixeira, A.: Tecnologias de Fala para Pessoas Idosas. Laboratório Vivo de Usabilidade (Living Usability Lab), pp. 167–181. ARC Publishing (2013)
5. Stephanidis, C., Akoumianakis, D., Sfyrakis, M., Paramythis, A.: Universal accessibility in HCI: process-oriented design guidelines and tool requirements. In: Proceedings of the 4th ERCIM Workshop on User Interfaces for all, Stockholm, pp. 19–21 (1998)
6. Fox, S.: Are "wired seniors" sitting ducks? Pew Internet & American Life Project (2006)
7. Teixeira, V., Pires, C., Pinto, F., Freitas, J., Dias, M.S., Rodrigues, E.M.: Towards elderly social integration using a multimodal human-computer interface. In: Proceedings of International Living Usability Lab Workshop on AAL Latest Solutions, Trends and Applications (AAL 2012), pp. 3–13 (2012)

8. Jessen, M.: Speaker classification in forensic phonetics and acoustics. In: Müller, C. (ed.) Speaker Classification 2007. LNCS (LNAI), vol. 4343. Springer, Heidelberg (2007)
9. Linville, S.E.: Vocal Aging. Singular Thomson Learning, CA (2001)
10. Wilpon, J.G., Jacobsen, C.N.: A study of speech recognition for children and the elderly. In: IEEE International Conference on Acoustics, Speech and Signal Processing (ICASSP 1996), pp. 349–352. IEEE (1996)
11. Helfrich, H.: Age Markers in Speech. Cambridge University Press, Cambridge (1979)
12. Pellegrini, T., Hämäläinen, A., de Mareüil, P.B., Tjalve, M., Trancoso, I., Candeias, S., Dias, M.S., Braga, D.: A corpus-based study of elderly and young speakers of european portuguese: acoustic correlates and their impact on speech recognition performance. In: Proceedings of (INTERSPEECH 2013), pp. 852–856 (2013)
13. Stover, S.E., Haynes, W.O.: Topic manipulation and cohesive adequacy in conversations of normal adults between the ages of 30 and 90. Clin. Linguist. Phon. **3**, 137–149 (1989)
14. Albuquerque, L., Oliveira, O., Teixeira, T., Sá-Couto, P., Freitas, J., Dias, M.S.: Impact of age in the production of european portuguese vowels. In: 15th Annual Conference of the International Speech Communication Association (INTERSPEECH 2014), Singapore (2014)
15. Xue, S.A., Hao, G.J.: Changes in the human vocal tract due to aging and the acoustic correlates of speech productiona pilot study. J. Speech Lang. Hear. Res. **46**, 689–701 (2003)
16. Pellegrini, T., Trancoso, I., Hämäläinen, A., Calado, A., Dias, M.S., Braga, D.: Impact of age in asr for the elderly: preliminary experiments in European Portuguese. In: Torre Toledano, D., Ortega Giménez, A., Teixeira, A., González Rodr\'ıguez, J., Hernández Gómez, L., San Segundo Hernández, R., Ramos Castro, D. (eds.) IberSPEECH 2012. CCIS, vol. 328, pp. 139–147. Springer, Heidelberg (2012)
17. Schultz, T.: Speaker characteristics. In: Müller, C. (ed.) Speaker Classification 2007. LNCS (LNAI), vol. 4343, pp. 47–74. Springer, Heidelberg (2007)
18. Anderson, S., Liberman, N., Bernstein, E., Foster, S., Cate, E., Levin, B., Hudson, R.: Recognition of elderly speech and voice-driven document retrieval. In: IEEE International Conference on Acoustics, Speech, and Signal Processing (ICASSP 1999), pp. 145–148. IEEE (1999)
19. Baba, A., Yoshizawa, S., Yamada, M., Lee, A., Shikano, K.: Elderly acoustic model for large vocabulary continuous speech recognition. IEICE Trans. Inf. Syst. **J85-D-2**(3), 390–397 (2002)
20. Vipperla, R., Wolters, M., Georgila, K., Renals, S.: Speech input from older users in smart environments: challenges and perspectives. In: Stephanidis, C. (ed.) UAHCI 2009, Part II. LNCS, vol. 5615, pp. 117–126. Springer, Heidelberg (2009)
21. Hämäläinen, A., Avelar, J., Rodrigues, S. Dias, M., Kolesinski, A., Fegyó, T., Németh, G., Csobánka, P., Lan, K., Hewson, D.: The EASR corpora of European Portuguese, French, Hungarian and polish elderly speech. In: LREC, pp. 1458–1464 (2014)
22. Hämäläinen, A., Pinto, F., Dias, M., Júdice, A., Freitas, J., Pires, C., Teixeira, V., Calado, A., Braga, D.: The first European Portuguese elderly speech corpus. In: Proceedings of IberSPEECH, Madrid, Spain (2012)
23. Olincy, A., Ross, R.G., Youngd, D.A., Freedman, R.: Age diminishes performance on an antisaccade eye movement task. Neurobiol. Aging **18**, 483–489 (1997)
24. Munoz, D.P., Broughton, J.R., Goldring, J.E., Armstrong, I.T.: Age-related performance of human subjects on saccadic eye movement tasks. Exp. Brain Res. **121**, 391–400 (1998)
25. Munoz, D.P., Everling, S.: Look away: the anti-saccade task and the voluntary control of eye movement. Nat. Rev. Neurosci. **5**, 218–228 (2004)

26. Bowling, A., Draper, A.: Using saccadic eye movements to assess cognitive decline with ageing. In: Horsley, M., Eliot, M., Knight, B.A., Reilly, R. (eds.) Current Trends in Eye Tracking Research, pp. 237–244. Springer International Publishing, Switzerland (2014)

27. Trick, L.M., Enns, J.T.: Lifespan changes in attention: the visual search task. Cogn. Dev. **13**, 369–386 (1998)

28. Scialfa, C.T., Thomas, D.M., Joffe, K.M.: Age differences in the useful field of view: an eye movement analysis. Optom. Vis. Sci. Official Publ. Am. Acad. Optom. **71**, 736–742 (1994)

29. Beurskens, R., Bock, O.: Age-related decline of peripheral visual processing: the role of eye movements. Exp. Brain Res. **217**, 117–124 (2012)

30. Kliegl, R., Nuthmann, A., Engbert, R.: Tracking the mind during reading: the influence of past, present, and future words on fixation durations. J. Exp. Psychol. Gen. **135**, 12–35 (2006)

31. Rayner, K.: Eye movements in reading and information processing: 20 years of research. Psychol. Bull. **124**, 372–422 (1998)

32. Rayner, K., Pollatsek, A., Ashby, J., Clifton, C.: The Psychology of Reading, 2nd edn. Psychology Press, Abingdon (2012)

33. Holmqvist, K., Nyström, M., Andersson, R., Dewhurst, R., Halszka, J., van de Weijer, J.: Eye Tracking: A Comprehensive Guide to Methods and Measures. Oxford University Press, Oxford (2011)

34. Rayner, K., Castelhano, M.S., Yang, J.: Eye movements and the perceptual span in older and younger readers. Psychol. Aging **24**, 755–760 (2009)

35. Rayner, K., Yang, J., Schuett, S., Slattery, T.J.: The effect of foveal and parafoveal masks on the eye movements of older and younger readers. Psychol. Aging **29**, 205–212 (2014)

36. Maltz, M., Shinar, D.: Eye movements of younger and older drivers. Hum. Factors **4**, 15–25 (1999)

37. Ho, G., Scialfa, C.T., Caird, J.K., Graw, T.: Visual search for traffic signs: the effects of clutter, luminance, and aging. Hum. Factors **432**, 194–207 (2001)

38. Schieber, F., Gilland, J.: Age differences in the useful field of view during real-world driving. In: Proceedings of the Human Factors and Ergonomic Society Annual Meeting, vol. 49, pp. 182–185. Sage Publications (2005)

39. Cantin, M.L.M.T.V., Teasdale, M.S.N.: Aging yields a smaller number of fixations and a reduced gaze amplitude when driving in a simulator. Adv. Transp. Stud. Int. J. Special Issue, 21–30 (2006)

40. Bitsios, P., Prettyman, R., Szabadi, E.: Changes in autonomic function with age: a study of pupillary kinetics in healthy young and old people. Age Ageing **25**, 432–438 (1996)

41. Kuchinsky, S.E., Ahlstrom, J.B., Vaden, K.I., Cute, S.L., Humes, L.E., Dubno, J.R., Eckert, M.A.: Pupil size varies with word listening and response selection difficulty in older adults with hearing loss. Psychophysiology **50**, 23–34 (2013)

42. Mather, M., Carstensen, L.L.: Aging and motivated cognition: the positivity effect in attention and memory. Trends Cogn. Sci. **9**, 496–502 (2005)

43. McGurk, H., MacDonald, J.: Hearing lips and seeing voices. Nature **264**, 746–748 (1976)

44. Oviatt, S.: Ten myths of multimodal interaction. Commun. ACM **42**, 74–81 (1999)

45. Quek, F., McNeill, D., Bryll, R., Duncan, S., Ma, X.-F., Kirbas, C., McCullough, K.E., Ansari, R.: Multimodal human discourse: gesture and speech. ACM Trans. Comput. Interact. **9**, 171–193 (2002)

46. Hakkani-Tür, D., Slaney, M., Celikyilmaz, A., Heck, L.: Eye gaze for spoken language understanding in multi-modal conversational interactions. In: Proceedings of the 16th International Conference on Multimodal Interaction, pp. 263–266. ACM (2014)

47. Cooke, N.J., Russell, M.: Gaze-contingent automatic speech recognition. Signal Process. IET **2**, 369–380 (2008)

48. Cooke, N., Shen, A., Russell, M.: Exploiting a "gaze-Lombard effect" to improve ASR performance in acoustically noisy settings. In: IEEE International Conference on Acoustics, Speech and Signal Processing (ICASSP 2014), pp. 1754–1758. IEEE (2014)
49. Prasov, Z., Chai, J.Y.: What's in a gaze? the role of eye-gaze in reference resolution in multimodal conversational interfaces. In: Proceedings of the 13th International Conference on Intelligent User Interfaces, pp. 20–29. ACM (2008)
50. Heck, L.P., Hakkani-Tür, D., Chinthakunta, M., Tür, G., Iyer, R., Parthasarathy, P., Stifelman, L., Shriberg, E., Fidler, A.: Multi-modal conversational search and browse. In: SLAM Workshop, pp. 96–101 (2013)
51. Slaney, M., Rajan, R., Stolcke, A., Parthasarathy, P.: Gaze-enhanced speech recognition. In: IEEE International Conference on Acoustics, Speech and Signal Processing (ICASSP 2014), pp. 3236–3240. IEEE (2014)
52. Vertanen, K.: Efficient correction interfaces for speech recognition (2009)
53. Vertanen, K., MacKay, D.J.C.: Speech dasher: fast writing using speech and gaze. In: Proceedings of the SIGCHI Conference on Human Factors in Computing Systems, pp. 595–598. ACM (2010)
54. Vertanen, K., MacKay, D.J.C.: Speech dasher: a demonstration of text input using speech and approximate pointing. In: Proceedings of the 16th International ACM SIGACCESS Conference on Computers & Accessibility, pp. 353–354. ACM (2014)
55. Slaney, M., Stolcke, A., Hakkani-Tür, D.: The relation of eye gaze and face pose: Potential impact on speech recognition. In: Proceedings of the 16th International Conference on Multimodal Interaction, pp. 144–147. ACM (2014)
56. Malins, J.G., Joanisse, M.F.: The roles of tonal and segmental information in Mandarin spoken word recognition: an eyetracking study. J. Mem. Lang. **62**, 407–420 (2010)
57. Mitterer, H., Reinisch, E.: No delays in application of perceptual learning in speech recognition: evidence from eye tracking. J. Mem. Lang. **69**, 527–545 (2013)
58. Kennington, C., Kousidis, S., Schlangen, D.: Interpreting situated dialogue utterances: an update model that uses speech, gaze, and gesture information. In: Proceedings of the SIGDIAL 2013 (2013)
59. Misu, T., Raux, A., Lane, I., Devassy, J., Gupta, R.: Situated multi-modal dialog system in vehicles. In: Proceedings of the 6th Workshop on Eye Gaze in Intelligent Human Machine Interaction: Gaze in Multimodal Interaction, pp. 25–28. ACM (2013)
60. Dalmaijer, E.S.: Is the low-cost EyeTribe eye tracker any good for research? PeerJ PrePrints (Preprint, 2015).http://dx.doi.org/10.7287/peerj.preprints.585v1, https://peerj.com/preprints/585/, Accessed 25 Jan 2015
61. Dowiasch, S., Marx, S., Einhauser, W., Bremmer, F.: Effects of aging on eye movements in the real world. Frontiers Hum. Neurosci. **9**, 46 (2015)

Design Engineering and Human Computer Interaction: Function Oriented Problem Solving in CAD Applications

Gisela S. Bahr[✉], Stephen L. Wood, and Anthony Escandon

Florida Institute of Technology, 150W. University Blvd, Melbourne,
FL 32901, USA
{gbahr, swood}@fit.edu

Abstract. CAD Software such as CREO and SolidWorks are used to develop mechanical parts and assemblies and do not explicitly support the function of the feature, component, part or assembly. Therefore, the reasoning of why and how a design is developed has not been incorporated into current CAD systems. At the same time, CAD systems support sophisticated functions such automated routing, modelling and simulation of dynamic and geometric properties and design solutions tracking. In this paper we investigate (a) to what degree CAD tools have advanced beyond drafting tools to include cognitive supports that facilitate problem solving and (b) which possibilities exist to enhance CAD with cognitive tools that with focus on the intersection between cognitive psychology, interaction design and design engineering remain unexplored.

Keywords: Engineering design · Design reasoning · Design support · Design cognition · Problem solving · Creo · SolidWorks · Functional fixedness

1 Introduction

Design engineers rarely have the opportunity to use algorithmic approaches, but solve ill-defined problems with creative and novel solutions. For example, the design of an Autonomous Underwater Vehicle (AUV), such as the Bluefin AUV used to look for Malaysian Flight 370 that was lost March 8, 2014, requires thousands of design decisions that are based on (often changing and poorly defined) customer requirements. Mechanical components, electrical circuits, computer code, and all of the connections are interwoven by mechanical, electrical and computer design engineers to create the AUV. It is easy to see from this example that the task of the design engineer is not to reproduce prior solutions but to develop a novel approach and a creative solution to design an innovative, complex vehicle.

When conceptualizing design engineering as a creative problem solving process, the question arises as to the underlying cognition, specifically, how information processing of the design engineer can be supported during the development of solutions. In addition to traditional drawing and sketching, CAD (computer assisted design) software is a primary tool of design engineers to develop and articulate their solutions. CAD tools are sophisticated and popular as computerized drafting tools but questions

© Springer International Publishing Switzerland 2015
M. Antona and C. Stephanidis (Eds.): UAHCI 2015, Part I, LNCS 9175, pp. 13–24, 2015.
DOI: 10.1007/978-3-319-20678-3_2

remain unanswered whether CAD applications support the cognitive aspects of problem solving. As early as 1989 [1] observed that CAD tools provide computerized versions of traditional drafting and that these approaches had not yet realized the possibility of supporting the design process beyond the mechanics of drawing. Furthermore, he observed that CAD applications did not support problem solving and solutions finding, specifically in the context of function based thinking, which is instrumental to design engineering. In this paper we investigate (a) to what degree CAD tools have advanced beyond serving as drafting support and include cognitive tools that facilitate problem solving, and (b) which implementation possibilities remains in CAD for cognitive tools that are supported by interdisciplinary research in cognitive psychology, interaction design and design engineering. In addition to this introduction and the conclusion, this paper has four parts. Part 1 is an overview of problem solving including human biases and cognitive artifacts that impede ill-defined problem solving. Part 2 is a review of that state of the CAD software and which tools are provided, including possible cognitive tools. Part 3 integrates the cognitive psychological findings with the state of CAD. Part 4 reviews the seminal study on function based problem solving in the design process and presents research opportunities for enriching CAD application with cognitive tools. We conclude that the state of CAD as cognitive support tool for the design engineer is in its infancy and substantial cognitive research of the design process and software development is still to be done.

2   Review of Cognitive Phenomena in Problem Solving

To answer the question whether CAD tools have advanced to include cognitive tools that facilitate problem solving for engineers, we first present a review of cognitive phenomena that apply to design engineering.

Developing a solution to an engineering task, such as to "build an autonomous underwater vehicle that can do these things" is an instance of solving an ill-defined problem. Unlike well-defined problems, ill-defined problems lack definition, which may be a somewhat elusive goal or uncertainty how to reach a goal, i.e., not knowing which necessary steps and what resources are available [2]. In design engineering the lack of problem definition is expressed by a lack of specific or generic requirements and uncertainty about the tasks that need to be performed to reach the goal. To support the design process and productive thinking [3], strategies such as the House of Quality model have been developed [4]. Such strategies encourage perspective taking and the discovery of dependencies and expectations and tend to be paper or whiteboard based. They are primarily used as communication tools between customers and the engineering team and aide in defining the goals of the project but are less useful and not intended to support creative problem solving during the design process.

2.1   Functional Fixedness

A well-studied phenomenon that occurs during ill-defined problem solving is a fixation of the typical use of an object. For example, a hammer is made for hammering, a toothbrush for cleaning teeth, etc. Karl Duncker discovered the phenomenon that people tend to limit the uses of previously encountered objects in 1945 and termed his observation Functional Fixedness [5].

The research may seem dated but the phenomenon of functional fixedness persists as an artifact of human information processing. Examples in recent history are the terrorist attacks that occurred on September 11, 2001 in metropolitan areas of the USA [6, 7]. Four planes (commercial jets, which are generally considered means of transport for goods and people) were used as weapons and killed thousands of people. The realization that the function of a plane is not limited to preconceived notions but that its uses depends on the characteristics of the object, was obvious to the terrorist who used the planes as airborne, target finding bombs.

Duncker's original study investigated functional fixedness using ill-defined problems that required productive as opposed to *re*productive, or algorithmic thinking [3]. For example, he invented the candle-wall problem, which is now well known inside and outside of cognitive psychology. The problem description follows: Seated at a table facing the wall, the participant is given a candle, a box of matches, a box of tacks and a task: attach the candle to the wall so that it can be lighted and burn without dripping wax.

This goal is clearly stated but how to reach it is unclear. The results of the study indicate that participants, unless they are already familiar with the solution, tend to struggle. However, when the matches and/or the tacks are on the table, rather than contained in the box, the solution becomes obvious [5]: The box can be used as a candle sconce that is fixed to the wall using the tacks. The critical observation of the research is that problem solvers implicitly place limits on the functions of an object that are related to its current use, context and prior knowledge. This is related to schema use in cognition where a previously learnt framework guides recall based on a set of cues [8, 9]. In this context cues are the current function or usage of an object which appears to inhibit the exploration of alternative uses, i.e., functions or functionalities. By making alternative uses of the object more obvious, i.e., taking the tacks out of the box, problem solvers are more likely to find solutions.

2.2 Analogical Problem Solving

Research related to the obstacles of ill-defined problem that require productive thinking have been also investigated in analogical problem solving. Analogical problem solving refers to the transfer of a solution from one problem to another problem that seems initially unrelated.

For example, [10] presented participants with a fictitious military problem. The problem description follows: The only way to reach a fortress is by road. Many roads radiate out from the fortress and each road is mined so that only a small number of people can traverse them safely. A general is tasked to capture the fortress and plans launch a full attack. Consequently, the number of people needed to take the fortress exceeds the number of people who can safely traverse the roads. The solution to the problem is based on a convergence strategy: Divide the troops into groups that are small enough to use the roads safely, join forces at the fortress and make the conquest.

After receiving the problem and the solution, participants were given another problem, originally described by Duncker [5]. The problem description follows: A patient is suffering from a malignant tumor but surgery is not an option. A high intensity X-ray could destroy the tumor but at the same time would destroy to the healthy surrounding tissue. A low intensity laser would preserve all tissue including the tumor. Without surgery, is it possible to develop a procedure possible that destroys the tumor without destroying the healthy, surrounding tissues? The solution is to use multiple low power lasers that converge on the site of the tumor.

The results show 10 % of the participants who did not receive any additional information or irrelevant information before the radiation problem, solved it. However, 75 % of the participants who received the radiation problem after studying the military problem and receiving the convergence solution with a hint to apply the solution to the next problem, solved the radiation problem. Without specific hints it appears that participants have difficulty in noticing similarities between problems. Research [11] suggests that failure to recognize the commonalities between the problems is the result of deep vs. surface structure processing [12], where surface refers to appearance and deep refers to an abstraction of structural organization. In the current study, the impression that military strategy and cancer treatment seem unrelated prevents participants to shift their focus from the surface to the common, deep structure of the problems unless explicitly instructed to do so. The failure mechanism is simple: dissimilar domains create different appearances (surface structures) and these differences imply that the problems have nothing in common, hence analogical search is not conducted.

It appears that appearances, whether they take the form of a problem context or the current usage of an object, lead problem solving to adopt a particular mindset (Einstellung) [13]. This finding by itself does not seem surprising except that the consequences extend beyond the laboratory, as seen in the 9–11 example.

2.3   Solution Fixation in Design Engineers

Similar to Einstellung and Functional Fixedness, solution fixation is a common cognitive artifact affecting design engineers from the novice to the expert. Prior research [14, 15] focused on professional mechanical design engineers and found that they became fixated upon preliminary solution ideas and failed to consider alternative design concepts. The phenomenon was seen both at the level of the overall design problem and at the level of each individual sub-problem. In addition, [14, 15] observed that if the designer discovered weaknesses in original design later in the process, they were solved by 'patching' the design rather than discarding the idea and developing a new concept. According to [14, p. 15]: "The first idea was almost sacred, and sometimes even highly implausible patches would be applied to make it work." Similarly, [16] in a study of pre-expert electronics designers observed that individuals rarely generated and modelled alternative solutions but focused upon initial ideas that were iteratively improved until they reached a state that was adequate.

In summary, previous studies indicate the design engineers "patch" and "repair" solution ideas instead of questioning or exploring alternative uses of the parts and assemblies they created. From an information processing perspective this means that design engineers tend to limit the functionality of the design elements to the originally conceived design context. This is an instance of functional fixedness.

The findings that the problem context and the current object usage create cognitive artifacts such as surface structure processing, solution fixation and functional fixedness, are likely to have implications for the presentation and organization of CAD tools and the way they are presented in a graphic user interface. Hence we proceed to the next section which is a review of the state of CAD.

3   Review of CAD: SolidWorks and Creo 3.0

We reviewed current CAD packages that are the most widely used in the engineering community: SolidWorks developed by Dassault Systèmes Solidworks Corporation and CREO developed by Parametric Technology Corporation (PTC). Other CAD applications, such as CATIA, AutoCAD, Inventor and TurboCAD offer comparable functionalities.

3.1   SolidWorks

SolidWorks is self-described as a user-friendly CAD program in that it offers a wide range of real-time support in the form of interactive prompts, automatic button descriptions, and tutorial options. Variations of the SolidWorks software packages offer the user varied levels of design and analysis capabilities. They include standard 2D and 3D design capabilities, design and drawing interference checks, automated cost estimation, and online parts and components library, as well as reverse engineering capabilities and wiring and piping design tools.

Design Library. The SolidWorks design library structure relies on a variety of categorization methods of user solutions. The library is organized in a cascading dropdown format with increasing specificity as presented in Fig. 1.

The design library contains a wide range of basic mechanical and geometric objects that can be modified and built upon. These objects range from very basic washers and screws to fairly complex injection mold bases and assemblies. The library incorporates object and form-based cascading menu structures. Menu options can be categorized into the following groups:

- Specific Objects: Object or assemblies of objects too complex to be generalized in menus. Vendor libraries and SolidWorks add-ons offer a range of additional complex objects. Examples are mold base, valve assembly, fittings, etc.
- General Objects: Objects (physical parts) are categorized generally. Each category has its own more specific parts catalog. The library add-on called toolbox is also organized in this manner. Examples are hardware, sheet metal, knobs.
- Forms: While less common, there are a few library menu options that are organized based off of form. Examples are basic sheet metal forms, embosses, flanges, and ribs.

The library also contains a toolbox that has imported screw standards and sizes for 10 different countries. Also, the user has the option to add a file or object to the parts library. In addition, *Partner Products Online Resources* provide functionalities such as vendor libraries (providing object prototypes), automated analysis of the design geometry for piping routing and circuits, plug-ins for computer aided manufacturing (CAM) and computer numerical control (CNC) machining and sheet-metal designs. Perhaps not surprisingly given the number of option and contributors, the library does not have a search feature.

Workflow Enhancements. SolidWorks supports the drafting process with automation, such as auto-sizing and auto-routing tools. For example, if the user drags a generic flange onto an existing fluid tank outlet, the flange automatically sizes and forms into the type of flange necessary to make the proper connection. The auto routing suggests the spatial location where pipes and wires should be positioned and can generate piping layout after an inlet and outlet are specified. An example of "designed by software" is an image of an orthogonally routed solution in Fig. 2.

Fig. 1. SolidWorks design library cascade menu [screenshot].

SolidWorks also provides electrical wire routing tools. For example, the wire auto-bundler can automatically bundle a group of wires and route them through a space given a specified origin and endpoint, fixing the wires to structures for support as needed. Moreover, the auto-routing wire feature can detect ports between components that require wire connections. The software can then automatically add and route the wire connections. In addition, SolidWorks offers software package that is specifically for the design of electrical systems. This software platform is capable of importing electrical schematics and components and converting the layout into 3D space with all the necessary connections.

3.2   Creo 3.0

The Creo design platform is an evolution of the Pro/Engineer software. The software lets the designer "perform analysis, create renderings and animations, and optimize productivity across a full range of other mechanical design tasks, including a check for how well the design conforms to best practices" [17]. Creo has a number of modelling & simulation tools that assist the design engineer. Examples are: Simulate, a structural,

Fig. 2. SolidWorks' auto-route feature [tutorial screenshot]

thermal and vibration analysis tool for the evaluation of 3D virtual prototypes; Mechanism Dynamics, a tool that enables the designer to simulate the forces and accelerations in systems with moving components; Manikin Extension, a tool to test designs against a number of quantitative human factors, workplace standards and guidelines. Similar to SolidWorks, Creo 3.0 offers piping and cabling automation. Other aides include a Tolerance Analysis Extension that analyzes geometric tolerances to verify that components fit together correctly (Fig. 3).

CREO also has import/export compatibility with around 30 common CAD platforms. CREO lacks internal tutorials but has a link to an online tutorial website. Some of the content on the tutorial website is "how to" organized. For example, the home page on the tutorial website contains instructional videos on how to: control tangency, move and rotate, manage chamfers etc. In summary, CREO does not contain a built-in design library and is compatible with wide range of CAD software programs, allowing for access to many external libraries.

Design Libraries. The vendor libraries are extensive and are accessed on a broad object-basis. For example, Creo links to a 3D model database of over 750,000 basic CAD designs available for purchase http://www.3dmodelspace.com/ptc. Models are searchable based on a two-tier menu of objects. Specifically, the 3D Model Space database is hierarchically structured, from broad to narrow. Some of the sub-categories within the menus are organized by type that can suggest the primary function of the object. For example the selection, "mechanical components > springs" gives the user the option of choosing from "compression spring, tension spring, and torsional spring".

Workflow Enhancements. CREO Design Exploration Extension (DEX) saves critical design mile stones to create design branches so the designer can move back and forth between design alternatives; It is based on a design tree structure that allows for alterations to a design while storing the original design files separately. The feature variation is not automated and each version or change to the design needs to be created by the design engineers. A related product, the Advanced Assembly Extension allows critical design information to be shared with individual team members enabling them to complete their tasks concurrently while working within the context of the full assembly.

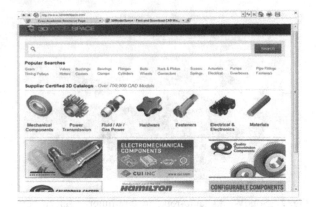

Fig. 3. Online vendor library [3DModelSpace screenshot]

4 Relating Cognitive Psychological Findings to CAD

CAD systems have made strides over the last 25 years to make the designing of products easier and more intuitive. Companies have been integrating new analysis tools and automation into their products to aid the designer (e.g., Solidworks' fluid flow analysis, and AutoRouting and CREO 3.0's Design Exploration Extension that provides the capability to explore and save design alternatives without committing any changes to the original model [18]). Whether or not these enhancements support the solving of ill-defining problems during the design process remain empirical questions. This section make provides an initial interdisciplinary integration by examining the cognitive artifacts such as functional fixedness and problem fixation in the context of SolidWorks and CREO 3.0 functionalities.

SolidWorks as a Cognitive Tool. SolidWorks is a highly sophisticated drafting tool that supports 2D and 3D creation of design images, libraries that support prototypes of objects to reduce the need for "drafting from scratch", the automation of geometric problems such as layouts and path design. It may be argued that such tools provide cognitive support by reducing the workload of the user: they allow the design engineer to construct less during object creation by selecting a prototype and to think less or differently by disengaging from the solutions' reasoning process by selecting from automatically generated geometric solutions.

In the context of functional fixedness and solutions fixation, the interaction with object organized libraries has the following implications for the information processing of the design engineer:

The artifacts of functional fixedness seem to be preserved libraries that are organized by object type and to some extent by primary object use. Object types do not prompt the user with usage options or alternatives and that they are organized by primary use reinforces functional fixedness and lack of consideration for alternatives. The current level of implementation does not provide the user with alternative functions or usage of the object, or the capability to search by functionality. Likewise, since functionalities are not available, cross-referencing of multiple usages for the same is not an option. The question arises how functional fixedness can be alleviated in the context of design libraries rather being reinforced.

The automation of solutions appears as a time saving innovation by alleviating workload. However, it can be argued that this feature shifts the designer's task from creation and productive thinking to a selection task which may or may not be supported by well-reasoned analyses to determine the best option. While automation may alleviate the fixation on a single solution, it introduces complexity and choice options while detaching the engineer from the reasoning process. This raises the issue of reliance and trust in automation and to what degree automation can reasonably support the creative process of problem solving, without impairing human cognition. This topic awaits investigation and implications for the design process are likely profound.

4.1 Creo 3.0 as a Cognitive Tool

CREO 3.0 provides a number of sophisticated modelling and simulation tools, as well as vendor libraries and workflow management. It includes automation features and libraries similar to SolidWorks and the implications of these features for the occurrence of Functional Fixedness, creativity and reasoning need not be duplicated here. In addition CREO offers the Design Exploration Extension (DEX) a version tracking system that allows the designer to move back and forth between design alternatives; it seems possible that the facilitation of version tracking and the ability to preserve and track multiple solutions unencumbers the design engineer who wishes to explore alternative solutions without losing track. In that sense, DEX may alleviate working memory limitations and aide retrieval. Moreover, the memory extension provided by DEX could diminish the occurrence of solution fixation by implicitly supporting the memory of design engineers and reducing the workload associated with managing alternatives. Whether CREO users are less likely to exhibit solution fixation is an empirical question.

5   Cognitive Tools for CAD Using Function Based Retrieval

To capture the basic reason of a design, the designer's reasoning and design development must be understood in addition to generic human information processing artifacts.

Over the last 30 years, design cognition has been investigated by a small subset of mechanical, industrial, and electrical engineers, and computer scientists who have limited training in psychology. At the same time cognitive psychologists with limited or no training in engineering have investigated creative problem solving. It is easy to see that both research areas are highly related and that interdisciplinary investigations would be positioned optimally to address the underlying questions of design cognition. However, to date studies how to support the problem solving of the design engineer using the CAD system remain scarce and the implementation of tools that aide designers offers greater enhancements.

It been argued [1] that to integrate design needs into a CAD system various important aspects must be obtained and preserved:

1. The ability to track, capture and store design engineering concepts as they are developed along with the design reasoning (e.g., why, how etc.);
2. The ability to track all design solution possibilities and supply comparisons and advise, and have the ability to learn new solutions with the design engineer's assistance;
3. Standardized components are already are integrated in CAD systems (e.g., screws, bolts, belts, bearings, etc.), but the potential functionalities of these components need to be included and supplied with respect to their potential functionality;
4. The ability to retrieve any previously designed feature, part or assembly along with known functionality and design reasoning (and design history) of a given a component, and when new functionality is devised that this too is added to the component's stored database design reasoning information. In other words, the CAD system must be able to obtain and preserve the design reasoning while the design process is underway, while saved solutions need be retrieved to the CAD system through the functional parameters of the design and be able to transfer the retrieved solution's information, and capture the reasoning or intent of the design during development.

It is easy to see that design needs 1, 2 and 3 are mostly addressed by current systems. With respect to need to retrieval (item 4), Wood [1] was the first to develop a function driven mechanical design solution library that was capable of being implemented in an object-oriented or relational database. This system was targeted as a design assistant and advisor for the plastic injection molding domain, but was developed for other applications such as sheet-metal or casting designing. Wood's system (1) preserves the information of interfacing features within the product's database, (2) maintains a database of features with their fundamental properties and corresponding functions used by experienced design engineers, and (3) transfers the information within the solution's database to the design under development [1]. Wood also developed the structure called a "function-object" that is used as the search tool for his developed library that also serves to "maintain functional information of the solution that relates-to or interacts-with other objects" [1]. Wood's system documented plastic injection primary feature selection from the functions that drive a product's development or in other words Form follows Function. As stated by [1, p. 2].

"The use of functions for the search for solutions is not new, prominent design theory researchers have suggested solution library contexts revolving around complete design solutions. Other researchers have investigated designing-with features by using feature-based solution libraries... These investigations are relevant because they are the first step towards designing with features, but they either have not made a complete use of the functional attributes or have not modelled the entire solution in a functional way."

To summarize Wood's findings, the capturing of the basic reasoning of how and why a design engineer designs a product is necessary to fully preserve and document an object or object assembly. Therefore, capturing design information and being able to reuse these objects through a retrieval system in a CAD system requires different types of information transferal and preservation than those traditionally used. The design engineer develops and retrieves solutions through functional properties, transfers the retrieved solution's information, and consequently captures the design rationale or intent of the design during development. This approach is likely to support analogical problem solving and alleviate functional fixedness by preserving the reasoning and making a variety object uses available during the design process.

Overall, it seems that much empirical research remains to investigate the complex interaction between the design engineer and how to enhance CAD to provide optimal information processing and problem solving support. In addition to the function based design as a cognitive tool, other considerations that require investigation of the relationship between the representation of the design and design engineer's actions must take into account the aspects composing a design situation. For example a design engineer's design creativity using 2D or 3D shapes depends upon the discipline in which the designer is trained [19]. Similarly, [20] noted that different levels of abstraction (where cues for idea generation are represented) stimulate creative design outcomes differently depending on whether the designer is an expert or a novice. Additionally, different designers undertake design tasks in different ways ending-up with different designs even when given the same design specifications, and the same designer is likely to produce different designs at later times for the same specifications. The relationship between design representations and design actions is complex. Consequently, future cognitive CAD tools need to be sensitive to the diversity of experience, interpretation and goals of the users.

6   Conclusions

In the current paper we approached the complexity of the interaction between the design engineer and the CAD package from a cognitive psychological processing perspective. We conceptualized the design process as the creative solving of an ill-defined problem and integrated cognitive psychological findings with the state of CAD. Current software supports a number of design needs however it falls short of enhancing design cognition during ill-defined problem solving. Wood's function based reasoning architecture is presented as an approach to a cognitive CAD tool that alleviate functional fixedness and enhances analogical problem solving. Other interdisciplinary research domain should address individual differences in experience, training, and user goals. We leave the exploration of these topics to future papers and the implementation of current and future research findings in the capable hands of software *design engineers* as a somewhat ill-defined problem.

References

1. Wood, S.L.: Function driven design selection of plastic injection molding features. In: 1996 ASME Design for Manufacturing Conference, DFM A W2, Los Angeles, CA

2. Reisberg, D.: Cognition: Exploring the Science of the Mind, 5th edn. W.W. Norton & Company, Norton (2012)
3. Wertheimer, M.: Productive Thinking. Harper & Brothers Publishers, New York (1959)
4. Hut, P.M.: House of Quality Matrix. The Project Management Hut, 29 June 2008. http://www.pmhut.com/house-of-quality-matrix
5. Duncker, K.: On Problem Solving, vol. 58. Psychological Monographs, Washington, DC (1945). Whole no. 270
6. Schmemann, S.: Hijacked Jets Destroy Twin Towers and Hit Pentagon, Section A, pp. 1–14. New York Times, 12 September, 2001
7. Grunwald, M.: Washington Post, Terrorists Hijack 4 Airliners. 12 September, 2001
8. Bartlett, F.: Remembering. Macmillan, New York (1932)
9. Marshall, S.P.: Schemas in Problem Solving. Cambridge University Press, Cambridge (2007)
10. Gick, M.L., Holyoak, K.J.: Analogical problem solving. Cogn. Psychol. **12**, 306–355 (1980)
11. Holyoak, K.J.: Problem solving. In: Osherson, D., Smith, E.E. (eds.) Invitation To Cognitive Science, vol. 3, pp. 267–296. MIT Press, Cambridge (1990)
12. Chomsky, N.: Deep Structure, Surface Structure, and Semantic Interpretation. Indiana University, Bloomington (1969)
13. Luchins, A.S.: Mechanization in Problem Solving, vol. 54. Psychological Monographs, Washington, DC (1942). Whole no. 248
14. Ullman, D.G., Stauffer, L.A., Dietterich, T.G.: Preliminary results of an experimental study on the mechanical design process. Technical Report X6-30-9, Oregon State University (1987)
15. Ullman, D.G., Dietterich, T.G., Stauffer, L.A.: A model of the mechanical design process based on empirical data. AI EDAM **2**, 33–52 (1988)
16. Ball, L.J., Evans, J.St.B.T., Dennis, I.: Cognitive processes in engineering design: a longitudinal study. Ergonomics **37**(11), 1753–1786 (1994)
17. CREO (2014). http://store.ptc.com
18. Spaulding, B.: Experts Explore PTC CREO Design Exploration Extension in New Webinar Series, 28 January, 2015. http://CREO.ptc.com/
19. Kokotovich, V., Purcell, T.: Mental synthesis and creativity in design: an experimental examination. Des. Stud. **21**(5), 437–449 (2000)
20. Ball, L.J., Ormerod, T.C., Morley, N.J.: Spontaneous analogising in engineering design: a comparative analysis of experts and novices. Des. Stud. **25**(5), 495–508 (2004)

Assessing the Inclusivity of Digital Interfaces - A Proposed Method

Michael Bradley[✉], Patrick Langdon, and P. John Clarkson

Engineering Design Centre, Department of Engineering, University of Cambridge,
Trumpington Street, Cambridge, CB2 1PZ, UK
{mdb54,pml24,pjc10}@eng.cam.ac.uk

Abstract. In the assessment of the inclusivity of products with interfaces for digital devices, there are difficulty and validity issues relating the cognitive demand of using and learning an unfamiliar interface to the capabilities outlined in the population source data. This is due to the disparity between the types of cognitive tasks used to create the source data, and those needed to operate a digital interface.

Previous work to understand the factors affecting successful interactions with novel digital technology interfaces has shown that the user's technology generation, technology prior experience and their motivation are significant. This paper suggests a method which would permit digital interfaces to be assessed for inclusivity by similarity to known interaction patterns. For a digital device interface task that contained a non-transparent or novel interaction pattern, then the resulting cognitive workload could also be assessed.

Keywords: Inclusive design · Exclusion audit · Errors · Older user · Usability · Prior experience

1 Introduction

1.1 Inclusive Design

Inclusive design is a general approach to designing in which products and services address the needs of the widest possible audience, regardless of age or ability [1]. Implicitly it recognises that ageing, capability impairment and disability should be designed for wherever possible in the goods and services for use by the mainstream population. It has been shown that adoption of inclusive design approaches during the design and development of mainstream products and services can not only improve the uptake for those with capability impairment, but also improve the user experience for those who do not consider themselves impaired [2]. From the authors' experiences it seems that many people prefer tasks that require less of their capabilities (typically: visual acuity, dexterity, cognitive ability) to be achieved successfully.

© Springer International Publishing Switzerland 2015
M. Antona and C. Stephanidis (Eds.): UAHCI 2015, Part I, LNCS 9175, pp. 25–33, 2015.
DOI: 10.1007/978-3-319-20678-3_3

1.2   Digital Interfaces

It has been recognised for some time that interfaces for technological devices can be difficult to use, and particularly for older people. Docampo Rama [3] defined the technology generations that cohorts of people fell into based on the dominance of a style of technology interaction when those people were in their formative years. For example someone born in 1930 would be considered to be a member of the electro-mechanical generation, due to the dominance of this interface technology in their life experience until age 25. In this paper, we shall use the expression 'digital interfaces' to refer to any type of interface that incorporates electronic controls with an electronic display screen ('display style' and 'menu style' interfaces) including the most recent style: touchscreen interfaces. Interfaces for digital devices are continuing to become more prevalent including for devices that previously were analogue, e.g. domestic heating thermostats and timers, fixed line telephones, automobile climate controls, household appliances etc. This prevalence does not come without a cost: some people find digital interfaces difficult, and in some cases impossible, to learn and to use [4]. This is perhaps best summarised by Bjarne Stroustrup, author of the C++ programming language:

> "I have always wished that my computer would be as easy to use as my telephone.
> My wish has come true. I no longer know how to use my telephone."

However, extrapolating the difficulties individuals face using digital interactions to population exclusion is currently problematic, as the currently available tools are insufficiently developed and population data sets inadequate to do so, although recent work has attempted to fill this gap [5].

The University of Cambridge's Inclusive Design Group within the Engineering Design Centre (EDC) has developed a method of estimating UK population exclusion [6] by reference to a UK nationwide disability survey which assessed the abilities of over 7,000 randomly surveyed people [7]. However the current exclusion calculation does not take into account the prior technology experience of the users nor their expectations and familiarity with the ever increasing possible number of digital interaction types and styles [8]. For example, until the widespread adoption of capacitive touchscreens on mobile devices, the idea of 'swiping' a screen to effect an event was very unfamiliar.

The fragility of learning of newly acquired heuristic and procedural knowledge is also not currently addressed in the exclusion calculator. These effects have a very strong impact on the success or otherwise of the interactions that any user will have with digital interfaces. Older users in particular, are likely to exhibit perceptual, sensory and motor skill variability [5, 9] which will affect their interactions with technology devices, and in particular technology devices which are new to them, and/or exhibit unfamiliar interaction styles.

Exclusion Calculation. The proportion of the adult UK population who are unable to achieve certain interactions due to degradation of perceptual and motor skill performance can currently be estimated using the Inclusive Design Toolkit's exclusion calculator [6], by comparison of task difficulty to data collected in 1996/7, the Disability

Follow-Up Survey [7]. For example, the exclusion calculator is able to estimate the percentage of UK adults who would not be able to read a small sized font used on a display by comparison to whether the task would be capable by someone who can read a newspaper headline, a large print book, or ordinary newsprint. By use of similar comparisons, the calculator helps estimate a prediction of the proportion of the UK adult population excluded through the visual, hearing, thinking, dexterity, reaching and loco-motion demands of the interaction required to achieve a goal. This process has been used successfully to estimate exclusion in categories as diverse as food packaging, vehicle maintenance tasks, kitchenware and domestic appliances. However, the thinking criteria used to create the dataset were developed to assess the consequences of cognitive impairment on daily living, and consequently have little face validity to apply to inter-action with digital interfaces. For example, attempting to relate the extent to which someone 'who cannot watch a 30 min television programme and tell someone what it was about' affects their ability to operate a digital interface interaction element, is prob-lematic.

1.3 Difficulties with Digital Technology Interaction

There are many people with sensory and cognitive capabilities which are more than sufficient to enable them to successfully interact in the non-digital world. However, many of these people will struggle to use some forms of digital technology, such as computers, tablets and mobile devices to varying degrees. For example, in a national study carried out to assess UK population abilities only 72 % of 35–44 year old adults were successful in carrying out a paper mock-up of a 'number navigation' task, and 85 % were successful with the more common 'select and confirm' interaction pattern. Older participants had substantially worse success rates, but the contribution of age related capability impairments to this cannot be isolated [10]. A Microsoft survey from 2003, found only 21 % of working age adults reported being able to operate ICT equipment without difficulty [2].

Some users complain that digital technology is not for them, and hence that they don't want to engage with digital technology [11]. It is suggested that for people who don't have much digital interface 'prior experience', this perception is at least partially true: they do not have the skill with the interaction patterns to engage with interfaces that seem almost always primarily designed for people with a reasonable level of digital technology experience.

In studies with older low technology literate people using digital technology, the usual user performance measures such as time to task completion are not as important as the ability for the user to be able to make error-free progress to their goal achievement [4]. Error making tends to reinforce the negative feelings of confusion and stress, and frequently puts the device into a state from which the user is unable to recover [13].

1.4 Interaction Design and Patterns

Interaction design (IxD) is the practice of designing interactive digital products, envi-ronments, systems and services [14]. It is closely related to the fast emerging disciplines of user experience (UX) design, which attempts to take a broader view of the content, form and behaviour of interaction, and information architecture (IA), which focuses on the navigational structural aspects of predominantly web design.

The individual interaction elements within interaction design are frequently referred to as 'patterns', and has been a strong focus of interest for this research in the context of older novice users. Zajicek [15] generated a pattern language for a speech system for older people, and advocates the principle for communicating solutions to developers and designers.

This approach has been adopted for use in interaction design for reasons of programming efficiency as well as user centred goals [16]. The major operating system manufacturers, Microsoft, Google and Apple [17, 20] have released through their software developer kits (SDKs) for external developers, their user interface guidelines which incorporate some of their versions of interaction patterns, elements, user interface elements. In addition, there are defined sources of interaction patterns for touchscreens from Saffer [21], and basic gestural interaction patterns from Van Welie [22].

Despite the available advice and patterns from the Apple iPad Human Interface Guidelines [18], Budiu and Nielsen [23] found that for applications written by developers external to Apple, the implementation of the simplest touchscreen action, the tap on an image, provided no less than five different responses on five different iPad applications. The responses included hyper-linking to a more detailed page about the item, flipping the image to reveal further images, enlarging the image, popping up a set of navigation choices to no response whatsoever. From a novice older user perspective, this does not sound encouraging; however it may be that as long as there is sufficient prior experience and/or 'exploratory desire' to initiate a tap action and that the response provides sufficient cues as to the available functions, this may provide a bounded route to follow.

In interaction design the design pattern approach has great benefit from the user's perspective, as the interface elements and patterns (combination of elements) should be used in a consistent way, which offers the opportunity for ease of recall once the user is familiar, and the much greater chance that the user will be faced with a well-developed interface. However, many interaction patterns exist – and as new technologies emerge to permit their evolution, more are added, and in the un-regulated mobile device app domain, human creativity seems to be the only limit to the novelty of new interactions. Of course, for these novel interactions, and in particular the less transparent (both perceptually salient, of obvious function, and operation) will require either trial and error to have a chance of learning (and hence an interaction which is liable to be exclusive) or prior experience of that learning to use successfully.

1.5 Other Methods of Predicting Interaction Issues

As most readers of this paper will probably be aware, there are a huge number of methods available in the literature, in addition to almost certainly many more proprietary variations used in industry, to enable an early view on the cognitive modelling methods (e.g. GOMS [24]), heuristic evaluation or usability inspection [25], error identification (e.g. TAFEI [26]), understandability (e.g. cognitive walkthrough [27]), etc. of an interface design. It is not the purpose of this paper to critique the strengths and weaknesses of each of these, other than to say that the exclusion audit process (and the proposed prior experience addition) is most similar to the cognitive walkthrough method [27], as it builds on a task analysis for a particular user goal, and requires an assessment at each of those task steps.

2 Method Proposal

2.1 User Task Flow for Unfamiliar Interaction

When users engage in activities with unfamiliar interactions, it is quite common for them to need to adopt trial and error strategies (for extreme examples see [13]), which do not necessarily end in a successful outcome. Figure 1 shows a users' task flow for a simple temperature control task and an assessment of which of the visual, hearing, dexterity and cognitive processes are required in each of the steps. For the cognitive assessment, Rasmussen's Skills, Rules and Knowledge (SRK) framework has been used to give an indication of how much conscious activity is needed to be used to carry out each step [28]. In this example, it suggests that the user will have to employ significant cognitive resources when there is an incompatibility between the expected control appearance and mode of operation, and the available controls and modes of operation. Where this requires decision making in the Knowledge level, it is deemed that this will lead to exclusion due to the errors that will be made. Future work in this area could look at assessment of the cognitive demand of coping with this incompatibility, and determining the exclusion based on population cognitive characteristics.

Figure 2 provides a structure for assessment of exclusion for a selected user journey, building on the current process for exclusion calculation. Where the assessment process needs to deviate from the conventional one, is when the task requires a digital interface or digital interaction pattern to be used. At this point, the assessor needs to determine the explicitness of the interaction for someone with no prior digital experience. If it is not completely explicit (i.e. clear that this function is available, is likely to do the required function and that the operation to invoke the function is obvious), then the assessor would need to identify where such an interaction pattern were to normally reside in the list of technology devices that are in the technology prior experience list [6]. If it is not explicit, and not found in any of the technology devices listed, then it would be deemed to incur 'mainstream exclusion', i.e. people without any impairments would need to engage in a conscious trial and error strategy to have a chance of operating successfully. Since this process is by definition very susceptible to errors, and there is no guarantee of successful goal completion it is classified as a step causing mainstream exclusion.

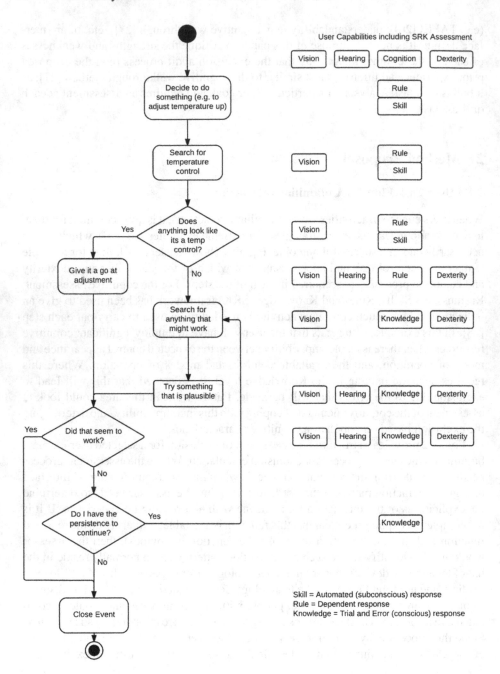

Fig. 1. User steps for carrying out an example digital interaction with the goal of increasing temperature including Skills, Rules, and Knowledge framework assessment. Exclusion assessment flow for digital interfaces.

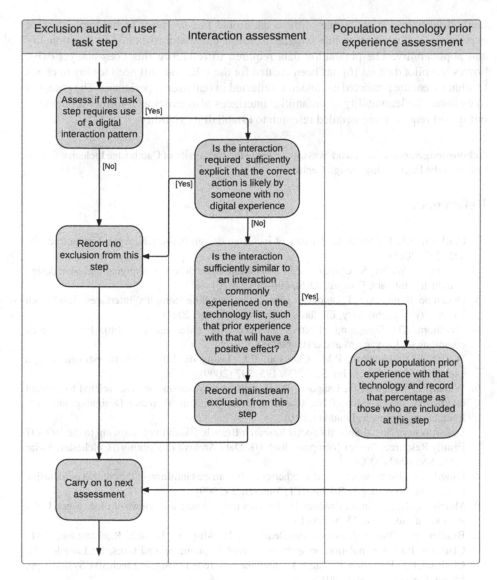

Exclusion audit - of user task step	Interaction assessment	Population technology prior experience assessment

Assess if this task step requires use of a digital interaction pattern — [Yes]

[No]

Is the interaction required sufficiently explicit that the correct action is likely by someone with no digital experience

[Yes]

[No]

Record no exclusion from this step

Is the interaction sufficiently similar to an interaction commonly experienced on the technology list, such that prior experience with that will have a positive effect? [Yes]

[No]

Look up population prior experience with that technology and record that percentage as those who are included at this step

Record mainstream exclusion from this step

Carry on to next assessment

Fig. 2. Assessment steps for carrying out a digital interaction exclusion audit

3 Discussion and Conclusion

The exclusion audit technique has shown great potential to highlight not only the potential issues, but also the potential magnitude of the consequences of those issues expressed as a percentage of the UK population who are excluded from achieving that task step [29]. In the digital interface arena however, there are many factors both from a user's perspective and the characteristics of a digital interface (in addition to the context and scenario of use) that affect the potential for a successful task completion. The proposed method takes into account one of these additional factors: prior technology interface experience, and attempts to link it to the exclusion calculator to extend its functionality and applicability. The population data required to reference this does not yet exist, however a pilot data set [6] has been created for the UK, and will need testing to check to what extent the predicted exclusion is reflected in real user experiences. The potential to evaluate the learnability of unfamiliar interfaces also exists as a further refinement, but would require more detailed research to establish its viability.

Acknowledgements. This work was carried out in the University of Cambridge Inclusive Design Group in the Engineering Design Centre.

References

1. Clarkson, P.J., Coleman, R.: History of inclusive design in the UK. Appl. Ergonomics **46**, 235–247 (2015)
2. Hosking, I., Waller, S., Clarkson, P.J.: It is normal to be different: applying inclusive design in industry. Interact. Comput. **22**(6), 496–501 (2010)
3. Docampo Rama, M.: Technology generations handling complex interfaces. Eindhoven University of Technology, Eindhoven, The Netherlands (2001)
4. Hawthorn, D.: Designing effective interfaces for older users (2006). http://research commons.waikato.ac.nz/handle/10289/2538
5. Waller, S.D., Langdon, P.M., Clarkson, P.J.: Using disability data to estimate design exclusion. Univ. Access Inf. Soc. **9**(3), 195–207 (2009)
6. Waller, S., Williams, E., Langdon, P.: Quantifying exclusion for tasks related to product interaction. In: Langdon, P.M., Clarkson, P.J., Robinson, P. (eds.) Designing Inclusive Interactions. Springer, London (2010)
7. Department of Social Security Social Research Branch: Disability Follow-up to the 1996/97 Family Resources Survey [computer file]. UK Data Archive [distributor], Colchester, 3 Mar 2000. SN: 4090 (2000)
8. Langdon, P., Hurtienne, J.: Is prior experience the same as intuition in the context of inclusive design? In: Workshop at British HCI Conference (2009)
9. Morris, A., Goodman, J., Brading, H.: Internet use and non-use: views of older users. Univ. Access Inf. Soc. **6**(1), 43–57 (2006)
10. Bradley, M., Waller, S., Goodman-Deane, J., Hosking, I., Tenneti, R., Langdon, P.M., Clarkson, P.J.: A population perspective on mobile phone related tasks. In: Langdon, P., Clarkson, P.J., Robinson, P., Lazar, J., Heylighen, A. (eds.) Designing Inclusive Systems, pp. 55–64. Springer, London (2012)
11. Milner, H. (ed.): Does the internet improve lives? UK Online & Freshminds (2009)
12. Bradley, M., Langdon, P., Clarkson, P.: Older user errors in handheld touchscreen devices: to what extent is prediction possible? In: Stephanidis, C. (ed.) Universal Access in HCI, Part II, HCII 2011. LNCS, vol. 6766, pp. 131–139. Springer, Heidelberg (2011)
13. Murad, S., Bradley, M., Kodagoda, N., Barnard, Y., Lloyd, A.: Using task analysis to explore older novice participants' experiences with a handheld touchscreen device. In: Anderson, M. (ed.) Contemporary Ergonomics and Human Factors 2012, pp. 57–64. CRC Press, Boca Raton (2012)
14. Cooper, A., Reimann, R., Cronin, D.: About Face 3: The Essentials of Interaction Design, Revised edn. Wiley, New York (2007)

15. Zajicek, M.: Successful and available: interface design exemplars for older users. Interact. Comput. **16**(3), 411–430 (2004)
16. Van Welie, M., Trætteberg, H.: Interaction patterns in user interfaces. In: Seventh Pattern Languages of Programs Conference, pp. 13–16 (2000)
17. Apple Inc.: iPhone Human Interface Guidelines. Apple Inc. (2010)
18. Apple Inc.: iPad Human Interface Guidelines. Apple Inc. (2010)
19. Fulcher, R., Nesladek, C., Palmer, J., Robertson, C.: Android UI Design Patterns Presented at the Google 2010 Conference (2010)
20. Microsoft: UX Guide Windows Style Guide (2009)
21. Saffer, D.: Designing Gestural Interfaces: Touchscreens and Interactive Devices, 1st edn. O'Reilly Media, Sebastopol (2008)
22. Van Welie, M.: Interaction design pattern library - Welie.com. Interaction design pattern library: http://www.welie.com/patterns/. Accessed 23 Aug 2010
23. Budiu, R., Nielsen, J.: Usability of iPad apps and websites: first research findings. Nielsen Norman Group. http://www.nngroup.com/reports/mobile/ipad/. Accessed 17 Aug 2010
24. Baskin, J.D., John, B.E.: Comparison of GOMS analysis methods. In: CHI 1998 Conference Summary on Human Factors in Computing Systems, p. 262 (1998)
25. Nielsen, J., Mack, R.L.: Usability Inspection Methods. Wiley, New York (1994)
26. Baber, C., Stanton, N.A.: Task analysis for error identification: a methodology for designing error-tolerant consumer products. TERG **37**(11), 1923–1941 (1994)
27. Wharton, C., Rieman, J., Lewis, C., Polson, P.: The cognitive walkthrough method: a practitioner's guide. In: Nielsen, J., Mack, R.L. (eds.) Usability Inspection Methods. Wiley, New York (1993)
28. Rasmussen, J.: Skills, rules, and knowledge: signals, signs, and symbols, and other distinctions in human performance models. IEEE Trans. Syst. Man Cybern. **SMC-13**(3), 257–266 (1983)
29. Waller, S., Langdon, P., Clarkson, P.: Visualizing design exclusion predicted by disability data: a mobile phone case study. In: Stephanidis, C. (ed.) Universal Access in HCI, Part I, HCII 2009. LNCS, vol. 5614, pp. 644–653. Springer, Heidelberg (2009)

Socio-Technical Barriers Induced by the Design of Emerging Technologies

A Perspective Situated in iDTV Applications

Samuel B. Buchdid[✉], Roberto Pereira, Heiko H. Hornung,
and M. Cecília C. Baranauskas

Institute of Computing, University of Campinas, Av. Albert Einstein N1251,
Campinas, SP, Brazil
{buchdid,rpereira,heiko,cecilia}@ic.unicamp.br

Abstract. Emerging technologies may impose barriers on groups of people or even the whole society. These barriers are of a socio-technical nature and impact the acceptance, adoption and use of technology. In this paper we investigate Interactive Digital TV (iDTV) as an example of such emerging technology. We identify and discuss socio-technical barriers that arise in the domain of iDTV. As our method, we present, analyze and discuss a study of iDTV application design situated in the real context of a Brazilian broadcasting company. News and documents from the Brazilian Digital TV Forum portal were used to understand external forces that act on Digital TV and the society. Our findings indicate that iDTV acceptance is negatively influenced by project decisions that do not consider socio-technical constraints, and also the beneficial of the "Socially Aware Computing" perspective to propose design solutions that make sense for stakeholders, including end users.

Keywords: Interactive Digital TV · Human-Computer Interaction · Socially Aware Computing · Organizational Semiotics · Participatory Design

1 Introduction

When trying to access or use emerging technologies, people often face socio-technical barriers that range from affordability to social and technical acceptance and that include cultural and (socio-) cognitive aspects such as values and motivation. As Bannon [4] argues, "the sophisticated and complex technologies available to us" can "confuse us— or even worse, disable us". These barriers have their roots in the outset of ideation and design. Few theoretical and methodological references are available to inform design and evaluation of emerging technologies in the scenario of a society mediated by information and communication technologies [10].

These barriers tend to increase when the design decisions to solutions are motivated mainly by the interests of governments, industry and service providers in detriment of potential benefits or drawbacks for direct and indirect users [6]. In situations where the introduction of a new technology is imposed by norms and laws, the population may

© Springer International Publishing Switzerland 2015
M. Antona and C. Stephanidis (Eds.): UAHCI 2015, Part I, LNCS 9175, pp. 34–45, 2015.
DOI: 10.1007/978-3-319-20678-3_4

not be prepared to receive such technologies, especially those most in need, such as the elderly, disabled, and people in unfavorable socio-economic situations [13].

In this paper, we discuss such barriers and show how they appear in a real design context, how they are identified, influence design decisions, and how designers might deal with them to minimize their impact. The background scenario of our study is interactive Digital TV (iDTV) in the Brazilian context. Digital TV is an emerging technology in Brazil and many other countries [14], and the Brazilian government considers it a promising medium for the dissemination of information and for fostering social and digital inclusion by reducing barriers that prevent the participatory and universal access of Brazilian citizens to knowledge [5].

Our study is situated in the real context of EPTV [17] – a Brazilian broadcasting company with an audience reach of more than ten million people. The study resulted in a prototype for an iDTV application that aims at encouraging and motivating viewers to interact with the TV. The main goal of the discussion presented in this paper was to understand the challenges that arise during the design of an emerging technology in a situated perspective. To understand challenges that are external to the company we used documents and news available in the Brazilian Digital TV System Forum website [14], an entity that brings together the main stakeholders concerned with Digital TV in Brazil.

The paper is organized as follows: Sect. 2 introduces the background scenario of our study, including the socially aware approach proposed to design an iDTV application in the situated context of a TV show. Section 3 describes the study for identifying barriers to be addressed during the design of an iDTV application. Section 4 presents the barriers found in the study. Section 5 shows the design solution proposed by the EPTV team to address the barriers found; it also presents and discusses the main findings from the study, Sect. 6 presents our final considerations and directions for further research.

2 Background

Digital TV was launched in Brazil in 2007. The city of São Paulo was the first city to receive the digital technology, which gradually extended to other cities and metropolitan areas. However, in most Brazilian cities digital transmission is still being offered by a few broadcasters, depending on the population density, market prospects and feasibility inherent to local broadcasters [14].

The implementation of Digital TV in Brazil was conducted in collaboration with the SBTVD Forum. The SBTVD Forum's important mission is to support and stimulate the standardization and quality assurance of the transmission and reception of digital signal (e.g., audio, video and protocols) and data (e.g., iDTV applications). Moreover, it promotes and coordinates technical meetings among receiver and transmission industry, broadcasters, software companies, and also representatives of the research entities, education and federal government that develop activities in Terrestrial Digital TV (e.g., technical, marketing, and promotional issues). The Forum is also responsible for an information portal with news and documents, and it is the main communication channel with the population [14].

EPTV (Portuguese acronym for "Pioneer Broadcasting Television Stations") is affiliate of a large Brazilian broadcaster that is member of SBTVD Forum. Currently, EPTV reaches part of national population that includes 300 cities with more than 10 million people. EPTV provides for this region both regional programming (e.g., journalism, documentaries, programs, and regional advertisers) produced by itself and national programming (e.g., soap operas and national journalism) produced by its parent broadcaster [17]. For instance, EPTV produces the "Terra da Gente" (TdG, "Our Land", in English) program, which is focused on ecotourism, regional cuisine and sport fishing [16].

Since 2007 EPTV has been producing digital programs with high quality of video and audio. In 2008, EPTV began broadcasting its programming in the digital format to some regions, which was gradually extended to all its regions. EPTV wants to add interactive content associated with its various programs in order to increase the viewer interests, and the first EPTV program to receive interactivity will be the TdG program. Interactivity aims to add useful content to complement the program's content, without competing for the audience's attention [17].

Aiming at promoting interactivity with TV as something that makes sense to all stakeholders, and for addressing the complex challenges involved in design of iDTV applications, we adopted a theoretical-methodological background that favors the identification and understanding of the different forces that govern iDTV development at different abstraction levels. Following we present the adopted referential.

2.1 Socially Aware Computing (SAC)

"Socially Aware Computing" (SAC) [2, 3] is a design approach that seeks to understand the complex relationship of signs that govern an organization in its complex social context in order to design a technical system that fits this organization. Therefore, Baranauskas [2] argues that the design of a system involves a cyclical, interactive and iterative movement that begins with understanding the society in which the organization operates, and then goes through the informal and formal layers of this organization towards reaching a technical solution.

SAC is grounded in Organizational Semiotics (OS) [12] as the main theoretical framework articulated with techniques from Participatory Design (PD) [15]. On one hand, while OS provides artifacts that can look systemically for socio-technical layers of an organization, on the other hand, PD allows different stakeholders to discuss their concerns about the system in a participatory way. To understand the organization situational context and the role of a technical system on it, the SAC proposes workshops that bring together the main stakeholders, an heterogeneous group of people who influence and are influenced by the system to be developed, not only the end user [3]. In this sense, it is essential start with stakeholders from technical (iDTV examples: engineers and technicians), formal (e.g., producers, journalists and designers) and informal layers (e.g., audience). Figure 1 shows the semiotic onion and how SAC design approach acts on it.

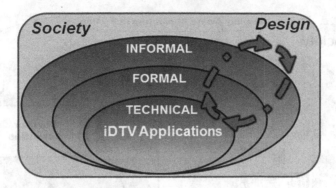

Fig. 1. SAC design approach

3   Practical Study

In order to identify barriers faced during the design of iDTV applications, we mainly used two sources of knowledge:

1. EPTV workshops: 4 workshops conducted inside EPTV in order to design an iDTV application for TdG TV program.
2. SBTVD News: Documents and news produced by the SBTVD Forum [14].

Inside EPTV, we conducted four participatory workshops grounded on SAC approach [2, 3]. The workshops encompassed different design stages spanning problem clarification, solution prospection, requirements identification, content and prototyping ideas, the creation of the user interface for the prototype, and prototype evaluations (see Fig. 2). Ten workshop participants were directly involved in the problem domain, including different profiles such as designers, engineers, researchers, TV program director and interns. The interested reader may consult [7–9] for detailed results and discussions related to these activities.

Complementing the knowledge from EPTV workshops, we reviewed news and documents shared in SBTVD Forum website since 2008. In total, we analyzed around 700 news distributed over the 8 years. Some news are related to the locations where the TV companies began operating in digital signal; and other news are about the status, updates and decisions about Digital TV in Brazil and Latin America. The Forum website has also the presidential decrees and technical standards (ABNT) on Digital TV. Documents are open to public access, and were also used to identify barriers for iDTV applications design.

These two knowledge sources (SBTVD Forum and EPTV workshops) feature information with different nature. On the one hand, the knowledge from the EPTV workshops focuses on the barriers that a TV company may face on situational context that involve from technical to social layers, including society. On the other hand, the knowledge gained from the SBTVD Forum [14] website applies to technical and formal contexts of the focal problem (iDTV application design); it considers all the necessary infra-

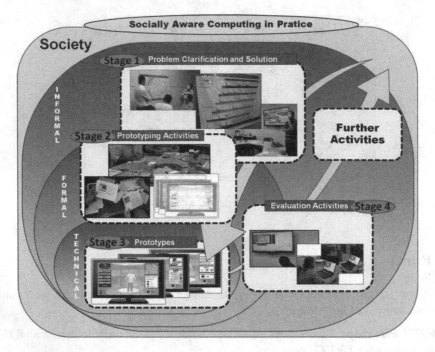

Fig. 2. The design process as an instance of socially aware computing

structure for production and transmission of Digital TV in Brazil, including iDTV applications. For example, this infrastructure defines transmission constraints (e.g., types of modulation), and the basic requirements (minimum and maximum features) receivers must attend to receive the digital signal. This infrastructure also encompasses the entire definition of protocols, languages and hardware configurations for the transmission and reception of iDTV applications.

In the next section, we describe some of the barriers faced for designing iDTV applications encountered during both EPTV workshops and analysis of new and documents produced and posted in the SBTVD's Forum portal.

4   Preliminary Findings and Discussion

This section presents and discusses barriers found in both contexts (SBTVD Forum and EPTV workshops). Barriers marked with the letter "E" (External) came from the knowledge from SBTVD Forum, while barriers marked with the letter "S" (Situational) were identified in the context of EPTV and came from the situational context.

Geographical Barriers (E): On December 2014, the SBTVD Forum reported that "the Japanese-Brazilian digital TV system reaches more than 89 million Brazilians in 425 municipalities, including all the country's capitals, according to the Ministry of Communications" [14]. Brazil is the 5th largest country in terms of territory and population (around 200 million people); 89 million people represent around 44 % of the population receiving the digital signal. This shows that 64 % of the population does not receive the digital signal yet; this represents a barrier once people that do not receive the digital signal will not be able to interact with iDTV applications.

Economic Barriers (E + S): Economic barriers prevent the viewer to receive the digital signal and access television applications. According to news published in September 2014: "Public broadcasters receive government support, but private companies, which are the vast majority, need resources to make the investment." In addition, "the high tax burden was also cited as an obstacle" and "30 % of the final value of the product is the result of taxes. A reduction of the tax burden could speed the deployment of transmission equipment in the cities" [14]. In summary, this kind of news shows that although 44 % of the population are reached by the digital signal, only part of TV companies are transmitting digital signal to certain places.

For the Reception Industry there are economic challenges in order to develop high quality receivers with a competitive cost. These receivers must be economically viable for viewers but also have to be compatible with the Brazilian standard for Digital TV (ABNT). In this regard, the industry has to customize production costs and also the chipsets that compose the receivers.

For TV companies, new technologies also involve financial resources for development and for maintenance. The workshop participants commented that "it is not difficult to find qualified professionals to develop iDTV applications, but to find resources to hire employees to perform services that are outside the scope of TV company production chain." In this sense, investing in new technology should involve the prospect of financial and knowledge return to the TV company.

Viewers also have to deal with economic challenges. In 2007, São Paulo was the pilot city to receive digital signal. However, as reported in news published in September 2014: "1/3 of the São Paulo population still use tube televisions" in the analog version [14]. News published in February 2015 report that the Federal Government created an assistance program to distribute "digital signal receivers to families enrolled in the assistance program". There are government and industry forces to these receivers "mandatory incorporate the interactive capacity" within their features [14].

Socio-Political and Socio-Cultural Barriers (E + S): Digital TV was influenced by political strategies and presidential decrees that established the SBTVD. Among other things, the SBTVD was created to "promote social inclusion, cultural diversity of the country" and to "stimulate the research and development, and encourage the expansion of Brazilian technologies and national industry related to information and communication technology" [5]. Another objective, as reported in SBTVD Forum news published in December 2014, is related to release of bandwidth used by analog TV signal so that it would be possible to create the "infrastructure to support the sign for the fourth-generation Internet (4G)" [14]. Thus, the iDTV in Brazil is an initiative of both government and industry, not necessarily a necessity claimed by society. Thus, these barriers are limiting, although not preventing the design of iDTV applications.

In addition, the Brazil is a country with high level of socio-cultural inequalities. The high diversity of users (regarding age, skills, gender, intentions, literacy, special needs) may influence directly on the design of iDTV applications. In the EPTV workshops, the participants have argued that "considering the diversity of the target audience is an issue that would hardly be treated". These barriers improve the challenges to designing iDTV solutions.

Technical Barriers (E + S): Infrastructure to digital TV should be flexible so that different manufacturers (receivers and transmitters), TV companies and viewers could use the digital TV according to their needs. This technical diversity ensures that manufacturers produce receivers and transmitters of different types and a "set of essential features required by devices" [1]. A technical barrier faced during design came from iDTV receivers' companies: to gain economic advantage, they produce devices with limited processing and memory capacity. For the workshop participants "receivers from some brands not are in accordance with Brazilian Digital TV standard". Thus, "iDTV applications may run incorrectly or even block the receiver". For Kunert [11] other technical challenge is related to the absence of input resources (keyboard and mouse). In this sense, the application should have few resources and functionalities that would enable users to interact with it in a pleasant way.

Kunert [11] also argues that every emergent technology suffers from a lack of references, processes and artifacts for supporting their design. For workshops' participants, designing iDTV applications is a novelty activity, and a design process to guide them is essential to develop the first iDTV applications for TdG TV program.

The interactive channel, which is the communication channel between viewers and broadcasters via the Internet, is not a reality for part of national population yet. This problem comes from geographic and economic barriers and is directly reflected in the technical solutions to be implemented for the design of iDTV applications. For example, if the TV company wants to create a poll in order to identify the satisfaction of viewers regarding a particular program, the interactive channel will be necessary. On the one hand, while some workshop participants were against the use of the interactive channel, on the other hand, other participants pointed out the usefulness and benefits of functionalities that might be obtained with the interactive channel.

Use Barriers (E + S): Workshop participants argued that "an iDTV application for the TdG program must use features that the TV offers and should not need any additional resource from viewers". This barrier is directly related to economic barriers and diversity of users that may affect users with different economic profiles.

An additional use barrier is the diversity of devices surrounding the TV, and competing for the users' attention. Currently, as devices are even more present in our everyday lives it is difficult to build attractive solutions that are restricted to a single device. Thus, analyzing the potentialities and resources from these technologies and bringing these resources and knowledge can be a differential to design solutions that have a good acceptance by their target audience.

Kunert [11] also mentions the lack of habit to interact with television content and the usual presence of other viewers in the same physical space as habits of use from analogical TV that impact negatively on iDTV usage.

Organizational Barriers (S): Workshop participants reported that "any iDTV television created by the parent company or subsidiaries must follow a set of premises that work as a pattern to be followed by the companies. These premises define constraints on the layout type to be used by the iDTV application. Moreover, the participants defined a premise that the application should complement the program content". This barrier partially limits the design options for an iDTV application. In this case, the participants should propose creative solutions that attract the audience and do not disperse the attention of conventional viewers.

Figure 3 shows the identified barriers according to the layers of the Semiotic Onion it operates. For instance, while use and geographic barriers are located in the Semiotic Onion's outside layer, technical and organizational barriers are closer to the Semiotic Onion's core layer.

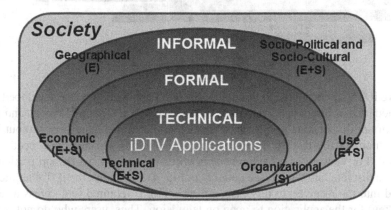

Fig. 3. Barriers mapped to the layers of the Semiotic Onion

5   Designing Solutions to Address the Barriers

In this section we present the solutions proposed by participants from EPTV workshops to lower the barriers pointed out in the previous section. Figure 4 shows some elements of a prototype of the first designed application. The design of the prototype was informed by participatory workshops with the EPTV team. In the remainder of this section, we use this prototype to illustrate design solutions that have been proposed by the participants in order to address the identified barriers.

Geographical Barriers (E): To face geographical barriers, TV companies should have access to the infrastructure of digital technology. Thus, new production and transmission equipment must be purchased to replace analog technology. Currently, EPTV reaches the full coverage area with a digital signal. Therefore, the design of an iDTV application for the TdG program would not suffer from this kind of geographic barriers.

Economic Barriers (E + S): EPTV is a pioneer in the production and transmission of the digital TV signal. Thus, the economic constraints come from the receiver industry and viewers. Accordingly, some viewers still use analog technology or use digital receivers that do not support the interactive channel. Thus, only some viewers are able

Fig. 4. Prototype screenshot

to receive iDTV applications. In this sense, the TdG application being developed must accommodate both users that want and can interact with iDTV applications and those who cannot or do not want to interact with such applications. Receivers without inter-activity automatically discard data regarding applications and no action needs to be performed. For viewers who have receivers with interactivity, workshop participants opted for a discrete initial icon (see detail D in Fig. 4) that shows the iDTV application is loaded into the receiver. In this case, a user action is required (e.g., press a remote control key) for the application to open on television. Thus, users who do not want to interact will not feel uncomfortable with an iDTV application opening without their consent.

Regarding financial resources for the development and maintenance of the iDTV application, the workshop participants stressed the importance of easy maintenance. Thus, the application must be maintained by the engineering or production team without the need to hire new employees.

Technical Barriers (E + S): The strategy adopted by the participants in order to deal with limited processing and memory capacity during the application design was to propose a simple application with clean layout and few images (see details A and B in Fig. 4), compatible with the hardware performance. This application is also easy to broadcast as it is small and will not require a large bandwidth. Furthermore, the iDTV application must be able to automatically customize functionalities as Pool or Quiz after identifying the existence or absence of the interactive channel. These functionalities should be present or absent from the application interface depending on the existence of the interactive channel.

To deal with the receptors that are not in accordance with the Brazilian Digital TV standard, the workshop participants suggested that applications must strictly follow the standard. Final application must also be tested in receptor of several brands before being transmitted with the TdG TV program.

Socio-Political and Socio-Cultural Barriers (E + S): A social-cultural barrier is related to diversity (cognitive, educational, physical, socio-economic, cultural) of Brazilian viewers. In this case, the participants chose to work with few menu options (to reduce cognitive load – see detail A in Fig. 4) and attractive features (for people with high technology affinity – see details B and C in Fig. 4) to attract and motivate different profiles of viewers. For instance, detail C in Fig. 4 shows a Fishing Game: a ludic game to maintain attention from viewers while they watch the TdG TV program. In this case, fishes will appear on the screen and the viewers must select a different remote control key to fish them.

Use Barriers (E + S): Workshop participants established that "the remote control should be the main interaction device." Although the remote control presents several problems regarding the lack of inputs and the difficulty of interaction, it comes with the TV and everyone has access to it. In relation to concurrence with other devices, the iDTV application must have mechanisms and features to attract viewers to interact and/or attract the audience to the TV program. For instance, participants select contents (e.g., making of – see detail B in Fig. 4) and functionalities (e.g., fishing game – see detail C in Fig. 4) that are essential for the TdG program.

Organizational Barriers (S): The participants decided to follow the constraints determined by the parent company. For example, the layout on the screen corners is a suggestion from the parent company so that the application does not disturb users who want to see the television content while another user is interacting with the iDTV application. IDTV application content that complements the TV show with information was another suggestion followed by the participants.

5.1 Discussion

Identifying barriers in the design of iDTV applications is fundamental to propose design solutions compatible with the technology constraints and also with the interests of the organization. In this study, we pointed out barriers of different nature and situated in different levels (from technical to informal level) those were considered and influenced the design of an iDTV application for the TdG program.

When these barriers are neglected, and when no design solutions are proposed to minimize them, the end users may suffer the consequences. Minimizing these barriers is a challenge for most designers of such applications. In this sense, design approaches, such as SAC, can make the difference as there are dynamics that allow looking at the problem from different perspectives and levels of abstraction. In this sense, to propose solutions that made sense to all participants of EPTV workshops it was necessary to involve different stakeholders in discussions. For example, the interactive channel, which allows for direct communication between the TV company and viewers, is not present in every viewer's house. Thus, technical participants were against the use of the interactive channel, while other participants, who enjoy new features, argued by the use of the interactive channel functionalities to attract the target audience. A customizable interface was the solution that pleased the two participant groups.

The use of the SAC approach in a situated context seemed efficient and effective regarding the identification of barriers and proposal of solutions to overcome them. Some of these barriers (e.g., lack of human resources to create and maintain iDTV applications) would only be identified in the real context of an organization.

6 Conclusion

In this paper we discussed the importance of identifying and considering different barriers that may exist in the design of emerging technologies. We situated our discussions in the practical context of a Brazilian broadcast TV organization, where an iDTV application was designed for one of its TV shows. The results presented and discussed in this paper include the identification and situated discussion of the internal and external barriers related to iDTV applications design. We organized these barriers according to the different layers of information systems (informal, formal, technical). We furthermore showed that the barriers influence the design of iDTV applications and indicated how they might be considered during the design process.

Results showed that interaction design in this situated context does not involve only the relationship between humans and computers, but also social, technological, political, cultural, and motivational issues. Ignoring these issues during software design might result in solutions that do not make sense to stakeholders and end users. Discussions also pointed out the effective contribution of SAC to understand this scenario (audience, interests and barriers) in techno-social dimensions. In addition, we argue that industry, government and investors impose iDTV technology and its ecosystem, and decide on solutions for their own benefit, neglecting the interests of the most important stakeholder group: the end users' who buy and use iDTV products. In this sense, adopting the SAC perspective showed to be potentially beneficial to end users.

As further work, we intend to test the design solution with end users, and to verify the application acceptance with the TdG TV program's audience.

Acknowledgment. This research is partially funded by CAPES, CNPq (#165430/2013-3) and FAPESP (2013/02821-1; 2014/01382-7). MCCB receives a Productivity Research Fellowship from CNPq (grant #308618/2014-9). The authors specially thank the EPTV team, and the all participants who collaborated and authorized the use of their data in this paper. This work is part of a project that was approved by Unicamp Institutional Review Board CAAE (#37341414.4.0000.5404).

References

1. ABNT, Brazilian Association of Technical Standards. http://www.abnt.org.br. Accessed on 13 Feb 2015
2. Baranauskas, M.C.C.: Socially aware computing. In: Proceedings of VI International Conference on Engineering and Computer Education (ICECE 2009), pp. 1–5 (2009)
3. Baranauskas, M.C.C.: Social awareness in HCI. ACM Interact. **21**, 66–69 (2014)
4. Bannon, L.: Reimagining HCI: toward a more human-centered perspective. Interactions **18**(4), 50–57 (2011)

5. Presidential decree No 4.901, Brasil. http://www.planalto.gov.br/ccivil_03/decreto/2003/d4901.htm. Accessed 31 July 2014
6. Van den Broeck, W., Bauwens, J.: The promises of iDTV: between push marketing and consumer needs. In: Proceedings of the 7th European Conference on Interactive TV and Video (EuroITV 2009), pp. 41–48 (2009)
7. Buchdid, S.B., Pereira, R., Baranauskas, M.C.C.: Creating an iDTV application from inside a TV company: a situated and participatory approach. In: 15th International Conference on Informatics and Semiotics in Organisations (ICISO 2014), pp. 63–73 (2014)
8. Buchdid, S.B., Pereira, R., Baranauskas, M.C.C.: Playing cards and drawing with patterns: situated and participatory practices for designing iDTV applications. In: 16th International Conference on Enterprise Information Systems (ICEIS 2014), pp. 14–27 (2014)
9. Buchdid, S.B., Pereira, R., Baranauskas, M.C.: You can interact with your TV and you may like it an investigation on persuasive aspects for an iDTV application. In: Marcus, A. (ed.) DUXU 2014, Part IV. LNCS, vol. 8520, pp. 208–219. Springer, Heidelberg (2014)
10. Harrison, S., Tatar, D., Sengers, P.: The three paradigms of HCI. In: Alt.CHI, CHI 2007, pp. 1–18. ACM Press (2007)
11. Kunert, T.: User-Centered Interaction Design Patterns for Interactive Digital Television Applications. Springer, New York (2009)
12. Liu, K.: Semiotics in Information Systems Engineering. Cambridge University Press, Cambridge (2000)
13. Quico, C., Damásio, M.J., Henriques S.: Digital TV adopters and non-adopters in the context of the analogue terrestrial TV switchover in Portugal. In: Proceedings of the 10th European Conference on Interactive TV and Video, EuroITV 2012, pp. 213–222. ACM, New York (2012)
14. SBTVD Forum, Brazilian Digital TV Forum. http://www.forumsbtvd.org.br. Accessed on 15 Feb 2015
15. Schuler, D., Namioka, A. (eds.): Participatory Design: Principles and Practices. Erlbaum, Hillsdale (1993)
16. Terra da Gente, Terra da Gente news portal. http://www.terradagente.com.br. Accessed 15 Jan 2015
17. Via EPTV, EPTV news portal. http://www.viaeptv.com. Accessed 10 Feb 2015

Consideration of Measuring Human Physical and Psychological Load Based on Brain Activity

Hiroaki Inoue[1]([✉]), Shunji Shimizu[1], Ishihara Hirotaka[1], Yuuki Nakata[1], Hiroyuki Nara[2],
Takeshi Tsuruga[3], Fumikazu Miwakeichi[4], Nobuhide Hirai[5], Senichiro Kikuchi[6],
Satoshi Kato[6], and Eiju Watanabe[6]

[1] Tokyo University of Science, SUWA, Nagano, Japan
jgh12701@ed.tus.ac.jp, shun@rs.suwa.tus.ac.jp
[2] Hokkaido University, Sapporo, Japan
nara@ssc.ssi.ist.hokudai.ac.jp
[3] Hokkaido Institute of Technology, Sapporo, Japan
tsuruga@hit.ac.jp
[4] The Institute of Statistical Mathematics, Tachikawa, Japan
Miwake1@ism.ac.jp
[5] Tokyo Medical and Dental University, Bunkyo, Japan
nobu@nobu.com
[6] Jichi Medical University, Shimotsuke, Japan
{skikuchi,psykato}@jichi.ac.jp,
Eiju-ind@umin.ac.jp

Abstract. In Japan and developed countries, it has become aged society, and wide variety welfare device or system have been developed. But these evaluation methods of welfare device or system are limited only stability, intensity and partial operability. Because of, it is not clear to determine the standard to evaluation for welfare device or system of usefulness. Therefore, we will attempt to establish the standard for evaluation about usefulness for objectively and quantitatively for including non-verbal cognition. We examine the relationship between human movements and brain activity, and consider the evaluation method of welfare devices and systems to measure the load and fatigue which were felt by human. In this paper, we measure the load for sitting and standing movement using NISR. We tried to make sure for the possibility of the quantitatively estimation for physical or psychological load or fatigue by measuring of brain activity using NIRS (Near Infra Red Spectroscopy). As results, when subjects perform the movement task, the statistical significant difference was shown in the specific part of the brain region.

Keywords: NIRS · EMG · Welfare technology · Useful welfare device evaluation

1 Introduction

As it has been known widely, aging population in Japan and world-wide countries has been increasing. Thereby the number of care worker has been increasing. Care is very

© Springer International Publishing Switzerland 2015
M. Antona and C. Stephanidis (Eds.): UAHCI 2015, Part I, LNCS 9175, pp. 46–53, 2015.
DOI: 10.1007/978-3-319-20678-3_5

hard work. Welfare devices and systems reducing a burden of the care work are required. In this background, welfare systems and device are rapidly developing, and various devices are manufactured based on the increased popularity of welfare device and system. Also, the market of welfare devices and systems is expanding. However, the evaluation method is limited respectively to stability, strength and a part of operability for individual system or device. It means that evaluation methodology for usefulness of them was not established. Therefore, we will attempt to establish a standard to evaluate the usefulness for objectively and quantitatively on the basis of cognition such as physical load, reduction of fatigue and postural stability. Especially, in considering universality, it is necessary to measure human movement in daily life. Movement was not measured by using particular device, but routinely-performed movement in daily life.

Recently, technology of measuring brain activity is progressed. Previous measurement apparatus limited subject's posture and experimental condition. NIRS has little such limitation in posture and the experiment condition. Because there was such advantage, we used NIRS in this study (Fig. 1).

2 Experimental Method

2.1 Evaluation by Using NIRS

We measured brain activity during motion with the purpose of establishing evaluation method based on generality (Fig. 2).

Subjects were six males aged twenties. They were asked to read and sign an informed consent regarding the experiment. Measurement apparatus was NIRS (SHIMADZU CO. Ltd products-FOIRE3000 [4]). Measurement region was at right and left prefrontal cortex.

Measuring Brain Activity During Transfer with Standing Position (Task1). At this measurement, the subjects used welfare device to perform transferring in a standing position. In this measurement, subject sat on seating face of welfare device appeared on the top of chair after raising hip until sitting posture in an invisible chair. Also, subject performed inverse transferring from seating face to chair. Time design was rest(5 s), task(10 s), and rest(5 s). This time design was repeated 30 times. Rest time is to stabilize the brain activity. In the measurement NIRS, we have started to measure brain activity of the subject becomes stable. Therefore, rest of the most first is least 5 s. It also applies to the measurement of other experiments.

Measuring Brain Activity During Transfer with Sitting Posture in an Invisible Chair (Task2). At this measurement, the subjects used welfare device to perform transferring in a sitting posture in an invisible chair. In this measurement, the subjects sat on seating face of welfare device appeared on the top of chair after raising hip until sitting posture in an invisible chair. Also, the subject performed inverse transfer from seating face to chair. Time design was rest(5 s), task(10 s) and rest(5 s). This time design was repeated 30 times.

In experiments of task1 and task2, operation of welfare device was performed by operator other than subject. Before this measuring, subjects adjusted to transferring by use of welfare device.

3 Experimental Results

3.1 Evaluation by Using NIRS

As the common result of all subjects, oxy-Hb tended to increase during task and to decrease in resting state. Therefore, it was thought that change of hemoglobin density due to task was measured. Figures 3 and 4 show trend of the channel in which significant different was shown. Analysis was performed via one-sample t-test [5–9] by a method similar to previous researches [5–9]. In this analysis, it was necessary to remove other than change of blood flow due to fatigue. So, our method was mainly focused on resting state to compare with the 1st trial and other trials of brain activity.

In task1, 1 and 2, each of sample data for analysis was 4 s after the task (Fig. 2). In the t-test of the same task, we performed t-test with first time trial and other trial which was from second times to thirty times, and examined relationship the number of trials and significant differences.

In task 1, significant different could be found from the about 10th trials. Figure 5 show the region confirmed significant difference. In task 2, significant different could be found from the about 10th trials too. Figure 6 shows region confirmed significant difference.

At first, we performed t-test using 4 s during first trial and 4 s during other trials, which were from second to fifteenth in same position.

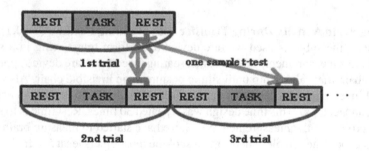

Fig. 1. T-test of sample data in task1 and 2

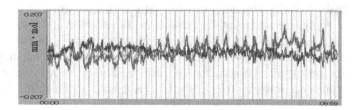

Fig. 2. Measuring result of task1

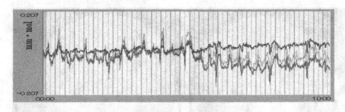

Fig. 3. Measuring result of task2

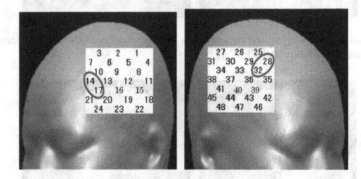

Fig. 4. Signififant difference of task1 (Color figure online)

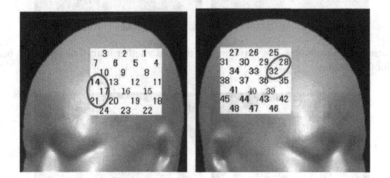

Fig. 5. Significant difference of task2 (Color figure online)

Results of Brain Activity Measurements When the Load was Applied to the Subjects.
Analysis method was one-sample t-test of brain activity data as with above analysis.
Figure 7 shows the result of one sample t-test between first trial of rest data and another
trial of rest data. This analysis method was same with Fig. 2. Figures 8 and 9 shows the
result of one sample t-test with brain activity data of different movement in the same
number of trials. Red circle is the brain region that has seen a statistically significant difference in 5 of 6 subjects. Yellow circle show the brain region that has seen a statistically
significant difference in 4 subjects. Green circle show the brain region that has seen a statistically significant difference in 3 subjects.

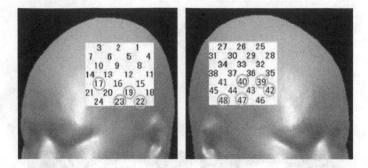

Fig. 6. Result of one sample t-test between first tial and another trials when subjects had no additional load (Color figure online)

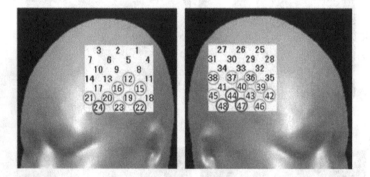

Fig. 7. Result of one sample t-test between first tial and another trials when subjects had 5 kg load (Color figure online)

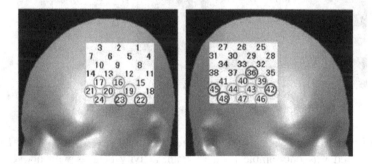

Fig. 8. Result of one sample t-test between first tial and another trials when subjects had 10 kg load (Color figure online)

In the both t-test, there were significant difference on the prefrontal cortex. These results were similar to above experiments. However, significant differences were found randomly regardless of the number of trials. As the cause of these results, there is a possibility that t-test could not remove the changes in scalp of blood flow.

t-test [5–9] by a method similar to previous researches [5–9]. In this analysis, it was necessary to remove other than change of blood flow due to fatigue. So, our method was mainly focused on resting state to compare with the 1st trial and another trials of brain activity.

In task1 1 and 2, each of sample data for analysis was 4 s after the task (Fig. 4).

In the t-test of the same task, we performed t-test with first time trial and other trial which was from second times to thirty times, and examined relationship the number of trials and statistically significant differences.

In task 1, significant different could be found from the about 10th trials. Figure 9 show region confirmed statistically significant difference.

In task 2, significant different could be found from the about 10th trials too. Figure 10 show region confirmed statistically significant difference.

Next, we performed t-test with case of standing position (task 1) and sitting posture in an invisible chair(task 2). In this analysis, significant different could be found at prefrontal area(14ch, 17ch, 28ch and 32ch). Figure 11 shows region confirmed significant different.

4 Discussion

4.1 Evaluation by Using NIRS

In this experiment, we tried to measure quantitatively the physical and psychological strain on the basis of brain activity. Also, we think that brain activity disclose human cognitive including non-verbal. As a result, it was shown that there were differences at brain activity due to number of trials and postural. In this time, analysis was performed via one-sample t-test using sample of brain activity in resting state during task or after task. Hence, analysis method was to remove disturbance such as body motion and angular variation of neck to the extent possible although there was the possibility to measure skin blood flow. Therefore, it was thought that strain due to tasks was quantitatively measured by being recognized significant differences. Also, in previous research, it was reported to decrease in activity in the brain around #10, 11 [10], as the result of measuring brain activity during Advanced Trial Making Test using PET [11]. Therefore, this result came out in support of previous research in no small part.

Results of Brain Activity Measurements When the Load was Applied to the Subjects. As a step to make the evaluation method, we performed additional experiment, which is imposed to subjects the load other than using the welfare devices. Significant difference was observed in the brain region similar to previous experiments. And, each time the load increases, brain regions found statistically significant differences became widespread. And, the frequency of showing the statistical significant difference became the higher. We think that there are the possibility of happen this results by the additional load.

Of course, it is necessary to increase number of subject at the present stage. In addition, there are problems associated with experiment, number of subject, method and measured region. However, in terms of being recognized significant differences at brain activity due to movement, it was thought to show useful result in evaluating quantitatively daily movements.

5 Conclusion

In this paper, we tried to measure physical and psychological load with measuring brain activity. And there were significant differences due to number of trials. In this experiment, analysis method was to remove disturbance such as body motion and angular variation of neck to the extent possible by using the measurement result in resting state as sample. Therefore, it was thought to show the useful result in evaluating quantitatively load due to movement task by being recognized difference in brain activity caused by number of trials.

Main purpose in this study is to evaluate physical load and fatigue quantitatively. So, we tried to evaluate change of muscle load due to difference of motion by simultaneous measuring with 3D motion analysis System and EMG quantitatively.

However, evaluation of psychological load is necessary, too. In terms of using welfare device, prolonged use must be taken into account. In this case, it is important to consider not only physical load but also psychological load due to prolonged use from standpoint of developing welfare device and keeping up surviving bodily function.

Also, in previous research, separation between physical and psychological load has been performed. But, our view is that there is correlation with physical and psychological load. So, we tried to measure psychological load including physical one based on brain activity and quantitatively evaluate both load.

References

1. Inoue, H., Shimizu, S., Tkahashi, N., Nara, H., Tsuruga, T., Miwakeichi, F., Hirai, N., Kikuchi, S., Watanabe, E., Kato, S.: Fundamental study to new evaluation method based on physical and psychological load in care. In: IARIA COGNITIVE 2012, Nice, France, pp. 101–106 (2012)
2. Shinoda, Y.: Considertion of feature extraction based on center of gravity for Nihon Buyo dancer using motion capture system. In: SICE Annual Conference, Tokyo, Japan, pp. 1874–1878 (2011)
3. Yamaguchi, Y., Ishikawa, A., Ito, Y.: Development of biosignal integration analysis system for human brain function and behavior, Organization for Human Brain Mapping, China pp. 329–336 (2012)
4. Inoue, H., Shimizu, S., Takahashi, N., Nara, H., Tsuruga, T.: Fundamental study for evaluation of the effect due to exercise load, assistive technology, Bio Medical Engineering and Life Support, Japan (2011)
5. Watanabe, E., Yamashita, Y., Ito, Y., Koizumi, H.: Non-invasive functional mapping with multi-channel near infra-red spectroscopic topography in humans. Heurosci. Lett. **205**(1), 41–44 (1996)
6. Takahashi, N., Shimizu, S., Hirata, Y., Nara, H., Miwakeichi, F., Hirai, N., Kikuchi, S., Watanabe, E., Kato, S.: Fundamental study for a new assistive system during car driving. In: Proceedings of International Conferrence on Robotics and Biomimetics, DVD-ROM, Tenjin, China (2010)

7. Takahashi, N., Shimizu, S., Hirata, Y., Nara, H., Inoue, H., Hirai, N., Kikuchi, S., Watanabe, E., Kato, S.: Basic study of analysis of human brain activities during car driving. In: The 14th International Conferrence on Human-Computer Interaction, USA (2011)
8. Shimizu, S., Takahashi, N., Nara, H., Inoue, H., Hirata, Y.: Fundamental study for human brain activity based on the spatial cognitive task. In: The International Conference on Brain Informatics-BI, China (2011)
9. Shimizu, S., Takahashi, N., Nara, H., Inoue, H., Hirata, Y.: Basic study for human brain activity based on the spatial cognitive task. In: The Third International Conference on Advanced Cognitive Techonologies and Applications, Italy (2011)
10. Shimizu, S., Takahashi, N., Inoue, H., Nara, H., Miwakeichi, F., Hirai, N., Kikuchi, S., Watanabe, E., Kato, S.: Basic study for a new assitive system based on brain activity associated with spatial perception task during car driving. In: Proceedings of International Conferrence on Robotics and Biomimetics, Thailand (2011)
11. Watanabe, Y.: Molecular/neural mechanisms of fatigue, and the way to overcome fatigue. Folia Pharmacol. Jpn. **129**, 94–98 (2007)
12. Kuratsune, H., Yamaguti, K., Lindh, G., Evengard, B., Hagberg, G., Matsumura, K., Iwase, M., Onoe, H., Takahashi, M., Machii, T., Kanakura, Y., Kitani, T., Langstrom, B., Watanage, Y.: Brain regions involved in fatigue sensation: reduced acetylcarnitine uptake into the brain. Neuroimage **17**, 1256–1265 (2001)
13. Maruta, K.: The influence of seat angle on forward trunk inclination during sit-to-stand. J. Jpn. Phys. Ther. Assoc. **31**(1), 21–28 (2004)

Defining Acceptable Interaction for Universal Access

Simeon Keates[✉]

University of Greenwich, Medway Campus, Central Avenue, Chatham Maritime,
Kent, ME4 4TB, UK
s.keates@gre.ac.uk

Abstract. Many new assistive input systems developed to meet the needs of users with functional impairments fail to make it out of the research laboratory and into regular use by the intended end users. This paper examines some of the reasons for this and focuses particularly on whether the developers of such systems are using the correct metrics for evaluating the functional attributes of the input technologies they are designing. In particular, the paper focuses on the issue of benchmarking new assistive input systems against a baseline measure of useful interaction rate that takes allowance of factors such as input success/recognition rate, error rate, correction effort and input time. By addressing each of these measures, a more complete understanding of whether an input system is practically and functionally acceptable can be obtained.

Keywords: Interaction rate · Universal access · HCI · Input technologies · Error rate · Assistive technologies · Acceptability

1 Introduction

Much of the research into Universal Access, both past and present, has focused on the development of new and innovative assistive input device and interface design technologies for users with functional impairments. It is widely accepted that the traditional keyboard and mouse input arrangement does not serve those with a range of functional impairments well [1].

For example, a person with severe vision impairment will experience significant difficulties in using a mouse, not least because the feedback on the position of the cursor on the screen is invariably visual only. Similarly, users with motor impairments will typically experience comparable levels of difficulty, because of the challenges presented in generating the quality of limb and digit control usually required to position a mouse, click on its buttons or type on a keyboard [2]. Consequently, many researchers have taken the view that perhaps a new input device/user interface arrangement [e.g. 3] or a re-design of the device/interface [e.g. 4] may alleviate or remedy the difficulties faced by many such users.

However, while the motivation for developing new assistive input and interaction technologies is clear, the success of such devices has been mixed. It is still a common problem that many of the new technologies developed rarely progress beyond the

© Springer International Publishing Switzerland 2015
M. Antona and C. Stephanidis (Eds.): UAHCI 2015, Part I, LNCS 9175, pp. 54–63, 2015.
DOI: 10.1007/978-3-319-20678-3_6

research laboratory. Of those that do, many end up simply collecting dust on shelves, never really used to the extent anticipated by their developers [5].

There are many reasons why individual assistive input technologies suffer this fate, but there are a few that are reliably useful indicators of the likely success or otherwise of such developments. Jakob Nielsen, for example, has identified that the success of a product depends on it meeting both practical/functional acceptability and social acceptability criteria [6]. He defines practical acceptability as including factors such as cost, reliability, utility/functionality and usability. Social acceptability considers factors such as brand identity, stigma, etc.

There is a large body of work looking at usability theory and overall acceptability of products and systems. This paper focuses on one aspect in particular, that of the challenge of establishing whether the practical acceptability offered by assistive input systems has genuinely been met.

It is accepted that one of the principal reasons for the failure of the uptake of these new solutions is that their development has typically focused on the functional/technical issues, i.e., getting the solution to work, often to the detriment of the softer/social issues, i.e., does it meet the wants, needs and/or aspirations of the users [7].

It is also correct, though, to recognize that a failure to meet the practical acceptability criteria will also translate to a failure of the product or system to succeed in the real world. For assistive input systems, one of the major difficulties has been that the functional aspect of the development often only considers a narrow part of the interaction process as the metric of success. In many cases, this is usually input recognition rate [e.g. 8]. This paper explores the possibility of developing more complete measure of the functionality of new input devices.

2   Functional Impairments and Computer Access

There are several approaches to categorizing types of functional impairment. One of the most straightforward was inspired by the work of Card, Moran and Newell on the Model Human Processor [9]. Effectively, they proposed a model of interaction that consists of three elements:

$$\text{Total time} = x\,\tau_p + y\,\tau_c + z\,\tau_m \qquad (1)$$

In this equation, x, y and z are integers and τ_p, τ_c and τ_m correspond to the times for single occurrences of the perceptual, cognitive and motor functions respectively. It is possible to categorize impairments along these lines of functionality.

Perceptual impairments are those that affect a user's ability to perceive the state of the world around them and are principally focused on the five senses. In the case of computer access, the human senses of most interest are vision and hearing [10]. Indeed, vision impairments have received arguably the lion's share of research effort and also have the most successful assistive technologies to facilitate better interaction, with products such as JAWS achieving strong market positions [11]. Blindness and low vision present challenges with most stages of human-computer interaction, from input actions, such as text entry and cursor control, to perceiving output, such as reading text on a screen or interpreting a figure or diagram.

Cognitive impairments are those that affect the user's ability to understand or respond to the state of the world around them. Such impairments can include memory loss or reduction, learning and communication difficulties and executive function limitations [12]. It is often argued that cognitive impairments are the most "hidden" ones, since their presence is often more difficult to identify and, once identified, to also diagnose. However, they are beginning to be researched more frequently [e.g. 13] than, say, 10 years ago. Typical solutions can include personalized diaries and reminders for medication and other reminders, assistive word processors for help with typing and dialogue structures, etc. More innovative solutions include emotion and affective state recognition to assist people with Asperger's and forms of autism [14] and also deep question and answer systems, such as IBM Watson [15].

Finally, motor impairments can create difficulties with both text entry and cursor control in a typical computer interaction scenario [1]. Symptoms such as tremor, spasm, restricted range of motion and weakened muscles can make both gross and fine motor control a challenge [1].

Text entry assistance typically focuses on making keyboards more accessible through physical assistance, for example adding keyguards, or using "soft" on-screen keyboards or replacements, such as Dasher [16]. On-screen, soft keyboards are usually activated by a dwell time function (in the case of a cursor control replacement system) or some form of binary switch/scanning combination [5].

Cursor assistance can be in the form of adapted mouse replacement devices, such as tablets or specially design mice/joysticks/trackballs [1]. One area of particular promise is that of haptic assistance, such as through the addition of "gravity" to on-screen targets [17]. Other approaches include adapting or altering the processing of the cursor input stream to make targets more "sticky" by slowing the cursor down over the targets or by fixing a mouse button activation to the location of the button down event, not the button up one [18]. More radical solutions involve changing the input paradigm from the usual windows/icons approach to that of using gestures for the input [19], for example.

As can be seen, there are many forms of functional impairments that can affect human-computer interaction adversely and present specific challenges to particular users. There are also many forms of potential assistance, each of which offer their own particular combination of strengths and weaknesses. As discussed earlier, not all of these assistive solutions are successful in the wild, so the question then becomes whether there are more effective methods for identifying or predicting whether a particular solution has a genuine chance of successful adoption by users in real world circumstances.

As regards determining the social acceptability of a new technology or product, approaches such as focus groups, user evaluations, etc., would usually be used [20]. These methods are generally well understood and widely accepted. However, there is less of a consensus on methods of evaluating the practical acceptability of novel interaction technologies.

3   Establishing a Measure of "Acceptable" Interaction

Most research papers addressing the development of novel input systems or interaction paradigms usually focus on only one or two measures of success, principally the rate of successful completion of a specified task, such as clicking on a target or producing a particular gesture that is recognized correctly by the computer. While clearly a very important measure, focusing on this metric only can lead to an exaggerated view of the efficacy of the new input system/interface. There are other important factors to consider, such as the definition of usability used by ISO [21]:

- Efficiency – i.e. the time taken and effort expended to complete a task.
- Effectiveness – i.e. the ability to complete the task.
- Satisfaction – i.e. user contentedness with the interaction.

Using these definitions, satisfaction is typically measured through user surveys, interviews, questionnaires, etc., after completing a series of tasks using the new technology [7]. Efficiency is usually calculated by looking that the task completion rates and times. Measuring effectiveness involves looking at error rates and effort expended to correct for any errors that occur as well as proportion of tasks completed [22]. However, while research papers addressing the development of assistive input systems that include some form of user evaluation with the prototype system usually include a summary of task completion times (i.e. a variant of the efficiency metric above) and task completion rates (i.e. a partial treatment of the effectiveness metric), it is less common to find an exploration of the frequency of errors. It is even less common to find an analysis of the impact of those errors, with some experimental designs not even recognizing the presence of errors.

Even in the comparatively rare instances where such analyses exist, it can be argued that the final piece of the jigsaw is still missing – i.e. a comparison with an accepted baseline measure. Fundamentally, even where the developers do such analysis, they often fail to reflect on whether the assistive input system that they have developed meets an acceptable level of interaction. It is all well and good to say that it takes x seconds to complete a task, with an error rate of y %, but the real question is whether those task completion and error rates are acceptable to the intended end users [23]. Basically, the question that really needs to be asked is:

- *Does this new assistive input system equal or outperform the other systems available to the end users?*

If the answer to this question is negative then that immediately casts doubt upon the likely successful adoption of the system being developed by users outside of the research laboratory. Fundamentally, if users can obtain better interaction rates using an existing, and most likely proven, assistive input system then they are less likely to wish to switch to a new or different one.

Even where the answer to the question above is positive, there is still a further question to be asked:

- *Does this new assistive input system meet the full needs, wants and aspirations of the end users?*

A simpler, more direct formulation of this question is:

- *Is this new assistive input system good enough?*

The reason for asking this second question is that for users with more severe impairments there may not be a suitable or practical input system readily available. However, in all but the most extreme cases, some form of input is usually possible through the use of simple binary, i.e. on/off, switches and a scanning on-screen keyboard. Consequently, it can be argued that the very minimum target for user acceptance of a new assistive input system is that it should at least outperform the scanning/binary switch input approach.

3.1   Measuring Text Input

Text input is typically reported in terms of words per minute [e.g. 24]. It may also be reported as characters per minute, if that is a more meaningful metric, such as when typing rates are unusually slow or where a more detailed analysis is required [25].

However, defining a "word" is not straightforward. Many approaches simply assume that a word is 5 characters in length, with a following space implicitly (5 characters) or explicitly (5 + 1 characters) associated with it. In many modern systems, the impact of word prediction systems needs to be considered. It is not clear how often users need to actually enter all 5 characters to make a word when a predictive system is also being used, thus raising a question over the calculations made using the 5 or 5 + 1 assumptions.

There is a choice to be made over how to handle errors. Some researchers simply choose to ignore that errors may exist, e.g. by not supporting or allowing error correction in the design of the experiment. Others remove words with errors in them from the data analysis. Neither of these are ideal solutions when looking at users with motor impairments where errors will most often carry a significant correction penalty, i.e. the amount of effort required to correct any errors will be non-trivial, and also where the frequency of errors can be expected to be significant.

Where errors are identified, they are typically reported through metrics that capture deviations from the expected minimum, error-free input, such as Mean String Distance (MSD) or Keystrokes per Character (KSPC) [26]:

$$MSD \approx \frac{INF}{C + INF} * 100\% \tag{2}$$

$$MSD \approx \frac{C + INF + IF + F}{C + INF} \tag{3}$$

where INF = Incorrect and Not Fixed character entries, IF = Incorrect but Fixed, F = Fixing non-character entries (e.g. a backspace or other edit function) and C = Correct character entries. Other measures are possible [26], but are not used as often as MSD and KSPC.

3.2   Measuring Cursor Input

The most common approach to measuring cursor input is to use a Fitts' Law type experiment. Fitts' Law has undergone a number of modifications since first proposed and one of the more common formulations is the Shannon one [e.g. 27]:

$$Movement\_Time = a + b * ID \tag{4}$$

where a and b are constants and the Index of Difficulty (ID) is:

$$ID = \log_2 \left(\frac{A}{W} + 1 \right) \tag{5}$$

in which A is the distance travelled towards the target and W is the width of the target along the direction of travel.

Although experiments have confirmed that Fitts' Law can be applied to users with motor impairments, there is again little explicit handling of errors. A more sophisticated set of cursor measures has been developed to look at the detail of the quality of cursor control [28] and these measures have been applied successfully to examine the quality of cursor control for users with severe motor impairments [29]. Again, though, while these measures can tell a lot about what is happening to the cursor input, they do not necessarily help researchers and designers determine if the quality of the input is sufficiently good by themselves. There is a clear need for a baseline measure to compare against.

3.3   Measuring Overall Interaction Rate

As can be seen from the discussion above, there are many ways of examining the details of human-computer interaction. However, while those methods may make good research tools, they do not typically answer the question raised earlier – specifically: *is the input system good enough*?

To answer this question succinctly, a simple metric needs to be considered, one that can help a developer or researcher know immediately if the new system is operating in the correct ballpark. A likely candidate for such a measure is the bit rate of useful information transfer between the user and the computer utilizing the assistive input system.

An example of how such a calculation can be made is illustrated by a gesture recognition system [30]. In that experiment, users were able to generate a range of possible gestures (the vocabulary). Rather than using a simple recognition rate, a scoring system was implemented where correctly recognized gestures were scored as +1, non-recognized gestures were scored as a 0 or null return and misrecognized gestures were scored as −1 to reflect that a corrective action would be needed to fix the error. The overall input samples gathered from each user were then normalized and scaled to a range of −100 to +100 to remove any data collection inconsistencies.

That score was then combined with the vocabulary size and the time taken to produce and recognize each gesture into a single measure, the bit rate of useful information transfer between the user and the system:

$$Bit\_rate = \frac{\log_2 (Vocabulary\_size) * \frac{Score}{100}}{Time\_taken} \qquad (6)$$

It can be seen from the formulation of Eq. (6) that a system scoring 0 or less will not generate any useful bit rate since the user will be permanently trying to correct incorrect inputs, which is intuitively correct.

3.4 Benchmarking the Interaction Rate

If the notion of the bit rate of useful information transfer is taken as the most appropriate measure for benchmarking the practical acceptability of an assistive input system, then it is further possible to establish a baseline to compare the bit rate against.

As discussed earlier, the most basic working input system for almost all users with severe motor impairments is the simple binary switch used in conjunction with a scanning on-screen keyboard. Each successful binary switch input will generate 1 bit of information by definition. It is known from the work on the Model Human Processor [9] that for an able-bodied user the typical response time to a stimulus is ≈ 250 ms, where the perceptual response time (τ_p) ≈ 100 ms, cognitive cycle time (τ_c) ≈ 70 ms and motor response time (τ_m) ≈ 70 ms. Thus, if we assume no prediction, the idealized input interaction for an able-bodied user would look something like:

$$Time\_per\_input = \tau_p \text{ [see the choice]} + 2\tau_c \text{ [identify each of the options]}$$
$$+ \tau_c \text{ [decide on which option]} + \tau_m \text{ [operate the switch]} + f(t) \qquad (7)$$

where f(t) is the mean time for the scanning input to land on the option to be selected. In the limiting case, and without the ability to predict ahead, the fastest scanning speed possible is anticipated to be 250 ms per target. If standard able-bodied performance parameters are used in Eq. (7), the mean idealized time per bit of useful information using such a scanning keyboard is approximately 100 ms + 140 ms + 70 ms + 70 ms + 250 ms = 630 ms, giving a useful information transfer bandwidth of (1/0.63) = 1.59 bits/s. For comparison, the bits rates seen for the gesture recognition system used in [30] ranged from 0.56 bits/s to 0.77 bits/s.

Of course, the values used in (7) above were derived for able-bodied users. The comparable values for motor impaired users have also been determined empirically [31]. Typical values for each of the Model Human Processor parameters were found to be: perceptual response time (τ_p) ≈ 100 ms, cognitive cycle time (τ_c) ≈ 110 ms and motor response time (τ_c) $\approx 110, 210$ or 310 ms, depending on the severity of the impairment. From these values, it can be seen that a baseline idealized interaction time for the binary switch/scanning input is approximately 100 ms + 220 ms + 110 ms + 110|210| 310 ms + f(t). Note that f(t) may have to be varied to allow for the range of reaction times, i.e. 320 ms, 420 ms or 520 ms depending on the severity of the impairment and thus also the associated motor function time.

Consequently, using these assumptions, the best-case interaction rate for a user with a motor impairment is (1/0.86) = 1.16 bits/s (based on τ_m = 110 ms). For users with severe motor impairments, that rate decreases to $(1/1.05) = 0.95$ bits/s. It can be seen from these calculations that the binary switch and scanning input outperforms the gesture input system described in [30].

4   Conclusions

To improve the success of assistive input systems outside of the research laboratory, it is necessary for researchers and developers to take a more sophisticated view of how well the systems that they are developing genuinely meet the needs of the users. While methods for assessing the social acceptability of such systems are widely understood, although not necessarily undertaken, there is much more variability over the approaches to measure the practical acceptability of such systems.

This paper has discussed the notion of focusing on a single measure, *the bit rate of useful information transfer*, as a possible more sophisticated metric than measures such as recognition rate. It has also introduced a method for establishing a straightforward baseline for such a measure to be compared with.

The measure and baseline can be further improved – this paper proposes them as a work in progress and not as a definitive set of baselines. For example, the scoring system used in [30] could be modified to penalize incorrect recognitions further to better reflect the effort required to correct an error. Equally, the approximations for f(t) in Eq. (7) should be determined empirically and an error rate could be introduced. In practice, it would be rare for a user to be faced with an unexpected choice for the scanning input. An element of t prediction and anticipation would usually be expected, where f(t) could perhaps tend to significant reductions in the times used above.

Overall, though, the use of such a metric would help designers and researchers understand the likely success or otherwise of a new assistive input system more clearly than the metrics that currently prevail.

References

1. Keates, S.: Motor Impaired Users and Universal Access. Universal Access Handbook, pp. 5.1–5.14. Taylor and Francis, London (2009)
2. Paradise, J., Trewin, S., Keates, S.: Using pointing devices: difficulties encountered and strategies employed. In: Proceedings of the 3rd International Conference on Universal Access in Human-Computer Interaction, Las Vegas, NV, July 2005, pp. 22–27 (2005)
3. Keates, S., Trewin, S.: Effects of age and Parkinson's disease on cursor positioning using a mouse. In: Proceedings of 7th International ACM SIGACCESS Conference on Computers and Accessibility (ASSETS 2005), Baltimore, MD, October 2005, pp. 68–75 (2005)
4. Hanson, V., Brezin, J.P., Crayne, S., Keates, S., Kjeldsen, R., Richards, J.T., Swart, C., Trewin, S.: Improving web accessibility through an enhanced open-source browser. IEEE/IBM Syst. J. (Spec. Ed. Accessibility) 44(3), 573–588 (2005). IEEE
5. Keates, S., Potter, R., Perricos, C., Robinson, P.: Gesture recognition - research and clinical perspectives. In: Proceedings of RESNA 1997, Pittsburgh, PA, pp. 333–335 (1997)
6. Nielsen, J.: Usability Engineering. Morgan Kaufman, San Francisco (1993)

7. Keates, S.: Designing for Accessibility: A Business Guide to Countering Design Exclusion. CRC Press, Boca Raton (2007)
8. Tsourakis, N.: Using hand gestures to control mobile spoken dialogue systems. Int. J. Univ. Access Inf. Soc. **13**(3), 257–275 (2014). Springer
9. Card, S.K., Moran, T.P., Newell, A.: The Psychology of Human-Computer Interaction. Lawrence Erlbaum Associates, Hillsdale (1983)
10. Keates, S., Clarkson, P.J.: Countering design exclusion: bridging the gap between usability and accessibility. Int. J. Univ. Access Inf. Soc. **2**(3), 215–225 (2003). Springer
11. Freedom Scientific: JAWS for windows: screen reading software (2014). http://www.freedomscientific.com/Products/Blindness/JAWS
12. Keates, S., Adams, R., Bodine, C., Czaja, S., Gordon, W., Gregor, P., Hacker, E., Hanson, V., Kemp, J., Laff, M., Lewis, C., Pieper, M., Richards, J., Rose, D., Savidis, A., Schultz, G., Snayd, P., Trewin, S., Varker, P.: Cognitive and learning difficulties and how they affect access to IT systems. Int. J. Univ. Access Inf. Soc. **5**(4), 329–339 (2007). Springer
13. Keates, S., Kozloski, J., Varker, P.: Cognitive impairments, HCI and daily living. In: Stephanidis, C. (ed.) Universal Access in HCI, Part I, HCII 2009. LNCS, vol. 5614, pp. 366–374. Springer, Heidelberg (2009)
14. El Kaliouby, R., Robinson, P., Keates, S.: Temporal context and the recognition of emotion from facial expression. In: Proceedings of HCI International 2003, Crete, Greece, pp. 631–635 (2003)
15. Keates, S., Varker, P., Spowart, F.: Human-machine design considerations in advanced machine-learning systems. IEEE/IBM J. Res. Dev. **55**(5), 4:1–4:10 (2011). IEEE
16. Welton, T., Brown, D.J., Evett, L., Sherkat, N.: A brain-computer interface for the Dasher alternative text entry system. Int. J. Univ. Access Inf. Soc. Springer, (Springer online first) (2015)
17. Hwang, F., Keates, S., Langdon, P., Clarkson, P.J.: Movement time for motion-impaired users assisted by force-feedback: effects of movement amplitude, target width, and gravity well width. Int. J. Univ. Access Inf. Soc. **4**(2), 85–95 (2005). Springer
18. Trewin, S., Keates, S., Moffatt, K.: Individual responses to the steady clicks cursor assistance technique. Disabil. Rehabil. Assist. Technol. Informa Healthcare **3**(1&2), 2–21 (2008)
19. Keates, S., Perricos, C.: Gesture as a means of computer access. Commun. Matters **10**(1), 17–19 (1996)
20. Keates, S.: A pedagogical example of teaching universal access. Int. J. Univ. Access Inf. Soc. **14**(1), 97–110 (2015). Springer
21. International Standard Organization (ISO) ISO 9241-11: Ergonomic requirements for office work with visual display terminals (VDTs), Part 11: Guidance on Usability Specification and Measures. Technical report, ISO, Geneva (1998)
22. Frokjaer, E., Hertzum, M., Hornbaek, K.: Measuring usability: are effectiveness, efficiency and satisfaction really correlated? In: Proceedings of CHI 2000, The Hague, NL, pp. 345–352 (2000)
23. Keates, S., Clarkson, P.J.: Countering Design Exclusion: An Introduction to Inclusive Design. Springer, London (2003)
24. Rodrigues, E., Carreira, M., Goncalves, D.: Enhancing typing performance of older adults on tablets. Int. J. Univ. Access Inf. Soc. Springer (Springer Online First) (2014). doi:10.1007/s10209-014-0394-8
25. MacKenzie, I.S., Soukeroff, R.W.: A character level error analysis technique for evaluating text entry methods. In: Proceedings of the Second Nordic Conference on Human-Computer Interaction (NordiCHI 2002), pp. 243–246. ACM (2002)

26. Soukoreff, R.W., MacKenzie, I.S.: Metrics for text entry research: an evaluation of MSD and KSPC, and a new unified error metric. In: Proceedings of the ACM Conference on Human Factors in Computing Systems (CHI 2003), Fort Lauderdale, FL, pp. 113–120 (2003)
27. Hwang, F., Keates, S., Langdon, P., Clarkson, P.J.: A submovement analysis of cursor trajectories. Behav. Inf. Technol. (BIT) **24**(3), 205–217 (2005). Taylor & Francis
28. MacKenzie, I.S., Kauppinen, T., Silfverberg, M.: Accuracy measures for evaluating computer pointing devices. In: Proceedings of CHI 2001, Seattle, WA, pp. 9–15 (2001)
29. Keates, S., Hwang, F., Langdon, P., Clarkson, P.J., Robinson, P.: The use of cursor measures for motion-impaired computer users. Int. J. Univ. Access Inf. Soc. (UAIS) **2**(1), 18–29 (2002). Springer
30. Keates, S., Robinson, P.: Gestures and multimodal input. Behav. Inf. Technol. **18**(1), 36–44 (1999). Taylor and Francis Ltd.
31. Keates, S., Langdon, P., Clarkson, P.J., Robinson, P.: User models and user physical capability. User Model. User-Adap. Inter. (UMUAI) **12**(2–3), 139–169 (2002). Wolters Kluwer Publishers

The Bridge Connecting Theory to Practice - A Case Study of Universal Design Process

Yilin Elaine Liu[✉], Seunghyun (Tina) Lee, Ljilja Ruzic Kascak,
and Jon A. Sanford

Center for Assistive Technology and Environmental Access (CATEA),
Georgia Institute of Technology, Atlanta, USA
{y.elaineliu,tinalee,ljilja}@gatech.edu,
jon.sanford@coa.gatech.edu

Abstract. In a typical design process, the decision making process by which desirable and predictive outcomes are achieved is clearly defined by problem definition, goals and objectives setting, design criteria development, design solution generation and evaluation of the solutions. In contrast, the current literature on Universal Design typically jumps from Universal Design as an ideal and set of principles to Universal Design as an artifact. Without interpreting Universal Design principles into specific design criteria, it is not possible to understand design intent, reliably evaluate design outcomes, replicate design processes or outcomes, or generalize findings to other products and environments. In this paper, an universal design process has been proposed and illustrated in a case study of a universally designed voting system in which Universal Design has been applied throughout the design process in a consistent and explicit way to produce a desirable Universal Design outcome.

Keywords: Universal design · Design process · User interface

1   Introduction

Universal Design is a well-accepted concept for designing and evaluating products and environments that are accessible to and usable by all people regardless of their abilities. It has often been referred to more as a design process rather than a product/environment itself [1]. Since it begins with considering all users, the outcome of universal design is less stigmatizing because the design solutions would reduce or eliminate barriers so that all users can use it without requiring additional device or service. The benefits of universal design make it being used as an approach to solve certain design problems and evaluate designs of products as well as environment, however, the process of how universal design is applied to design decision making and evaluation of products is vague. In contrast of everyday design process where an explicit design process is documented through certain phases as problem definition, goals and objectives setting, design criteria development, design solution generation and evaluation of the solutions [2], the

© Springer International Publishing Switzerland 2015
M. Antona and C. Stephanidis (Eds.): UAHCI 2015, Part I, LNCS 9175, pp. 64–73, 2015.
DOI: 10.1007/978-3-319-20678-3_7

UD literature fails to document a similar or even detailed design process that demonstrates how universal design informed design decision-making, what decisions were made and why during the design process. Without a clear understanding of how UD impacted the design outcome through the design process, there is neither a way for others to understand how to apply or appreciate the value of universal design in making design decisions or evaluating design outcomes.

From the design process perspective, Universal Design process is merely a process of designing a product or environment. Thus, the process of Universal Design should be no different than it in typical everyday design. In a typical everyday design process, development of design criteria is a key step in the design process. Design criteria not only reflect project goals, but also determine the starting point for the generation of design solutions, guide design decisions and in some cases are used to evaluate how well the outcome achieves project goals. To this extent, design criteria are the bridge between project goals and outcomes. Compare to everyday design process, the documented UD process repeatedly fails to provide information about design criteria and other phases of the design process. Rather, generic Principles of Universal Design and their associated guidelines are typically substituted for specific perspective or performance-based criteria, leaving a wide gap between design intent and design outcome. Without clearly articulated perspective and/or performance-based design criteria, there is no way to make informed and replicable design decisions, determine whether design goals have been achieved or reliably evaluate the outcome of the design process. In universal design process, to ensure the design outcome being universal design as well as meeting the project-specific design goals, design criteria should be explicitly established and how they impact design process throughout different design phases should be documented.

In this paper, a case study of a universally designed voting system - EZ Ballot, is used to illustrate how project-specific design criteria were interpreted from generic universal design principles and guidelines. These UD-based design criteria demonstrate how design decisions were made to meet the design criteria and how design solutions were generated based on the criteria and clearly articulated design decision-making process. Moreover, because design criteria transcend the UD Principles, they represent the relationship between different guidelines within the same principle and the relationship between different principles. More specifically, the paper will demonstrate how certain principles and guidelines are associated with different aspects of ballot design (i.e., input, output and system logic), yet the design criteria are specific to one of the three aspects.

2 Background

2.1 Application of Universal Design: Principles and Guidelines

Successfully applying Universal Design in a design process to achieve the desirable outcome of design for all abilities can be challenging. First, universal design is a broad concept that different researchers have interpreted it in different ways. It has been elaborated as an information society being more participatory, cooperative and sustainable, are based on a set of principles developed from both social and individual perspectives in economic, political and culture dimensions [3]. It has also been elaborated as an approach to allow people with disabilities to be able to use standard products because they are generally cheaper and more accessible marketwise than those specialized products [4]. Finally, it has been divorced from the typical everyday design process, often being introduced toward the end of the process, which results in "extra" design features driven by the consideration of "all people". As a result, universal design features appear as add-ons to a previously well-designed product [5]. Moreover, without a consideration of universal design from the beginning of the design process, the potential for achieving a universal design outcome that accurately reflects user needs is difficult [4] Like the process used to create typical everyday design, the process used to create universal design should be applied from the very beginning to the end, where it will contribute to defining problems, setting goals and objectives, defining design criteria and evaluating the outcome.

In operationalize universal design so it can be applied in the design process, seven principles and sets of guidelines were developed by 10 experts in 1997 [6]. Nonetheless, these principles and guidelines are intentionally broad and vague so as to be applied to the design of any interface, product or environment. As a result, the application of the principles and guidelines in any specific design necessitates the development of tangible project-specific design criteria. The progressive interpretation of principles and guidelines into design criteria/recommendations is illustrated in a design process focusing on Universal Accessibility in HCI (Fig. 1) [7].

Within the world of information technology, design features are manifested as functionalities of a system (e.g., visual display or audio output). However, embedding considerable functionalities does not ensure usability of the system [8]. Rather, usability is defined by the characteristics of those features (e.g., high contrast display or loud audio output). As illustrated in the figure, generic principles have been interpreted into specific design recommendations that are not only tied to design features but also tied to characteristics that direct how the feature is manifested. Based on this model, universal

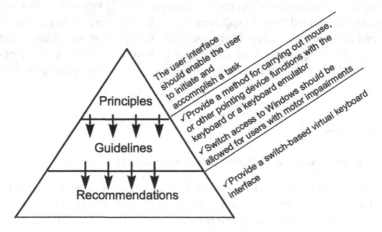

Fig. 1. Progressive interpretation of principles and guidelines into design criteria/recommendations.

design principles and guidelines can be applied to generate more project-specific design criteria that could better guide the generation of design solutions to meet the project goals. In addition, developing more concrete, project-specific design criteria would make evaluation of the design more explicit since clear measurements have been established as in the design criteria.

2.2 Lack of Design Criteria Development in Universal Design Process

Although universal design has been extensively discussed in the literature at the conceptual level of principles and guidelines, documentation of how universal design has been operationalized and integrated into the design process is lacking. Clearly, the development of design criteria that articulate the specific characteristics of a design is a necessary condition for operationalizing universal design. However, the literature is either silent on the design criteria or criteria are insufficiently defined to determine whether the design outcome is universal. Moreover, where the development of universal design criteria is documented in the literature, it has been based on the needs of special populations, rather than the whole population [9–11].

In addition, studies that documented design criteria were, most often, focused on general recommendations for characteristics of generic design features such as large text size and high contrast elements, without regard for the design context as a whole. As a result, the design criteria are isolated from each other in terms of their relationship to the different functionalities they are supposed to accommodate. These design criteria have also failed to associate accommodations with project-specific context. For example, in a study of designing mobile phones for older adults, [9] the functional limitations of older adults have been examined separately and design criteria which were proposed to accommodate those functional limitations are only associate with one functionality each. This approach of developing design criteria overlooked the fact that to complete most of the mobile phone use tasks, different functionalities will need to work together. Focusing on accommodations of each individual functionality without associating them with task-related requirements and considering the interaction between different functionalities can result in a set of insufficiently developed design criteria which is only accommodating individual functionalities without considering how would users complete the task. Furthermore, although the group of older adults is an good sample to practice universal design with since they usually have multiple deficits of functionalities, the design criteria developed from the studies of older adults do not sufficiently imply that other groups of users have been included for a product or environment to be universally designed.

2.3 Universal Design-Informed Criteria for Evaluation

Universal design principles have not only been applied to the design process to achieve more universally designed outcome, they have also been applied to the evaluation process to assist users, designers, and researchers to assess the usability and inclusivity of products and environments. However, using the generic universal design principles to assess products does not provide sufficient evidence of a product being universally designed [12]. In addition, while such generic evaluation might determine the universality of a design, unless it is linked to the characteristics of design features, the evaluation is not useful for modifying the design or informing the design of future products.

Linking Universal Design with specific design features and characteristics can be very helpful for identifying ideal solutions to a design problem. The report, *International Best Practices in Universal Design* reviewed standards from all over the world that were used as design/evaluation criteria for to determine best practices of Universal Design [13]. Using task-relevant scenarios to develop an association between specific design characteristics (as the tangible manifestation of design criteria) and human functionality to determine the usability of each design, the report was able to determine the extent to which a set of design criteria was universal. Although it is merely the examination of standards to identify the best practice of Universal Design, the methodology provides insight into the way universal design can be seen as a set of considerations regarding human functionality, task context and the design features/characteristics.

Another successful example [14] of applying universal design into the evaluation process is an evaluation for universal building design in which experts from different disciplines gathered to evaluate a building based on Universal Design principles. In this case, experts were asked to apply the seven principles of universal design through a consideration of tasks, human functionality and design characteristics to assess five main categories of features within the building. As a result there were profound increases in the number of usability issues found in the evaluation compare to the evaluation where experts were asked to identify usability issues based only on construction drawings. It has been proven, once again, that Universal Design can become useful to a great extent when it is used in a way that tasks, human functionalities and characteristics of features have been all taken into consideration.

2.4   Proposed Universal Design Process

Without the development of project-specific design criteria based on universal design existing literature has failed to document how universal design can be operationalized so that it can be applied to the design process. To overcome that shortcoming, the Universal Design Process proposed here (Fig. 2) demonstrates how Universal Design can be applied to design process through developing project-specific criteria based on seven Universal Design principles. In the proposed process, the design criteria are developed based on the consideration of not only the usability aspects (Principles 2–7), but also the equitability aspect (Principle 1) of universal design. Principle one, which is about equitable use, is the most important principle that distinguishes universal design from assistive technology, accessible design or other usability principles. The uniqueness of universal design is the idea of providing the same means of use for all users is embodied in principle one [15]. This should be considered through the design criteria development phase to ensure that all users could be able to use the product or environment that has been designed. In addition to that, the design criteria should be as explicit as possible to associate with specific design decisions. The design decisions, in turn, are typically represented by one or several design characteristics. Associating design criteria with characteristics allows designers to deal with design problems in a more tangible and contextual way that it provides the opportunities to articulate the interaction between different design features and characteristics according to the task context to maximize usability for all. Compared to the existing universal design process in which design decisions were guided by theoretical universal design principles/guidelines that served as implicit (albeit generic) design criteria or criteria were developed to accommodate human functionality individually without considering the task context, the proposed process connects the theory of universal design to design decisions through the development of explicit design criteria.

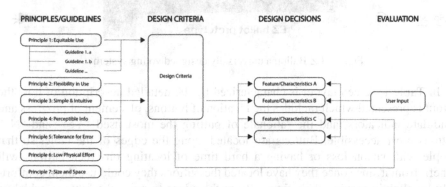

Fig. 2. Proposed universal design process

3 Case Study: EZ Ballot

EZ Ballot is a universally designed voting system with multimodal input and output that facilitates participation of voting by allowing voters to go through the voting process by simply answering "yes" and "no" questions [16] (Fig. 3). It simplifies the voting process conceptually that voters can vote on this system regardless of their abilities. The proposed Universal Design Process was employed in the design of EZ Ballot to maximize universality of the design outcome. In the design process, design criteria associated with characteristics of features in the voting system were developed based on the seven Principles (specify the version of UD Principles have been used for assessment) of Universal Design. By linking design decisions with Universal Design Principles, the design rationale was revealed through the illustration of the interaction between design features and characteristics. Details of the interaction between design features and their characteristics are described in the tables along with the principles from which each of these design decision were derived. The design criteria have been embodied into the relationship between the characteristics within a design feature as well as the relationship between characteristics and Universal Design principles.

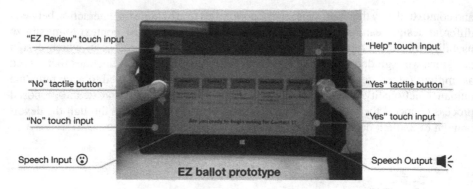

Fig. 3. EZ Ballot, a universally designed voting system

In Table 1, screen layout is characterized by the detailed description of how the layout is presented which includes the location of buttons, placement of progress and candidate indicators, and the rationale of putting the most used "Yes" and "No" buttons most accessible. Buttons are located along the edges of the tablet so that people with vision loss or having a hard time of locating onscreen buttons will benefit from it since once they have located the buttons they could use them comfortably by slightly moving their fingers from the edges to press the buttons, which is derived by Universal Design guideline 6a and 7b about allowing users to maintain a neutral body position and make comfortable reach to all components regardless whether they are sitting or standing. The rest of design features and characteristics (Tables 1 and 2) basically followed the same rule that characteristics are described explicitly to explain how design features are presented and followed by the corresponding principles and guidelines that a characteristic is derived from.

In categorizing the characteristics and design features, it is interesting to note that the characteristics associated with a feature are not always a characteristic of the feature itself, but may be a characteristic that links a feature to the larger context. For example, size, color and shape are characteristics of interface buttons, whereas the location of buttons is a characteristic of screen layout at a larger scale. This relationship provides designers and researchers a deeper insight of how different elements interact with each other at different scales.

4 Discussion

Developing a clear association among design features, universal design-based criteria, design decisions derived from the design criteria and design characteristics that result from those decisions, illustrates how universal design can be operationalized within the typical everyday design process. Within any design feature, different characteristics may meet universal design principles in different ways. For example, the feature of touchscreen buttons in Table 1 has five different characteristics such as being sensitive to force, being big in size and so on that were derived from five different Universal Design principles. It is the characteristics of design features that describe how Universal

Table 1. Relationship between system input/output(i/o) features, characteristics and universal design principles.

Feature	Characteristic directed by Design Criteria	Principle /Guideline
Screen Layout	Locating buttons by the edges of tablet	6a, 7b
	Ballot Progress Indicator is on the top but with different background color	3d
	Candidate indicator is at the side of candidate box	3d
	Most used "Yes" and "No" buttons are located by the sides of tablet	3d, 5a
	Secondarily important "Help" and "Review" buttons are located at the corners of the tablet	5a
Touchscreen Buttons	Sensitive to force	6b
	Redundant in icon, text and color	4a
	Touchable Look (with colored background, text label and icon on the button)	3b
	With big size	2c, 7c
	Locations of buttons are left with enough space between each other	2c, 7c
Physical Buttons	It can be pushed down and bounce back to ensure the intentional input	5d
	It can be push down and bounce back to give feedback of action	4a
	Regular button look to offer affordance	3b
Audio	Simultaneous with visuals	4a
Text	Big in size and in high contrast	4c
	Descending in size for different information	3d
Touchscreen Cover	With cut-outs to show locations of "yes" and "no" buttons	4a
Stylus	Compatible with touchscreen	3b
Input Methods	Offering different input methods, i.e. touchscreen, stylus, physical buttons	2a

Table 2. Relationship between system logic features, characteristics and universal design principles

Feature	Characteristic	Principle /Guideline
Under-voting Reminder	Provided at the end of each contest	5b
Verification Prompt	Instant	5c, 3e
Instruction	Context-sensitive; constant (is offered all the time)	3a
Process	Piece-by-piece (question-by-question)	3a
	User-controlled pace of proceeding	2d
Review	EZ Review (which offers real-time ballot review)	3e
Progress Indicators	Color-coded, numeric, such as "1 of 3"	3e

Design has been applied, which is to say that the key of achieving a universally designed outcome is to use Universal Design to inform design decisions on design characteristics. By explicitly describing the characteristics of a design feature with related Universal Design principles, it also allows other designers and researchers to examine the design rationale behind the outcome so they can benefit from knowing how Universal Design can be applied.

References

1. Iwarsson, S., Ståhl, A.: Accessibility, usability and universal design-positioning and definition of concepts describing person-environment relationships. Disabil. Rehabil. **25**(2), 57–66 (2003)
2. Portillo, M., Dohr, J.H.: Bridging process and structure through criteria. Des. Stud. **15**(4), 403–416 (1994)
3. Fuchs, C., Obrist, M.: HCI and society: towards a typology of universal design principles. Int. J. Hum.-Comput. Interact. **26**(6), 638–656 (2010)
4. Abascal, J.: Human-computer interaction in assistive technology: from patchwork to universal design. In: 2002 IEEE International Conference on Systems, Man and Cybernetics, vol. 3, p. 6. IEEE (2002)
5. Newell, A.F., Gregor, P.: User sensitive inclusive design—in search of a new paradigm. In: Proceedings on the 2000 Conference on Universal Usability, pp. 39–44. ACM (2000)
6. Mace, R.: What is universal design. The Center for Universal Design at North Carolina State University (1997). Accessed 19 Nov 2004

7. Stephanidis, C., Akoumianakis, D., Sfyrakis, M., Paramythis, A.: Universal accessibility in HCI: process-oriented design guidelines and tool requirements. In: Proceedings of the 4th ERCIM Workshop on User Interfaces for all, Stockholm, Sweden, pp. 19–21 (1998)
8. Goodwin, N.C.: Functionality and usability. Commun. ACM **30**(3), 229–233 (1987)
9. Pattison, M., Stedmon, A.W.: Inclusive design and human factors: designing mobile phones for older users. Psychol. J. **4**(3), 267–284 (2006)
10. Kim, H.-J., Heo, J., Shim, J., Kim, M.-Y., Park, S., Park, S.-H.: Contextual research on elderly users' needs for developing universal design mobile phone. In: Stephanidis, C. (ed.) HCI 2007. LNCS, vol. 4554, pp. 950–959. Springer, Heidelberg (2007)
11. Johnson, R., Kent, S.: Designing universal access: web-applications for the elderly and disabled. Cogn. Technol. Work **9**(4), 209–218 (2007)
12. Beecher, V., Paquet, V.: Survey instrument for the universal design of consumer products. Appl. Ergon. **36**(3), 363–372 (2005)
13. Canada, Canadian Human Rights Commission Staff, and Betty Dion Enterprises Staff. International best practices in universal design: a global review. Betty Dion Enterprises Ltd. (2006)
14. Afacan, Y., Erbug, C.: An interdisciplinary heuristic evaluation method for universal building design. Appl. Ergon. **40**(4), 731–744 (2009)
15. Sanford, J.A.: Universal Design as a Rehabilitation Strategy: Design for the Ages. Springer, New York (2012)
16. Lee, S.T., Liu, Y.E., Xiong, X., Sanford, J.: Development of a more universal voting interface. Proc. Hum. Factors Ergon. Soc. Annu. Meet. **57**(1), 1624–1628 (2013). SAGE Publications

Camera Mouse + ClickerAID: Dwell vs. Single-Muscle Click Actuation in Mouse-Replacement Interfaces

John Magee[1]($\boxtimes$), Torsten Felzer[2], and I. Scott MacKenzie[3]

[1] Math and Computer Science Department, Clark University, 950 Main Street, Worcester, MA 01610, USA
jmagee@clarku.edu
[2] Institute for Mechatronic Systems, Technische Universität Darmstadt, Otto-Berndt-Str. 2, 64287 Darmstadt, Germany
felzer@ims.tu-darmstadt.de
[3] Department of Electrical Engineering and Computer Science, York University, Toronto M3J 1P3, Canada
mack@cse.yorku.ca

Abstract. Point-and-click interface modalities are a pervasive method of interacting with graphical user interfaces. Users of mouse-replacement interfaces use alternative input devices to replace the mouse for pointing and clicking. We present a comparison of click actuation modalities with users of the Camera Mouse, a motion-tracking mouse interface. We compare dwell-time click generation against detecting a single intentional muscle contraction with an attached sensor (ClickerAID). A preliminary evaluation was conducted as well as an in-depth case study with a participant with the neuromuscular disease Friedreich's Ataxia. The case study shows modest temporal differences among the test conditions in movement time and throughput, though the participant subjectively favored the ClickerAID interface.

Keywords: Human-computer interaction · Mouse-replacement interfaces · Camera mouse · ClickerAID · Dwelling · Intentional muscle contractions · Neuromuscular diseases · Friedreich's ataxia

1 Introduction

Users of mouse replacement interfaces must perform two disjoint tasks while using graphical user interfaces. These tasks involve first positioning the mouse pointer ("pointing") followed by selecting the user interface element under the pointer ("clicking"). Here we investigate two alternative mouse selection techniques in the context of a mouse-replacement interface: dwell-time selection and single-muscle contraction activation.

© Springer International Publishing Switzerland 2015
M. Antona and C. Stephanidis (Eds.): UAHCI 2015, Part I, LNCS 9175, pp. 74–84, 2015.
DOI: 10.1007/978-3-319-20678-3_8

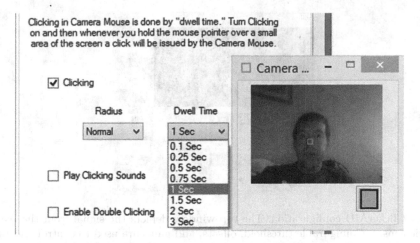

Fig. 1. CameraMouse dwell-time click configuration options. The feature tracking is selected in the video window. The click configuration can select the dwell radius and dwell time as well as single- or double-clicking.

Our investigation evaluates selection options for people who use the Camera Mouse[1] [1,7] – a computer-vision-based mouse-replacement interface that tracks head motion to move a mouse pointer on the screen. The Camera Mouse allows clicking via a configurable dwell-time selection. In order to use dwell selection, the user must keep the mouse pointer relatively still over the target for a specified period of time. Users with different motor abilities have varying levels of success with dwell-time selection. Configuration options are shown in Fig. 1.

One common issue is the "Midas Touch" problem [5], the unintentional selection of a target. This can be due to a short dwell duration or to the user resting or reading information on the screen. It is particularly a problem when a user interface contains interactive elements that take up a large portion of a screen, thus leaving only a few "rest areas" on the screen.

Another common problem with dwell-time selection is the inability to select small user interface elements. This may be due to a dwell-time setting that is longer than the user can comfortably maintain. In addition, users with involuntary motions may have difficulty holding the pointer still for *any* period of time.

ClickerAID [4] is an alternative selection modality. It uses intentional muscle contractions to actuate a mouse event. It is not limited to any one particular muscle; rather, the user decides what works best for him or her (eyebrow, jaw, cheek, chin, etc.). This makes the system very flexible. The ClickerAID configuration interface is shown in Fig. 2.

The user chooses a suitable muscle group that he or she is able to reliably control (e.g., the brow muscle). The muscular activity of that muscle group is acquired using a piezoelectric sensor in contact with the skin directly over

---

[1] The Camera Mouse is freely available as a download at http://www.cameramouse.org/.

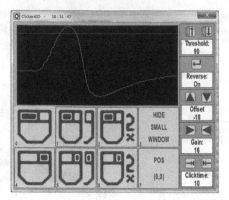

Fig. 2. ClickerAID configuration. The top window depicts the signal from the piezo-electric sensor. Configurable threshold, offsets, and gains are used to control and tune event actuation. The type of click functionality can be selected by the user. Image credit Felzer and Rinderknecht [4].

the muscle and, in the brow example, kept in place with a flexible headband. ClickerAID compares the intensity of the input signal to an adjustable threshold. Whenever the threshold is exceeded, the software detects a contraction event and executes a corresponding code segment (resulting in the emulation of a mouse click). ClickerAID was developed to provide mouse click functionality based on a previous system: HaMCoS (HAnds-free Mouse COntrol System) - which used the same single-muscle actuation to provide all mouse functionality [3].

In the following sections, we present an evaluation of Camera Mouse's visual tracking of a user's head motion combined with ClickerAID's muscle contraction actuation. With this combination, the Camera Mouse is used to position the mouse pointer and the ClickerAID interface is used to actuate selection. This is compared against dwell-time selection from the Camera Mouse alone.

2   Preliminary Evaluation

2.1   Participants and Apparatus

We performed a preliminary evaluation of dwell-time selection versus ClickerAID selection while participants used the Camera Mouse. Ten participants, five female, mean age 29, participated in the preliminary evaluation. Half performed the dwell-time condition first, while the other half performed ClickerAID first. All performed a baseline Touchpad condition last.

The interface test was conducted on a 13-inch laptop screen set to a resolution of 1366 × 768, viewed from a distance of approximately 2.5 feet. For the Camera Mouse, a Logitech® HD Pro Webcam C920 was used, and ClickerAID was operated with the help of a headband sensor monitoring the muscular activity of the brow muscle. The following Camera Mouse settings were used for all participants: medium horizontal and vertical gain, very low smoothing, and dwell-time click area was set to "Normal" and 1.0 s.

Fig. 3. FittsTaskTwo - User interface test software highlights a target circle. When the user clicks on the target, the next circle is highlighted. The test software is configurable for different size targets and distance between targets. The overlaid arrows indicate the order that targets are highlighted.

2.2 Procedure and Design

The preliminary investigation employed an interactive evaluation tool called FittsTaskTwo[2] ([6], p. 291). Users performed selection tasks that required them to first position the mouse pointer over a target and then select the target before moving to the next target (Fig. 3). We performed a comparative experiment using this interactive tool to analyse the performance of users with the different interaction modalities. A log file recorded the mouse trajectory and click events.

Each participant's session contained four sequences of thirteen targets at amplitudes 300 and 600 and widths 50 and 80 pixels. The main independent variable was input method with the following three conditions:

- CM_DWELL – Camera Mouse with 1.0 s dwell time,
- CM_CA – Camera Mouse with ClickerAID,
- Touchpad – standard pointing method.

The experimental protocol therefore included 156 trials ($3 \times 4 \times 13$) for each participant. The dependent variables were movement time (speed), throughput (speed and accuracy – bits/s), error rate (%), and target re-entries.

2.3 Results and Discussion

The Touchpad baseline was clearly the better method for the dependent variables movement time and throughput. The mean movement time was lower for the Touchpad (1302 ms) compared to CM_CA (2226 ms) and CM1000 (2609 ms). The differences were statistically significant ($F_{2,18} = 49.4$, $p < .0001$). Bonferroni-Dunn post hoc comparisons revealed significant differences between all pairs ($p < .05$). See Fig. 4a.

For throughput (speed and accuracy), the Touchpad had a better mean (2.10 bits/s) compared to CM_CA (1.43 bits/s) and CM1000 (1.28 bits/s). The differences were statistically significant ($F_{2,18} = 12.3$, $p < .0005$). Pairwise,

---

[2] The software is freely available as a download at http://www.yorku.ca/mack/HCI book/.

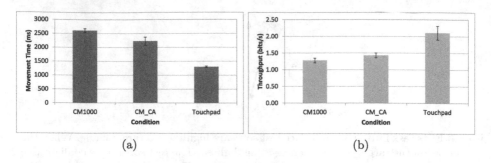

Fig. 4. Preliminary evaluation: (a) movement time; (b) throughput, which combines speed and accuracy. Error bars show ±1 *SE*.

CM_CA had 11.7 % higher throughput than CM1000. Figure 4b summarizes these results. Bonferroni-Dunn post hoc comparisons show significant differences only between the Touchpad condition and the CM conditions ($p < .05$), but not between the CM_CA and CM1000 conditions. Nine out of ten participants had faster movement time with CM_CA than CM1000, and eight out of ten had higher throughputs in those respective conditions.

For the accuracy measures, the dependent variable error rate again favors the Touchpad baseline, while target re-entry favors the CM_CA condition (see Fig. 5). The Touchpad condition averaged 0.12 re-entries/trial compared to 0.10 for CM_CA and 0.15 for CM1000. There was no significant effect on target re-entries ($F_{2,18} = 0.9$, ns). Error rate demonstrated larger differences with means of 3.8 % for Touchpad, 8.1 % for CM1000, and 10.8 % for CM_CA. The differences were statistically significant ($F_{2,18} = 4.2, p < .05$). However, Bonferroni-Dunn post hoc pairwise comparisons did not show statistically significant differences in either error rate or target re-entries.

Although CM1000 had slightly lower error rates than CM_CA on average, individual participant performance was not consistent in comparison to the throughput measures. Some participants had larger error rates in one or the other condition, while others had equal error rates. While observing the trials, we noted that a few participants attempted to quickly click in the CM_CA condition without stopping long or at all, causing them to miss the target. In the CM1000 condition the dwell-time clicking forced them to stop and hit the target. With the Touchpad, some participants had zero errors, while others had errors caused by inadvertently moving (i.e., dragging) the pointer while attempting to tap the touchpad.

On subjective measurements, all but one participant said that the ClickerAID was either "somewhat easier" or "much easier" compared to dwell-time clicking. Almost all participants felt they had more control with ClickerAID and the ability to intentionally click rather than waiting for a click to happen. Many mentioned that it was difficult to keep the mouse moving to avoid unintentional clicks and then to hold still in a small area to intentionally click. The one user who preferred dwell-time clicking stated that the sensory feeling of the headband

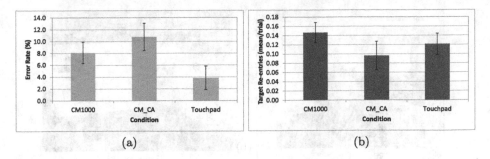

Fig. 5. Preliminary Evaluation - Accuracy measures (a) error rate; (b) target re-entries (a low value generally means good cursor control). Error bars show ± 1 *SE*.

made her uncomfortable and that she worried her face movements might trigger an unintended click. This participant was not the same participant with faster movement time or higher throughput in that condition.

Several years of experience with Camera Mouse users with various abilities suggest that individual user's abilities may be the determining factor in efficacy and preference between the two click actuation modalities evaluated here. For users of the Camera Mouse who have difficulty holding the head still to activate the dwell-time clicker in a small region, the ClickerAID activation may provide a more reliable and intentional activation option. However, users who have difficulty actuating the muscle required by the ClickerAID sensor may have better performance with the dwell-time option. The preliminary evaluation included only subjects with typical motion abilities.

3   Case Study

In addition to the preliminary evaluation with multiple participants, a case study documenting the experiences of a single 44-year-old male computer user, the second author, who has the neuromuscular disease Friedreich's Ataxia, has been conducted. The purpose of the study was to determine whether there are any (objective or subjective) advantages for this particular user of Camera Mouse with ClickerAID compared to the usual dwell method, or to the participant's ordinary pointing technique.

3.1   Apparatus

The study took place in the participant's work environment. The click targets were displayed on a 33-inch TV monitor, set to a resolution of 1920 × 1080, viewed from a distance of approximately 2 feet. For the Camera Mouse, the same webcam was used as in the preliminary evaluation, and ClickerAID was again operated with the help of a headband sensor monitoring the muscular activity of the brow muscle.

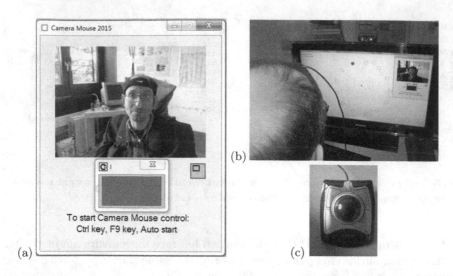

Fig. 6. Experimental setup: (a) Camera Mouse window during the generation of a click with ClickerAID; (b) view from behind; (c) trackball used as ordinary pointing device.

Figure 6 shows the entire setup. Figure 6a depicts the exact moment when the participant raised his eyebrow to generate a click; the ClickerAID window flashes red as a confirmation. The ClickerAID window is shown on top of the Camera Mouse window, and normally illustrates the muscular activity of the brow muscle as a green curve on black background. To interact with a PC, the second author regularly uses OnScreenDualScribe [2], which efficiently replaces both the standard keyboard and mouse with a small manually-operated keypad. He infrequently uses the trackball device depicted in Fig. 6c for pointing; however, to make the case study as comparable as possible to the preliminary evaluation, this standard device was chosen as a baseline.

Furthermore, the second author is currently developing a pointing-driven variant of OnScreenDualScribe for users who cannot employ their hands. The idea is as follows. OnScreenDualScribe reduces operating the entire keyboard to pressing just a few keys. Obviously, not all of those keys can always emulate the same functionality. To remind the user of the currently valid associations, an "avatar" of the keypad is displayed on screen. Making the buttons of the avatar clickable naturally leads to a point-and-click keyboard replacement.

Compared to conventional onscreen keyboards, this extension has the advantage of needing less screen space. In particular, users of non-manual mouse-replacement interfaces might appreciate that they have to span smaller distances between keys. Although being able (within limits) to use both hands, the second author had the additional goal when doing the case study to look into potential benefits for himself and people with similar symptomatologies. The manual device was the natural choice since the on-screen clickable version of OnScreen-DualScribe requires external mouse control.

3.2 Procedure and Design

The case study employed the same evaluation tool as in the preliminary evaluation. It consisted of two sessions, each containing four sequences of thirteen targets at amplitudes 400 and 800 and widths 50 and 100 pixels. The main independent variable was input method with the following conditions:

- CM1500 – Camera Mouse with 1.5 s dwell time,
- CM2000 – Camera Mouse with 2.0 s dwell time,
- CM_CA – Camera Mouse with ClickerAID,
- Trackball – standard pointing method.

The experimental protocol therefore included 416 trials ($2 \times 4 \times 4 \times 13$) plus any sequence repeats. The participant's subjective evaluation of the Camera Mouse configurations resulted in the following settings: low horizontal gain, a medium vertical gain, and high smoothing. He used these settings in all trials. The difference between the two sessions was that the dwell-time click area was set to "Normal" in the first session and "Small" in the second. The dependent variables were the same as in the preliminary evaluation.

3.3 Results and Discussion

While developing the experiment, the participant tried shorter dwell times, but these resulted in frequent sequence repeats due to unintended clicks. A zoomed camera image was also tried, but the quick motion made it too sensitive for accurate dwell-time clicking.

Despite attempts to configure the input methods to optimal settings, the evaluation may not lead to a clear outcome among the conditions. Results showed better performance with the 1.5 s dwell-time setting of CM1500 compared to the 2.0 s dwell-time of CM2000. Here, we will compare the better of the dwell-time conditions against the ClickerAID condition. When considering the dependent variable movement time, CM1500 had the lowest mean movement time of 5960 ms compared to CM_CA (6713 ms, 13 % slower). For throughput, CM1500 again had the better mean of 0.488 bits/s compared to CM_CA with 0.454 bits/s (7 % less). Figure 7 summarizes the results of all four conditions.

When considering the accuracy of user input, the dependent variables error rate and target re-entry favor the Trackball condition (see Fig. 8). The Trackball condition averaged 0.375 re-entries/trial compared to 0.894 for CM1500, and 0.692 for CM_CA. Error rate demonstrated the largest differences with mean percentage of 1.9 for Trackball, 19.2 for CM1500, and 18.3 for CM_CA. Pairwise comparisons between the dwell-time and ClickerAID conditions shows CM1500 had 29 % higher target re-entry rate and 4.9 % higher error rate than CM_CA. The accuracy of the trackball is not surprising given that it was the slowest input condition – it is a well-known trade-off that users make fewer mistakes when given more time. In addition, since the pointer stops moving when the trackball is not being touched, it's likely that the user would not click the button when the pointer is off the target – contributing to the low error rate.

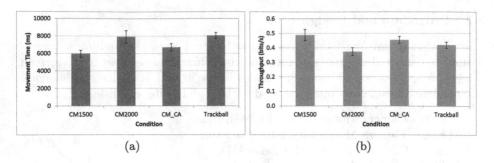

Fig. 7. Case Study - Temporal performance for the four conditions: (a) movement time; (b) throughput, which combines speed and accuracy.

While differences in these four dependent variables were considerable, we note that tests for statistically significant differences could not be performed given that there was only one participant. The differences for movement time and throughput were modest compared to those for target re-entries and error rate.

Subjectively, the participant preferred the ClickerAID condition, as it demanded less physical effort than the trackball, while allowing him to "stay in control". This feeling of control was in contrast to the dwell-time conditions where the user must wait for a click to occur, and is similar to what was noted by participants in the preliminary evaluation. The difference in this effect is illustrated in Fig. 9. When using the Camera Mouse, the participant is unable to keep the mouse pointer completely still; it is constantly moving, with sometimes larger, sometimes smaller amplitudes. When near the desired target, the pointer often drifts out of the intended area while – in the dwell-time conditions – waiting for a click to be issued. When that happens, the pointer has to be repositioned quickly, which regularly results in overcorrections. An extreme example is the four circled targets in Fig. 9a. With ClickerAID, the participant does not have to wait for a click to be issued by the dwell timer; instead, he can intentionally actuate a click. This ability allows the participant to correctly actuate a click on

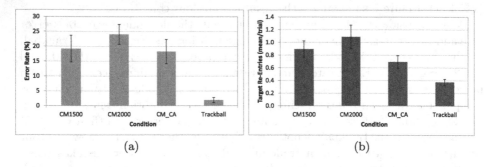

Fig. 8. Case Study - Accuracy measures (a) error rate; (b) target re-entries (a low value generally means good cursor control).

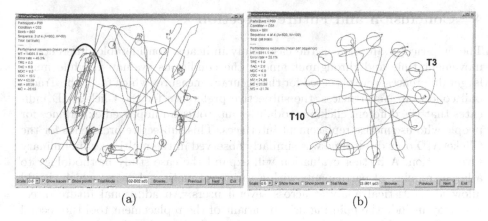

(a)   (b)

Fig. 9. Staying in control: (a) Waiting for a click to be invoked while dwelling; (b) intentional clicks in the CM_CA condition.

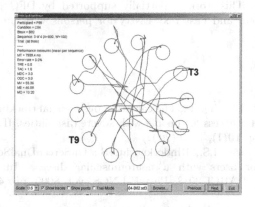

Fig. 10. Several "strokes" needed to maneuver the mouse pointer from one target to the next in the Trackball condition.

a target and move directly to the next target, as shown in Fig. 9b near targets T3 and T10 and the path between.

Given that the participant in the case study is able to use both hands, it might not have been expected that the Trackball condition would be so slow. The loss of speed is related to the physical size of the trackball (about two inches diameter); when moving across the screen, especially in the large outer radius sequences, the participant usually needs several "strokes" to span the required distance. This means that he must roll the ball all the way in one direction, then lift his hand and move it back in the opposite direction, and then put his hand down and roll again – very cumbersome. This pattern is evident in the path between targets T3 and T9 in Fig. 10.

4   Conclusion and Future Direction

The empirical evaluation in the case study indicates considerable difference in movement time and throughput among the conditions evaluated, while much larger differences were observed for the accuracy measures which favor the Trackball condition. Nevertheless, the subjective preference for the ClickerAID indicates that the different clicking modalities may offer an improved experience for people who use mouse-replacement interfaces. This subjective preference for the ClickerAID over dwell-time was similarly observed in the multi-user preliminary investigation. A further evaluation will expand the case study methodology to a larger number of participants with a variety of motion abilities, which should allow for statistical analyses across several users. An additional future direction may include the pointing-driven variant of the replacement tool the second author is currently developing for users who cannot employ their hands.

Acknowledgments. This work is partially supported by DFG grant FE 936/6-2 "EFFENDI – EFficient and Fast text ENtry for persons with motor Disabilities of neuromuscular orIgin".

References

1. Betke, M., Gips, J., Fleming, P.: The camera mouse: visual tracking of body features to provide computer access for people with severe disabilities. IEEE Trans. Neural Syst. Rehabil. Eng. **10**(1), 1–10 (2002)
2. Felzer, T., MacKenzie, I.S., Rinderknecht, S.: OnScreenDualScribe: a computer operation tool for users with a neuromuscular disease. In: Stephanidis, C., Antona, M. (eds.) UAHCI 2013, Part I. LNCS, vol. 8009, pp. 474–483. Springer, Heidelberg (2013)
3. Felzer, T., Nordmann, R.: Evaluating the hands-free mouse control system: an initial case study. In: Miesenberger, K., Klaus, J., Zagler, W.L., Karshmer, A.I. (eds.) ICCHP 2008. LNCS, vol. 5105, pp. 1188–1195. Springer, Heidelberg (2008)
4. Felzer, T., Rinderknecht, S.: ClickerAID: a tool for efficient clicking using intentional muscle contractions. In: Proceedings of the ACM SIGACCESS Conference on Computers and Accessibility (ASSETS 2012), pp. 257–258. ACM (2012)
5. Jacob, R.J.K.: What you look at is what you get: eye movement-based interaction techniques. In: Proceedings of the SIGCHI Conference on Human Factors in Computing Systems (CHI 1990), pp. 11–18. ACM (1990)
6. MacKenzie, I.S.: Human-Computer Interaction: An Empirical Research Perspective. Elsevier, New Delhi (2013)
7. Magee, J.J., Epstein, S., Missimer, E.S., Kwan, C., Betke, M.: Adaptive mouse-replacement interface control functions for users with disabilities. In: Stephanidis, C. (ed.) Universal Access in HCI, Part II, HCII 2011. LNCS, vol. 6766, pp. 332–341. Springer, Heidelberg (2011)

Analyzing the Design Space of Personal Informatics: A State-of-practice Based Classification of Existing Tools

Fredrik Ohlin[1,2]($\boxtimes$), Carl Magnus Olsson[1,2], and Paul Davidsson[1,2]

[1] Department of Computer Science, Malmö University, Malmö, Sweden
{fredrik.ohlin,carl.magnus.olsson,paul.davidsson}@mah.se
[2] Internet of Things and People Research Center, Malmö University, Malmö, Sweden

Abstract. We are presently seeing a rapid increase of tools for tracking and analyzing activities, from lifelogging in general to specific activities such as exercise tracking. Guided by the perspectives of collection, procedural, and analysis support, this paper presents the results from a review of 71 existing tools, striving to capture the design choices within personal informatics that such tools are using. The classification system this creates is a contribution in three ways: as a standalone state-of-practice representation, for assessing individual tools and potential future design directions for them, and as a guide for new development of personal informatics tools.

Keywords: Personal informatics · Quantified self · State-of-practice · Design choices · Classification

1 Introduction

The field of personal informatics, although unified by a common theme of individuals recording and analyzing personal data, remains quite heterogeneous as to why and how this is done. This is especially clear when looking at the broad spectrum of tools used in personal informatics practices. On one end of the spectrum, we find general purpose tools such as pen, paper, and spreadsheet applications [23]. These tools allow for logging and analysis of most kinds of data but are not designed for any one type of logging or analysis, and thus require significant effort from the user. On the other end of the spectrum, we find highly customized tools designed by expert users themselves (cf. [7]). These are very particular to the individuals who created them, and trade a higher up-front time investment for increased customizability, possibilities for insight, or simpler everyday use.

Motivated by the heterogeneity as to why and how individual recording and analysis of personal data, this paper presents an analysis of current personal informatics tools. As the range of available tools continues to grow, it is becoming increasingly difficult to compare and contrast the available alternatives. This is not only a concern for end user adoption of appropriate tools – it also holds

© Springer International Publishing Switzerland 2015
M. Antona and C. Stephanidis (Eds.): UAHCI 2015, Part I, LNCS 9175, pp. 85–97, 2015.
DOI: 10.1007/978-3-319-20678-3_9

concerns for the design of and research on digital tools supporting personal informatics.

Establishing a common understanding of the field, determining the state of the art, and identifying areas of opportunity, all depend on having clear descriptions of key features of the design space. Consequently, there is a prominent need for a consistent vocabulary which establishes a common frame of reference for both analysis and design within personal informatics. We thus use our analysis to define a classification system of digital personal informatics tools that describes key similarities and distinctions among them. This classification system is a contribution in three ways. One, as a standalone state-of-practice representation of aspects that presently are emphasized in personal informatics tools, two, as a catalyst for assessing individual tools and potential future design directions for them, and three, as a guide for new development of personal informatics tools.

2   Central Aspects of Personal Informatics

Personal informatics is the primary term within academia to describe activities aimed at self-understanding through collection and analysis of personal data. As part of personal informatics, we include terms that are used synonymously such as *quantified self, self-surveillance, self-tracking,* and *personal analytics* [23]. While personal informatics is certainly related to *lifelogging* it does not capture the whole of personal informatics as lifelogging could be viewed as the act of logging, rather than including potential interest in informing and adapting behavior based on the analysis of the logged data.

In examining the available research on personal informatics, there is a general consensus as to what the field is, regardless of the term used for describing the area. The available descriptions are focused on describing the practice of personal informatics, however, rather than what makes up a personal informatics tool. The oft referred to definition by Li et al. [23, p. 558] is representative of this: "We define personal informatics systems as those that help people collect personally relevant information for the purpose of self-reflection and gaining self knowledge. There are two core aspects to every personal informatics system: collection and reflection." Recent research [22, 29, 32, 38] also regard *collection* of data and *analysis* of this data that promotes reflection as central aspects. This always yields *participatory personal data* [36] which is data accessible to the subject it describes. We also see that these practices are distinct from tracking that is not managed by the individual [4, 36].

Furthermore, *procedural support* can be argued as a third central aspect of support that has been left largely implicit so far. Such procedural support dictates ways that the tool drives, controls, shapes, or otherwise strives to affect the personal informatics practice. The goal with such procedural support is to promote engagement, motivation, or goal commitment and fulfillment. As an example of procedural support, the study by Bentley et al. [3] observed that tool-provided interjections in the form of smartphone notification promoted engagement through a significantly increased user logging frequency. Procedural support can take many shapes in personal informatics tools. Rewards provided by the tool, such as performance-based badges, have been found to influence people's behavior [16]. In such cases, the tool has built-in notions of what constitutes appropriate or beneficial behavior, quite similar to the design goals found in persuasive computing (c.f. [15]). The overlap is apparent in some cases – such as when Fritz et al. [16] refer to fitness trackers as both being persuasive technology and personal informatics tools. The design of personal informatics tools has also been suggested to benefit from lessons from persuasive technology [23]. There can however be a conflict between promoting a specific type of behavior, and embracing the "reflective capacities" [4] of users – and individual agency may be denied through restrictive technologies [32].

3   Classifying Personal Informatics Tool Support

3.1   Procedure

In this study, our scope is to explore digital tools that have been designed specifically to support personal informatics. This implies that we have limited ourselves to tools that have explicit functionality for data collection and analysis (thereby e.g. excluding pure visualization tools), as well as support continuous use (thereby e.g. excluding snapshot analyses). The selection of tools for analysis was made by combining the public list from personalinformatics.org [28] with tools the authors already had experience with. This resulted in 71 current and accessible personal informatics tools that were studied further.

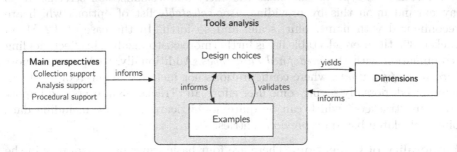

Fig. 1. Approach to generating the classification system

To form our classification system, we analyzed individual tools according to the open coding technique often used in grounded theory research [9]. This meant that we started from the central aspects of personal informatics acting as perspectives on our analysis of tools. This analysis was an iterative processes (Fig. 1), wherein specific examples from tools enabled the identification of design choices in these tools. Similar design choices were then grouped into overarching dimensions. Emerging dimensions then informed further analysis of tools, resulting in additional refinement of design choices and examples, which subsequently yielded additional dimensions, and so forth. This iterative process was repeated until the dimensions reached a stable state, in the sense that further examples did not yield additional design choices or new dimensions.

3.2 The Classification System

The process of analyzing specific personal informatics tools resulted in classification system containing nine dimensions with a total of 53 design choices. These are summarized in Table 1 and described below with example from well-known tools. Relying on more well-known tools is a purposeful choice as these are more likely to be known by readers also.

Selection of Data to Collect. Control over which data to collect varies among current tools. In the most flexible of tools, this selection is completely *user-defined*. An example of this can be seen in DailyDiary [10], which prompts users on any custom-defined question. On the other extreme, the selection of data may be *predefined* in tools that allow for no customization – such as collection by hardware sensors (e.g. Withings Smart Body Analyzer [42]). It should be noted, however, that updated display of collected data may give users a different experience, even though the underlying data is the same.

There are also variants on user-defined selection which place some additional constraints on how data selection is made. With *predefined data types*, the user freely names what is being collected, but maps it to a particular data type supported by the tool. The Reporter application [30] exemplifies this in using the selected data type to customize the entry and visualization screens. Tools may expand upon this by providing *user-selectable* list of options which are preconfigured with name, unit, scale, and so forth. In the case of T2 Mood Tracker [39], the user-selectable list is furthermore customizable, in effect yielding a combination with the *predefined data types*. Additionally, tools may support *sharable configurations*, where configurations not included in the tool itself can be imported, possibly saving some user effort. In rTracker [33], users can import and share 'trackers', which can be quite sophisticated, e.g. by including data points calculated based on previous entries.

Temporality of Collection. There are four basic types of temporality in the collection of data: continuous, session-based, single entries, and post hoc edit. *Continous* collection is ongoing, requiring no interaction to maintain. Location logging applications such as Moves [26], along with fitness trackers that are always-on, fall in this category. *Session-based* collection implies that data is collected over a period of time delimited by an explicit (and often manually controlled) start and stop. Exercise tracking applications such as RunKeeper [34] are typical examples of this, with collection only occurring during each specific training sessions. *Single entries* are made at one particular moment in time, as in self-survey applications such as Reporter [30]. *Post hoc edit* differs from the other three types, in that it concerns modification of already entered data. In Jawbone's UP Coffee [20] application, this enables batch collection of several entries, which can then be backdated through the edit feature. The post hoc edit may also be used to allow users that have forgotten to turn on for instance a fitness tracker, the chance to enter estimated activities as such omissions may otherwise prevent users from reaching goals they have set due to a handling mistake during use of the tool.

Granted, in some cases it may be difficult to distinguish between the types of temporality. Some tools that ongoingly (e.g. several times a day) prompt the user for manual entry are in effect providing procedural support to collect *single-entries* either in a *continuous* or in a *session-based* manner.

Support During Manual Entry. Tools that rely on manual entry from users can provide various forms of support for this step. Although in some cases, *no support* is given, such as with your.flowingdata. This tool relies on direct messages via Twitter for collection, which inherently is free form text, separate from the tool's user interface. A simple form of manual support is *previous entries shown*, exemplified by Joe's Goals [21] where the collection and analysis user interfaces are one and the same. Other tools support *re-entry*, either by making *previous entries selectable* (e.g. Reporter [30]) or by suggesting previous entries through *autocomplete* (e.g. Toggl [40]). Another form of making manual entry easier is *inline calculator*, where simple arithmetic operations are added to number inputs (e.g. Loggr [24]).

Different types of data can also be shown to assist the user in their manual entry, possibly increasing the validity of the entry. The mood tracking application Expereal [12] exemplifies two such forms of support, by showing both a *personal aggregate* and a *collective aggergate* as the user is asked to input the current mood. Another form of support is *automatic calculation of derived value*, where part of the recorded data is calculated based on manual input and displayed to the user. Such calculations could conceivably be done as part of later analysis also, but tools such as rTracker [33] include the results of the calculation in the collection stage as an aid for manual data entry.

Data Collection Control. The control over initiating data collection differs greatly between tools, and inherently carries qualities of procedural support depending on the design choice made. Tools such as e.g. i.strive.to [18] rely on *user-initiated* collection, placing the responsibility solely on the user. To alleviate some of the potential downsides of user-driven collection, such as the risk of forgetting collect on, other tools provide procedural assistance. *Scheduled notifications* remind the user at predefined intervals or times, and in the case of rTracker [33] the user can configure multiple notifications of each type. *Randomized notifications* also remind the user, but varies the exact times. In the case of Reporter [30], this is described as a feature that facilitates more accurate data through random sampling. Some tools also analyze user data to trigger *behavior-determined notifications*. RunKeeper [34] exemplifies a simple form of this through push notifications in the form of "Lets work out! You thought this was the perfect time a while back... remember?". Furthermore, RunKeeper also supports *social notifications*, where the user is prompted to engage in an activity based on the explicit request of a contact. Finally, tools may use fully *automatic collection*, such as what the location logging application Saga [35].

Form of Goal Setting. The form of goal setting is a central concern to tools that strive towards behavior change, and dictates how the tool handles how user goals are created. With *manual goal setting*, goals are handled separately from the tool, meaning that it does not provide any explicit support (e.g. Loggr [24]). One form of support is *predefined goal types*, where the tool provides a list of goals it supports tracking towards, and lets the user select among them. Fitness and activity trackers commonly have these, such as running a particular distance over a fixed period (e.g. RunKeeper [34]). Some tools provide *personalized goals*, where the achievement for reaching a goal is determined based on previous user data. When starting Breeze [5], as an example, it uses the step count data already available through the smartphone to generate a user-specific daily step goal (which also continues to update).

Another form of goal setting is through *crowdsourced goals*, where goals defined by others are available for the individual user to adopt. This is the core model of Coach.me [8], which also uses shared goals as social objects around which the users can interact. *Default goals* are also visible among the reviewed tools, to which the user is automatically committed to rather than actively reflecting on and subscribing to specific goals. An example of this is Fit Simply [13], which by default includes and tracks a series of challenges of (designer defined) increasing difficulty. *Expert plans*, such as the "professional training plans" of Garmin Connect [17], is also a form of goal setting, wherein a sequence of steps or targets are prescribed.

Data Analysis Control. Analysis in personal informatics has traditionally been *user-driven*, in that the user has responsibility in engaging with the collected data. Many tools fall into this category, such as ChartMySelf [6], which can track many kinds of data, but relies on users actively seeking out the analysis interface. Some tools take on part of the responsibility, and provide *notifications to check status*. Breeze [5] does this through push notifications in the form "Morning! Curious how yesterday went? We can shed some light!".

Other tools go further and include pertinent information in the notifications themselves. Jawbone UP [19] provides *self-contained data notifications*, e.g. "You got 8 h 31 m of sleep last night, 106 % of your goal", while Fitbit [14] provides *self-contained achievement notifications*, e.g. "Nailed it! You met your step goal for today." These enable the user to get a status update without any further interaction with the tool. *Goal-keeping notifications* are similar, but proactively focused. Basis [1] supports these through alerts if the user must hit a daily target to meet a weekly goal. A *periodic report* is more detailed than a notification, but is still a self-contained representation of some aspect of user data. The Basis weekly sleep email report exemplifies this.

Form of Comparison. Personal informatics tools can support comparisons in different ways. A tool can have *no comparison support*, meaning that it provides

Table 1. Design choices in current personal informatics tools

Dimension	Design choice	Example
Selection of data to collect	User-defined	DailyDiary [10]
	User-defined (pre-defined data types)	Reporter [30]
	User-defined (quantitative only)	Loggr [24]
	User-selectable (from predefined list)	T2 Mood Tracker [39]
	Sharable configurations	rTracker [33]
	Predefined	Withings [42]
Temporality of collection	Single entries	Reporter [30]
	Session-based	RunKeeper [34]
	Continuous	Move [26]
	Post hoc edit	Jawbone UP Coffee [20]
Support during manual entry	No support	your.flowingdata [43]
	Previous entries shown	Joe's Goals [21]
	Re-entry (selectable)	Reporter [30]
	Re-entry (autocomplete)	Toggl [40]
	Inline calculator	Loggr [24]
	Personal aggregate shown	Expereal [12]
	Collective aggregate shown	Expereal [12]
	Automatic collection of derived value	rTracker [33]
Data collection control	User-initiated	i.strive.to [18]
	Scheduled notification	rTracker [33]
	Randomized notification	Reporter [30]
	Behavior-determined notification	RunKeeper [34]
	Social notification	RunKeeper [34]
	Automatic collection	Saga [35]
Form of goal setting	Manual	Loggr [24]
	Predefined goal types	RunKeeper [34]
	Personalized goals	Breeze [5]
	Crowdsourced goals	Coach.me [8]
	Default goals	Fit Simply [13]
	Expert plans	Garmin Connect [17]
Data analysis control	User-driven	ChartMySelf [6]
	Notification to check status	Breeze [5]
	Self-contained achievement notification	Fitbit [14]
	Self-contained data notification	Jawbone Up [19]
	Goal-keeping notification	Basis [1]
	Periodic report	Basis [1]

(Continued)

Table 1. *(Continued)*

Dimension	Design choice	Example
Form of comparison	None	rTracker [33]
	Top list	Fitbit [14]
	To projection	Beeminder [2]
	To facets of data	Strava [37]
	According to user-defined categories	Toggl [40]
	According to automatic categories	Mint [25]
Subject(s) of comparison	To self	Drinking Diary [11]
	To specific other	RunKeeper [34]
	To group	Strava [37]
	To collective aggregate	Saga [35]
	According to detailed demographics	Fitbit [14]
Appraisal	None (raw data displayed)	rTracker [33]
	Relative data	Withings Health Mate [41]
	General encouragement	Basis [1]
	Social encouragement	Strava [37]
	Abstract score (fixed)	Nike+ [27]
	Abstract score (customizable)	RescueTime [31]

no such functionality beyond displaying the collected data (e.g. rTracker [33]). Other tools allow for *comparison according to user-defined categories*. Toggl [40] is one such example, where entries belong to projects which themselves can belong to clients, i.e. a classification used for subsequent analysis. There are also tools that support *comparison according to automatic categories*. This is typified by Mint [25], which classifies expenditures of the user, placing them automatically into categories.

Data can also be *compared to projection* – a core feature of Beeminder [2]. This allows the user to evaluate how current performance will progress. Some tools break down data to support *comparison of facets*. In Strava [37], user are automatically compared according to overlapping "segments" (where the user can also create new segments which affect future comparisons for others). Complete activities or entries can also be compared in *top lists*, exemplified in Fitbit [14] through a seven day steps leaderboard.

Subject(s) of Comparison. Not only the form of comparison is relevant to consider, however, as a separate dimension of comparison concerns with whom the comparison is made. A tool may support *comparison to self*, such as Drinking Diary [11] does when listing several personal averages (last 7 days, last 100 days, etc.) alongside current values. Another design choice exemplified in RunKeeper [34] is *comparison to specific other*, where "compare friends" is an option in the reports page. There is also *comparison to group* where a specific set of people are included. This is visible when viewing a "Club" in Strava [37], for instance, as members are automatically compared based on multiple aspects. Tools may also support *comparison to collective aggregate*, concerning e.g. a generalized average. Saga [35] does this by providing a comparison with its "average user" over aspects such as "Time spent in transit each week". Finally, *comparison according to detailed demographics* allows for very specific comparisons. This is a feature of Fitbit's [14] premium service, which can give insights such as "You are in the 33rd percentile of all men and women aged 35 to 44 who are overweight".

Appraisal. The appraisal dimension concerns ways that the performance visible in the user data is evaluated or judged. In instances where when raw data is simply displayed, as e.g. rTracker does, the design choice is to use *no appraisal*. *Relative data* is a form of appraisal where the current data is evaluated based on previous performance. The Withings Health Mate app [41] does this in the form of ":(Taking only 6235 steps is the least active you've been on a Wednesday", where the sad smiley makes the desirable direction visible. Some tools provide *general encouragement* not directly referencing user data, i.e. are based on predefined designer interpretation of what is in the best interest of the user. With Basis [1], when completing a weekly habit (i.e. a recurring goal), it remarks "Keep on keepin' on; clearly it's paying off". The risk involved here is obviously that the predefined interpretation of what is good may not be as relevant to all users. Other tools, such as what Strava [37] uses through its activity feed, allow for *social encouragement*, where other users give positive feedback (e.g. by giving a "like" or "kudos").

Furthermore, evaluation of user data may be according to an abstract scoring system. One variant of this, *fixed abstract score*, is represented by Nike+ [27] which uses "NikeFuel" as a portable measurement of physical activity. We consider this as fixed because it is entirely determined by the tool (and in the NikeFuel case even according to a secret algorithm). Another variant is *customizable abstract score*, represented by RescueTime's [31] "Productivity Score", which classifies user activities according to predefined but customizable categories, yielding a 0–100 score.

4 Discussion of Implications

In the previous section, a total of nine dimensions and 53 design choices found in current personal informatics tools – indicating how user practices are enabled, constrained, and shaped presently. It has previously been recognized that personal informatics places a strong emphasis on personal reflection [22,23,29,32, 38]. Aligning intentions of the individual with the design intentions inscribed in the tools is therefore particularly important within personal informatics tools. Failure to do so is likely to cause disruption in the self-reflection process, thus causing breakdown in the central purpose of the tool use. The classification system described in this paper represents a contribution towards the design of

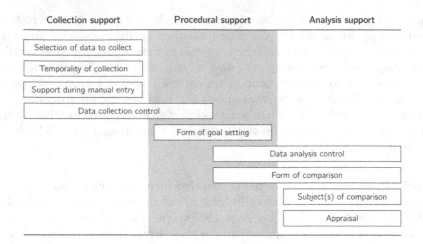

Fig. 2. Relating the classification system to the main perspectives

personal informatics tools by outlining the current design space. In itself, the examples provided may also act as inspiration for researchers that are considering which tools to use in their own inquiries.

Three perspectives set the outer boundaries for the design space of personal informatics: data collection support, procedural support, and analysis support. As evident in the examples of the previous section, the specific dimensions within these perspectives - depending on the design choices made - may result in the dimensions starting to overlap the perspectives (Fig. 2). Notably, *data collection control* and *data analysis control* contain examples of tools actively driving the personal informatics process, i.e. clearly have procedural elements. With design choices such as *goal-keeping notifications* and *behavior-determined notifications*, a tool may proactively look to engage with the user to affect the user behavior rather than simply monitor or analyze it. While such design choices are explicitly trying to affect user behavior, procedural support can also be more subtle. By supporting or promoting a certain *form of goal setting* such as Breeze's [5] automatically suggested *personalized goals*, a tool can also look to shape user behavior. Similarly, by supporting a particular *form of comparison*, a tool emphasizes aspects of the personal informatics practice and may push user behavior towards these, similar to Strava's [37] segments.

An important way of evaluating design choices in personal informatics is the type of engagement with personal data that is promoted. As an example, consider a traditional pedometer which simply displays the number of steps since last reset. One can argue that just being aware of this number promotes a certain kind of engagement, in that the user now has potential to engage with the data though the choices of if, how, and when, remain with the user. The traditional pedometer does not contribute with any form of appraisal, comparison, or procedural support. In contrast, current fitness trackers may make such contributions in very nuanced ways. This ranges from making the numbers of steps relative (e.g. to the previous day or an average), to driving data analysis (e.g. actively notifying of progress during the day) or doing tracking and evaluation on a meta level (e.g. providing points for using various aspects of the tool).

At a basic level, designers must consider the intention of a tool and whether it should promote a specific kind of behavior from the user. Placing logging on one end of a construct and behavior regulation on the other, a continuum for the identified types of engagement with informatics data may be outlined (Fig. 3). On the scale this creates, a classic pedometer would be placed as supporting logging, while a smart and proactive fitness tracker with training programs to follow would rate highly in the supporting behavior regulation.

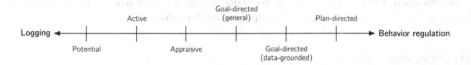

Fig. 3. Types of engagement with personal informatics data

A further observation that can be made is for the potential conflict between convenience and flexibility. Previous research has shown that enthusiasts and expert users often rely on custom tools [7], and conscious evolution of practices is a key theme in the enthusiast community [4]. Many of the tools included in our analysis are however activity-specific and quite inflexible – in effect examples of restrictively designed technologies. Such design may lead to denying user agency and control over what and how to track (cf. [32]). Taking a restrictive approach may however be understandable since this may increase product clarity and initial ease of use, something that may be harder to achieve in fully generic and customizable tools.

Striking a balance in the conflicting design ideals of convenience and flexibility may be one of the harder design decisions to take, simply as there are no dominant best practices. Early attempts to address this include design choices such as *sharable configurations*, i.e. where a user can configure and share a tracker suitable for some metric (exemplified by rTracker [33]). Another attempt is appraisal according to *customizable abstract score* (exemplified by RescueTime [31]), which initially is completely system-driven but can be customized as personal needs emerge. Exploring new forms of such gradual personalization mechanisms – that embrace the user engagement indicative of personal informatics (cf. [4]) – is a promising future development.

5   Conclusions

In this paper, we have proposed a classification system for design choices within personal informatics that is based on an analysis of current personal informatics tools. The classification system thus holds an in-practice use emphasis, and may be used as a standalone state-of-practice representation, for assessing individual tools and potential future design directions for them, and to guide new development of personal informatics tools. The overall results furthermore have implications for personal informatics in showing that end-user practices may be enabled or restricted through the selection of particular design choices.

Future research direction of this work includes establishing design considerations and similar guidelines that promote improved flexibility in personal informatics tools, as well as improved responsiveness to needs of the individual user. We believe this involves further studying procedural support primarily, as this perspective is currently dominated by the goal-setting dimension, with few examples of individualized and tailored behavior support.

Acknowledgments. This work was partially financed by the Knowledge Foundation through the Internet of Things and People research profile.

References

1. Basis. http://www.mybasis.com
2. Beeminder. https://www.beeminder.com
3. Bentley, F., Tollmar, K., Stephenson, P., Levy, L., Jones, B., Robertson, S., Price, E., Catrambone, R., Wilson, J.: Health mashups: presenting statistical patterns between wellbeing data and context in natural language to promote behavior change. Trans. Comput.-Hum. Inter. (TOCHI) **20**(5), 1–27 (2013)
4. Boesel, W.E.: What is the Quantified Self now? May 2013. http://thesocietypages.org/cyborgology/2013/05/22/what-is-the-quantified-self-now/
5. Breeze. http://breezeapp.com
6. Chartmyself. https://www.chartmyself.com
7. Choe, E.K., Lee, N.B., Lee, B., Pratt, W., Kientz, J.A.: Understanding quantified-selfers' practices in collecting and exploring personal data. In: Proceedings of the SIGCHI Conference on Human Factors in Computing Systems, CHI 2014, pp. 1143–1152. ACM, New York (2014)
8. Coach.me. http://www.coach.me
9. Corbin, J., Strauss, A.: Grounded theory research: procedures, canons, and evaluative criteria. Qual. Sociol. **13**(1), 3–21 (1990)
10. Dailydiary. https://www.dailydiary.com
11. Drinking diary. http://www.drinkingdiary.com
12. Expereal. http://expereal.com
13. Fit simply. http://www.fitly.io
14. Fitbit. http://fitbit.com
15. Fogg, B.J.: Persuasive Technology. Morgan Kaufmann, San Francisco (2003)
16. Fritz, T., Huang, E.M., Murphy, G.C., Zimmermann, T.: Persuasive technology in the real world: a study of long-term use of activity sensing devices for fitness. In: Proceedings of the SIGCHI Conference on Human Factors in Computing Systems, CHI 2014, pp. 487–496. ACM, New York (2014)
17. Garmin connect. http://connect.garmin.com/
18. i.strive.to. http://i.strive.to
19. Jawbone up. https://jawbone.com/up
20. Jawbone up coffee. https://jawbone.com/up/coffee

21. Joe's goals. http://www.joesgoals.com
22. Khovanskaya, V., Baumer, E.P.S., Cosley, D., Voida, S., Gay, G.: "Everybody knows what you're doing": a critical design approach to personal informatics. In: Proceedings of the SIGCHI Conference on Human Factors in Computing Systems, CHI 2013, pp. 3403–3412. ACM, New York (2013)
23. Li, I., Dey, A., Forlizzi, J.: A stage-based model of personal informatics systems. In: Proceedings of the SIGCHI Conference on Human Factors in Computing Systems, CHI 2010, pp. 557–566. ACM, New York (2010)
24. Loggr. http://www.loggr.me
25. Mint. https://www.mint.com
26. Moves. https://www.moves-app.com
27. Nike+. http://nikeplus.nike.com
28. Personal informatics tools. http://www.personalinformatics.org/tools/, Retrieved 2014-06-06
29. Pirzadeh, A., He, L., Stolterman, E.: Personal informatics and reflection: a critical examination of the nature of reflection. In: CHI 2013 Extended Abstracts on Human Factors in Computing Systems, pp. 1979–1988. ACM, New York (2013)
30. Reporter. http://www.reporter-app.com
31. Rescuetime. https://www.rescuetime.com
32. Rooksby, J., Rost, M., Morrison, A., Chalmers, M.C.: Personal tracking as lived informatics. In: Proceedings of the SIGCHI Conference on Human Factors in Computing Systems, CHI 2014, pp. 1163–1172. ACM, New York (2014)
33. rtracker. http://www.realidata.com/cgi-bin/rTracker/iPhone/rTracker-main.pl
34. Runkeeper. http://runkeeper.com
35. Saga. http://www.getsaga.com
36. Shilton, K.: Participatory personal data: an emerging research challenge for the information sciences. J. Am. Soc. Inform. Sci. Technol. **63**(10), 1905–1915 (2012)
37. Strava. https://www.strava.com
38. Swan, M.: The quantified self: fundamental disruption in big data science and biological discovery. Big Data **1**(2), 85–99 (2013)
39. T2 mood tracker. http://t2health.dcoe.mil/apps/t2-mood-tracker
40. Toggl. http://toggl.com
41. Withings health mate. http://www.withings.com/health-mate.html
42. Withings smart body analyzer. http://www.withings.com/smart-body-analyzer.html
43. your.flowingdata. http://your.flowingdata.com

Eye Tracking Evaluation of User Experience on Large-Scale Displays

Andrew Schall[✉]

Key Lime Interactive, Miami, FL, USA
andrew@keylimeinteractive.com

Abstract. Recent advancements in technology have made eye tracking less expensive, much easier to use, and flexible enough to track a variety of display sizes and configurations. Larger high-resolution displays have become an increasingly prominent format for many users. New user behavior patterns have been emerging between primary and secondary (also known as second screen) displays. This paper describes a new research approach in order to understand what attracts user attention and identifies what they see when interacting with these devices. A case study is presented that demonstrates the procedures and findings for a study that involves eye tracking of a large-screen television display. The study described is a user experience evaluation of dynamic on-screen content presented as a part of the display during a television program.

Keywords: Eye tracking · Large-scale displays · Television · User experience · Second screen · Study design · Case study

1 Introduction

Eye tracking is now more accessible to UX researchers than ever before. Recent advancements in technology have made eye tracking less expensive, much easier to use, and flexible enough to track a variety of devices. However, few UX researchers are aware that eye tracking isn't just for computer screens anymore. Eye tracking technology and its uses are evolving. The ability to accurately and unobtrusively conduct eye tracking research on large-scale displays was nearly impossible until only very recently. Larger high-resolution displays have become a dominant interface for our users and we need to be able understand what attracts their attention and what they see when interacting with these devices.

Conducting eye tracking on large displays can be complex. Eye tracking needs to be carefully considered during the planning of a user research study. Testing these displays with eye tracking can be daunting if the study objectives are not carefully selected, and if plans have not been made to make the necessary accommodations required to obtain reliable and accurate data.

Large display experiences are highly contextual and it can be difficult to recreate the user's environment within a lab setting. It is critical to establish the optimal distance between the user, the eye tracker and the display being evaluated. This can be complex

© Springer International Publishing Switzerland 2015
M. Antona and C. Stephanidis (Eds.): UAHCI 2015, Part I, LNCS 9175, pp. 98–108, 2015.
DOI: 10.1007/978-3-319-20678-3_10

due to limitations of the eye tracking hardware which often requires a relatively short distance between the user and eye tracker. This distance can also impact the trackability of the display itself. The larger the screen, the greater the needed distance between the participant and the display.

New user behavior patterns have been emerging between primary and secondary (also known as second screen) displays. These second screens often display content unrelated to what is being shown on the larger display and can be a source of distraction for the user. Researchers need to understand the tradeoffs associated with allowing participants to use a second display, which tends to be more natural, versus the ability to collect as much eye tracking data from the primary display as possible. It is important to understand the different eye tracking configurations available to create a balance between a realistic environment and the need to collect comparable data across participants.

Other considerations for conducting eye tracking studies with large displays include carefully planning out areas of interest for analysis. Manual segmenting of video clips can be necessary when comparing highly dynamic media across different screen regions across many participants. Large high-resolution displays also require additional computing power for capturing, analyzing and storing eye tracking data.

A case study is presented that demonstrates the study design, lab configuration, and analysis procedures for a recent study involving eye tracking of a large-scale display. The study involved the user experience evaluation of dynamic content presented as a part of the display during a television segment.

2   Using Eye Tracking to Measure User Experience

In nearly all cases, the user experience of digital interfaces is driven by visual output. These days, user experience designers are creating visual content for everything from wall-mounted displays to laptops to mobile devices.

Our visual field is constantly being bombarded by many concurrent stimuli. We are overloaded and overwhelmed by visual information, and we constantly resort to prioritizing what we pay attention to. To measure the effectiveness of content, researchers need to determine what users are looking at and what they choose or do not choose to engage with [1].

The user experience of television has been studied for numerous decades and more recently through the use of eye tracking. A fundamental difference between television and other digital media is that it tends to be more passively experienced. This puts greater weight on the viewing rather than interacting experience. User engagement becomes less about what the user is doing and instead becomes predominately about what they are visually engaging with. This makes eye tracking a natural fit for studying the user behavior of television programs.

2.1   Related Work

Eye tracking has been used to evaluate the user experience of websites to understand how users perceive and work the interface. However, eye tracking has been used in little research on television [2]. Several studies have explored the presentation of on-screen information overlaying television programs including research by Josephson and Holmes in 2006.

Researchers have found3 that individual looks at the TV vary in length and people develop different watching strategies to follow content on TV. For example, people may look at the TV only at the right times, just enough to be aware of what is happening, while being engaged in some other activity.

In the late nineties Jakob Nielsen published an article [4] based on his work comparing the experience of watching television with interacting with a computer. The diagram below summarizes the key differences between these two mediums.

	Television	Computer
Screen resolution (amount of information displayed)	relatively poor	varies from medium-sized screens to potentially very large screens
Input devices	remote control and optional wireless keyboard that are best for small amounts of input and user actions	mouse and keyboard sitting on desk in fixed positions leading to fast homing time for hands
Viewing distance	several meters	a few inches
User posture	relaxed, reclined	upright, straight
Number of users	social: many people can see screen (often, several people will be in the room when the TV is on)	solitary: few people can see the screen (user is usually alone while computing)
User engagement	passive: the viewer receives whatever the network executives decide to put on	active: user issues commands and the computer obeys

Nielsen highlights key differences between the two devices that imply how the user is likely to experience and interact with each medium. While this article was written prior to the widespread adoption of smartphones and tablets it helps to establish basic operating parameters that guide how television studies should be conducted.

Brown et al. [5] take this a step further by applying these facts to the design of a user research study. TV viewing typically occurs in a relaxed environment, quite different to that of a typical usability lab. This environment complicates experimental setup compared to an office/desktop computer scenario, with even basic challenges such as viewing distance potentially making data capture difficult.

2.2 Understanding Eye Movement Behavior While Watching TV

Holmes et al. [6] compiled key findings from several researchers who studied visual attention of the television experience using eye tracking. Based on this research, it was determined that the amount of uninterrupted sustained eye gaze on the television is only about 7 s long at a time. An even shorter period of time (less than 2 s) reflects active, informed monitoring of content that they equate to "checking in" for those familiar with the program.

Financial and news programming contains an assortment of ever changing content.

This type of viewing for frequent, yet very short periods of time also makes sense for those watching financial and news programming where the information changes very quickly. Viewers of this particular type of content are used to obtaining small fragments of information at a time with frequent periods of looking towards and away from the screen.

2.3 Use of a Second Screen

Many users today do not sit down and entirely focus their attention on the television screen. The ubiquitous nature of mobile devices has created the phenomena of a two-screen experience. In 2014, 84 % of smartphone and tablet owners said that they use their devices as second-screens while watching TV at the same time [7]. To better understand the second-screen experience Holmes et al. performed an eye tracking study where participants were asked to watch a program on a television and also use a companion app on a tablet computer. They found that on average only 63 % of the participants' attention went to the television during the program, and 30 % to the tablet (and 7 % off of both screens).

The effects of a second device should be a major consideration for any studies involving the study of real world television viewing experiences.

3 Case Study: Evaluating the Effectiveness of a Financial TV Segment

Many news and financial television networks utilize on-screen visualizations complementary to their standard programming. These can include news alerts, stock performance, and additional details related to a story. One particular organization, which shall be referred to as "Financial Network 1" for the purposes of this paper, wanted to better understand the viewing behaviors of their audience. The executives and producers of the network's programming had several assumptions related to typical viewing patterns and areas of attention. They believed that by providing a screen with less visually complex information it would encourage viewers to engage more with the content displayed. They also believed that the type of content displayed is the information that their audience most wanted to see.

The research team involved also theorized that many of the audience members would likely multitask while watching the network, which may include the use of smartphones, tablets, laptops and non-digital media as well. The team wanted to be able to understand typical viewer behavior while they watched live television as opposed to prerecorded programs.

3.1 Research Goals

A series of research objectives were established in order to better understand user behavior while watching the network. The goals included:

- How quickly do they notice each of the on-screen elements?
- How long do they spend looking at certain Areas of Interest (AOIs)?
- How many times do they look at an AOI during the viewing period?
- Do they read the bullets and headlines? How many do they read?

Another goal of the study was to compare the results with a competing television network's programming to see if the different design layout contributed to the consumption of different types of information.

3.2 Stimulus Materials

All of the network programming contains the same types of onscreen elements such as a dedicated box for news stories and stock information. The various elements of the on-screen displays were categorized into a series of Areas of Interest (AOIs) that were then later used during analysis.

3.3 Participants

Given the distinctive type of content provided on both television networks it was critical to obtain participants that would normally watch financial news programs. This included both members of the general public with personal portfolios as well as professional investors who manage the portfolios of their clients. Participants were asked about their current viewing behaviors including which specific networks they watch and how often they watch them. Our study included a total of 35 participants.

Talking head content	Top News
	Bottom News
Stock Information	

Layout of Financial Network 1.

Stock Markets	
Talking Head Content	Right News
Individual Stock Information	

Layout of Financial Network 2.

3.4 Test Protocol

All participants watched live TV programming, so they saw different programming depending on their session times. All sessions took place between 7 am and 6 pm. Viewers were asked to simulate their normal TV viewing behavior by using the desktop PC or their own personal devices (e.g. phones, tablets, laptops); they were not required to watch TV the entire time.

Participants watched each channel, Network 1 and Network 2, for 15 min (total of 30 min TV viewing). The order of the two channels was alternated (e.g., P1 watched Network 1 then Network 2, P2 watched Network 2 then Network 1, etc.) in order to eliminate any order bias. Each session in total lasted approximately 45 min to 1 h

After watching both networks, participants were asked a series of questions about their viewing experience. This provided a qualitative perspective on why participants were interested in certain content and areas of the display.

The research team made efforts to create as natural an environment as possible for participants. The setting used was meant to emulate a typical home office or desk at an office. The environment included commonly found elements such as a desktop computer, telephone, large working surface, and also a television.

Time (1 hour in length)	Section Description
0:00-0:10 (10 minutes)	Section I. Introduction and background questions • What do you do for a living? • When are you normally watching TV? • What do you do while watching TV? • Why do you watch ' and/or '
0:10-0:15 (5 minutes)	Section II. Eye Tracking Calibration
0:15-0:30 (15 minutes)	Section III. Live video segment #1 • / or (randomized) • Allowed to multi-task and use computer and/or personal device
0:30-0:45 (15 minutes)	Section IV. Live video segment #2 • √ or (randomized) • Allowed to multi-task and use computer and/or personal device

0:45-1:00
(15 minutes)
	Section V. Qualitative feedback and follow-up questions
	• Overall feedback regarding on-screen content and news programming
	• Ranking screen content areas
	• Comparative rankings between ' anc
	  • Stock and market information
	  • On-screen readability
	  • Overall usefulness of screen data

Test session breakdown.

Participants were encouraged to use their own personal devices throughout the test session including tablets (e.g. iPads) and smartphones (e.g. iPhones). They also were given access to a desktop computer with dual monitors in order to browse the Internet.

1. Participants viewed media on a 46-inch TV.
2. The eye tracker was placed on the desk in front of viewers.
3. A computer was available for participants to use while watching TV.
4. A ceiling mounted camera was used to capture the participant's face

One of the most challenging technical aspects of the study setup involved the eye tracker itself. We used a Tobii X2 Eye Tracker [8] to track the participant's eyes while looking at the television monitor. The eye tracker can only do accurate tracking of a person's eyes if the visual angle, as seen from the person's eyes, does not exceed 36°, between the center of the eye tracker and any point on what the person is looking at. This is valid as long as the person stays within the area in front of the eye tracker defined as the area of freedom of head movement, which is roughly between 40 and 90 cm from the center of the eye tracker when seen from the side. This means that depending on the position of the eye tracker in relation to the display, it can track different sizes of displays. If the display is positioned further away from the user, a larger area can be tracked.

Another feature is the aspect ratio of the display. Since the optimally tracked area is about half circle, the eye tracker can track displays with a large width to height ratio better than displays where this ratio is small. This was ideal for our setup, which included a typical widescreen HD television display.

The limitations of the technology required that we place the eye tracker on a small tripod directly in front of the participant with the television display set up approximately 1.8 m further away. The setup was also limited by the distance the television could be from the participant. In an ideal setting, the television would have been wall-mounted and placed a greater distance from the participant, however this was not possible due to the limitations of the lab space.

3.5 Analysis

The analysis included a qualitative aspect focusing on general user viewing patterns and areas of engagement as well as a quantitative aspect focusing on predefined areas of interest.

Due to the nature of eye tracking user interfaces over video content, traditional automated and aggregated eye tracking analysis methods (such as heat maps) could not be generated for the television interfaces tested. Instead, we relied on a more time-consuming qualitative analysis method: watching videos of each session. While watching each session, we looked for recurring patterns of usage behavior, paying special attention to participants' eye fixations and saccades.

3.6 Results

Not surprisingly, the most amount of viewing time was spent watching the primary news story (72 %). However, a significant amount of time was spent viewing the other onscreen information. It was determined that over a quarter of viewing time (28 %) on

Network 1's programming was spent reading news content on the side of the screen. This area was separated out into two areas. The top section received 20 % of attention while the bottom half received only 8 % of viewer's attention. Participants also looked at the top news section more frequently (every 13 s compared with the bottom (every 27 s). By using the time to first fixation metric we were able to determine that participants noticed the news area early on in their viewing experience. On average, they first viewed the top news area within the first 13 s and the bottom news area within 18 s. In comparison, it took participants much longer to notice other onscreen elements such as the stock ticker (42 s), market data (46 s) or date/time (60 s).

Measure	Definition	What it indicates?	Unit of measurement
Total Visit Duration	Cumulative amount of time spent looking at a particular area	Fixed attention and attraction to a given area	seconds % of total time spent
Visit Count	The number of times a person looks at a particular area	Usefulness and attraction to a given area	# of times visited
Visit Duration	The average length of time per look in a particular area	Fixed attention and usefulness of a given area	seconds
Time to First Fixation*	The amount of time before a person looks at a particular area	Noticeability of a given area	seconds

*Fixation is a pause in eye movement. Saccade is rapid eye movement between fixations.

On average participants looked at the main story most frequently (11 s). In comparison, the news headlines attracted their attention approximately every 19 s. Participants looked at the market data the least (53 s).

In our post experience debriefs participants said that they found the news on the right side to be informative, in proportion to their interests, and that the information stayed on the screen long enough to understand what the story was about. The real-time eye gaze data supported this by showing clearly defined left to right reading patterns across each of the bullets of information displayed in the news box. Most participants appeared to read at least two of the bullets before the content changed. We were surprised by how quickly participants were able to scan over the content. The average viewing time for the top news box was only 2 s on average per visit, however this was sufficient time to read the contents of a bullet or a headline.

Participants were least interested in viewing the market data. During the debriefs participants said that they only wanted to see general market trends such as whether the major markets were trending up or down. Most were not interested in seeing individual stocks because they would normally look this information up on their computer and would not want to wait for a specific stock to appear on the TV screen. This was supported by the eye tracking data that showed attention on the market data to last no more than a second or two at a time.

The news information performed better overall on Network 1 than on Network 2. Participants spent 61 s longer reading news content on Network 1 than Network 2 (a total viewing time of 28 % compared with 15 %). However, out of the total viewing time participants spent more time looking at Network 2's stock information (46 s compared to 25 s total).

4 Conclusion

Recent advancements in technology have made eye tracking less expensive, much easier to use, and flexible enough to track a variety of devices. Eye tracking technology and its uses are evolving. Larger high-resolution displays have become a dominant interface for our users and we need to be able understand what attracts their attention and what they see when interacting with these devices. Eye tracking needs to be carefully considered during the planning of a user research study. Large display experiences are highly contextual and it can be difficult to recreate the user's environment within a lab setting. New user behavior patterns have been emerging between primary and secondary displays. Researchers need to understand the tradeoffs associated with allowing participants to use a second display, which tends to be more natural, versus the ability to collect as much eye tracking data from the primary display as possible. It is important to understand the different eye tracking configurations available to create a balance between a realistic environment and the need to collect comparable data across participants.

References

1. Bergstrom, J.R., Schall, A. (eds.): Eye Tracking in User Experience Design. Elsevier, Waltham (2014)
2. Ali-Hasan, N.F., Harrington, E.J., Richman, J.B.: Best practices for eye tracking of television and video user experiences. In: Proceedings of the 1st International Conference on Designing Interactive User Experiences for TV and Video, pp. 5–8. ACM, October 2008
3. Vatavu, R.D., Mancas, M.: Visual attention measures for multi-screen TV. In: Proceedings of the 2014 ACM International Conference on Interactive Experiences for TV and Online Video, pp. 111–118. ACM, June 2014
4. Nielsen, J.: TV meets the web. Alertbox for February 15 (1997)
5. Brown, A., Evans, M., Jay, C., Glancy, M., Jones, R., Harper, S.: HCI over multiple screens. In: CHI 2014 Extended Abstracts on Human Factors in Computing Systems, pp. 665–674. ACM, April 2014

6. Holmes, M.E., Josephson, S., Carney, R.E.: Visual attention to television programs with a second-screen application. In: Proceedings of the Symposium on Eye Tracking Research and Applications, pp. 397–400. ACM, New York (2012)
7. What's empowering the new digital consumer? Nielsen.com, http://www.nielsen.com/us/en/insights/news/2014/whats-empowering-the-new-digital-consumer.html. Accessed 1 Feb 2015
8. Tobii X2-60 Eye Tracker User's Manual V.1.0.3. Tobii, 2014. Web, 1 February 2015

Design and Development of Multimodal Applications: A Vision on Key Issues and Methods

Samuel Silva[1,2]([✉]), Nuno Almeida[1,2], Carlos Pereira[1,2], Ana Isabel Martins[1,2], Ana Filipa Rosa[1,2], Miguel Oliveira e Silva[1,2], and António Teixeira[1,2]

[1] IEETA – Institute of Electronics and Informatics Engineering, University of Aveiro, Aveiro, Portugal
sss@ua.pt
[2] DETI – Department of Electronics, Telecommunications and Informatics Engineering, University of Aveiro, Aveiro, Portugal

Abstract. Multimodal user interfaces provide users with different ways of interacting with applications. This has advantages both in providing interaction solutions with additional robustness in environments where a single modality might result in ambiguous input or output (e.g., speech in noisy environments), and for users with some kind of limitation (e.g., hearing difficulties resulting from ageing) by yielding alternative and more natural ways of interacting. The design and development of applications supporting multimodal interaction involves numerous challenges, particularly if the goals include the development of multimodal applications for a wide variety of scenarios, designing complex interaction and, at the same time, proposing and evolving interaction modalities. These require the choice of an architecture, development and evaluation methodologies and the adoption of principles that foster constant improvements at the interaction modalities level without disrupting existing applications. Based on previous and ongoing work, by our team, we present our approach to the design, development and evaluation of multimodal applications covering several devices and application scenarios.

Keywords: Multimodal interaction · Design and development · Evaluation

1 Introduction

Multimodal user interfaces (MMUI) allow the user to interact with the machine recurring to natural communication modalities such as speech, pen, touch and gesture. This provides a more robust and stable solution than a single modality interface, due to the mutual disambiguation inherent to an MMUI [7]. One of the most pervasive applications of MMUIs is in the accessibility and inclusion area where some studies [10,31] show that they improve the user experience by disabled, elderly and not so technologically-savvy users [25,26].

© Springer International Publishing Switzerland 2015
M. Antona and C. Stephanidis (Eds.): UAHCI 2015, Part I, LNCS 9175, pp. 109–120, 2015.
DOI: 10.1007/978-3-319-20678-3_11

The multimodal interaction scenario poses several challenges for designers and developers. It is not just the possibility of using different modalities to interact with the applications and devices, it is also the continuously changing plethora of modalities that are proposed, need to be tested and possibly supported by existing applications. Several modalities are already part of everyday activities, such as touch, but what about evolving modalities such as eye gazing or emerging approaches such as silent speech [14] or emotions?

In this article we discuss several aspects which we deem important to the design, development and evaluation of multimodal systems. These, derive from our experience gathered from continued work on multimodal applications in the context of several projects such as S4S[1], AAL4ALL[2] and Paelife.[3]

The contribution of this article is a vision of the full multimodal application design and development cycle, for which we have made contributions, at different levels, along with our perspective on what are the some of the key issues to address. At the onset of our proposals are concerns regarding how traditional methods need to be adapted, to serve the more complex scenario of multimodality, and what needs to be proposed, to tackle new challenges and provide users with the best possible experience of usable and useful applications.

In our discussion, we consider three aspects: (1) the system architecture, to flexibly support multimodality, not only to deploy applications, but also to support research in, for example, interaction modalities; (2) the design and development methodologies, to account for proper gathering and fulfilment of requirements, adapted to the target users; and (3) the evaluation, at the different stages of development, considering the increasing complexity of the application, its possibly distributed nature and the importance of context.

The focus of this article is not on a detailed descriptions of all aspects, but in providing an integrated view of the full range of what we have been considering and adopting for the design, development and evaluation of multimodal applications, providing examples, and, where applicable, directing the reader to additional literature. With this, we hope to contribute to show how a set of methods and tools can be put together to support research and development in multimodality, in a wide range of scenarios. This is not to be understood as the only way to do it, nor the methods are presented as the best, but as the possible instruments to serve a set of long-term research goals.

The remainder of this article is organised as follows: Sect. 2 briefly discusses multimodal interactions and presents our high level research goals; Sect. 3 concerns the rationale and advantages deriving from adopting a multimodal architecture aligned with the W3C recommendations; Sect. 4 describes the adopted iterative user-centred development methodology; Sect. 5 explains the methods used for system evaluation, how they blend with the development methods and adapt to the different development stages; finally, Sect. 6 presents conclusions and ideas for further work.

---

[1] http://www.smartphones4seniors.org/.

[2] http://www.aal4all.org.

[3] www.paelife.eu.

2   Multimodal Interaction

Multimodal interaction research looks for more natural communication channels [24] and for ways to deal with certain context restrictions or user limitations (e.g., reduced motor and cognitive abilities as a result of ageing) by adding
redundancy to the interfaces or by providing the chance to perform different
tasks using the most suitable modality [3]. This can improve accessibility and
user performance, but we are no longer designing for a fixed keyboard and mouse
setting and the essence of multimodal interaction raises different challenges if we
want to harness its full potential.

First, designing multimodal interfaces requires following a set of principles
that concern the applicability of the different modalities to specific tasks and
data and needs to consider how to perform modality combination and adaptability (e.g., to context) [32]. Second, interaction modalities are often improved
or new modalities can be proposed and need to be tested in a context that favours
a perception of their real potential and flaws. Third, any application should be
designed with a strong focus on its potential users and application contexts and
be subject of thorough evaluation. For multimodal applications it is particularly relevant to pay attention to how different modalities might interact or how
cognitive load or task complexity might influence performance [35] or modality
choice. Finally, developing a multimodal application, if it includes many features
and interaction modalities, might be a complex task and its modularity might
enable parallel development efforts.

Each of these aspects is a challenge in itself and contributions to each are
required. When addressing research on multimodality, we consider a set of high-
level goals:

- Specifically address the particularities of the target user groups (e.g., elderly)
  and contexts;
- Develop and improve interaction modalities, with a particular emphasis on
  speech related interaction given its importance for human communication and
  usefulness for interaction with small/vanishing devices;
- Develop multimodal systems for different devices and application scenarios;
- Foster evaluations that account for the maturity level of the application, for
  the characteristics of the end-users and for multimodal interaction and the
  context in which it should happen;
- Collaboratively develop complex applications e.g., by different partners in a
  research project;

Based on these high-level goals we made a set of choices, adopting or evolving methods already described in the literature and started research on aspects
we felt were not conveniently covered by the state-of-the-art as detailed in the
following sections.

3   Architecture

Some approaches to accomplish multimodal interactions have been proposed in
the literature, such as Mudra [16] or HepaisTK [11]. One notable effort we have

been following attentively is being performed by the World Wide Web Consortium (W3C). The W3C recommendation for multimodal architectures [4] defines four major components of a multimodal system (as depicted in Fig. 1) and defines how the communication between the components and data modules should work. Notable modules in the architecture are modalities and the interaction manager. The W3C recommendations, even though they are originally proposed for web scenarios, encompass the potential to support a wider range of applications as we advocated in Teixeira et al. [39]. Therefore, we adopted its view and extend it for the general multimodal interaction scenario encompassing mobile devices (e.g., smartphones, tablets) and different application contexts, e.g. AAL [36]. This is enabled by the versatile nature of the architecture and provides a direct answer to a significant part of the envisaged requirements, easing the creation and integration of new modules or their improvements.

Therefore, having a standard for multimodal architecture helps application developers to avoid the unpractical situation of having to master each individual modality technology. This is particularly problematic as the number of technologies that can be used with multimodal interaction is increasing rapidly. This standard architecture gives experts the possibility to develop standalone components [9] that can be used in a common way.

This architecture has already been tested as the basis for the development of a multimodal personal assistant application [36], in the scope of project PaeLife, involving the development of different modules (messaging services, agenda, weather report, news) by multiple European partners and supporting speech interaction in multiple languages (Portuguese, French, Hungarian, Polish and English). The adoption of this architecture allowed a collaborative effort from all partners and a seamless integration of all modules, including increasingly refined versions of the speech modality [1, 38].

Another line of research we are following, supported on this architecture, is multimodal multi-device applications development [2]. It consists in interacting with an application using more than one device with each device providing a set of interaction modalities and presenting the user with the same or

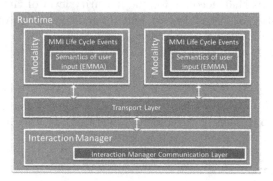

Fig. 1. The W3C multimodal architecture diagram depicting its main components.

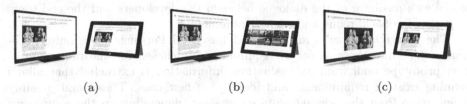

(a)   (b)   (c)

Fig. 2. Using a news reader in a multi-device setting. The two devices can present: (a) the same content; (b) content and navigation pane; or (c) detail and full content.

complementary views of the application. In a particular instantiation of this concept, in project PaeLife, the personal assistant application can be accessed through a tablet and, if near the television, use its display to provide detailed news contents, while the user keeps browsing the news list on the tablet. When the user moves away, all interaction and output are performed using the tablet. Figure 2 shows different ways of accessing the same application using two devices: a TV and a tablet.

4 Design and Development

The adoption of the architecture, as described in the previous section, defines the organization for the different components required to develop a multimodal application and provides the structure to support research at its different levels, but how can we use it to develop applications tailored to specific audiences and scenarios?

First of all, it is our view that interaction and interaction modalities need to be developed considering real application contexts that allow the definition of realistic requirements and the assessment of their performance [12]. Therefore, we do not separate modality development and tuning from applications [1]. This view benefits from the adopted architecture since any developed modality is not hard coded onto the application, but is a module that can then be reused in any other of our applications.

Since one of our goals is dealing with different age groups, particularly those presenting strong heterogeneity [34], whether age-related or deriving from other disabilities impeding communication and interaction, it is important to adopt a methodology that includes the end-users in the whole process. Furthermore, given the complexity of the envisaged systems and interaction modalities, it makes sense to have multiple development stages [19] and assess progress along the way, to guaranty that the system evolves towards the defined requirements and is usable and useful for its users. Therefore, and inheriting from user-centred design (UCD), we adopted an iterative, user-centred methodology aligned with Martins et al. [21]. After obtaining the requirements (phase 1), a prototype is proposed (phase 2) and evaluated (phase 3), in order to refine the requirements. This iterative methodology continues with additional prototypes and evaluations towards an increasingly refined application. In this methodology, the prototype works as a mediator of the dialogue between the developers and the end users to gather feedback, refine and elicit requirements.

The first requirements are gathered based on Personas and context scenarios [8]. From these, a set of requirements is chosen for the first application prototype and, from its evaluation, information is extracted that allows refining existing requirements and identifying new ones. These, and possibly a few more from the original requirements list, depending on the complexity involved in addressing any of the problems identified or refinements needed, are used as requirements for the new prototype and a new development iteration is performed.

Note that, since this methodology is grounded on fast prototyping, and significant additions or changes might be required from one prototype to the other, the adopted architecture plays a key role in reducing the development effort. Its modularity provides a decoupling among the different aspects (modalities, fusion, graphical user interface, etc.) minimizing the cascade effect when changes are required.

Examples of applications developed by adopting this methodology are those of Medication Assistant [13], an application devoted to address different factors contributing to medication non-adherence in the elderly; Trip4All [33], a gamified tourism application that provides users with information and Telerehab, a telerehabilitation service [37] that allows a patient to perform a remote physiotherapy session supervised by a physiotherapist.

5   Evaluation

The previous section already presented evaluation as intrinsic to the adopted iterative design and development methodology, but how should this evaluation be performed?

The design and development of complex multimodal systems, working in multiple devices and deployed in dynamic environments, poses several challenges. Beyond the technical aspects, designing user experience in this context is far from being simple. At this level, tasks and interaction modalities cannot be looked at as isolated phenomena. For example, the use of several modalities simultaneously, as a result of a more complex use of the system, might result in sensory overload; or particular modalities, which in abstract seem suitable options, are disregarded in some (e.g., stressful) situations. Furthermore, these concerns are particularly relevant when the target users might present some level of disability, physical or cognitive, which directly influences how they use the system: an audio warning might not be heard by the user, due to a hearing disability, or multiple tasks crossing might leave the user disoriented. Therefore, integration of proper evaluation, in the development cycles, covering different contexts of use and complex tasks, running in its intended (real or simulated) environment, is of paramount importance and should be increasingly introduced, from early on, as a tool to support the development of such systems.

In Martins et al. [21] a method is described that reflects this need to intertwine evaluation with iterative design and development and considers three phases: conceptual validation, prototype test, and pilot test. The first phase of evaluation, conceptual validation, aims to determine if an idea of a system is sustainable in terms of interface and functions. In the prototype test, the second phase of the evaluation, the goal is to collect information regarding the usability and user satisfaction. At this phase there is already a physical implementation of the system prototype in order to be tested by users. The prototype test is conducted in a controlled environment and can be repeated the number of times judged necessary, e.g., to fulfil the defined requirements. Finally, the third phase of evaluation, the pilot test, and the goal is to evaluate, in addition to usability and satisfaction, the meaning that a system has on users lives. For this reason, this last phase of testing differs from the prototype phase in the context where it happens. The system should be installed in user's homes and integrated into their daily life routines.

It has been discussed, in the literature, that users tend to increase their use of multimodality if cognitive load or task difficulty increase [27] and context plays an important role in how systems are used and modalities selected [42]. The advantages of deploying systems in the field are also an important aspect for evaluating multimodal systems [5,30] and might be an entry point to the long term assessment of user experience as advocated, for example, by Ickin et al. [17] and Wechsung [40]. Therefore, adding complexity, context and naturalness to the usability evaluation seems an important route to follow. Nonetheless, and even though some of the usual usability evaluation approaches can be used [40], accounting for all the environmental factors is not a simple task and might profit from a supporting framework.

Facing these issues and considering evaluation scenarios such as those of a telerehabilitation application [37], or where evaluating the system during context changes is important such as in multi-device scenarios, we have proposed Dynamic Evaluation as a Service (DynEaaS) [28] that is an evaluation platform providing the means to evaluate user performance in dynamical environments by allowing evaluation teams to create and conduct context-aware evaluations. The platform allows evaluators to specify evaluation plans which are triggered at precise timings or only when certain conditions are met, thus gathering better contextualized data. DynEaaS follows a distributed paradigm allowing the evaluator to run multiple evaluations at different locations simultaneously. At each location, the plan is instantiated and applied taking into account user preferences, current context and the environment itself. When applying the plan, DynEaaS constantly evaluates the current context and chooses the best suited conditions to interact with the user. Results are synchronized in real time. By having access to them, the evaluator is able to analyze current data and have a better grasp on the evaluation current status making small changes to it, if required (Fig. 3).

The major difference of DynEaaS, when compared to other evaluation frameworks, such as those proposed by Navarro et al. [22], Ickin et al. [17] and Witt [44] is that it specifically addresses the context of use and emphasizes the need to collect the data at the best possible time, or at least contextualizing it as best as

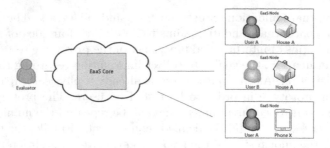

Fig. 3. DynEaaS allows the instantiation of local nodes in each of the envisaged evaluation contexts, based on evaluation plans defined by the evaluator, and adapts the application of the defined evaluation tools to the local ecosystem.

possible. For example, it makes far more sense to ask a user about an application feature right after he has used (or had problems with) it than to do the same questions at the end of the evaluation session, when most of the impressions have probably faded; or it might not be a good time to enrol the user in providing feedback if he/she is leaving for an appointment. Furthermore, by using ontologies, DynEaaS is highly flexible and can be used in different domains without core changes.

Another aspect that is also important, beyond the stages at which evaluation is performed and the support framework described above, is which methods to use to actually measure the quality of service (QoS) and quality of experience (QoE) and Wechsung et al. [41] propose a taxonomy of the factors defining each one of these measures. Usability questionnaires are also an important tool for evaluation and a set of works has been presented assessing the applicability of existing questionnaires (AttrakDiff [15], System Usability Scale (SUS) [6], USE [20] and QUESI [23]) to the evaluation of multimodal systems [18]. Despite the great number of usability questionnaires, none of them adequately addresses user functionality when interacting with technology solutions. Existing questionnaires are technology-oriented instead of user centred. To address this issue, members of our team [21] proposed assessment tools based on the International Classification of Functioning, Disability and Health (ICF) [43] addressing the individuals' functionality and assessing environmental factors according to an ICF approach. The ICF brought the concepts of functionality and disability into a multidimensional understanding of human functioning, such as biological, psychological, social and environmental. The surrounding environment is crucial in multimodal systems in the attenuation or elimination of the disability. In ICF, an environmental factor is classified as a facilitator if contributes to increase users performance and participation.

Technologies, including multimodal systems, should be considered as environmental factors in an ICF approach. Accordingly, the ICF may arise as a conceptual model for the holistic development of a methodology for evaluation of environmental factors and, consequently, multimodal systems. The assessment tools were created based on the first qualifier of the ICF environmental factors. Using the ICF as a framework to develop instruments for the evaluation of environmental factors permits that the terminology, concepts and coded information can be aggregated with the available in-formation, and can also be used as a comprehensive model to characterize users and their contexts, activities and participation [21]. Applying these tools at the proper time, in the relevant context maximizes their utility and their integration with DynEaaS has been performed [29].

6   Conclusions

This article provides an overview of our approach to the design and development of multimodal applications, covering the full cycle, from architecture definition to evaluation. In the different lines of work involved there is still room for improvement. On the subject of the multimodal architecture, we are currently exploring how to integrate fusion in our multimodal framework, producing fusion of events, and how to dynamically discover and register new interaction modalities.

In terms of the evaluation process, more research is needed in the consolidation of the ICF evaluation method. However, despite of the operational difficulties in the evaluation using the ICF as a conceptual framework, it is still an added value because it focuses the assessment in the users functionality. The ICF seems to be useful to identify what to change in the product and what to consider as a good practice.

The usage of ontologies on DynEaaS opens the door to automatic data evaluation which is able to trigger new questions based on domain ontologies. Such a feature would enable evaluation plans to inquire the user without the evaluator specifically setting the questions. In such a scenario, this would enable the evaluator to simply indicate a domain ontology from which DynEaaS would extract knowledge and combine it with already gathered data to enhance the evaluation plan on its own. On the subject of evaluation the use of DynEaaS paves the way to improved in-context evaluations, but also brings forward an infrastructure that might be used to gather data that allows continuously measuring user performance and detecting changes in behaviour. This might be due, for example, to some environmental changes or a sign of difficulties in dealing with the system or particular features. Proper handling of such information can lead to improved adaptability of the system [44].

To conclude, we do not claim this to be the only (or the best) possible approach. Instead, we aim to provide an integrated view of the whole pipeline, currently in use, along with the rationale supporting our choices. Along the way, we refer to concrete examples that have been put together using this same methods and discuss where they can/need to evolve and where the literature provides further information.

Acknowledgments. Research partially funded by IEETA Research Unit funding (PEst-OE/EEI/UI0127/2014), project Cloud Thinking (funded by the QREN Mais Centro program, ref. CENTRO-07-ST24-FEDER-002031), Marie Curie Actions IRIS (ref. 610986, FP7-PEOPLE-2013-IAPP), project Smart Phones for Seniors (S4S), a QREN project (QREN 21541), co-funded by COMPETE and FEDER, project PaeLife (AAL-08-1-2001-0001) and project AAL4ALL (AAL/0015/2009).

References

1. Almeida, N., Silva, S., Teixeira, A.: Design and development of speech interaction: a methodology. In: Kurosu, M. (ed.) HCI 2014, Part II. LNCS, vol. 8511, pp. 370–381. Springer, Heidelberg (2014)
2. Almeida, N., Silva, S., Teixeira, A.: Multimodal multi-device application supported by an SCXML state chart machine. In: Proceedings of EICS Workshop on Engineering Interactive Systems with SCXML (2014)
3. Basson, S., Fairweather, P.G., Hanson, V.L.: Speech recognition and alternative interfaces for older users. Interactions 14(4), 26–29 (2007)
4. Bodell, M., Dahl, D., Kliche, I., Larson, J., Porter, B.: Multimodal architecture and interfaces. In: W3C (2012). http://www.w3.org/TR/mmi-arch/
5. Bonsignore, E., Quinn, A.J., Druin, A., Bederson, B.B.: Sharing stories "in the wild": a mobile storytelling case study using storykit. ACM Trans. Comput.-Hum. Interact. 20(3), 18:1–18:38 (2013)
6. Brooke, J.: SUS-A quick and dirty usability scale. In: Thomas, B., Weerdmeester, B.A., McClelland, A.L. (eds.) Usability Evaluation in Industry, vol. 189, pp. 189–194. Taylor & Francis, London (1996)
7. Chen, F., Sun, Y.: An efficient unification-based multimodal language processor for multimodal input fusion. In: Multimodal Human Computer Interaction and Pervasive Services, pp. 58–86 (2009)
8. Cooper, A., Reimann, R., Cronin, D.: About Face 3: The Essentials of Interactive Design, 3rd edn. Wiley Publications, New York (2007)
9. Dahl, D.A.: The W3C multimodal architecture and interfaces standard. J. Multimodal User Interfaces 7(3), 171–182 (2013)
10. D'Andrea, A., D'Ulizia, A., Ferri, F., Grifoni, P.: A multimodal pervasive framework for ambient assisted living. In: Proceedings 2nd International Conference on PErvasive Technologies Related to Assistive Environments, New York, pp. 39:1–39:8 (2009)
11. Dumas, B., Lalanne, D., Ingold, R.: HephaisTK: a toolkit for rapid prototyping of multimodal interfaces. In: Proceedings of International Conference on Multimodal Interfaces, pp. 231–232 (2009)
12. Ferreira, F., Almeida, N., Rosa, A., Oliveira, A., Teixeira, A., Pereira, J.: Multimodal and adaptable medication assistant for the elderly: a prototype for interaction and usability in smartphones. In: Proceedings of 8th Iberian Conference on Information Systems and Technologies (CISTI), pp. 1–6, June 2013
13. Ferreira, F., Almeida, N., Rosa, A.F., Oliveira, A., Casimiro, J., Silva, S., Teixeira, A.: Elderly centered design for interaction - the case of the S4S medication assistant. Procedia Comput. Sci. 27, 398–408 (2014)
14. Freitas, J., Teixeira, A., Dias, M.S.: Towards a silent speech interface for Portuguese: surface electromyography and the nasality challenge. In: Proceedings International Conference on Bio-Inspired Systems and Signal Processing (BIOSIGNALS), pp. 91–100 (2012)
15. Hassenzahl, M., Monk, A.: The inference of perceived usability from beauty. Hum.-Comput. Interact. 25(3), 235–260 (2010)

16. Hoste, L., Dumas, B., Signer, B.: Mudra: a unified multimodal interaction framework. In: Proceedings of 13th International Conference Multimodal Interfaces, pp. 97–104. ACM, New York (2011)
17. Ickin, S., Wac, K., Fiedler, M., Janowski, L., Hong, J.H., Dey, A.: Factors influencing quality of experience of commonly used mobile applications. IEEE Commun. Mag. **50**(4), 48–56 (2012)
18. Kühnel, C.,Westermann, T., Weiss, B., Möller, S.: Evaluating multimodal systems: a comparison of established questionnaires and interaction parameters. In: Proceedings of 6th Nordic Conference on HCI: Extending Boundaries, NordiCHI 2010, pp. 286–294. ACM, New York (2010)
19. Lemmelä, S., Vetek, A., Mäkelä, K., Trendafilov, D.: Designing and evaluating multimodal interaction for mobile contexts. In: Proceedings of 10th International Conference Multimodal Interfaces, pp. 265–272. ACM, New York (2008)
20. Lund, A.M.: Measuring usability with the USE questionnaire. Usability Interface **8**(2), 3–6 (2001)
21. Martins, A.I., Queirós, A., Cerqueira, M., Rocha, N., Teixeira, A.: The international classification of functioning, disability and health as a conceptual model for the evaluation of environmental factors. Procedia Comp. Sci. **14**, 293–300 (2012)
22. Mateo Navarro, P., Hillmann, S., Möller, S., Sevilla Ruiz, D., Martínez Pérez, G.: Run-time model based framework for automatic evaluation of multimodal interfaces. J. Multimodal User Interfaces **8**(4), 399–427 (2014)
23. Naumann, A., Wechsung, I., Hurtienne, J.: Multimodality, inclusive design, and intuitive use. In: Proceedings of British Computer Society HCI Workshop and Conference (2009)
24. Obrenovic, Z., Abascal, J., Starcevic, D.: Universal accessibility as a multimodal design issue. Commun. ACM **50**(5), 83–88 (2007)
25. Oviatt, S.: Designing robust multimodal systems for universal access. In: Proceedings of Workshop on Universal Accessibility of Ubiquitous Computing: Providing for the Elderly, pp. 71–74. ACM, New York (2001)
26. Oviatt, S., Cohen, P., Wu, L., Vergo, J., Duncan, L., Suhm, B., Bers, J., Holzman, T., Winograd, T., Landay, J., Larson, J., Ferro, D.: Designing the user interface for multimodal speech and pen-based gesture applications: state-of-the-art systems and future research directions. Hum.-Comput. Interact. **15**(4), 263–322 (2000)
27. Oviatt, S., Coulston, R., Lunsford, R.: When do we interact multimodally?: cognitive load and multimodal communication patterns. In: Proceedings of 6th International Conference on Multimodal Interfaces, New York, pp. 129–136 (2004)
28. Pereira, C., Teixeira, A., Oliveira e Silva, M.: Live evaluation within ambient assisted living scenarios. In: Proceedings of 7th ACM Conference on Pervasive Technologies Related to Assistive Environments (PETRA) (2014)
29. Pereira, C., Ferreira, N., Martins, A.I., Silva, S., Rosa, A.F., e Silva, M.O., Teixeira, A.: Evaluation of complex distributed multimodal applications: evaluating a telerehabilitation system when it really matters. In: Proceedings of HCII, LA, CA, USA, August 2015
30. Ramsay, A., McGee-Lennon, M., Wilson, G.A., Gray, S.J., Gray, P., De Turenne, F.: Tilt and go: exploring multimodal mobile maps in the field. J. Multimodal User Interfaces **3**(3), 167–177 (2010)
31. de Salces, F.J.S., England, D., Llewellyn-Jones, D.: Designing for all in the house. In: Proceedings of the 2005 Latin American Conference on Human-Computer Interaction, CLIHC 2005, pp. 283–288. ACM, New York (2005)

32. Sarter, N.: Multimodal Information Presentation in Support of Human-Automation Communication and Coordination, vol. 2, pp. 13–35. Emerald Group Publishing Limited, UK (2002)
33. Signoretti, A., Martins, A.I., Almeida, N., Vieira, D., Teixeira, A., Costa, C.M.M.: Trip 4 All (T4A): a gamified app to provide a new way to elderly people traveling. In: Proceedings of DSAI (accepted) (2015)
34. Silva, S., Braga, D., Teixeira, A.: AgeCI: HCI and age diversity. In: Stephanidis, C., Antona, M. (eds.) UAHCI 2014, Part III. LNCS, vol. 8515, pp. 179–190. Springer, Heidelberg (2014)
35. Stevens, C.J., Gibert, G., Leung, Y., Zhang, Z.: Evaluating a synthetic talking head using a dual task: modality effects on speech understanding and cognitive load. Int. J. Hum.-Comput. Stud. **71**(4), 440–454 (2013)
36. Teixeira, A., Hmlinen, A., Avelar, J., Almeida, N., Nmeth, G., Fegy, T., Zaink, C., Csap, T., Tth, B., Oliveira, A., Dias, M.S.: Speech-centric multimodal interaction for easy-to-access online services - a personal life assistant for the elderly. In: Proceedings of DSAI 2013, Procedia Computer Science, November 2013
37. Teixeira, A., Pereira, C.: e Silva, M.O., Alvarelhão, J., Silva, A., Cerqueira, M., Isabel, M., Pacheco, O., Almeida, N., Oliveira, C., Costa, R., Neves, A.J.R., Queirós, A., Rocha, N.: New telerehabilitation services for the elderly. In: Miranda, I., Cruz-Cunha, M. (eds.) Handbook of Research on ICTs for Healthcare and Social Services: Developments and Applications. IGI global, USA (2013)
38. Teixeira, A., Francisco, P., Almeida, N., Pereira, C., Silva, S.: Services to support use and development of speech input for multilingual multimodal applications for mobile scenarios. In: Proceedings of 9th International Conference on Internet and Web Applications and Services (ICIW) (2014)
39. Teixeira, A.J.S., Almeida, N., Pereira, C., e Silva, M.O.: W3C MMI architecture as a basis for enhanced interaction for ambient assisted living. In: Get Smart: Smart Homes, Cars, Devices and the Web, W3C Workshop on Rich Multimodal Application Development. New York Metropolitan Area, US (2013)
40. Wechsung, I.: An Evaluation Framework for Multimodal Interaction: Determining Quality Aspects and Modality Choice. Springer, Switzerland (2014)
41. Wechsung, I., Engelbrecht, K.P., Kühnel, C., Möller, S., Weiss, B.: Measuring the quality of service and quality of experience of multimodal human-machine interaction. J. Multimodal User Interfaces **6**(1–2), 73–85 (2012)
42. Wechsung, I., Schleicher, R., Möller, S.: How context determines perceived quality and modality choice. Secondary task paradigm applied to the evaluation of multimodal interfaces. In: Proceedings of the Paralinguistic Information and Its Integration in Spoken Dialogue Systems Workshop, pp. 327–340 (2011)
43. WHO: The international classification of functioning, disability and health. In: World Health Organization, vol. 18, p. 237 (2001)
44. Witt, S.: A set of quantitative user experience metrics for multi-modal dialog systems. In: Proceedings of ITG Symposium Speech Communication, pp. 1–4, September 2014

Creating Forms and Disclosures that Work: Using Eye Tracking to Improve the User Experience

Jonathan Strohl[✉], Christian Gonzalez, Jacob Sauser,
Soodeh Montazeri, and Brian Griepentrog

Fors Marsh Group, Arlington, VA, USA
{jstrohl,cgonzalez,jsauser,smontazeri,bg}
@forsmarshgroup.com

Abstract. Forms and disclosures are a central component of business and customer interactions. However, they often lack good visual organization or clear and concise language, highlighting a distinct need for more extensive usability testing and research. In particular, eye tracking serves as an excellent tool for evaluating and improving paper and electronic forms. In this paper, we present numerous examples of the benefits of eye tracking for form usability as well as practical considerations for conducting eye tracking on paper forms. In addition, we provide two case studies of paper form eye tracking. One involves a paper diary designed to track users' television viewing habits and the other is a multi-page government form. Our experiences suggest that paper forms are amenable to traditional usability testing practices and also benefit from the additional insights gained through eye tracking.

Keywords: Eye tracking · Usability testing · Form design · User experience research

1 Importance of Forms

Business forms and disclosures have become central to customer relationship management. Forms are used to solicit information from the customer in a standardized manner, and disclosures are used to communicate rights, facts, risks, and other important information to the customer. Anyone who has ever completed a medical history form at a hospital or accepted the terms and conditions of a new software download has interacted with a business form or disclosure and, more than likely, the unnecessary jargon, redundancy, ambiguity, and obscurity associated with many of these documents. It should therefore come as no surprise to learn that most consumers are unable or unwilling to read these documents [1].

2 Importance of Usability Testing for Forms

Although some may speculate that businesses deliberately make forms opaque, there are just as many benign causes related to the difficulty in organizing and presenting large

© Springer International Publishing Switzerland 2015
M. Antona and C. Stephanidis (Eds.): UAHCI 2015, Part I, LNCS 9175, pp. 121–131, 2015.
DOI: 10.1007/978-3-319-20678-3_12

amounts of information to a wide variety of audiences. In fact, this situation led the U.S. Government to pass the Plain Writing Act of 2010 [11], which requires federal executive agencies to use plain writing in all documents agencies issue to enhance citizen access of Government information and services.[1] The latter part of this requirement is essential because it highlights the need to collect and assess information from users on their experience with forms and their language.

Typically, when we consider the application of usability testing, it is in regard to complex technologies such as websites, software, or applications, but usability can apply to any context where specific users are interacting with a product or information in order to reach a specific goal [5]. In this respect, forms and disclosures are no different from applications or websites. In general, the goals of forms and disclosures are to extract accurate information from users and convey important, necessary information. In order to meet these goals, these documents must comply with the same usability principles that are used in more complex applications. Peter Moorville [8], in particular, expanded upon the concept of usability and illustrated the facets of user experience. Table 1 shows each facet, its general application, and how it applies to form usability.

Table 1. Facets of the user experience with products

Facet	Application
Useful	The product needs to be a solution to a problem.
Usable	The product needs to be easy to use. Usability is necessary but not sufficient.
Accessible	Content needs to be accessible to people with disabilities.
Credible	Users need to believe the information that is provided.
Findable	Content needs to be navigable and locatable on-site and off-site.
Desirable	Image, identity, brand, and other design elements are used to evoke emotion and appreciation.

3   Role of Eye Tracking in Usability Tests of Forms

Because the user experience is multi-faceted and complex, the use of multiple metrics is often advocated for when conducting a usability test [15]. The two most common group of metrics are self-report (e.g., satisfaction questionnaire ratings, verbal comments) and performance (e.g., time on task, task accuracy). The third, and less often discussed, group of metrics is implicit (e.g., eye tracking, pupil dilation, electrodermal activity). Some aspects of form usability and findability are directly related to users'

---

[1] The Plain Writing Act of 2010 is not the first declaration of this type, but it does represent a high-profile, high-impact piece of legislation.

attentional capture and engagement, making eye tracking an attractive tool to capture these behaviors. These same data gathered through other means may be biased or unreliable, given that users are not fully conscious of their attentional focus. Eye tracking has been used extensively in many other usability contexts, but has only recently been adopted for use with physical forms and notices [7]. Eye-tracking data informs us about the allocation of attention on design elements as well as the language in the form. It can be used to provide an additional level of insight—over and above self-report and performance metrics—into the optimal design and language.

3.1 Web Forms

Forms can take on two mediums: electronic and physical. Both mediums are used for a multitude of purposes. Electronic forms are used for site registration, email and service subscriptions, customer feedback, checkout, and data input to search or share information [6]. Electronic forms are critical to e-product success because poor design would likely result in lost data, lost conversions, and uninterested users. Much of the usability testing literature has focused on optimizing the design of web forms and, in a few examples, eye tracking has also been incorporated [7].

One such study tested the effectiveness of twenty web-form design heuristics [2, 14]. The researchers selected forms from actual commercial websites and applied their twenty heuristics to improve upon the design. The primary aim of the study was to examine the differences in usability between the original and redesigned versions of the forms. Eye tracking was included to provide further insight on users' processing and comprehension. The original version of one of the forms displayed the labels on the side of the open fields, while the redesigned version contained labels directly above the text fields. Usage of the original version of the form with side-by-side labels and text fields resulted in more fixations, longer total fixation duration, and longer total saccade duration than in the redesigned version. These results suggest that completing the redesigned form was more efficiently done and less cognitively demanding. Furthermore, not only did performance-based outcomes improve, but researchers also saw improvement in self-report-based outcomes such as satisfaction questionnaire ratings and verbal responses during follow-up interviews.

In a separate study, Redline and Lankford [12] tracked participants' eyes while they completed a complex questionnaire with extensive branching between questions. The researchers found that many completion errors could be attributed to participants failing to read branching instructions, especially when instructions were presented long before or after participants responded to the origin question. In addition, they found that participants did not read linearly and skipped around looking at the survey. In this case, eye tracking provided insight into the sequential processing undertaken by participants in addition to their overall performance.

3.2 Physical Forms

Though there is some literature related to the usability of physical forms [6] —mostly voting ballots—the vast majority of work has concerned their electronic counterparts.

Furthermore, this disparity is even more apparent regarding the application and value derived from eye tracking in usability tests of physical forms and notices [7]. Nonetheless, due to the ubiquity and importance of physical forms, it is essential to update the methods and tools that improve their efficiency and effectiveness.

Eye tracking of users while they interact with a physical form provides researchers access to important cues about where users are in the process that would be otherwise unavailable. For example, when users complete a web form, they make frequent mouse movements and clicks that cue the researcher about progress they made on the task. However, when users complete a paper form, there are large gaps and absences of their observable behavior. During this time, the researcher is unaware of progress made on completing the form, making it difficult to ascertain the level of difficulty that is being experienced. These gaps in user behavior are precisely where eye tracking provides critical insight and value. During this time interval, the researcher can observe whether certain areas of the form are fixated on as well as the frequency and duration of those fixations.

Challenges with Eye Tracking Physical Forms. Before introducing eye tracking into the usability test of a form, researchers must determine whether the goals of the study merit its use, because many research questions can be addressed more efficiently and directly through alternative measures [3]. Further, using eye tracking for exploratory purposes can be a rather long and arduous fishing expedition given the sheer quantity of data collected by most contemporary tracking equipment. However, once specific hypotheses and outcomes related to users' visual behavior have been established, the practical and methodological concerns can be minimized.

The demands of extracting eye-tracking data from users interacting with paper forms are rather different from those of electronic forms. For example, paper forms are manually manipulated and often require interaction with other environmental elements, making their eye tracking more complicated than that of well-contained electronic forms. However, in order to maintain ecological validity, it is important to try to reflect the natural context in which physical forms are completed during the usability test. Because there is no human-computer interface for the eye tracker to communicate with, an external scene camera must be used to map the eye movements to the environment.

There are two tools to choose from when eye tracking with paper: one is a fixed-position setup and the other is a head-mounted setup. With the fixed-position setup, the form is affixed to a mounted stand and the eye tracker is mounted below it. The stand keeps the scene camera and form in the same positions for each participant in the study. Because the form and eye tracker remain in the same position, the frame of reference never changes. As a result, eye-tracking data points are mapped to the same coordinates. This greatly simplifies data aggregation and analysis after the study is completed. However, the fixed-position configuration comes with a significant trade-off in external generalizability. The stand prevents participants from being able to hold the form, forcing them into an unnatural and contrived experience and restricting the available area to lay out multiple pages.

Eye-tracking glasses provide an alternative head-mounted option to paper form eye tracking. The glasses integrate a scene camera in the eyewear that continuously records the field of view. The eye-tracking technology is mounted into the glasses itself. The trade-off with the head-mounted option is extensive time during data aggregation. Because the scene camera is not in a fixed position, the field of view is continuously changing. As a result, the coordinates for the data points are constantly changing while the participant interacts with the form. This requires researchers to map individual fixations to a still image of the stimulus. Although this option requires more labor, it permits users to hold the form, creating a more natural and realistic experience.

4   Case Studies of the Application of Eye Tracking in Our Paper Form Usability Test Work

4.1   Usability Test of a Paper Diary

Introduction. The Nielsen television diary is a paper-based booklet that allows participants in Nielsen's panel to record their television viewing habits. Members of the Nielsen panel receive these diaries in the mail and are asked to record their television watching behavior during a specified interval. Despite the increased availability of other modes of entering television behavior (i.e., Nielsen desktop websites and mobile applications), the paper diary is still a heavily relied upon source for data collection. Although desktop websites and mobile applications are more prevalent among higher-income households, mailed paper diaries are necessary for a representative sample, because lower-income households are less likely to have access to electronic resources. Nielsen, at the time, was in the process of redesigning their paper diary form. Full details of this study have been presented by our colleagues [16, 17].

Stimulus. The diary was printed on double-sided saddle-stitched 8½″ × 11″ sheets of paper. The cover displayed the title of the diary and the Nielsen name. Inside the diary, Step 1 asked participants to answer questions about the number of TV sets and people in their household. Step 2 asked participants to list the local channels they received as well as the method (i.e., cable, satellite, antenna) and list their local television stations. Step 3 asked participants to answer questions about who watches TV in their household by entering this information in specified slots. Step 4 asked participants to record their daily TV viewing. Step 5 instructed participants on how to seal and submit the diary.

Method. Seventy-four people (29 male, 45 female), with an average age of thirty seven, and diverse demographics participated in the study. Participants were randomly assigned to use one of three versions of the paper diary: an "Old" diary, a "New" diary, and a "Prototype" diary. The backing of the diary was mounted to a stand above a Tobii X2-60 eye tracker. In additional to the eye tracking, we collected conventional performance and self-report metrics. Participants were asked to complete Steps 1 through 5 of the diary. After completing the task, participants were asked to complete a satisfaction questionnaire. The moderator then conducted a debriefing interview with each participant.

Example Cover Findings. The original version of the paper diary had the words "Nielsen Television Viewing Diary" in the center of the front cover. The "New" and "Prototype" versions of the cover page contained motivational phrases in the center, such as "Your viewing matters...Tell us what YOU watch!" as well as faces of people from diverse backgrounds. For the redesigned versions, the Nielsen name and logo was moved to the bottom left corner of the cover. Participants fixated more on the center of the cover than on the other areas of the page for all three designs. This resulted in an issue with the two redesigned versions of the cover page because participants did not fixate on the name and logo. Self-reported data supported the eye tracking: Participants who received the original version of the diary made comments such as, "It [Nielsen logo] is the first thing I looked at." Participants who received the redesigned versions made comments such as: "I noticed [the Nielsen logo] only when you pointed it out. It is not clear that it had any important information" (Fig. 1).

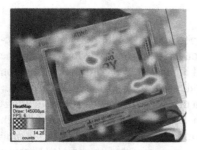 

Fig. 1. Left to right: "Old" and "New" diaries. Mean fixation count heat maps show more fixations in the center of the page for both designs.

This finding highlights the importance of designing for desirability and credibility of a form, as well as how eye tracking helped inform this finding. Without noticing the name and logo of the sender, respondents are unlikely to find mail material trustworthy, and they will often quickly discard it. And without a desirable cover, respondents are unlikely to open the diary to get started with the process. Here, eye tracking was able to inform designers about the elements on the cover that were most likely to be missed. As a result, we recommended moving the logo and name to the center of the cover, where it would be more visible.

Example Step 3 Findings. Step 3 asked participants to answer questions about who watches TV in their household by entering this information in specified slots at the top of the page. The "Old" diary and "Prototype" diary contained an example directly below the fillable slots, while the "New" diary contained an example beneath the fold. Unlike Steps 1 and 2, which progressed linearly from top to bottom and left to right, Step 3 forced participants to start at the bottom of the page and move to the top in order to progress in the correct sequence. The "Old" diary and "Prototype" diary, performed poorly in regard to noticeability. Eye tracking showed that 45 % of participants did not fixate on the example until after they had completed the fillable areas—a finding that exemplifies the importance of the "findable" facet of user experience. We recommended that the example be placed before the actual content, where users will be more likely to notice it before they are asked to input information.

Example Step 4 Findings. Eye tracking also provided relevant insights into how participants processed the fillable fields in Step 4. The "Old" diary and "New" diary had a column order that listed the station and channel number earlier in the sequence. The subsequent columns requested that participants enter the name of the program and the people in the household who watched it. Gaze plots indicated that participants were confused about this order, because they did not look in an orderly left-to-right pattern as one would expect. Gaze plots indicated that participants did not look in an orderly left-to-right pattern— a result that demonstrated the inefficiency with processing information in this layout. The "Prototype" diary had a different column order which had participants enter the name of the show before the other information. Gaze plots revealed a more F-shaped pattern [8] of participants looking down the page and then looking in a linear left-to-right pattern when entering information, — a result that demonstrated a marked improvement in processing efficiency. We recommended the ordering of the "Prototype" diary, with the television show entry field occurring earlier in the progression (Fig. 2).

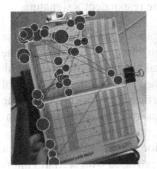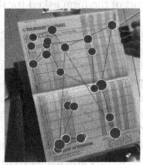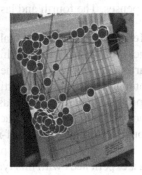

Fig. 2. Three fixation gaze plots that exemplify eye movement-patterns when using the three different diaries. The "Prototype" diary grid (right) resulted in more linear gaze patterns than the "Old" (left) and "New" diary grids (middle).

Practical Considerations. Our first challenge with conducting the study was selecting the placement of the eye tracker. At first, we tested the usability test setup with an older and larger eye tracker (Tobii X120) and mounted it above the form. We encountered issues with this setup when we found that participants' eyelids were more likely to block the eye tracker from collecting data. Before data collection began, a newer and more compact eye tracker (Tobii X2-60) was launched. The size of this eye tracker allowed us to place it below the form. This placement resulted in a considerably higher rate of capture.

Other challenges with implementing eye tracking into this study related to the interactive nature of the form. Responding to the form resulted in head movement; consequently, during this interaction, the eye tracker was less likely to collect eye movement data. As a result, we focused on providing results from data collected while the participant was not moving his or her hand to respond. Participants also tended to block the eye tracker while they wrote on the form. To overcome this, we delineated an area below the form so participants had a cue as to where not to place their hands.

4.2 Usability Test of a Multi-page Government Form

Introduction. This multi-page form is completed to report discrepancies in personal finances to the Federal Government. The purpose of this study was to determine the issues associated with completing the form and provide recommendations to correct those issues. Full details of this study have been presented by our colleagues [13].

Stimulus. Before the form began, there were three pages of instructions with text and tables. The first part of the form was a series of "yes" and "no" questions to help respondents self-assess whether they should continue with completing the form. The second part of the form asked respondents to enter their personal information and the information for a family member. The third part of the form was a grid format that asked participants to account for different amounts of items associated with their income and expenses. The fourth and last part of the form asked for the respondent's signature.

Method. Nine people (4 male and 5 Female), with an average of forty two, and diverse backgrounds from the Washington, DC, area participated in this study. Eight of the nine participants reported that they typically complete this form themselves by hand or with computer software; one participant reported to complete the form with the assistance of a professional. The form was mounted to a flat vertical surface for viewing and writing above a Tobii X2-60 eye tracker. In additional to the eye tracking, we collected conventional performance and self-report measures.

Before starting the task, participants completed a questionnaire that asked about their past experiences with this type of form. Participants were provided with scenario information so they did not enter their own personally identifiable information. Participants were also provided with supporting documents that helped them complete the form.

Example Findings. Eye-tracking gaze plots demonstrated that participants read most information on the first page of instructions, skimmed through the second and third pages of instructions, and then began working on the form. An analysis of the quantified fixation data demonstrated that, although most of the first page instructions were fixated, certain areas of the page, particularly the information that came later on the first page, tended to be skipped.

Most of the sections on the second page of instructions were not fixated. However, the center of the second page, which was a numbered section, had higher counts of fixations. This is consistent with research that has shown that users tend to read numbers and bulleted, bolded items [4, 9]. Participants had very minimal fixations on the third page of instructions.

Participants' self-reported comments during the debriefing interview supported the eye-tracking and performance data about the use of instructions. One participant commented on the length of the instructions by saying, "I feel like the instructions were so long and perilous that I could really only retain about 10 %." On the satisfaction questionnaire, participants, on average, responded that they read "some of the instructions." In debriefing, we asked participants about the way they usually interact with tax form instructions. Responses indicated that, consistent with the session observations and eye-tracking data, participants tended to skim and skip instructions. For example, one participant said: "[I used them] the way I usually do. I read the first page and then I skip the rest. It's typical of how I do it. I read about 30 %, and I know that the information is there and that I can go back. But I don't ever finish the whole instruction booklet." Another participant said: "I usually skim through it. Usually [these types of] forms are laid out the same way."

The evidence suggested that the instructions are not being used as intended and highlights the importance of the "usable" facet of user experience. The instructions were presented in narrative format, which suggested that respondents should read through the full instructions before they start the form. However, our research suggested that most respondents will visually scan the information on these pages before they start. The later the information appears in the instructions, the less likely it will be read. Because the instructions are lengthy, they are more likely to be used as a reference when working on the form, and less likely to be read before getting started.

We recommended moving instructions to sections of the form where the specific information. For example, we recommended placing a condensed version of the instructions for completing the line items next to their respective fillable lines in the form. We also recommended that the remaining information in the instructions should be reformatted to facilitate an efficient scan pattern, such as reformatting text by chunking different pieces of information together into bulleted lists with bolded items.

Practical Considerations. We faced similar challenges to those in our first case study. In this study, we also used the more compact eye tracker (Tobii X2-60) and placed it below the form. In the first case study, the form was mounted at a 45° angle. In this study, we mounted the form to a vertical flat viewing service at a 90° angle. This resulted in a trade-off: we collected a higher rate of eye movement data samples, but it made the form more difficult to write on. In this study, the emphasis was on the use of the instructions, so we proceeded with the vertical setup. As in the first case study, we focused on providing results from data collected while the participant was not moving his or her hand to respond.

5 Conclusion

Despite playing an important role in organizations and customer relationships, forms and disclosures are often poorly organized and difficult to complete. Principles of usability testing commonly employed in more interactive and complex applications provide significant value to improving the design and organization of forms. In particular, the use of eye tracking provides an additional level of insight into users' attentional allocation and progress through a form or disclosure. In this paper, we have summarized and synthesized relevant literature related to electronic forms and presented two case studies demonstrating the efficacy of usability testing paper forms and emphasized the value derived from including eye tracking in these tests. In addition, we have provided practical guidance for user experience researchers considering using eye tracking for paper forms. In summary, we have shown that forms regardless of medium can benefit from the same usability methods and measures implemented in more interactive environments. In the future, we hope businesses and organizations recognize the value of usability testing and the additional insight eye tracking delivers in creating useful, usable, accessible, credible, findable, and desirable forms.

References

1. Bakos, Y., Marotta-Wurgler, F., Trossen, D.: Does anyone read the fine print? consumer attention to standard-form contracts. J. Legal Stud. **43**(1), 1–35 (2014)
2. Bargas-Avila, J.A., Brenzikofer, O., Roth, S., Tuch, A.N., Orsini, S., Opwis, K.: Simple-but-crucial user interfaces in the world wide web: introducing 20 guidelines for usable web form design. In: Matrai, R. (ed.) User Interfaces, pp. 270–280. INTECH, Croatia (2010)
3. Bojko, A.: Eye Tracking the User Experience: A Practical Guide to Research. Rosenfeld Media, New York (2013)
4. Graham, G.: White paper article: five tips on writing better bullets. http://www. thatwhitepaperguy.com/copywriting-article-five-tips-on-writing-better-bulleted-lists.html
5. ISO Standard 9241-11. https://www.iso.org/obp/ui/#iso:std:iso:9241:-11:ed-1:v1:en
6. Jarrett, C., Gaffney, G.: Forms that Work: Designing Web Forms for Usability. Morgan Kaufmann, Boston (2009)
7. Jarrett, C., Bergstrom, J.R.: Forms and surveys. In: Bergstrom, J.R., Schall, J.A. (eds.) Eye Tracking in User Experience Design, pp. 111–137. Morgan Kaufmann, Waltham (2014)
8. Moorville, P.: User experience design. http://semanticstudios.com/user_experience_design/
9. Nielsen, J.: F-shaped pattern for reading web content. http://www.nngroup.com/articles/f-shaped-pattern-reading-web-content/
10. Nielsen, J.: Show numbers as numerals when writing for online readers. http://www. nngroup.com/articles/web-writing-show-numbers-as-numerals
11. Plain Writing Act of 2010. Public Law 111-274 (2010). http://www.gpo.gov/fdsys/pkg/ PLAW-111publ274/pdf/PLAW-111publ274.pdf
12. Redline, C.D., Lankford, C.P.: Eye-movement analysis: a new tool for evaluating the design of visually administered instruments (paper and web). In: Proceedings of the Section on Survey Research Methods, American Statistical Association. Paper presented at 2001 AAPOR Annual Conference, Montreal, Quebec, Canada (2001)
13. Bergstrom, J.R., Strohl, J., Hale, A., Keaton, S.: Improving federal forms with user experience testing and eye tracking. Paper presented at 2014 American Association for Public Opinion Research Annual Conference, Anaheim, CA, USA (2014)
14. Seckler, M., Heinz, S., Bargas-Avila, J.A., Opwis, K., Tuch, A.N.: Designing usable web forms – empirical evaluation of web form improvement guidelines. In: CHI 2014, pp. 1275–1284 (2014)
15. Tullis, T., Albert, B.: Measuring the User Experience: Collecting, Analyzing, and Presenting Usability Metrics. Morgan Kaufmann, Burlington (2008)

16. Walton, L., Bergstrom, J.C., Hawkins, D.C., Pierce, C.: Eye tracking on a paper survey: implications for design. In: Stephanidis, C., Antona, M. (eds.) UAHCI 2014, Part II. LNCS, vol. 8514, pp. 175–182. Springer, Heidelberg (2014)
17. Walton, L., Bergstrom, J.R., Hawkins, D., Pierce, C.: User experience and eye-tracking study: paper diary design decisions. Paper presented at 2014 American Association for Public Opinion Research Annual Conference, Anaheim, CA, USA (2014)

Using Interpretive Structural Modeling to Make Decisions for Direction of Caring Design

Ming-Tang Wang[(⊠)]

The Department of Education, National Kaohsiung Normal University,
Kaohsiung, Taiwan, R.O.C
mtwang2000@gmail.com

Abstract. Interpretive structural modelling (ISM) is a well-established methodology for identifying relationships among specific items, which define a problem or an issue. The natural caring is born with human beings; besides caring persons the natural environment is also important. In this research, Interpretive structural modeling (ISM) is used to make decision for design direction of rescuing injury in landslide disaster, recognized the main target to solve ease of use and independent problems (level 1) and the main problem are reliability issues (level 2), the safe issue (Level 3), the security issue (level 4) for the proposed stretcher. Finally, the design direction is concluded, new stretcher structure was proposed to be independent and confident for conveying, and collecting the scenario for ATV drag rescue stretcher.

Keywords: Caring design · Design direction · ISM · Make decision

1 Background

It is generally felt that individuals or groups encounter difficulties in dealing with complex issues or systems. The complexity of the issues or systems is due to the presence of a large number of elements and interactions among these elements. Owing to fact of the junction of the plate has a new significant structural movement; it becomes a mountainous region with steep terrains from outcropping strata generally young and fragile lithology, structural complexity, and rock crushing (Fig. 1). Due to the plate's movements, it leaves natural disasters, such as: earthquakes, typhoons, floods, and surface deformation. The natural landslides disaster has become a major accident to mountainous residents. It leads one to consider suitable facilities to convey patient, especially the emergency patient has to transport to hospital when landslides cause injuries to people in mountainous area. Who will care these issues for preventing the disaster to cause an accident death? ATV (All-terrain vehicle) can be a motorized vehicle for natural disaster in short time preparation.

Human beings are born with a natural feeling of caring, it is called "natural caring" [1] that is, others can naturally emit emotion, which is derived from the parents care for their children born of love, and to take care of incapacitated baby, the baby's feelings and learning will be issued smile. Her care ethics in the statement of contents of the

© Springer International Publishing Switzerland 2015
M. Antona and C. Stephanidis (Eds.): UAHCI 2015, Part I, LNCS 9175, pp. 132–142, 2015.
DOI: 10.1007/978-3-319-20678-3_13

Fig. 1. Mudslide disaster point [3]

object, the more focus on the carers need to be open-minded expression of emotion "are carers" (cared for), and will involve carers between the two need to give full attention to put in, in order to establish such a good relationship. The design issue can have a chance to purpose some ideas for rescuing.

Noddings [2] proposed caring for people, offered to care for themselves as the starting of the six levels of care: (1) yourself, (2) intimate and familiar persons, (3) the strangers and distant persons, (4) the plants, animals and the natural environment, (5) artificial world, (6) care concept. In this research, the stranger and natural environment will be discussed to find a solution for preventing in the main purpose is for achieving result of caring design; it needs to make a design direction decision for proposing ideas. Design is conceiving and planning, and presents a creative action with a target.

2 Literature

ISM is an interactive learning process. In this technique, a set of different directly and indirectly related elements are structured into a comprehensive systematic model [4, 5]. This methodology is used to evolve mutual relationships among information barriers. The information KM (Knowledge management) barriers have been classified, based on their driving power and dependence power. The objective behind this classification is to analyze the driving power and dependence power of these barriers [6]. People usually judge based on their intuition and experiences when they study complex, divisive issues, conducting problem analysis and assessments. Interpretive structural modeling (ISM) is used for ideal planning, which is an effective method because all elements can be processed with a simple matrix [7–9], is a well-established methodology for identifying relationships among specific items, which define a problem or an issue [10]. It is also a well-established methodology for identifying relationships among specific items, which defines a problem or an issue [11], and a suitable modeling technique for analyzing the influence of one variable on other variables [10], often using to provide fundamental understanding of complex situations, and putting together a course of action for solving a problem. Its mathematical foundations of the methodology can be found in various reference works [12].

The ISM can be used to help groups of people in structuring their collective knowledge [13]; and its systematic application of graph theory in a way that is theoretical, conceptual, and computational leverage is exploited to efficiently construct a directed level graph for referencing [13, 14]. Some design planning [15, 16], and productivity issues [17] have provided the adequate ground to begin with ISM research to induct a solution. Owing to this method, it can supply a direction from complex and unconfirmed information.

3 Methodology

Warfield [8] developed this methodology that uses systematic application of some elementary notions of graph theory and Boolean algebra in such a way that when implemented in a man machine interactive mode, theoretical, conceptual and computational leverage is exploited to construct directed graph (a representation of the hierarchical structure of the system). It was to construct hierarchical interaction graph of the system and area detail of the main problem and the main target to propose design thinking by ISM. (1) VOA (Value of analysis): It can the original design proposal can be divided into 7 different categories from iNPD (integrated New product design) [18]: emotion, human factors engineering, aesthetics, product image, influence, core technology and quality. They are magnified for explanation into 22 issues to search possible conditions for design, (2) finding the fuzzy front: Integrating higher value of VOA from Interpretive structural modeling (ISM) defines problem to be an issue as design guideline. (3) Proposing innovative caring design direction: planning from fuzzy front to present scenario to present picture of LEF (Life style, Ergonomics, Feature) for describing the design solution.

ISM methodology suggests the use of the expert opinions based on various management techniques such as brain storming, nominal group technique, etc. in developing the contextual relationship among the variables [19, 20]. The principal of ISM as below: One simple way to do that in this case is to assign weights w_i for the ith element according to its relative position in individual hierarchy. By summing over the individuals, a collective score w_{ij} can be assigned to each element, constructed the matrix [A] to present the related relationship of each element (formula 1, 2).

$$[A] = \sum_{j=1}^{n_j} w_{ij} \tag{1}$$

$$[A] = \begin{bmatrix} w_{11} & \cdots & w_{i1} \\ \vdots & \ddots & \vdots \\ w_{1j} & \cdots & w_{ij} \end{bmatrix} \tag{2}$$

Malone [14] showed that a matrix is termed the adjacency matrix of D, and is constructed by setting $a_{ij} = 1$, wherever there is an arc in D directed from element s_i to element s_j, and by setting $a_{ij} = 0$, elsewhere. The Element s_j is said to be reachable from element s_i if a path can be traced on D from s_i to s_j. By convention, an element s_i is said to be reachable from itself by a path of length 0. The reachability matrix M of a digraph is defined as a binary matrix in which the entries m_{ij} are 1 if element s_j is reachable from element s_i; otherwise $m_{ij} = 0$. It can be shown that the reachability matrix can be obtained operationally from the adjacency matrix by adding the identity matrix and then raising the result matrix to successive powers until no new entries are obtained.

That is:

$$[M] = ([A] + [I])^n \tag{3}$$

Where n is determined such that

$$([A] + [I])^{n-1} < ([A] + [I])^n = ([A] + [I])^{n+1} \tag{4}$$

4 Result

4.1 Selected VOA

VOA is surveyed by questionnaire, derived from 7 different categories: emotion, human factors engineering, aesthetics, product image, influence, core technology and quality which has 22 original items (Table 1) from iNPD. This surveyed result is selected 9 items: reliability, ease of use, sense of independence, security, safe, location, power, confident and durability as center of Table 2.

4.2 Finding the Fuzzy Front

The fuzzy front can be constructed a matrix from Table 2 (right) which the original matrix is checked for all items to find out each pair relation. The '1' and '0' mean to describe 'Yes' or 'No' relation between items of row and column which decisions were decided by assessed persons are three rescue experts, they discussed together to decide their relations and follows majority decision.

(1) Constructs a correlation matrix: to conduct logical operations and analyze the resulting hierarchical structures of the most important VOA from iNPD process. To compare the relationships of a directional correlation matrix [A] (Fig. 1) is formed using the relationship (aij) between one element and another.

(2) Generating a reachability matrix: the reachability matrix [R] (Fig. 2) is deducted from the incidence matrix [A] if a Boolean n-multiple product of [A] + [I] uniquely converges to R for all integers n > n0, where n0 is an appropriate positive integer, [I] is a Boolean unity matrix, and + is an addition in the Boolean sense [8]. Matrix [R] represents all direct and indirect linkages between components. Relation transitivity is a basic assumption in ISM, representing the reachability matrix [R] derived from matrix [A], in which an entry rij = 1 if component j is reachable by i, although the path

Table 1. Issues in product value opportunities analysis [18]

Category	Item	Description
Emotion	Courage	Rescuers can be inspired when using.
	Independence security	Rescuers can operate independently and the equipment has the versatility on other tasks.
		Rescuers can feel safe.
	Sensibility	The equipment can make rescuers feel confident himself.
	Confident	Easy using equipment increases rescuers' confident.
	Power	Rescuers can handle situations by using equipment.
Human factors engineering	Comfortable	Feel comfortable and no pressure when using rescuing equipment.
	Safe	It's safe to use and won't danger users.
	Usability	Simple and easy to use.
Aesthetics	Sight	The equipment is good looking.
	Sense of touch	Feels smooth with no discomfort.
	Auditory sense	Equipment doesn't make noises.
	Nose	The material has no peculiar smell.
	Sense of taste	Is not harmful or uncomfortable to mouth.
Image	Time	Able to meet the time or frequency when local disaster happens.
	Location	Fit local rescuing demand.
Influence	Society	Adaptable equipment to fit various environments and situations.
	Environment	Do not have any harmful influence to environment.
Core technology	Reliability	Product can use for a long time stable without fault.
	Availability	The core tech must meet the product's function and be easily accessible when needed
Quality	Craft	Product must have high quality.
	Durability	Product must achieve the high durability.

length may be one or more. 'Reachability' in graph theory is the ability to move from one vertex in a directed graph to some other vertices (formula 4). This is sufficient to find the connected components in the graph.

(3) Generate a rearranged matrix: cluster elements that affect one another in the output matrix of the reachability matrix. Rearranged matrix and retrieval of clusters Step by step of ISM (Fig. 3) reveals that hierarchical interaction graph of the system has four clusters, namely, {2, 3, 6, 8}, {1, 7, 9}, {5}, and {4} the clustered components are integrated and treated as a single entity.

(4) Illustrate the hierarchical relationships of elements: the hierarchy graph is then obtained by identifying a set of components in matrix [R] (Fig. 2) that cannot reach or be reached by other components outside the set itself. Hierarchical interaction graph of the system: the oriented links then connect the nodes from source to sink, based on the incidence matrix. In this step, the elements' hierarchical relationships are illustrated

Table 2. Original matrix for ISM from VOA

level	description of no.	No.	1	2	3	4	5	6	7	8	9
2	reliability	1	1	0	1	0	0	0	0	0	1
1	ease of use	2	0	1	1	0	0	0	0	1	0
1	sense of inde-pendence	3	0	1	1	0	0	1	0	1	0
4	security	4	1	0	0	1	1	0	1	1	0
3	safe	5	0	0	1	0	1	0	1	1	0
1	location	6	0	1	1	0	0	1	0	0	0
2	power	7	0	1	1	0	0	0	1	1	0
1	confident	8	0	0	1	0	0	0	0	1	0
2	durability	9	1	0	0	0	0	0	1	1	1

$$[A] = \begin{array}{c} \\ 1 \\ 2 \\ 3 \\ 4 \\ 5 \\ 6 \\ 7 \\ 8 \\ 9 \end{array} \begin{array}{ccccccccc} 1 & 2 & 3 & 4 & 5 & 6 & 7 & 8 & 9 \\ \left[\begin{array}{ccccccccc} 1 & 0 & 1 & 0 & 0 & 0 & 0 & 0 & 1 \\ 0 & 1 & 1 & 0 & 0 & 0 & 0 & 1 & 0 \\ 0 & 1 & 1 & 0 & 0 & 1 & 0 & 1 & 0 \\ 1 & 0 & 0 & 1 & 1 & 0 & 1 & 1 & 0 \\ 0 & 0 & 1 & 0 & 1 & 0 & 1 & 1 & 0 \\ 0 & 1 & 1 & 0 & 0 & 1 & 0 & 0 & 0 \\ 0 & 1 & 1 & 0 & 0 & 0 & 1 & 1 & 0 \\ 0 & 0 & 1 & 0 & 0 & 0 & 0 & 1 & 0 \\ 1 & 0 & 0 & 0 & 0 & 0 & 1 & 1 & 1 \end{array}\right] \end{array}$$

Fig. 2. Original incidence matrix [A]

according to the rearranged matrix, providing decision makers with the procedures and hierarchical structures to use in the deconstruction of a problem.

Conclusion of Figs. 2 and 3 show that the main target is level one ({2, 3, 6, 8}) 'ease of use', 'sense of independence', 'location', 'confident', the main problems are the level two ({1,7,9}): 'reliability', 'power', 'durability' and level 3 ({5}): 'safe', and the level four ({4}): 'security' (left of Table 2). Figure 6 shows $D + R$ and $D - R$ element distribution graph that the rescue stretcher must achieve confident for patient and driver, solving the problem of safety (level 2) and the usability (level 3) (Fig. 4).

(5) Draw the $D + R$ and $D - R$ element distribution graph: based upon the reachability matrix [R], the user must add up the scores of the elements in each row to generate D and the elements in each column to generate R. After this, calculate the values of $D + R$ and $D - R$ to generate a reachability matrix determinant and then

$$[R] = \begin{array}{c} \\ 1 \\ 2 \\ 3 \\ 4 \\ 5 \\ 6 \\ 7 \\ 8 \\ 9 \end{array} \begin{array}{ccccccccc} 1 & 2 & 3 & 4 & 5 & 6 & 7 & 8 & 9 \\ \left[\begin{array}{ccccccccc} 1 & 0 & 1 & 0 & 0 & 0 & 0 & 0 & 1 \\ 0 & 1 & 1 & 0 & 0 & 0 & 0 & 1 & 0 \\ 0 & 1 & 1 & 0 & 0 & 1 & 0 & 1 & 0 \\ 1 & 0 & 0 & 1 & 1 & 0 & 1 & 1 & 0 \\ 0 & 0 & 1 & 0 & 1 & 0 & 1 & 1 & 0 \\ 0 & 1 & 1 & 0 & 0 & 1 & 0 & 0 & 0 \\ 0 & 1 & 1 & 0 & 0 & 0 & 1 & 1 & 0 \\ 0 & 0 & 1 & 0 & 0 & 0 & 0 & 1 & 0 \\ 1 & 0 & 0 & 0 & 0 & 0 & 1 & 1 & 1 \end{array}\right] \end{array}$$

Fig. 3. Reachability matrix [R]

$$\bullet \; [R] \bullet [R]^T = \begin{array}{c} \\ 2 \\ 3 \\ 6 \\ 8 \\ 1 \\ 7 \\ 9 \\ 5 \\ 4 \end{array} \begin{array}{ccccccccc} 2 & 3 & 6 & 8 & 1 & 7 & 9 & 5 & 4 \\ \left[\begin{array}{cccc|ccc|c|c} 1 & 1 & 1 & 1 & 0 & 0 & 0 & 0 & 0 \\ 1 & 1 & 1 & 1 & 0 & 0 & 0 & 0 & 0 \\ 1 & 1 & 1 & 1 & 0 & 0 & 0 & 0 & 0 \\ 1 & 1 & 1 & 1 & 1 & 0 & 0 & 0 & 0 \\ 1 & 1 & 1 & 1 & 1 & 1 & 1 & 0 & 0 \\ 1 & 1 & 1 & 1 & 1 & 1 & 1 & 0 & 0 \\ 1 & 1 & 1 & 1 & 1 & 1 & 1 & 0 & 0 \\ 1 & 1 & 1 & 1 & 1 & 1 & 1 & 1 & 0 \\ 1 & 1 & 1 & 1 & 1 & 1 & 1 & 1 & 1 \end{array}\right] \end{array}$$

Fig. 4. Rearranged matrix and retrieval of clusters step by step of ISM

demonstrate $D + R$ and $D - R$ on a binary scale to interpret both the problem and the target areas. This system can also be employed to analyze independent elements according to their hierarchical relationships. After the element level has been determined, draw the $D + R$ and $D - R$ element distribution graph to find out the main problem and main target (Fig. 5).

To ensure a stretcher mechanism is designed to sit on ATV for landslide disaster. It should comply with the principle of operation as simple and easy, be suitable to operate independently and confidently, and it needs reliability and power to confirm structure, and will keep the injury be safe, does not happen the risk.

4.3 Proposing Innovative Caring Design Direction

The planning of fuzzy front to present scenario is from picture of LEF (Life style, Ergonomics, Feature). The injury often caused death from mountain accident (Fig. 6), it needs to transport to hospital. The usability and reliable security are essential elements

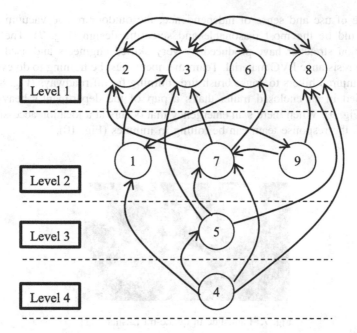

Fig. 5. Hierarchical interaction graph of the system

of rescue stretcher. Stretcher can be for an ATV is mainly used to retrieve an injured patient in harsh terrain during hurricane on broken pavement.

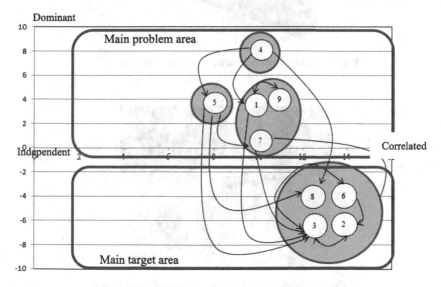

Fig. 6. $D + R$ and $D - R$ element distribution graph

For ease of use and sense of independence, the outdoor rescue vacuum mattress stretcher could be the most reasonable and scientific design (Fig. 7). The vacuum immobilization stretcher have produced by very skilled engineers and used the best quality cold resistance PVC material. Team members must be training to do everything from assist injured hikers to douse brush fires burning far off roadways (Fig. 8). All of this is carried in an enclosed trailer that's a part of the department's heavy rescue operation (Fig. 9). When there's an emergency that occurs at a location accessible only by an ATV, the response team can be rolling in minutes (Fig. 10).

Fig. 7. Landslide in quake-hit Lushan [21]

Fig. 8. Outdoor rescue vacuum mattress stretcher [22]

Fig. 9. Rescue stretcher for ATV in off road [23]

Fig. 10. AO fire department launches ATV rescue squad [24]

5   Conclusion

Landslides are a main secondary fatalities source of earthquakes. Especially in hilly rain forest areas or in the middle of a monsoon season, landslides can be disastrous. For the caring natural environment, it needs to some equipment for preparing landside. The complex structure of Taiwan geology, rock crushing which its geology is still active, causing very often nature disasters: earthquakes, typhoons, floods, surface deformation and subsidence. In this study, we focused on decisions making to recognize research target and design to be a product to construct an ISM process to decrease black-box design thinking.

The ATV has shown to be a more suitable vehicle for rescuing. Then, it must be with a stretcher to vehicle injury, to conclude nine important issues for searching design direction, security is main problem then the safe, the main target is level one: 'ease of use', 'sense of independence', 'location', 'confident', it can be noted that this stretcher is required to easily use and need a location to rescue urgent patients. It can be proposed a good solution for natural disaster for emergent injury patient or seriously ill patients when the general truck or helicopter cannot transport emergency. The ATV drag rescue stretcher becomes easy and flexible.

http://www.ncbi.nlm.nih.gov.

References

1. Noddings, N.: Educating Moral People: A Caring Alternative to Character Education. Teachers College, Columbia University Press, New York (2002)
2. Noddings, N.: Caring: A Feminine Approach to Ethics and Moral Education, p. 170. University of California Press, Berkeley (1984)
3. Mudslide disaster point. http://www.moi.gov.tw/print.aspx?print=news&sn=8675&type_code=01
4. Sage, A.P.: Interpretive Structural Modeling: Methodology for Large Scale Systems. McGraw-Hill, New York (1977)
5. Warfield, J.N.: Developing interconnected matrices in structural modelling. IEEE Trans. Syst. Men Cybern. **4**(1), 51–81 (1974)

6. Singh, M.D., Kant, R.: Knowledge management barriers: an interpretive structural modeling approach. Int. J. Manag. Sci. Eng. Manag. **3**(2), 141–150 (2008)
7. Warfield, J.N.: An Assault on Complexity. Battelle Monograph, vol. 3. Battelle Memorial Institute, Columbus (1973)
8. Warfield, J.N.: Structuring Complex Systems. Battelle Monograph, vol. 4. Battelle Memorial Institute, Columbus (1974)
9. Warfield, J.N.: Implication structures for system interconnection-matrices. IEEE Trans. Syst. Man Cybern. **6**(1) (1976)
10. Agarwal, A., Shankar, R., Tiwari, M.K.: Modeling agility of supply chain. Ind. Mark. Manag. **36**, 443–457 (2007)
11. Attri, R., Dev, N., Sharma, V.: Interpretive structural modelling (ISM) approach: an overview. Res. J. Manag. Sci. **2**(2), 3–8 (2013)
12. Harary, F., Norman, R., Cartwright, D.: Structural Models. Wiley, New York (1965)
13. Faisal, M.N., Banwet, D.K., Shankar, R.: Supply chain risk mitigation: modelling the enablers. Bus. Proc. Manag. J. **12**(4), 535–552 (2006)
14. Malone, D.W.: An introduction to the application of interpretive structural modeling. Proc. IEEE **63**(3), 397–404 (1975)
15. Lee, Y.C., Chao, Y.H., Lin, S.B.: Structural approach to design user interface. Comput. Ind. **61**, 613–623 (2010)
16. Hsiao, S.W., Ko, Y.C., Lo, C.H., Chen, S.H.: An ISM, DEI, and ANP based approach for product family development. Adv. Eng. Inform. **27**, 131–148 (2013)
17. Jharkharia, S., Shankar, R.: IT-enablement of supply chains: understanding the barriers. J. Enterp. Inf. Manag. **18**(1), 11–27 (2005)
18. Cagan, J., Vogel, C.M.: Creating Breakthrough Products: Revealing the Secrets that Drive Global Innovation. Pearson Education Inc., Upper Saddle River (2013)
19. Hasan, M.A., Shankar, R., Sarkis, J.: A study of barriers to agile manufacturing. Int. J. Agile Syst. Manag. **2**(1), 1–22 (2007)
20. Ravi, V., Shankar, R., Tiwari, M.K.: Productivity improvement of a computer hardware supply chain. Int. J. Prod. Perform. Meas. **54**(4), 239–255 (2005)
21. Deng, Z.Y., Wang, Q.Y.: Landslide in quake-hit Lushan kills 3. http://en.people.cn/90882/8239004.html
22. Outdoor rescue vacuum mattress stretcher. http://www.ambulancetrolleystretchers.com/sale-2070024-outdoor-rescue-vacuum-mattress-stretcher-medical-first-aid-stretcher.html
23. Rescue stretcher for ATV in off road. http://my.firefighternation.com/photo/east-pierce-wa-atv-training?q=photo/east-pierce-wa-atv-training
24. Huffman, S.: AO fire department launches ATV rescue squad. http://www.thetimesnews.com/polopoly_fs/1.47873!/fileImage/httpImage/image.jpg_gen/derivatives/landscape_445/ao-atvs-1.jpg. Accessed 10 Nov 2012

How to Construct UX and Story in HCI or Service Design

Toshiki Yamaoka[✉] and Misako Sakamoto

Faculty of Home Economics, Kyoto Women's University, Kyoto, Japan
{tyamaoka6, null}@gmail.com

Abstract. The three attributions of products, the four stories, the ten feelings and the six experiences are important items in HCI or service design. The three attributions of products: usefulness, usable-ness and desirableness, the four stories: historical story, newest story, fictitious story and actual story, the ten feelings: joy, familiarity, surprising, satisfaction, lovely, longing, expectation, com-fort, interest, impression, experience: experience of obtaining something, unusual experience, experience of getting something after doing tasks, experience of getting convenience, experience of longing for something, experience of feeling through the five senses. These items are integrated into a basic or applied UX-Story system diagram. These relationship are clarified and UX designer or engineer can construct a flame of UX design or service design.

Keywords: UX · Story · UX-Story system diagram · HCI · Service design

1 Introduction

UX (User Experience) and story are now very important items for constructing UI. ISO has been examining UX to apply in Human Centered Design. The reasons why UX and story become to be important in manufacturing are that users want to have a good experience and sympathize the story included in products or GUI and so on. They are satisfied by not only functions but also experience and story.

When people moved up to self-actualization needs of Maslow's hierarchy of needs or become rich, they seem to sympathize products or GUI by UX or story in order to fulfill the self-actualization needs.

This paper shows method to construct UX and story in HCI or Service design.

2 Study 1

2.1 Purpose

When we usually experienced, we got a feeling through a sensation. As the elements of UX are sensations and feelings, the combinations of them are important parts to construct UX. The combinations are examined in study 1.

M. Antona and C. Stephanidis (Eds.): UAHCI 2015, Part I, LNCS 9175, pp. 143–150, 2015.
DOI: 10.1007/978-3-319-20678-3_14

2.2   Method

As six kinds of user experience were extracted [1, 2], 42 respondents from 20's to 70's were asked to fill out questionnaires.

The questionnaires are as follows.

- What is your experience regarding experience of obtaining something such as purchasing, unusual experience, experience of getting something after doing tasks, experience of getting convenience, experience of longing for something, and experience of feeling through the five senses.
- What kinds of feeling such as joy, surprise and excitement do you get from the experiences.

2.3   Results and Discussion

206 experiences and 75 keywords related to feeling were extracted (Tables 1 and 2).

Table 1. 206 experiences

Respondents	Experiences	Feeling	Note
No. 31	I bought Sony's RX-1 camera.	Feeling of stir	
No. 31	I went to Finland	Excited feeling	

Table 2. Keywords (adjective)

Joy	Feeling of stir	Excitement	Satisfaction
Enjoyment	Sense of superiority	Respect	Fortune
Novelty	Open feeling	Relief	–

75 keywords were classified and finally 15 keyword were selected.

15 keywords: Joy, love, expectation, interest, excitement, enjoyment, relief, delight, astonishment, impression, accomplishment, satisfaction, comfort, gratitude, interest.

3   Data Analysis

The data were analyzed from viewpoint of relations between experiences and feeling. The relations between experiences and feeling were shown in Fig. 1.

The strong relation of the six experiences and feeling are as follows.

- Experience of obtaining something: Joy, expectation, delight, excitement, satisfaction.
- Unusual experience: Joy, surprising, astonishment.
- Experience of getting something after doing tasks: Joy, accomplishment, satisfaction, comfort.

- Experience of getting convenience: Joy, surprising.
- Experience of longing for something: expectation.
- Experience of feeling through the five senses: Joy, surprising, excitement, satisfaction.

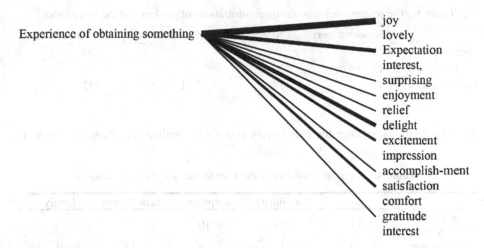

Experience of obtaining something

joy
lovely
Expectation
interest,
surprising
enjoyment
relief
delight
excitement
impression
accomplish-ment
satisfaction
comfort
gratitude
interest

Fig. 1. Relations between experiences of obtaining something and feeling (Bold line means strong tie).

4 Study 2

4.1 Purpose

As we usually feel stories in Starbucks, Ace hotel, Clif bar and REI, we feel sympathy for objects. The relation among three aspects of product, four stories and ten feelings are clarified in this chapter.

4.2 Method

- The three aspects of product, four stories and ten feelings are as follows.

- Three attributions of products: Usefulness, usableness and desirableness
- Four stories: Historical story, newest story, fictitious story and actual story
- Ten feelings: Joy, familiarity, surprising, satisfaction, lovely, longing, expectation, comfort, interest, impression (Table 5).

- 62 respondents from 20's to 80's were asked to connect lines among the three aspects of product, the four stories and the ten feelings.

4.3 Results and Discussion

(a) The relations between the three aspects of product and the four stories are shown in Table 3.

Table 3. The relations between the three attributions of product and the four stories

	Historical story	Newest story	Fictitious story	Actual story
Usefulness	12	36	2	34
Usableness	13	20	1	46
Desirableness	42	19	41	11

(b) The relations between the four stories and the ten feelings are shown in Table 4.

Table 4. The relations between the four stories and the ten feelings

	joy	familiarity	surprising	satisfaction	lovely
historical story	11	25	10	15	19
newest story	16	1	36	17	0
fictitious story	21	7	15	5	14
actual story	10	29	1	29	7

	longing	expectation	comfort	interest	impression
historical story	28	11	11	6	16
newest story	13	27	7	12	15
fictitious story	21	15	3	27	25
actual story	3	13	35	8	6

(c) The relations between the three aspects of product and the four stories were analyzed by correspondence analysis and cluster analysis.

- First group: historical story, fictitious story and desirableness.
- Second group: newest story, actual story, usefulness and usableness.

(d) The relations between the four stories and the ten feelings were analyzed by correspondence analysis and cluster analysis.

- First group: historical story, lovely, longing.
- Second group: fictitious story, impression, interest and joy.
- Third group: newest story, expectation, surprising.
- Fourth group: actual story, familiarity, comfort and satisfaction.

5 The Relation Among the Four Aspects

5.1 The Four Aspects

The four aspect previously described are as shown below.

- The three attributions of products: Usefulness, usableness and desirableness
- The four stories: Historical story, newest story, fictitious story and actual story
- The ten feelings: joy, familiarity, surprising, satisfaction, lovely, longing, expectation, comfort, interest, impression
- The six experiences:

    - experience of obtaining something such as purchasing
    - unusual experience
    - experience of getting something after doing tasks
    - experience of getting convenience
    - experience of longing for something
    - experience of feeling through the five senses.

5.2 The Relation Among the Four Aspects

The data previously described in Sects. 3 and 4 were integrated into UX-Story system diagram (Fig. 2). As 15 feelings in UX and 10 feelings in story are examined, the 10 feelings are selected as the common feelings.

5.3 How to Use the UX-Story System Diagram

When UX designers design HCI designs, service design or product designs, they can construct designs with UX or story as shown below.

- Designers plan to imagine feeling of HCI, service design or products based on the concept of them.
- They can select keywords of feelings in the basic or applied UX-Story system diagram according to the feeling of HCI, service design or products.
- They select the attribution of product (usefulness, usableness and desirableness) which are suitable for the feelings based on the concept.
- The UX or story are decided based on the attribution.

5.4 Examples Using the UX-Story System Diagram

- How does a hospital receive a high evaluation?
  When it has good equipment as an actual story, the actual story is selected according to the UX-Story system diagram. As the actual story can connect experience of get-ting convenience with familiarity and satisfaction easily.

TOYOTA MIRAI Hydrogen Fuel-cell Sedan[3]

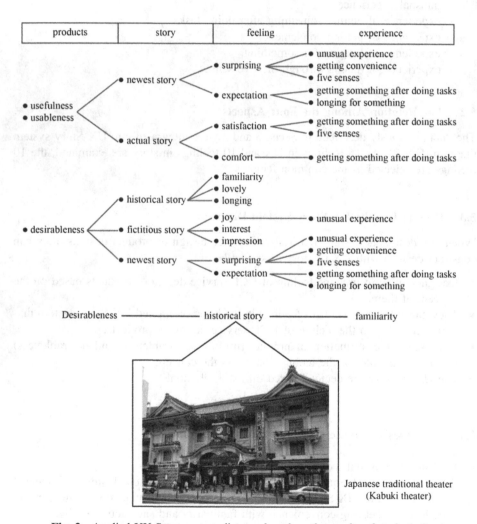

Fig. 2. Applied UX-Story system diagram based on the results of study 1, 2

Table 5. Basic UX-Story system diagram

Product	Story	Feeling	Experience
1. Usefulness 2. Usableness 3. Desirableness	1. Historical story 2. Newest story 3. Fictitious story 4. Actual story	1. Joy 2. Familiarity 3. Surprising 4. Satisfaction 5. Lovely 6. Longing 7. Expectation 8. Comfort, 9. Interest, 10. Impression	1. Experience of obtaining something 2. Unusual experience 3. Experience of getting something after doing tasks 4. Experience of getting convenience 5. Experience of longing for something 6. Experience of feeling through the five senses

– The usableness of a GUI design connects UX (experience of getting something after doing tasks) with feelings (satisfaction and comfort).

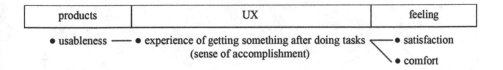

products	UX	feeling

• usableness ——— • experience of getting something after doing tasks ⟨ • satisfaction
(sense of accomplishment)   • comfort

6 Summary

The three attributions of products, the four stories, the ten feelings and the six experiences are important items in HCI or service design, and integrated into an UX-Story system diagram. These relationship are clarified and UX designer or engineer can construct a flame of UX design or service design.

- 3 attributions of products: usefulness, usableness and desirableness.
- 4 stories: Historical story, newest story, fictitious story and actual story.
- 10 feelings: joy, familiarity, surprising, satisfaction, lovely, longing, expectation, comfort, interest, impression.
- 6 experience: experience of obtaining something, unusual experience, experience of getting something after doing tasks, experience of getting convenience, experience of longing for something, experience of feeling through the five senses.

The procedure to construct UX or Story is as follows.

- Designers plan to imagine feeling of HCI, service design or products based on the concept of them.
- They can select keywords of feelings in the basic or applied UX-Story system diagram according to the feeling of HCI, service design or products.
- They select the attribution of product (usefulness, usableness and desirableness) which are suitable for the feelings based on the concept.
- The UX or story are decided based on the attribution.

References

1. Yokoyama, K.: Extraction of the type of emotion for user experience design. Master's Thesis of Wakayama University (2013)
2. Yamaoka, T., Kanbara, k.: Experience design/examining service engineering design and evaluation items. Bull. Jpn. soc. Sci. 1, 262–263 (2006)
3. http://toyota.jp/mirai/grade/

Universal Access to the Web

Social Networks: Technological and Social Aspects of Social Network-Mediated Interaction of Elderly People

Laura Burzagli[✉], Paolo Baronti, and Lorenzo Di Fonzo

Institute of Applied Physics "Nello Carrara", National Research Council of Italy,
Florence, Italy
{l.burzagli,p.baronti,l.difonzo}@ifac.cnr.it

Abstract. Services for the social interaction of elderly persons are here considered here and described. After an initial analysis, the implementation within the framework of an existing Social Network Site, such as Facebook, is proposed.

Keywords: Social network sites · Elderly people · Social interaction

1 Introduction

Social interaction, for combating feelings of loneliness and isolation, is an essential aspect of inclusion for elderly people. A number of services for social interaction based upon ICT solutions have been created in different contexts and tested in different projects, even if they are often not particularly efficient and effective and sometimes even trivial. This contribution starts from an accurate analysis of the main elements involved in this process, considering both social and technological aspects and then describes the set-up of a specific service on an existing platform for Social Network Sites.

2 Social Aspects

Social interactions are one of the fundamental human activities, the features of which have been carefully studied and classified. For example, in the WHO ICF classification (International Classification on Functioning and Disabilities) [1] many references to social interactions can be found in both the Activities and the Environmental Factors sections. Chapter 7 (Interpersonal Interactions and Relationships) describes in detail all tasks and actions required for simple and complex interactions among people.

Even a preliminary analysis of the ICF classification clearly shows the difficulties of the problems connected with social interactions. First, the list of interpersonal communications (d730-d779) is of interest from the perspective of exemplifying the complexity of the social network of each person, as it makes possible the formal identification of how many types of relationships it is necessary to consider and the possible problems of all of them. In a preliminary examination, the d750 (d7500-d7504) and d760 (d7601-d7603) classes can be considered. For example, for the Family Relationships

© Springer International Publishing Switzerland 2015
M. Antona and C. Stephanidis (Eds.): UAHCI 2015, Part I, LNCS 9175, pp. 153–161, 2015.
DOI: 10.1007/978-3-319-20678-3_15

class (d760), the Parent-child and Child-parent relationships (d7600, d7601), the Sibling relationships (d7602), and the Extended family relationships (d7603) can be examined. These imply relationships between people of different ages, which is one of the points of discussion when network-mediated interactions are considered. Another element in this analysis is the group of Informal social relationships (d7500-d7504). Five different groups of people are considered: friends, neighbors, acquaintances, co-inhabitants, and peers. The groups in the social life of people outside the family are completed with groups that are part of the formal relationships (d740). In this group of particular relevance is the group of service providers. Even if the social interactions of people are probably reduced when they grow old, some of them are important for social integration. One example is the group of service providers, public as the ones dealing with certifications or hospital reservations or private, as shops where e.g. food can be ordered or bought. If people may be kept connected to their social environment, particularly when they leave their home to be recovered in an institution, this can significantly contribute to their well-being [2] (Fig. 1).

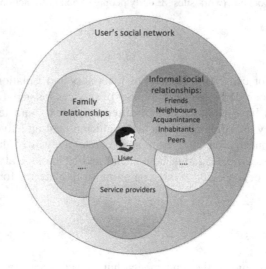

Fig. 1. User social network representation

The complexity of the interaction can also be considered. For example, in Chapter 7 of ICF, there is a division into General Interpersonal Interactions (d710-d729) and Particular Interpersonal Relationships (d730-d779). In the first group, the interaction elements are structured, considering e.g. Tolerance (d7102) and Criticism (d7103) in relationships. These factors could be particularly critical when dealing with old people, who are often very sensitive to criticisms, particularly when dealing with the use of technology. From this perspective, the presence of a moderator in services dealing with group social interactions should probably be taken into consideration.

Finally, in ICF it is also taken into account that personal interactions involve communication processes that can be defined as [3] "the exchange of information, feelings and meanings through verbal and non-verbal messages including two or groups of people".

Therefore, other chapters in the classification could be relevant, such as Chapter 3, which deals with communications. The definition of d360 (Using communication devices and techniques) "Using devices, techniques and other means for the purposes of communicating, such as calling a friend on the telephone" can also be considered to be a direct link of social interactions with the use of ICT technology.

In modern society, when social interactions are considered, the concept of distance should also be taken into account. The physical distance between people can cause a feeling of loneliness that has an influence on the physical and psychological well-being of people. In addition, health problems, even if minor, or a slight reduction in mobility can reduce contacts including also those with relatives [4]. Therefore, interpersonal communication, even if nor face-to-face but mediated by a telecommunication system, can contribute to individual well-being. An old and simple type of telecommunication equipment, as the telephone, is a testimony to this fact, even if only the audio component is available to transfer information and communicate feelings. The telephone allows a single-synchronous channel. It is very far from the potentials offered by modern computer-mediated communications systems, able to transport synchronously or asynchronously all information components: texts, audios, pictures, videos. An example of advanced systems with the above characteristics is Skype.

The main problem dealing with old people is the acceptability of such systems, including as part of acceptability also the concepts of usability and accessibility. One of the aspects to be discussed is that each of the above outlined social relations can be taken care of independently or can be integrated as uniformly as possible in a common communication platform. The second option can give to the person the idea of being really part of a social network and can favor the use of the available services due a coherent approach and interface.

As a preliminary conclusion, it can be observed that:

- The set of relationships that constitute the social network of people is very extensive, much more so than can be identified simply by focalization on a specific angle;
- The concept of community in a physical space is progressively being replaced by the concept of an on line community;
- The use of technology to cancel out physical distance at an interpersonal communication level is positive. It has also been widely used in the past (telephone);
- The adoption of a common platform that unifies access and interaction procedures may be in principle useful in facilitating its use.

3   Technological Aspects

Technological aspects require a careful analysis. In the previous section a number of preliminary observations have already been offered. Examples are the use of telephone as an existing device for technology-mediated communication between people, and the advantage of a uniform platform and interface for the social network of any person, extending from relationships with family and friends, up to the ones with service providers. However, additional analyses are necessary about modifications of interpersonal communication processes, due to the recent technological developments. A first crucial aspect is the different role that Internet is assuming in the Information Society. Internet is no longer solely a source of information, but more and more an interpersonal communication platform and a channel for social relationships. Moreover, the increasing use of Social Network Sites (SNS) is leading a new definition of community, no more limited by proximity, but also including distributed networks of people, which offer new opportunities for social connections.

From the point of view of technological implementation, for the design of a social network service at least two different approaches can be adopted:

- The development of specific product;
- The Use of currently available platforms according to the specific requirements of the service.

The first solution implies, for example, the addition of a specific chat channel for interpersonal communication in an application where other service components are already available. An example is the food application developed in the FOOD (Framework for Optimizing the prOcess of feeDing) project, active in the framework of the European Ambient Assisted Living (AAL) program [5]. On the interface tablet, where the kitchen lists all shopping items, the user may also find a chat to ask her friends if an ingredient is necessary in a recipe. With this approach, accessibility and usability aspects can be optimized, if the application developers have a sufficient knowledge about these topics. Moreover, it probably requires an easier and faster phase of training for the use of the application functionalities and the interface components. Anyway, the implementation is limited to a specific application, and therefore to only a component of her social connections.

An additional critical aspect of this solution is represented by stability and robustness: if the product does not present high levels of these characteristics, it introduces heavy barriers to elderly people, because they are unable to distinguish between an error in the procedure and a bug in the software.

The second approach is the adoption of already existing platforms as a basis for the implementation of the necessary application, the so-called Social Network Sites. Even if many of them are available, in this contribution the more widespread i.e. Facebook, is considered. As for the use, from http://newsroom.fb.com/company-info/ the following information is available:

- 890 million daily active users on average for December 2014;
- 745 million mobile daily active users on average for December 2014;
- 1.39 billion monthly active users as of December 31, 2014;
- 1.19 billion mobile monthly active users as of December 31, 2014.[1]

From a technological perspective, this implies a robust and affordable platform, which is not comparable with ad hoc implementations. Even if many people still believe that such platforms are only used as an entertainment by the young generations, the actual dimensions of the phenomenon are clearly expressed by the reported figures. Data relative to user

---

[1] Approximately 82.4 % of daily active users are outside the US and Canada.

age distribution are also available. Publications, such as [6, 7], confirm a wide distribution of the user age, while outlining differences in the use of the application. A different importance, for example, is attributed to the various communication channels, but no rejection by specific categories is reported.

A second concern of utmost importance in the field of e-inclusion is accessibility. Facebook takes also care of this aspect, with a specific page oriented to the problem: http://www.facebook.com/help/contact/169372943117927. The page assembles all observations in a structured way, so guarantying, at least in principle, an interest to the problem and an extended network that works on it.

3.1 Presentation of the Platform to Elderly Users

When the use of general-purpose platforms for the implementation of social interaction services is considered, an aspect appears particularly crucial, i.e. the presentation and introduction of these communication systems to persons who are not acquainted with the use of the new telecommunication environments or only use few of their features. With reference to [8], first it is necessary to present the goal of the platforms, with a clear description of the basic underlying concepts, which have to be discussed with the users before starting any activity on them. Then, how to create an account must be described, showing the way to modify the personal profile with some example about how to add data to it. Finally, support should be offered in the identification of groups of interest connected to the specific activities of each user. Reactions coming from the user and showing their needs and difficulties should guide the support actions. The training is much more crucial if the users do not present a natural attitude towards the use of the systems. The learning phase may result significantly heavier for them.

4 A Practical Example

In the FOOD project, a community of about 30 families of elderly users are testing services related to feeding. While these elderly people are already using an application specifically developed for managing services related to food and cooking, the project consortium is discussing the adoption of a general-purpose social network application, as Facebook, for social interaction, which results of particular importance in this context.

Most of the scenarios describing new services are often written without specific references to currently available technologies and tools. This is due to the lack of a language that can be easily understood by people with different expertise, to allow fruitful discussions on multidisciplinary aspects. When this discussion about a useful scenario is made possible, in order to translate the description of the scenario in a product to be tested by users, several approaches can be adopted. In FOOD a solution based on the use, as much as possible, of already widely available tools and applications has been proposed.

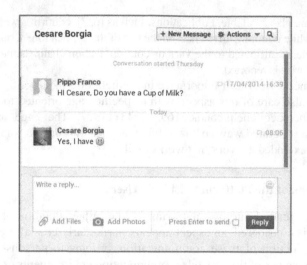

Fig. 2. Chat example

One of the scenarios discussed in the project is based on a social network, which involves friends, neighbors and, at least in principle, other actors such as shopkeepers, with the aim to organize a lunch. The corresponding service can be decomposed in a list of tasks. After these tasks have been clearly described from the perspective of technological implementation, their features can be compared with the features available in existing applications, such as Facebook, and translated as specifications for this specific environment. When the feasibility of all tasks has been checked, the service can be reformulated in the language of the adopted tool.

The organization and management of a service as the one foreseen in the above scenario, requires that the adopted system is able to perform three main tasks:

- To allow the creation and management of a group of people, such as an on-line room;
- To facilitate discussion;
- To help in the organization of an event.

The first task is easily implemented within Facebook, which allows the creation of a group, with the selection of a name, a list of members and a specific level of privacy. The second task is also easily available, because members of each group can have a direct communication with individual members of the group through a chat or with the entire group through the post. In Fig. 2 an example of the chat is presented. In this case, the chat is used to ask a friend an ingredient for the lunch that the group is organizing. A video communication, if necessary, is also possible using the option of linking Skype, provided in the chat menu. Finally, in Facebook (see Figs. 3 and 4), a member can create an event and other members can adhere or not. The name, the context, the location, date, and people to be invited can be introduced. A poll about how many people are available ("Ask Question" button) can also be included.

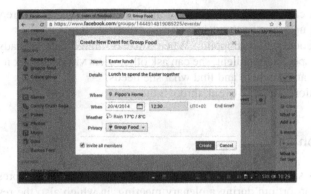

Fig. 3. Event creation

Fig. 4. Event visualisation

Therefore, after having tested the technical feasibility, in order to set up the service the pilot leaders have been asked to proceed with the following steps:

1. Create an account for each user, if this has not yet been done. It is possible to use the language of the country;
2. Create a group for each pilot, for example called FOOD_countryname_1, FOOD_countryname_2, FOOD_countryname_3. The task can be implemented by the pilot team responsible, with just a few settings[2];
3. Fill the list of contact with the names of pilots' participants;
4. Start with an exchange of messages among users;
5. Create an event, for example a lunch together. All users can reply to the invitation and see the list of people, who are involved. With the help of other available applications, a menu can be decided, according to different needs and preferences. A draft

---

[2] Data to be set: privacy options, contacts to be added. Among the three different privacy option (open - the group is visible to all Facebook contacts, closed - the group is visible to all, but the posts can be seen only by members of the group, secret - only group's members can see the group), it was suggested to start with "Secret option".

of the menu can be posted by the host and other participants can reply with their suggestions, up to the final version;

6. Simulate a cooperative shopping. When a list of ingredients is ready, if the chef needs some special ingredient, she can ask other users via Facebook to check shops and markets around them and find what she needs;

7. Collect opinions after the event, through the chat.

5 Discussion

The idea of this specific implementation on Facebook has been first presented to the whole FOOD consortium during a plenary meeting, in which also the responsible for the three pilot sites were present. The greatest barrier turned out to be just the adoption of a Social Network Site. The vast majority of partners considered these platforms too complex, not secure enough and distracting for elderly people. These reactions are probably due to an insufficient knowledge of the systems and their technological possibilities. Partners only associate these products to social entertainments for younger generations, while the products are usable in complex environments. This phenomenon is quite common in the field of ICT services, where many people limit the use only to the most common features, without asking if and how different modalities are conceivable. A careful analysis of the technological components leads to the identification of different uses, especially when different categories of potential users are considered.

A second reaction was collected when the service was presented to a limited group of users, asking the question: "Do you agree on a trial with Facebook?", with the only option Yes or No. In this case the reaction was not again completely positive, probably because, as described in Sect. 3.1, a more accurate introduction of the service is required. Presently, different approaches to describe this approach to the final users is under study. Other platform will be studied and tested, but the fundamental idea is to try the use of existing, robust tools with a large number of features already available.

6 Conclusion

Social Network Sites present elements of interest not only for young people, but also for people with limitations to their activities and abilities, and also for elderly people, especially as far as social interaction services are concerned. An analysis of the classifications, the surveys and the examples already available is required before the core methodology to be applied in this specific field can be defined. An example within an ongoing project was presented. The future work will be devoted to verify the actual response of people to such services and to extend the use to other activities of social networking.

References

1. WHO: ICF International Classification of Functioning, Disability and Health. World Health Organization, Geneva (2001)
2. Bothorel, C., Lohr, C., Thépaut, A., Bonnaud, F., Cabasse, G.: From individual communication to social networks: evolution of a technical platform for the elderly. In: Abdulrazak, B., Giroux, S., Bouchard, B., Pigot, H., Mokhtari, M. (eds.) ICOST 2011. LNCS, vol. 6719, pp. 145–152. Springer, Heidelberg (2011)
3. Ismail A.: Interpersonal Interaction. http://www.slideshare.net/drarif89/interpersonal-interaction
4. Baker, P., Bricout, J., Moon, N., Coughlan, B., Pater, J.: Communities of participation: a comparison of disability and aging identified groups on Facebook and LinkedIn. Telematics Inform. **30**, 22–34 (2013)
5. FOOD project website. http://www.food-aal.eu/
6. Kneidinger, B.: Intergenerational contacts online: an exploratory study of cross-generational Facebook "friendships". Stud. Commun. Sci. **14**, 12–19 (2014)
7. Braun, M.: Obstacles to social networking website use among older adults. Comput. Hum. Behav. **29**, 673–680 (2013)
8. How to Teach Facebook to Seniors. http://www.wikihow.com/Teach-Facebook-to-Seniors

Accessibility in E-Commerce Tools:
An Analysis of the Optical Inclusion of the Deaf

Maria Eduarda de Araújo Cardoso[1(✉)], Daniela de Freitas Guilhermino[1],
Rafaella Aline Lopes da Silva Neitzel[1], Laura Sanchéz Garcia[2],
and Roberto Elero Junior[1]

[1] Center of Technological Sciences, State University of Paraná,
Bandeirantes, Brazil
{mariaeduarda,danielaf,rafaella,robertoej}@uenp.edu.br
[2] Informatics Department, Federal University of Paraná, Curitiba, Brazil
laura@inf.ufpr.br

Abstract. The deaf communities are members of a unique culture and language, the Sign Language. Worldwide, the spoken/oral language is predominant, however, Deaf may encounter several hindrances to establish social relationships using spoken/oral language. E-commerce systems are significantly important not only to the listeners, but also to the Deaf, as E-commerce systems are the main vehicle for online shopping. Currently, the majority of the population shops online; nevertheless, the conditions in which information is disclosed in such systems may not appropriately respect the particularities of the Deaf. In this context, this paper supports the hypothesis that, identifying the accessibility requirements for the Deaf, the development of inclusive E-commerce systems is feasible and, thus, ensuring that the benefits and utilities provided by E-commerce systems are also accessible by deaf people. Therefore, in order to prove our hypothesis, the implications that the Sign Language (first language of the Deaf infers to the communication, to improve the accessibility of such environments, must be identified. This paper investigates the necessities of the deaf community when accessing Web systems, and based on evaluation mechanisms, analyses the environments developed using E-commerce tools concerning accessibility aspects.

Keywords: Accessibility · Web accessibility · Deaf community · E-commerce tools

1 Introduction

The way deaf people interact with the world is mainly visual (by means of visual experiences), thus, the Deaf regularly endures several difficulties, not only regarding information access, but also regarding the basic person-to-person interaction and transport (via public transportation).

Based on the aforementioned difficulties, the necessity of developing accessible and inclusive systems that provide equal opportunities to the Deaf grows considerably.

E-commerce is a category of trading in which financial transactions are performed via mobile devices and computing platforms. There are many advantages in using

M. Antona and C. Stephanidis (Eds.): UAHCI 2015, Part I, LNCS 9175, pp. 162–173, 2015.
DOI: 10.1007/978-3-319-20678-3_16

E-commerce tools, for instance, such tools are constantly online, providing quick propagation of new products and the anticipation of market tendencies at a relatively low cost. In fact, the adoption of E-commerce tools is reasonably expanding worldwide.

Therefore, the deaf communities' necessity of acquiring access to E-commerce systems in Brazil, aiming to diminish the struggle of locomotion as a result of their communication conditions, becomes evident.

The World Web Consortium (W3C) states "accessibility means achieving a vast percentage of people at distinct sensorial conditions, including visual, auditory, physical, speaking, cognitive and neurologic". However, due to the lack of accessibility of current computational tools, the information technology is by far not appropriate to the Deaf.

Hence, in this paper, not only E-commerce tools, but also deaf-oriented systems are analyzed aiming to promote accessibility improvements towards E-commerce environments. Normally, the accessibility required by the Deaf is not provided by E-commerce tools, and as a consequence, the deaf user's experience is quite defective when using E-commerce websites, especially in terms of lack of content in Sign Language and the necessity of utilizing a simple, but sufficient language.

The scenario above motivated the research described in this paper, which analyzed the requirements of E-commerce tools and the challenges concerning the inclusion of the Deaf in the virtual environment.

2   Accessibility Recommendations for the Deaf

Currently, the Deaf not only endure several prejudices from the society and are commonly misconceived, for instance, as "deaf-mute". Furthermore, the deaf community also experiences social problems, once many people are not able to use Sign Language. Consequently, the Deaf may suffer from isolation, low self-esteem and discrimination [1], which may prevent deaf communities from growing and evolving.

Deaf communities have fought hard for the recognition of their own language. The recognition of the Sign Language must be achieved, however, this language has a lot ahead to be studied, taught and disclosed [2].

In addition, the Deaf experiences several hindrances in Brazil, as in other countries, once the communication and interaction are commonly performed using the mother language of each country while most of the Deaf have not achieved satisfactory understanding of the language [3].

The W3C highlights several barriers that the Deaf may find when accessing the Internet, for instance: lack of alternative subtitles and audio, the use of not clear and not simple language, and lack of video content. The aforementioned barriers demonstrate the importance of the research in such fields in order to prioritize the necessities of the Deaf, and waken the deaf communities' hindrances in the information and communication access.

In order to advance the state of deaf-oriented technologies, computational research has examined applications that assist collaborative activities and promote the digital inclusion of the Deaf. Generally, collaborative systems focus on users not only able to orally communicate, but also users acquainted with Information and Communication Technologies (ICTs) [4], disregarding accessibility aspects required to the digital inclusion of disabled people.

Accessibility recommendations for the Deaf according to the view of distinct authors have been examined in this section. The recommendations are mainly related to the following aspects: content creation, visual representation of information, media alternatives, resources for Web browsing and communication leveraging [5–12].

Corradi [5] describes Sign Language requisites for the development of virtual environments focused on deaf people. In addition, she highlights the importance of using video subtitles in Sign Language to improve the comprehension of the Deaf and auditory disabled people on the interpreted content, promoting the distinction of colors between visited links and other contents to facilitate the navigation of disabled users on the Web page, and adopting dictionaries in Sign Language in case disabled users are not aware of certain signs utilized by the interpreter.

Bueno [6] highlights guidelines to create engaging and expressive content using rather visual than verbal features. The aforementioned guidelines are mostly related to multicultural aspects and the different ways to represent information. The author also recommends that the environment should be multicultural, thus, the content should not be restricted to the deaf community. The environment also should explore visual resources due to the fact that the visual sense is the cornerstone of the communication between the Deaf. Bueno [6] also states that the Brazilian Sign Language, LIBRAS, should be the main communication language of the user; the visual vocabulary (signs and arrows) should be utilized on the interface for the user navigation; regarding the interpreter mediation, the interpretation should not only respect rules of the environment, but also be well planned and organized, taking into account adverse situations, clothing, and accessories.

Debevec et al. [1] describe how technologies utilized in videos may be applied to E-commerce systems, highlighting the main criteria to ensure satisfactory quality of videos and images. The minimum frame rate should be greater than 15 frames per second. The author also affirms that the comprehension rate may be optimized in order to keep an appropriate recognition of the movements of the hands and facial expressions, taking into account the Sign Language is completely gestural. Moreover, the image delay should be lower than 1, 2 s when utilizing video resources in Sign Language. Blurry fingers during the movement are tolerable, although clearly visible fingers are preferable.

Kitunen [8] affirms that the facial recognition is significantly important to the Deaf, once they rely on facial features to communicate, thus, respective people's pictures should follow their names. Kitunen [8] also trusts that videos in Sign Language, which is used to translate the content to the Deaf, should not replace subtitles. Moreover, the author suggests the adoption of a pure written transcription of the audio followed by visual representation, e.g. illustrations. Regarding the user navigation, the author suggests the use of symbols and icons to improve the recognition of different sections on the website, and thus, assist users in the exploration of the webpage content. However, symbols and icons should be employed only upon important section/menus of the page, otherwise, the layout page may become crowed and unpleasant for any types of users.

Abreu [9] maintains that certain recommendations such as user interface adaptation for the Deaf, alternative texts for images, and how to present the content in a comprehensible fashion. The author reinforces that the creation of content requires not only the adaptation of interface resources for the Deaf, but also the division of large information blocks in smaller groups, to enhance the comprehension of the content by the Deaf. In addition, the author suggests that users should be provided with meaningful information so they are able to acquire documents according to their preferences.

Kosec et al. [10] find out that, to create accessible video to the Deaf, the speed of execution should be slow, so the user is able to follow the gestures of the Sign Language interpretation. The author also highlights that, for the same reason previously mentioned, the use of content (for creation, presentation or utilization) has to be mild and clear. Kosec et al. [10] also recommend that, to improve the visual presentation of the content, it is important to provide mechanisms to enable users to increase the screen size of the video, and as a result, they are able to easily recognize facial expressions and gestures presented in the videos, as long as the quality of the video is not compromised when the screen size is increased.

e-MAG [11] identifies recommendations focusing on the presentation of Web pages. The author recommends that a standard of page division should be applied in order to assist not only the visualization of the target audience, but also the reading and comprehension, not requiring substantial prior knowledge. In addition, supplementary information must be provided to illustrate the main content when the reading of complex text is necessary. The author restates that besides alternative texts and subtitles, video content should also provide Sign Language support. Moreover, in order to present the content, it is recommended that information areas should be divided in groups to simplify the management of the content. Generally, the information areas are divided in four groups: "top", "content", "menu", and "footer".

WCAG 2.0 [12], W3C guideline, recommends the control and temporization of media, so deaf-users are able to clearly and comprehensively read and utilize the content. The author also highlights ways to facilitate the navigation of deaf-users, to locate contents and determine the location of the user itself on the web page. To appropriately create content, the content should be allowed to be present in distinct ways, without affecting the information presented in the content or structure of the content. To visually present the content, the foreground and background should be separated to facilitate the visualization of the content. Moreover, media resources should provide users with sufficient time to read and make use of the content.

Mostly, usability problems on the web concern finding, reading, and understanding the information [13]. The diverse situations and features are required to be taken into account by the content creators during the web page conception.

3 Methodology of the Accessibility Evaluation

To develop the present analysis, the following steps were necessary: 1-Selection of development tools to assess the environments developed from such tools, aiming the evaluation of accessibility; 2-Selection of mechanisms to support the evaluation of accessibility; 3-Evaluation of E-commerce environments using the previously selected mechanisms of evaluation; 4-Combination of results obtained from the analysis of the recommendations provided in the literature review and also from the evaluation of the E-commerce environments (performed in the previous item).

3.1   E-Commerce Development Tools

The most popular tools to develop E-commerce web pages have been selected and analyzed. They are OpenCart [14]; PrestaShop [15]; OsCommerce [16]; and Magento [17].

Opencart is a E-commerce solution of easy use containing a friendly and intuitive interface. Opencart presents the function of expanding its functionalities via extensions (plugins and add-ons) and customizing its design using templates. The main functionalities provided by the tool are: free documentation, open source platform, security socket layer (SSL) support, users are able to rate and comment products, among others.

PrestaShop is an Open Source tool. The tool provides an interface in which the administrators of the store are able to manage their products in stock, orders, clients and payments. There are no boundaries regarding the number of categories, sub-categories, and images, among others. As mentioned, the tool is open source, thus, the user is provided with access to the source code of the virtual store.

OsCommerce is also an open source solution, providing a large set of functionalities. The tool allows users of the online page to keep their stores at no cost, taxes or limitations. The tool is simple and relatively fast, however, being familiarized with the tool is preferable to configure the OsCommerce.

Magento is an E-commerce platform built under an open source license that provides users with flexibility, design management, content management, among other functionalities. Magento is also distributed under an Enterprise version. The tool presents hundreds of extensions and an open architecture allowing users to add even more functionalities. Moreover, additional features are: friendly URL, URL rewrite, 100 % customizable design, and multilingual support, among others.

The aforementioned tools present limitations regarding accessibility in general, especially towards the deaf community. Therefore, it is proven that improvements could be proposed in order to provide the accessibility required by the Deaf, which would allow them to access the environments built upon such tool without negatively affecting the content and information access.

3.2   Support Mechanisms to the Accessibility Evaluation

In order to analyze accessibility of E-commerce websites, four evaluation mechanisms have been chosen. The mechanisms are based on accessibility guidelines proposed by W3C/WAI and allow us to evaluate all pages contained in a website, indicating page errors in contrast to accessibility features. In the set of analyzed mechanisms, four have been chosen to perform the evaluation: CynthiaSays [18], Hera [19], Examinator [20] and DaSilva [21].

CynthiaSays is a mechanism focused on web accessibility and is considered the most used mechanisms by disable people. The mechanism is intended for personal use and not commercial use and it is mainly used to demonstrate how satisfactory web designs and accessible content are achieved. Cynthia also assists users to identify content errors concerning the Section 508 of accessibility guidelines in WCAG Web, which presents accessibility standards of the USA government to a vast variety of sources and information technologies. The mechanism not only allows users to test individual pages in their website, but also provides feedback in a clear and straight-forward report format.

HERA is a mechanism to review the accessibility of Web pages according to the recommendations of the WCAG/W3C. HERA performs an automatic pre-analysis of the page and provides information of the errors presented by the page (errors detected automatically) and in which points of verification should be reviewed manually. The HERA mechanism returns a summary containing the quantity of errors found, the verification time, how long the analysis takes and the total of analyzed elements. In addition, HERA returns a table containing the name of the "state of the verification points" showing all errors, rights, and the points that should not be changed in the page.

eXaminator is an automatic validator in accordance with Web Content Accessibility Guidelines 1.0, developed by W3C targeting a given page on the Internet. The tool is developed by the UMIC – Agency to the Knowledge Society, and could be utilized in the accessibility evaluation of all web pages of a website. This mechanism analyzes the webpage and returns a log screen containing information on errors and provides a quantitative report using tables to demonstrate accessibility errors and rights in the page.

DaSilva, web version, is a mechanism developed by Brazil Accessibility in partnership with the company W2B Internet Solutions. DaSilva is the first evaluator of accessibility of sites in Portuguese, based on principles of the E-MAG document, which is developed by the Brazilian electronic government in partnership with Brazil Accessibility. This mechanism not only allows us to analyze all pages contained in a website, but also indicates page errors in contrast to accessibility. The accessibility verification in the tool DaSilva is not greatly different than the previous tools, however, as opposed to the previous tools; users are able to choose priorities for the evaluation, so the tool returns accessibility reports focusing on errors and warnings conforming the elected priorities.

According to Queiroz [1], the aforementioned automated tools generally are fast, although not capable of identifying all features of accessibility. Therefore, the validation of accessibility should also be performed by direct revision. The human validation may assist to ensure language clarity and navigation easiness [1]. As a consequence, after the use of such tools, it was necessary to complement the evaluation by directly reviewing the analyzed websites aiming to check additional accessibility features.

3.3   Accessibility Requirements

The present evaluation process elects the following accessibility requirements: language, visual representation, interpreter mediation, technologies adopted in videos, content language, media duration, alternative text in images and other elements, destination addresses of links and keyboard utilization. The previous requirements have been identified according to data collected from accessibility guidelines. The mechanisms for automatic analysis, in general, allow us to evaluate all the aforementioned requirements. Certain mechanisms may not present results for a given requirement nevertheless, such details will be cited throughout the present paper.

Table 1. The relevancy of each requirement in E-commerce websites

Aspects evaluated	Environment implications	Relevancy
Language	When the website does not indicate the language in use, usually, the user is not able to determine the language of the website.	Low
Visual Representation	Deaf people may encounter hindrances when interpreting plans, thus, the page format should be easily perceived, and as a result, the user may familiarize with the website structure quickly. Thus, it is important to discern colors on different contents and visited links and the text should be divided in information blocks.	High
Interpreters Mediation	Deaf people are pleased to recognize other members, thus, they may feel confident when accessing a website that endorses their communication in Sign Language. As a consequence, the interpreter mediation is quite important in web pages.	High
Technologies Adopted in Videos	It is important to ensure a satisfactory video quality, in order to maximize the comprehension by deaf people, namely, ensuring a satisfactory visual detection of gestures and facial expressions. The image delay should be the lower than 1,2 seconds when employing video resources in Sign Language.	Medium
Content Language	Clear language assists deaf people to better interpret the content, thus, the content of the text should be well structured and with simple language. It is also important to employ titles, subtitles, paragraphs, and lists. The excessive information blocks may hinder the comprehension of the content. Thus, information blocks should be divided in convenient and small groups.	High
Media Duration	Deaf people need sufficient time to read, interpret and utilize the content in a way that the users are able to establish control under	Medium
	the media execution. In addition, it is important to provide controllers for the media execution such as: stop, continue, cancel, start, previous, next, among others.	
Alternative Texts	Deaf people requires subtitle to associate images and elements of the page.	Medium
Aspects evaluated	**Environment implications**	**Relevancy**
Destination Addresses of Links	Links should clearly indicate their destination addresses. Users are not able do distinguish links once they are bind to each other, without any separator in between them. Furthermore, navigation bars comprised by link lists should be provided to organize links and facilitate their location.	High
Keyboard Utilization	Shortcuts and additional functionalities should be made available from the keyboard.	Low

A relevancy parameter regarding accessibility has been attributed to each requirement. These requirements assisted the classification of development tools. Thus, three relevancy parameters are taken into account for each requirement: low, medium, and high. Table 1 demonstrates the environment implications and relevancy of each requirement.

4 Accessibility Evaluation for the Deaf in E-Commerce Systems

According to the methodology, an accessibility evaluation has been performed on websites developed using the aforementioned E-commerce tools. Namely, six E-commerce websites have been analyzed, in addition, each website was developed from a different development tool, aiming to identify the accessibility requirements offered by each tool. The evaluated websites embrace distinct trading categories, such as books, supplements, clothes and men's and women's accessories. Diversified websites have been chosen in order to achieve the manifold interests of the deaf community.

As the aforementioned websites are comprised by most of the resources provided by the development tools, the analysis of the accessibility issues became possible. Next, our analysis results are described. The results are grouped by the E-commerce development tools and highlight the most relevant positive and negative points found.

- **OpenCart:** systems developed using OpenCart present several positive points, such as: the indication of language is present in all information blocks, all images are captioned, all images and links are clearly discerned (character separators are employed); links alter colors to indicate a visit, which assists the navigation of deaf people, the user is informed about moving information in displacement or in automated update before the time expires, furthermore, the user has at least 20 s to extend the time limit and pause, stop or hide if necessary; information blocks are appropriately summarized, and in average 9 words are highlighted in each block, which facilitates the comprehension by deaf people, the content language is declared via Doctype (DTD), indicating a satisfactory page structure. In contrast, the main negative points of OpenCart are: the aspect of visual representation of the page, as notation of structure for visual formation effects should not be used; interpreter's mediation is not adopted and certain links containing equal content lead to distinct destination addresses; no shortcuts for important links on the keyboard; no media synchronization during multimedia presentations.
- **PrestaShop:** the main positive points are: style control for page presentation, which assists the comprehension by deaf people; 72 % of the links are organized in lists, helping on the navigation by deaf people; every link is clearly discerned; the words are separated in information blocks; the content language is declared on the DTD; tables are not used to format the page (important to users who utilize browsers based on text and read line by line, which is the deaf people's case. The main negative points are: the language in use is not presented; titles for the frames are not employed; no interpreter mediation; the language is not presented in a clear and

simple way in order to facilitate the comprehension by deaf people; images are not captioned; and the shortcuts for important links are not enabled.

- **OsCommerce:** the positive points presented by the systems are: simple header, facilitating the comprehension and identification of the language in use. The main negative points highlighted are: images not containing alternative texts, elements are presented and arranged without control attributes; printable characters are not used in links; no keyboard shortcuts for links; no interpreter mediation; media are not synchronized; and the Doctype is not provided.

- **Magento:** the main positive points presented by the systems are: visual presentation of the page using the correct structure and the elements arrangement present appropriate controls; main language identified; information blocks are summarized using in average 8 words, which facilitates the comprehension by deaf people; DTD is properly declared; images are captioned; and all adjacent links contain printable characters. The main negative points addressed are: the use of pop-up images; no keyboard shortcuts are presented; certain icons of the page are useless; no interpreter mediation; links containing equal content lead to distinct destination addresses; captions are not used in 36 % of the images; and media is not synchronized.

Table 2 presents a summary of evaluated aspects, described above, and classified in: (0) Bad – the page fails in the given aspect; (1) Regular – the aspects are ordinarily met; (2) Good – the aspect are mostly met and (3) Great – the page fully met the evaluated aspect.

Table 2. Summary of the accessibility evaluation of the E-commerce tools

Aspects evaluated	OpenCart	PrestaShop	Magento	OsCommerce
Language	3	0	3	3
Visual representation	1	1	1	1
Interpreter mediation	0	0	0	0
Technologies adopted in videos	–	–	1	–
Content language	2	1	1	0
Media duration	2	–	1	1
Alternative texts	0	0	0	1
Destination addresses of links	2	1	1	–
Keyboard utilization	1	1	1	1

After the evaluation of the websites developed using the development E-commerce tools, OpenCart presented the most satisfactory results in terms of accessibility for deaf people. OpenCart presents the requirements of higher relevancy and lower percentage of negative points. The functionalities of the tool are the most appropriate to obtain an accessible system, accordingly to the way deaf people interact: in a visual way. It is also important to reiterate that deaf people present several difficulties to use Portuguese, thus, certain requirements are essential to their inclusion in computational environments.

In the analysis, the mechanism HERA has been shown to be the most complete, as the tool presents a straightforward table, which is complete and easily comprehended. Figure 1 presents an evaluation performed via the mechanism HERA. The results are presented by the tool in Portuguese (Brazil).

The Hera mechanism presents results according to three WCAG priory levels. Priority 1 (P1) implies that web developers must satisfy the guidelines of level 1, otherwise, groups of disable users (e.g. deaf, bling, among others) will be unable to access web content. Priority 2 (P2) implies that once the guidelines are not satisfied, the access to web content is hindered and Priority 3 (P3), once satisfied, infers greater ease on the content access. The Hera shows positive points, negative points, points not applied and the points that require manual verification in the context of accessibility to the Deaf. Figure 1 highlights one of the three identified negative points regarding P1.

Furthermore, the tool details all aspects concerning each accessibility requirement, pointing out the rights and wrongs (when clicking on the point). Hera also presents a summary containing the total of errors found and the total of verified elements.

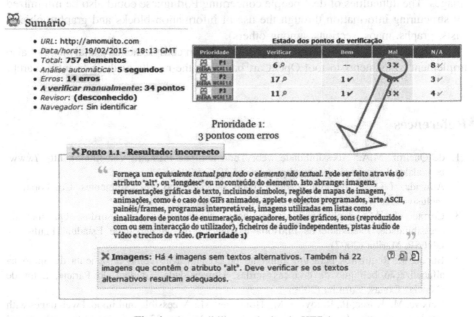

Fig. 1. Accessibility analysis via HERA

5   Conclusion

Deaf people require computation environments that take into account their peculiarities aiming to leverage the inclusion of the Deaf in such environments. Interactions via activities leveraged by computers are relevant to the development of the Deaf and may contribute to their identity creation.

Based on the results of the present evaluation, it is observed that the accessibility towards deaf people in the E-commerce websites is minimum, thus, the need of not only promoting reforms focusing on accessibility features, but also awareness of accessibility features is evident. The promotion of reforms and accessibility awareness is vital for the deaf community to be able to access computational environments.

It is also important to highlight that the E-commerce tools have been analyzed from websites developed through them. Therefore, the E-commerce tool may present resources or features not utilized, which may prejudice its evaluation regarding accessibility.

The fact that the deaf community fully and solely communicates using Sign Language is a valid presupposition and, as long as the computational environments meet the special language condition of the Deaf, such environments are more likely to include the deaf community. In this sense, an ideal accessibility condition would imply in the mediation of an interpreter fluent in Libras, allowing effective interaction in computational environments.

Regarding the visual representation, providing strong visual mechanisms to provide feedback to participants, enhancing their comprehension on the progress of the activities and increase the cohesion, presenting information via videos, Sign writing and images. The difficulties of deaf people concerning Portuguese could also be minimized by structuring information through the use of information blocks and graphic objects (lists, graphs, maps, sections, among others).

As future work, it is intended to not only perform complementary analysis, but also implement adjustments to tool OpenCart based on the results of the present research.

References

1. de Queiroz, M.A.: Acessibilidade web: Tudo tem sua Primeira Vez (2006). http://www. bengalalegal.com/capitulomaq.php. Acessed 10 Jan 2015
2. Almeida, L.D.A.: Awareness do Espaco de Trabalho em Ambientes Colaborativos Inclusivos na Web. Universidade Estadual de Campinas (2011)
3. Corradi, J.A.M.: Ambientes informacionais digitais e usuários surdos: Questões de acessibilidade. Faculdade de Filosofia e Ciências da Universidade Estadual Paulista – UNESP, Marília (2007)
4. Bueno, J.: Requisitos para um ambiente de comunicação como ferramenta de apoio na alfabetização belíngue de crianças surdas. Universidade Estadual do Paraná, Setor de Ciências Exatas, Curitiba (2009)
5. Debevc, M., Kosec, P., Rotovnik, M., Holzinger, M.: Accessible multimodal web pages with sign language translations for deaf and hard of hearing 72 users. In: 20th International Workshop on Database and Expert Systems Application, pp. 279–283 (2009)
6. Kitunen, S.: Designing a deaf culture specifc web site: Participatory design research for knack. University of Art and Design Helsinki, Finlândia (2009)
7. de Abreu, P.M.: Recomendações para projetos de TICs para apoio a alfabetização com libras. Universidade Federal de Minas Gerais - Instituto de Ciências Exatas, Belo Horizonte (2010)
8. Kosec, P., Debevc, M., Holzinger, A.: Sign language interpreter module: accessible video retrieval with subtitles. In: Miesenberger, K., Klaus, J., Zagler, W., Karshmer, A. (eds.) ICCHP 2010, Part II. LNCS, vol. 6180, pp. 221–228. Springer, Heidelberg (2010)
9. e-MAG: Modelo de acessibilidade em governo eletrônico (2011). http://www. governoeletronico.gov.br/acoes-e-projetos/e-MAG

10. WCAG, 2.0: Web content accesssibility guidelines. Web Accessibility Initiative (WAI) (2013). http://www.w3.org/TR/WCAG20/
11. CynthiaSays. http://www.cynthiasays.com. Accessed 15 Oct 2014
12. DaSilva. http://www.dasilva.org.br/. Accessed 15 Oct 2014
13. Examinator: eXaminator Validador de Acessibilidade Web. http://www.acessibilidade.gov.pt/webax/examinator.php. Accessed 15 Oct 2014
14. HERA. http://www.sidar.org/hera. Accessed 15 Oct 2014
15. Magento. http://magento.com/. Accessed 17 Oct 2014
16. Debevc, M., Kosec, P., Rotovnik, M., Holzinger, A.: Accessible multimodal web pages with sign language translations for deaf and hard of hearing users. In: 20th International Workshop on Database and Expert Systems Application, pp. 279–283 (2009)
17. OpenCart. http://www.opencart.com/. Accessed 17 Oct 2014
18. OsCommerce. http://www.oscommerce.com/. Accessed 17 Oct 2014
19. PrestaShop. http://www.prestashop.com/pt/. Accessed 17 Oct 2014
20. W3C/WAI: Web Accessibility Initiative (WAI). WAI guidelines and techniques. http://www.w3.org/WAI/guid-tech.html
21. Loranger, N. J.: Usabilidade na Web: Projetando Websites com Qualidade. Rio de Janeiro (2007)
22. Monteiro, M.S.: História dos movimentos dos surdos e o reconhecimento da Libras no Brasil, pp. 292–302 (2006)
23. Trindade, D.F.G.: InCoP: Um Framework conceitual para o design de ambinetes colaborativos inclusivos para surdos e não surdos de cultivo á comunidades de prática. Curitiba (2013)
24. da Silva, R.A.L.: Recomendações para Acessibilidade aos surdos de auxilio aos desogners a criação e na implementação de ambientes Web. Curitiba (2013)

Generating User Interfaces for Users with Disabilities Using Libraries of XSLT, UIML, and Stylesheet Files

Lawrence Henschen[1(✉)], Julia Lee[1], Ning Li[2], and Xia Hou[2]

[1] Northwestern University, Evanston, IL, USA
henschen@eecs.northwestern.edu, julialee@agep.northwestern.edu
[2] Beijing Information Science and Technology University, Beijing, China
{lining,houxia}@bistu.edu.cn

Abstract. We describe a method for reconfiguring and reformatting documents, in particular web pages, to meet the needs of users with different abilities. The method merges our previous work on semantic markup [1] and presentation of intelligent documents [2] with a new approach to interoperability of document processing [3]. Semantic markup provides information about the purpose of elements in a document, in the spirit of HTML5 [4]. The work on intelligent documents provides means for dynamically adding functionality to a presentation system. The first new concept in this paper is to use XSLT [5] to reformat and reconfigure the material in a document to better meet the needs of a user. The second new concept is to create public libraries of XSLT, UIML, and stylesheet files for classes of users with different needs. A user then configures his or her browser for that user's abilities. When the browser opens a document, it retrieves an appropriate publicly accessible library to use in transforming and presenting the document.

Keywords: Universal access · XSLT translation · UIML · Semantic mark-up · Document presentation

1 Introduction

In this work we merge two lines of research presented in previous HCII conferences. In [1] we described an approach to universal access based on the idea of using semantic markup in web pages to describe the purposes of the various elements on the page - functionality, author intent, etc. We proposed that these could be used by more sophisticated browsers of the future to reorganize the presentation of the material to users with different disabilities, such as visually impaired users or deaf users. In [2] we showed how UIML could facilitate easy extension of browser display features and functionality to match the needs of a particular application area. In [2] the application area was extension of capabilities of document processing systems. Now we want to apply the techniques from [2] and a new idea in document processing [3] to our approach to universal access presented in [1], specifically to solve the problem of actually implementing the new meta-level markup in browsers without the need for the browser companies to modify their software.

© Springer International Publishing Switzerland 2015
M. Antona and C. Stephanidis (Eds.): UAHCI 2015, Part I, LNCS 9175, pp. 174–182, 2015.
DOI: 10.1007/978-3-319-20678-3_17

The use of semantic tags and attributes allows the author of a document to specify his or her purpose as well as the content. This can be used to adjust the presentation based on the medium, as in the use of HTML5 [4] to achieve platform independence. It can also be used to adjust the presentation to the needs of users with different abilities, as proposed in [1]. While HTML5 emphasizes the semantic aspects of its elements and attributes, we believe it is not sufficiently rich for universal access. Some elements, such as "article" and "section", convey semantic intent of the author and do have semantics that is the same for all users, and HTML5 encourages the content of these to be presented in ways that are appropriate for both the medium and the user. On the other hand, the attributes and elements are not rich enough to distinguish some kinds of semantic intent. For example, the "em" element (indicating emphasis) in HTML5 is more semantically meaningful than "font_size = 40" and allows different platforms to display the corresponding information in a way most relevant for the medium. However, there could still be different types of information whose emphasis is strong, such as warning or section heading or even just ordinary emphasis, and these would need to be presented differently to visually impaired or hearing impaired users. The "role" attribute in ARIA [6] approaches this idea, but the role attributes in ARIA are not sufficient to distinguish content to the degree we feel is needed for impaired users. Therefore, a much richer set of semantic tags and attributes is needed to address the needs of users who are visually impaired, hearing impaired, manually impaired, combinations of these, etc. The need for special mark-up for special classes of users has been used in many different contexts, among these for example the DAISY system [7] for reading text out loud to visually impaired users in a more naturally sounding way.

This need for a rich set of tags and attributes places stronger requirements on the presentation systems and precludes simply adding a few new capabilities through modest additional programming. We propose in this paper to combine the techniques of [2, 3] to solve this problem. XSLT is a well-known technology for reformatting information in XML documents. Through XSLT translation the information can be restructured and reorganized, and new tags and attributes can be added. An XSLT library could use the semantic information in a document to restructure the document for presentation to and interaction with a user with special needs. The techniques of [2] can then be used to map the elements, attributes, and functionality of the restructured document to appropriate presentation and interaction implementations. In [2] it was shown that the applications that implement the functionality could be anywhere that is accessible on the internet and need not be tied to an individual browser or document system. This achieves a very high degree of platform independence.

There are many different kinds of users with special needs. Therefore, a single XSLT library will not suffice. Furthermore, corresponding libraries of style sheets will be needed to present the reorganized content properly. Therefore, a set of libraries is needed that can be accessed every time a document is loaded. Reference [3] proposes a technique for maintaining a dynamically expanding set of such libraries. It also proposes that a document system determine a suitable library to retrieve each time a document is opened. In the case of word processors, the document processor examines the document type, for example OOXML or UOF. For the purpose of universal access, we suggest that the processor be configured for the intended user by specifying that user's special needs.

After that, the system can retrieve a suitable XSLT and style sheet library based on both the user's configuration and the document type.

In Sect. 2 we review the three references that form the foundation of this proposal. In Sect. 3 we give a few examples of how documents might be restructured to be more presentable to users with some disabilities. In Sect. 4 we make concluding remarks.

2   Motivation and Review of the Three Main References

In [1] we proposed the use of semantic information representing author intent as a means to help reorganize web page presentation for users with different impairments. For example, simply reading the textual content of a web page is not sufficient for a visually impaired user. Some portions of the content, for example major headings or warnings, on a page are more important than others, and some important material is not presented in text form. Inclusion of semantic information is consistent with the philosophy of HTML5 in moving away from visually oriented elements and attributes. However, HTML5 does not include a sufficient set of elements and attributes to address the needs of universal access. In [1] we showed examples of additional elements and attributes and how they could be used to present web pages to users with different abilities. Examples included:

- An attribute "purpose" with a value like "site_running_title". With this information a browser might read the corresponding content to a blind user once but not every time the user navigated to a different page.
- An element "navigation". This element would include the navigation information for the page, and a browser could read the choices to a blind user as soon as the page was opened.
- An attribute value "warning" for the attribute "purpose". This informs the browser to render the content in special circumstances and in a way suitable for the kind of user.

As noted, the role, property, and state attributes in ARIA [6] help, but they are not rich enough in our opinion.

While browsers may implement HTML5, they would not be expected to handle much richer sets of elements and attributes as proposed in [1]. Moreover, HTML5 is still oriented towards browser display rather than general document display and would therefore not be sufficient for general document-processing systems; for example, the common word-processing systems use different XML schemas such as OOXML and UOF. A more general means of translating a marked-up document to a target processing system (browser, cell phone, word processing system, etc.) and in a way that accounts for users with differing abilities is needed. XSLT [5] is designed to accomplish such transformations. Improved algorithms for performing such transformations, such as [8], make on-load or dynamic translation of even large documents feasible without introducing delays for the user.

The techniques of [2], particularly the use of UIML, were proposed to allow document processing systems to dynamically generate user interfaces with expanded capabilities and functionality that could be accessed anywhere on the web. We propose to adapt these techniques to universal access. In [2] we showed a specific example of how UIML, and in particular the "interface" section of a UIML document, can be used to map the vocabulary used in a document to a new vocabulary in preparation for presentation to a user. When combined with semantic information this could allow transformation of orig-inal document elements into forms suitable for users with various disabilities. For example, an HTML5 "input" element marked with role "command" could be mapped to an ordinary button with on_click function for regular users but mapped to a voice command input system for blind users. Note that it is important to know both that it is an input element and also that its purpose is a command. Other input elements, such as basic information entry, could still be mapped to ordinary keyboard input rather than voice input, while the command inputs might be collected together and handled by a separate part of the system that monitors for any voice input. In [2] we also showed how operations mentioned in the document can be mapped to services anywhere on the web through the "peers" section of the UIML document. For example, a blind user who is also hearing impaired may need a special voice output service, not just the one built into the computer's browser. An element like

```
<uiml:d-component id="TextToSpeechService"
    location ="http://MyPersonalServer/TextToSpeechService/Speaker.svc">
    <uiml:d-method id="speaker" maps-to="speak">
        <uiml:d-param id="speakertext" type="string" />
    </uiml:d-method>
</uiml:d-component>
```

in the "peers" section of a UIML document would map the voice-to-text function to the user's own speech software on the user's own server, thus allowing that user to access the web using his or her special speech software from a laptop from anywhere in the world.

There are many audiences with special needs because there are many disabilities and combinations of disabilities. Therefore, a set of translations is needed that can map, say, a semantically marked-up HTML5 document to a particular kind of user (e.g., blind, hearing impaired, manually impaired, combination, etc.) and perhaps even a platform (PC web browser, cell phone, etc.). While there would be a large number of such transformations, generating XSLT libraries for each situation is much more feasible than reprogramming browsers and document processing systems to meet all the variety of needs. Moreover, the XSLT transformations can be refined as more experience with real users is gained and as HTML itself expands and progresses toward richer sets of semantic mark-ups, whereas hard-coded implementations are not likely to adapt to such learning.

Once such a library of transformations is developed, the work in [3] can be applied. In [3] the goal is to obtain interoperability among document processing systems. The idea is that a set of libraries be developed that provide stylesheets suitable for rendering documents written in one of the major document processing formats – for example, OOXML, UOF, ODF, etc. - in a document system designed for a different one of those formats. A document processing system would check the type of a document being opened and retrieve the appropriate stylesheet library before actually rendering the document. Style sheets for various element types would be grouped into sub-libraries to provide better access and higher reusability. For example, paragraph styles for different document formatting systems might be stored as

http://public.styles.lib/public/paragraph/normal/1/uof
http://public.styles.lib/public/paragraph/normal/1/ooxml
...
http://public.styles.lib/public/paragraph/table/uof
http://public.styles.lib/public/paragraph/table/ooxml...

The first of these, for example, would contain information about styling the first paragraph in a section in a uof document. Document systems could retrieve appropriate ones of these and incorporate into larger stylesheets for a given document in a given system.

In [3] the focus was on office documents, and the libraries contained style sheets only. We propose to extend this concept by adding XSLT translation files and UIML files to the libraries. A user would configure his or her system, for example browser, with parameters specifying that user's situation - hearing impaired, visually impaired, etc. Then, when the system opens a new document it uses the configuration to determine a suitable transformation and style library to retrieve, translates the original document into a format suitable for that user, and then uses the style sheets to actually present the content and manage the interaction. We note that for universal access styling alone is not enough. As we illustrate in the next section, it will likely be necessary to a restructure a document, sometimes drastically, before presenting it to users with a disability. Therefore, the libraries we are proposing would contain both XSLT files and regular style sheet files. Moreover, functions used by regular users, such as mouse motions or clicks, may also need to be replaced, perhaps by special software not available on the user's machine. Therefore, our libraries will also include UIML with information like that indicated in a previous paragraph.

3   Examples

In this section we present a number of examples of how content and interaction might be presented to different users. Space precludes showing complete XSLT and UIML files. Therefore, our presentation here focuses on how the information in a semantically marked up document should be reorganized and presented. These are only suggestions; detailed studies of actual users should be made to determine how best to reorganize and present web content and handle interaction. These examples are only meant to illustrate the kinds of reorganization that are possible and the wide variety of presentation styles that will be needed to achieve universal access.

Much web page content is generated dynamically, for example by executing Javascript either on page load or in response to an event. Thus, all of the transformations that would be applied to a static page must also be applicable to content generated on the fly. This might be accomplished by modifying the Javascript as well as the static page content through XSLT when the page is first loaded. It might also be accomplished by allowing the Javascript to operate on the original form of the web page and then pass the Javascript output through the translation process before rendering. The point is that any techniques that are proposed for transforming content must be applicable to both static and dynamically generated files.

We consider a small set of disabilities - blind, color blind, deaf, manually impaired (cannot use a mouse or keyboard) - and how content and interaction might be changed to accommodate users with those disabilities.

3.1 Blind Users

Presentation to blind users will likely require the most reorganization and the most changes in the interaction methods. Here are some ideas on changes that would help blind users.

Sighted users can easily comprehend the organization of most web pages and can scroll to areas of interest. Blind users need to be told what kinds of information are on the page and must have a different means to access, or "scroll to", the desired content. HTML5 elements, like article and section, can be used to inform the bind user about the content, especially if the author has added attributes in these elements that give descriptive information about the content and purpose. When the page is retrieved, a system like the one proposed here can extract such information from the article, section, and possibly other elements and present that information by voice as the page is actually loaded into the browser. The user could then navigate the page by voice input and could request the organization information to be repeated, perhaps by a voice input such as "page organization", if the user needed to refresh his or her memory. Other voice command inputs, such as "next section" or "previous paragraph", would simulate ordinary navigation by mouse scrolling/clicking.

Many pages contain input elements representing commands, such as submit, clear-form, buttons that activate Javascript functions, etc. Sighted users can easily identify and locate these, but blind users need to be told that the page has such inputs. One approach is to notify the blind user by voice output that the page contains such inputs when the page is first loaded. The user can then request a list of the available commands by voice, say by speaking the word "commands", at which point the browser can present the list of available commands by voice output. The user could speak the desired command, thus simulating a mouse click, or say "done".

Many pages contain input boxes for normal text, for example first and last name in a form or feedback to the web author or server. Many blind users are proficient typists, and those users may prefer to use the keyboard for normal text entry. These users need help bringing such input boxes into focus. A sighted user would just mouse over the box or use the tab key to move to the next box. For blind users a method similar to the one in the preceding paragraph could be used. To accomplish this, the list of text input boxes would be identified when the html file was retrieved from the server, as suggested for command inputs. On page load the list of these input boxes could be read out to the user. The user could focus on a text input by speaking the name of the input box and could indicate when he or she had finished text entry by speaking a word like "done". Alternatively, the user could speak commands like "first input box" or "next input box". Of course, some blind users may prefer voice input for both normal text and command inputs. Thus, even for a single class of impaired users there would be a need for multiple types of preprocessing to allow for the preferences and abilities of individuals within that class.

Visually-oriented elements, like img and video, are of little direct use to a blind user. If the purpose of the element is purely decorative, the element can simply be removed before the page is loaded into the browser. If the element has a non-decorative purpose and the page author has added additional information through suitable attributes on the element, the element can be changed into a different form, for example into an audio element that contains the alternate information from the "alt" attribute value of an img element.

These are but a few suggestions of how information can be presented to blind users and how a web page might interact with a blind user. But it is enough to illustrate several points. First, obviously not every browser manufacturer is going to build all of these features and many more into their browsers. Likely, in fact, none of them will. However, the above can be accomplished by a system as proposed here. Extracting content from an HTML5 file (or any XML file) can be accomplished through XSLT transformation. An XSLT transformation can find the command elements in a suitably marked-up HTML5 file and generate suitable Javascript, for example, to accomplish the voice read-out and voice input. UIML files can be used to map functionality, such as voice output and voice recognition for verbal command input, to appropriate software either in the browser itself or on the user's computer or anywhere on the web.

3.2   Color Blind Users

Section 3.1 illustrates the main ideas proposed in this paper. We now present a few additional examples to illustrate the need for a large collection of libraries and also to illustrate the flexibility and adaptability of the method we propose.

Users who are color blind do not need drastic reorganization and presentation of the material. These users are able to locate and mouse-over the elements on the page. They are also able to see the organization of the page and locate both textual and non-textual information as easily as sighted users. Therefore, the elements of the original HTML5 page can be retained with little if any modification. Uses of color on the page would need modification, and this could probably be accomplished by transforming the styles sheets for the page rather than the HTML itself. An obvious example is the use of color to highlight links. For a color blind user links could be highlighted by emphasis plus underlining rather than color plus underlining. Other uses of color specified by the author of the page could be replaced by combinations of font size and style. If the author had followed the guidelines of HTML5, all the color information would have been included in a stylesheet. XSLT could be used to transform that stylesheet before the page was loaded into the browser. Alternatively, the whole stylesheet could be replaced by one from the library for color-blind users.

3.3 Hearing Impaired Users

Users who were hearing impaired but had normal sight would only need to have the sound elements modified. For video or voice audio one approach would be to import voice-to-text software or software that provides closed-captioning from video. UIML could provide the connection between the web page that was loaded by the browser and such software, again either on the user's own machine or from anywhere on the web.

3.4 Manually Impaired Users

Users who cannot use a mouse and keyboard could interact with the page by voice input. Again, assuming the user had normal sight, the elements of the page would not need reorganization. However, voice input and output would be used, and UIML would provide the link between elements on the page and appropriate software.

4 Conclusion and Future Work

Achieving universal access is extremely difficult. It is not enough just to read the text to a blind user or just to replace sounds by text for a deaf user. In many cases the content needs to be completely reorganized, and often the interaction also needs to be drastically modified. And, because there are many diverse groups of users with a variety of combinations of disabilities, this reorganization needs to be done in many different ways. It is unrealistic to expect browsers to be implemented that could achieve such a diversity of functionality, much less to expect that to be done on the variety of platforms ranging from PC browsers to cell phones to book readers to.... Further, the variety of platforms will increase over time, and it is not likely that all these new platforms will implement the presentation and functionality required for the many kinds of users. We have proposed an approach, based on reformatting marked up documents, that is feasible to implement, expandable as future platforms and document systems are introduced, and that provides usable access to a much wider array of users.

We close by noting that an important aspect of universal access has yet to be addressed by the HCI community. Prior work, including our work in this paper, has focused on the technology. There is little work on understanding how different types of users can best interact with the web. We have hinted in Sect. 3 at some plausible ways a few kinds of users might want to receive the content and interact with it, but we make no claims that our suggestions there are exhaustive or are the best ways for those users. We only presented those ideas to illustrate the method. What is needed is an interdisciplinary effort involving HCI professionals and also psychologists, sociologists, medical professionals, and others to gain a deep understanding and model of different types of users and what are the best ways for each type to interact with our machines.

Acknowledgements. This work was supported in part by the Project of Construction of Innovative Teams and Teacher Career Development for Universities and Colleges under Beijing Municipality (IDHT20130519).

References

1. Henschen, L., Lee, J.: Using semantic-level tags in HTML/XML Documents. In: Proceedings of the 13th HCII International Conference, pp. 683–692 (2009)
2. Henschen, L., Li, N., Shi, Y., Zhang, Y., Lee, J.: Intelligent document user interface design using MVC and UIML. In: Proceedings of the 16th HCII International Conference, vol. 1, Part I, pp. 423–432 (2014)
3. Li, N., Hou, X., Fang, C.: Harmonization of office document format and web page format driven by separating presentation from content. Submitted to The 15th ACM Symposium on Document Engineering, Lausanne, Switzerland
4. W3C.HTML5. http://www.w3.org/TR/html5
5. W3C XSL Transformation (XSLT) Version 2.0. http://www.w3.org/TR/xslt20
6. World Wide Web Consortium. http://www.w3.org/TR/wai-aria
7. DAISY. http://www.daisy.org
8. Henschen, L., Lee, J., Li, N., Hou, X., Gao, X.: Parallelization of the XSLT transformation process by XSLT stylesheet partitioning. Submitted to ACM Transactions on the Web

Medium-Fidelity Usability Evaluation
for the American Community Survey Website

Using Eye-Tracking Data to Examine
Fixation Differences by Task Performance

Temika Holland[✉] and Erica Olmsted-Hawala

U.S. Census Bureau, Center for Survey Measurement, 4600 Silver Hill Road,
Washington DC 20233, USA
{Temika.Holland,Erica.L.Olmsted.Hawala}@census.gov

Abstract. The American Community Survey (ACS) website provides supplementary information about ACS participation and about ACS data (e.g., data collection, data utilization, survey procedures, etc.). Additionally, the ACS website is a portal to the American Fact Finder (AFF) for access to ACS data. The U.S. Census Bureau is undergoing a new initiative to change the look and feel of Census sites, and various design features have been modified on a web based prototype for the redesigned American Community Survey (ACS) website, including navigational tools and layout. Feedback on whether users of the site would be able to obtain the information they need given the new design features was warranted. The site was tested in its early stages of development using a web-based prototype with limited functionality (i.e., medium-fidelity). Eye tracking was incorporated in the evaluation of the site to gain an in-depth understanding of users' visual interaction and to add support to observed findings. In addition, differences in eye-fixation duration on Areas of Interest during optimal task performance and non-optimal task performance were explored.

Keywords: Usability · Eye tracking · Task performance · Fixation duration

1 Introduction

During the spring of 2014, the U.S. Census Bureau's Human Factors and Usability Research Group conducted a medium-fidelity usability evaluation of a web-based prototype for the redesigned American Community Survey (ACS) website. The ACS website is a public site providing information about the American Community Survey, an ongoing national survey that is administered to nearly 3 million households per year and assists in the allocation of more than $450 billion in federal and state funds.

Disclaimer: This report is released to inform interested parties of research and to encourage discussion. Any views expressed on the methodological issues are those of the authors and not necessarily those of the U.S. Census Bureau.

M. Antona and C. Stephanidis (Eds.): UAHCI 2015, Part I, LNCS 9175, pp. 183–192, 2015.
DOI: 10.1007/978-3-319-20678-3_18

The site also provides supplemental information about ACS data (e.g., data collection, data utilization, survey procedures) and serves as a portal to the American Fact Finder (AFF) for access to ACS data. The U.S. Census Bureau is undergoing a new initiative to change the look and feel of its websites. As a result, various design features have been modified in a prototype for the redesigned ACS website, including its navigational tools and layout, warranting a usability evaluation.

The web-based prototype used during the medium-fidelity evaluation of the ACS site was limited in its functionality and navigational capabilities (e.g., not all links were functional). The web pages were housed on a CD-ROM and up-loaded to the computer for testing. This type of medium-fidelity testing is often a preferred usability method when exploring design alternatives or when requiring guidance on layout and functionality of a site [1]. This is essential in the user-centered design process because feedback regarding the design can be obtained early on. It allows changes to be made during the design phase, which may in turn be less burdensome for developers of the site.

In addition to obtaining accuracy, efficiency, confidence in navigation decisions, and satisfaction data (common usability metrics) [2], eye-tracking data were also collected in the usability evaluation to gain a deeper understanding of participants' visual interaction with the site. The use of eye-tracking technology has emerged in usability testing as a way to inform the design of an interface [3]. Eye tracking is a method used to study eye movements with the assumption that the data provide information on the human-computer interaction. For example, knowing where users are looking can help developers of a site know which features of a site are being noticed and which are being overlooked. It can also be used to understand emotional states and cognitive processes [3].

Data obtained from eye tracking, such as fixation duration captures how long a users' eyes are relatively still as they look at specific content [3]. Research suggests that greater mean eye-fixation duration can be indicative of information complexity and task difficulty [4]. Other research has found that longer fixation duration was associated with difficult words in a reading task and decreased discriminability of a target [5]. The present study seeks to assess whether these findings will hold for data captured in the usability evaluation of a web-based information-rich prototype. Our hypothesis is that, given findings from previous research, there will be longer fixation duration on links and on the ACS main page overall, during non-optimal task performance-in which users are less accurate in completing the task, take longer to complete a given task, and less confident in their navigation decisions- than during optimal task performance (where users are more accurate in task completion take less time to complete a task, and are more confident in navigation). The rationale for this hypothesis is that poor performance on tasks using the web-based prototype is an indicator of cognitive challenges and task difficulty which would warrant additional eye fixations.

2 Methodology

2.1 Participants

Twelve participants (four males, eight females) took part in the medium-fidelity usability evaluation for the ACS website. All participants were from the public and recruited from local advertisements (newspapers, Craigslist, etc.). The participants selected for the medium-fidelity evaluation self-reported that they had little to no experience with Census Bureau sites (including the ACS website), had at least one year Internet experience, and spent on average about 44.33 h on the Internet per week. The mean age of participants was 40.67 years (range 23–63 years), and 8 out of 12 participants (67 %) had a Bachelors' degree or greater. (See Table 1 for a complete description of participant demographics.)

Table 1. Characteristics of participants

Total Participants (n)	12
Gender	
Male	4
Female	8
Average Age (standard deviation)	40.67(14.90)
Education	
High School	3
Some College	1
Bachelor's degree	5
Post Bachelor's degree	3
Race	
White	4
Black	8
Hispanic Origin	
Yes	3
No	9

2.2 Procedure

In each individual usability session, the participant entered the testing area and was informed about the purpose of the study and the uses of data that were to be collected. The moderator asked the participant to read and sign a consent form stating that they understood their rights and were voluntarily taking part in the study. The test administrator began video/audio recording after the participant signed the consent form. The participant completed a demographic and computer and Internet experience questionnaire. The participant was positioned in front of a Tobii X120 computer monitor equipped with infra-red cameras. A brief calibration procedure was performed to ensure the quality of eye-tracking data collected.

The test administrator gave the participant randomized task questions and instructed him/her to think aloud while using the American Community Survey site to complete each task. Tasks consisted of common reasons people would visit the site. For example, *You just received the American Community Survey in the mail, and none of your neighbors did. Find out why your address was selected.* (See Appendix A for a complete listing of tasks). The participant was instructed to read each task aloud, and the test administrator loaded the ACS main page on the screen for the task to begin. At the end of each task, the participant was instructed to rate his/her confidence that their link selection(s) led/would lead them to the correct page to complete the task. After completing all tasks, the participant answered a satisfaction questionnaire about their overall experience with the site. The test administrator asked the participant a set of debriefing questions to obtain more information about his or her experience. The session concluded, and the participant was given a $40 cash honorarium.

2.3   Metrics

Eye-tracking data were analyzed using t-test procedures to determine whether there were significant differences in eye-fixation duration, on optimal links located on the main page or on the ACS main page overall (Fig. 1), for tasks that had a higher percentage of users perform with accuracy, efficiency, and confidence in navigation decisions (optimal task performance) and those that did not (non-optimal task performance).

Fig. 1. ACS web-based prototype tested during the medium fidelity usability evaluation (main page)

Fixation Duration. Fixation duration is defined as the amount of time (in seconds) of fixations within predefined areas, also known as Areas of Interest [6]. In this analysis, Areas of Interest consist of optimal links from the main page needed for task completion and the ACS main page overall. As previous research suggests, users would likely need to fixate longer on these areas during non-optimal task performance because the task is complex and difficult to complete. See Appendix B for highlighted Areas of Interest for the ACS web-based prototype.

Accuracy. Accuracy was based on users' ability to successfully click on the optimal link to successfully complete a given task. A task was coded as having "high accuracy" if 85 % or more of the participants were able to successfully navigate to the optimal link, without assistance. Otherwise, the task was coded as having "low accuracy"

Efficiency. Each task was timed from when the ACS web page prototype loaded until the participant clicked on their last link on the ACS page to complete a given task. Time duration was averaged for each task. A task was coded as a "high efficiency" task if 70 % or more participants were able to complete the task in the average time duration or less. Otherwise, the task was coded as a "low efficiency" task. It is important to note that efficiency is not typically captured in low- and medium-fidelity testing due to the limited functionality of the site, which may not reflect accurate timing of task completion. Therefore, given the range of efficiency scores overall, more leniency was given to what constituted a "high-efficiency" measure than might occur if it were a high-fidelity study.

Confidence. Participants were asked to select links that they felt would direct them to the correct information needed to successfully complete tasks. Following their link(s) selection, they answered the following question to assess the level of confidence they had in their navigation decisions to obtain the information:

On a scale of 1 to 9 where 1 is confident and 9 is not confident, *"How confident are you that you would be able to find the information you were looking for based on your selection?"*

Participants' rating for each task was noted as their level of confidence in their navigation behaviors. Confidence ratings were individually coded such that, those who chose 1 or 2 were confident and those rating a 3 or greater were less confident. Similarly to the accuracy coding, a task was coded as having "high confidence" if 85 % or more participants were confident in their link selection. Otherwise, the task was coded as having "low confidence".

3 Results

Task categorizations are presented below in Table 2. In addition, the number of participants included in the analysis of each task and the average fixation duration for optimal links and the ACS main page (AOI's) is noted.

When examining the average fixation duration on optimal links, there were no significant differences in the fixation duration between tasks that had low accuracy $(M = 1.78, SD = .63)$ and high accuracy $(M = 1.48, SD = .64)$; $t(7) = 0.72, p = .49$. There were no significant differences in the fixation duration between tasks that had low efficiency $(M = 1.45, SD = .59)$ and high efficiency $(M = 2.04, SD = .54)$; $t(7) = -1.43, p = .19$. Lastly, there were no significant differences in the fixation

Table 2. Average fixation duration for AOI's and performance categorization by task

[a]Task (n)	Average fixation duration (in seconds) for AOI's		Performance categorization		
	Optimal link(s)	Main page	Accuracy	Efficiency	Confidence
Task 1 (n = 9)	1.25	27.07	Low	Low	Low
Task 2 (n = 10)	2.47	7.43	**High**	**High**	**High**
Task 3 (n = 5)	2.12	14.87	Low	Low	Low
Task 4 (n = 10)	3.08	11.82	Low	**High**	**High**
Task 5 (n = 8)	1.48	9.58	**High**	**High**	**High**
Task 6 (n = 10)	2.12	16.20	Low	Low	Low
Task 7 (n = 10)	0.60	10.31	**High**	Low	**High**
Task 9 (n = 12)	1.79	25.47	**High**	Low	Low
Task 10 (n = 8)	1.17	24.42	Low	Low	Low

[a]Tasks were randomly assigned and not all tasks were given to participants due to time constraints. In addition, task 8 was excluded from the eye tracking analyses as there was no optimal link defined.

duration between tasks that had low confidence ($M = 1.63$, $SD = .45$) and high confidence ($M = 1.68$, $SD = .85$); $t(7) = -.11$, $p = .91$.

When examining the average fixation duration on the ACS main page, there were no significant differences in the fixation duration between tasks that had low accuracy ($M = 18.88$, $SD = 6.54$) and high accuracy ($M = 13.20$, $SD = 8.27$); $t(7) = 1.15$, $p = .28$. However, there were significant differences in the fixation duration between tasks that had low efficiency ($M = 19.72$, $SD = 6.84$) and high efficiency ($M = 9.61$, $SD = 2.20$); $t(7) = 2.43$, $p = .05$ and between tasks that had low confidence ($M = 21.60$, $SD = 5.64$) and high confidence ($M = 9.79$, $SD = 1.83$); $t(7) = 3.97$, $p = .01$.

4 Conclusion

While research suggests that increased fixation duration can be indicative of information complexity or task difficulty [4], our results are mixed. Contrary to our hypothesis, we did not find differences in fixation duration on optimal links by task performance. It appears that the links needed to successfully complete a given task captured the same amount of attention from participants regardless of whether the task had a high or low accuracy rate, was high or low in efficiency, or whether there was high or low confidence in navigation decisions.

However, in support of our hypothesis, our results for the fixation duration on the ACS main page showed that increased fixation duration did correspond with task difficulty. Tasks that were more difficult to complete based on non-optimal task performance measures (i.e., low in efficiency, low in confidence) required participants to spend more time looking at content on the ACS main page to find the information they needed. There were significant differences in the fixation duration between tasks that had high efficiency and low efficiency and tasks that were high in confidence and low in confidence. Tasks for which participants were confident in their navigation decisions and tasks that were higher in efficiency had a shorter fixation duration. For these less challenging tasks, participants were able to quickly sort through the content on the ACS main page and proceed. However, whether or not participants were able to more accurately identify the optimal link needed for successful completion did not vary the amount of time they had to spend looking through the ACS main page content.

Given these mixed results, it may be the case that increased fixation duration is not indicative of only confusion, task difficulty or negative aspects of the user interface design. Perhaps, similar to other studies, fixation duration could be indicative of greater interest and engagement with a target [7]. In addition, perhaps the optimal links themselves may not have been difficult for participants to understand or identify for task completion.

There are various limitations in the present study including, having a small sample size that was based on convenience sampling, using very few tasks in the analyses, and analyzing only fixation duration. Future research should analyze eye-tracking data from a larger sample of participants and perhaps a greater number of tasks or websites. In addition, separate analyses based on participants' individual performance and charac-teristics should also be considered, as research suggests that there may be differences in eye behaviors based on gender [4] and age [8], to name a few.

Lastly, other types of eye-tracking data can be incorporated in the analyses of eye behaviors to better understand eye patterns as it relates to task performance. For example, gaze time has been shown to be negatively related to task difficulty and saccade rates have been found to decrease when task difficulty or mental load increases [4]. These are two examples of future research with information-rich prototypes that are underway in our lab.

Overall, the present study presents a framework on which future research can build. Our results are preliminary and we hope to elicit future research in exploring the meaning of eye behaviors. Given the emerging uses of eye tracking in usability evaluations, it is important to develop a clearer understanding of what these eye-tracking data mean as it relates to the design of a user-interface and task difficulty.

Appendix A: User Tasks

1. You just received the American Community Survey in the mail, and none of your neighbors did. Find out why your address was selected.

2. Your aunt has been contacted about responding to the American Community Survey (ACS). She would prefer to fill the form out online with your help. Find out if there is an online option.

3. You are interested in seeing what kind of information the American Community Survey has collected. Specifically, does it collect information on the number of people who speak languages other than English in the United States?

4. You are a researcher who will begin using the American Community Survey website on a regular basis, and you want to stay up-to-date on any changes or news items. Is there a way to subscribe to email updates? If so, subscribe to it.

5. Your Vietnamese neighbors received the American Community Survey in the mail and have asked for your help. They want to know if there is any information in their native language. Check the website to see if there is anything available in Vietnamese to help your neighbors understand the basics.

6. You are filling out the survey but feel uneasy about Question 33 - What time did this person usually leave home to go to work? Find out why this question is being asked.

7. You have heard that the American Community Survey has data about your community. Find out how many children are enrolled in elementary education (grades 1–8) in your state.

8. At the request of your Statistics instructor, you are giving a presentation on the American Community Survey. Are there any prepared materials that you can use for this purpose? Based on information on the site, please name at least one example of these materials.

9. Use the site to find:

a. What is the estimated number of grandparents who are caring for their grandchildren in Maryland in 2012?

10. You just got mailing materials in the mail inviting you to complete the American Community Survey online, but you aren't sure if this is real or a scam (e.g., is it legitimate?) What would you do?

Appendix B: Defined Areas of Interest on the ACS Web-Based Prototype

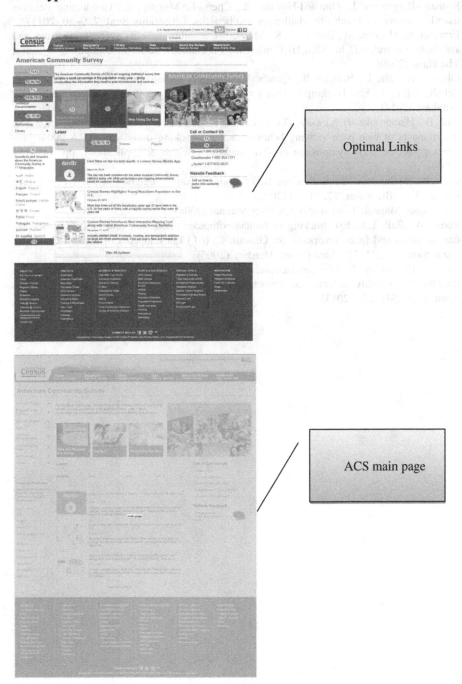

References

1. Romano-Bergstrom, J., Olmsted-Hawala, E., Chen, J., Murphy, E.: Conducting iterative usability testing on a web site: challenges and benefits. J. Usability Stud. **7**, 9–30 (2011)
2. Frøkjaer, E., Herzum, M., Hornbaek, K.: Measuring usability: are effectiveness, efficiency and satisfaction correlated? In: SIGCHI Conference on Human Factors in Computing Systems, The Haag (2000)
3. Olmsted-Hawala, E., Holland, T., Quach, V.: Usability testing. In: Romano-Bergstrom, J., Schall, A.J. (eds.) Eye Tracking in User Experience Design, pp. 49–80. Morgan Kaufmann, Waltham (2014)
4. Pan, B., Hembrooke, H.A., Gay, G.L., Granka, L.A., Feusner, M.K., Newman, J.K.: The determinants of web page viewing behavior: an eye-tracking study. In: ETRA 2004: Proceedings of the 2004 symposium on Eye tracking research & applications, pp. 147–154 (2004)
5. Guo, K., Mahmoodi, S., Robertson, R.G.: Longer fixation duration while viewing face images. Exp. Brain Res. **17**, 91–98 (2006)
6. Tobii: User Manual: Tobii studio 1.X User Manual (2008)
7. Poole, A., Ball, L.J.: Eye tracking in human-computer interaction and usability research: current status and future prospects. In: Ghaoui, C. (ed.) Encyclopedia of Human Computer Interaction, pp. 211–219. Idea Group, Hershey (2005)
8. Romano-Bergstrom, J., Olmsted-Hawala, E., Jans, M.E.: Age-related differences in eye tracking and usability performance: website usability for older adults. Int. J. Hum.-Comput. Interact. **29**, 541–548 (2013)

Effects of Facebook Like and Conflicting Aggregate Rating and Customer Comment on Purchase Intentions

Yu-Hsiu Hung[✉] and Hsueh-Yi Lai

Department of Industrial Design, National Cheng Kung University, Tainan, Taiwan
{idhfhung,P36024116}@mail.ncku.edu.tw

Abstract. The conflict between an aggregate rating and a customer's comment oftentimes cause consumers' negative feelings on the quality of a product. The purpose of this study was to investigate whether such conflict influenced an individual's purchase intentions. Particularly, this study looked at how social influence mediated the effects of a conflicting aggregate rating and a customer's comment on purchase intention. To achieve the goal, an online mixed factorial experiment was conducted with one hundred and eighty-four student volunteers. The independent variables of interest were: consistency of aggregate rating and customer comment and number of Facebook likes. The dependent variable was purchase intention. In this study, participants were mainly recruited through the social groups on Facebook. Participants were instructed to provide their degrees of purchase intentions to snack food on our experimental website (containing pages reflecting differing treatment conditions under the independent variables). Results of the experiment showed that the conflict between a aggregate rating and a customer's comment, as well as the number of Facebook likes respectively had significant impacts on purchase intentions. Results of this study have implications on the design of social interfaces on social commerce websites.

Keywords: Aggregate rating · Customer comment · Purchase intention

1 Introduction

Web 2.0 has transformed e-commerce from a product-oriented environment to a social environment [1]. The transformation resulted in the birth of social commerce consisting of communities of customers with similar interests, passions, and goals [2]. In a social commerce environment, customers have access to social knowledge and experiences to support better understanding of purchase intentions and purchase decisions [3]. According to Ng. [4], social commerce involves the use of social media to support social interactions and communications on user generated content (e.g., customer's ratings and reviews). Sellers want to convert customers into brand advocates (e.g., turning Facebook likes into paying customers), whereas customers want to make better informed purchase decisions (e.g., getting a good deal from checking Facebook likes). The aims of the two parties can be achieved through customers' sharing and expressing experiences [5]. These social interactions and communications enable word-of-mouth marketing, product advocacy for a brand, and social capital building.

© Springer International Publishing Switzerland 2015
M. Antona and C. Stephanidis (Eds.): UAHCI 2015, Part I, LNCS 9175, pp. 193–200, 2015.
DOI: 10.1007/978-3-319-20678-3_19

Customer reviews are an important resource for users to buy a product, do business, and/or choose a hotel. These reviews became a useful asset for purchase decisions [6]. They typically supplement the product descriptions and/or expert reviews provided by electronic commerce companies. They have been shown to have a positive influence on product sales [6].

The presence of customer reviews on a website has been shown to improve customer perception of the social presence of a website [7]. They create a sense of community among frequent shoppers [8]. A customer review typically consists of a numerical star rating and an open-ended consumer-authored comment. Both information provide valuable product information to a web shopper.

- **A numerical star rating** usually ranges from one to five stars. A very low rating (one star) indicates an extremely negative view of a product, whereas a very high rating (5 stars) reflects an extremely positive view of a product. A three star rating reflects a moderate view of a product. Re-search has demonstrated that customer ratings have the potential to add value for a prospective customer. Positive ratings can positively influence the growth of product sales [9].
- **Consumer-authored comments** are written in a free-text format that reflects decision-making process of product purchases, and experiences and preferences of product usages, etc. Research showed that consumer-authored comments are not presented properly and are technologically poor. Web users/shoppers oftentimes need to browse massive amount of text information in order to find a particular piece of product information [10].

In social commerce, not all customer reviews are helpful to a user in making a purchasing decision [8]. What makes web users/shoppers frustrated is that a comment is not reflective of its corresponding numerical star rating. Research showed that a negative consumer comment may become unfavorable while the aggregate rating is positive. For example, Qiu et al. [11] found that the presence of a conflicting aggregated rating decreased comment credibility and diagnosticity. However, early re-search in social cognition held an opposite stance. Borgida and Nisbett [12] showed that people tended to regard base rate data (statistical summaries) as if they were uninformative and relied more on individuating data (people's comments) if both data were presented at the same time. In other words, social cognition researchers believed that the presence of a conflicting aggregate rating has little impact on comment adoption.

In fact, people are most confident in decisions when information is highly diagnostic. The consistency between a particular comment and other comments influenced customers' perception credibility perception and adoption intention of a target comment [13]. The inconsistent findings of Qiu et al. [11] and Borgida and Nisbett [12] suggest that more research are needed to discern the effects of the consistency of aggregate rating and consumer comment on purchase decisions and behavior.

In the field of social commerce, one of the most influential models for illustrating the intention–behaviour relationship is Ajzen's theory of planned behaviour (TPB) [14–16]. This theory proposes that behaviour is influenced by intention, and that intention is determined by attitudes, subjective norms, and perceived behaviour control. Generally speaking, individuals will intend to perform a behavior when they evaluate it positively and/or when they are influenced by social pressure. The relationships among attitude, intention, and behavior proposed by TPB were applied in many fields. For example, Kim and Njite [17] applied TPB to investigate why people chose eco-friendly restaurant. Kim and Njite found that subjective norm played an important role in purchase intention. Shin [14] analyzed consumer behaviours in social commerce from the perspective of social influence. Shin created a model to validate the relation-ship between the subjective norm and trust, social support, attitude, and intention. Shin found that the subjective norm is a key behavioural antecedent to use social commerce. The above research suggests that social pressure and influence play a key role in enabling successful purchases. In current social commerce, such influence could have come from the "like" buttons (e.g., Facebook's like, Google's +1, Twitter's follow) [18, 19].

From the above, it is imperative to understand whether social influence comes into play in affecting purchase intention when customer ratings and comments are inconsis-tent. The aims of this study are as follows: (1) investigate whether the conflicts between an aggregate rating and a consumer comment influenced an individual's purchase inten-tions; (2) examine how Facebook likes impacted purchase intentions when there was a conflict between an aggregate rating and a consumer comment. An online experiment was conducted with one hundred and eighty-four participants. Participants were engaged in buying snack on our developed social commerce website. Results of this study show implications on the design of social interfaces on social commerce websites. Our work takes a novel approach to study how Facebook likes (i.e., social influence) mediated the effects of a conflicting aggregate rating and a consumer comment on purchase intention.

2   Method

2.1   Participants

Purposeful sampling was used to select information-rich participants for the experiment. In our study, participants were required to have experiences of purchasing products on social commerce websites and visited relevant websites for at least once per month. To recruit participants, the information about the experiment was posted on differing social groups on Facebook. A total of 184 student participants (82 males, 102 females, average age: 23) voluntarily joined the experiment. No compensation was provided for partici-pating in the experiment.

2.2   Experimental Design and Equipment

The independent variables of the study were: (1) consistency of aggregate rating and customer comment (with two levels, consistent, and inconsistent); (2) number of Face-book likes (with four levels, zero, five, ten, and fifteen). The dependent variable was purchase intention. Participants' ratings on purchase intentions were analyzed with SAS 9.4 software.

The experimental design is shown in Table 1. In our study, eighty-seven participants were exposed to the "consistent rating-comment" condition. Ninety-seven participants were exposed to the "inconsistent rating-comment" condition. Figure 1 shows an example of the experimental condition. As illustrated in Fig. 1, every condition contained (1) an image of snack, (2) an aggregate 5 star rating, (3) a Face-book like icon with the number on the side (either 0, 5, 10, or 15), (4) product descriptions, and (5) a customer's comment (either positive or negative).

Table 1. The experimental design of the study (mixed factorial design)

		Number of Facebook likes			
		0	5	10	15
Consistency of aggregate rating and customer comment	Consistent: 5 stars with a positive customer comment	P1–P87	P1–P87	P1–P87	P1–P87
	Inconsistent: 5 stars with a negative customer comment	P88–P184	P88–P184	P88–P184	P88–P184

Note: P denotes participant

Fig. 1. An example of the experimental page: snack with a high aggregate rating, a positive customer comment, and 0 Facebook like).

2.3 Procedure

An online experiment was conducted. All experimental conditions were transformed into differing web pages. To increase the response rate and to reduce the effort for completing the experiment, we separated all experimental conditions into two sub-categories with two separate links under our posts on Facebook. One link contained all "inconsistent rating-comment" conditions. The other contained all "consistent rating-comment" conditions. The following describes the procedure of the experiment:

After clicking on the link of our experiment, participants were shown an instructional page containing the purpose of the study, descriptions of the experiment, as well as the information about the risks, benefits, and compensation for joining the study. After agreeing to participate in the experiment, participants were randomly presented with web pages containing differing experimental conditions. Participants were asked to take their time to respond to each of the conditions with their degrees of purchase intentions (from 1 to 5, 1 being very low, 5 being very high). Two questions associated with purchase intention were presented:

- I will buy this snack.
- Buying this snack is a good choice.

Every condition was shown on a web page one at a time. Participants were notified the end of the experiment as soon as they responded to all questions.

3 Results and Discussion

Descriptive statistics were conducted on the treatment conditions. Results are shown in Table 2. It appears that participants gave lower ratings if an aggregate rating did not match with a customer comment (Mean $= 2.8$, SD $= 0.94$). With regards to the number of Facebook likes, it appears that, no matter whether or not an aggregate rating and a customer comment were conflicted, participants provided higher purchase intentions to higher numbers of Facebook likes.

A mixed two way ANOVA was conducted with PROC GLM in SAS 9.4. Results of the analysis showed that both Consistency of aggregate rating and customer comment and Number of Facebook likes significantly influenced participants' purchase intentions. There was no interaction between Consistency of aggregate rating and customer comment and Number of Facebook likes. This suggests that the number of Facebook likes did not mask the effect of Consistency of aggregate rating and customer comment.

In other words, if an aggregate rating is consistent with a customer's comment, a product received higher purchase intentions no matter whether the number of Facebook likes was high or low. Results of the analysis also suggest that no matter whether an aggregate rating conflicted with a customer comment, a higher number of Facebook likes increased an individual's purchase intentions (Table 3).

Table 2. Descriptive statistics: mean ratings of the treatment levels under the independent variables.

Independent variables		n	Mean (Standard deviation)	
Consistent: 5 stars with a positive customer comment	0 Facebook like	87	3.20 (0.82)	3.33 (0.88)
	5 Facebook likes	87	3.23 (0.83)	
	10 Facebook likes	87	3.33 (0.85)	
	15 Facebook likes	87	3.55 (0.97)	
Inconsistent: 5 stars with a negative customer comment	0 Facebook like	97	2.77 (0.98)	2.80 (0.94)
	5 Facebook likes	97	2.68 (0.90)	
	10 Facebook likes	97	2.85 (0.93)	
	15 Facebook likes	97	2.91 (0.95)	

Table 3. Statistical output for the mixed two-way ANOVA

Source	DF	Type III SS	Mean square	F value	p value
Consistency of aggregate rating and customer comment	1	50.390	50.390	29.31	0.000
Participant	182	312.904	1.719		
Number of Facebook likes	3	8.429	2.810	5.32	0.001
Consistency of aggregate rating and customer comment * Number of Facebook likes	3	1.121	0.374	0.71	0.548
Number of Facebook likes * Participant	546	288.296	0.528		
Total	735	661.14			

Overall, the consistency of an aggregate rating and a customer comment as well as Facebook likes are the driving force for purchase intentions. To increase the revenue, social commerse websites should prevent the happening of the conflict. A good example can be found in the Amazon rating-review system. For every customer comment, Amazon places an interface at the bottom, "Was this review helpful to you?" If a comment does not reflect the true aggrgate rating from most customers and shoppers/web users answer no to the question, it could be pushed downwards on the product review page.

In addition, social commerce websites could develop interfaces to let customers being aware of other customers' feedback, opinions, comments, or even impressions on a product of interest. The idea here is to introduce social influence. An example could be that if an individual wants to buy a particular skateboard, social commerce websites might want to show the number of likes/dislikes from people who are extreme sports athletes, instead of general shoppers/users on the websites.

4   Conclusion

The purposes of this study were to (1) investigate whether the conflicts between an aggregate rating and a consumer comment influenced an individual's purchase intentions; (2) examine how Facebook likes impacted purchase intentions when there was a conflict between an aggregate rating and a consumer's comment. An online experiment was conducted with one hundred and eighty-four participants. Participants were engaged in buying snack on our developed social commerce website.

Results of the study indicated that consistency of an aggregate rating and a customer's comment, as well as the number of Facebook likes significantly affected participants' purchase intentions. Particularly, if an aggregate rating is consistent with a customer's comment, a product received higher purchase intentions (no matter whether the number of Facebook likes was high or low).

Research showed purchase intention is highly correlated with purchase behavior. Although other factors could have influenced purchase behavior, the insight obtained from this study was valuable to the design of social interfaces on social commerce websites. Social commerce websites should put more emphasis on designing for social influence. The benefit is not simply the sales revenue for the websites. Customers also get an idea of the quality of products, decision supports, and even prevent the lose for buying unwanted products.

Our work takes a novel approach to study how Facebook likes (i.e., social influence) mediated the effects of a conflicting aggregate rating and a consumer comment on purchase intention. The outcomes of this study are limited by the type of product used in the experiment. The product price was fixed in the experiment which could have affected our results. In addition, the participants were mainly college students. To improve the ecological validity, further studies are needed to recruit other groups of participants and look at more variables that might also influence online purchase intentions and behavior.

References

1. Huang, Z., Benyoucef, M.: From e-commerce to social commerce: a close look at design features. Electron. Commer. Res. Appl. **12**(4), 246–259 (2013)
2. Jin, C.: The perspective of a revised TRAM on social capital building: the case of Facebook usage. Inf. Manage. **50**(4), 162–168 (2013)
3. Kim, Y.A., Srivastava, J.: Impact of social influence in e-commerce decision making. In: Proceedings of the Ninth International Conference on Electronic Commerce, Minneapolis, MN, pp. 293–302. ACM Press, New York, August 2007
4. Ng, C.S.P.: Intention to purchase on social commerce websites across cultures: a cross-regional study. Inf. Manage. **50**(8), 609–620 (2013)
5. Kaplan, A.M., Haenlein, M.: Users of the world, unite! the challenges and opportunities of social media. Bus. Horiz. **53**(1), 59–68 (2010)
6. Chevalier, J.A., Mayzlin, D.: The effect of word of mouth on sales: online book reviews. J. Mark. Res. **43**(3), 345–354 (2006)
7. Kumar, N., Benbasat, I.: The influence of recommendations on consumer reviews on evaluations of websites. Inf. Syst. Res. **17**(4), 425–439 (2006)

8. Mudambi, S.M., Schuff, D.: What makes a helpful review? a study of customer reviews on Amazon. com. MIS Q. **34**(1), 185–200 (2010)

9. Clemons, E., Gao, G., Hitt, L.: When online reviews meet hyperdifferentiation: a study of the craft beer industry. J. Manage. Inf. Syst. **23**(2), 149–171 (2006)

10. Ganu, G., Elhadad, N., Marian, A.: Beyond the stars: improving rating predictions using review text content. WebDB **9**, 1–6 (2009)

11. Qiu, L., Pang, J., Lim, K.H.: Effects of conflicting aggregated rating on eWOM review credibility and diagnosticity: the moderating role of review valence. Decis. Support Syst. **54**(1), 631–643 (2012)

12. Borgida, E., Nisbett, R.E.: The differential impact of abstract vs. concrete information on decisions. J. Appl. Soc. Psychol. **7**(3), 258–271 (1977)

13. Cheung, M.Y., et al.: Credibility of electronic word-of-mouth: informational and normative determinants of on-line consumer recommendations. Int. J. Electron. Commer. **13**(4), 9–38 (2009)

14. Shin, D.-H.: User experience in social commerce: in friends we trust. Behav. Inf. Technol. **32**(1), 52–67 (2013)

15. Dutta-Bergman, M.J.: Theory and practice in healthcommunication campaigns: critical interrogation. HealthCommun. **18**, 103–122 (2005)

16. Chan, R.Y.-K., Lau, L.: A test of the Fishbein-Ajzen behavioral intentions model under Chinese culturalsettings: are there any differences between PRC and HongKong consumers? J. Mark. Pract. Appl. Mark. Sci. **4**(3), 85–101 (1998)

17. Kim, Y.J., Njite, D., Hancer, M.: Anticipated emotion in consumers' intentions to select eco-friendly restaurants: augmenting the theory of planned behavior. Int. J. Hospitality Manage. **34**, 255–262 (2013)

18. Bachrach, Y., Kosinski, M., Graepel, T., Kohli, P., Stillwell, D.: Personality and patterns of Facebook usage. In: Proceedings of the 3rd Annual ACM Web Science Conference, pp. 24–32 (2012)

19. Harris, J.K., Mueller, N.L., Snider, D.: Social media adoption in local health departments nationwide. Am. J. Public Health **103**(9), 1700–1707 (2013)

(Digital) Social Innovation Through Public Internet Access Points

Christoph Kaletka and Bastian Pelka(⊠)

TU Dortmund University, Dortmund, Germany
{kaletka, pelka}@sfs-dortmund.de

Abstract. The post-industrial innovation system with its distinct focus on social innovation allows for theoretical and conceptual connections between innovation research and new fields of social practice. In this article we elaborate on the potential of social innovation and especially digital social innovation to tackle digitally excluded persons' needs. Public internet access points are key infrastructures driving the digital inclusion of marginalized persons. Empirical results presented in this paper shows that these players act socially innovative by creating collaborative spaces for digital inclusion, by developing hybrid staff competence profiles and by creating community-based, intergenerational learning content. The paper relates research perspectives from the social innovation and the digital inclusion discourse and argues against the background of research and development results of six EU funded projects on social innovation and/or digital inclusion in the years 2011–2015.

Keywords: Telecentre · Digital gap · Digital inclusion · Social innovation · Digital social innovation

1 Introduction

As of today, there is a growing consensus among practitioners, policy makers and the research community that technological innovations alone are not capable of overcoming the social and economic challenges modern societies are facing. This is why the task of understanding and unlocking the potential of social innovation is on the research and policy agenda alike. The social innovation discourse is being driven by new projects, initiatives and policies, and by fields of practice which recognize SI theory and methods as useful drivers, and social innovators as powerful allies. The field is practice led. In this text we explore the common ground of social innovation and digital inclusion. Existing approaches and empirical findings on the role of telecentres as offline support structures for digital inclusion are introduced and discussed, with special attention being paid to their socially innovative character. A generic understanding of social innovation, as developed in ongoing research projects, is distinguished from a functional understanding in a concrete field of application. This leads to a better understanding the complementarity and the collaborative potential of social innovation and digital inclusion as two important fields of social research.

M. Antona and C. Stephanidis (Eds.): UAHCI 2015, Part I, LNCS 9175, pp. 201–212, 2015.
DOI: 10.1007/978-3-319-20678-3_20

2 Background: (Digital) Social Innovation

2.1 Social Innovation

With the change from the industrial to post-industrial society, the innovation system shows an increasing appreciation of the "social" as a field of new ideas. Recent years have seen a new form of innovation emerging, both as an object of research and development: Social innovations (SI) appear in a variety of forms and influence our lives. They change the way we live together (flat sharing), work (tele-working) or handle crises (short-time work instead of layoffs). They enable new types of cooperation (co-working bureaus) and organizations (public-private partnerships). They are driven by civil society (urban farming), politics (parental leave), the economy (micro-credits), or in-between sectors (dual studies, sharing economy).

As a first step, it is important to differentiate between two levels on which SI can be defined: a generic one, valid for all types and areas of application, and a definition referring to a specific area of action. On a generic level, the term "social innovation" in this paper is referring to a combination or figuration of practices in areas of social action, prompted by certain actors or constellations of actors with the goal of better coping with needs and problems than is possible by existing practices. An innovation is therefore social to the extent that it varies social action, and is socially accepted and diffused [1]. Taking into account that society changes through innovation, Howaldt/Schwarz [2] have pointed out that this understanding of innovation on the level of social action has an ever-increasing influence on society in the post-industrial era – while innovation after Schumpeter [3] had focused almost exclusively on technological innovation. Howaldt/Schwarz [2] conclude that "the contours of a new innovation paradigm are becoming visible and causing social innovation to grow in importance. This is accompanied by an exploration of the question of what (new) roles social sciences can play in analyzing and shaping social innovation" (ibid, p. 2). Recent research within the project "SI-Drive" has tried to identify drivers and barriers as well as means to support and foster them [4].

Project name	SI-Drive
Funding provided	EU, 7th Framework Programme
URL	http://www.si-drive.eu/
Research question	How does social innovation relate to social change?
Main outcomes	World wide mapping of social innovations; SI case studies and database; policy dialogue and recommendations

In addition to the generic understanding presented above, there are numerous definitions applied in different parts of the world and in different areas of application [5].

A definition for this specific sub-set of SI which is compatible with the generic definition and at the same time conducive to better understanding SI's potential for the (digital) inclusion of vulnerable target groups – as targeted in the project "SIMPACT" - is the following: SI "refer to new ideas (products, services and models) that simultaneously meet the needs of socially or economically marginalised groups more effectively and enable the society to create new or improved social relationships or collaborations leading to a better use of societal assets and resources" (ibid: p. 3).

Project name	Boosting the Impact of Social Innovation in Europe through Economic Underpinnings ("SIMPACT")
Funding provided	EU, 7th Framework Programme
URL	http://www.simpact-project.eu/
Research question	How can social innovation for vulnerable people be economically underpinned
Main outcomes	Insights in economical drivers and barriers for social innovation for marginalised persons

Several aspects of the generic and specific definitions of social innovation presented above are of special interest also in the context of digital or electronic inclusion ("eInclusion"). Public internet access points (PICs) or telecentres are institutions that provide free internet access and help to raise the competences of digitally excluded persons - typical examples are public libraries, senior residences, youth clubs or dedicated public internet cafes that offer free internet access and support to their clientele. These institutions have shaped new practices of supporting vulnerable target groups by creating places in which to learn and spend leisure time, by creating new learning opportunities and principles (such as community-based learning), by creating local networks for promoting digital and social inclusion on the local level, and finally by supporting staff competences matching the multi-faceted profile needed to do the job. As Sect. 3 will show, this development did not happen randomly or in few places, but well-planned and on a major scale. Through a continuous and transnational diffusion of the telecentre concept, they have become a widespread phenomenon meeting the needs of (digitally) excluded target groups and improving their capabilities.

The diffusion concept of social innovations as mentioned above almost always has a strong spatial component, meaning that a social innovation is implemented in different communities, cities or regions. This understanding of diffusion is closely related to traditional innovation research's concept of scaling [6]. One example for diffusion in this sense would be the emerging social practice of car sharing, which can be found all over the world, but which is organized differently in every city or community, not speaking about the fundamental differences of car sharing in first-world and third-world contexts. This concept of adaptive diffusion is important in order to understand the large-scale diffusion of telecentres throughout the world and, as analyzed by Rissola/Garrido [7], specifically in Europe. This diffusion resulted in a broad functional diversity of both the learning centres and their staff (cf. Section 3.2).

Social Innovation and Cross-Sector Collaboration at Local Level. Although digital technologies are often used to connect people with similar intereststt, the telecentres' mission to digitally and socially include vulnerable target groups has a strong emphasis on the local level and is focused on establishing or re-activating local communities. One reason is certainly that exclusion and inadequate policies become visible in cities, suburbs and villages in the first place.

Social innovation perspectives on local development, in this context, have some distinct characteristics setting them apart from traditional innovation models. They focus on the increase of social capital facilitated by cross-sectoral collaborations between actors from policy, research, economy and the civil society. This collaborative principle is picked up by at least two different heuristic models, the quadruple helix [8] on the one hand, where government, industry, academia and civil society work together to co-create the future and drive specific structural changes, and the social innovation ecosystem [9] on the other hand, which also asks for interactions between the helix actors, adds the notion of systemic complexity and looks at both the serendipity and absorptive capacity of a system as a whole. In this system, civil society is considered increasingly important for developing new processes and collaborations in such helix structures aimed at social change on the local level [10], which can be exemplified by telecentres promoting social and digital inclusion (see Sect. 3.1).

A Small-Scale Stakeholder Experiment. In a small-scale stakeholder experiment conducted in the SIMPACT project in September 2014 such cross-sector collaborations were highlighted as a central driver - understood as all factors which stimulate or facilitate the emergence of social innovation - for the inclusion of disadvantaged target groups through SI. The participants of this exercise (stakeholder organisations for vulnerable people, social policy makers, social innovators and researchers) pointed out:

1. A society's openness to change and the emergence of a "social innovation eco-system" is crucial for SI promoting the inclusion of disadvantaged target groups. Supporting factors were seen in an intimate relation between society and innovation, naturally perceived co-operations and a policy framework supporting SI.
2. A rich, trust based and powerful collaboration environment promotes innovation processes. Features of this environment include the involvement of all actors of the quadruple helix in policy making processes and new and effective ways of knowledge creation and sharing.
3. Social media play a dominant role in the communication infrastructure of social innovators. Social media are used as cheap and easy-to-use tools for interlinking actors, exchanging knowledge and empowering vulnerable people to articulate their opinion and support the diffusion of good practices.

2.2 Digital Social Innovation

Many social innovation activities are driven by the use of ICT and cooperation supported via social media [22], which prompted research activities and the emerging research domain of "digital social innovation" [11]. Digital social innovation (DSI) is understood as "a type of social and collaborative innovation in which final users and communities collaborate through digital platforms to produce solutions for a wide range of social needs and at a scale that was unimaginable before the rise of internet-enabled networking platforms" [12, p. 4].

This definition, again, is more specific than the generic understanding of SI presented in Sect. 2.1 and describes another sub-set of social innovations: While DSI are still social innovations in the first place, it stresses the collaborative and participatory character of problem-solving enabled by the use of ICT and digital media. The specific role of digital media in social innovation varies from case to case. In line with our results of the small-scale stakeholder experiments introduced before, digital media can be a central driver, but sometimes also a barrier for SI on several layers. Three such layers will be introduced and commented on the basis of our research results here: (1) the supporting or enabling character of ICT in general, (2) the use of standard or bespoke software solutions, and (3) the concept of spaces and place-making.

A central distinction is whether digital media have a supporting or an enabling role. "'Enable' implies that the SI wouldn't happen without ICT and could even mean that new types of SI appear (i.e. doing new things). A supporting role implies that SI is taking place anyway but also that it is, in some way or other, improved by ICT (i.e. doing existing things better, faster, cheaper, etc.)." [13, p. 135]. Earlier we elaborated on the settings needed for a telecentre operating as a social innovation incubator [23].

For example, ICT in telecentres can help jobseekers identify a larger number of potential employers and speed up the job seeking process (supporting character). On the other hand, blended-learning opportunities offered by telecentres help to include groups of learners who otherwise could not participate in the course at all (enabling character). This includes people with disabilities, people who live in remote rural areas and employed people who cannot attend courses at regular hours.

Another important distinction is whether social innovations make use of standard or customized/bespoke ICT. Many DSI cases use off-the-shelf ICT solutions, which are available and relatively cheap [13, p. 4]. Such affordable solutions can enhance the speed of diffusion for two reasons: budgets for promoting social innovations are usually limited, so off-the-shelf software limits necessary expenses, and also the time needed for adapting software to one's own requirements is manageable. Telecentres generally use standard office solutions, easily accessible leaning platforms like moodle to implement distance- and blended-learning courses, and promote the use of open software. Without such easily replicable and adaptable solutions, the inclusion of new learning opportunities in the telecentres' curricula on a large scale and the diffusion of the telecentre concept throughout the world would have been severely impeded.

Although digital media support transnational cooperation and network-building, many cases of digital social innovation make use of place-related infrastructures and facilities. These spaces help to create local partnerships, build capacity in local communities and facilitate volunteer activities by using digital media. Examples of such local spaces are Fablabs, Social Innovation Labs, Hackerspaces, Living Labs, Impact Hubs, and also telecentres (cf. Section 3.1). Millard/Carpenter conclude that such spaces "need to be multi-sectoral and comprehensive at the local level to ensure good impacts [...]. Relationship building based on trust, ethics, transparency and clear, often shared responsibilities are also hallmarks of these cases" [13, p. 30].

3 Telecenters for Digital Inclusion

This chapter is dedicated to the question where social innovation for the digitally excluded actually can take place. Following our initial puzzle of how digital inclusion could be supported, we earlier [14] differentiated three dimensions of digital inclusion instruments: In a first dimension, technology can be designed to avoid barriers and invite people with special needs; universal design is regarded as a fruitful approach here [15]. Secondly, online media themselves can be used to mediate and stipulate competences, solutions and assistance – online training or peer support networks are examples here. With this article we elaborate on the third dimension: "brick and mortar" welfare institutions (like senior residences or welfare centers) as "traditional" instruments, discovering the digital world as a new field of exclusion. Drawing from a series of research and development projects on telecentres, we can describe three ingredients necessary to make these "spaces" successful in reaching vulnerable target groups: A pedagogical concept of "space", skilled pedagogical staff and an appropriate learning methodology; a pedagogy for digital inclusion.

3.1   Space

The need for "offline" support structures for digital inclusion is obvious: As 22 % of Europeans [16] do not use the internet regularly and 18 % never accessed it, online support cannot reach them. This target group – predominantly elderly, unemployed or people with disabilities– can only be empowered through offline instruments addressing their special needs. A comparison on the European level shows that the percentage of "offliners" in a society is not set in stone, but strongly depends on the national context: Some European countries - as Denmark, Iceland, Norway or the Netherlands - see only 3–6 % of their population never using the internet; in other countries - like Romania or Greece - numbers reach 39 % [16]. With ICT entering everyday life in most countries, welfare organizations and public institutions (like libraries, cultural centers and youth clubs for example) have acknowledged the risks but also the potentials of the digital society for inclusion and empowerment of their target groups. They offer IT infrastructure, internet access, courses and individual support for disadvantaged persons on their way to the digital society as a new branch of their empowerment services. These institutions often have an established expertise in supporting these target groups and add "ICT knowledge" to their agenda. Other organizations were founded just recently and with the explicit aim of raising ICT competences. Both types – public internet access points as parts of existing welfare institutions with a broad variety of offers, and dedicated "telecentres" – can be understood as a third dimension of support for digital inclusion which is using "space" and "proximity" as key factors in a low-threshold target group approach. The physical space of a telecentre is therefore used to establish proximity to persons who are not profiting from ICT. These spaces serve as learning and community centres alike.

Rissola/Garrido [7] estimate that there are "almost 250,000 eInclusion organizations in the EU27, or an average of one eInclusion organization for every 2,000 inhabitants". More than a quarter of these (25.8 % of the public and 28.4 % of the third sector funded institutions) are targeting individuals with physical disabilities. 18.8 % of the public and 24.1 % of the third sector funded organisations are targeting individuals with mental disabilities (ibid: p. 59). These institutions usually operate with less than 10 employees and a budget of less than 100,000 EUR per year (ibid) – leading to a "physical" digital inclusion support structure in Europe which is widely spread, but consisting of small units. There is a huge variety in the quality of those "spaces": They can be distinguished by the support they offers and the proximity to their target group. There are four levels of empowerment services [17]:

Level 1: On demand assistance	Passive role; the telecentre only reacts to user's demand of help.
Level 2: Level 1 + Training	Provider of digital literacy training, the telecentre can also look for/attract the users and give a social orientation to his/her intervention.
Level 3: Level 2 + User empowerment	Provider of social inclusion services, the telecentre promotes the digital autonomy of the users and their achievement of personal goals taking advantage of the many resources available at the information society.
Level 4: Level 3 + Active participation in community	Provider of community service-learning, the telecentre promotes the critical use of ICT and the engagement of the users with their local communities/social belonging groups through their active participation of community/social projects.

Telecentres on levels 3 and 4 understand themselves as active social innovation actors in local communities - they empower local communities via digital media and build networks and unlikely alliances with other education providers, public employment services and companies. An overview of telecentre activities shows [18] the broad variety of social activities these spaces provide for local communities, including occupational training, local network facilitation, digital literacy support, child care services during parents' learning hours, and more. Accordingly, telecentres do not only consider themselves providers of digital literacy, but also social innovation and inclusion agents. They articulate the need of additional competences for facilitating social co-construction processes, such as "socio-cultural animation" or "job guidance", as results of an online survey of 252 telecentre staff suggest [18, p. 46].

3.2   Staff

Project name	Vocational training and education solutions for e-Facilitators for social inclusion (vet4e-I")
Funding provided	EU, Lifelong learning programme, 2011-2013
URL	http://www.efacilitator.eu
Research question	Which competences should people working in a telecentre have in order to empower their target groups for eInclusion?
Main outcomes	Learning material for eFacilitators

The four levels of services offered by telecentres demonstrate that "space" is working as an anchor for discourse between vulnerable people and professional staff addressing their needs. This staff - recently named "eFacilitators" [19] - is combining competences in target group specific approaches and digital skills. As those 250,000 institutions comprise such different "spaces" as internet cafes, workshops for disabled or public libraries, it is difficult to estimate the number of staff actually involved in digital inclusion activities. But taking 250,000 organisations as a basis, it seems safe to argue that around 250,000–375,000 persons in the EU are working on digital competences for disadvantaged persons. The "vet4e-I" and "TeF" projects' initial research [18] has revealed the socio-demographic characteristics of this occupational field: The results show that eFacilitators are mostly young, female and highly educated, 70 % have an educational background in different fields of social work [20, p. 13]. Men or staff with an ICT background are a minority. Telecentre staff are persons with a high interest in social innovation. Strong links between this group and social innovators can be traced. Against this background, eFacilitators can be considered social innovators in the field of digital inclusion.

DSI research is still too young to produce insights into innovators' motivations, but Millard/Carpenter suggest that "hubs" of opinion makers are playing a significant role in their spreading [13, p. 14]. Telecentres could play the role of such hubs, as they provide a sphere of social action and bring together people with a high motivation to care for vulnerable people. On the other hand, eFacilitators are no natural ICT professionals - 67 % of 252 eFacilitators participating in a survey in 2012 [18] indicated they were in need of ICT skills. Easy to use ICT seems to be a prerequisite for supporting DSI, as Millard/Carpenter point out [13, p. 47]. Other job requirements requested by eFacilitators are managerial and sustainability aspects. The projects "vet4e-I" and "TeF" provided these competences by developing training curricula for telecentre staff. The "TeF" training course consists of twelve modules, addressing management, sustainability, communication and ICT competences. All learning materials are available online and free and have been disseminated to telecentre staff all over Europe.

Project name	Training for e-facilitators ("TeF")
Funding provided	EU, Lifelong learning programme, 2012-2014
URL	http://www.trans-efacilitator.eu
Research question	Which competences should people working in a telecentre have in order to empower their target groups for eInclusion?
Main outcomes	12 modules of e-learning course for eFacilitators

3.3   Learning Content

Making use of the trust-building low-threshold functions of "space" and approaching vulnerable target groups with skilled staff, telecentres are a powerful instrument for providing digital skills. But being a relatively new phenomenon, in many countries telecentres cannot build on a long standing experience in providing digital competences. Therefore, the European Commission started two projects aiming at developing learning materials and pedagogical approaches for telecentres. The project "Key competences for all" addressed the learning needs and interests of digitally excluded people. Empirical research identified labour market participation and participation in social networks as two key reasons for acquiring ICT competences [21]. The project developed a toolkit of learning materials, structured in three modules: The first part helps users to choose a profession based upon their skills and interests. Two workshops are available in this section, improving own skills assessment and the ability to search the web and use word processing software. The second part offers online resources and three workshops to help them apply for a job by developing job search skills using IT, to compare vacancies, and to prepare a professional CV. The workshops also improve the general ability to use word processing and spreadsheet software. The last part raises users' awareness of social networks' possibilities to create new professional opportunities.

Project name	Key Competences for all (KC4all)
Funding provided	EU, Lifelong learning programme, 2011-2013
URL	http://www.keycompetences.eu
Research question	Which learning content should telecentres offer their target groups?
Main outcomes	Learning material for disadvantages persons, facilitators' handbook, guidelines for stakeholders and policy makers

Another challenge telecentres are facing is the fact that pedagogical approaches of traditional welfare institutions do not consider ICT as a key factor of empowerment and lack a pedagogical methodology to raise ICT competences. This was addressed by the EU funded project "eScouts" [20]. Initial research found a broad variety of approaches to empower vulnerable target groups in Europe. Another key finding was that welfare organisations articulated interest in intergenerational learning methodologies, as ICT seems to be both a binding and a separating phenomenon between generations. The project identified two distinct learning methodologies and brought them together in an approach to support ICT-driven intergenerational learning. A main outcome is a blended learning course which empowers seniors to support the labour market related skills of young people and at the same time empowers the young to support ICT competences of the elderly. eFacilitators take the role of innovators community innovators (elderly and youth), stipulating peer empowerment processes.

Project name	Intergenerational learning circle for community management ("eScouts")
Funding provided	EU, Lifelong learning programme, 2011-2013
URL	http://escouts.eu/
Research question	Which pedagogical approaches are useful for mediating digital skills to marginalised target groups?
Main outcomes	Learning approach for intergenerational peer support for digital inclusion

4 Conclusion

Two distinct research contexts have been introduced: (digital) social innovation on the one hand, public internet access points and telecentres as drivers of digital inclusion on the other. First, a generic definition of social innovation and two specific definitions (SI for vulnerable and DSI) were presented, offering a new approach to observe and construct digital inclusion instruments. Secondly, public internet access points (PICs) or telecentres as institutions providing free internet access and helping to raise the competences oft digitally excluded persons were described, drawing on diverse survey results.

While the research discourses on digital social innovation and digital inclusion have not been linked systematically yet, both fields can profit from an integrated debate. We have argued that telecentres as infrastructures for digital inclusion show clear characteristics of both social and digital social innovation. While these support structures, despite their impressive numbers, have yet to overcome their pioneer status, they have initiated and sustained new practices of supporting vulnerable target groups. New learning opportunities and principles (such as community-based learning) were developed and diffused, local networks and "unusual" actor constellations were facilitated, with an underlying focus on the empowerment of local communities and unlikely alliances with education providers, public employment services, companies and other local stakeholders. These telecentres do not only consider themselves providers of digital literacy, but also social innovation and inclusion agents. The complex qualificational staff profile ("eFacilitators") seems to be a key enabler for this mission and was already addressed in several projects.

In order to better understand the complementarity and the collaborative potential of the two fields of research as well as the related communities in the field, the following questions should be addressed in future research:

1. How can new pedagogic approaches and materials and local networking solutions be scaled up, and how can an efficient process of adaptive diffusion look like which is sensitive to different local, organizational and pedagogic requirements?
2. How can small-scale innovations involving digital technology be applied in telecentres, and how can the most powerful ones be better identified in order to promote digital inclusion on a larger scale?
3. How can the use of innovative digital means and interpersonal relations be balanced and managed in the telecentre context, harnessing the best from both sides?
4. How can eFacilitators' and social entrepreneurs skills and learning programmes be exchanged and combined in order to empower both sides to do their job better?

Answering these questions will not only help to promote the scientific debate on the two respective topics, it will also drive very concrete collaborations of the two communities of practice working in the field. Telecentres can join and valorize the emerging group of DSI intermediaries with their mission of empowerment, and at the same time they may profit from the other side's vast experience in promoting (digital) social entrepreneurship, which creates new opportunities for telecentres' curricular development and their capacity to promote digital literacy.

Acknowledgements. This paper builds on the results of the research project SIMPACT – "Boosting the Impact of Social Innovation in Europe through Economic Underpinnings". SIMPACT has received funding from the EU's 7th Framework Programme for research, technological development and demonstration under GA No. 613411.

References

1. Howaldt, J., Butzin, A., Domanski, D., Kaletka, C.: Theoretical approaches to social innovation - a critical literature review. A Deliverable of the Project: 'Social Innovation: Driving Force of Social Change' (SI-DRIVE), European Commission – 7th Framework Programme. SFS, Dortmund (2014)
2. Howaldt, J., Schwarz, M.: Social innovation: concepts, research fields and inter-national trends. In: Henning, K., Hees, F. (eds.) Studies for Innovation in a Modern Working Environment - International Monitoring, vol. 5 (2010). http://www.sfs-dort-mund.de/odb/Repository/Publication/DocC1289CIMO_Trendstudie_Howaldt_Schwarz_englische_Version.pdf
3. Schumpeter, J.A.: Theorie der wirtschaftlichen Entwicklung. Duncker & Humblot, Berlin (1964)
4. Howaldt, J., Kopp, R., Schwarz, M. (eds.): Zur Theorie sozialer Innovationen. In: Tardes vernachlässigter Beitrag zur Entwicklung einer soziologischen Innovationstheorie, Wiesbaden (2014)
5. Rehfeld, D., Terstriep, J., Welschhoff, J., Alijani, S.: Comparative report on SI framework. Deliverable D1.1 of the Project: 'Boosting the Impact of SI in Europe Through Economic Underpinnings' (SIMPACT), EC – 7th Framework Programme. European Commission, DG Research & Innovation, Brussels (2014)
6. Gabriel, M.: Making it Big: Strategies for Scaling Social Innovations. National Endowment for Science, Technology and the Arts (NESTA), London (2014)
7. Rissola, G., Garrido, M.: Survey on eInclusion Actors in the EU27 (2013). http://www.jrc.es/EURdoc/JRC84429.pdf
8. Wallin, S.: The co-evolvement in local development - from the triple to the quadruple helix model. In: Conference Paper at Triple Helix VIII, Madrid, October 2010. www.triplehelix8.org
9. Sgaragli, F.: Enabling Social Innovation Ecosystems for Community-led Territorial Development. Fondazione Giacomo Brodolini, Rome (2014)
10. Sinnergiak Social Innovation & Innobasque, Regional Innovation Index. Innobasque Publishing (2013)
11. Casebourne, J., Armstrong, K. (eds.): Digital social innovation. Second Interim Study Report (2014). http://content.digitalsocial.eu/wp-content/uploads/2014/09/FINAL-2ND-INTERIM-STUDY-REPORT.pdf
12. Bria, F.: Digital social innovation. Interim Report (2014). http://content.digitalsocial.eu/resource-category/research/
13. Millard, J., Carpenter, G.: Digital technology in social innovation: synthesis, gaps and recommendations. A Deliverable of the Project: 'The Theoretical, Empirical and Policy Foundation for Building Social Innovation in Europe' (TEPSIE), European Commission – 7th Framework Programme. EC, Brussels (2014)
14. Bühler, C., Pelka, B.: Empowerment by digital media of people with disabilities, three levels of support. In: Miesenberger, K., Fels, D., Archambault, D., Peňáz, P., Zagler, W. (Hrsg.) 14th International Conference on Computers Helping People with Special Needs, ICCHP 2014, Paris, France, 9–11 July 2014, Proceedings, Part I (2014)

15. Bühler, C.: Universal design – computer. In: International Encyclopedia of Rehabilitation, Chapter. 146. Center for International Rehabilitation Research Information and Exchange (CIRRIE) (2010). http://cirrie.buffalo.edu/encyclopedia/en/article/146/

16. Eurostat, Internet use by individuals. Code: tin00028, % of individuals aged 16 to 74 Last internet use: within last 3 months (2014). http://ec.europa.eu/eurostat/tgm/refreshTableAction.do?tab=table&plugin=1&pcode=tin00028&language=en

17. Kaletka, C., Pelka, B., Diaz, A., Rastrelli, M.: eScouts: Intergenerational Learning In Blended Environments And Spaces (ILBES) for social inclusion. In: European Distance and eLearning Network (EDEN) (2012). www.eden-online.org/system/files/Annual_2012_Porto_BOA.pdf

18. eFacilitator: Results of a multi-country analysis: context in four countries (2012). http://www.efacilitator.eu/wordpress/wp-content/uploads/2010/12/VET4e-i_Multi-Country_Context_AnalysisDEF.pdf

19. Pelka, B., Kaletka, C.: eFacilitators: functional hybrids between ICT teaching and community management. In: Proceedings of the ECER VETNET Conference (2012). http://www.b.shuttle.de/wifo/vetnet/ecer12.htm, http://vetnet.mixxt.org/networks/files/file.111156

20. eScouts: Deliverable 3.2: context analysis, Part 2: Facilitators (2012). http://escouts8.files.wordpress.com/2012/04/escouts-context-analysis-facilitators.pdf

21. Keycompetences: online employment toolkit. In: Guidelines for stakeholders and new actors (2012). http://www.keycompetences.eu/wordpress/wp-content/uploads/2011/09/booklet_English_guidllines_r2.pdf

22. Pelka, B.; Kaletka, C.: Web 2.0 zwischen technischer und sozialer Innovation: Anschluss an die medientheoretische Debatte. In: Howaldt, J.; Jacobsen, H. (eds.) Soziale Innovation. Auf dem Weg zu einem postindustriellen Innovationsparadigma, pp. 143–161. VS Verlag, Wiesbaden (2010)

23. Pelka, B., Kaletka, C.: Blended learning spaces as a social innovation for Local Inclusion. In: EIRP Proceedings on Integration and Employability, vol. 7 (2012). http://www.proceedings.univ-danubius.ro/index.php/eirp/article/view/1362/1308

On the Need for Assistance in HTML5 Web Authoring Systems

Julia C. Lee and Lawrence J. Henschen[✉]

Northwestern University, Evanston, IL 60208, USA
Julialee@agep.northwestern.edu, henschen@eecs.northwestern.edu

Abstract. HTML5 incorporates semantics, including among others the purpose and intention of the web author, as an integral part of the language and specification. The goal is to allow more sophisticated browsers to render the content in ways that are appropriate for both the platform and the abilities of the user, thereby achieving universal access. However, achieving that goal depends on web authors using the elements and attributes correctly. We illustrate why this will be difficult for most web authors. We propose that web editors be enhanced to provide guidance to web authors in the correct and proper usage of the HTML5 features and give some examples of how this might work.

Keywords: HTML5 · WAI-ARIA · Semantic web · Universal access

1 Introduction

HTML5 became an official recommendation on Oct. 28 2014 [1]. HTML5 inherits and improves on many features of the previous versions of HTML but also embraces many new ideas and philosophies. Among the new features that HTML5 offers are: homogenize HTML and XHTML into one specification; make DOM the "official" in-memory model of an HTML document; and hide the complexities of multithreading from web authors. But the feature that is perhaps the most important one for the HCI community is the giant step towards the separation of formatting and presentation from the content and semantics.

To clearly convey ones thoughts in a presentation and to correctly understand the thoughts conveyed by presentations from others are critical issues for successful communication between parties. As the internet becomes an increasingly indivisible part of our daily life, HTML becomes one of the most important languages used for communication among humans. Much research in the information technology field has been devoted to understanding the semantic meaning of human presentations and to providing tools that facilitate the correct presentation of peoples' meaning. The Semantic Web and universal access are hot topics in the Web development/research area [2, 3, 8, 9]. HTML5 is a major step forward in supporting these trends. In particular, the separation of presentation from content and semantics, the introduction of new elements that explicitly give the intended purpose of the content, and the use of WAI-ARIA roles [5] greatly improves the ability to present content on arbitrary platforms and to users with arbitrary

© Springer International Publishing Switzerland 2015
M. Antona and C. Stephanidis (Eds.): UAHCI 2015, Part I, LNCS 9175, pp. 213–220, 2015.
DOI: 10.1007/978-3-319-20678-3_21

abilities and needs in ways that facilitate human understanding of the content, that is, that greatly improves the chances for universal access to web content.

However, the degree to which HTML5 can lead to increased access depends heavily on web authors using the language properly. Languages, such as HTML5, are the tools used to present human thoughts. Good tools need users that have good understanding about the tools in order to fully utilize the good attributes that are built in. Many of the wonderful new features of HTML5 are difficult for web authors, particularly non-professional web authors who may produce the majority of web pages, to understand and use properly. We suggest in this article that, in order to achieve the promise of universal access inherent in the philosophy and design of HTML5, intelligent web authoring tools will be needed. We describe some of the subtleties of HTML5 and then suggest several ways in which web authoring tools and HTML5 editors can aid authors in properly using the language.

2 Related Work on the Semantic Web

W3C has contributed much in this area by developing a number of recommendations related to the semantic web and universal access. W3C published a specification of RDF (The **Resource Description Framework**) and its data model and an XML serialization as a recommendation in 1999 [4]. This is one of the earliest efforts focused on "semantic web", and efforts by W3C and others have continued vigorously since then. There is now a suite of standards, recommendations, and tools related to RDF initiatives. One of the most important contributions by W3C is the recent WAI-ARIA specification [5].

"This specification provides an ontology of roles, states, and properties that define accessible user interface elements and can be used to improve the accessibility and interoperability of web content and applications".

The role taxonomy defined by this specification makes direct connection between semantic meaning and HTML mark-up elements, as described in [6]. The role taxonomy is primarily defined for universal accessibility aimed for people with disabilities. HTML5 incorporated the role attribute into its element definition. The role taxonomy includes specific roles, such as "button", "banner", "checkbox", etc., and abstract roles, such as "composite", "command", "range", etc., that can express semantics of elements that are not directly represented by the element itself.

3 Semantic Aspects of HTML5

In this section we illustrate by example how HTML5 incorporates semantics. We point out in advance that web authors could express their content without using these HTML5 features, but this would make it difficult or impossible for renderers to understand the author's meaning and thereby be able to render the content well on different platforms and to different kinds of users. We encourage the reader to think to him- or herself how much easier it is to understand content when the appropriate element or attribute is used.

3.1 New Elements with Semantic Meaning

HTML5 introduced many new elements that convey certain semantic meanings by the name itself – for example: video, address, legend, aside, blockquote, small, etc. The need and use of some of these is obvious; modern web pages often include video, and it is natural to have a special element for that purpose. The need for other elements, especially elements whose content is mainly text, is less obvious until one considers the rendering of text to, for example, a blind user or an application. A block of text in a document might be difficult to recognize as being address information or a side comment not part of the main subject, even if additional intelligent technology is applied to that text. And yet users with different abilities will need to have those texts presented in different ways, and applications would need signposts to identify the portions of the page they want to use. With the meaningful tag/element names an application program or a screen reader for blind people will know immediately the semantics of the text block. Here are some simple examples.

"data" elements mark up blocks of text made of machine readable data values. Application programs may be able to read the text directly, but blind users will likely need the content present in a special way.

"main" elements point out the main contents related to the central topic. Blind readers can be informed that this text contributes to the main idea of the page, and sighted readers will benefit by knowing the author's intent for this portion of the page.

"blockquote" elements contain quoted material. Using the "blockquote" element allows the renderer to distinguish that content from a simple quoted word, such as at the beginning of these points. It also alerts the renderer to look for a "cite" element that contains the citation for the quoted material. Without the "cite" element it would be impossible in general for a renderer to find the citation information.

These are very much semantic markups rather than structural markups. Only the author of the document can correctly say in all cases which parts of the text are which; document processing systems and artificial intelligence have not yet evolved to a level that could match the author's knowledge. If used correctly, these new semantic HTML5 elements will enhance the understanding of the semantics of documents and improve accessibility to those documents.

3.2 Element Attributes

Using attributes to note special issues, including semantic issues, for element usage is not unique to HTML5; attributes have been a feature of HTML from the beginning. However, prior to HTML5 there were no official guidelines for how to use attributes to specify semantics relating to the element in which it was used. For example, an author could assign a value to the "name" attribute of a "div" element, but there was nothing in earlier HTML versions indicating that this attribute should specify the element's role in the context of the document.

However, unlike previous versions of HTML, HTML5 has placed great emphases on using element attributes correctly and intelligently. The "title" attribute was a required element in every HTML5 document as a child element of the "head" element.

Now it can also be an attribute of other elements such as "abbr", "dfn", and others. The HTML5 specification [1] specifically tells what kind of "advisory" information this attribute should provide for each element. For example, in an "abbr" element the "title" attribute should be used to provide an expansion of the abbreviation being defined. For the "dfn" element the value of the "title" attribute is the term being defined. As another example, consider the new keyword "cite". When used as an element it should contain the title of the reference, but when used as an attribute in a "blockquote" or "q" element it must be a valid URL potentially surrounded by spaces. Authors writing HTML5 documents should not use attributes arbitrarily but rather use them for exactly those purposes prescribed in the HTML5 specification.

More importantly, HTML5 allows ARIA roles, states, and properties [5] as attributes on any HTML5 element. The role attribute allows the author to annotate markup languages with machine-extractable semantic information about the purpose of an element. The presence of the "role", or purpose, information can lead to increased accessibility, as described in [5] or in other literature on universal access (for example, [10]), as well as better presentation on different platforms, increased processing flexibility for applications, etc. WAI-ARIA [5] defines a specific role taxonomy for web elements focusing on the widget elements. This specification also defines the supported states, representing more dynamic aspects of a role, and properties, representing more stable aspects of a role, for the roles in the taxonomy. Figure 1, taken from [7], gives an example of how this might be used. The 'aria-flowto' attribute allows the author to specify alternative navigation through the document that might be useful for, say, a blind user. The "aria-flowto" overrides the default ordering based on the occurrence of the text in the document and also serves to group related items that may be physically separated in the text by other elements.

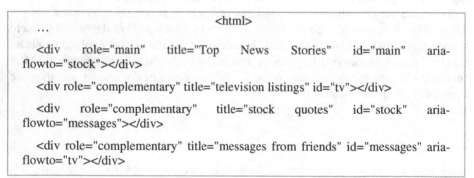

```
                                      <html>
    ...
    <div    role="main"    title="Top    News    Stories"    id="main"    aria-
flowto="stock"></div>

    <div role="complementary" title="television listings" id="tv"></div>

    <div    role="complementary"    title="stock    quotes"    id="stock"    aria-
flowto="messages"></div>

    <div role="complementary" title="messages from friends" id="messages" aria-
flowto="tv"></div>
```

Fig. 1. Example of ARIA attributes

3.3 Subtleties in HTML5 Semantics

The HTML5 specification emphasizes "Elements, attributes, and attribute values in HTML are defined (by this specification) to have certain meanings (semantics)" [1]. The semantics of the elements allows different browsers, screen readers, search engines, etc. to present and interpret the HTML document closely to the intention of the author. Unfortunately, there are many subtleties in the semantics of the various elements and attributes that are difficult for even a professional web developer to understand, much less a novice. Therefore, the goal of HTML5 to make the web more accessible will be difficult to achieve without tools that aid web authors in correctly using the HTML5 language. We illustrate the difficulty with a brief discussion of two sets of HTML5 elements - a set of section/grouping elements and a set of text-level elements.

The HTML5 specification includes several elements that group larger portions of content. These include, among others, "main", "article", and "section". The specification gives brief descriptions of the semantics and proper usage of each of these. For example, an "article" is a portion of content that could stand on its own or be extracted from the web page and still be meaningful. But, how is that different from "main"; and often times a "section" in a major work has the same property. The situation is made more confusing by the fact that in many (perhaps even most) browsers the text content of these three elements will appear in identical font and style. Even experienced web authors will need guidance in deciding which of these to use at any given point in an HTML5 document. Another example in this category is the "aside" element, whose content should be related to but not part of the main subject of the content surrounding it [1]. Web authors may think this can be used for parenthetical remarks in the content itself because in ordinary writing tangentially related comments are often written as parenthetical text. However, the HTML5 specification explicitly states that "aside" is not to be used for that purpose. And to further confuse the issue, the text-level element "small" is to be used for side comments.

Several text-level elements will also lead to confusion. For example, "em", "strong", and "b" all indicate some kind of stress, but the HTML5 specification gives slightly different semantics to these.

- The em element represents stress emphasis of its contents.
- The strong element represents strong importance, seriousness, or urgency.
- The "b" element represents a span of text to which attention is being drawn.

It is difficult to fully understand the differences or to appreciate how the content would be presented differently to impaired users. Moreover, web authors experienced in using earlier versions of HTML would be tempted to use the "span" element with suitable attributes for most of these purposes, but this would not be in the spirit of HTML5. In addition to helping impaired users, proper usage of elements such as these will facilitate the development of more sophisticated applications, such as search engines and data miners.

4 How HTML5 Editors Can Improve the Quality and Universal Accessibility of Web Pages

To overcome the difficulties mentioned in the preceding section, particularly Sect. 3.3, we propose that HTML5 editors provide help for web authors. It is not enough for editors to merely check for syntactical correctness or compliance or even to provide syntactically-oriented auto-correct features like automatically closing elements. Authors need help in understanding the subtle semantic differences and connections between closely related elements and attributes so that the resulting web pages accurately reflect the HTML5 semantics and the author's intent. We present examples of how editors could give such help at several different levels of sophistication.

4.1 Simple Guidance and Crosschecking

At the simplest level editors can provide guidance in the use of the various elements and attributes. A simple scheme would be to alert an author to alternate elements or attributes when the author used one of the HTML5 items. For example, the editor could pop up a window explaining the difference between "main", "article", "section", "span", etc. whenever a user selected one of those (either by typing it explicitly in a primitive editor or selecting it from a menu in one of the more sophisticated web authoring environments). Similarly for when the user types or selects one of "em", "strong", "u", "i", etc. The help might be several levels deep. For example, the first pop-up help window could remind the author of the differences and link to a second level help window with simple examples. Depending on the particular element or attribute group involved, there could be deeper levels explaining in great detail the differences and how those differences would impact impaired users.

Many of the semantic aspects of HTML5 elements have a closely related syntactical aspect that can easily be checked. For example, the presence of a "blockquote" should indicate the need for a "cite" element, and "li" elements should appear inside a list group element ("ol" or "ul"). HTML5 web authoring systems can easily check whether or not the document satisfies these and can suggest to the author how to fix errors.

As authors become better at writing semantically correct HTML5 documents, the need for such proactive help would reduce. Therefore, systems should allow users to specify the level of help and guidance and whether to present it during document preparation or only at certain times (for example, on request or at document save).

4.2 Templates

A somewhat more sophisticated and proactive approach is for the web authoring system to know about templates for various kinds of web documents and to provide templates based on the kind of web page the author is developing. In this kind of system the user might be asked at the beginning to select a web page type from a drop-down menu or through a more complex dialogue. For example, the user might select "business" or "newsletter" or "scientific-article" from a list of basic web-page types. The system might then prompt for additional information, for example the kind of business page (simple advertisement, shopping, information only, etc.) Once the author has specified the type, the system proposes a structure and gives help and guidance aimed specifically at that type of web page. In some cases the choice of HTML5 elements and attributes will be quite clear, while in others there may be much more flexibility based on what the web author intends. We illustrate with two examples.

If the author indicates this is a moderate to extensive news page, the overall structure would be quite well defined. The bulk of the content would be organized as "article" elements, and there should be "head", "title", and possibly "link" and "meta" elements for the document as a whole. In this situation the system would simply advise the author about the need for each of these and perhaps provide empty elements for the author to simply fill in. There would still be some issues involving choice. For example, while print news (e.g., printed newspapers) rarely have sections, web-based news may well benefit by the extra organization the "section" element provides. An authoring system should explain the benefits to the author but let the author make the final choice.

Other contexts would allow more flexibility, and the system would be more advisory in nature. For example, if the type was shopping page for a business, then the system might propose the author use either header elements (e.g., "h1", "h2", ...) or "article" for major areas of the web site (company overview, contact information, billing, shipping, product lines). Each of these choices has consequences in terms of presentation on different platforms and to different users as well as for applications that process the web page. Similarly, individual products might be presented in any of "p", "ol", "ul", or "div" elements, optionally with "hr" elements. Again, each of these will have consequences for both presentation and processing by applications. The system should suggest these alternatives and explain the consequences so that the author not only achieves his or her purpose but also does it in a way that matches the semantics of HTML5.

Of course, the choices made by the author when the system presents alternatives, the specific content, and the actual look of the page (color schemes, logos, etc.) would still be left to the author. However, the actual HTML5 coding would comply with the semantics of HTML5.

4.3 Guidance for Universal Access

Very few web authors understand the difficulties encountered by web users with disabilities. So, while understanding the semantic of HTML5 is already a difficult matter, understanding the impact of the choices of HTML5 elements and attributes is even harder for most web authors. Moreover, web authors may not even be aware that there are special tools in HTML5 for use by assistive technology. Because they do exist in HTML5, this would be a good time for web authoring tools to take proactive measures to ensure authors use those features. Here are some samples of the kinds of help and guidance that could be provided.

- When the editor detects sequences of major sections or navigation points on a page it can suggest to the author that alternate navigations for impaired users should be provided. We have already illustrated how aria-flowto attributes can aid blind users.
- Authors should be prompted to use aria role types so that assistive technology can help impaired users understand web pages. For example, "img" elements being used in the role of "separator" should be handled differently than "img" elements with other roles. Similarly for "div" elements with role "alert" vs. role "banner" vs. role "definition", etc.
- In [10] we proposed the development of new kinds of roles specifically for presentation to impaired users. Web authoring systems could add such roles to their libraries.

We also suggest that web developing systems incorporate the same assistive technologies that are available for web browsers so that authors can experience for themselves how impaired users will feel when using the documents being developed.

4.4 Artificial Intelligence, Natural Language Processing, and the Future of Intelligent Web Authoring Tools

Artificial intelligence, and in particular natural language processing, has progressed to the point where useful tools that analyze text are now becoming available. For example, see [11] for a system that analyzes web content, aggregates information, and automatically generates news stories. Techniques from AI and NL could be applied to recognition of text within an HTML5 document, and the results could be used with rule systems and corresponding reasoning systems to recognize non-compliance with the semantics of HTML5. For example, text representing a citation that is not included in a "cite" element could be recognized and flagged. Such techniques could also be incorporated into HTML5 compliance checkers so that authors who do not use a sophisticated editing tool could still be helped to write semantically correct HTML5 documents.

5 Conclusion

We have shown by example how it will be difficult for web authors to understand the subtle semantics of HTML5 and therefore difficult for them to use HTML5 properly so that the goal of universal access can be achieved. We then proposed that web editors that can inform authors about the semantics and guide the authors as they develop web pages to correctly use the elements and attributes. The types of help from such editors can range from relatively simple explanation to sophisticated help using artificial intelligence and natural language understanding.

References

1. World Wide Web Consortium. http://www.w3.org/TR/2014/REC-html5-20141028/
2. Berniers-Lee, T., Hendler, J., Lassila, O.: The semantic web. Sci. Am. **284**, 29–37 (2001)
3. Hendler, J.: Agents and the semantic web. IEEE Intell. Syst. **16**, 30–37 (2001)
4. World Wide Web Consortium. http://www.w3.org/TR/1999/REC-rdf-syntax-19990222/
5. World Wide Web Consortium. http://www.w3.org/TR/wai-aria/
6. World Wide Web Consortium. http://www.w3.org/TR/2011/WD-role-attribute-20110113/
7. World Wide Web Consortium. http://www.w3.org/WAI/PF/aria-practices/
8. Cameron, D., Smith, G., Daniulaityte, R., Sheth, A., Dave, D., Chen, L., Anand, G., Carlson, R., Watkins, K., Falck, R.: PREDOSE: a semantic web platform for drug abuse epidemiology using social media. J. Biomed. Inform. **46**, 985–997 (2013)
9. Dinh, D., Reis, J., Pruskia, C., Da Silveira, M., Reynaud-Delaitre, C.: Identifying relevant concept attributes to support mapping maintenance under ontology evolution. Web Seman. Sci. Serv. Agents World Wide Web **29**, 53–66 (2014)
10. Henschen, L., Lee, J.: Using semantic-level tags in HTML/XML documents. In: Proceedings of the 13th HCII International Conference, pp. 683–692 (2009)
11. Iacobelli, F., Birnbaum, L., Hammond, K.: Tell me more, not just more of the same. In: Proceedings of the 14th International Conference on Intelligent User Interfaces, pp. 81–90 (2010)

A WYSIWYG Editor to Support Accessible Web Content Production

Hedi Carlos Minin[1], Javier Jiménez Alemán[1],
Carolina Sacramento[2,3](✉), and Daniela Gorski Trevisan[1]

[1] Universidade Federal Fluminense, Niterói, Brazil
{hminin, jjimenezaleman, daniela}@ic.uff.br
[2] Fundação Oswaldo Cruz, Rio de Janeiro, Brazil
carolina.sacramento@uniriotec.br
[3] Universidade Federal do Estado do Rio de Janeiro, Rio de Janeiro, Brazil

Abstract. In a world where lay users on web languages and standards are responsible to produce content to web, it's essential the presence of tools which support the creation of accessible content. This paper proposes to make Web accessibility concepts more understandable to these users with the incorporation of WCAG 2.0 accessibility guidelines in HTML WYSIWYG editors they use. For that we designed and prototyped such Editor and performed preliminaries usability tests with target users. Results shown that accessibility warnings were easy to understand and to apply but difficult to perceive them.

Keywords: Accessibility guidelines · WYSIWYG HTML editor · WCAG 2.0 · ATAG 1.0

1 Introduction

The main advantage of Web 2.0 is the possibility of Web content creation by lay users. In this context, we can find authoring tools such as CMS (Content Management Systems) which allows the publication of content without knowledge about languages, web standards or accessibility guidelines. On the other hand, initiatives such as WCAG 2.0 [1] (Web Content Accessibility Guidelines 2.0) and ATAG 1.0 [2] (Authoring Tool Accessibility Guidelines 1.0) can guide developers in creating authoring tools that produce accessible Web content for disabled people.

Even with these guidelines and specific laws for accessibility in many countries, recent researches indicate that adherence to accessibility standards on web sites is still low [3–5]. According to these, although the version 2.0 of WCAG has been designed to make the accessibility guidelines more understandable and testable, non-experts and even experts in web accessibility have found problems in use them. Brajnik *et al.* [3] demonstrated that experienced evaluators differed in interpreting the success criteria based in the WCAG 2.0.

Our work proposes to make Web accessibility concepts more understandable to lay users that produce Web content. To do that we suggest the incorporation of accessibility guidelines in HTML WYSIWYG editors. The HTML WYSIWYG (pronounced "wiz-ee-wig") - an acronym for "what you see is what you get" - editor is a tool built-in

M. Antona and C. Stephanidis (Eds.): UAHCI 2015, Part I, LNCS 9175, pp. 221–230, 2015.
DOI: 10.1007/978-3-319-20678-3_22

the CMS that allows users to create content without HTML code knowledge and shows to these users exactly how the content should appear on screen.

For a better understanding of the objectives and results of this study, this article is organized as follows: Sect. 2 presents the related work and the advantages of the proposed concept in relation to the state-of-the-art in the field. Section 3 describes the methodology used in the design of the proposed HTML WYSIWYG editor interface. Section 4 presents the results of a preliminary evaluation with target users and, finally, in Sect. 5, are shown the conclusions and future works.

2   Related Work

Accessibility guidelines is a theme often approached by researches of the Human-Computer Interaction area.

Researches show that adherence to accessibility standards is still low due to its complexity [3–5]. Even experts in web accessibility have difficulty understanding the guidelines. Brajnik et al. [3] demonstrated that even experienced evaluators differed in interpreting the success criteria based in the WCAG 2.0.

Power et al. [6] developed an empirical study of the problems encountered by 32 blind users that evaluated a set of 16 sites. One of evaluation result denoted low degree of guidelines implementation in the evaluated sites, which made the researchers concluded that web developers still have to make great efforts to create accessible sites, possibly due to the low understanding the guidelines or the lack of support tools.

Concerning evaluation of authoring tools, Bittar et al. [7] evaluated 5 desktop tools (not Web) about support they offer to Web developers in the implementation of accessibility standards. In this work were evaluated tools as Adobe Dreamweaver, Eclipse and Netbeans, which support the developer on site construction but not in content producer. The authors selected relevant guidelines from ATAG1.0 and WCAG 2.0 and evaluated the adherence of the tools. Although the work is not related to HTML WYSIWYG editors, provides an analysis methodology for the WCAG 2.0 and ATAG 1.0 standards in authoring tools.

Lopez et al. [8] presents a methodology for identifying and resolving Web accessibility issues in Content Management Systems (CMS). The methodology proposes the production of an HTML document using the CMS and then validate it with rules of WCAG and ATAG. The article mentions that HTML editors do not consider some aspects of accessibility and users can manage content without considering accessibility.

Iglesias et al. [9] compares the ability to create accessible content according to WCAG and ATAG guidelines in three different learning environments (Moodle, ATutor and Sakai). They concluded that, in practice, the creation of accessible content depends more of the experience and knowledge of the user on Web accessibility.

Developers of the Portal of Casa de Oswaldo Cruz/Oswaldo Cruz Foundation [10] and winners of Brazilian National Accessibility Award[1] [11], concluded, with their

---

[1] Awards organized by Brazilian government and W3C's local office to encourage the development of accessible websites.

experience, that is a challenge keeping site content accessible. According to them, more difficult than building an accessible site is to keep the same standard of accessibility over time, especially when the content producer has little or no knowledge of Web languages and standards, including accessibility [12].

This entire scenario reinforces the relevance in development of tools to support the construction of accessible content, especially considering the complexity of the WCAG 2.0 guidelines in contrast to the strong presence of lay users on creating web content.

3 Methodology

The study was conducted in three main stages. The first stage called Context Analysis, focused on the accessibility evaluation of the most used HTMLs Editors and its target audience. In the second, called Design, we developed a prototype in JavaScript language, considering the key features observed in the first stage. Finally, in third step, we conducted a usability evaluation in the prototype developed. All stages will be detailed below.

3.1 Context Analysis

In order to better understand the typical users of WYSIWYG editors, we designed an online questionnaire composed mainly of closed questions.

The questionnaire was answered by 15 people, including 8 women and 7 men. All participants had between 16 and 49 years old. They were asked about the Content Management System (CMS) used and results shown that the Joomla! and Wordpress were the most mentioned (80 % of responses). The user experience on this CMS's was considered medium by 86 % of participants. The main HTML editor features used by participants can be observed in Fig. 1. Although all participants have declared interest in producing Web content accessible, 56 % reported not to know accessibility guidelines. Finally, 87 % of people considered it relevant that the HTML editor could assist and provide help about how to create accessible Web content.

Next, we analyzed the adequacy of the main HTML WYSIWYG editors to WCAG 2.0 and ATAG 1.0 Guidelines. The objective was to know how HTML editors meet the accessibility requirements. We considered from the questionnaire responses that HTML WYSIWYG editors built-in in the CMSs are more accepted. By default, the editor installed in Joomla! is the TinyMCE and Visual Editor is the Wordpress default editor. Besides these, the CKEditor was also evaluated because it can be incorporated in both mentioned CMS and it is considered one of the most accessible WYSIWYG editors according to an informal web search [13–15].

After defining which WYSIWYG editors will be evaluated, we analysed the WCAG 2.0 and ATAG 1.0 Guidelines. In this study, we have identified some accessibility guidelines, those that are considered relevant for the production of Web content. For the WCAG 2.0, we selected only success criteria that the WYSIWYG editor could use to help the user to comply with them. For the ATAG 1.0 were selected guidelines related to the ability to produce accessible content by the WYSIWYG editor.

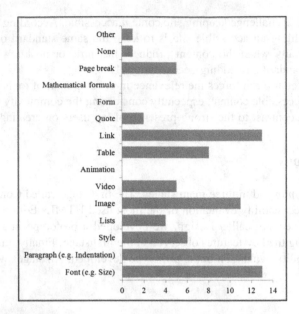

Fig. 1. HTML WYSIWYG editor resources used by participants of survey

For each question, the answers were classified as "No agreed", "Partially agreed" or "Fully agreed". This standard was used by [16], when they analyzed the accessibility of computer games. Tables 1 and 2 show the results of the evaluation of WYSIWYG editors.

CKEditor showed the best results with respect to the support and the production of accessible content (WCAG 2.0: 60 % and ATAG 1.0: 40 %). As this is an open source application, maintained by an international community [17], we considered the possibility of including accessibility features in this editor. However, due to time for implementation and the lack of qualified staff to customize WYSIWYG editor's source code, we decided to develop an independent prototype. Our proposal is that accessibility features could, subsequently, be incorporated into others HTML WYSIWYG editors.

3.2 Design

The prototype was developed in *JavaScript* and HTML languages considering the key features observed in the previous questionnaire. It can be viewed at: http://www.ifrocolorado.com.br/uff/taes/ (only in Portuguese).

It was designed to show, in real time, if a specific accessibility guideline was violated. The current prototype version is taking into account images, tables and titles tags checks. When the user is inserting content not according to the expected standard the WYSIWYG editor shows alerts at the interface including contextual examples to help content producers better understand and solve the problem. Figure 2 shows accessibility guidelines provided by the prototype.

Table 1. Editors' evaluation with the WCAG 2.0 success criteria (X = No agreed, V = Partially agreed, VV = Fully agreed).

Level	Success criteria	TinyMCE	CKEditor	Visual editor
A	Has features to insert alternate text (alt) into images? (CS 1.1.1)	V V	V V	V V
	When inserting an image, the alt attribute is inserted with a blank value (alt = "") when its content is not specified? (CS 1.1.1)	V V	V V	X
	Has resources to insert long descriptions (longdesc) in complex images? (CS 1.1.1)	X	X	X
	It checks whether semantic markup titles (H1, H2,...) is properly used? (CS 1.3.1)	X	X	X
	It uses correctly semantic markup (blockquote) in quotes? (CS 1.3.1)	V V	V V	V V
	Has the resources to set headers in tables and relate them to their content? (CS 1.3.1)	X	V	N/A
	Has the resources to enter summary (summary attribute) in tables? (CS 1.3.1)	X	V V	N/A
	Has the resourses to incorporate anchors in the content? (CS 2.4.1)	X	V V	X
AA	Has the resources to set the language (lang) in quotes? (CS 3.1.2)	X	V V	X
AAA	Has the resources to insert abbreviations (abbr)? (CS 3.1.4)	X	X	X

Table 2. Editors' evaluation with ATAG 1.0 checkpoints (X = No agreed, V = Partially agreed, VV = Fully agreed).

Level	Checkpoints	TinyMCE	CKEditor	Visual editor
A	Does not the tool generate equivalent alternatives automatically? (PV 3.4)	V V	V V	X
	Does the tool automatically generate markup (HTML) valid? (PV 2.2)	V V	V V	V V
AA	Does the tool support the production of content through context-sensitive help or documentation on creating accessible content, including examples? (PV 6.2)	X	X	X
AAA	Does the tool report the author if the marking is not produced according to the W3C specifications. (PV 2.3)	X	X	X
	Does the tool provide the author a summary of the status of the document accessibility? (PV 4.4)	X	X	X

226   H.C. Minin et al.

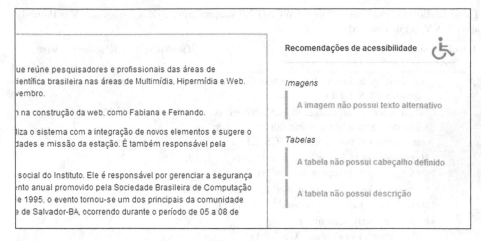

Fig. 2. Example of accessibility guidelines provided by WYSIWYG editor prototype (in Portuguese).

For the images, our prototype analyses if there is an alternative text, which is the text alternative for non-textual elements on a Web page. Every time an image is added without alternative text, the editor displays a warning to fill the text.

Tables of data should have headers and description. For non-blind users, the information contained in tables of data are easily understood visually, across columns and rows. However, for blind people, understanding and obtaining data from a table isn't an easy task [18]. In this context, headers to identify the contents of a given table cell containing a description of its purpose and general structure are fundamental. The editor prototype alerts the user to the absence of these information.

And, finally, for the title tags, our prototype analyses whether the levels of title were specified correctly and alert if there is any hierarchy violation. For example, if a user selects a level 3 title tag in the middle of a text only to create a paragraph with letters larger than the other, without having defined title tags levels 1 and 2 before, the prototype will warning.

For all three situations, help resources will be provided with examples of how to meet the guidelines. Figure 3 illustrates the help feature relating to the image description.

At the end of the creating content process, if user decided for not adjust the items indicated by the editor and try to save the work, a warning appears on the screen asking if the user really wants to save without correcting accessibility issues detected.

3.3   Evaluation

Usability tests was used as evaluation methodology, from Think-Aloud technique proposed by [19]. The objective of the evaluation was assess whether the accessibility features provided by the prototype helped the content producers on creation of accessible Web content.

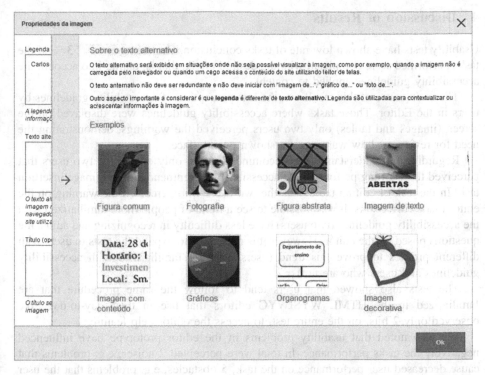

Fig. 3. Help feature with examples of alternative text (in Portuguese)

Five persons participated of usability test: 3 men and 2 women with an average age of 33 years, among them journalists and secretaries. Four of five participants self-declared as graduate degree and reported having more than 5 years of experience with web content production. The participants highlighted that "font", "tables" and "images" are the more used HTML WYSIWYG editor's resources by them. Three of five participants indicated do not have knowledge of Web content accessibility guidelines.

The test consisted of three tasks related to creation of textual content, content with images, texts with table of data and texts with well defined titles hierarchy. In every task, the participant should insert a pre-defined content in the editor. When the texts were long or had associated images, it was supplied by an appraiser to facilitate the activity execution. It was expected that participants would use the accessibility guidelines supplied by the editor to create accessible content, so these guidelines were not included in the material provided by appraiser. Upon completion of each task, the user was directed to press the "Save" button and call the appraiser.

After the usability testing, users completed a satisfaction questionnaire which contained a set of questions based on the System Usability Scale methodology (SUS) [20] and other questions related to the editor accessibility features.

4   Discussion of Results

Usability tests have shown low rate of tasks conclusion. On average, only 53 % of the tasks performed were completed with the desired effect, that is, taking into account the accessibility guidelines applied to content.

The main cause of this result was the low perception of accessibility guidelines by users in the Editor. Those tasks where accessibility guidelines were displayed on the screen (images and tables) only two users perceived the warnings, demonstrating the need for review of how warnings are shown on interface.

Regarding the understanding of recommendations, only one of the two users that perceived the warning performed the accessibility recommendation on image insertion task. In the task of editing table data, the two users who perceived the warning on the editor made corrections. It was possible to see a trend of people more familiarized with the accessibility guidelines (two users) have less difficulty in recognizing and adjust the questions posed by the editor. However it is necessary to expand the tests to users with different profiles to prove this trend (users who are familiarized with accessibility guidelines and users who are not).

The tests also showed that users tend to follow the same procedure that are familiarized in the HTML WYSIWYG editors that use in their day-to-day. We observed only 2 hits, on the entire test, to access the editor help feature.

We also noted that usability problems in the editor prototype have influenced negatively the tasks performance. In total were perceived 2 noises, e.g. problems that cause decreased user performance on the task, 5 obstacles, e.g. problems that the user experiences a few times but eventually overcome them and 2 barriers, that means problems that user can't overcome. Because of these problems, 20 % of the task executions were not completed.

The post-test questionnaire indicated a level of satisfaction of 68.1 points in the SUS scale, which is considered slightly below the average of 68.2 points to Web interfaces, according to the Usability Professionals Association [21]. Participants who perceived accessibility guidelines classified as satisfactory the quality of guidelines and stated that the recommendations brought much contribution to their learning on Web accessibility theme.

5   Final Remarks and Future Works

Taking into account that 40 % of users did not perceive the accessibility recommendations it is necessary to rethink the way that the editor is delivering the warnings at the interface. The authors believe due the fact that the equipment used in the test has widescreen may have contributed to this result. At this point, is needed a further investigation of how the user's visual attention behaves in HTML WYSIWYG editors.

Even with the low percentage of recommendations perception, 75 % of users who noticed the warnings performed the corrections proposed. This finding indicates that the editor tends to meet its goal of supporting the accessible Web content creation. However, we point out that these corrections were made by users who knew, even superficially, the WCAG 2.0 recommendations.

In order to improve the tests results we are adjusting the usability problems detected to submit it to new tests, increasing the number of participants and dividing them into two distinct groups: those without knowledge about WCAG 2.0 recommendations and those that know the recommendations.

As future work, we want to expand the items checked by the editor, incorporating new accessibility guidelines and trying different kinds of alerts, with sounds and blinks for instance. Also, we intended to make the editor available as a plugin for others HTML WYSIWYG Editor and to expand the HTML editor accessibility for disabled people, since the current prototype does not consider the use by this public.

Acknowledgement. The Brazilian Students-Agreement Program Graduate (PEC-PG).

References

1. W3C: Web Content Accessibility Guidelines 2.0 (2008). http://www.w3.org/TR/WCAG20/
2. W3C: Authoring Tool Accessibility Guidelines 1.0 (2000). http://www.w3.org/TR/WAI-AUTOOLS/
3. Brajnik, G., Yesilada, Y., Harper, S.: Is accessibility conformance an elusive property? a study of validity and reliability of WCAG 2.0. ACM Trans. Access. Comput. **4**(2), 28 (2012). Article 8
4. Lazar, J., et al.: Potential pricing discrimination due to inaccessible web sites. In: Campos, P., Graham, N., Jorge, J., Nunes, N., Palanque, P., Winckler, M. (eds.) INTERACT 2011, Part I. LNCS, vol. 6946, pp. 108–114. Springer, Heidelberg (2011)
5. Hanson, V.L., Richards, J.T.: Progress on website accessibility? ACM Trans. Web **7**(1), 30 (2013). Article 2
6. Power, C., Freire, A., Petrie, H., Swallow, D.: Guidelines are only half of the story: accessibility problems encountered by blind users on the web. In: SIGCHI Conference on Human Factors in Computing Systems (CHI 2012), pp. 433–442. ACM, New York (2012)
7. Bittar, T.J., Amaral, L.A., Faria, F.B., Fortes, R.P.M.: Supporting the developer in an accessible edition of web communications: a study of five desktop tools. In: Workshop on Information Systems and Design of Communication (ISDOC 2012), pp. 3–9. ACM, New York (2012)
8. López, J.M., Pascual, A., Menduiña, C., Granollers, T.: Methodology for identifying and solving accessibility related issues in web content management system environments. In: The International Cross-Disciplinary Conference on Web Accessibility (W4A 2012), Article 32, 8 p. ACM, New York (2012)
9. Iglesias, A., Moreno, L., Martínez, P., Calvo, R.: Evaluating the accessibility of three open-source learning content management systems: a comparative study. Comput. Appl. Eng. Educ. **22**(2), 320–328 (2014)
10. Casa de Oswaldo Cruz. http://www.coc.fiocruz.br/
11. Todos @Web: Prêmio Nacional de Acessibilidade. http://premio.w3c.br/2013/
12. Sacramento, C.C., Silva, C.S., Conceição, F.I., Moraes, F.L.D., Castro, I.M., Zorzanelli, L. P., Barros, Y.S.: Portal da Casa de Oswaldo Cruz e o Prêmio Nacional de Acessibilidade na Web. In: 13th Brazilian Symposium on Human Factors in Computing Systems. Brazilian Computer Society, Foz do Iguaçu (2014)
13. 10 Best WYSIWYG Text and HTML Editors for Your Next Project. http://www.1stwebdesigner.com/design/10-best-wysiwyg-text-and-html-editors-for-your-next-project

14. Top 5 Latest Javascript and HTML5 WYSIWYG Advanced HTML Editors. http://www.typeerror.com/index.php/top-5-latest-jquery-wysiwyg-advanced-text-editors
15. 10 Best Free Javascript/jQuery WYSIWYG HTML Editors. http://medleyweb.com/resources/10-best-free-javascript-or-jquery-wysiwyg-html-editors
16. Porter, J.R., Kientz, J.A.: An empirical study of issues and barriers to mainstream video game accessibility. In: The 15th International ACM SIGACCESS Conference on Computers and Accessibility (ASSETS 2013), Article 3, 8 p. ACM, New York (2013)
17. About CKEditor. http://ckeditor.com/about
18. Modelo de Acessibilidade em Governo Eletrônico. http://emag.governoeletronico.gov.br/
19. Lewis, C.: Using the 'thinking aloud' method in cognitive interface design. Technical report, IBM, RC-9265 (1982)
20. Brooke, J.: SUS: a quick and dirty usability scale. In: Jordan, P.W., Thomas, B., McClelland, I.L., Weerdmeester, B. (eds.) Usability Evaluation in Industry, pp. 189–194. CRC Press, London (1996)
21. Bangor, A., Kortum, P., Miller, J.: Determining what individual SUS scores mean: adding an adjective rating scale. J. Usability Stud. 4(3), 114–123 (2009)

Video Accessibility on the Most Accessed Websites - A Case Study Regarding Visual Disabilities

Johana M. Rosas-Villena[✉], Bruno Ramos, Rudinei Goularte,
and Renata P.M. Fortes

Computer Science Department, Institute of Mathematics and Computer
Sciences at University of São Paulo (USP),
Av. Trabalhador São Carlense - 400, São Carlos, São Paulo, Brazil
{johana,rudinei,renata}@icmc.usp.br
brunolol@gmail.com
http://www.icmc.usp.br

Abstract. The availability of video content has increased along with the popularity of the Web due to the large amount of interactive systems and video sharing. This scenario should be carefully considered by video authors since the content needs to be accessible to a variety of final users (including people with disabilities). Although efforts have been made to improve accessibility for embedded videos on webpages, there still the need to develop accessibility solutions for video content. In this study we aim to analyze the video accessibility on the most accessed websites, identify the accessibility controls they had or not and which navigation mode they used to help people with visual disabilities. We analyze each video player of the top 50 websites to identify which controls they use. Also, we made a case study with a blind user, who was interviewed too. As results we realize that the most accessed websites are not accessible. Additionally, the blind user reported the problems he has to understand video content, to navigate through webpages and to use video players. The most accessed websites did not have accessible controls, only two sites allow to watch videos with captions. The blind user has reported main issues and barriers that he usually faced while trying to access video contents in the websites, and these comments are specially lessons that all video developers should have in mind.

Keywords: Facilitas player · Video accessibility · Blind users

1 Introduction

Every day, more and more video content is made available on the Web, driven by the popularization of interactive systems supporting video sharing (YouTube and Vimeo, for instance). In order to ensure that the IT advances allow our society to be actually inclusive, the scenario of the availability of a huge amount

© Springer International Publishing Switzerland 2015
M. Antona and C. Stephanidis (Eds.): UAHCI 2015, Part I, LNCS 9175, pp. 231–241, 2015.
DOI: 10.1007/978-3-319-20678-3_23

of video contents should be carefully considered by video authors. The content needs to be accessible to a variety of final users, including people with disabilities.

In order to improve the video interaction on the Web, mainly by people with disabilities, general guidelines were designed and published by the Web Accessibility Initiative (WAI) of W3C (World Wide Web Consortium), such as the Web Content Accessibility Guidelines (WCAG) and the User Agent Accessibility Guidelines (UAAG). ISO 9241-171:2008 provides ergonomics guidance and specifications for the design of accessible software [6]. In addition, laws and regulation were defined to protect the user rights, and people from different cultures have proposed their own recommendation like the eMag 3.1 model in Brazil [5] and the Sect. 508 in the USA [8]. The eMag refers to a set of accessibility guidelines and the ones for multimedia are specified based on success criteria of WCAG 2.0, such as:

– Provide alternatives for videos,
– Provide alternatives for audio,
– Provide audio description for prerecorded video,
– Provide audio control for any audio,
– Provide pause, stop and hide controls for any dynamic content.

The Sect. 508 presents the requirements to make the most accessible products; there are requirements for podcast, audio, videos and multimedia presentations, software to play videos, audio and multimedia, tips for implementing and key areas to test for accessibility. Also, the 21st Century Communications and Video Accessibility act, signed in October 2010 in the USA, promotes expanded access to Internet-based video programming [4].

However, although efforts have been made to improve accessibility for videos on webpages, there still the need to develop accessibility solutions for video content.

In this study we aim to analyze the video accessibility on the most accessed websites. We searched websites that play videos into the top fifty (50) websites, the most accessed ones according to www.Alexa.com; navigating the selected sites with video content, issues like how many steps are necessary to achieve the video were examined and the barriers identified, regarding to each type of deficiency.

Given this context, we have identified the key aspects that influence people with disabilities to interact with video. In this investigation we conducted a case study to understand how a person with visual disabilities might use a resource of assistive technology or another means to:

1. Watch and comprehend video content;
2. Accomplish tasks, related to video players, and
3. Recover from task failures using workarounds.

We reported the problems and situations that the blind user has faced when watching video content on some of the websites. As a result, we have summarized a set of problems found in the websites.

The paper is organized as follows: Sect. 2 presents the video accessibility on the most accessed websites; Sect. 3 addresses the case study with a blind user; finally, Sect. 4 concludes the paper and suggests future work.

2   Video Accessibility on the Most Accessed Websites

In this section, we present an analysis of video's accessibility on the most accessed websites. The analysis aimed to identify the usual resources that websites implement to help people with disabilities.

We started by making a search in www.Alexa.com [2] website looking for clues about how video accessibility is being approached. Alexa website provides web analytics services as a global traffic rank, measuring how a website is doing relative to all other sites on the Web over the past 3 months. We analyzed the top 50 most accessed websites.

From those 50 websites, 34 were excluded from further analysis because they did not show any video or because the language was different from English, Spanish or Portuguese. Other 6 sites (Twitter, Linkedin, Blogspot, Hao123, Wordpress and Reddit) were also excluded because they show videos hosted in other sites like YouTube or Vimeo.

The 10 remaining websites were selected - they allow watch or upload videos (Facebook, YouTube, Yahoo, Vk, Msn, Instagram, Tumblr, Apple, Xvideos and Microsoft). All of them present play and pause controls. Three of them (Instagram, Tumblr and Microsoft) do not have volume control. Only one site (Microsoft) does not have screen size configuration. Currently, Microsoft only has two basic functionalities: play and pause. There are four sites (YouTube, Vk, Msn, Xvideos) that have quality configuration.

At this point it is worth to mention that more important for accessibility purposes are special features than the basic controls. The basic controls are necessary to obtain an accessible media player: play, stop, resize and volume [9]. The special features can assist to control and to understand videos [10], based on the following characteristics:

- closed captions (CC),
- highlighting,
- text configuration,
- keyboard access,
- search,
- preference settings, and
- toolbar configuration.

Other controls, such as: play/pause, rewind, forward and full screen, are still important to most users, but, do not address special needs of those with special disabilities.

Only two websites (YouTube and Yahoo) present caption configurations, even though few videos present captions. We have made five YouTube searches analyzing what proportion of the returned videos have captions or closed captions.

Table 1. Youtube videos comparison - with and without caption

Searched text	Total results	Results filtered by subtitles/CC	Percent
"Sesame street"	1,010,000	35,000	3.5 %
"Gangnam Style"	6,360,000	102,000	1.6 %
"The Simpsons"	1,190,000	15,900	1.3 %
"Barney"	1,940,000	15,100	0.8 %
"Teletubbies"	798,000	3,320	0.4 %

Table 2. Video Controls that the websites have: Facebook (S1), YouTube (S2), Yahoo (S3), Vk (S4), Msn (S5), Instagram (S6), Tumblr (S7), Apple (S8), Xvideos (S9) and Microsoft (S10)

Controls	S1	S2	S3	S4	S5	S6	S7	S8	S9	S10
Play/pause	Yes	Yes	Yes	Yes	Yes	Yes	Yes	Yes	Yes	Yes
Stop	no	no	no	no	no	no	no	no	no	no
Volume	Yes	Yes	Yes	Yes	Yes	no	no	Yes	Yes	no
Screen size	Yes	Yes	Yes	Yes	Yes	Yes	Yes	Yes	Yes	no
Quality configuration	no	Yes	no	Yes	Yes	no	no	no	Yes	no
Caption configuration	no	Yes	Yes	no	no	no	no	no	no	no
Video download	Yes	no	no	no	no	no	no	no	Yes	no
Video comments	Yes	Yes	no	Yes	no	Yes	no	no	Yes	no
Video rotation	Yes	no	no	no	no	Yes	no	no	no	no

Table 1 summarizes the results, showing that the proportion is between 0.4 and 3.5. One reason for this could be that YouTube and Yahoo need a caption file to be inserted/uploaded and common users may not know how to do such task.

As we can observe, in Table 1 only 3.5 percent of the videos have captions, although YouTube have the resource to add captions. In Table 2 we can observe that the websites developed only basic controls and social controls (comments, share, etc.) leading to lack of accessibility. Table 2 shows the video player controls provided by the 10 mentioned websites, indicating that the controls do not guarantee that the video player is accessible.

There are a wide range of diversity of people and abilities, and there are web accessibility barriers that people commonly encounter from poorly designed video players. There are many reasons why people may be experiencing varying degrees of auditory, cognitive, neurological, physical, speech, and visual disabilities. For instance, a disability may be present from birth, or occur during a person's lifetime, as a result of an illness, disease, or accident, or they may develop impairments with age. Some may not consider themselves with disabilities even if they do experience such functional limitations [1].

In these paper we focused on visual disabilities. According to [1], there are guidelines for visual disability that should be followed, such as:

- video content need to have text or audio alternatives, or an audio-description track;
- the navigation mechanisms and page functions need to be consistent, predictable and simple;
- controls and other structural elements need to have equivalent text alternatives;
- text over the video need to have enough contrast between foreground and background color combinations;
- websites, web browsers, and authoring tools need to support use of custom color combinations;
- websites, web browsers, and authoring tools need to provide full keyboard support.

There are some types of visual disabilities, as color blindness, that include difficulty distinguishing between colors such as between red and green, or between yellow and blue, and sometimes inability to perceive any color; low vision includes poor acuity (vision that is not sharp), tunnel vision (seeing only the middle of the visual field), central field loss (seeing only the edges of the visual field), and clouded vision; blindness is a substantial, uncorrectable loss of vision in both eyes and deaf-blindness is a substantial, uncorrectable visual and hearing impairments [1].

Blind people usually use screen readers to navigate on the Web. One example of screen reader is the NVDA (NonVisual Desktop Access). The screen reader has two navigation modes: the Virtual Mode and Focus Mode.

In the Virtual Mode, NVDA converts the HTML of an webpage into a flat document with semantic information. Links, headings, form fields, images and other information being spoken along with the actual text of the page. The conversion is done in the order the HTML appears in the source document loaded by the browser. Navigation through the document is possible in a character-by-character and line-by-line basis, using arrow keys or word-by-word, using the Ctrl key with the arrow keys.

In the Focus Mode, NVDA focus is set to the control at hand to interact using the keyboard, as if NVDA was not running at all. To invoke focus mode Enter must be pressed when the virtual caret is on the relevant field. Using Escape ables to switch back to reading inside the virtual document. In order to navigate the page with the Tab key, focus mode will automatically be switched on.

We chose two sites (Facebook and YouTube) to analyze the access to the videos using the two navigation modes of NVDA, and we could know which type these sites developed. To navigate in Facebook using focus mode navigation, 24 Tabs are necessary to achieve the timeline, if the video is the first publication. Twenty two (22) more Tabs are necessary to achieve the video to then press the Enter key in order to access to the video (the video plays immediately), but there is no way to pause or stop the video. Using virtual mode navigation is impossible to access to the video.

The initial YouTube focus is located in Search box. After searching a video and press the search button, sometimes the focus goes to the link bar and the screen reader reads the JavaScript code. Using focus mode navigation, we started in the search box, entering a word and pressing the search button, the next links that screen reader reads are: upload, account, what to watch, my channel, my subscriptions, history, watch later, playlists, subscriptions, browse channels and manage subscriptions. After visited these links, the number of videos is read, then each video can be visited. The virtual mode navigation is confuse, having no order to navigate.

We can observe that both sites were developed to navigate using focus mode navigation, but the blind users do not use the focus navigation, as we can explain in the next section.

3 Case Study

We conducted a case study to understand how a person with visual disabilities might use a resource of assistive technology or other means to watch and comprehend video content, accomplish tasks and recover from task failures using workarounds. Our goal is to report the problems and situations that blind users face when watching video content on the websites. We tested using Facilitas Player [7] but the user always compare with his experience.

We made an interview with David (not his real name) and after that we tested the Facilitas Player. We used Morae software[1] to record the interview and the interaction with Facilitas Player. The study protocol (482.306/2013) and informed consent form received ethics approval from the Ethic Committee on Human Experimentation. Written informed consent of the survey was obtained from the participant. Complete anonymity of the participant was assured since he is not identified in any of the reports. Participation was voluntary and it was explained that the volunteer could leave the study whenever he wanted without suffering any loss or consequence. The results will be disseminated to the participating volunteer.

To allow more contributions during the development of the accessibility features, we created a new version of Facilitas Player, and anyone can use the plugin Facilitas player to play a video on a webpage. To download Facilitas Player visit the link http://facilitasplayer.com/ and download the packages.

David is 31 years old, married, pursuing a Bachelor in Information System degree in a undergraduate distance education course. He is a blind software developer and he usually has access to the videos on the Web. The websites he is used to watch videos are YouTube and ESPN – Entertainment and Sports Programming Network – (he is interested in news about soccer). When playing videos, he explores all functionalities that he has access.

When David studied the subjects of Information System course, he developed a video player that supports closed caption functionality, used specially for people with auditory impairment.

---

[1] www.techsmith.com/morae.html - Morae is a software solution for usability testing, including recording of the screen, user, and keystrokes.

We asked him about the difficulties that he usually has when accessing videos at the Internet. He said *"Some time ago I thought YouTube invested in an interesting way to provide accessibility in a video player, but sometimes I go there to see something and it is difficult to access the videos because the player is implemented in Flash, and the controls do not have any accessibility."*

He also said *"One thing I miss in many players is the possibility of forward or rewind the video, to control the playback. For example, when you are hearing something and lose what the person spoke, you cannot listen again, then you have to click to play the video from the beginning to get to that point where the person was talking about. This is something that I miss."*

We asked about how accessibility works with closed captions, he said:

- *"If it is accessible, no, honestly I do not remember a player that it is accessible in the popular websites, which have an accessible caption for visual disabilities. The YouTube used to have that feature, I was able to read the captions, but after a while, I was not anymore. I do not know if YouTube changed his player code or if the screen reader I was using does not had support or does not work well with YouTube Flash applications. Currently I cannot access it anymore"*. He used the NVDA as screen reader.

To test, we used a researcher's notebook with Windows 8 and NVDA screen reader. He used to set up the configurations. The researcher's notebook keyboard has some differences with his notebook, it took some time to recognize the key position and when he asked about an specific key (`home` and `function` keys), we help him. He wanted to use the headphone to listen the NVDA explanations. He asked for disable the touchpad.

After that, we have tested the Facilitas Player [7] with David. The researchers explained to him all functionalities. He reported issues about navigation and the common problems founded in other websites players. We asked him to explore all Facilitas Player functionalities and comment while navigate.

About the button's name, we used the `title` attribute in Facilitas Player. David commented that using these attribute is a problem because he did not read the button's name using the arrow keys. `Title` attribute can be read only using `Tab` key. And depend on the person, `Tab` key cannot be common to use, therefore it can be confuse to understand.

David used virtual mode to navigate, for these reason he had difficulties using the Facilitas Player. He said *"when I navigate by the virtual mode the NVDA did not read button's names, he read 'button, button, button'. Then I need to navigate with Tab key to read the names. It is confuse."*

He continued testing the functionalities, but suddenly the focus disappeared from screen. We asked him which part of the website he was located. He said that he was navigating by the hidden menus (search and configuration) and the transcript. He said *"I will need to enable that option. I was just navigating with arrow keys, then eventually lost focus in that area. Are you hidden it?"*. The answer is yes, we hidden that options and we need to modify using `display:none`. He said *"the audio description is playing with the NVDA captions, that is cool, are you using aria-live?"*. The answer is yes.

We developed the audio description (AD) using aria-live property. These property indicates that an element will be updated, and describes the types of updates the user agents, assistive technologies, and user can expect from the live region [11]. The aria-live attribute is the primary determination for the order of presentation of changes to live regions.

We asked him if he was using the audio description. He said *"yes, the audio description belongs to the player or the video?"*. We explained that the audio description belongs to the player, it is a mp3 file that we created and play along with the video. To create the mp3 file we went through the following steps: (1) create the text that will be the audio description and put it on the caption file (srt) to mark the time that will be used to play the audio; (2) copy each sentence created in step 1 without the time; (3) if some word requires special pronounce, it is necessary to write as the word is spoke to guarantee the right pronunciation by the TTS; (4) use any tool to convert the text into audio, we used Soar[2] because is a free online tool that converts text into audio (mp3 file); and to finish, (5) it is necessary to edit the original audio and add the audio description audios in the correct time. The final mp3 file needs to have the same time of the video. To edit the audio we used GoldWave[3] editor.

When he navigated using virtual mode, he found the close button and he did not understand why need to close something that he did not open. This problem happen because we hidden the search and configuration windows back to the video using opacity. David commented *"If you use opacity does not work, because it is visible to the screen reader, you need to hidden by the display to really take away of the document flow"*. We used Google Chrome browser at the beggining, but after 20 min David asked if he could use the Mozilla Firefox. He said that NVDA adapts better to Mozilla Firefox because is the browser most accessible to the people with visual disabilities.

Facilitas has help functionality. We instructed David to navigate to help to read the shortcuts. He navigated to the help button and pressed enter. The help window opens over the video, but he did not detected. We asked him if he can access the help content. He said *"I can not find the help content. You told me that a window is open over the video. The sighted people saw the dialog automatically but when we navigate, we interact with the document in a linear way, for these reason, when I pressed enter on the help button I have the sensation that nothing happen. You need to put the focus on the dialog, but also the dialog need to be marked with the correct roles. You can use JQueryUI dialog, it is very well developed. There is another ARIA property called ARIA-PopUp, you set with true value and the screen reader announce that the button has a pop-up, it is intuitive"*.

He also said *"as we are visually impaired, something that is fundamental in webpages is semantics. A signed person press the button and open a window as a dialog, for these person is clear that it is a dialog, is visible to him, by the shape, the colors, the layout, behavior, finally, the person can identify it quietly. But for*

---

[2] www.soarmp3.com - Soar is a free tool to convert text to audio.

[3] www.goldwave.com - GoldWave is a tool to edit audio.

*people who are visually impaired, the screen reader always plays the semantic role
that the* html *element has in the document, for example, if this dialog has been
implemented with only a* div *, the* div *in the* html *does not have any semantic
role, then for us, when we access the button, the content appears anywhere in the
document, we can not tell that it is a dialog or it is separate from the document
in some way or that it has a specific role in the document. For these reason, the
W3C created ARIA, ARIA is actually a way to assign specific semantic roles to*
html *components".*

David could not read the help content, we said that he can press the P key
to pause and play the video. He said *"P?, interesting"*, he tested and using a lot
during the rest of the test.

We asked his opinion about the annotation functionality, he tested three
annotations and said *"very interesting, very nice, it is an interesting idea. It
facilitates a lot, help navigation, when you want to go to some point, you did not
need to control the reproduction time, you can go by the shortcut (talking about
the annotation links). This functionality is really relevant"*.

David gave us important contributions about how web can improve Facilitas player and how we can develop other accessible web applications for visual
impaired people.

Fig. 1. Facilitas Player with the answer of the task.

We prepared a task to present to David which is a question about the video
content. He needed to show the part of the video where the answer was, using any
Facilitas player control. We used the first 5:49 min of Sintel film [3], see Fig. 1.
The question was "The dragon had an injury. In which part of the body?". He
used NVDA search and we saw that the annotation "The dragon in the fair"
was selected, he accessed the annotation and played the video until it finished.
Then he said that did not find the part of the video with the dragon injury.

We said that the scene appears before of the selected annotation. He clicked on "Old town" annotation and found the answer. The researchers asked him if he was searching using NVDA or the search functionality of Facilitas. He said *"oh yes, I was using the NVDA search, it is intuitive. I went to annotations, I could have gone to the search control and search into the caption. I did not think about that"*.

4   Conclusions and Future Work

Nowadays, the context of the use of video contents is very popular in websites, and there are many attractive IT solutions that enhance and boost the potential of their dissemination. The users should be considered, with their specifics, to enjoy all the available resources and contents. However, many users have faced barriers when are interested in watching contents in a video player. For example, a blind user who would like to watch something has difficult to access videos because sometimes the video player is implemented in Flash, and the controls do not have any accessibility, since the user adopts a screen reader to have access to the video content.

Although efforts have been made to improve accessibility for videos on web-pages, there is still the need to develop accessibility solutions for video content.

In this paper we aimed to analyze the video accessibility on the most accessed websites. The selected sites, that include video content, were studied based on the issues like how many steps are necessary to achieve the video and the bar-riers identified, regarding to each type of deficiency. We analyzed the video player characteristics of the 10 most accessed websites. Only two sites have caption configuration - just one of the many necessary accessibility special fea-tures/characteristics and controls discussed at Sect. 2.

We have also developed an accessible video player called Facilitas Player following the W3C guidelines.

We described a case study that was conducted with a blind user and, regard-ing to the observed aspects, we have identified that the blind user usually navigates using virtual mode and many sites are not prepared for this type of navigation, usually they use the focus mode. A limitation of our test is that we tested only with one user with visual disability.

As future work we will improve Facilitas player functionalities, for instance, improve help functionality, facilitate navigation when the arrow keys are used and increase other functionalities, like transcript and language.

Finally, we will develop a framework with guidelines to create accessible videos.

Acknowledgements. The authors would like to thank to the program Estudantes-Convênio de Pós-Graduação PEC-PG, of CAPES/CNPq Brazil for the finantial sup-port provided to this project.

References

1. Abou-Zahra, S.: How people with disabilities use the web. http://www.w3.org/WAI/intro/people-use-web/Overview. Accessed: 28 November 2014
2. Alexa. Alexa. http://www.alexa.com/topsites. Accessed: 15 December 2014
3. Blender. Sintel. https://durian.blender.org/. Accessed: 03 December 2014
4. Federal Communications Commission. 21st Century Communications and Video Accessibility Act (CVAA). http://www.fcc.gov/guides/21st-century-communications-and-video-accessibility-act-2010. Accessed: 05 December 2014
5. eMAG. eMAG - Modelo de Acessibilidade em Governo Eletronico. http://emag.governoeletronico.gov.br/. Accessed: 19 December 2014
6. ISO. ISO 9241–171:2008, Ergonomics of human-system interaction - Part 171: Guidance on software accessibility. http://www.iso.org/iso/iso_catalogue/catalogue_tc/catalogue_detail.htm?csnumber=39080. Accessed: 08 October 2014
7. Rosas Villena, J.M., Goularte, R., de Mattos Fortes, R.P.: A user test with accessible video player looking for user experience. In: Stephanidis, C., Antona, M. (eds.) UAHCI 2014, Part IV. LNCS, vol. 8516, pp. 623–633. Springer, Heidelberg (2014)
8. Section508. Making multimedia section 508 compliant and accessible. http://www.digitalgov.gov/2013/06/26/making-multimedia-section-508-compliant-and-accessible/. Accessed: 08 October 2014
9. Rosas Villena, J.M., Ramos, B.C., Fortes, R.P.M., Goularte, R.: An accessible video player for older people: Issues from a user test. Procedia Comput. Sci. **27**, 168–175 (2014). 5th International Conference on Software Development and Technologies for Enhancing Accessibility and Fighting Info-exclusion, DSAI 2013
10. Rosas Villena, J.M., Ramos, B.C., Fortes, R.P.M., Goularte, R.: Web videos concerns about accessibility based on user centered design. Procedia Comput. Sci. **27**, 481–490 (2014). 5th International Conference on Software Development and Technologies for Enhancing Accessibility and Fighting Info-exclusion, DSAI 2013
11. W3C. Accessible rich internet applications (wai-aria) 1.0. http://www.w3.org/TR/wai-aria/states_and_properties. Accessed: 08 February 2015

The Accessibility of Web-Based Media Services – An Evaluation

Norun C. Sanderson[1(✉)], Weiqin Chen[1,2], and Siri Kessel[1]

[1] Oslo and Akershus University College of Applied Sciences, Post box 4 St.
Olavs plass, 0130 Oslo, Norway
{Norun-Christine.Sanderson,Siri.Kessel}@hioa.no,
Weiqin.Chen@uib.no
[2] University of Bergen, Post box 7802, 5020 Bergen, Norway

Abstract. Online digital media is becoming the most important arena for general information sharing and public debate. Making this arena accessible to all is essential for equal participation in today's society. However, the accessibility of web-based media services has not been given much attention despite their importance for the democracy of our society. The overall objective for this research is to gain knowledge on universal design of websites containing complex multimedia, in order to ensure equal access for diverse groups operating different devices in various situations. To achieve this objective, we have conducted heuristic evaluations of the news web pages at the Norwegian Broadcasting Corporation (NRK), the authoring tools for journalists, and focus group interviews on the accessibility of NRK.no. The preliminary results show that although participants expressed general positive attitude towards the design of NRK.no, many accessibility challenges remain to be addressed.

Keywords: Universal design · Web accessibility · Media service · Heuristic evaluation · Focus group · WCAG · ATAG

1 Introduction

In recent years, digital newspapers are outdoing the traditional newspaper [1] and digital media has become the most important arena for general information sharing and public debate. In the emerging e-society, this trend will likely continue, with even more of the media content and public debate taking place online. Thus, media plays a key role in ensuring freedom of expression, an essential foundation for democracy [2]. Consequently, ensuring accessibility for all to these digital arenas is essential for equal participation in society.

In Norway, citizens' rights to access Internet services are stated in the Discrimination and Accessibility Act (DAA) [3], the regulation for section 14 in DAA [4] and in governmental Information and Communication Technology (ICT) policy. The objective is equal access to the e-society for all citizens. The Norwegian government has allocated large funds to increase broadband coverage and improve the level of digital knowledge in the population. In 2013, 99.9 % of Norwegian households had possibilities for broadband access. Only less than 2000 households lack this opportunity [5].

© Springer International Publishing Switzerland 2015
M. Antona and C. Stephanidis (Eds.): UAHCI 2015, Part I, LNCS 9175, pp. 242–252, 2015.
DOI: 10.1007/978-3-319-20678-3_24

In primary schools as well as lower and upper secondary schools ICT skills is defined as one of five skills which form the basic conditions for learning and development in school, work and society [6]. However, despite of the fast growing e-society, little attention has thus far been paid to accessibility concerns in the arena of digital media and public debate.

NRK.no is the second biggest website in Norway [7] and the official website for the state-owned Norwegian Broadcasting Corporation (NRK) which is the largest media house in Norway. The website contains several sections, including a news section, an online TV player, radio player, and dedicated content for children. Our research focuses on the digital news section of the NRK.no. It has been conducted in cooperation with NRK New Media, the department responsible for publishing and rendering content at the NRK.no website.

We have previously published, in [8], a summary of findings from end user group interviews and heuristic evaluation of the accessibility of the content creation and management (CMS) tool, Polopoly, in NRK. The evaluation mainly used Authoring Tool Accessibility Guidelines (ATAG) 2.0, focusing on accessibility of the CMS tool for journalists, as well as to what extent it supports the authors create accessible content.

In the current paper, we present a heuristic evaluation of selected web pages on NRK.no using Web Content Accessibility Guidelines (WCAG) 2.0, i.e., from the end users' perspective, as well as elaborate and discuss our earlier findings in relation to this. In addition, we look into important considerations that need to be addressed when evaluating large and complex websites from large organizations.

The following sections are organized as follows. In Sect. 2 we describe the workflow for publishing content on NRK.no as well as the environment and applications for the publishing process. In Sect. 3, we provide a short summary of our previous research on Polopoly, approaching the publishing process from the journalists' perspective. In Sect. 4, we take the end users' perspective, presenting results from focus group interviews and heuristic evaluations of NRK.no. In Sect. 5 we discuss our findings and provide recommendations for improving the accessibility of the web sites. Finally, in Sect. 6, we conclude the paper and discuss future work.

2 NRK.no Applications and Workflow

NRK is a large organization and the website is complex, offering a wide selection of multimedia content. Several applications are part of the publishing process in addition to the CMS and rendering tools, and the process is part of a large environment, both technological and organizational. When evaluating the accessibility of NRK.no website, we need to take into consideration the framework of software tools involved in content creation and publishing, as well as the publishing process itself.

In this section, we give an overview of the workflow for publishing web content on NRK.no and the relevant software tools involved in this workflow.

2.1 Relevant NRK Applications

Two systems are used together to publish content on NRK.no: Polopoly and Panorama. Polopoly, used for content creation and content management, is an external system from Atex[1]. The users of Polopoly are mainly journalists who write articles for NRK, about 400 in total, according to NRK, producing over 250 articles daily. The Panorama rendering system, developed in-house at NRK, is used for rendering the web pages for NRK.no. Figure 1 shows an overview of the relevant applications.

Polopoly stores metadata and content (articles, media objects) in a database, while Panorama retrieves metadata and content from this database and renders the content on the web page. Thus, Panorama handles presentation and appearance of content at NRK. no, while Polopoly handles editing and managing content. In consequence, to be able to conduct a thorough evaluation using ATAG B.1, which largely concerns WCAG 2.0, we need to include Panorama in the evaluation.

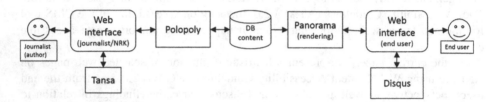

Fig. 1. Overview of environment and applications

In addition to Polopoly and Panorama, there are other applications involved in publishing content on NRK.no. These are Tansa[2] for spell checking and Disqus[3] for discussions/comments. Tansa is used as a plug-in or extension to the web browser, and does not work directly with Polopoly. Tansa is available to NRK journalists and mainly used as a spell checker. Disqus is a widely used, free community tool for handling comments. End users log in to Disqus when posting comments to articles open for discussion on NRK.no. Both Tansa and Disqus are third party tools that are used by NRK. Consequently, NRK is not responsible for the accessibility issues related to these tools. To be able to evaluate NRK.no satisfactorily, we will have to take these other applications and tools into consideration, preferably also conducting heuristic evaluation and user testing on these.

2.2 Publication Work Flow

When a journalist creates a new article item, s/he first logs on to the Polopoly web interface and creates a new article in the category where the new article is to appear, for example "Distrikt (Regional pages)" or "Viten (Knowledge)". Panorama will use this

---

[1] Atex, http://www.atex.com/.

[2] Tansa Systems AS, http://www.tansasystems.com/.

[3] Disqus, https://disqus.com/.

information to render the article using the corresponding template for the given category.

In addition to the category of the article, journalists normally provide the following elements: a headline as the main title, an alternative title to be displayed in article lists, a lead paragraph, and body text of the article. Polopoly provides a text editor for adding lead paragraph and body text. During this process of creating and writing an article, Tansa monitors the text typed into Polopoly, and discovers misspellings.

A variety of article elements may be added to an article such as audio/video objects, fact boxes, citations, images, links, and maps. When adding images, journalists may add a description of the image, which Polopoly will use to generate a caption and alternative text. The journalists also typically add their name(s). There are several other optional settings available to the journalist, such as running head, language, and geo-positioning. Once the article is ready for publishing, the journalist can choose to promote an article on the front page.

The activities of journalists in Polopoly concerns mainly adding and editing content, as well as setting options that will add metadata to the article. The page layout on NRK.no, for instance, the number of columns for a given type of article on NRK.no, is defined and decided by specialists, not journalists. Panorama renders web pages before they are sent to the browser. The pages are rendered according to predefined layout templates created for different page categories, e.g., regional pages, "Viten (Knowledge)", and "Ytring (Opinions)". This includes the placing of content as well as choice of colours, font sizes, etc. The design is responsive, thus images, for instance, are scaled on the fly.

3 Summary of Previous Research

The main objective of the evaluation reported in [8] was to discover to what extent the content management system for publishing content on NRK.no, Polopoly, is compliant to Part B of the Authoring Tool Accessibility Guidelines (ATAG 2.0). Although the rendering tool Panorama was taken into consideration where necessary, it was not fully included in the evaluation.

Our evaluation of Polopoly included the criteria in B.2, B.3, and B.4. In addition, we evaluated B.1.2.2 (Copy-Paste Inside Authoring Tool) and B.1.2.4 (Text Alternatives for Non-Text Content are Preserved) which we considered relevant. In total, 26 success criteria were evaluated. Our findings show that Polopoly is not compliant to most of the criteria. Furthermore, we found that Polopoly does not provide enough support for journalists to create accessible content. For example, Polopoly does not have an option to add alternative text to pictures. Instead, Panorama combines caption and title of the picture, name of photographer and bureau as the alternative text for the picture. This creates an unnecessarily long and seldom relevant description.

Experiences and results from this evaluation show that in order to further investigate the accessibility of NRK.no it is necessary to conduct heuristic evaluation and user testing on the web pages.

4 Evaluating the Accessibility of NRK.no

For this evaluation we have carefully selected a set of web pages at NRK.no. These pages are "Ytring (Opinions)", "Distrikt (Regional pages)", "Nyheter Beta (News Beta)", "Kultur (Culture)", and "Viten (Knowledge)". The content for these pages is edited in Polopoly and rendered by Panorama as described earlier. The front page has not been included in our evaluations, as NRK uses a different tool for editing this page.

In the following, we first present the focus group interviews, a brief summary published in [8], and then we describe the heuristic evaluation of the selected pages based on WCAG 2.0.

4.1 Focus Group Interviews

Participants and Procedure. In order to ensure that the participants represented the diversity of potential users, we recruited participants through various non-governmental and non-profit organisations. The participants sampled a broad variety in age, education level and work experience. The groups of participants included: (1) people with visual impairment, including blind and partially sighted, (2) people with hearing impairment, including hard of hearing and sign language users, (3) people with cognitive impairment, (4) people with foreign language background, (5) elderly/seniors, and (6) volunteers in an organisation for underprivileged people. In total 19 participants took part in the interviews. The participants were given a list of links to selected web pages on NRK.no in advance so they could prepare for the group interviews.

Five focus group interviews were conducted in March 2014. Two researchers from the project were present: one facilitating the focus group interview and the other observing and taking notes. The interview sessions were audio recorded in agreement with NSD[4] requirements.

The interview sessions were organised into two main sessions. The first session focused on the participants' general use of Internet and NRK.no, personal preferences and use of devices. The second focused specifically on their experiences with different functions and design of NRK.no, including general design, structure, layout, navigation, text content, language, multimedia, and debate. For each topic, the interview facilitator opened the discussion with appropriate questions and/or showed examples from the website.

Findings. From the interviews, it is clear that users experience a variety of challenges when using NRK.no. Some identified issues were common across several groups of participants. Regarding structure, layout and design, all groups of participants expressed they experienced navigation elements to be generally adequate.

Despite of the general positive experience, there were several challenges reported in relation to navigation, particularly when using a screen reader or navigating by keyboard. The main issues include menu items not accessible to the screen reader, menu

---

[4] NSD: Norsk Samfunnsvitenskapelig Datatjeneste (Norwegian Social Science Data Services), http://www.nsd.uib.no/.

items that do not expand, submenus that cannot be reached using tabulator, unlabelled buttons, and buttons named "…". Other navigation issues not related to screen readers or keyboard navigation include inconsistent use of names in menus and page title, and inconsistent use of county names in the pages for regional news. The main challenges experienced in relation to videos include the lack of subtitles, and play-buttons not being accessible to screen readers or not visible when using inverted colours/high contrast.

Regarding the use of colours and colour contrast, the challenges concern the use of soft colours, i.e., colours of low saturation, which results in poor contrast and makes it difficult to perceive some elements or areas on the page. This was particularly evident for participants that need to use settings for high contrast or inverted colours. Some participants reported that setting options in the Operative System (OS) for high contrast or inverted colours might even aggravate this effect, so that some elements cannot be seen at all unless moving the mouse over it. Examples of such elements are play-arrows, menu-arrows, and logos. Apart from these issues, participants reported that using high contrast settings and inverted colours (OS settings) works relatively well with NRK.no.

Personal settings allowing users to specify their preferences were communicated as an important feature by several groups of participants. Some of the visually impaired participants reported they were dependent on such settings.

Another comment, common among the participants, is that the debate opportunities were not widely used by the groups. Most people we interviewed had never posted any comments, although some had read posts from other commenters. Participants using screen readers reported that comments posted in discussions were not accessible to screen readers.

Individual groups of users also reported other important issues. For example, participants with visual impairments reported missing keyboard navigation support for menu items and videos, where the play button was not accessible through keyboard. Their comments also included occasions of the image text (caption or alternative text) being needlessly long and sometimes even irrelevant to the image content or containing links. The group of hearing impaired participants commented on the importance of showing whether a video has captions or not, which would save users the frustration of downloading and open a video just to find out it does not have captions. Other participants reported inconsistent use of font or text style for the same text element in some articles, e.g., using italics or quotation marks (" ") for direct quotation. The elderly users found that some icons were not easily recognizable and that for some menus, the element names and their corresponding page titles were not consistent with each other.

Although the identified issues did not completely prevent individual participants from using NRK.no, they resulted in low efficiency and sometimes created confusion, frustration and irritation. Addressing these issues will likely improve the overall user experience of the NRK.no webpages.

4.2   Heuristic Evaluation Using WCAG 2.0

The purpose of WCAG 2.0 is to ensure accessible web content. It consists of four principles, each organised into a set of guidelines with success criteria that has to be fulfilled for conformance.

The evaluation of selected pages at NRK.no took place in May/June 2014. The pages included in the evaluation were the same as in the focus interviews. The evaluation was conducted using an HP Laptop (Intel Core i5 vPro) or a PC (Intel i3), both with Windows 7 operative system, Firefox Version 27/28 browser, ZoomText 10 and Infovox screen reader. ZoomText and Infovox are used regularly by one of the researchers who conducted the evaluation.

All 61 success criteria in WCAG 2.0 have been evaluated. Nine criteria were met, 43 criteria were found not met, and the remaining nine were not applicable since NRK.no does not cover all the features in WCAG 2.0. Table 1 shows the results from the evaluation.

In particular, news headings generally appear after images and captions, which makes the content difficult to follow, and time-consuming to find what one is looking for. In addition, the top image of articles is so huge that only a part of it is shown in the browser window. This is particularly confusing for orientation and navigation (WCAG 3.2.3).

The identified navigation issues related to Guideline 2.4 may be regarded as severe. Only two out of the 10 success criteria are met: one in four at level A and one in three at level AA. Issues such as lack of bypass blocks, links with uninformative names, inconsistent use of headings and heading levels, almost invisible focus indicators, and lack of breadcrumb tails make the pages in NRK.no difficult for users to navigate, find content, and determine where they are.

Another issue that needs to be highlighted is Readability (Guideline 3.1). NRK.no does not have a "Plain Language" text alternative. Nor does it have mechanisms for explaining unusual words and abbreviations or possibilities for pronunciation of word with ambiguous meanings.

As Table 1 shows, the selected pages in NRK.no do not fully comply with WCAG 2.0. Since the selected pages are representative in NRK.no, we can assume that the results are valid for the whole NRK.no website. The findings clearly indicate that much work needs to be done in order for NRK.no to be fully accessible. It is, however, important to note that due to NRK's continuous effort in improving their websites, some of the issues identified in the heuristic evaluation have already been rectified. For example, dropdown menus can now be accessed by keyboard (Guideline 2.1), page sections are adjustable to screen size when zooming with bowser (Guideline 1.4), and an informative label has been added to the search field (Guideline 3.3).

5   Discussion and Recommendations

From the focus group interviews and the heuristic evaluation using WCAG 2.0, we can see that issues related to image captions and alternative text are experienced by users as sometimes long and even irrelevant to the image content. The selected pages in NRK.no are not compliant to WCAG 2.0 Guideline 1.1 (Text alternatives).

When considering how image captions and alternative text are created using Polopoly and rendered through the rendering tool Panorama, and relating this to our evaluation of the CMS Polopoly and the NRK publishing process, we may find a possible explanation. Our heuristic evaluation using ATAG 2.0 show that Polopoly is

Table 1. Results from heuristic evaluation with WCAG2.0

Guidelines	Comments
1.1 Text alternatives	• Lack of or inappropriate text descriptions for images, audios and videos
1.2 Time-based media	• Lack of or inappropriate text descriptions, captions, or sign language description for pre-recorded time-based media
1.3 Adaptable	• Much use of coding for structure of content, also within tables
	• Programmatically incorrect reading sequence
	• Inconsistent use of heading and title styles
	• Lack of semantic structure in "Ytring (Opinions)"
1.4 Distinguishable	• Text links do not fulfil the contrast requirement
	• No possibility to resize text
	• No option for choosing foreground and background colours
	• Page sections do not adjust to screen size when resized without assistive technology
2.1 Keyboard accessible	• Some functions are not accessible by only keyboard
	• Keyboard trap exists in YouTube videos
2.2 Enough time	• No possibility for users to control the frequency of the automatic update of NRK.no
2.3 Seizures	• One blinking (red) icon exists and lasts longer than one second. The frequency seems to be less than three times per second
2.4 Navigable	• Pages have descriptive titles
	• No bypass blocks
	• Links are sometimes not informative and purpose not clear
	• Inconsistent use of headings and heading levels
	• Keyboard focus indicators are hardly visible
	• No breadcrumb trail
3.1 Readable	• Code for language is specified with "lang" attribute
	• No mechanisms for explanation of unusual words, abbreviations
	• No mechanisms for pronunciation of word with ambiguous meanings
	• No "Plain Language" alternative for textual content
3.2 Predictable	• Cursor may automatically activate dropdown menus in the menu bar
	• Some links automatically change names without notification
	• Pages automatically update without warning
3.3 Input assistance	• Input fields have no spelling check
	• Search field lacks of descriptive title
4.1 Compatible	• Pages tested with W3C Markup Validator show from 16 to 64 errors
	• Not all user interface components have names, roles or value.

not compliant to criteria B.1.2.4 (Text Alternatives for Non-Text Content are Preserved) and B.2.2.1 (Accessible Option Prominence). Although Polopoly does allow journalists to add a description for an image, the CMS generates both an alternative text and an image caption from this description. It does not allow journalists to distinguish between an alternative text and an image caption. Nor does it allow them to add a dedicated alternative text. Furthermore, when rendered, Panorama creates another yet different alternative text by combining the generated image caption, photographer's name, and the name of the photo bureau into an "associated text", ignoring the original alternative text altogether. Consequently, the combination of Polopoly and Panorama does not give journalists any real opportunity to distinguish between captions and alternative text for images. Nor do they allow them to create separate image caption and alternative text.

Most participants in the focus group interviews commended the quality of article content in NRK.no and there were no comments regarding the use of foreign words or particular challenges regarding textual content. According to the 2013 OECD PIAAC survey of adult skills, Norway scores significantly higher than OECD average in literacy in adults aged 16-65, and the mean score is high both among immigrants and across different educational levels in the population [9]. Further, only 9.3 % of the adult population in Norway has a literacy score of Level 1 in literacy proficiency. Level 1 literacy proficiency equals to being able to read relatively short digital or printed texts to locate a single piece of information that is identical or synonymous with information given in a question or directive [10]. Nevertheless, many people in the general population will benefit from content, especially text, designed to be easy to understand and read, particularly people with cognitive disabilities, people with low language skills, and people with auditory disabilities that may impact reading and perception of written language [11]. Considering possibilities in Tansa for customising dictionaries and looking at text in context, we presume that using these functions in Tansa may increase the accessibility and usability of published textual content.

Participants who are screen reader users in the focus group interviews commented that participating in discussions on NRK.no is extremely difficult, if not impossible, when one cannot see the screen visually. As mentioned in Sect. 2, NRK.no uses Disqus as a plug-in discussion tool. Disqus is written in JavaScript and works on platforms that can handle JavaScript. However, a known drawback when using JavaScript is that it may introduce accessibility problems unless measures are taken to ensure that generated content and functionality are accessible to assistive technologies.

Subtitles on NRK videos is on the wishlist of many participants, including the deaf, hard of hearing, elderly, dyslectics, immigrants, and "language trainers", regardless of noisy or quiet environments. As many of the posted videos are produced for TV and have captions when shown on TV, we assume that the subtitles issues for the videos on NRK.no can be easily solved technically. It is therefore difficult to understand why the videos do not have subtitles when posted at NRK.no. Today, more and more information is conveyed through videos. Therefore giving all users and potential users of NRK.no possible alternatives for supplementary information is of great importance. The deaf and hard of hearing participants suggsted that marking subtitled videos with a dedicated symbol would save them from having to download the video in order to find out whether it has subtitle.

Participants in the focus group interviews, particularly seniors, commented that they found inconsistent use of names across menu elements and page titles both annoying and confusing. One such example is the menu element named "Oslo" which takes the user to a regional page titled "Østlandssendingen". Consistency, which relates to WCAG 2.0 Guidelines 2.4 and 3.2, is an important principle for ensuring that the user knows where s/he is and where to find content. We therefore recommend that NRK ensure consistency in their use of names across menu elements and page titles.

As we have shown, Polopoly and Panorama in combination can cause some of the issues identified in NRK.no, and the use of third party application such as Disqus may influence users' possibility to take part in discussions. Thus it becomes important to take the context, including the environment and applications, as well as the publishing process itself into consideration when evaluating large and complex websites in large organizations, as accessibility issues may be introduced during the publishing process itself, and third party applications may influence the accessibility of the content presented to end users.

6 Conclusion and Future Work

In this research we have conducted heuristic evaluations of the content creation and management (CMS) tool, Polopoly and selected web pages on NRK.no, as well as focus group interviews with diverse user groups. Results from our evaluations show that Polopoly is not compliant with ATAG 2.0 Part B, and that the evaluated pages on NRK.no not fully compliant with WCAG 2.0. We have learned that evaluating a web site containing complex multimedia requires taking the larger environment of applications into consideration, including the publishing process workflow, as these may influence accessibility, usability, and user experience. Further, results from conducted focus group interviews have shown that users in general have positive attitudes towards NRK.no, despite several groups of users experiencing challenges when operating and using content on the website.

NRK has a long history of accessibility awareness and focus on offering accessible content, and they are continually working on improving accessibility of their website and media services. Most recently NRK TV has implemented visual interpretation (audio description) of films and audio caption (captions read by synthetic speech). The technology and solutions could be transferred to NRK.no, thus improve accessibility of NRK.no.

Findings from our research have provided recommendations for improving the accessibility. The results have also indicated that many challenges remain and further research is necessary. In order to gain deeper insight into how end users experience the accessibility of NRK.no, we are currently performing user testing of the same selected pages with the same groups of people who participated in the focus group interviews. We have also recruited people with mild intellectual disability, as well as elderly (age 70 +) who are at the beginning stage of dementia.

To learn more about how NRK can better support the production of universally designed web content, future research needs to include the following aspects:

Journalists' Perspective: we need to understand how the content creation tool can support the creation of accessible content without disturbing the journalists' workflow. We also need to understand how increased awareness among journalists about how to create accessible content can be achieved through training and increased knowledge.

The Rendering Process: A closer study of how Polopoly and Panorama works together, particularly the automatic changes made by the rendering tool, Panorama, as some of the issues resulting in lack of compliance to WCAG 2.0 success criteria seem to be introduced in rendering process.

Other Applications: We need to study how the use of Tansa may affect the published content, as well as how NRK can utilise Tansa better for improving accessibility and usability of the web content. The tool used for comments, Disqus, strongly influences users' opportunity to participate in any discussions at NRK.no, and therefore needs to be evaluated for accessibility issues.

Acknowledgement. This project is funded by The Delta Centre on behalf of the Norwegian Ministry of Children, Equality and Social Inclusion. We would like to thank Helge Kaasin and NRK for their collaboration and support. We would also like to thank all the participants for their valuable feedback.

References

1. Medienorge. http://medienorge.uib.no/statistikk/medium/avis/360. Accessed 10 Feb 2015
2. European Convention on Human Rights. Article 10
3. LOV-2013-06-21-61, Barne-, Likestillings- og Inkluderingsdepartementet (in Norwegian)
4. FOR-2013-06-21-732, Kommunal- og moderniseringsdepartementet (in Norwegian)
5. NEXiA: Bredbåndsdekning 2013, p. 12. Fornyings-, administrasjons- og kirkedepartementet (2013). https://www.regjeringen.no/globalassets/upload/fad/vedlegg/ikt-politikk/bredband sdekning_2013.pdf (in Norwegian)
6. Utdanningsdirektoratet: Rammeverk for grunnleggende ferdigheter, P3. Kunnskaps departementet (2012). http://www.udir.no/Upload/larerplaner/lareplangrupper/RAMMEVERK_grf_2012.pdf (in Norwegian)
7. Fordal, J.A.: A Gigantic Small Broadcaster, http://www.nrk.no/about/a-gigantic-small-broadcaster-1.3698462. Accessed 5 Jan 2015
8. Kessel, S., Sanderson, N., Chen, W.: Public media on the web for everyone – an evaluation of the Norwegian broadcasting cooperation's website. In: Stephanidis, C. (ed.) HCI 2014, Part II. CCIS, vol. 435, pp. 32–36. Springer, Heidelberg (2014)
9. OECD Skills Survey: Country specific-material. http://www.oecd.org/site/piaac/country-specific-material.htm. Accessed 19 Feb 2015
10. OECD: OECD: Skills Outlook 2013 First Results from the Survey of Adult Skills. OECD Publishing, Paris (2013). doi:http://dx.doi.org/10.1787/9789264204256-en
11. Miesenberger, K., Petz, A.: Easy to read on the web – state of the art and research directions. Procedia Comput. Sci. **27**, 318–326 (2014)

Interactive Software Technology for Deaf Users: Mapping the HCI Research Landscape that Focuses on Accessibility

Alexandros Yeratziotis[✉] and Panayiotis Zaphiris

Department of Multimedia and Graphics Arts, Cyprus University of Technology,
Lemesos, Cyprus
{alexis,pzaphiri}@cyprusinteractionlab.com

Abstract. The purpose of this paper is to chart research developments in HCI literature that focuses on accessibility for the deaf user group. A map for this particular landscape has been constructed based on a review of the four most relevant sources in HCI that focuses on accessibility, from 2000 to 2013. The map describes topics of research that are covered under the umbrella of Interactive Software Technology (IST) for deaf users in HCI literature that focuses on accessibility. To construct the map and identify these topics a systematic approach was applied, involving a number of stages and employing several research methods (literature review, focus group and card sorting). The resulting map, which underwent three revisions, consists of 23 code categories in total: 3 main categories, 8 subcategories, 7 second-level subcategories and 5 third-level subcategories. This paper can act as a guide for other researchers interested in conducting research within this landscape.

Keywords: Map · Deaf user · HCI · Accessibility · Interactive software technology

1 Introduction

Deaf people have been at an unfair disadvantage with regards to education, employment and access to technology [1]. This is due to the fact that limited interactive technologies address usability and accessibility concerns, stemming mainly from the literacy-related barrier they experience. Accessing content on the Internet is problematic for many deaf people since as pupils, many leave school with severe reading and writing inadequacies [2]. Equally important is the fact that the first language for many deaf people is the sign language of their country and not the oral one [2, 3]. Providing information in sign language can alleviate these types of barriers and impact positively in the integration of deaf people into the IT society [2]. In an attempt to make deaf people full citizens, the European Union of the Deaf (EUD) declares three objectives [1]: recognition of the right to use sign language, the use of communication and information for empowerment, and equality in education and employment. Support for the right to use sign language is recognized in international and European legal documents too, such as the Brussels Declaration on Sign Languages in the EU (2010) and the United Nation Convention on the Rights of Persons with Disabilities (2006) [2].

© Springer International Publishing Switzerland 2015
M. Antona and C. Stephanidis (Eds.): UAHCI 2015, Part I, LNCS 9175, pp. 253–264, 2015.
DOI: 10.1007/978-3-319-20678-3_25

Using websites and online services requires a level of literacy and technology competency. Literacy issues and content not being presented in sign language are just two reasons that prevent many deaf people from having positive user experiences when accessing technology. Several past projects that have investigated such issues are Dicta-Sign, eSign, ViSiCAST and the South African Sign Language (SASL) machine translation project of Stellenbosch University [4]. The need for more research that can lead to the design and development of more accessible and usable IST for deaf users is stressed [2]. A definitive description of published manuscripts in the field of IST for deaf users in the discipline of HCI that focuses on accessibility will contribute in classifying topics that new researchers can undertake within the field. In support of this classification, this paper will address the following objectives:

1. Construct a map of existing research topics in the field of IST for deaf users in the discipline of HCI that focuses on accessibility
2. Summarize the purpose of each code category of the map
3. Identify the least and most researched topics of the map

2   Method

A validated and existing systematic approach was applied to construct the map of IST for deaf users in the discipline of HCI that focuses on accessibility (see Fig. 1).

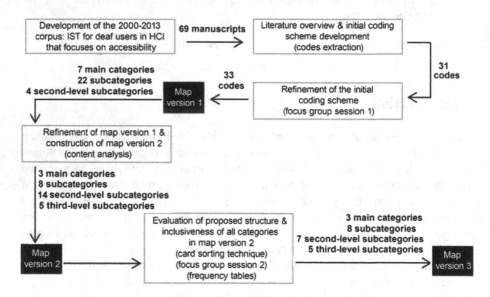

Fig. 1. The process adopted for the construction of the map

The approach has been applied to other areas before, such as to develop web design guidelines for the elderly [5] and to construct a map for the field of Computer Assisted Language Learning [6]. Figure 1 presents the process supporting the approach that was adopted to construct the map for this study. A more detailed discussion on each stage of the process and how it was considered in this study follows:

Stage 1: Build the Corpus. According to [6] it is in this stage that a corpus of literature for the particular research field must be determined. This corpus will be thoroughly reviewed in order to construct the map for the field under investigation. The corpus in this study included 69 manuscripts that were published from 2000 to 2013 and which had a specific focus on IST for deaf users. All main sources of HCI literature that focuses on accessibility were studied. The small number of manuscripts can be considered as an indication that this area of research is understudied. Four main research sources devoted to the field of HCI with a focus on accessibility were reviewed to select the manuscripts for inclusion into the corpus. The manuscripts were extracted from two journals and two conferences. These included the journals' of Universal Access in the Information Society (UAIS) and the ACM Transactions on Accessible Computing (TACCESS). Conferences that were reviewed are the ACM CHI Conference on Human Factors in Computing Systems and the ASSETS conference. The distribution of manuscripts from the four sources is presented in Table 1. The corpus does not include introductions to special issues or editorials.

Table 1. Distribution of manuscripts based on source

Journal/conference title	Number of manuscripts
UAIS	18
TACCESS	6
CHI	9
ASSETS	36
Total number of manuscripts	69

Stage 2: Literature Overview and Initial Coding Scheme Development. According to [6] it is in this stage that an overview of the built corpus, which was determined in stage 1, is conducted to elicit basic themes and to develop a coding scheme with code categories. The overview is based on reviewing the title, keywords and abstract from all the manuscripts of the corpus. To elicit the basic themes, an initial overview of the corpus's manuscripts was conducted by the authors. The overview was based on extracting codes from the title, abstract and keywords of each manuscript. The output from this stage was the identification of 31 keywords, which represent the basic themes discussed in the manuscripts of the corpus. The initial coding scheme was consequently developed, consisting of 31 code categories.

Stage 3: Refinement of the Initial Coding Scheme. According to [6] it is in this stage that a focus group session is conducted to verify, expand or limit the initial coding scheme that was created in stage 2. A selection of manuscripts from the corpus are reviewed, discussed and classified within existing or new code categories, which are created if required. The outcome from the focus group session is a revised coding scheme. A focus group session was conducted to refine the initial coding scheme that consisted of the 31 code categories, which were extracted from the initial overview conducted in stage 2. Three independent HCI and accessibility experts participated in this focus group session. The experts were required to randomly select twelve manuscripts (17 %) from the indexed corpus. Time was provided to the experts to read the title, abstract and keywords from a selected manuscript. After overviewing a manuscript, consensus-based discussions followed between experts and the moderator, who was facilitating the discussions. The consensus-based discussions focused on the classification of a selected manuscript into an existing code category or if necessary into a new code category that would need to be established during the focus group session. If classification could not be determined or consensus not be agreed by reading the title, abstract and keywords of a selected manuscript, its introduction and conclusion sections were then also reviewed. This process was followed twelve times, in order to classify each selected manuscript into a code category. A total of 2 new code categories were added during manuscript classification, increasing the total number of code categories from 31 in the initial coding scheme to 33 in the revised coding scheme. The revised coding scheme was the next topic of discussion. In order to proceed from the revised coding scheme in this stage to the construction of the first version of the map in the next stage, the 33 code categories had to be organized into logical structures. The construction of logical structures for the code categories was likewise determined in the focus group session with the experts. Code categories were required to be divided into categories and subcategories. The division of code categories was imposed by the data (manuscripts). Subcategories are defined when differences with other subcategories in the same main category are apparent.

Stage 4: Construction of Map Version 1. According to [6] it is in this stage that the first version of a map is constructed. The structure of the map is based on the revised coding scheme, which was the outcome of stage 3. By constructing logical structures from the code categories of the revised coding scheme in stage 3, it is now possible to construct the first version of the map in this stage. The first version of the map for this study consists of 7 main categories, 22 subcategories and 4 second-level subcategories. The map must be organized in a manner that complies with two criteria: internal homogeneity within the generated categories and external heterogeneity among categories [6]. Reference to code categories in the focus group sessions includes main categories and all levels of subcategories.

Stage 5: Refinement of Map Version 1 and Construction of Map Version 2. According to [6] it is in this stage that the first version of the map, which was created in stage 4, is revised and assessed for its meaningfulness and accuracy. It is therefore necessary to work back and forth between the manuscripts and conduct a content analysis to ensure that all manuscripts can be assigned to the map's categories/subcategories (the logical structures of the code categories). In addition to title, abstract and keywords that were reviewed in stage 2, it is also required to comprehensively review the introduction, conclusion and future implications (if any) sections of each manuscript during this stage. An important factor contributing to classification is saturation; the classification of the corpus manuscripts into code categories without incongruity [6]. The outcome from the refinement of the first version of the map is map version 2. Based on results collected from stages 3 and 4, refinements were made to the first version of the map. Meaningfulness and accuracy of categories and all levels of subcategories for the first version of the map were further examined by classifying all the corpus manuscripts within these. As previously mentioned, it was necessary to work back and forth between the manuscripts and the map. A content analysis that included a review of the introduction, conclusion and future work (if any) sections of all manuscripts was conducted. Following the content analysis, each manuscript had to be classified into a single code category of the map. Therefore, in order to assign a manuscript to a single code category, it is imperative to consider the objective of the manuscript. This provided a means to determine its main focus and to likewise reach saturation, by classifying all manuscripts of the corpus into a single code category. The second version of the map is the outcome of refinements done to the first version of the map (see Table 2).

Stage 6: Evaluation of the Proposed Structure and Inclusiveness of all Categories in Map Version 2. According to [6] it is in this stage that the card sorting technique is applied to independently cross-check the code categories of the second version of the map, which was created in stage 5. Furthermore, it also assists in the procedure of implementing new refinements to the map (if necessary). A new panel of experts will participate in the card sorting technique. Disagreements on classification (if any) are resolved by discussing classification differences and identifying the purpose and contribution of the manuscripts until consensus can be reached. The second version of the map was evaluated by applying the card sorting technique. In addition, to ensure the validity of the results, a second focus group session was also conducted to further refine the second version of the map on the basis of cross-checking and reflective discussions. Frequency tables were also applied to summarise the experts' classifications as frequency counts and percentages. They are the simplest method for representing categorical and ordinal data. They are commonly used as exploratory procedures, with an attempt to establish how the different categories of values are distributed within the sample. Similar to the first focus group session that was conducted in stage 3, three new independent experts in HCI and accessibility were participating in this stage too. They were required to randomly select fifteen manuscripts (21 %) from the indexed corpus. The classification of the selected manuscripts into code categories proceeded. Following classification, experts shared insightful opinions regarding the revised map and the classification of selected manuscripts within it. These were largely influenced by their research background and expertise in the field of HCI and in the area of accessibility. Consolidation and consensus was reached through meaningful discussions in several cases where different opinions and classifications surfaced. In addition, results from the frequency tables also supported the course of determining the final classifications of the selected manuscripts and likewise supporting the reflection of these refinements into the third version of the map. Including the author's classification of the selected manuscripts with those of the three independent experts, an overall percentage agreement of 71.6 % is reported for manuscript classification. This percentage is determined by measuring each participant's classification for a selected manuscript against the consolidated and consensus-based classification (if required), which was the outcome of discussions. Simply stated, classification differences were ultimately resolved by means of discussions that were supported by the results indicated in the frequency tables. It entailed discussing the reasoning motivating each expert's classification for a selected manuscript in alignment with the manuscript's objective. Once agreement was reached regarding classification, consensus and saturation is likewise achieved. A more in-depth analysis of the frequency tables indicates that for 33.3 % of the selected manuscripts evaluated there was 100 % agreement regarding classification. For another 33 % of the selected manuscripts evaluated there was 75 % agreement regarding classification. For the remaining 33 % of the selected manuscript evaluated there was 50 % or less agreement regarding classification. It is for this set of manuscripts in particular (50 % or less agreement) that more extensive and meaningful discussions were conducted in order to reach consensus regarding classification. The third version of the map is the outcome of refinements done to the second version of the map, based on the results from the evaluation that was conducted in this stage (see Table 2). The final map (version 3) is presented in Fig. 2.

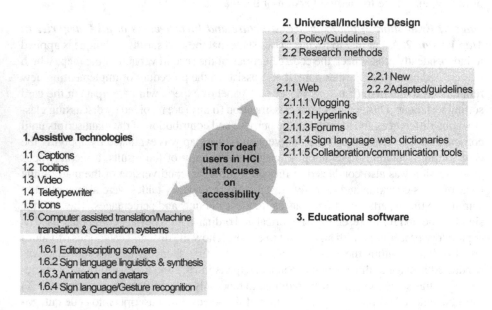

Fig. 2. IST for deaf users in the discipline of HCI that focuses on accessibility - Map version 3

3   Results

Results are discussed in terms of the 3 paper objectives mentioned in the Introduction.

3.1   Objective 1: Construct a Map of Existing Research Topics in the Field of IST for Deaf Users in the Discipline of HCI that Focuses on Accessibility

Table 2 summarizes the refinements that were made to the map from its initial first version until its improved third version (see Fig. 2). Map version 2 represents refinements that were based on the outcomes from the first focus group session, conducted in stage 3 of the process. Map version 3 represents refinements that were based on the outcomes from the second focus group session, conducted in stage 6 of the process.

In Table 2, *Category integration* occurs when an existing code category (main or sub) is integrated into another existing code category. A *Rename* occurs when the name of a code category has been rewritten. When a subcategory has been removed from the map it is listed in the column *Removed subcategory*. *Reclassified manuscripts* represent those manuscripts that had to be reclassified into different code categories in comparison to those that they were initially classified in. It must be noted that the total number of reclassified manuscripts does not relate specifically to the manuscripts that were selected for evaluation in the focus group sessions alone. The reclassification also occurs from refinements made to the actual map versions. For example, when a subcategory has been removed from a map version it is necessary to reclassify the manuscripts that were included in the removed subcategory into a different code category (main or sub).

Table 2. Refinements during map construction

Refinement	Version 1	Version 2	Version 3
Main category	7	3(−4)	3
Subcategory	22	8(−14)	8
2nd-level subcategory	4	14(+10)	7(−7)
3rd-level subcategory		5(+5)	5
Category integration		4	3
Rename		2	2
Removed subcategory		3	4
Reclassified manuscripts		2	14

3.2 Objective 2: Summarize the Purpose of Each Code Category of the Map

HCI literature that focuses on accessibility was reviewed to develop the map. This section provides an overview of its main categories, highlighting key issues covered in their subcategories. It is notable that subcategories classified within a main category can consist of a limited number of manuscripts, yet are regarded worthy of individual separation based on topic, need and prospect of attracting new researchers.

Assistive Technologies. The main category of Assistive Technologies focuses on tools and software that can assist deaf users experience technology in a more positive and usable manner. It supports them in performing tasks that were formerly difficult to accomplish or not accomplishable. This is possible due to technology enhancements or due to the alteration of interaction methods with technology and software. Assistive technologies must promote social inclusion, autonomy, independence and life quality. This main category includes six subcategories. The first subcategory focuses on *captions*. These are real-time textual alternatives for audio, which can also include descriptions of sound. They are regarded as the most common type of assistive technology used by deaf users since they transform aural into visual information [3]. The second subcategory focuses on *tooltips*, which are used to make icons more comprehensible. Deaf users prefer visual information since they are visual learners; therefore tooltips can have a positive effect. The third subcategory focuses on *video*. As an assistive technology, video is significant for deaf users. Video for mobile communication is mainly discussed. The fourth subcategory focuses on *teletypewriters*. Teletypewriter (TTY) technology enables deaf individuals to have direct and equal access to emergency call centers. Users can type, send and receive messages for communication. Regarding the corpus, this subcategory had a poor representation of manuscripts. Nevertheless, it presents potential for new research. The fifth subcategory focuses on *icons*. This entails investigating the design and use of iconographic touch interfaces on mobile applications. The sixth subcategory focuses on *Computer Assisted Translation (CAT)*, also referred to as Machine Translation (MT) or Generation systems. Their aim is to provide deaf users with the capabilities to translate text/voice of vocal languages into sign languages and to produce, modify and review online avatar-based sign language contributions. It requires expertise in several related topics, including sign language linguistics and synthesis to create system vocabularies, knowledge-based sign synthesis architecture [7], and sign language animation and recognition to present manual and non-manual means of expressions in sign language translations using avatars. This subcategory is further divided into four second-level subcategories that are interrelated; it is however possible for research to be conducted in a single second-level subcategory only. Each of these second-level subcategories can be highly technical components. The first second-level subcategory is *editor/scripting software*, which is an additional capability to intervene and correct translations that are error-prone. The second is *sign language linguistics and synthesis* that focus on the study of sign language as a natural language. This can include its history, structure, acquisition of language, morphology, syntax, semantics and pragmatics. Examining the linguistics is required to ensure to the best extent possible, the linguistic adequacy of sign generation tools and to support robust conversions [7]. Sign synthesis is methods/techniques that are applied to provide fluid mediums of sign language, for conversation synthesis, by converting sign language from a stored and textual medium. The third is *animation and avatars* that are used to display sign language translation representations to the users. The synthesis of signed speech/text can therefore be portrayed through the movements of a human signing figure. In order to provide translations, an avatar is required to display the synthesized sign language. The fourth is *sign language/gesture recognition* that mainly focuses on the technical approaches implemented to capture and recognize sign language gestures. In broad-spectrum, gesture recognition utilizes mathematical algorithms to interpret human gestures.

Universal/Inclusive Design. The main category of Universal/Inclusive design focuses on the design of services, products, software and environments that are usable and accessible for as many people possible, despite their differences in abilities, gender, education, age or cultural backgrounds. The aim is to provide equal opportunities for people to participate in economic, social, technological, cultural, recreational and entertainment activities. With regards to the IST map, this main category discusses manuscripts that emphasize Universal/Inclusive design in general. In overview, apart from the manuscripts categorized with the main category, two more specific subcategories are determined. The first subcategory focuses on *policy/guidelines*. Policies are intended to inform stakeholders and policymakers about the adaption and use of technology by people with disabilities. Guidelines and acknowledged standards (e.g. W3C, ISO) intend to guide developers in the design of accessible software [8]. The development of guidelines and the transformation of technical specifications into international standards are also discussed in this context. Policies and guidelines pertaining to the Web are specifically identified. Hence, the *Web* is defined as a second-level subcategory. This second-level subcategory is further divided into five third-level subcategories: *vlogging*, *hyperlinks*, *forums*, *sign language dictionaries* and *collaboration/communication tools*. *Vlogging* investigates the use of video technology and techniques by the Deaf community to post video content on websites. Alternative forms of *hyperlinks* are compared and new forms of hyperlinking, which are based on video material that enable browsing without written language, are discussed. *Forums* empower online participation and deliberations on various topics. Video is used as the communication medium and forums can accommodate several user types, such as advanced contributors' and lurkers. *Sign language dictionaries* provide online translations for spoken and sign languages. The interfaces of such web dictionaries must be designed applying user centered design methodologies and it is required that composition rules of signs be encoded. *Collaboration/communication tools* are browser based systems that support face-to-face communication between deaf and hearing members of a team.

The second subcategory focuses on *research methods*. The objective of manuscripts categorized within this subcategory is to either provide insights into new methods for conducting research with deaf participants or to modify existing research methods in a manner that accommodates the needs of deaf users. Henceforth, two second-level subcategories have been created within this subcategory; *new* and *adapted/guidelines*. Example of a new method is a remote testing technology to conduct user studies in sign language at a lower cost or the use of drawing software with set stories to conduct evaluations with deaf children [9]. In the *adapted methods/guidelines*, it is acknowledged that impairments can impact how researchers will design questionnaires, user interviews, focus group sessions and user evaluations to elicit more reliable and valid data.

Educational Software. The main category of Educational Software focuses on using technology software to teach or self-learn. Software, web tools, mobile applications, games and e-learning environments are the types of platforms discussed within this context. Learners include deaf and hard-of-hearing individuals, as well as hearing parents of deaf individuals. Providing tools that can improve the literacy levels of deaf children and students who are native signers of a particular sign language is the main focus.

3.3   Objective 3: Identify the Least and Most Researched Topics of the Map

In Table 3, the total distribution of manuscripts for each of the three main categories is presented. In order to identify the least and most researched topics within each of the main categories, the total number of manuscripts for their subcategories are also provided. Regarding Table 3, it must be noted that manuscripts can be classified into main categories, without necessarily being classified into a subcategory. Second- and third-level subcategories are not included in the table.

Table 3. Distribution of corpus manuscripts into code categories (main and sub) of the map

Category type	Code category	Total manuscripts
Main	Assistive technologies	36
Sub	Captions	3
Sub	Tooltips	1
Sub	Video	4
Sub	Teletypewriter	1
Sub	Icons	1
Sub	Computer assisted translation/Machine translation/Generation systems	26
Main	Universal/Inclusive design	21
Sub	Policy/Guidelines	9
Sub	Research methods	5
Main	Educational software	12

It can be concluded from the results presented in Table 3 that emphasis is being devoted mainly to the *CAT/MT/Generation systems* subcategory. It is seen as a crucial area for deaf accessibility, particularly over the web. Despite it being the most researched topic from the corpus however, it is relatively unexplored considering the sources reviewed to create the corpus and the time period that was covered. The *Universal/ Inclusive design* main category is likewise crucial and unexplored. Contributions in this category in the form of *policies/guidelines* and *new research methods* will be most valuable to designers and developers so that they can provide deaf users with products and services that are accessible, useful and provide positive user experiences. Researchers will also benefit by knowing how to implement different and the most appropriate research methods with deaf users, ensuring that the participants have been properly considered. The data collection process and analysis of the collected results will also have increased validity. In terms of the *educational software* main category, research is needed to provide deaf people with solutions that can assist them in learning and improving their sign language and vocal language skills. Work conducted in the *CAT/MT/Generation systems* subcategory will prove invaluable in this regard. It is also important to remember that people who are not deaf, particularly parents of deaf children, require solutions as well to improve their sign language skills in order to communicate with their children. This is critical because the longer it takes for deaf children to start communicating with their parents; the more their language modality is affected.

4 Conclusion and Future Work

This paper presents an inventory of research into IST for deaf users in the discipline of HCI that focuses on accessibility, on the basis of four relevant sources. It provides guidance to new researches who are interested in conducting research within this landscape. In addition, the paper attempts to stress the need for more research activity in this discipline. This need is voiced by considering the number of deaf people worldwide that are required to use technology that is not accessible and usable for them. Noteworthy is the limited number of sources available discussing IST for deaf users in HCI literature that focuses on accessibility. The limited number of manuscripts from these sources that were relevant for the review over a period of more than ten years, further support the call for more research activity.

A systematic approach based on a six-stage process was considered to conduct the inventory. The process assisted in achieving the three objectives of the paper. The first objective was to present a map of existing research topics in the field of IST for deaf users in the discipline of HCI that focuses on accessibility. This was achieved with map version 3 (see Fig. 2). The second objective was to summarize the purpose of each code category within the map. This is achieved in Sect. 3.2, which synthesizes the findings of the map. An overview of the type of research conducted in each main category and all their levels of subcategories is provided. The third objective was to identify the least and most researched topics of the map. This is achieved with Table 3, which lists the distribution of manuscripts from the corpus based on main and subcategories.

Considering the map for IST for deaf users in the discipline of HCI that focuses on accessibility, future directions have been identified. Researchers can position themselves in this landscape and contribute to new work in the identified areas. Addressing the problems of non-accessible technology and the educational and employment disadvantages that deaf people experience are areas that require further and immediate exploration. The authors' future work will be directed towards improving web accessibility for deaf users. In particular, efforts will be directed towards the construction of a new research method that can support HCI experts and developers when evaluating and respectively designing websites for deaf users. Based on the map for IST for deaf users in the discipline of HCI that focuses on accessibility (see Fig. 2), such work would be classified into the *Universal/Inclusive Design* (2) main category. Within this main category, it is further classified into the *Research methods* (2.2) subcategory. As a second-level subcategory it is classified into the *New* (2.2.1) subcategory, since it will provide a new method of evaluation that is specifically for the deaf user group.

Acknowledgments. The financial assistance of the National Research Foundation (NRF) of South Africa towards this research is hereby acknowledged. Opinions and conclusions expressed in this paper are those of the author and are not necessarily to be attributed to the NRF.

References

1. European Union of the Deaf. http://www.eud.eu/Statutes-i-216.html
2. Debevc, M., Kožuh, I., Kosec, P., Rotovnik, M., Holzinger, A.: Sign language multimedia based interaction for aurally handicapped people. In: Miesenberger, K., Karshmer, A., Penaz, P., Zagler, W. (eds.) ICCHP 2012, Part II. LNCS, vol. 7383, pp. 213–220. Springer, Heidelberg (2012)
3. Gulliver, S.R., Ghinea, G.: How level and type of deafness affect user perception of multimedia video clips. J. Univ. Access Inf. Soc. **2**(4), 374–386 (2003)
4. Van Zijl, L.: South African sign language machine translation project. In: Proceedings of the 8th International ACM SIGACCESS Conference on Computers and Accessibility, pp. 233–234, ACM (2006)
5. Zaphiris, P., Kurniawan, S., Ghiawadwala, M.: A systematic approach to the development of research-based web design guidelines for older people. J. Univ. Access Inf. Soc. **6**(1), 59–75 (2007)
6. Parmaxi, A., Zaphiris, P., Papadima-Sophocleous, S., Ioannou, A.: Mapping the landscape of computer-assisted language learning: an inventory of research. J. Interact. Technol. Smart Educ. **10**(4), 252–269 (2013)
7. Fotinea, S.E., Efthimiou, E., Caridakis, G., Karpouzis, K.: A knowledge-based sign synthesis architecture. J. Univ. Access Inf. Soc. **6**(4), 405–418 (2008)
8. Gulliksen, J., Harker, S.: The software accessibility of human-computer interfaces—ISO Technical specification 16071. J. Univ. Access Inf. Soc. **3**(1), 6–16 (2004)
9. Mich, O.: E-drawings as an evaluation method with deaf children. In: Proceedings of the 13th International ACM SIGACCESS Conference on Computers and Accessibility, pp. 239–240. ACM (2011)

Universal Access to Mobile Interaction

Speech Recognition Native Module Environment Inherent in Mobiles Devices

Blanca E. Carvajal-Gámez[1]([✉]), Erika Hernández Rubio[2],
Amilcar Meneses Viveros[3], and Francisco J. Hernández-Castañeda[2]

[1] Instituto Politécnico Nacional, Unidad Profesional Interdisciplinaria y Tecnología
Avanzada, México D.F., Mexico
becarvajal@ipn.mx
[2] Instituto Politécnico Nacional, SEPI-ESCOM, México D.F., Mexico
ehernandezru@ipn.mx
[3] Departamento de Computación, CINVESTAV-IPN, México D.F., Mexico
ameneses@cs.cinvestav.mx

Abstract. Applications on mobile devices have been characterized for their usability. The voice is a natural means of interaction between users and mobile devices. Traditional speech recognition algorithms work in controlled media are targeted to specific population groups (e.g. age, gender or language to name of few), and also require a lot of computational resources so that the algorithms are effective. Therefore, pattern recognition is performed in mobile applications as web services. However, this type of solution generates high dependence on Internet connectivity, so it is desirable to have an embedded module for this task that does not consume many computational resources and have a good level of effectiveness. This paper presents an embedded mobile systems for voice recognition module is presented. This module works in noisy environments, it works for any age of users and has proved that it can work for several languages.

1 Introduction

Applications on mobile devices have been characterized for their usability [1]. Developers try that interaction means for mobile devices are natural to the user [2]. Actually, the most common means of interaction based on gestures on touch screens [3]. It has explored the interaction through voice applications such as search and on tasks requiring multimodal interactions [4,5].

In hardware complies with those demands of speech recognition applications, because we can utilize parallel and pipelined architectures [6], which either reduce power with low operation frequency or speed up there cognition. With such knowledge, comprehensible human-like speech recognition can be obtained [6].

In automatic speech recognition systems (ASR) can be sorted into the following three categories [7]:

© Springer International Publishing Switzerland 2015
M. Antona and C. Stephanidis (Eds.): UAHCI 2015, Part I, LNCS 9175, pp. 267–278, 2015.
DOI: 10.1007/978-3-319-20678-3_26

1. First the ASR model converts the speech signal into a sequence of phonemes o words, and after wards the natural language processing (NLP) attempts to understand the given words.
2. The ASR model outputs more than one possible representation of the speech signal. These are then analysed with an NLP and the best one is chosen.
3. The ASR model and the NLP are combined, such that the ASR model can make use of the information and constraints provided by the NLP.

A popular application, which consists of a list of all possible words that one might encounter in a particular application. Current spoken language systems have limited vocabularies, since this is dependent on the available power and memory space of the central processing unit being used. As a result, one might encounter out-of-vocabulary (OOV) words, which the ASR system will either rejector consider it as an error [8].

Mobile devices have restrictions Battery, Memory and CPU [9,10]. Although a part of CPU has been thought that the increase in cores and incorporating parallel programs can help reduce energy consumption [11], although it is not clear that the incorporation of parallel programs on mobile devices really save energy [12]. Various techniques have been developed for offloading as a form of energy savings, improve response time, and avoid problems of storage and memory on the mobile device [9].

It has sought strategies that allow offloading the task of speech recognition. This has supported infrastructure for distributed speech recognition [13]. There are also a lot of support from below cloud-like structures [14,15]. However this creates a high dependency on the internet [10].

Additionally, there are restrictions on the systems automatic speech recognition (ASR) and performance problems with human-machine iteration are requiring extra learning to use. However, the biggest challenge for voice-based interfaces require: a more natural communication possible [8].

The main weakness of ASR systems is the use of the statistical principle: which looks for the best scenario of all possible candidates given a pre-defined dictionary [reference]. This gives rise to a problem called a grammarian OOV (out-of-vocabulary, OOV) [8]. This system takes words not recorded and added to the system. This system, however; is not always the best way in systems where the vocabulary is very large [8]. During the design phase of the dialogue should be clearly identified in the following conditions: Outreach, Level of naturalness, Strength and Length dialog [8].

In this paper the development of a native voice recognition module for mobile devices is presented. This type of solution avoids reliance on internet connectivity. The algorithm used has low complexity. It is inherent in the medium, recalling that the environment in which mobile devices are used are noisy. Not supervised so requires no training. Recognizes word of at least two languages: English and Spanish. It does not depend on the user type (adult, young, boy, man or woman).

2   Proposed Solution

The most significant problems in speech recognition systems are related to the individuality of the human voice (such as age or gender to name a few), dialect, speaking rate, the context of phonics, noise background, the characteristics of voice acquisition device (microphone), and the directional characteristics of the source speech signal, among others [16–18]. All these problems are considered in the proposed method, because the objective of this research is that the speech recognition is inherent to the environment and the people who use the application. The speech recognition module, based on the DWT-Haar, comprises three main blocks: encoding and compression, feature extraction and recognition, as shown in Fig. 1.

2.1   Pre-processing and Reduction Modules

Pre-processing module and reduction with a DWT. This reduces the complexity of calculation and does inherent to the medium. DWTs take into consideration the temporal information that is inherent in speech signals, apart from the frequency information. Since speech signals are non-stationary in nature, the temporal information is also important for speech recognition applications [7].

In this block, two vectors are obtained: The approximation vector (AV) and the fluctuations vector (FV). These vectors are obtained when DWT-Haar is applied in the original speech signal. The size of the vectors AV and FV is half the size of the original speech vector. The AV vector contains the low frequency components of the voice signal. The vector FV contains high frequency components of the speech original signal. For this work the AV was chosen, because this vector has the largest amount of information about the speech original signal. To encode speech signal through native methods of recording, signal compression is obtained through the AV with WAV format. Compression has a rate of 22050 samples per second with 16 bits per sample without encoding pulse code modulation (PCM).

2.2   Estimation Module

To increase the robustness of the designed system under noisy conditions [19]. We propose the CLCES analysis, when there cognition system is corrupted by noisy speech signals. This statement is confirmed through an evaluation made on four different noisy environments with different measure: standard deviation, variance, energy and mean value.

This block obtains the corresponding features of each input voice signal. This extraction is performed in the AV obtained in the previous block. Acquired characteristics are energy, Eq. 1, the standard deviation Eq. 2, variance Eq. 3 and the center frequency of the speech signal in the VA.

$$E[y_{Lo\_D}[n]] = \sum_{m=1}^{n} |y_{Lo\_D}[m]|^2 \qquad (1)$$

$$\sigma_{y_{Lo\_D}} = \sqrt{\sum_{m=1}^{n} \frac{\left(y_{(Lo\_D)_m} \bar{y}_{Lo\_D}\right)^2}{n}} \tag{2}$$

$$\sigma^2_{y_{Lo\_D}} = \sum_{m=1}^{n} \frac{\left(y_{(Lo\_D)_m} \bar{y}_{Lo\_D}\right)^2}{n} \tag{3}$$

where $\bar{y}_{Lo\_D} = \sum_{m=1}^{n}(y_{Lo\_D})/n$ represent de mean value of AV, and $n = w/2$.

2.3   Classification Module

Three renowned methods that were used at the classification stage of ASR systems are the HMM (Hide Markov Models), the ANN (Artificial neural network) and the SVMs (Suport Vector Machine) [7]. These three classifiers usually have prior training which is sometimes tedious and energy-intensive. In this paper, simple classification techniques were incorporated, such as fuzzy logic classifier and K-neighbors distance variations and techniques to obtain additional distance. These techniques are supported although simple largely this stage prior to preprocessing. Thus ensure satisfactory accuracy with low power consumption.

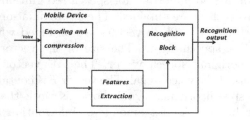

Fig. 1. Block diagram of the proposed method

This block is determined by the spoken word. The words used are suggested: "*Hola*" and "*Adios*", and also "*High*" and "*Potato*". The words "*Hola*" and "*Adios*" in particular were chosen in order to show that the system works with high statistical dependence as shown in Fig. 3(a), contained in the green circle overlapping of these two words is observed.

Unlike the words "*High*" and "*Potato*", which in Fig. 3(b), the statistical independence is observed. This task is accomplished by using speech recognition. The entries in this block are the characteristics of the speech signal.

Fuzzy Logic Method. A fuzzy logic system (FLS) is unique in that it is able to simultaneously handle numerical data and linguistic knowledge [20]. It is a nonlinear mapping of an input data (feature) vector into a scalar output. Fuzzy set theory and fuzzy logic establish the specifics of the nonlinear mapping. For many problems two distinct forms of problem knowledge exist: (1) objective knowledge, which is used all the time in engineering problem formulations (e.g., mathematical models), and (2) subjective knowledge, which represents linguistic

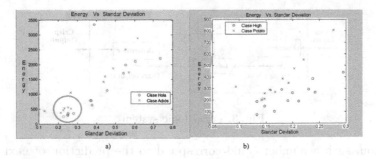

Fig. 2. Graphic of energy vs. standard deviation, (a) words *"Hola"* and *"Adios"*, (b) *"High"* and *"Potato"*.

information that is usually impossible to quantify using traditional mathematics (e.g., rules, expert information, design requirements) [20].

Fuzzy logic was used for word recognition in speech signal. This technique allows determining whether a spoken word in the set of speech signal features vector.

Fuzzy logic system (FLS), Fig. 2, maps crisp inputs into crisp outputs. It contains four components: rules, fuzzifier, inference engine, and defuzzifier. Once the rules have been established, a FLS can be viewed as a mapping from inputs to outputs (the solid path in Fig. 2, from "Crisp Inputs" to "Crisp Outputs"), and this mapping can be expressed quantitatively as $y = f(z)$.

Rules may be provided by experts or can be extracted from numerical data. In either case, engineering rules are expressed as a collection of IF THEN statements e.g.

IF *"Hola"* is very near *"Adios"* is very far, THEN turn somewhat to the right.

This one rule reveals that we will need an understanding of: (1) linguistic variables versus numerical values of a variable; (2) quantifying linguistic variables, which is done using fuzzy membership functions; (3) logical connections for linguistic variables (e.g., "and", "or", etc.); and (4) implications, i.e., "IF A THEN B". Additionally, we will need to understand how to combine more than one rule.

The fuzzifier maps crisp numbers into fuzzy sets. It is needed in order to activate rules which are in terms of linguistic variables, which have fuzzy sets associated with them.

The inference engine of the FLS maps fuzzy sets into fuzzy sets. It handles the way in which rules are combined. Just as we humans use many different types of inferential procedures to help us understand things or to make decisions, there are many different fuzzy logic inferential procedures. Only a very small number of them are actually being used in engineering applications of FL.

In many applications, crisp numbers must be obtained at the output of a FLS. The defuzzifier maps output sets into crisp numbers. In a controls application, for example, such a number corresponds to a control action. In a signal processing

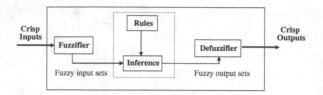

Fig. 3. Fuzzy logic system

application, such a number could correspond to the prediction of next year?s sunspot activity, a financial forecast, or the location of a target.

Crisp Sets. Recall that a crisp set A in a universe of discourse U (which provides the set of allowable values for a variable) can be defined by listing all of its members or by identifying the elements $x \in A$; thus A can be defined as $A = \{x|x$ meets some condition$\}$. Alternatively, we can introduce a zero-one membership function (also called a characteristic function, discrimination function, or indicator function) for A, denoted $\mu_A(x)$ such that $A \Rightarrow \mu(x) = 1$ if $x \in A$, and $\mu_A(x) = 0$ if $x \notin A$. In this paper the universe is the user's speech block, i.e. the input signal. In this universe must define members that belong to the class.

Fuzzy Sets. A fuzzy set F defined on a universe of discourse U is characterized by a membership function $\mu_F(x)$ which takes on values in the interval $[0, 1]$. A fuzzy set is a generalization of an ordinary subset (i.e., a crisp subset) whose membership function only takes on two values, zero or unity. A membership function provides a measure of the degree of similarity of an element in U to the fuzzy subset. Fuzzy logic is performed using the membership functions [21] for each of the features extracted from the Eqs. (1), (2) and (3). The membership function indicates the degree to which each element of a given universe belongs to a set. If the set is crisp, the membership function (characteristic function) take the values $\{0, 1\}$, while if the set is blurred, it will take in the interval $[0, 1]$. If the result of the membership function is equal to 0, then the element is not in the set. In contrast, if the result of the membership function is 1, then the element belongs to the set completely [21]. Gaussian membership, Eq. (4), is used for the purpose of this word recognizer in the speech signal by using fuzzy logic. The Gaussian membership is specified by two parameters c, σ to determine the boundaries of the speech signal, and also to determine where the greatest amount of information is presented in the spectral content of the word to be identified [22].

$$Gaussian(x; c, \sigma) = e^{-\frac{1}{2}(\frac{x-c}{\sigma})^2} \tag{4}$$

The Gaussian function is determined by the values they take σ and c. Where c represents the center of the function and σ is the standard deviation (2). For this case, c is the mean value, and each value is the mean average of each standard sample, and σ is the standard deviation (2) of each test pattern [22].

From define boundaries of membership function can determine whether or not the word issued by the user is the search word in the inference system.

K-Nearest Neighbors Method. In many pattern recognition problems, the classification of an input pattern is based on data where the respective sample sizes of each class are small and possibly not representative of the actual probability distributions, even if they are known. In these cases, many techniques rely on some notion of similarity or distance in feature space, for instance, clustering and discriminant analysis [3,23]. This decision rule provides a simple nonparametric procedure for the assignment of a class label to the input pattern based on the class labels represented by the K-closest (say, for example, in the Euclidean sense) neighbors of the vector.

The nearest neighbor classifiers require no preprocessing of the labeled sample set prior to their use. The crisp nearest-neighbor classification rule assigns an input sample vector y, which is of unknown classification, to the class of its nearest neighbor [24].

This idea can be extended to the K-nearest neighbors with the vector y being assigned to the class that is represented by a majority amongst the K-nearest neighbors. When more than one neighbor is considered, the possibility that there will be a tie among classes with a maximum number of neighbors in the group of K-nearest neighbor exists. One simple way of handling this problem is to restrict the possible values of K [24]. A means of handling the occurrence of a tie is as follows. The sample vector is assigned to the class, of those classes that tied, for which the sum of distances from the sample to each neighbor in the class is a minimum. This could still lead to a tie, in which case the assignment is to the last class encountered amongst those which tied, an arbitrary assignment. Clearly, there will be cases where a vector's classification becomes an arbitrary assignment, no matter what additional procedures are included in the algorithm [24].

3   Test and Results

The test module for voice recognition were performed on a smartphone android, words that have used statistical dependence and a population was considered with varied age. Also sought experiments were made in noisy environments.

The module for speech recognition embedded was implemented on a mobile device. This module identifies words, two in Spanish Languagem *"Hola"* and *"Adiós"*, and two in English language, *"High"* and "Potato", applying Fuzzy Logic and KNN methods. The words *"Hola"* and *"Adiós"* have high statistical dependence. It seeks to do the tests with this type of words to prove that this does not affect the method proposed in this paper. The English words were chosen for their statistical independence.

A population with diverse gender and age were chosen for testing. Samples are shaped with a total population of 12 people, 6 men and 6 women. The ages are classified as follows. People over 50 years old: 3. People between 30 and 50 years old: 3. And people between 20 and 30 years old: 6.

The speech recognition system was tested in a smartphone with Android 4.3, 1 GB of RAM, Quad-core processor Qualcomm Snapdragon 400 MSM8226 @1200 Mhz. To execute the embedded module, the audio is acquired through the microphone of the mobile device, with active noise cancellation. It should consider the disadvantages of this type of device on a mobile device, where its main objective is the correct management of energy consumption. Since microphones with active noise cancellation is that they require external power to cancel outside noise with continuous presence as people laughing noise, sounds of cars, music, etc. So you have as the detector active noise within the mobile device applies more energy for canceling outside noise, reduces efficiency calculations in the mobile processor. So this is one of the main challenges to overcome in identifying words without dependence on internet for any gender and age of the user.

The speech files that were used have different environmental conditions, because they want to test the robustness and accuracy of the identification of the word within the audio file. The module was also tested in different languages. Tables 1 and 2 show the results obtained from the two algorithms applying in the embedded module. In these tables you can see the quantitative results of this algorithm. Also a comparison between the signal acquired and processed audio signal is shown.

Table 1. Results obtained by the embedded module to identify "Hola" and "Adiós"

	Embedded module							
	Fuzzy logic method				Knn method (0.15)			
Age range	Processing time (seg)	Sp (%)	Se (%)	ACC (%)	Processing time (seg)	Sp (%)	Se (%)	ACC (%)
Age > 50	0.109	69.35	93.33	71.08	0.128	60.12	63.33	56.66
30 ≤ Age ≤ 50	0.116	71.87	96.66	66.66	0.114	66.66	51.66	57.76
20 ≤ Age < 30	0.106	69.49	100	70.55	0.122	67.29	56.30	58.33
Avegrage	0.110	70.23	96.66	69.43	0.121	64.49	57.09	57.58

Table 2. Results obtained by the embedded module to identify "High" and "Potato"

	Embedded module							
	Fuzzy logic method				Knn method (0.15)			
Age range	Processing time (seg)	Sp (%)	Se (%)	ACC (%)	Processing time (seg)	Sp (%)	Se (%)	ACC (%)
Age > 50	0.107	68.25	98.90	73.34	0.150	46.66	51.33	53.33
30 ≤ Age ≤ 50	0.120	64.82	97.56	72.22	0.130	81.33	73.09	80.00
20 ≤ Age < 30	0.120	63.22	100	73.33	0.119	54.33	54.33	65.00
Avegrage	0.115	65.43	98.82	72.96	0.133	60.77	59.58	66.11

Performance results are calculated from the speech signal processing through the mobile device. To test the performance of the proposed method, we consider four cases: two for correct classifications and two for misclassification. The classifications are: true positive (TP), false positive (FP), false negative (FN) and true negative (TN). By using these different measures of performance metrics as the following relation is obtained [19]:

$$Specificity = \frac{TN}{TN + FP} \tag{5}$$

$$Sensitivity = \frac{TP}{TP + FN} \tag{6}$$

$$Precision = \frac{TP + TN}{samples\,of\,speech\,signal} \tag{7}$$

Specificity (Sp) is the ability to detect samples that do not correspond to the audio signal. The sensitivity (Se) reflects the ability of an algorithm to detect the sample audio signal. Accuracy (ACC) measures the ratio between the total number of correctly classified samples (sum of true positives and true negatives) by the number of samples of audio signal [19]. The positive predictive value, and accuracy rate, gives the proportion of samples of the audio signal identified which are true. That is, the probability that a sample of the audio signal is identified as true positive. From the results of tests concentrated in Tables 1 and 2, we note the following. The module embedded on the mobile device detects up to 70 % of search word (Sp) and up to 96.66 % for detecting those who have the search word in the audio file (Se) for the Spanish language. For English language, the embedded module detects up to 65.43 % the search word (Sp) and up to 98.82 % for detecting those who have the search word in the audio file (Se). In the case of the Spanish language, an accuracy greater than 69.43 % is obtained at a time of 0.110 s. And for English, an accuracy of 72.96 % is obtained in a time of 0.115 s, with applying the Fuzzy logic method.

The module embedded on the mobile device detects up to 64 % of search word (Sp) and up to 57.09 % for detecting those who have the search word in the audio file (Se) for the Spanish language. For English language, the embedded module detects up to 60.77 % the search word (Sp) and up to 59 % for detecting those who have the search word in the audio file (Se). In the case of the Spanish language, an accuracy greater than 57 % is obtained at a time of 0.133 s. And for English, an accuracy of 66.11 % is obtained in a time of 0.133 s, with applying the Knn method.

4   Discussion

From the results, it can be seen that although there are variations in gender and age, the precision of the embedded system remains constant. This causes that the system will not need a re-training every time to capture the variations of voice that can occur with age. This job requires increasing values of Sp and Se, this is in progress with the investigation.

The range of ages, regardless of gender, who presented the best accuracy for word recognition within the mobile device is above 50 years old, for the Spanish language, Table 1. In the case of English language, the same behavior was presented. The greatest accuracy was obtained with the elderly 50 years old, Table 2. In the case of the Spanish words that begin or end with the same phoneme, such as cases that were used in this research as "*Hola*" and "*Adiós*" as well as the noisy environment of the cell itself and the age range of the people, causing the rate of Sp, and Acc is, decrease its performance.

In [22], a module for recognizing isolated words, in real time, on a mobile device is presented. In this study conducted with a sample population of 10 people in total. This population consists of 5 men and 5 women, and the age range of the members of the population is not mentioned. Replays of the audio signals on the mobile performed 3 times to create an average error. The tests in this work were attacked with white noise with SNR, Eq. 8, between 15 and 30 db [22].

$$SNR = \frac{\bar{y}_{Lo\_D}}{\sigma_{y_{Lo\_D}}} \tag{8}$$

The SNR has a uniform distribution, so that altering the signal audio not affected and a substantial modification of this signal is taken. This is different to present audio signal to ambient noise, because in this case the signal is affected by impulsive noise. And this kind of noise no predictable distribution, generating in certain sections of audio are altered significantly. The results presented in [22], are returned in a time of 11.61 ms and with an average of 61.4 % in the worst case, when the signal is changed to white noise. And an average of 90.2 % is obtained when the audio file is in a controlled environment.

The average processing time for the words used is in a range between 0.11 and 0.133 s. This is relevant because the voice processing does not exceed 0.2 s required for the user to have an answer during interaction with the mobile device.

5   Conclusion

The proposal presented in this research for isolated word recognition in a mobile device in uncontrolled environments gives yields higher than 70 % in less than the time 0.120 s, in the Spanish language. In the case of American English language, results over 66.11 % are obtained in an average time of 0.133 s. The voice recognition system is implemented on a mobile device with a microphone type active voice cancellation. This causes, as the tests are performed in uncontrolled ways, some mobile resources are limited by the energy due to design own mobile forces you to pay attention to the noise cancellation. In some works present results but not so bi-lingual, unlike the proposal presented here. The processing time is good for the tasks of interaction between the mobile device and the user.

This embedded word recognizer module requires no prior training or generation of a dictionary as those currently commercially. Also the so-embedded module works offline, i.e.; not require a connection to the network in order to perform their job recognition. This streamlines its use and management, adding portability and the generation of an App to be used as a tool in voice commands or support systems in any treatment such as Luria tests. We note also that being a working embedded system offline use so the battery is not as affected in the performance of this. The word recognition system achieves work for any genre and any age group not presenting any difficulty, to be altered or amended by voice acuity or severity of the tone of speech signal for the gender of the user, as well as the possible echo the voice generated by age. Concluding finally that although in some cases the performance is not expected, than the results shown in [22], embedded system mounted on an FPGA, where the processing is done faster and transparent manner.

Finally, for the voice recognition module is not necessary voice retraining determined by a period of time. This behavior is due to natural variations in the voice over time.

References

1. Love, S.: Understanding Mobile Human-Computer Interaction. Elsevier, Amsterdam (2005)
2. Jacko, J.A.: Human-Computer Interaction Handbook: Fundamentals, Evolving Technologies, and Emerging Applications, 3rd edn. CRC Press Inc., Boca Raton (2012)
3. Bragdon, A., Nelson, E., Li, Y., Hinckley, K.: Experimental analysis of touch-screen gesture designs in mobile environments. In: Proceedings of the SIGCHI Conference on Human Factors in Computing Systems, pp. 403–412. ACM (2011)
4. Turk, M.: Multimodal interaction: a review. Pattern Recogn. Lett. **36**, 189–195 (2014)
5. Tzovaras, D.: Multimodal User Interfaces: From Signals to Interaction. Signals and Communication Technology. Springer, Heidelberg (2008)
6. Choi, J., You, K., Sung, W.: An fpga implementation of speech recognition with weighted finite state transducers. In: 2010 IEEE International Conference on Acoustics Speech and Signal Processing (ICASSP), pp. 1602–1605. IEEE (2010)
7. Cutajar, M., Gatt, E., Grech, I., Casha, O., Micallef, J.: Comparative study of automatic speech recognition techniques. IET Sig. Process. **7**(1), 25–46 (2013)
8. Fábián, T.: Confidence Measurement Techniques in Automatic Speech Recognition and Dialog Management. Der Andere Verlag, Tönning (2008)
9. Kumar, K., Liu, J., Lu, Y.H., Bhargava, B.: A survey of computation offloading for mobile systems. Mob. Netw. Appl. **18**(1), 129–140 (2013)
10. Kumar, K., Lu, Y.H.: Cloud computing for mobile users: can offloading computation save energy? Computer **43**(4), 51–56 (2010)
11. Hill, M.D., Marty, M.R.: Amdahl's law in the multicore era. IEEE Comput. **41**(7), 33–38 (2008)
12. Isidro Ramírez, R., Meneses Viveros, A., Hernándes Rubio, E., Torres Hernández, I.M.: Differences of energetic consumption between java and jni android apps. In: International Symposium on Integrated Circuits (ISIC 2014). IEEE (2014)
13. Pearce, D.: Enabling new speech driven services for mobile devices: an overview of the etsi standards activities for distributed speech recognition front-ends. In: AVIOS 2000: The Speech Applications Conference, pp. 261–264 (2000)

14. Bahl, P., Han, R.Y., Li, L.E., Satyanarayanan, M.: Advancing the state of mobile cloud computing. In: Proceedings of the Third ACM Workshop on Mobile Cloud Computing and Services, pp. 21–28. ACM (2012)
15. Di Fabbrizio, G., Okken, T., Wilpon, J.G.: A speech mashup framework for multimodal mobile services. In: Proceedings of the 2009 International Conference on Multimodal Interfaces, pp. 71–78. ACM (2009)
16. Husnjak, S., Perakovic, D., Jovovic, I.: Possibilities of using speech recognition systems of smart terminal devices in traffic environment. Procedia Eng. **69**, 778–787 (2014)
17. Oviatt, S.: Multimodal interfaces. In: The Human-Computer Interaction Handbook: Fundamentals, Evolving Technologies and Emerging Applications, pp. 286–304 (2003)
18. Ons, B., Gemmeke, J.F., et al.: Fast vocabulary acquisition in an nmf-based self-learning vocal user interface. Comput. Speech Lang. **28**(4), 997–1017 (2014)
19. Carvajal-Gamez, B.E., Gallegos-Funes, F.J., Rosales-Silva, A.J.: Color local complexity estimation based steganographic (clces) method. Expert Syst. Appl. **40**(4), 1132–1142 (2013)
20. Mendel, J.M.: Fuzzy logic systems for engineering: a tutorial. Proc. IEEE **83**(3), 345–377 (1995)
21. GEORGE, J.K., Bo, Y.: Fuzzy sets and fuzzy logic, theory and applications (2008)
22. Carvajal-Gamez, B.E., Hernándes Rubio, E., Meneses Viveros, A., Hernandez-Castaneda, F.J.: Feature extraction for word recognition on a mobile device based on discrete wavelet transform. In: Advances in Computing Science, vol. 83. Instituo Politénico Nacional (2014)
23. Sears, A., Jacko, J.A.: The Human-Computer Interaction Handbook: Fundamentals, Evolving Technologies and Emerging Applications. CRC Press, USA (2007)
24. Keller, J.M., Gray, M.R., Givens, J.A.: A fuzzy k-nearest neighbor algorithm. IEEE Trans. Syst. Man Cybern. **4**, 580–585 (1985)

Advances on Breathing Based Text Input for Mobile Devices

Jackson Feijó Filho[✉], Wilson Prata, and Thiago Valle

Nokia Technology Institute, Av. Torquato Tapajós, 7200 – Col Terra Nova,
Manaus, AM 69093-415, Brazil
+55 92 98134 0134
{jackson.feijo,wilson.prata,thiago.valle}@indt.org.br

Abstract. This paper highlights the progress of exploring a puffing activated keyboard for mobile phones. This approach aims to stand as an assistive technology for users with motor disabilities. From the implementation of prior versions we were able to identify recurring and persistent issues, such as ambient noise handling and keyboard layout. Some of these issues were detected during the experiments and some were reported by users. The advances achieved in this work are narrated from the outcomes of the implementation and experimentation of a mobile phone application that handles e.g. background noise by performing signal processing and a new keyboard layout.

1 Introduction

People with disabilities have restricted opportunities in a lot of areas, and the field of mobile technologies is no exception. A virtual environment offers the option to operate or to function in the real world, reducing physical boundaries. Technology users are likely to use their arms, hands, and fingers when using a mobile phone. Nonetheless, for people with motor disabilities, the need for movements that require dexterity can be a barrier for them to be able to interact with the phone [9].

Assistive technologies have been demanded, generally targeting users with severe motor disabilities such as motor neuron disease (MND), amyotrophic lateral sclerosis (ALS), spinal muscular atrophy, spinal cord injury, cerebral palsy, locked-in syndrome and Guillain-Barrè Syndrome (GBS) [8]. There are many types of physical disabilities that affect a pleasant human-computer interaction. As mentioned above, these diseases cause muscle deterioration and/or neurological disorders and consequently result in physical weakness, loss of muscle control, paralysis, and even amputation. In this context, the central issue for these users is the capacity to access computer controls (i.e. power/volume switch, menu items selection) and the aptitude to type on the regular keyboard or move pointing devices like a mouse cursor.

Assistive solutions have been investigated and established as an important field in human–computer interaction. Several forms of assistance have been produced for technology consumers with particular disabilities that lessen their capabilities to achieve inputting text on some devices. Several alternative interfaces for users with motor disabilities have been developed and reported. Frequently, these solutions include procedures that implement speech recognition methods, eye-trackers and

M. Antona and C. Stephanidis (Eds.): UAHCI 2015, Part I, LNCS 9175, pp. 279–287, 2015.
DOI: 10.1007/978-3-319-20678-3_27

sip-and-puff controllers. Speech recognition software is well accepted to be useful as textual input aid, while additional hardware are usually employed as pointing devices, allowing the control of e.g. the mouse pointer [2].

2 Related Work

Textual input and other interaction for people with motor disabilities and their phones have challenged the academy and industry to investigate alternative software and hardware solutions. These solutions will not depend on any manual interaction e.g. keystroking, screen-touching. Text input through other physiological signals [1, 4] is often considered. Speech recognition is also a solution used by the targeted audience.

2.1 Interaction Through Physiological Signals

Common physiological measures already used in previous Human Computer Interaction (HCI) and Accessibility works include: cardiovascular, electrodermal, muscular tension, ocular, skin temperature, brain activity and respiration measures [2]. These solutions typically require extra hardware, which makes these alternatives more expensive to final users. Not to mention they are 'immobile' computer oriented solutions (desktops, laptops, etc.) and do not cover mobile phones. Some works present sip-and-puff controlling that aims mobile devices, but requiring extra hardware.

2.2 Voice/Speech Recognition

Speech recognition is able to present itself as software based solution, which means no extra hardware is needed. But it affects the privacy of the user, as it implies the representation of whatever is being commanded through the form of speech to the periphery auditory. Consider the use case where one has to perform a phone call from within a bus. The user will obviously say out loud "call". This may cause an unpleasant situation when the user is not willing to share e.g. the contact being called. Some hardware work has been developed to minimize peripheral representations of speech and improve privacy, as in [1] but again this requires not only extra and expensive hardware but the burden of wearing cochlear implants.

2.3 BLUI: Low-Cost Localized Blowable User Interfaces

BLUI [4] presents a form of hands-free interaction that can be implemented on laptop/desktop computing platforms. This approach supports blowing at a laptop or computer screen to directly control certain interactive applications. Localization estimates are produced in real-time to determine where on the screen the person is blowing. This work relies on a microphone, such as those embedded in a standard laptop or one placed near a computer monitor. Even though this approach is: very cost-effective, since no extra-hardware is required; silent and discrete, since no voice/speech is needed, it may not fit some mobile 158 computing platforms because: mobile phones need simpler computing processes due to limited processing power, if compared to laptops, desktops; several mobile phone interfaces are not based on (mouse) pointers.

2.4   PuffText

This is an earlier version of the present solution. It proposes the use of a low-cost software-based puff controlled hands-free spinning keyboard for mobile phones as an alternative interaction technology for people with motor disabilities. It attempts to explore the processing of the audio from the microphone in mobile phones to select characters from a spinning keyboard. A proof of concept of this work is demonstrated by the implementation and experimentation of a mobile application prototype that enables users to perform text input through "puffing" interaction.

2.5   Text Entry Using Single-Channel Analog Puff Input

The purpose of this prototype [11] is to demonstrate a use of puff input for text entry. The entry method is based on hierarchical scanning like selection of characters located in a static table organized according to the letter frequency. The cursor is moved in a way similar to operating a claw crane machine with two buttons. To move the cursor to the target position the user needs to produce two puffs, the first selects the column, and the second selects the row. With a brief training the method is capable of entry rate of 5 WPM.

This work has inspired the grid layout approach and the column-row, two step selection.

3   Advances on Breathing Based Text Input for Mobile Devices

From the several experiments and interviews performed during [10, 12], we were able to identify significant and recurrent issues concerning puff-based interfaces for mobile devices, some of which we aim to address in this work, as an evolution from [7].

3.1   Ambient Noise

In [12] the detection of a puff was being performed with a simple sound level peak, using the phone's microphone. Whenever the solution was tested on rooms with a lot of noise, a high number of false positives was detected. Even when the sound level threshold was adjusted, if e.g. someone spoke with a 68–76 dB level (normal voice speaking [16]) the software would trigger a puff.

To address the proper detection of the puffs, we used a Fast Fourier Transform (FFT) algorithm, as implemented in [3, 17]. This has also enabled a puff calibration feature, in order to adjust the puff detection to a more customized use.

3.2   Using FFT to Process Signal from the Microphone on Mobile Phones

In this investigation, we are targeting a Windows Phone 8.1 enabled device to implement the system and perform experiments. The code below shows part of the sound matching procedure:

```
void microphone_BufferReady(object sender, EventArgs e)
{
        if (buffer.Length <= 0) return;

        // Retrieve audio data
        microphone.GetData(buffer);

        double rms = 0; double volume = 0;

        double cMagnitude = 0;
        double cPhase = 0;

        double[] sampleBuffer = new double[
FFT.FourierTransform.NextPowerOfTwo((uint)buffer.Length) ];
        double[] xre = new double[sampleBuffer.Length]; //
Real part
        double[] xim = new double[sampleBuffer.Length]; //
Imaginary part
        double[] spectrum = new double[sampleBuffer.Length /
sampleSize];

        for (int i = 0; i < 2048; i += 2)
        {
                sampleBuffer[index] = Con-
vert.ToDouble(BitConverter.ToInt16((byte[])buffer, i)); index++;
        }

        FFT.FourierTransform.Compute((uint)sampleBuffer.Length,
sampleBuffer, null, xre, xim, false);
        for (int i = 0; i < 512; i++)
        {
        rms += Math.Pow((10.0 *
Math.Log10((float)(Math.Sqrt((xre[i] * xre[i]) + (xim[i] *
xim[i]))))), 2);

                cMagnitude = (float)(Math.Sqrt((xre[i] *
xre[i]) + (xim[i] * xim[i]))); // Magnitude
                cPhase     = (float)(Math.Atan(xim[i] /
xre[i])); // Phase
                spectrum[i] = cMagnitude;
                cMagnitude = 0; cPhase = 0;
        }

        rms /= (double)512;
        volume = (int)Math.Floor(Math.Sqrt(rms));
}
```

At time of writing, in Windows Phone, the sample rate is fixed at 16.000 audio samples per second. According to the Nyquist sample theorem [14], this is appropriate for recording audio up to a frequency of 8 kHz. This is suitable for primitive simple sound sources, like human voice or puffs, but not so efficient with e.g. music.

Each sample is 2 bytes wide and monaural. This implies that each second of recorded sound requires 32 KB, and each minute requires 1.9 MB.

The TimeSpan value is the only option that microphone allows you to specify through the byte size of the buffer passed on GetData(). The BufferDuration property (which is of type TimeSpan) value, must range between 100 ms and 1000 ms (one second) in increments of 10 ms.

Assuming TimeSpan is 100 ms, this means that each time microphone.BufferReady is called we receive a buffer of size 3200 bytes/1600 audio samples.

FFT functions with a number of samples that is a power of two. Applying the FFT to the first 1024 samples means that the frequency resolution

$$\Delta f = 16000 / 1024 = 15.625$$

The magnitude of each FFT resulting element is referred to the frequencies

$$\Delta f, 2\Delta f, 3\Delta f, \ldots, (k/2 - 1)\Delta f \text{ (or } fs/2)$$

The most trivial form of sound pattern matching we might use would be to compare the two spectrum magnitudes, calculating the MSE. If the values differentiate within a determined threshold, the puff is detected. Unfortunately this simple approach may not be particularly effective – making puffs using more or less volume can affect the frequency components enough to fail the comparison.

This work uses a more advanced approach, named MFCC (Mel-frequency cepstral coefficients [15]) instead. This method extracts and compares key features in sounds. This approach is more efficient than the simple spectrum comparison - and it is less influenced by ambient noise or the volume of the tone.

The tutorial on [13] provide more in-depth information about FFT on Windows Phone devices.

3.3   Keyboard Layout

The keyboard layout on [7] helped us identify one recurrent issue during the experiments.

Figures 1 and 2 shows the user interface of the layout from [7], where that the keys are arranged linearly and in alphabetical order. This means that if the cursor is standing in front of e.g. "F" and the user wants to select the letter "E", he would have to wait until the cursor moves through the whole keyboard until he has another chance to select letter "E".

The work in [11] provides a grid layout of keyboard. The cursor is moved in a way similar to operating a claw crane machine with two buttons. To move the cursor to the target position the user needs to produce two puffs, the first selects the column, and the

Fig. 1. Screenshot of the first version of PuffText, with a linear round keyboard.

Fig. 2. Later version of PuffText, showing a graphical representation of audio volume.

second selects the row. We have reformed this layout and cursor movement pattern approach to the present work (Fig. 3).

Fig. 3. Grid layout and column-row selection of letters.

4 Experiments

For this round of experiments and interviews we have recruited the some of the same subjects as [7]. On the beginning of this round, we instantly noticed significant improvement in the subject's performance, due to training. Drafting repeated subjects also enabled us to reduce learning session's time and invest more time on training sessions with the new interface.

As soon as we reached the current implementation, 4 rounds of tests were conducted.

Each round consisted in one trying to perform the task of inputting a given text of 47 words.

Some text entry features, such as text prediction are still being tested, for preliminary evaluation simplification. Future works may include a more in depth analysis of the first 2 rounds were meant to be purely instructional. After that, 6 rounds of entering text using the present solution were timed. Three able-bodied and five disabled, high school students of $15 \sim 18$ years old, were tested.

The disabled group represented two types of disabilities: having no arms (birth defects) or lack of motor dexterity (due to accidents). The three subjects in this group are unable to handgrip a mobile phone manually.

The users were instructed to keep the distance of approximately 20, 30 and 50 cm during the first three rounds of tests.

These rounds of tests were meant to evaluate, emphatically:

- Puff accuracy at distance

- Background noise immunity – testing ambient noise handling with FFT algorithm
- Shortness of breath due to application usage
- Learnability of column-row letter selection interaction
- Memorability of column-row letter selection interaction
- Speed
- Typing mistakes

5   Results and Discussion

A proof-of-concept application was implemented to perform tests in order to support the argument of this work. The mobile application is able to deliver a way for users to perform text input with a hands-free, speech-free manner. This approach is software based, meaning it will not require extra hardware to function. It also presents itself as a rather discreet and private application, as it implies minimum representation (just puffs) of whatever is being inputted, to the periphery auditory.

The final fastest typing rate registered with this study group (able-bodied and disabled) and the given text was 8.8 words per minute and the average was 7.2. Compare to [6] were a Morse code typist makes 12.6 and a Mouth stick (hardware based) input solution gives 7.88 words per minute. The WPM was measured through logging character/timestamp in a text file on the phone and performing post-test calculation.

The distance of 20 and 30 cm from the user to the phone represented very little difference, although it was observed that the users tended to puff harder when the phone was moved slightly back (10 cm). Even though no shortness of breath episode was noted for these distances, an uninstructed user might report feeling winded. Future works may include a more in-depth analysis of shortness of breath due to puff controlled interfaces.

At the distance of 50 cm we were able to note various unsuccessful attempts, false positives due to background noise and minor shortness of breath. Users described feeling "far from the phone, even for reading".

Background noise handling algorithm adapts sound level peak threshold and microphone gain to reduce false positives and increase overall performance. The puffs – from a controlled distance of < 25 cm, were detected to a nearly zero false positive performance.

References

1. Arroyo-Palacios, J., Romano, D.M., Exploring the use of a respiratory-computer interface for game interaction. Paper presented at the IEEE Consumer Electronics Society Games Innovation ICE-GIC 2009, London, pp. 154–159 (2009)
2. Sibert, L.E., Jacob, R.J.K.: Evaluation of eye gaze interaction. In: Proceedings of CHI 2000 Conference on Human Factors in Computing Systems. ACM Press, The Hague, pp. 281–288 (2000)

3. Patel, S., Abowd, G., BLUI: Low-cost localized blowable user interfaces. In: Proceedings of the 20th Annual ACM Symposium (2007)
4. Jones, M., Grogg, K., Anschutz, J., Fierman, R.: A sip-and-puff wireless remote control for the apple iPod. Assist. Technol. Off. J. RESNA **20**(2), 107–110 (2008)
5. Sporka, A.J., Kurniawan, S.H., Slavík, P.: Whistling user interface (U3I). In: The 8th ERCIM International Workshop "User Interfaces For All", Vienna, Austria (2004)
6. Levine, S., Gauger, J., Bowers, L., Khan, K.: Comparison of mouth stick and morse code text inputs. Augment. Altern. Commun. **2**(2), 51–55 (1986)
7. Filho, J.F, Valle, T., Prata, W.: Explorations on breathing based text input for mobile devices. In: Proceedings of the 16th International ACM SIGACCESS Conference on Computers and Accessibility, pp. 345–346, ACM (2014)
8. Majaranta, P., Räihä, K.J.: Text entry by gaze: Utilizing eye-tracking. In: MacKenzie, I.S., TanakaIshii, K. (eds.) Text Entry Systems: Mobility Accessibility, Universality. Morgan Kaufmann, San Francisco (2007)
9. Stéphane, N., Lobo, F.G.: A virtual logo keyboard for people with motor disabilities. ACM SIGCSE Bull. **39**(3), 111–115 (2007)
10. Filho, J.F., Prata, W., Valle, T.: Breath mobile: a low-cost software-based breathing controlled mobile phone interface. In: Proceedings of the 14th International Conference on Human-Computer Interaction with Mobile Devices and Services companion, pp. 157–160, ACM (2012)
11. Sporka, A.J.: Text entry using single-channel analog puff input. In: Proceedings of the 16th International ACM SIGACCESS Conference on Computers and Accessibility, pp. 359–360, ACM (2014)
12. Filho, J.F., Prata, W., Valle, T.: PuffText: a voiceless and touchless text entry solution for mobile phones. In: Proceedings of the 15th International ACM SIGACCESS Conference on Computers and Accessibility, p. 63, ACM (2013)
13. Galazzo, S.: Sound pattern matching using Fast Fourier Transform in Windows Phone, (2013). http://developer.nokia.com/community/wiki/Sound_pattern_matching_using_Fast_Fourier_Transform_in_Windows_Phone
14. Nyquist-Shannon Sampling Theorem. http://en.wikipedia.org/wiki/Nyquist%E2%80%93Shannon_sampling_theorem
15. Mel-frequency Cepstrum. http://en.wikipedia.org/wiki/Mel-frequency_cepstrum
16. American Speech-Hearing Association. http://www.asha.org/public/hearing/Noise/
17. Sakamoto, D., Takanori, K., Takeo, I.: Voice augmented manipulation: using paralinguistic information to manipulate mobile devices. In: Proceedings of the 15th International Conference on Human-Computer Interaction with Mobile Devices and Services, pp. 69–78, ACM (2013)

BeaconPass: A Location Based APP Game for Traveler

Tsung-Yuan Ho[1], Chien-Hsu Chen[1(✉)], Sheng-Fen Chien[2], Yi-Hsuan Chen[1], Su-Yu Liu[1], and Juan Sebastian Bayona[2]

[1] Department of Industrial Design, National Cheng Kung University, Tainan, Taiwan
{ap313620,huokzv,suyu77121}@gmail.com,
chenhsu@mail.ncku.edu.tw
[2] Institute of Creative Industry Design, National Cheng Kung University, Tainan, Taiwan
schien@mail.ncku.edu.tw, sebasbayona@gmail.com

Abstract. BeaconPass is a smartphone/tablet application inspired by shared problems among travelers. Following our previews research; lack of internet access, GPS inaccuracy, battery life and insufficient site-specific information, reflect on travelers getting lost and missing on their touring expectations. Thus it was decided that the application's goal is to narrow the gap between previously planned activities and the exploration of a city. Beacon technology was selected as the means, from which the application would develop, to ease the exploration of a city. Given the potential that beacon technology holds for showcasing a wide offer of visiting alternatives, on a site-specific basis, the application has been packaged into a game that seeks to encourage the traveler to meet unplanned locations. Graphically, the game uses a "pirate's journey" metaphor that allows the user to level up while engaging in an open exploration of the city.

Keywords: Ibeacon · Location based game · APP · Traveler · Service design · Mobile application

1 Introduction

Within its planning dimension the application allows the user to design a trip by choosing desired visiting locations and setting a time and a start point from which the trip is going to develop into a complete traveling schedule. It was observed that inter-net is a recurrent source for travelers seeking guides and information regarding traveling tips. Also, social networks become a mean for validation of found information and play a role on gathering personal recommendations.

As a result of these practices, travelers tend to accumulate several desired visiting locations that applicationear unarticulated to the physical contexts that allocate them. For this reason, the application helps the process by suggesting alternative destinations relative to the places that have been chosen, allowing the user to fix the order in which the visit is going to be conducted under proximity based organization. As a result of this activity, the user will have created a visiting plan that can be shared on social networks in join the trip.

M. Antona and C. Stephanidis (Eds.): UAHCI 2015, Part I, LNCS 9175, pp. 288–297, 2015.
DOI: 10.1007/978-3-319-20678-3_28

The exploration dimension of the application starts when a previously conceived plan is set to action, providing site-specific information such as: directions, relative site information and schedule (among other), in an attempt to reduce the gap be-tween previously planned activities and unplanned situations that might applicationear along the exploration phase. This feature of the application is also designed to integrate different activities that are intrinsic to traveling practices (taking pictures, getting lost, exploring, finding food, sharing the experience, etc.) and encourages the traveler to find unplanned locations or scenes by their demand, or just randomly choosing their next stop.

2   Literature Review

2.1   Location-Based Games

These new game type take place normal virtual game's action in some dimension [1]:

- Players interacting object from simulators producing events to true events in real worlds.
- Player join the game themselves in location-based game instead of avatars and other characters interacting with each other.
- Player doing riddle and puzzle in virtual games, and chase some object or area in real world in location-based game.
- Players generating information in digital form associated with physical objects.

We using Google Scholar on March 20th, 2014 returned 483 publications. This is a full text index, so the publications found may have these keywords anywhere in their body, thus more thorough search in their content is needed. We view about 10 games in this result and make a list to observe and categorize them.

- *Area occupied games*

These games goal is occupy or collect some real-world's area virtually to gain score and keep some award, the service provider usually use these goal to reach their objection such like user data collection or crowdsource the area's information. For example:

- Team-It: Each player is assigned a number of skills; they have to use their own skill to rescue the virtual people in given city as much as you can [2].
- Urbanopoly: Player can occupy some spot by record "venues" picture, sold it and trade it to build a monopoly area [3].
- Frequency 1550: Players are told that they can earn citizenship in Amsterdam by collecting as many of the required 366 so-called Days of Burghership as possible. These 366 points refer to the medieval year-and-a-day rule, which is how long you had to be living inside the city walls to earn citizenship rights. Groups of four students each – two located at the headquarters at the Waag, the other two walking the streets of Amsterdam – are randomly assigned the identity of beggars or merchants, who have – as in the Middle Ages – a different social status in the game, causing merchants to win a confrontation in the city [4].

- *Treasure hunting games*

These games goal is finding several objectives in a given area, once you found these objectives; you can get some virtual award or collection. This type of action can persuade users unconsciously, and change user behavior by go to their unknown area. For example:

- iDetective: Players try to makes searching out a photo shooting location from one photograph, and go to the place where photograph was taken [5].
- See It: players use ambiguous visual clues in the form of images and video clips to find locations containing a hidden container. Players can also create and hide game content in order to help promote long-term engagement and an increasing numbers of players [6].

- *Learning games*

These game usually is a guide to learning something in given area, The services are tend to add some virtual data at some specific area, when player trigger the function in this area, a surrounding information context will pop up on your device. These application usually used in museum or area guide, and package it like a game to persuade user to use it. For example:

- Foursquare: automatically provide contextually relevant content in the world's major cities, user can learn local language when they entered some educational area [7].
- Tidy city: players need to physically explore their city by interpreting clues to find the correct target destination. And enable historical riddle provider walk around the city and collecting notes, images and GPS data for potential riddles [8].

2.2 Key Technologies in Location-Based Games

- *Locating people*

To get the location of the user there are several methods that can be used. The most common is to use the Global Positioning System (GPS) on smartphones as this is known to be more accurate than other methods. These include the WiFi-based positioning system (WPS) from Skyhook and Global System for Mobile Communications (GSM) based positioning. In 2010 ~ 2012's mobile location-based games, most of them are using GPS for their game's location technology. At that time, iBeacon and NFC technology are still not wide use in Location-based service game.

But there are some location-based game start using the ibeacon and NFC to build there system, such like CES 2014, CNET company use ibeacon technology to ask user in CES download their application to find hidden treasure in the exhibition. By the iBeacon supported devices increasing, that will be a potential indoor-location-based game technology [9].

- *Storing and accessing data*

Once the location has been established the application needs to use this to provide information about the location in the game. This data can be sourced in many ways. Two examples of these are: using open linked data or crowdsourced data.

Open linked data is when data sets are produced and are then made freely available to all over the internet. It must also be free of all copyright and in a format that is not owned by anybody. Linked data is when data is published in a structured logical manner so that different data sets can be easily combined as they are in the same format and it is easily queried.

Crowdsourcing is using the collective knowledge of a large group of users to decide on facts. If contributors can be kept involved crowdsourced data sets can grow rapidly. It is a good way of pooling the resources of a collection of people especially for mundane tasks. It is easier for lots of people to do a little bit each than for one person to do a lot as they will get bored. However this can only be claimed to have a validation rate of about 40 %.

Some treasure hunting game and learning game will use crowdsourcing to ask user to help service to collect big amount of data or generate the new treasure for found. Such like Urbanopoly or Tidy city.

Finally, for the fair of the competition games, area-occupied games usually use static context, and usually unable end user to change their data or add game content.

3 User Studies

The development of the application started with a field recognition on the assigned perimeter within the city of Tainan, Taiwan. From our observation exercise, the commercial and touristic attributes of the neighborhood caught our attention, reason for which a semi-structured interview was designed to bring light to our project. Tourists had been decided as our point of departure based on the analysis of our previous application oxidation in which their recurrence along the streets presented an opportunity for further research. This led us to raise questions regarding the ways in which tourists engage their touristic experience, how they organize their trips and how they make sense of spatial relations while exploring the city. Based on the information collected, activities surrounding tourist undertakings were identified and separated into "Planning" and "Visiting" as major umbrella categories under which, related activities were organized using POEMS [10]. This allowed us to get a better image of how tourists were conducting their experience and what other elements were involved in each of the major activities.

To put this information under perspective, activity theory [11] served as a tool to highlight the contradictions between planning and exploring in touristic endeavors; issues such as internet access, GPS, landmarks, language barriers, touristic offer and unplanned events, built into our project's attempt to diminish the above mention gap between planning and exploration (Fig. 1).

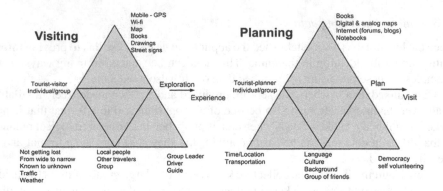

Fig. 1. Planning and visiting activity diagrams

After several discussions and fast prototyping alternatives to the identified problems, our project had developed into a location based application that would guide our user to easily reach a preset listing of desired visiting locations. The application posed the use of Beacon technology as an alternative to the technological issues that had been previously identified, also it seek to allow and encourage the user's exploration of the surroundings. Nevertheless the design of our application was still on a conceptual stage, reason for which, five personas were designed as a mean to put our application under perspective, realizing how different target customers were to use our application and how its succeeded or failed to satisfy their needs. Each of them was followed by a case scenario in which our application was to help them achieve a determined goal. From there the design of our project took off, and each of the required steps in order to complete the task was designed so that we then had a comprehensive product (Fig. 2).

Andy's scenario

	Planning	Sailing to next stop	Developing new spot	Get lost	Fill the diary
Internet	●				●
Mobile Phone	1. road			3. spot	
Digital Camera					●
iBeacon of Mapping		●		●	
iBeacon of Spot		●	●	●	
iBeacon of Shop			●		

6. shop

Fig. 2. Actor Andy's scenario

Adding to it, a follow up evaluation was done by abstracting each of the touch points within the personas' journey, meaning, instances in which our application eared as a tool to solve a need or mediate our users' actions. This exercise reflected on fixing navigation problems within our application by defining shortcuts and coherent pathways.

4   Game Design

4.1   Structure

Because our Application allow users to upload their interesting photos in the trip, and also the user can share his/her traveling plans with friends, the first way for people to know this Applications through some attractive sharing on the social network sites like FB. The second way to gain more users is through the shops that cooperate with us. We will set our "islands" (which has iBeacon inside it) in the counter of the shop. If a traveler enter in that shop and see the island, he/she may download our Application. After download the Application, the first screen of the loading applications should represent the pirates; portray an image that displays the ultimate goal of the pirate development on an action that could also relate to the function of the application. The game is designed for one player, in this sense he/she will play against the system or himself in order to grow within the application. There is only the role of the pirate, nevertheless this pirate will have many possible applications, in this way the player develops its own role or personality of the pirate. It is important to have a wide range of possible combinations and also place specific characteristics. In this way one user might "compete" by showing off the uniqueness of his character in relation to his traveling experiences. The use of the application in its planning or exploration modes reflects on points that will enable the user to access to more items for customization of the pirate (Fig. 3).

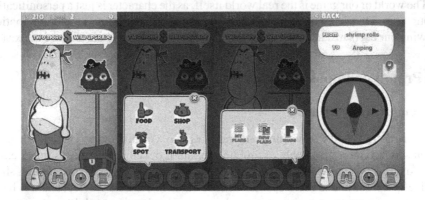

Fig. 3. Gameplays Screen

Users can customize and upgrade their own pirate by getting as many points as they can. Points are correlated to walked distances and fully accomplished plans. We encourage users to challenge their selves by setting an exploration plan (player de-fined) and find unplanned places along your way to collect as many points as you can finish your plans to upgrade. An exploration component, besides of the self-unplanned explo-ration, could be triggered by hiding treasures in our beacon islands setting in the whole city. In this game, gold (points) is presented as a currency within the game that is obtained by distances explored and can be traded for items. Stars represent levels of the pirate that will disclose different sets of purchasable items. Users will have their own inventory to save items like clothes, accessories, weapons and attributes.

4.2 Dramatic Elements

Traveling is an end for itself, nevertheless the way one person travels is subject to be modified, we challenge our players to engage in an exploration of their traveling spots by offering site specific opportunities of meeting unplanned locations. Our game is primarily chance based, although a preset plan might have been created by the user, the game encourages him to pursue unplanned visits, this is chance-based by the islands installed around the players' location and by the treasure alerts that might application near on the way. In this way our user falls in the category of the explorer player but also has a collector character in his pursue for character improvement. Our premise for exploration/tourism is done with the metaphor of pirates and their wondrous imaginary. In this sense our users start from a basic level or "lubber" (people not a sailor) growing with experience to become a professional traveler "Sea dog" (an experienced seaman), or a cap'n (captain). The story behind the game is the traveling experience of our user, for this reason our pirates should reflect on the user's story. This is done by providing site-related items that are inspired by the local culture. This allows that different vacations will result on different character possibilities that embody the stories behind them and that trigger the memory of our users.

The world of our game is the real world itself, as the character is just a personification of our user. This is made more evident on our integrated pirate to pictures option, allowing our users to add their pirates to pictures taken, giving them a world to exist in.

5 Prototype Implementation

5.1 Function Declaration

Our Core design is play on visiting and traveling. So we build the service in iOS application service cause it can able to mobile use and it develop difficulty is much easier than Android system for iBeacon support. The functions "Display surrounding shop/service/spot information at a stop." Is our core value in our LBS service, and it is based on several demands and restrictions inherent to exploration activities that can be answered when the application is implemented. Finally we select the iBeacon as our main LBS technology cause it has the longest sensor range. It's Also pair less, so we can receive a lot of information from different sensor at once.

5.2 Information Architecture

By spreading iBeacons in whole city, our mobile service can able to get the store and coordinate information by access nearest iBeacon, and merge with iOS's com-pass information and goal information in database, and display compass information—point the goal direction and distance. It will be used for "Get Lost" function and "Seek Island" function. Because our value is no WIFI reliable, and iBeacon must decode in client applications. That means we should build-in a large local database for map the iBeacon and Context or pre-download context when user has Internet access. The database store below data store coordination, store information, map coordinate information to map the real world's iBeacon spot to virtual map in mo-bile, it can be renewed by online database when user connect to Wi-Fi to ensure user can get the newest city information. We'll use the MySQL/PHP to implement online map server. It will combine the google map service and storage the map pin and re-late iBeacon mechanic unique ID, and it can be downloaded to client. Because of personal data, we should combine the account to share the plan, record the virtual character grow and upload the image. We can use a simple identified system or com-bine with Facebook.

We compose the "Trilateration positioning" and "Fingerprint positioning" in our method to get more accuracy location data. The localization technique used for positioning with wireless access points is based on measuring the intensity of the received signal (received signal strength in English RSS) and the method of "fingerprinting". Typical parameters useful to geo-locating the Wi-Fi hotspot or wireless access point include the SSID and the MAC address of the access point. The accuracy depends on the number of positions that have been entered into the database. The possible signal fluctuations that may occur can in-crease errors and inaccuracies in the path of the user. To minimize fluctuations in the received signal, there are certain techniques that can be application lied to filter the noise. In geometry, trilateration is the process of determining absolute or relative location points by measurement of distances, using the geometry of circles, spheres or triangles. In addition to its interest as a geometric problem, trilateration does have practical applications in surveying and navigation, including global positioning systems (GPS). In contrast to triangulation, it does not involve the measurement of angles. In two-dimensional geometry, it is known that if a point lies on two circles, then the circle centers and the two radii provide sufficient information to narrow the possible locations down to two. Additional information may narrow the possibilities down to one unique location.

We use fingerprint positioning method to measure the inaccuracy position in the city and use trilateration positioning by sensing multiple iBeacon and get RSSI for each beacons to get more accuracy position.

6   Evaluation

In this section, through one-on-one testing, we ask one subject to have a simple test of Beaconpass Application's paper prototype directly, and we recorded the problems he met in the test. After the game test, we had a brief interview with the subject, requesting for problems and suggestions during the game. Participant is two 23 years old student with design background. During the playing, one of the observers write down the problems he met, another one took respond for taking pictures and changing the pages of the interface for the user.

First in the preparation stage, we explain to the subject which Beaconpass applications a navigational application designed for serving outsiders or foreigners while traveling with pirate story as its content. We also set a task for him: suppose you are a stranger, travel to Tainan and using Beaconpass Application. During the process, you might get lost and need to plan your journey, and finally you can complete the task and upgrade your pirate. Through the observation of user testing, we could list out problems we found, and then arranged the result and the suggestions from our user with four aspects (four questions) in analysts of the Walkthrough proceeds.

7 Conclusion

After this project, we think the whole solution about foreigner taking trip to Tai-nan's Problem, and package in a game and user can solve these solution and take a trip in playing this application, feel yourself like a pirate. There are some part our team think we can improve in our games design. First, we can combine more Tainan's local element to fit the title "Tainan LBS games". Tainan is an ancient city and it has lots of culture element like sword lion, local sneak and ancient building in this city. Because our service is toward foreign tourist, we choose the element that foreign tourist will yearn for −pirate. And drop the element of Tainan. Although we can copy this business model to whole world cause we didn't use too much Tainan's local element, we still have to add some local element to make user more involved in Tainan City. Maybe make pirate wearing the local culture clothes is a good idea.

IBeacons are turned into islands that are installed inside local business in order to set a network of broadcasters. The islands are incorporated to our business model and also play with the pirate narrative and the larger brand construction. From our last public presentation in Tainan we received positive feedback, and good ideas were gathered from the public e.g., auto-sorting spots to minimize traveling distances when user managing locations, integrating local cultural elements into the app.

References

1. De Souza e Silva, A., Delacruz, G.: Hybrid reality games reframed: Potential uses in educational contexts. Games Cult. **1**(3), 231–251 (2006)
2. Frazier, S.: Location-Based Game Platform for Behavioral Data Collection in Disaster Rescue Scenarios (2012)
3. Celino, I.: Urbanopoly—a social and location-based game with a purpose to crowdsource your urban data. In: Privacy, Security, Risk and Trust (PASSAT), 2012 International Conference on and 2012 International Conference on Social Computing (2012)
4. Avouris, N.: A review of mobile location-based games for learning across physical and virtual spaces. J. UCS **18**(15), 2120–2142 (2012)
5. Yoshii, A.: A location based game to persuade users unconsciously. In: Embedded and Real-Time Computing Systems and Applications (RTCSA), 2011 IEEE 17th International Conference on, vol. 1, pp. 115–120, IEEE (2011)
6. Neustaedter, C.: See it: a scalable location-based game for promoting physical activity. In: Proceedings of the ACM 2012 conference on Computer Supported Cooperative Work Companion. ACM (2012)

7. Edge, D., Searle, E., Chiu, K., Zhao, J., Landay, J.A.: MicroMandarin: mobile language learning in context. In: Proceedings of the SIGCHI Conference on Human Factors in Computing Systems, ACM (2011)
8. Wetzel, R.: Tidy city: a location-based game supported by in-situ and web-based authoring tools to enable user-created content. In: Proceedings of the International Conference on the Foundations of Digital Games. ACM (2012)
9. Daniel Terdiman.: At CES, a hunt for hidden treasure, (2014). http://www.cnet.com/news/at-ces-a-hunt-for-hidden-treasure/
10. Kumar, V., Whitney, P.: Daily life, not markets: customer-centered design. J. Bus. Strat. 28(4), 46–58 (2007)
11. Uden, L.: Activity theory for designing mobile learning. Mobile Learn. Organ. 1(1), 81–102 (2007)
12. Brugnoli, G.: Connecting the dots of user experience. J. Inf. Architect. 1(1), 6–15 (2009)
13. Clatworthy, S., Service innovation through touch-points: development of an innovation toolkit for the first stages of new service development. Int. J. Des. 5(1) (2011)

Difference in Readability of Mobile Devices by Age Groups

Kohei Iwata, Yuki Ishii, Tatsuya Koizuka, Takehito Kojima,
Lege Paul, and Masaru Miyao[✉]

Nagoya University, Furo-Cho, Chikusa-Ku, Nagoya, Aichi 468-8603, Japan
kouoyashilv0@gmail.com, miyao@nagoya-u.ac.jp

Abstract. We carried out experiments to evaluate the readability of e-books under various conditions of illuminance. We used two types of e-paper, Amazon Kindle Paperwhite and Sony Reader, as well as plain paper as a reference. In this study, we focused on the effects of the contrast ratios between characters and background of e-book readers in terms of readability. This study found a dependency between the contrast ratio of the text of each device and their readability according to age groups.

Keywords: Evaluation of accessibility · Usability · Readability · User experience · Contrast ratio · E-books · E-paper · Kindle paperwhite · Sony reader

1 Introduction

In recent years, display technology has become widespread and highly developed. People are able to read or view high-quality content on e-readers and tablet devices. There are various methods of displaying texts on tablet devices which can affect readability. In an environment where illuminance is high, such as the outdoors, readability is reduced for liquid crystal display terminals such as the iPad because of the glare caused by the reflection that is likely to occur. On the other hand, the readability of e-book readers is less likely to decrease when the environmental illuminance is high because this display system is similar to paper. However, since e-book readers do not have a light source, readability is reduced in an environment with low illuminance. In order to solve such problems, manufacturers have inserted front lights into e-book readers.

In general, elderly people often have difficulty with reading because their eye lenses become cloudy with age and of presbyopia.

In this study, we focused on the effects of contrast ratios between characters and background of mobile devices in terms of readability. We carried out experiments with a reading test to evaluate how different age groups evaluated e-books under various conditions of illuminance.

© Springer International Publishing Switzerland 2015
M. Antona and C. Stephanidis (Eds.): UAHCI 2015, Part I, LNCS 9175, pp. 298–305, 2015.
DOI: 10.1007/978-3-319-20678-3_29

2 Method

2.1 Subjects

The subjects for this study included 107 healthy males and females between the ages of 15 and 78 years (mean: 46.9, SD: 15.5). We classified the subjects into three groups. Those individuals up to 44 years of as were placed in the "Younger" group, those who were 45–64 years old placed into the "Middle-age" group, and those who were 65 years old or older were in the "Elder" group. The subjects who usually wore glasses or contact lenses used them for the experiments. We obtained informed consent from all subjects and approval for the study from the Ethical Review Board of the Graduate School of Information Science at Nagoya University (Table 1).

Table 1. The age groups of the subjects

	Younger	Middle-age	Elder
Male	23	14	12
Female	18	35	5

2.2 Experimental Design

We carried out the experiment using an illumination box in a darkened room. The head-rest for the subject's forehead, which was on the illumination box, was kept at a visual distance of 40 cm. We carried out the experiment under conditions of 754 lx using a 6500 K LED light source with a fluorescent lamp that maintained the same color and temperature (Fig. 1).

Fig. 1. Experimental setting

We used two types of e-paper, the Amazon Kindle Paperwhite (released in 2013) [1] and the Sony Reader (released in 2013) [2], as well as plain paper (with the text printed on PPC paper of 69 % whiteness). Below, we will refer to the Paperwhite as PW, the Sony Reader as SR and the paper as Paper. The PW had an EPD (Electrophoretic Display) with front light, and the SR used a traditional reflective EPD. Since two of the electronic devices had different colored frames around their screens, we covered each frame with white Kent paper. Each device was raised to the same height as the subjects on the mounting board.

2.3　Task Design

The experimental task required subjects read silently the texts displayed on the devices. We used a random alphanumeric text. We used a PDF file for displaying the text, and a unified font size displayed on each device. The font type was Courier, and the font size was set at a uniform 8 pt. There were 30 characters per line, and 14 lines on each page. The display format conformed to those used for evaluation of electronic display devices in the International Organization for Standardization (ISO) [3]. Figure 2 shows an example of the text that subjects read.

We determined the contrast ratio for each display as the difference between the black text and the various changes in the shades of the colors for the different backgrounds. We calculated the contrast ratio from the measured values of the brightness of the background and the text. We set the contrast ratio at three levels by using three background colors in the grey level in which were numbered as 51 (dark gray), 153 (light gray) on the e 256 step scale between 0 (black) and 255 (white). We labelled the contrast ratio for, "Low" for the grey level of 51, "Medium" 153 and "High" at 255. We used 0 (black) for the text color. Table 2 shows the contrast ratio of each device.

```
eKRBg oK8onyo cB TO oyRj3 9Dco
qVqtKpI Mu zpjn4DsJ8 IuH6tg wh
BP MS bVLV5EbTm6 wW2Y 7IHnr 6f
Iat2V2kMTl MK zK Caza chPIkEvg
r4 hFSuMtGxd w5kpS M95Q yttZai
CRuNh8u t4 AMX 6gfKBM h9 nmAeh
9x 6Yx2JNx yS a5x0 oEw0891 YrA
26 fsDL vh IQVY Mi82 JXO6gL2Hr
tl fE2z O9 bupeh 9AqLJIFcUCpfB
hTDJ E3 QHQVK xkL hK2MEnC Y5Zt
tDE xcaelYf8e F4 Q1sXh GmOj xx
7L K8FnM a09GYy49S VfZXCJ78mHw
ta sV 3RvB bRKBmmr 3ntD2Iv 37R
Ee 9EJOB fi QM1n5 uQ3kYIItWFFq
```

Fig. 2. Example of text

Table 2. Contrast ratio of each device

	Low	Medium	High
PW	2.37	5.36	9.44
SR	1.83	4.38	9.01
Paper	1.31	6.62	14.37

We had subjects read the text silently from the top left. After reading, we had subjects evaluate the readability of text for case. This trial was carried out a total of nine times for each device and each contrast ratio. The order of device and contrast ratio was random for each subject.

We used subjective evaluations as an index for comparing the readability of the devices. After reading, we had subjects evaluate the texts using a visual analog scale (VAS). We converted the values of the VAS into a 100-*point* scale for analysis of the subjective evaluations (Fig. 3).

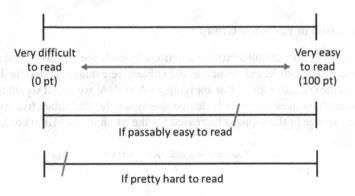

Fig. 3. Visual Analog Scale (VAS)

3   Results

3.1   Comparison of Each Device and Contrast Ratio

Figure 4 shows a graph of the subjective evaluations for each device according to the three contrast ratios. The vertical axis indicates the subjective evaluations, and the horizontal axis indicates the contrast ratio. After applying an ANOVA, there were significant differences in each device and each contrast ratio. Comparisons of the devices are shown by solid lines and comparisons of the contrast ratios are shown by broken lines. For all devices, the subjective evaluations decreased as the contrast ratios became lower. In particular, the evaluations of the Low contrast ratio were much lower than those of the Medium and High contrast ratios. Looking at each contrast ratio, evaluation of SR with a Medium contrast ratio was significantly lower than that of the other two devices.

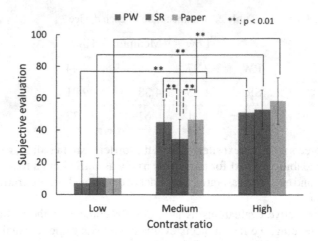

Fig. 4. Subjective evaluations for each device

3.2 Comparison of Each Age Group

Figures 5, 6, and 7 show the subjective evaluations by each age group divided according to each device. The vertical axis indicates the subjective evaluation, and the horizontal axis indicates the contrast ratio. After applying an ANOVA, we found significant differences between how ages rated each device. As a whole, the subjective evaluations decreased as the age of the subjects increased for the Medium and High contrast ratios.

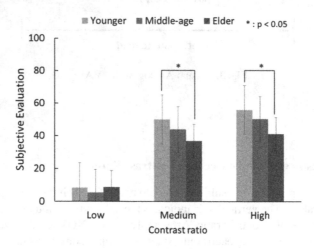

Fig. 5. Subjective evaluations of each age group (PW)

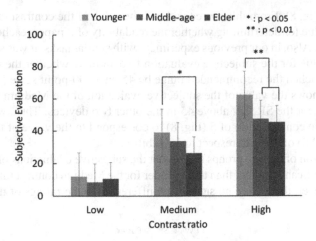

Fig. 6. Subjective evaluations of each age group (SR)

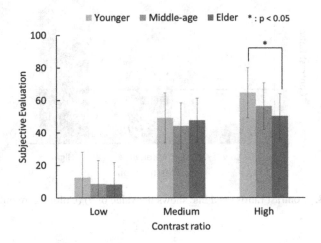

Fig. 7. Subjective evaluations of each age group (Paper)

4 Discussion

In this study, we evaluated the readability of e-paper and ordinary paper text. In the case of the Medium contrast ratios, the subjective evaluations of the SR were significantly lower than that of the other two devices (Fig. 4). This is explained by the fact that there was the boundary value of the contrast ratios that divided the evaluation between the contrast ratio of the SR and those of the other two devices. From a previous experiment, the contrast ratio of a display that can be used without discomforts was found to be a value of 5 or more [4]. On the other hand, the value of the Medium contrast ratio that we used in this experiment was lower than 5 for the SR, but greater than 5 for the other two devices (Fig. 8). From this, we considered the value of the contrast ratio of 5 to be a reference value for determining whether the readability of e-paper reached the recommended range. Also, in our previous experiment with similar tasks, it was suggested that a reference value for the subjective evaluation to determine whether the readability of e-paper has reached the recommended range be 45 on a 100-point scale [5].

Figure 9 shows the value of the subjective evaluation of the Medium contrast ratio is less than 45 for the SR, but above 45 in the other two devices. Thus, we considered the value of the contrast ratio of 5 (Fig. 8) to correspond to the value of the subjective evaluation (VAS) of 45 with respect to readability.

A comparison of the age groups shows that the subjective evaluations of the Younger group was significantly higher than that of Elder for the Medium contrast ratios of the PW and SR. However, there were no significant differences in the ratings of the Paper text.

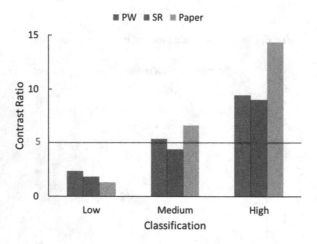

Fig. 8. Contrast ratios (Red line shows the value of 5) (Color figure online)

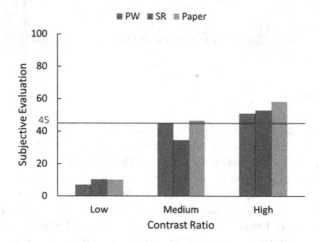

Fig. 9. Subjective evaluations (Red line shows the value of 45) (Color figure online)

The value of the contrast ratio for the Paper text was 6.62. This "Medium" value for paper is a value close to the contrast ratio of a newspaper [4]. Many elderly people are accustomed to this level of contrast ratio found in newspapers.

We found that the subjects tended to evaluate Paper higher than those of the other two devices for this experiment. For example, the subjective evaluations for Paper text were higher than those of e-paper devices in an environment of 750 lx. And this was consistent with the results of previous experiments [6]. Conventional paper has some advantages because of its various characteristics and long history [7].

5 Conclusions

In this study, we conducted a subjective experiment in order to compare and examine the differences in readability of mobile devices according to the contrast ratio of the text and background. For statistical processing, we divided subjects into three age groups. We used three devices in this experiment, Amazon Kindle Paperwhite, SONY Reader and plain paper text. We set the contrast ratios at three levels and asked subjects to evaluate the readability of each device using Visual Analog Scale.

From the experimental results, we found that there are positive and negative differences readability by the degree of the contrast ratio. Because the value of the contrast ratio of 5 corresponded to the value of the subjective evaluation (VAS) of 45, we think that the contrast ratio of 5 should be the criteria for determining whether e-paper has reached the recommended range of comfortable readability.

In terms of the age groups, the subjective evaluations decreased as the age of subjects increased for the Medium and High contrast ratios. We recognize that cloudiness in the eyes and cataracts reduces readability. For Low contrast ratios, the evaluations were low regardless of the device or age groups. Therefore, we feel that the values of Low contrast ratios are not suitable for any age.

References

1. Amazon – Kindle Paperwhite. http://www.amazon.com/gp/product/B00AWH595M
2. SONY – SONY Reader. http://www.sony.jp/reader/
3. ISO 9241–304: User performance test methods for electronic visual displays (2008)
4. Kubota, S.: Lightness and contrast requirements for legibility of reflective liquid cystal displays. J. Inst. Telev. Eng. Jpn. **50**, 1091–1095 (1996)
5. Koizuka, T., Ishii, Y., Kojima, T., Ishio, N., Lege, P., Miyao, M.: Proposing a baseline setup for readability using a visual analog scale. In: Proceedings of International Display Workshops (2014)
6. Koizuka, T., Sano, S., Kojima, T., Miyao, M.: Evaluating the effects of environmental illuminance on the readability of e-books. SID Symp. Digest Tech. Pap. **44**(1), 571–573 (2013)
7. Shibata, H., Takano, K., Omura, K.: Can electronic reading devices replace paper? Experiments to evaluate electronic reading devices. FUJI XEROX Technical Report, No. 21, 92012)

Mobile Assistive Technology Mapping and Integration

Luis Felipe Jimenez$^{(\boxtimes)}$ and Patricia Morreale$^{(\boxtimes)}$

Department of Computer Science, Kean University, Union, NJ 07083, USA
{jimluis,pmorreal}@kean.edu

Abstract. Assistive technology (AT) is designed to identify and provide individuals with disabilities independence and equal access to interact with their environment. With this type of assistance, people can maximize their independence and their performance of tasks they were not able to accomplish before. The research project illustrated here identifies one approach for an campus accessibility map to allow a population with mobility impairments to improve their daily experience when navigating through the Kean University campus. This project integrates an accessible campus map design with an interactive Android navigation mobile application to permit the identification of convenient accessible pathways within campus. In the project design phase, after a review of available accessibility maps elsewhere, usability studies were conducted in order to ensure that the application will meet the needs of the users. In the development phase, an accessibility layer was created on top of Google maps to display the accessible information on campus buildings, including convenient paths. This two-phase approach provides all students and visitors with critical accessibility information about the Kean University campus, while assisting researchers to design better overall user experiences in human computer interaction.

Keywords: Assistive technology · Accessibility · User experience · Navigation experience

1 Introduction

The majority of universities in the US have a mobile application campus map where students can find their location and building information. However, none of these university maps include sufficient accessibility information in their campus maps for students with mobility impairments. Unfortunately, these mobile map technologies are frequently designed without consideration of the needs of disabled and many other groups of people. Ideally all products would use a design-for-all approach [1, 7, 8].

This issue limits the independence of populations with mobility impairments and restricts their ability to freely interact with their environment. Developing a system that allows university community members with mobility impairments to locate accessibility information is imperative because they will feel confident and knowledgeable about where the accessibility locations are. Students will be able to take full advantage of the information regarding accessibility locations for their daily activities, and potentially improve their campus navigation experience.

© Springer International Publishing Switzerland 2015
M. Antona and C. Stephanidis (Eds.): UAHCI 2015, Part I, LNCS 9175, pp. 306–317, 2015.
DOI: 10.1007/978-3-319-20678-3_30

This research study investigated the design of a geo-location mobile application in order to assist Kean University students to locate campus accessibility locations. By creating a usability layer on top of Google maps, based on the accessibility features gathered from the design studies, members of the Kean University community with mobility impairments are able to identify important accessibility information such as: automated doors, handicap parking spots, elevators, accessibility restrooms and emergency doors, etc. Additionally, this project, called *NavKean*, includes the implementation a building-to-building routing path to provide individuals with disabilities alternative routes efficient paths. By designing an accessible user interface, this project takes into account usability and design principles for efficient and fast user interaction, keeping in mind that some users, due to their mobility levels, will have some issues when interacting with the application (i.e. pinching the phone display to zoom in or out).

This study is divided in two phases. In the first phase, usability studies and related work were evaluated in order to design a navigation mobile application for assistive technology to assist Kean University students and staff with disabilities, specifically mobility impairments. The second phase consists in the implementation of the application on a mobile phone. The scope of this project is limited, and the prototype presented here includes only accessibility information from Kean University's main campus.

2 Related Work

There are a variety of accessibility map applications for individuals with disabilities, which range from allowing users to rate the accessibility of individual buildings to displaying a map and its associated accessibility information. These applications have been created to provide individuals with disabilities a better experience when visiting a place by providing first hand information. One of the best examples of an accessibility application is University of New Hampshire (UNH) Campus accessibility map (Fig. 1) [2]. This is an interactive map, which allows users to click on every building, sidewalk and construction zone, to access the respective information. In addition, the map has convenient locate and zoom controls, as well as a map legend. This map also measures sidewalks and uses colors to identify slopes levels. Figure 1 illustrates the color code used to measure sidewalks' slopes. Green color identifies "Essential Level (0–2 %)"

Fig. 1. University of New Hampshire accessibility map

Fig. 2. Wesleyan University campus accessibility map

Yellow "Gentle Slope (3–5 %)", Orange "Moderate Slope (6–8 %)" and red "Steep Slope (9 %)". These slope percentages are taken from the ADA Act Standards for surface features [6]. These percentages allow individuals with disabilities to identify slopes levels and to determine how accessible a sidewalk is. In addition, the UNH accessibility map also identifies automated doors and constructions zones. Although this web-based map application, it has one of the best accessibility designs for campus navigation, however, the map lacks accessibility information for each building.

Wesleyan University (Fig. 2) has a campus accessibility map similar to UNH's [9]. An advantage over UNH campus accessibility map is that it identifies accessibility information for every building. In addition, this map has pre-drawn alternative routes on the map for pedestrians that use mobility chairs. One of the main disadvantages of this map is that it is not interactive. The only user-map interaction is a zoom magnifier that allows users to zoom in and out. The lack of interaction makes difficult to users to efficiently locate and access desired information. Another disadvantage is that accessibility information for individual buildings is displayed as a list of text on a different document (not on the map) and does not specify on what floor the accessibility features are located. In addition, the map does not have a legend to relate the map icons to their respective information on the same map. The information that is not on the same window, which makes users perform extra steps, which negatively impacts the user experience, due to the inefficiency of how the information is presented.

Yale University (Fig. 3) [10] also has a campus accessibility map. This university presents a partial interactive map. Once a user clicks on a building, a window pops out and describes how to access the building and if it has automated doors or not. The map identifies campus accessibility information such as: accessible routes within city blocks, indoor routes from accessible buildings, accessible building entrance with automatic door and elevators. Nevertheless, this map does not have ADA accessibility symbols, which are imperative to use because individuals with disabilities will be able to identify easily any type of accessibility information. Also, it lacks a legend to provide information on the map.

Fig. 3. Yale University campus accessibility map

Fig. 4. Truman State University campus accessibility map

Truman State University campus accessibility map (Fig. 4) is a Google Maps-based application. This map identifies handicap parking spots and how many there are. There is also an information icon on every building, which provides building's accessibility information such as: ramps, automatic doors, elevators and accessible bathrooms and their location of the building. Since this is a Google Maps-based application, it can actually provide directions by car, by public transit, walking and bicycling. This map uses ADA symbols. However, it does not identify sidewalks slopes [11].

Accessibility places (Fig. 5) [3] is a crowd sourcing mobile application for users primarily residing in the western region of India. The application requires users to input information pertaining to accessibility at places they are at. It allows users while at a place to determine if the place is accessible to people with different disabilities. This application is a great concept because the accessibility information is not just to a building, office or campus, but rather in general. The scope of the application is to simply display if the area is or is not accessible.

Fig. 5. Accessibility places app   **Fig. 6.** Accessibility map app

Accessibility map (Fig. 6) [4] is another crowd sourcing mobile application. This application goes into much more depth as opposed to the Accessible Places application. Information such as barriers and other possible obstructions are presented in a formal and very beneficial way. This is the type of application that the prototype presented here is modeled after because the goal is to give a user a great sense of the atmosphere, which is exactly what the NavKean application aims for.

3 Assistive Technology

Assistive technology (AT) is a system or product that is used to increase, maintain, or improve the functional capability of individuals with disabilities, ranging from mobility impairments and cognition to visual impairment and many others. The purpose of AT is to enable people to perform tasks that they were formerly unable to accomplish or may have had difficulty accomplishing, by interacting with specific technologies to accomplish such tasks. These technologies are made to improve functional capabilities in the everyday lives of those with disabilities.

4   Apps Evaluation

In order to design an accessible campus navigation mobile application, this research study is evaluating the accessibility interface and accessibility design features from the related work section (illustrated in Table 1). These features will be used to develop a high fidelity visual prototype to conduct usability testing; potential users will be able to interact with the application and suggest improvements.

Table 1. Accessibility features

Application	System features
University of New Hampshire	- Accessibility layers - Identifies slopes - Building names - Constructions zones
Wesleyan University	- Suggests pre-drawn routes for mobility chair students - Identifies building' accessibility information in a text form
Yale University	- Windows that display text with the building's accessibility information
Truman State University	- Google maps web-based application - Identifies buildings' accessibility information: routes, handicap parking spots and how many there are.
Accessibility places	- Users to rate how accessible a place
Accessibility map	- Identify accessibility information for buildings

The University of New Hampshire (UNH) web-based campus map application includes accessibility layers that allow users to locate accessible places on campus. This map identifies slopes, building names and constructions zones. However, this application lacks specific information regarding each building's floor accessibility, which is essential for students with disabilities in order to efficiently locate accessible restrooms, elevators, evacuation chair, etc. Also, this application lacks of a GPS-like route that suggests alternatives paths to avoid obstacles such as, slopes, stairs etc.

The UI of this application also makes complicated the user interaction. The mobile version of the web-based app has the zoom and the location buttons on the top left corner of the screen. This location makes harder to reach the buttons, keeping in mind the bottom right corner is more accessible since is closer to the thumb finger. In addition, if a user would like to access the search bar, s/he will have to tap a button and then the user will be taken away from the campus map to other search screen. Another accessible feature that is missing on the search bar is auto complete. This feature is important because it prevents error and improves search efficiency.

Truman State University and Wesleyan University web-based accessibility maps are not interactive. Even if a cell phone is used to open the map, users will not be able to locate themselves on the map. In addition, the map does not have any type of accessible controls to zoom in or out. Although these maps have accessibility information, they do not have enough information nor user interaction to improve a campus navigation experience. On the other hand, Yale University campus accessibility map is an interactive map where users can access buildings' information and directions. Although the map does not quantify the sidewalk levels nor suggest alternative accessibility routes, this map allows the users to find themselves on the map, if the application is used using a cell phone.

5 Visual Prototype Design

The objective of this research project is to identify the best design approach of a campus map mobile application that can assist Kean University students and staff with disabilities to identify accessibility information. For this purpose, a visual prototype was developed and is explained in this section.

To create and improve this application an iterative model was implemented with the goal of continuous improvement, dedicated to fixing any type of design issues that might affect the user navigation experience. Figure 7 indicates the life cycle of the application, which is explained as follows:

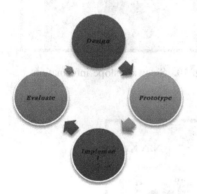

Fig. 7. Application usability life cycle   **Fig. 8.** Prototype main screen

Design: In order to develop an accessible mobile application, it is imperative to understand user needs and the tasks that they daily do when navigating through campus. With this in mind, to accomplish an accessible design, observations were made on how students with mobility impairments navigate through campus. Also, interviews with students and professionals on assistive technology were conducted, as well as an evaluation on related work to identified accessibility features. From the data gathered from these methods, ideas and requirements were identified to warranty an accessible design for a better campus navigation experience for students with disabilities.

Prototype: With the data gather from the design phase, a visual prototype was developed using an online tool [5]. The prototype is a concept that illustrates how the application will appear to the user. The advantage of creating a prototype in an early stage of the project is to get a better idea and understanding of how the stakeholders will interact with it. Once presented, the prototype encourages user feedback, which improves the design and development of the application. The prototype main screen has two buttons (Fig. 8), which will help users to select the best options to choose the map according to their mobility level. Each button will illustrate the same map and accessibility information; the only difference will be how the application will suggest routes to users.

The "I can walk short distances" button suggests accessible routes, but keeping in mind that a person that can walk short distances can still walk through some slopes. The "I use a mobility chair" button suggests paths that will avoid any types of slopes. Once any of the buttons is tapped, the user will be taken to the campus map (Fig. 9), where accessibility information such as: automated doors and accessibility parking spots are displayed on the map.

Fig. 9. Campus map   **Fig. 10.** Sidewalk slope information

Fig. 11. Building name   **Fig. 12.** Floor-by-floor accessibility information

As well, sidewalks with slope information are identified using colors to show slope incline levels. A yellow color indicates a 1 % slope, and a red color a 2 % slope (Fig. 10). If a user taps on any building, an information window will be displayed (Fig. 11), along with its name. Users will be able to tap on the window in order to access to the floor-by-floor accessibility information in that building (Fig. 12) This information includes automated doors, accessibility restroom, elevator and emergency evacuation chair.

Evaluation: As the evaluation is the heart of the process, after developing the visual prototype, it was evaluated for assistive technologies professionals, public safety officers at the university, including fire safety, and the focus group that included two individuals with disabilities and a student that was not familiar with the campus map. The feedback gathered was very positive. Some recommendations from the focus groups and professionals on the AT fields were made to improve the accessibility design of the project.

Implementation: Based on the data gathered from the design, prototype and evaluation a mobile application was developed, taking into account the requirements needed according to the related work and feedback from the focus group.

6 Prototype Evaluation

The purpose of the usability study is to evaluate how the stakeholders will interact with the application. This way, usability problems such as: Is the information valuable in the context provided? Is the interface accessible? Could be identified and fixed. An early usability study was conducted with a focus group and two professionals in the assistive technology field. The prototype was shown to these users to obtain feedback to improve the application, creating a usable and functional application that can best meet the needs of users with mobility impairments. During testing, users were asked to think aloud while they were interacting with the prototype. Throughout the process, the testers were making observations on users interactions and comments. Some of the features that were suggested during the tests were a routing feature that suggests paths to avoid slopes, individual floor accessibility information by building, a location button to identify handicap parking spots, and an automated door button, with a tracking position and a way to differentiate between automated door with sensor and a push button doors.

7 Prototype Development

Based on the apps evaluation and the prototype evaluation section, a mobile application prototype was developed with the accessibility features that this study considered as the best practices in accessible design, compared to existing applications from discussed in Sect. 2. For this application the Android SDK was used to develop a mobile application prototype. By creating a usability layer on top of Google maps, accessibility information was identified.

Figure 13 illustrates the user interface created for the mobile prototype. The first screen of the application is Kean University's campus map, on it; the evacuation zones are identified in case of an emergency. Also, if a user needs accessibility information from a building, s/he can tap on any (Fig. 14), and a window will be displayed with the building name. If a user taps on the window, s/he will be taken to building's floor-by-floor accessibility information (Fig. 16), which indicates in which floor accessible restrooms, elevators; automated door and emergency evacuation chair are located.

For accessibility purposes and an efficient navigation experience, a search bar was created and an auto complete feature was implemented (Fig. 15). This feature will reduce errors from users when typing information into the search bar. A locate button was created with the purpose of helping users to always find themselves on the map. For users with hands mobility impairments, to pinch in or out to zoom might be hard, for this reason, zoom buttons were created and conveniently located at the bottom ri-

Fig. 13. Campus map

Fig. 14. Building name

Fig. 15. Pre-filled accessibility information

Fig. 16. Floor-by-floor information

Fig. 17. Routing feature

Fig. 18. Number of parking spots

ght corner of the screen. This position is more accessible for users since the buttons are located closer to the thumb finger, which usually are used to reach these buttons.

Automated doors, handicap parking spots and the information buttons are located at the bottom of the screen for an easy access. If the automated doors or/and the handicap parking spots buttons are tapped, a little blue light will turn on in the button. This feedback will allow users to know that the button is working fine in the case of a delay when displaying doors or handicap parking spots. The application also distinguish between push button automated doors and doors with sensor. As well, if a user taps on any handicap parking spot, a window will display how many parking spots there are in that area (Fig. 18).

In addition there is a "Direction" button (Fig. 16), which will suggest a path from the user's current position to the desired building. The route will suggest the shortest path avoiding slopes and difficult pathways. Since the application is still under development there is a bug in the code that does not allow the direction feature to work properly (see Fig. 17).

8 Usability Studies

A second usability test was conducted with the focus group and a student that was not familiar with the campus. On this test users were asked to perform series of tasks and think aloud while performing them.

On the first task users were asked to interact with the application by locating the automated doors using the "Automated door" button. *Users said that the automated doors took too long to display.* Also, since the pushbutton doors and sensor-automated doors are being differentiated by colors, users suggested *using a better color to identify the sensor doors, since the current color does not have a good contrast with the map.* On the second task users were asked to identify parking spots by using the "parking spots" button, the suggestion on this task was *to show how many parking spots there are.* The third task was to tap on any building and to access to its respective information, according to one of the users, she was not sure if she had to tap on the window to access to building's information. Although there is an information icon inside of the window (Fig. 14), it seems that is not clear that in order to access to building's information, the user needs to tap on the window. The suggestion was to add a text that says, "Tap for more info". Once the user accessed to the building information, she was asked to comment about the relevance of the information and how it was presented. Her suggestion was that instead of having the building floors being the first floor on the top and fourth floor at the bottom, to have the floors starting from the button up, this way the presentation of the information would be more intuitive since the first floor is always on the bottom. Another suggestion was to have floor number as a text and numbers, this way, users will identify easier the information.

9 Discussion

After conducting an early usability testing with the visual prototype and a second test with the mobile application prototype, this study found that in order to create an accessible application two main designs factors need to be considered to deliver an integral application: the system design and the user interface design. The *system design* includes all the information that the application is going to provide such as: automated door and handicap parking spots locations, etc. The *user interface design* includes all the features that users will be controlling to interact with the application such us: buttons and controls.

By developing a system with clear information, individuals with disabilities will not only have first hand access to important accessibility information from their smart phones, but the relevance of this information might be the difference between a positive or a negative campus navigation experience. Parallel with the system design, it is imperative to create an accessible user interface design to ensure an efficient interaction between the users and the system. During the usability testing, one of the observations was that not only accessibility information is important, but also since this is an interactive application, user interaction needs to be efficient and joyful. For this reason when designing the user interface Fitt's law was used to determine the position and location of controls (i.e. buttons to display automated doors, parking spots and the legend, same as the zoom control buttons). Also, a Keystroke-Level model evaluation was performed to ensure an efficient user interface, this way, users can efficiently access to any information in less time.

By comparing the system discussed on the previous work section from a system and a user interface design perspective, most of those systems were lacking either system information or user interface features, keeping in mind that the target users are individuals with disabilities. The lack of this information makes a difficult interaction and user experience. In order to develop any system, requirements need to be identified to deliver a good product; in this project, this is done by taking into account users needs by conducting observations and usability studies. When users interacted with NavKean, they gave very positive feedback highlighting the importance of the development of this application and the positive impact that it will bring to their daily campus navigation experience.

The prototype was developed with the majority of features gathered from the apps evaluation and prototype evaluation sections. The purpose of this research project was to develop an accessibility mobile application to positively impact the campus navigation experience among individuals with disabilities, because Kean University did not have a campus accessibility map with accessibility information. This application benefits the Kean university community with disabilities and other visitors and new students.

10   Future Work

Future work on the application include features such as a parking reminder, building accessibility rating, bus route information, and speech recognition for blind people, with the overall goal being the assurance of a good accessible application for the Kean community. Also, a legend button (see Fig. 18) will be implemented to display icon information.

Plans for a third usability test to be conducted with the focus group to test the routing feature are also underway. This study will be conducted as follows: The application will be tested individually by participants in 45–60 min. During this time the testers will give to a participant a start location within the main campus (i.e. Downs Hall) and destination (i.e. Willis Hall). The testers will be walking alongside with the

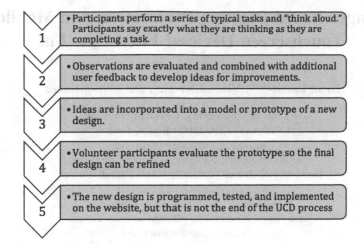

Fig. 19. Planned usability testing

participant, making observations to see how participants interact with the application. Also, the testers will ask participants questions before, during and after they finish testing the application. Figure 19 illustrates the testing process.

References

1. Nielsen, J.: Usability Engineering. Academic, New York (1993)
2. New Hampshire University Accessibility Map. http://facgismaps.unh.edu/Html5Viewer_1_3/?viewer=unhaccessibility
3. Accessible places. https://play.google.com/store/apps/details?id=com.celerapp.redpanda.accessibleplaces
4. Accessibility Map. https://play.google.com/store/apps/details?id=ru.articul.kartadostupnosti
5. Fluid. www.fluid.com
6. Americans with Disabilities ACT (ADA). http://www.ada.gov/regs2010/2010ADAStandards/2010ADAstandards.htm#pgfId-1006158
7. Petrie, H., Bevan, N.: The evaluation of accessibility, usability and user experience. In: Stepanidis, C. (ed.) The Universal Access Handbook. CRC Press, New York (2009)
8. Sharples, M., Corlett, D., Westmancott, O.: The design and implementation of a mobile learning resource. Pers. Ubiquitous Comput. **6**(3), 220–234 (2002)
9. Wesleyan University. Accessibility Information. http://www.wesleyan.edu/about/accessibility/map.html#top
10. Yale University Campus Access Map. http://www.yale.edu/rod/accessmap/
11. Truman State University Accessibility Map. https://maps.google.com/maps/ms?msid=216751922845241137356.0004e09d511ebe89003c1&msa=0&dg=feature

Finger-Based Pointing Performance on Mobile Touchscreen Devices: Fitts' Law Fits

Sandi Ljubic[1($\boxtimes$)], Vlado Glavinic[2], and Mihael Kukec[3]

[1] Faculty of Engineering, University of Rijeka,
Vukovarska 58, 51000 Rijeka, Croatia
sandi.ljubic@riteh.hr
[2] Faculty of Electrical Engineering and Computing,
University of Zagreb, Unska 3, 10000 Zagreb, Croatia
vlado.glavinic@fer.hr
[3] Polytechnic of Medimurje in Cakovec,
Bana Josipa Jelacica 22a, 40000 Cakovec, Croatia
mihael.kukec@mev.hr

Abstract. In this paper we investigate the utility of Fitts' law for predicting the performance of finger-based pointing on mobile touchscreens, by taking into account both different screen sizes and appropriate interaction styles. The experimental design bases on randomly generating pointing tasks in order to provide a wider range of both suitable target sizes and required finger movements, thus targeting a better representation of common pointing behavior with respect to the usual static test design with a smaller set of predetermined tasks. Data obtained from the empirical study was evaluated against Fitts' law, specifically its revision which defines target size as the smaller dimension of a 2D shape. Results show a strong model fit with our data, making the latter a fair predictor of pointing performance on mobile touchscreen devices. Altogether ten finger-based pointing models are derived, revealing Fitts' law pragmatic utility regarding various mobile devices, interaction styles, as well as real target sizes commonly found in mobile touchscreen interfaces.

Keywords: Fitts' law · Pointing performance · Mobile devices · Touchscreens · Finger input

1 Introduction

Since its proposal in 1954, Fitts' law [1] has became probably the most studied performance model in the area of Human-Computer Interaction. It denotes the movement time MT as a linear function of "index of difficulty" ID:

$$MT = a + b \times ID \tag{1}$$

$$ID = log_2\left(\frac{A}{W} + 1\right) \tag{2}$$

The expression (2), commonly known as *Shannon formulation* for ID [2], differs from the original Fitts' work, but is preferably used today because it provides better

© Springer International Publishing Switzerland 2015
M. Antona and C. Stephanidis (Eds.): UAHCI 2015, Part I, LNCS 9175, pp. 318–329, 2015.
DOI: 10.1007/978-3-319-20678-3_31

analogy with the underlying information theory and always provides positive *ID* values [3]. *MT* is the average time taken to complete the required movement in a pointing task, *A* stands for the movement amplitude (the distance from the starting point to the center of the target), *W* represents the target size (width), while *a* and *b* are slope and intercept coefficients typically derived using linear regression on data obtained from experimental testing.

2 Related Work on Fitts' Law: A Recapitulation

A number of Fitts' law revisions have been developed in HCI since its original introduction in 1954, targeting prediction improvement under particular conditions which include different pointing devices, interaction modalities, contexts of use, and experimental setups.

Weldorf [4] replaced the target width *W* with the *effective width* W_e $(W_e = \sqrt{2\pi e}\sigma)$ in order to tackle users' actual pointing precision i.e. "to reflect what a subject actually did, rather than what was expected" [2]. The proposed $W \rightarrow W_e$ adjustment, in which σ represents the standard distribution of endpoints, should be applied in cases when an error rate other than 4 % is observed [2]. MacKenzie and Buxton [3] extended Fitts' law to two-dimensional target acquisition tasks. They compared several interpretations of target width, and showed that the *smaller-of* model, which uses the smaller dimension of a rectangular area as the target width $(W = min(W, H))$, is both easy to apply and significantly better than the usual approach. On the other hand, Accot and Zhai [5] focused on the effect of target shape on pointing performance, and showed *H/W* ratio to be important as well. Their study resulted with Fitts' law revision involving the Euclidean model wherein unequal impact of *W* and *H* is included through a single weighting factor η.

One of the known Fitts' law limitations concerns pointing to particularly small targets, because the model's prediction accuracy then decreases. Oel et al. [6] argued that small targets (10–20 pixels, such as checkboxes or radio buttons on desktops) need above-average more time to be hit. Since the standard Fitts' law failed with their data, regarding small targets and low-valued IDs, they derived a new power law model that fits the reported data best. Chapuis and Dragicevic [7] also confirmed a deviation from Fitts' law for small target acquisition using a mouse, and declared both motor and visual sizes as limiting factors. They furthermore showed that the so called "tremor" model, originally developed by Weldorf et al. [8], can be used as a better predictor for small-target pointing tasks. The respective model uses $(W_e - c)$ instead of the effective width W_e, where *c* stands for the experimentally obtained constant assigned to human "tremor" (the case when cursor's hot spot changes its location in unpredictable ways).

Fitts' law small-target problem could be of particular importance when interacting with touchscreen devices, due to the well-known "fat finger" problem. Investigating Fitts' law relevance in the touchscreen domain has attained quite an interest in the HCI community. Albinsson and Zhai [9] proposed two techniques for finger-based pointing on a pixel level. For desktop-based pointing tasks they obtained a rather poor fit between the Fitts' law model and the actual collected data. Nevertheless, interaction techniques in their study were more complex, involving multiple steps for task completion, hence applying Fitts' law in their case can be questioned. Sasangohar and MacKenzie [10] evaluated mouse and touch input by emulating original Fitts' reciprocal tapping task on a 32″ touch-sensitive tabletop. The predictive power of Fitts' law was not considered in their work, but higher error rates in touch-based pointing was revealed, especially in the small-target scenario with $W = 8px$ (approximately 5 mm with the resolution used). Cockburn et al. [11] investigated performance of tap, drag, and radial pointing gestures using finger, stylus, and mouse. Finger input tapping was performed using a 23″ touch-capable all-in-one PC, the related results showing a strong fit ($R^2 = 0.97$) with the Shannon formulation of the Fitts' law. They also reported a finger pointing inaccuracy (13–14 % error rate), particularly for the smallest target size used ($W = 5$ mm on a 1920×1080 touch display).

When it comes to interaction with touchscreen mobile devices with generally smaller displays (namely smartphones and tablets), suitability of Fitts' law has recently been tested by Bi et al. [12]. A new model revision is proposed (called *FFitts*), basing on a dual-distribution hypothesis for interpreting the distribution of the endpoints in finger touch input. Such an approach assumes target width adjustment using both the standard distribution of endpoints (σ), and the absolute precision of the input finger (σ_a). In the respective study, small-target acquisition was specifically addressed by using tasks with circle-shaped targets with only three widths (2.4 mm, 4.8 mm, and 7.2 mm) on a 3.7″ smartphone display. Experimental results showed that the predictive power of *FFitts* model outperforms the conventional Fitts' law with either a target nominal width or a target effective width. Okada and Akiba [13] evaluated Fitts' law against different touchscreen sizes. For stylus-based pointing performance they proposed new model formulations that include raising factors α and β, reflecting the effect of screen size. Three mobile devices were used in their empirical research, namely two tablets with 10.2″ and 6″ screens, and one PDA with 2.8″ display. Finger-based input was not evaluated, however small-target pointing with stylus showed to be inaccurate as well (11 % error rate on PDA with 2–4 mm target widths).

Table 1 summarizes the abovementioned work on Fitts' law by presenting the model versions, related mathematical expressions, and the respective main properties.

3 Small Targets: Things Are not (Always) as They Appear

Although the problem of small-target pointing in mobile touchscreen interfaces is both well-known and well-studied, in this paper we argue against its overestimation. Specifically, we question the practical effect of involving particularly small target sizes ($W < 4$ mm) in empirical research of touchscreen pointing performance. The rationale originates from a simple fact: such targets are actually seldom in common mobile application GUIs. Mobile applications that inherently employ zoom-and-point interaction design can be considered as a special case. Selecting a tiny object from a highly populated geo-map (e.g. *Google Maps* application), or, sometimes, a particular link on a webpage (browser applications, usually with pages not optimized for mobile devices) can be considered as a difficult small-target pointing task. However, zoom-and-point enables users to adapt the content view in such scenarios, so as to make touch targets

Table 1. Fitts' law revisions

Author(s)	Mathematical expression for model	Focus/Properties
Fitts (1954) [1]	$MT = a + b \cdot \log_2\left(\frac{2A}{W}\right)$	Original; 1D pointing (reciprocal tapping) tasks
MacKenzie (1992) [2]	$MT = a + b \cdot \log_2\left(\frac{A}{W} + 1\right)$	*Shannon formulation*; 1D pointing tasks; *ID* > 0
Welford (1968) [4]	$MT_e = a + b \cdot \log_2\left(\frac{A}{W_e} + 1\right)$	1D pointing tasks; actual vs nominal performance (normalizing target width: $W \rightarrow W_e$)
MacKenzie and Buxton (1992) [3]	$MT = a + b \cdot \log_2\left(\frac{A}{\min(W,H)} + 1\right)$	*Smaller-of* model, 2D pointing tasks; focus on smaller dimension (*Width, Height*) of target rectangular shape
Accot and Zhai (2003) [5]	$MT = a + b \cdot \log_2\left(\sqrt{\left(\frac{A}{W}\right)^2 + \eta\left(\frac{A}{H}\right)^2} + 1\right)$	Euclidean model with one weight; effect of $W \times H$ target shape (taking into account both dimensions)
Oel et al. (2001) [6]	$MT = \left(a \cdot W^b\right) \cdot A^{c + d \cdot \log_2 W}$	Power law model; pointing tasks for small target areas and/or low *ID* values
Chapuis and Dragicevic (2011) [7]; Welford (1969) [8]	$MT = a + b \cdot \log_2\left(\frac{A}{W_e - c} + 1\right)$	"Tremor" model (motor inaccuracy modeled by subtracting a "tremor constant" c); small targets
Bi et al. (2013) [12]	$MT = a + b \cdot \log_2\left(\frac{A}{\sqrt{2\pi e\left(\sigma^2 - \sigma_a^2\right)}} + 1\right)$	*FFitts* model; touchscreens; finger-based pointing; dual-distribution interpretation of the endpoints; small targets
Okada and Akiba (2010) [13]	$MT = a + b \cdot \log_2\left(\frac{A^\alpha}{W} + 1\right)$ $MT = a + b \cdot \log_2\left(\frac{A}{W^\beta} + 1\right)$	Touchscreens; stylus-based pointing; device screen size (α – larger devices, β – smaller devices)

larger and thus easier to acquire. In other words, users will (probably) avoid selecting a few-pixels large target if there is a possibility to expand the underlying application content in the first place. When it comes to common mobile application interfaces, which consist of usual elements such as menus, lists, toolbars, icons, checkboxes, radio buttons and sliders, related target areas usually depend on a device's OS, screen size, and display density. On larger devices, extra screen real estate is commonly used to reveal more content and ease pointing; e.g., application launch screens on tablet devices contain larger icons than their counterparts on smartphones. In any case, mobile software developers are investing efforts to make actionable GUI elements appropriate in size for every display, often by following well-known design guidelines (e.g. iconography guidelines for Android devices [14]). Specifically, best practices in designing icons for Android OS assume the total touch-enabled area of a particular icon (full asset) to be larger than the icon picture itself (focal area).

While a certain image provides both the desired metaphor and a visual clue for related touch-target, icon pointing is facilitated in advance by allowing more actionable space around the used image. Nevertheless, end users can be (and often are) completely unaware of such discrepancy between the size of the imaged visual clues and the corresponding actual target areas. Visual clues are placed there on purpose – they inherently focus the user's attention and motor movement to touch-targets in question, but one must know that the related pointing tasks usually involve some "hidden extension" of real target proportions. Figure 1 presents several use cases in which visual clues do not exactly correspond to actual touch targets, with size differences given in both pixels and millimeters.

According to the above, our empirical research of finger-based touchscreen pointing performance does not involve particularly small targets; the task ID range is assigned in line with both particular screen size and commonly used target sizes instead.

4 Empirical Evaluation of Touchscreen Pointing Performance: Materials and Methods

For testing purposes, we implemented an Android application for gathering touch-screen pointing events and the corresponding timing data. The application stores in the CSV format on the device's internal SD card the measured results along with the information about user ID and utilized interaction style. When speaking of interaction style, we are referring to a combination of hands posture and device orientation while executing pointing tasks. Specifically we investigate thumb-based pointing performance on portrait oriented smartphones, as well as forefinger-based pointing on smartphones and tablets in both portrait and landscape orientation (Fig. 2). Forefinger-based pointing corresponds to the use case wherein one hand is holding the device, while the other – usually the dominant one – performs the pointing task.

Target pointing tasks for Fitts' law verification are easy to implement, as a single task instance only needs a designated starting point and a given target. However, unlike the usual approach which assumes predefined sets of distances A and target sizes W (cf. [5–7, 9–13]), our application randomly generates pointing tasks according to the: (i) mobile device screen size, (ii) position and size of the starting point, and (iii) defined margins for rectangular target width (Fig. 3).

Specifically, for five possible starting touch areas (four in the screen corners, and one in the middle) a random set of rectangular shapes is generated, representing pointing targets, whose distance from the starting point A and target size W jointly form particular ID values with a resolution of 0.5. The smaller dimension of the rectangular shape is considered as the actual target width, hence Fitts' law revision that we want to evaluate here is the well-known MacKenzie-Buxton *smaller-of* model. The example presented in Fig. 3 can be elaborated in more detail. If the task generator can produce 7 random tasks with ID values between 1.0 and 4.0 for each corner-positioned starting

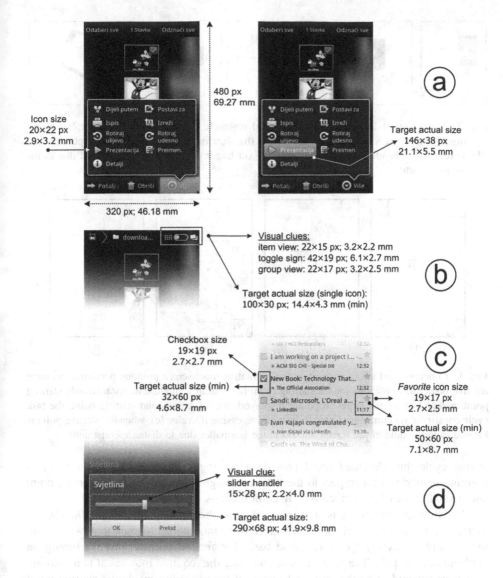

Fig. 1. Use cases in which visual clues do not exactly correspond to actual touch targets: choosing image management action in *Gallery* – actual target is list item, not an icon (a); changing display type in *Gallery* – the visual clue in question does not represent three actions/icons, instead a single action is assumed (b); marking items in *Gmail* – enabled through edge-positioned targets with sizes larger than one could anticipate (c); slider control can be activated by touching anywhere in the control space, it is not necessary to point the slider handler precisely (d). Snapshots are taken on *Samsung Galaxy Mini 2* (GT-S6500D).

point, as well as 6 random tasks with ID values between 1.0 and 3.5 for the starting point located in the middle of the screen, this makes a total of 34 pointing tasks covering a wider range of finger movements on a particular display. We believe that the

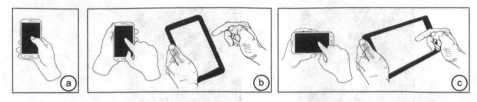

Fig. 2. Interaction styles used in our empirical research: thumb/portrait on smartphones (a), forefinger/portrait on smartphones and tablets (b), forefinger/landscape on smartphones and tablets (c). Single-handed thumb-based pointing on larger screens is not considered due to the tablets' form factor.

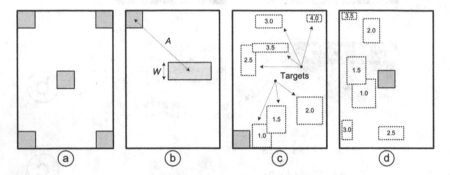

Fig. 3. Concepts used in our application for evaluating touchscreen pointing performance: there are five predefined positions for the starting point (a); within a single task instance only starting point area and generated target shape are displayed (b); for a particular starting point, the task cycle consists of randomly generated tasks with increasing ID value (c); when the starting point is located in the middle of the screen, the ID range is smaller due to distance constraints.

testing cycle thus designed could provide a better representation of the user's real pointing scenarios with respect to the "static" design including a single starting point and a smaller set of predefined $A \times W$ combinations.

The time measurement is implemented with the *SystemClock.elapsedRealtime()* method, as the respective clock is guaranteed to be monotonic, tolerant to power saving modes, and is anyway the recommend basis for general purpose interval timing on Android devices [15]. The time taken to complete the required movement in a pointing task is considered to be the interval between a *tap-up* action inside the starting point and a *tap-down* action within the target shape area (Fig. 4).

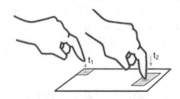

Fig. 4. Pointing task movement starts after losing touch contact within the starting point area (t_1), and lasts until contact is restored within the target rectangular shape (t_2). Pointing time is then calculated as (t_2-t_1).

In our empirical research 35 users were recruited (28 males, 7 females), their age ranging from 21 to 31, with an average of 23.1 years (SD = 2.2). Only two of them were left-handed. While every user confirmed her/his adequate experience in operating touchscreen smartphones and tablets, 80 % of them declared an Android-based device as their own personal gadget.

We used four different mobile devices (D1–D4) running the Android OS in the experiment, two of which were from the smartphone class (D1, D2), and two from the tablet one (D3, D4). For every form factor (smaller smartphone, larger smartphone, smaller tablet, and larger tablet) we defined configuration parameters for the pointing task random generator: dimensions of the starting point area and threshold values for target sizes. Both the display characteristics and suitable target dimensions were considered in this procedure, providing different task ID range for each device. As expected, larger devices enable pointing tasks with wider ID range. Details about all used devices and tasks configuration parameters are presented in Table 2.

Table 2. Touchscreen characteristics of mobile device models used in empirical research, and random task generator parameters assigned to each display. The last column includes both the ID range and related number of tasks presented in (X/Y) format. While X corresponds to the number of tasks for corner-positioned starting points, Y denotes the number of tasks for the center one.

Device class	Model	Display	Pointing tasks configuration parameters		
			Starting point area	Random target sizes [min - max]	ID range (# tasks)
D1 Smaller smartphone	*Samsung Galaxy Mini 2*	3.27" @ 320 × 480 176 dpi, capacitive	60 × 60 pixels 8.7 × 8.7 mm	25–100 pixels 3.6– 14.4 mm	1.0–4.0 (7/6)
D2 Larger smartphone	*Samsung Galaxy S II*	4.27" @ 800 × 480 218 dpi, capacitive	85 × 85 pixels 9.9 × 9.9 mm	38–150 pixels 4.4– 17.6 mm	1.0–4.5 (8/6)
D3 Smaller tablet	*Samsung Galaxy Tab 2*	7.0" @ 1024 × 600 170 dpi, capacitive	80 × 80 pixels 12 × 12 mm	30–150 pixels 4.5– 22.4 mm	1.0–5.0 (9/7)
D4 Larger tablet	*Samsung Galaxy Tab 2*	10.1" @ 1280 × 800 149 dpi, capacitive	80 × 80 pixels 13.6 × 13.6 mm	30–160 pixels 5.1– 27.3 mm	1.0–5.5 (10/8)

In order to familiarize with both available devices and testing application features, users were involved in a short practice session at the beginning of testing. In the actual experiment participants were instructed to input their unique identifier, and to complete a given cycle of randomly generated pointing tasks for each combination of available device (D1–D4) and appropriate interaction style (thumb/portrait, forefinger/portrait, forefinger/landscape). The time between two task instances within a cycle, when no actual pointing was performed, was not measured anyhow. Cycles consisted of 34, 38, 43, and 48 pointing tasks for each interaction style used on D1, D2, D3, and D4 respectively. If a particular target was missed, a new task instance with the same ID was generated. In order to further differentiate the starting point from the target area, related rectangles were being marked with numbers 1 (starting point) and 2 (pointing target). The start and the end of the testing cycle were acknowledged with appropriate application messages. Although the learning effect seemed to be negligible for simple touchscreen pointing tasks in our experimental setup, the sequence of experimental conditions, i.e. both device order and interaction style order, was nevertheless counterbalanced.

5 Results and Discussion

Participants provided 13930 (*Users* × *Tasks* × *Styles*) good hits in total: 3570 on D1 (35 × 34 × 3), 3990 on D2 (35 × 38 × 3), 3010 on D3 (35 × 43 × 2), and 3360 on D4 (35 × 48 × 2). Mean pointing times are calculated which, as expected, increase across levels of task ID. Linear regression was applied on data thus obtained, in order to evaluate the prediction power of Fitts' law, namely its MacKenzie-Buxton revision. Example pointing time models are shown in Fig. 5, one for the smaller smartphone and one for the larger tablet.

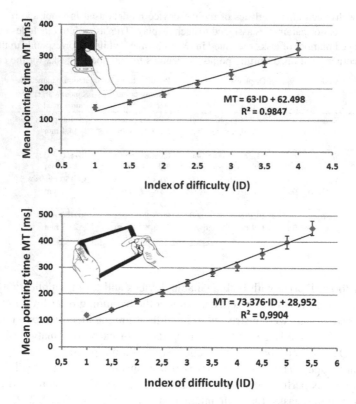

Fig. 5. Result examples: thumb-based pointing on portrait-oriented smaller smartphone (top), and forefinger-based pointing on larger tablet in landscape orientation (bottom). The graphs show mean pointing times, linear regression models, along with error bars with ± 1 standard error of the mean.

It can be seen that Fitts' law models for pointing tasks are actually very good, and that the *smaller-of* version of the law is appropriate to predict pointing times on touchscreen mobile devices. This holds not only for conditions shown in Fig. 5, but for every appropriate *Device × Style* combination. All the corresponding R^2 values are rather high, ranging from 0.969 to 0.993 (see Table 3).

Table 3. Mean pointing times expressed with Fitts' law (using derived slope and intercept coefficients). Linear regression on empirical data show strong fit with MacKenzie-Buxton *smaller-of* model.

Mobile device	Interaction style		
	thumb/portrait	forefinger/portrait	forefinger/landscape
D1	$MT = 62.49 + ID \cdot 63$	$MT = 65.10 + ID \cdot 55.48$	$MT = 60.88 + ID \cdot 55.15$
	$R^2 = 0.984$	$R^2 = 0.974$	$R^2 = 0.986$
D2	$MT = 19.55 + ID \cdot 86$	$MT = 36.05 + ID \cdot 60.76$	$MT = 30.79 + ID \cdot 60.12$
	$R^2 = 0.975$	$R^2 = 0.969$	$R^2 = 0.978$
D3	not appropriate	$MT = 19.88 + ID \cdot 68.78$	$MT = 37.42 + ID \cdot 63.74$
		$R^2 = 0.993$	$R^2 = 0.987$
D4	not appropriate	$MT = 30.12 + ID \cdot 74.38$	$MT = 28.95 + ID \cdot 73.37$
		$R^2 = 0.988$	$R^2 = 0.990$

The analysis of obtained slope coefficient values can tell much about touchscreen pointing performance. If pointing with particular interaction style is observed across different devices, then increasing slope values are observed with larger screen size. In general this means pointing will last longer on larger devices (for a task with given ID) if the same interaction style is assumed. This can be explained as the result of finger movement constraints that are inherently higher when operating a larger mobile device. Specifically, the thumb needs to be stretched more for reaching the far corners on a larger display. Forefinger-based pointing can be more troublesome on larger screens due to the handling effort for providing stability of a heavier mobile device. On the other hand, if pointing time on a specific device is examined against possible inter-action styles, we can conclude that the slope does not change significantly between forefinger/portrait and forefinger/landscape. Indeed, changing display orientation has no particular effect on pointing performance because both the screen size and the expected handling effort practically remain the same. However, slope values are con-siderably different between thumb/portrait and forefinger/portrait interaction styles. Predictive models assume larger pointing times on smartphones (D1, D2) if thumb-based interaction is applied. This is in line with higher level of interaction burden in single-handed smartphone usage, as opposed to the use case wherein one hand is holding the device, while the other performs pointing.

Although particularly small targets were not tackled in our experiment setup, it would be wrong to state that pointing tasks with small target sizes were not considered at all. On the contrary, the random task generator produced a number of task instances with W values being near (or exactly on) the defined lower threshold. Small targets were dominant in pointing tasks with higher ID. The example of target size distribution is presented in Fig. 6.

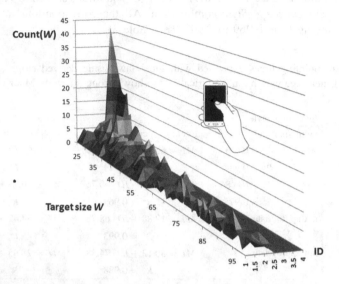

Fig. 6. Target size distribution obtained while testing thumb-based pointing performance on smaller smartphone (D1) in portrait orientation. Target size lower threshold, set to 25 pixels what equals 3.6 mm on D1 display, was actually included in 6.13 % of the tasks.

6   Conclusion

We have analyzed and compared the performance of finger-based pointing on mobile touchscreen devices, taking into account different screen sizes and appropriate inter-action styles. Pointing tasks were randomly generated in order to achieve a wider range of both suitable target sizes and required finger movements, thus targeting a better representation of common pointing behavior in everyday touchscreen usage. Data obtained from the empirical study was evaluated against Fitts' law, specifically its MacKenzie-Buxton revision which defines target size as the smaller of the two dimension of a 2D shape. Results revealed a strong model fit with our data, making this well-known form of Fitts' law a fair predictor of touchscreen pointing in the mobile. Altogether 10 finger-based pointing models are derived, each one with designated slope and intercept coefficients that can be used for particular combinations of device display size and interaction style. The validity of Fitts' law *smaller-of* model may be ques-tioned here regarding the case of finger input for particularly small target acquisition. Some existing model revisions can estimate pointing times better in this specific context (cf. [12]), however we find the conventional MacKenzie-Buxton model to be both easy to apply (well-known formulation with no additional parameters) and evi-dently strong for predicting overall pointing performance. Furthermore, we believe in its pragmatic utility regarding various mobile devices, different interaction styles, and real target sizes commonly found in mobile touchscreen interfaces.

The described empirical research is limited in scope since the related experiment took place in laboratory settings. Further work should investigate pointing performance in a real-life mobile context (walking scenarios, attention shifts, external distractions), as well as Fitts' law fit to data thus obtained.

Acknowledgments. The work presented in this paper is supported by the University of Rijeka research grant *Grant 13.09.2.2.16.*

References

1. Fitts, P.M.: The information capacity of the human motor system in controlling the amplitude of movement. J. Exp. Psychol. **47**(6), 381–391 (1954)
2. MacKenzie, I.S.: Fitts' law as a research and design tool in human-computer interaction. Int. J. Hum. Comput. Interact. **7**(1), 91–139 (1992)
3. MacKenzie, I.S., Buxton, W.: Extending Fitts' law to two-dimensional tasks. In: Proceedings of SIGCHI Conference on Human Factors in Computing Systems (CHI 1992), pp. 219–226. ACM Press, New York (1992)
4. Welford, A.T.: Fundamentals of Skill. Methuen, London (1968)
5. Accot, J., Zhai, S.: Refining Fitts' law models for bivariate pointing. In: Proceedings of SIGCHI Conference on Human Factors in Computing Systems (CHI 2003), pp. 193–200. ACM Press, New York (2003)
6. Oel, P., Schmidt, P., Schmitt, A.: Time prediction of mouse-based cursor movements. In: Proceedings of Joint AFIHM-BCS Conference Human-Computer Interaction (IHM-HCI 2001), vol. II, pp. 37–40. Cépaduès-Éditions, Toulouse (2001)
7. Chapuis, O., Dragicevic, P.: Effects of motor scale, visual scale, and quantization on small target acquisition difficulty. ACM Trans. Comput.-Hum. Interact. **18**(3), 1–32 (2011)
8. Welford, A.T., Norris, A.H., Shock, N.W.: Speed and accuracy of movement and their changes with age. Acta Psychol. **30**, 3–15 (1969)
9. Albinsson, P., Zhai, S.: High precision touch screen interaction. In: Proceedings of SIGCHI Conference on Human Factors in Computing Systems (CHI 2003), pp. 105–112. ACM Press, New York (2003)
10. Sasangohar, F., MacKenzie, I.S., Scott, S.D.: Evaluation of mouse and touch input for a tabletop display using Fitts' reciprocal tapping task. In: Proceedings of 53rd Annual Meeting of the Human Factors and Ergonomics Society (HFES 2009), pp. 839–843. Human Factors and Ergonomics Society, Santa Monica (2009)
11. Cockburn, A., Alhström, D., Gutwin, C.: Understanding performance in touch selections: tap, drag and radial pointing drag with finger, stylus and mouse. Int. J. Hum Comput Stud. **70**(3), 218–233 (2012)
12. Bi, X., Li, Y., Zhai, S.: FFitts law: modeling finger touch with Fitts' law. In: Proceedings of SIGCHI Conference on Human Factors in Computing Systems (CHI 2013), pp. 1363–1372. ACM Press, New York (2013)
13. Okada, H., Akiba, T.: Fitts' law index of difficulty evaluated and extended for screen size variations. In: Matrai, R. (ed.) User Interfaces, pp. 229–238. InTech, Rijeka (2010)
14. Android Developers: Iconography. http://developer.android.com/design/style/iconography.html
15. Android Developers: SystemClock. http://developer.android.com/reference/android/os/SystemClock.html

Behavioral Biometrics for Universal Access and Authentication

Liam M. Mayron(✉)

Arizona State University, Tempe, AZ 85281, USA
lmayron@asu.edu

Abstract. Behavioral biometrics, such as gait, voice, handwriting, and keystroke dynamics can provide a method of authenticating users that is both secure and usable, particularly on mobile devices. Behavioral biometrics can often be collected in the background, without requiring a specific security task to be completed by the user. Many behavioral biometrics can be recorded with hardware that has already been deployed in many mobile devices. In this paper, we consider the use of behavioral biometrics for authentication in systems designed for universal access. Requirements for security and authentication are discussed, and several behavioral biometrics are introduced. Considerations for universal access are presented.

Keywords: Biometrics · Behavioral biometrics · Security · Usability · Authentication

1 Introduction

Universal access has as its objective to provide access to information technology to as broad a range of people as possible [29]. Although universal access is a notable goal, it is important to keep security considerations in mind as we design such systems [2]. This work seeks to emphasize one of the security-related aspects of universal access – authentication.

Users can be authenticated in several ways. Typically, this is done using either one or a combination of something a user knows, possesses, and is (biometrics). Although something a user knows may be forgotten, and something a user possesses may be lost, biometrics are tightly associated with the individual and cannot be left behind, making them an appealing option for a system that is secure, usable, and universally accessible [3,7,8,19,26,27].

There are many types of biometrics, each with their own benefits and disadvantages. Physical biometrics include fingerprint, face, and iris recognition. Fingerprints are widely accepted and considered to be a reasonably usable option [1,30], although face recognition can be done without requiring direct contact between the user and the sensor.

Behavioral biometrics are a versatile method of collecting information about and, potentially, authenticating users. These biometrics include patterns of

© Springer International Publishing Switzerland 2015
M. Antona and C. Stephanidis (Eds.): UAHCI 2015, Part I, LNCS 9175, pp. 330–339, 2015.
DOI: 10.1007/978-3-319-20678-3_32

human behavior, including their gait, voice, handwriting, and keyboard typing patterns. In contrast to certain physical biometrics, many behavioral biometrics can be collected with common and inexpensive hardware. Behavioral biometrics do not necessarily require physical contact for collection and can often be collected without the user's awareness of the activity. This passive collection makes behavioral biometrics and intriguing option for securing systems in an accessible manner.

Today, behavioral biometrics deployed are more frequently, particularly for purposes of authentication and security. Additional information, such as the context within which the desired action is occurring within, may also be used to strengthen a user's case for access to protected resources. Whereas traditional passwords are cumbersome on a small mobile device's touch screen, and physical biometrics hardware (such as fingerprint readers) remains a premium feature, it may be tempting to employ behavioral biometrics to protect and restrict access to resources.

This paper examines the potential and challenges facing the widespread use of behavioral biometrics for authentication, particularly as it relates to universal access. We will introduce behavioral biometrics, discuss requirements for effectively realizing such schemes, and consider impediments to the universal use of behavioral biometrics.

This paper is organized as follows: Sect. 2 introduces key concepts in security. Authentication is discussed in Sect. 3. Behavioral biometrics are detailed in Sect. 4. Finally, discussion and concluding thoughts are shared in Sect. 5.

2 Security

It is challenging to separate *universal* access from *secure* access. If the objective is to provide access to as broad a range of individuals as possible, as is the case with systems designed for universal access, we must also seek to provide access in a secure manner, for all users. Furthermore, just as new features or capabilities should not degrade the usability for any individual or group of users, the purposeful incorporation of universal access should not degrade the security experience for other users. There is tension between the security and usability of a system [22].

Security serves as a barrier to a system's resources, whereas universal access seeks to provide multiple methods of use. Additionally, it is often the case that systems that must prioritize universal access also provide access to some of our most sensitive personal and health-related information [2].

Broadly, a secure digital system must provide confidentiality, integrity, and availability [14,24].

- Confidentiality: a system must only provide access to users who are authorized to view a certain resource.
- Integrity: only the intended parties should be able to modify the information contained within the system.
- Availability: the system must not deny access to legitimate users.

Thus, we have the challenge of designing systems that must provide access to a wide range of individuals, but in a secure way.

In some cases, systems have a primary method of authenticating, with one or more alternatives provided for users who are not able to use the primary method. For example, a user who cannot use a fingerprint reader may be able to present an identification card instead. System designers should be wary, however, as this opens a system's authentication mechanisms to potential abuse. It can be easier to forge an identification card than a fingerprint. Indeed, abusers may purposefully damage or circumvent the primary authentication mechanism in order to gain access using a less secure, alternative way.

One example is a version of Google's ReCaptcha authentication system [32]. ReCaptcha authenticates users as humans (as opposed to automated robots) by asking them to identify the text in an image. The intention is that the text in an image is easy (or at least, easier) for a human to understand and challenging for a computer to decipher. An alternative mode of access was provided for those who had difficulty with the visual cue – audio would play instead. However, audio CAPTCHAs have been shown to be vulnerable to automatic deciphering – perhaps even more vulnerable than text-based CAPTCHAs [6]. Instead of using a wide variety methods of authentication, our objective should be fewer, but more robust and well-test methods capable of authenticating a wide range of individuals.

3   Authentication

Authentication can be defined in terms of the states before and after authentication has occurred. After authentication, two entities (users, computers, or other systems) should be confident that they are communicating with one another [5]. In terms of universal access to information technology, we will focus on authentication of the user to the system (although the converse remains an interesting topic – how does the user know they are connected to the intended endpoint?).

There are three broad methods of authenticating an individual:

- Something a person knows: for example, a password, a passphrase, response to a secret question, or other piece of knowledge not readily known to others. Although this authentication scheme is the least resource-intensive for the system to implement, it is the most taxing on the user's mental abilities. Knowledge-based authentication schemes do not require specialized hardware, nor do they require a user to retain possession of a token. They shift the burden of proof to the user, who is responsible for memorizing a sequence of characters, numbers, and other tokens, or for responding to a question [4].
- Something a person possesses: this may include tokens such as an identification card or security token. In its simplest form, possession of a token is enough to gain access. In more sophisticated schemes, the token may require additional verification, such as checking if a picture on the security token matches that of the person requesting access.

– An intrinsic characteristic: biometrics. These may be physical traits that we
are born with, such as fingerprints or face structure, those that develop over
time due to uncontrollable factors, such as patterns in the iris, or learned
behaviors (behavioral biometrics). Generally, we seek to use biometrics that
exhibit both uniqueness and permanence – those that can uniquely identify
an individual and do not change much over time.

Table 1. Methods of authentication

	Something you know	Something you possess	Something you are
Convenience	*(Worse)* Requires memorization	*(Worse)* Must be on person for authentication	*(Better)* Part of the individual
Security	*(Worse)* May be shared, coerced, forgotten, or exposed	*(Worse)* May be shared, coerced, lost, or forged	*(Neutral)* Possible to forge, cannot be lost or forgotten
Suitability for mobile devices	*(Worse)* Long passwords are difficult to type on small devices	*(Worse)* Mobile devices may lack physical hardware needed to validate security tokens	*(Better)* Certain biometrics can be validated with hardware already incorporated into mobile devices
Risk	*(Better)* An exposed password can be invalidated and reset	*(Better)* A lost token can be invalidated and reissued	*(Worse)* We cannot change our biometrics if compromised

Table 1 presents a comparison of these high-level methods of authentication.
The three aforementioned methods (something you know, something you pos-
sess, something you are) are compared in terms of their convenience, security,
suitability for mobile devices, and risk. Each element is rated on a scale of worse,
neutral, or better with regards to the specified metric.

– Convenience: convenience is defined as ease of use to the user, not the system.
Memorizing passwords and securing tokens rank lower than biometrics, which
require no or minimal overhead of the user.
– Security: all three methods have security faults, although biometrics may be
more favorable as they cannot as easily be shared.
– Suitability for mobile devices: both passwords and tokens present challenges
on mobile devices (such as smartphones). These devices either make it incon-
venient to type lengthy passwords repeatedly (where lengthy passwords have
been shown to be more secure than shorter ones [36]) or lack hardware needed
to validate security tokens. Some biometrics, such as faces and fingerprints,
can be validated with hardware now available on mobile devices.

– Risk: we define risk as the risk to the user if their credentials are exposed. Passwords present minimal risk if they are not reused between systems (which, unfortunately, is typically not the case [17]). Lost tokens can be invalidated to prevent their use on systems. In both cases, it is possible for the user to move on with new credentials in the case of a breach. However, the major strength of biometrics – their inseparable association with the individual – makes them a liability if compromised (for example, if someone is able to replicate someone else's fingerprint). In this case, we cannot simply change our fingerprints. The user is dependent on the system implementing a biometric authentication scheme that does not directly store information that can be used to simulate the user's features.

Two-factor authentication is the use of two (or more) authentication modalities, such as requiring a password and a security token, or a fingerprint and a photo ID. While two-factor authentication can improve a system's security, it may impede usability by extending the duration and requirements of the authentication activity. Additionally, two-factor authentication still leaves vulnerabilities exposed [28].

Given the convenience to the user and security of the scheme, the remainder of this work focuses on biometrics as a single factor method of authentication. More specifically, this paper will present behavioral biometrics, which have the additional benefit of being able to be collected without necessarily requiring explicit user action, providing benefits for both security and usability.

4 Behavioral Biometrics

There are two types of biometrics: physical and behavioral. Physical biometrics include fingerprint, facial, and iris recognition. Physical biometrics are derived from unique physical characteristics that are usually determined prior to birth or formed through involuntary muscle movements. Behavioral biometrics are based on our activities and learned reactions, although they are heavily influenced by our physical characteristics. For example, a person's gait depends on their size, weight, and muscle mass.

Behavioral biometrics have a long history of acceptance as a means of verifying an identity. Signatures have been used from ancient to modern times in order to authenticate documents. Today, signatures are one of several options for behavioral biometrics.

Behavioral biometrics are appealing because they can be collected in a less intrusive manner than physical biometrics [13]. Some behavioral biometrics, such as keystroke dynamics (unique typing patterns made by users), can even be collected without any explicit user action. Keystroke dynamics can be recorded in the background as the user types. The wide variety of sensors available on mobile devices (touch, GPS, gyroscope, camera, microphone, among others) provide intriguing options for authentication using behavioral biometrics.

Although promising, behavioral biometrics have several potential pitfalls. From a security perspective, we must be prepared to allow a wide range of acceptable signals. Whereas, for example, a text password must match exactly,

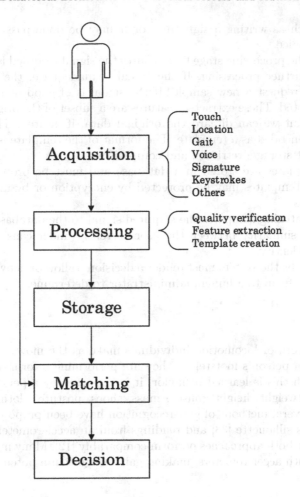

Fig. 1. Overview of a behavioral biometric system

behavioral biometrics can vary depending on a person's mood or stress [18]. Behavioral biometrics are also vulnerable to being imitated by a skilled attacker! [18]. In terms of usability, some behavioral biometrics may not apply to a wide range of users and may impede universal access.

The design of a behavioral biometric system is described in Sect. 4.1. Gait, voice, handwriting, keystroke dynamics, and other behavioral biometrics are presented in Sects. 4.2, 4.3, 4.4, 4.5, and 4.6, respectively.

4.1 Behavioral Biometric System Design

An overview of a behavioral biometric system is shown in Fig. 1. The system has the following stages:

– Acquisition: during the acquisition stage the system will sample signals derived from a user's behaviors. This may require the user to interact with a user interface, such as writing a signature, or it may be done passively, such as recording a voice.

– Processing: the processing stage first ensures the signal recorded is of sufficient quality for further processing. If the signal is inadequate, the system may immediately request a new sample. If the signal is of good quality, features will be extracted. These extracted features are a subset of the original signal – after this point we can discard the original data, if desired. The extracted features are encoded as a template. The format of the template is designed to allow efficient storage, retrieval, and comparison.

– Storage: templates are stored in a database and must be protected against adversaries. Templates may be protected by encryption or by more sophisticated schemes.

– Matching: matching compares the acquired signal to the database in order to compute the similarity between the user currently under consideration and the claimed identity.

– Decision: finally, the system must render a decision – allow or deny. Sometimes, this stage is left up to a human administrator to determine.

4.2 Gait

Gait is the pattern of locomotion individuals make as the move. When people can "recognize a person's footsteps", they are performing a form of gait recognition. Although this is learned behavior, it is impacted by a person's physical characteristics (weight, height, muscle mass, shoes, posture, clothing, motion, etc.) [11,20]. Several methods of gait recognition have been proposed, including using a person's silhouette [33] and readings from an accelerometer [12]. It has been shown that both approaches perform comparably [12]. Many mobile devices are equipped with accelerometers, making gait recognition a potential means of providing access.

4.3 Voice

Voice, or speech recognition is an intriguing behavioral biometric with applications including and beyond authentication. A user's voice can be used to determine their identity using simply a microphone. Performance can be used if the user dictates a specific phrase expected by the system (text dependent), but recognition can also be text-independent [25]. Speech is a natural part of many transactions and is not considered to be as intrusive as providing a fingerprint or even taking a picture. Furthermore, voice provides additional cues about a user's stress level that can be used to improve the performance of the system.

4.4 Handwriting

Handwriting, including signatures, can be used to identify users. This identification can be performed by identifying characteristics such as the number of strokes made, timing, count of pen up and pen down motions, and several proportions and areas formed by the written information [31]. As with several other behavioral biometrics, handwriting recognition can be vulnerable to attack [21]. However, handwriting is remarkably versatile and a natural input method for touch surfaces.

4.5   Keystroke Dynamics

Keystroke dynamics can be used to identify a person based on the timing between subsequent keystrokes. Although originally intended for physical, mechanical keyboards [23], keystroke dynamics have been implemented on mobile devices [16]. Interestingly, keystroke dynamics have also shown promise as a way for determining a user's emotional state (such as nervousness or tiredness) [10].

4.6   Other Behavioral Biometrics

Many other behavioral biometrics are available. Behaviors ranging from game strategy [34] to musical proficiency [9] can be used to authenticate individuals. A detailed survey of behavioral biometrics is available in [35]. While new schemes will continue to be developed, it is important to evaluate them on both their security and usability qualities.

5   Discussion and Conclusion

Many users do not use any or only minimal protection on their mobile devices [15]. Users to not seek to "do security", they aim to complete their intended tasks in the most efficient way possible. Generally, this relegates security to a burdensome task. Behavioral biometrics (and biometrics in general) are an attractive alternative. Behavioral biometrics can provide a degree of authentication for minimal user interaction.

However, we must also consider the implications widespread use of behavioral biometrics would have for universal access. Certain behavioral biometrics may exclude groups of people. For example, gait assumes a person is able to walk. Voice recognition requires a person who can speak. Poor usability of implementations of behavioral biometrics can lead to a high rate of false positive errors (allowing unauthorized users access). By definition, behavioral biometrics reflect the behavior of the user. The system must be able to guide the user's behavior in a consistent manner in order to achieve reliable authentication to as wide a range of users as possible.

Behavioral biometrics provide opportunities for universal access beyond authentication. For example, the ability to know the user's current emotional state can be incorporated into system behavior. Perhaps a user who is upset should have access to only a restricted set of features. Or, a user who is confused could be provided additional assistance.

This work discussed security and authentication considerations of universal access systems and then considered the utility of behavioral biometrics. Although behavioral biometrics provide intriguing opportunities for authentication users, their use must be moderated by security and usability requirements.

References

1. Al-Harby, F., Qahwaji, R., Kamala, M.: Users acceptance of secure biometrics authentication system: reliability and validate of an extended utaut model. In: Zavoral, F., Yaghob, J., Pichappan, P., El-Qawasmeh, E. (eds.) Networked Digital Technologies, pp. 254–258. Springer, Heidelberg (2010)
2. Bahr, G., Mayron, L., Gacey, H.: Cyber risks to secure and private universal access. In: Stephanidis, C. (ed.) Universal Access in Human-Computer Interaction. Design for All and eInclusion, Lecture Notes in Computer Science, vol. 6765, pp. 433–442. Springer, Berlin Heidelberg (2011)
3. Braz, C., Robert, J.: Security and usability: the case of the user authentication methods. In: Proceedings of the 18th International Conference of the Association Francophone d'Interaction Homme-Machine, pp. 199–203. ACM (2006)
4. Brostoff, S., Sasse, M.A.: Are passfaces more usable than passwords? a field trial investigation. People and Computers, pp. 405–424. Springer, London (2000)
5. Burrows, M., Abadi, M., Needham, R.M.: A logic of authentication. In: Proceedings of the Royal Society of London A: Mathematical, Physical and Engineering Sciences, vol. 426, pp. 233–271. The Royal Society (1989)
6. Bursztein, E., Bethard, S.: Decaptcha: breaking 75% of ebay audio captchas. In: Proceedings of the 3rd USENIX conference on Offensive technologies, p. 8. USENIX Association (2009)
7. Cohen, S., Ben-Asher, N., Meyer, J.: Towards information technology security for universal access. In: Stephanidis, C. (ed.) Universal Access in HCI, Part I, HCII 2011. LNCS, vol. 6765, pp. 443–451. Springer, Heidelberg (2011)
8. Cranor, L., Garfinkel, S.: Guest editors' introduction: secure or usable? IEEE Secur. Priv. 2(5), 16–18 (2004)
9. Dalla Bella, S., Palmer, C.: Personal identifiers in musicians' finger movement dynamics. J. Cog. Neurosci. 18, G84 (2006)
10. Epp, C., Lippold, M., Mandryk, R.L.: Identifying emotional states using keystroke dynamics. In: Proceedings of the SIGCHI Conference on Human Factors in Computing Systems, pp. 715–724. ACM (2011)
11. Gafurov, D.: A survey of biometric gait recognition: approaches, security and challenges. In: Annual Norwegian Computer Science Conference, pp. 19–21. Citeseer (2007)
12. Gafurov, D., Helkala, K., Søndrol, T.: Biometric gait authentication using accelerometer sensor. J. Comput. 1(7), 51–59 (2006)
13. Gamboa, H., Fred, A.: A behavioral biometric system based on human-computer interaction. In: Defense and Security, pp. 381–392. International Society for Optics and Photonics (2004)
14. Greene, S.: Security Policies and Procedures: Principles and Practices (Prentice Hall Security Series). Prentice-Hall Inc, Upper Saddle River (2005)
15. Harbach, M., von Zezschwitz, E., Fichtner, A., De Luca, A., Smith, M.: Itsa hard lock life: a field study of smartphone (un) locking behavior and risk perception. In: Symposium on Usable Privacy and Security (SOUPS) (2014)
16. Hwang, S., Cho, S., Park, S.: Keystroke dynamics-based authentication for mobile devices. Comput. Secur. 28(1), 85–93 (2009)
17. Ives, B., Walsh, K.R., Schneider, H.: The domino effect of password reuse. Commun. ACM 47(4), 75–78 (2004)
18. Jain, A., Ross, A., Nandakumar, K.: Introduction to Biometrics. Springer, US (2011)

19. Kumar, N.: Password in practice: a usability study. J. Global Res. Comput. Sci. **2**(5), 107–112 (2011)
20. Lee, L., Grimson, W.E.L.: Gait analysis for recognition and classification. In: Proceedings Fifth IEEE International Conference on Automatic Face and Gesture Recognition, pp. 148–155. IEEE (2002)
21. Lopresti, D.P., Raim, J.D.: The effectiveness of generative attacks on an online handwriting biometric. In: Kanade, T., Jain, A., Ratha, N.K. (eds.) AVBPA 2005. LNCS, vol. 3546, pp. 1090–1099. Springer, Heidelberg (2005)
22. Mayron, L.M., Hausawi, Y., Bahr, G.S.: Secure, usable biometric authentication systems. In: Stephanidis, C., Antona, M. (eds.) UAHCI 2013, Part I. LNCS, vol. 8009, pp. 195–204. Springer, Heidelberg (2013)
23. Monrose, F., Rubin, A.D.: Keystroke dynamics as a biometric for authentication. Future Gener. Comput. Syst. **16**(4), 351–359 (2000)
24. Pfleeger, C., Pfleeger, S.: Security in Computing. Prentice Hall PTR, Englewood Cliffs (2006)
25. Reynolds, D.A.: An overview of automatic speaker recognition. In: Proceedings of the International Conference on Acoustics, Speech and Signal Processing (ICASSP), pp. S.4072–S.4075 (2002)
26. Sasse, M.: Computer security: anatomy of a usability disaster, and a plan for recovery. In: Proceedings of CHI 2003 Workshop on HCI and Security Systems. Citeseer (2003)
27. Sasse, M., Brostoff, S., Weirich, D.: Transforming the weakest linka human/computer interaction approach to usable and effective security. BT Technol. J. **19**(3), 122–131 (2001)
28. Schneier, B.: Two-factor authentication: too little, too late. Commun. ACM **48**(4), 136 (2005)
29. Stephanidis, C.: The Universal Access Handbook. CRC Press, Boca Raton (2009)
30. Toledano, D., Fernández Pozo, R., Hernández Trapote, Á., Hernández Gómez, L.: Usability evaluation of multi-modal biometric verification systems. Interact. Comput. **18**(5), 1101–1122 (2006)
31. Vielhauer, C., Steinmetz, R., Mayerhofer, A.: Biometric hash based on statistical features of online signatures. In: Proceedings of 16th International Conference on Pattern Recognition, vol. 1, pp. 123–126. IEEE (2002)
32. Von Ahn, L., Maurer, B., McMillen, C., Abraham, D., Blum, M.: reCAPTCHA: Human-based character recognition via web security measures. Science **321**(5895), 1465–1468 (2008)
33. Wang, L., Tan, T., Ning, H., Hu, W.: Silhouette analysis-based gait recognition for human identification. IEEE Trans. Pattern Analy. Mach. Intell. **25**(12), 1505–1518 (2003)
34. Yampolskiy, R.V.: Mimicry attack on strategy-based behavioral biometric. In: Fifth International Conference on Information Technology: New Generations, ITNG 2008, pp. 916–921. IEEE (2008)
35. Yampolskiy, R.V., Govindaraju, V.: Behavioural biometrics: a survey and classification. Int. J. Biom. **1**(1), 81–113 (2008)
36. Yan, J., et al.: Password memorability and security: empirical results. IEEE Secur. Priv. **5**, 25–31 (2004)

Evaluation of the Android Accessibility API Recognition Rate Towards a Better User Experience

Mauro C. Pichiliani[✉] and Celso M. Hirata

Department of Computer Science, Instituto Tecnológico de Aeronáutica,
São José dos Campos, Brazil
{pichilia,hirata}@ita.br

Abstract. Mobile applications are based on interactive common UI elements that represents pointing targets visible on the screen. The usage of mobile applications in eyes-free scenarios or by individuals with vision impairments requires effective alternative access to visual elements, i.e. accessibility features. Previous works evaluated the accuracy of UI element's identification by accessibility APIs on desktop applications reporting that only 74 % of the targets were correctly identified, but no recent research evaluated the accuracy for similar mobile APIs. We present an empirical evaluation based on the Android accessibility API that computes the UI recognition accuracy rate on ten popular mobile applications. Our findings indicate that accessibility average recognition rate is 97 %.

Keywords: Accessibility · Android · Mobile · API · Evaluation · User interface · User experience

1 Introduction

The explosive growth of mobile devices is supported by the vast offer of applications available in online stores. The interaction model on these applications is primarily based on the touch and gestures performed on the screen representation of visual elements that compose the application's UI. However, there are special users, i.e. visually impaired, and circumstances that hinder or make the visual access to the display impossible, thus challenging application usage.

Accessibility features are one of the solutions used to allow access to visual elements and guide GUI interactions on computer platforms. Almost all operating systems provide guidelines and recommendations to make applications accessible based on existing accessibility APIs whose efficiency can be measured by their ability to recognize and identify UI elements.

This paper has the goal to evaluate the UI recognition accuracy rate of ten popular mobile applications by measuring how many UI elements are correctly identified by an accessibility API. The evaluation was based on the methodology that includes several observations of the UI elements and a special accessibility service that gatherers the location, size, type, and content data of the most common widgets found on mobile

© Springer International Publishing Switzerland 2015
M. Antona and C. Stephanidis (Eds.): UAHCI 2015, Part I, LNCS 9175, pp. 340–349, 2015.
DOI: 10.1007/978-3-319-20678-3_33

applications. Additionally, we also evaluated which events are captured by the API in order to create customized feedback notifications so the user can interact more consistently with the application being executed.

Identifying the properties of UI targets enables novel additions to existing technology and increases the support for development tasks. More specifically, the tasks that can benefit from accurate target identification of user interfaces include: (i) mobile accessibility services creation; (ii) automatic extraction of a task sequence; (iii) scripting of common actions; (iv) UI automation tests; and (v) support to collaboration frameworks.

The rest of the paper is organized as follows: Sect. 2 reviews the related work on evaluation of accessibility APIs. Section 3 presents the details of the mobile accessibility APIs and its applications. Section 4 discusses the methodology aspects employed to evaluate the recognition rate of UI elements along with details of the applications evaluated. Session 5 presents the results of the study. Session 6 provides a discussion and some examples of the UI interface elements that lack accessibility. Finally, Sect. 7 presents conclusions and possible developments for future work.

2 Related Work

The HCI literature has many research studies that collect data about the size, location, and other visual properties of UI interactive elements for usability evaluations [6], preference comparison [4], and pointing performance assessment [7]. Traditionally, data gathering is made on controlled laboratory settings with custom or adapted software techniques [4, 7, 8] that capture and hand code the interaction.

A recent previous work evaluated the accuracy of UI element's recognition by accessibilities APIs [5], which reports that only 74 % of the targets were correctly identified, i.e. the location and size indicated by the API matched the UI element's properties. This result is based on 1,355 targets covering real world usage of 8 arbitrary desktop applications on the Microsoft Windows XP Operating System with the Windows Automation API [11], formerly known as Microsoft Active Accessibility API (MSAA API).

On that study the authors did not evaluate the content of the element, which is the most important information needed by screen readers and other accessibility services that provide feedback to users. Additionally, the researchers did not studied the complexity of gestures and interactive UI elements found on mobile applications.

Despite the fact that there are approaches that increase the recognition rate of UI elements for desktop application [3, 5] and initiatives to define strategies, guidelines, and resources to make mobile web accessible [1], the recognition accuracy of native mobile OS accessibility APIs received little research attention.

3 Mobile Accessibility API

Accessibility APIs are designed to provide data regarding interactions on GUIs and are available on many operating systems and programming platforms. As an example, the Microsoft Active Accessibility API (MSAA API) [11] is a cross-application Windows operating system level solution for getting low-level information about targets, including push buttons, menus, textboxes, and other UI elements.

While the APIs can be extremely accurate at identifying some targets, Amant et al. [9] state, without formal evaluation, that in practice many real world targets are not supported by those accessibility APIs. In addition, not all applications support them in the same way. For example, two popular web browsers, Microsoft's Internet Explorer and Open-source Firefox, deal with content in a very different way, limiting the API's access to them [5].

While some mobile Operating Systems only provide ready to use accessibility services, i.e. screen reader or virtual magnifier glass, others provide a complete set of API and resources to develop accessibility services based on low-level hooks that capture OS events.

Among the three main mobile Operating Systems, Apple's iOS, Microsoft's Windows Phone, and Google's Android, the last is the only one that provides accessibility APIs [2] that gives developers a complete set of features to improve application usage to users who have special needs. With the APIs, all common visual controls have accessibility by default and developers can make their own application more accessible, or make their own accessibility services that provide enhancements for other applications.

Giving permissions from users, developers can access the on screen view hierarchy, accessibility events and enhance user experiences accordingly with the APIs. Those APIs act as a delegate between applications and the system exposing interface state so that an accessibility service can be aware of any interaction and interface changes triggered by the inputs. Developers can also leverage accessibility APIs to fire interaction events [10].

Besides the creation of accessibility services, the access to on screen interactions and elements provide technological support to frameworks that extract the sequence of tasks for scripting and resources to suits that automate UI testing without needing a real person to interact with an application. Another category of application that benefits from accessibility APIs are collaborative frameworks and groupwares that require instrumentation to capture and replay events on multi-synchronous collaboration scenarios found on the CSCW (Computer Supported Cooperative Work) area.

4 Evaluation Methodology

The evaluation methodology used to calculate the recognition rate of UI elements on mobile applications is based on the previous work [5] that automatically collects and compares screenshots of the interface elements with their real counterparts during real world tasks performed on selected desktop applications.

The approach that evaluates UI elements recognition rate may be biased due to the lack of developer's effort to implement accessibility properties on the desktop application's interfaces being tested. However, unlike the desktop scenario, all standard controls inserted on the UI of Android applications already have special properties, such as the *contentDescription*, filled with textual data that is passed over to events trigged by the accessibility API. This standard accessibility description reduces the bias probability on our rate recognition evaluation.

However, in many cases the default value for the *contentDescription* do not provide enough information to understand the element's content or function. For instance, picture containers used as buttons often lack a description that can be used to inform and assist the user interact with the UI on eyes-free scenarios.

The 10 applications selected for the evaluations were chosen by the popularity criteria, i.e. number of users shown on the Google Play store at February 16th, 2015. Table 1 shows the applications evaluated along with the total number of elements on all activities, which are similar to the window concept in desktop application.

Table 1. The 10 mobile applications evaluated.

Application	App. Version Date	Popularity (users)	Activities (windows)	Interactive elements	Non-interactive elements	Total UI elements
Facebook	02/14/2015	25,941,692	17	94	36	130
WhatsApp Messenger	02/10/2015	23,218,150	18	70	14	84
Clean Master	02/15/2015	21,386,769	13	105	30	135
Instagram	02/11/2015	19,379,612	15	69	29	98
Messenger (Facebook)	02/13/2015	14,197,755	26	112	23	135
Viber	02/15/2015	6,425,682	25	109	43	152
Skype	02/09/2015	6,177,881	27	160	26	186
YouTube	02/13/2015	5,818,561	18	77	23	100
Twitter	02/09/2015	4,799,044	14	64	26	90
Maps	02/11/2015	4,598,545	11	63	13	76

The total UI elements values of Table 1 were computed by manually highlighting the elements on top of the application's screen while performing real world tasks such as registering, typing a post, and changing an application setting. The UI elements were classified as interactive elements that trigger events, i.e. edit texts, buttons, hyperlinks, list items, or as non-interactive elements, i.e. text labels, layout grids, and images. Since the evaluated applications have elaborated, dynamic, and reused activities, the following criterion was used to account for the total number of elements.

4.1 Dynamic Content

A common pattern found on applications while analyzing their IU was the dynamic generation of control's elements from user data. For instance, several applications filled interactive lists with list items that correspond to the user's friends. When we found this pattern we account for only one element on the dynamic control.

4.2 Dialog Messages

Many applications used dialog pop-up windows that showed notifications or questions asking the users to choose options by touching buttons. We account for non-interactive (text) and interactive elements (buttons) when we found these dialog windows.

4.3 Web Pages

All evaluated applications were native, i.e. they did not require an internet web browser. However, when certain options are accessed the applications started a new web browser session and redirected the user to a specific web page. Since the web page is not officially part of the application, all the UI elements found on the page were not considered.

4.4 Common Android Activities

The Android platform allows developers to reuse common activities and controls via the definition of an intent that requests actions to be performed by a shared application or service once the correct permission was granted. The camera capture intent is a conventional example: developers register the intent to call a common shared activity that takes a photo or record a video instead of building their own logic to interact with the device's camera. These common activities are not part of the application and, therefore, their UI elements did not add up to the total number of elements.

4.5 Reused Elements on Distinct Activities

The interface of most applications reused basic navigation controls, such as back buttons, menus and clickable images, on more than one activity. If the element is the same, but it is located on distinct activities, it is accounted for only once.

The recognition of UI elements by and accessibly API was evaluated on an Intel tablet (codename Medfield) with the 4.0.4 Android version (Ice Cream Sandwich) that allowed the inspection of the element's properties. Contrary to previous work [5] that used image comparison techniques to identify the location and size of UI elements, we created a simple accessibility service that gathered the elements data properties when an event callback was triggered.

The accessibility service assumed the form of a class that extended the *AccessibilityService* class. Its main feature is the *onAccessibilityEvent()* callback method invoked when an accessibility event is triggered from a user interaction with the UI. Inside the event the *AccessbilityEvent* class was used to obtain the UI element represented by the *AccessibilityNodeInfo* class, which queries the view layout hierarchy (parents and children) of the target component that originated the accessibility event.

Once the instance of *AccessibilityNodeInfo* was obtained its public fields and methods allowed the access to the element's state and visual properties. The internal resource ID used to identify the element inside the application is also provided along with the value of the *contentDescription* property. However, the object received as a parameter of the callback method *onAccessibilityEvent()* is an instance of the *AccessibilityNodeInfo* class that do not correspond to an instance of the real control inserted on the activity.

The object instance of the *AccessibilityNodeInfo* class allows access to properties including the element's location, size, class, text and *contentDescription*. The *contentDescription* value is the element's content that is commonly used on accessibility services such as TalkBack, which is the default screen reader shipped with the Android OS.

5 Results

The location, size, and type provided by the accessibility layer are accurate and represent the correct properties of the element when an event is triggered. To calculate the recognition rate we focused on the API capability to trigger events that allows the access to the UI interactive element's properties and also the location, size, type, and content data recognition rate.

We evaluated the recognition rate only on interactive elements that allows the inspection of the *AccessibilityNodeInfo* object inside the *onAccessibilityEvent()* method. All non-interactive elements are obtained querying the view layout hierarchy once an event was triggered. While evaluating the API with this approach we found that when certain interactive elements were touched they did not generate any event at all. Although this lack of accessibility event generation is rare on the evaluated applications, we accounted for this fact and provided the Event Trigger Rate metric.

The most common type of event that triggered the *onAccessibilityEvent()* method was the TYPE_VIEW_CLICKED, which is a numeric constant that classify the event as a touch in any area of a View. Within this event an *AccessibilityNodeInfo* object can invoke the *getPackageName()* and *getClassName()* methods to identify precisely the type of target's element being clicked.

The methods *getBoundsInParent()* and *getBoundsInScreen()* allows the identification of the element's position relative to its container and on the real screen, respectively. The position of the element is obtained as a *Rect* object that has four coordinates, thus providing means to calculate the element's size.

The recognition of the content was evaluated by the presence of textual information that allows its identification. The methods *getText()* and *getContentDescription()* of the *AccessibilityNodeInfo* object returns the content information assigned manually by the developer or automatically by the accessibility API. Therefore, the Content Rate metric was calculated based on the presence of textual information provided by any of those two methods. Table 2 presents the values of the Event Trigger Rate and Content Rate metrics from the 10 Android applications evaluated. The Overall Recognition Rate is the average value of the two previous mentioned rates.

The evaluation of the recognition rate accounted for 923 interactive elements found on 185 activities across 10 applications. The average Event Trigger Rate was 99.69 % (*s.d.* 0.53) and the average Content Rate was 93.65 % (*s.d.* 3.35). The average Overall Recognition Rate was 96.87 % (*s.d.*1.88).

Table 2. Rates of the applications' trigger events and element content.

Application	Event Trigger Rate (%)	Content Rate (%)	Overall Recognition Rate (%)
Skype	100	98.75	99.37
WhatsApp Messenger	99.8	98.57	99.18
Viber	99.8	98.16	98.98
Instagram	100	94.20	97.1
Maps	100	93.65	96.82
YouTube	100	93.51	96.75
Twitter	99.8	92.19	96.00
Messenger (Facebook)	98.6	92.86	95.73
Clean Master	100	90.48	95.24
Facebook	99.8	88.30	93.55

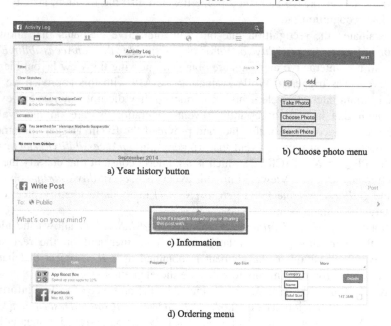

a) Year history button

b) Choose photo menu

c) Information

d) Ordering menu

Fig. 1. Highlighted interactive elements that did not triggered accessibility events: (a) Year history button on Facebook's Activity Log screen; (b) Phone menu items on messenger's new group screen; (c) Pop up information on facebook's write post screen; and (d) Ordering element items on clean master's app manager screen.

6 Discussion

The applications evaluated on this study have a high Event Trigger Ratio and five of them received the 100 % value for this metric, meaning that all interactive elements have triggered events that were captured by the accessibility API. The other applications lack events for elements such as buttons, menu items, list items, and check boxes. These elements did not raised events because they were created dynamically on execution time or are inside a pop up menu. Additionally, custom controls created by

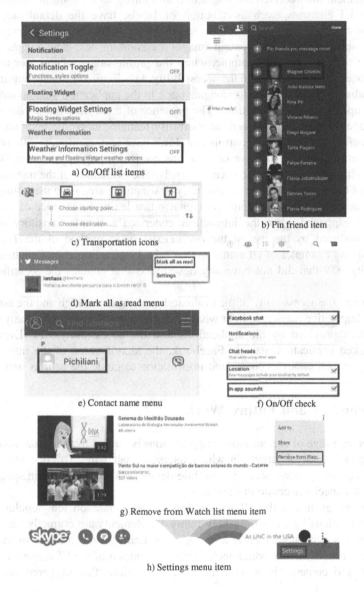

Fig. 2. Highlighted UI elements without textual content: (a) On and Off list items on Clean Master's Settings screen; (b) Pin friend item on Facebook's Pin friends screen; (c) Transportation icons on Map's Route start/destination screen; (d) Mark all as read menu item on Twitter's Messages screen; (e) Contact name item on Viber's Find contacts screen; (f) On and Off check items on Messenger Settings screen; (g) Remove from Watch list menu item on YouTube's History screen; (g) Settings menu item on Skype's home screen.

developers did not raised accessibility API callback events. Figure 1 highlights with rectangles some elements that were unreachable by the accessibility API layer.

The Content Rate metric evaluated the presence of textual information associated with the element that received the interaction and raised an accessibility event. Almost all simple UI elements, such as a button or labels, have the default accessibility description obtained from the element's name, text, caption, or title property.

Conversely, controls that contain images or combine text and images also had descriptive information. For example, when the profile image of the user received a touch the user's name was sent to the accessibility API. Similarly, image buttons shown on the toolbar to allow the user to navigate back to the application's home screen have "navigate up" or "back" descriptions. The presence of these descriptions demonstrates the developers' effort to implement accessibility features, since the texts are not provided by default for images or controls that don't have text, caption, or title properties.

The controls that did not have descriptions are icons, pop up menu items, custom list items with images, on/off and check controls. The evaluation of the interface shows that most of the controls without accessibility descriptions are inside the settings screen or on dynamic areas. Another common scenario that led to the absence of the element description happened when the interaction generated a simple transitory on screen message produced by the use of the *makeText()* static method of the *Toast* class. Figure 2 shows examples of UI elements that raised interaction events captured by the accessibility API that did not have any description that enables the identification of content.

In general, the accessibility of the evaluated applications is high and the authors did not found impeditive barriers to infer what is on the interaction focus by analyzing only the resources provided by the applications and the accessibility API. Even on the lowest ranked application, namely Facebook, the identification of the interactive UI elements provided enough context and information to guide the actions performed.

7   Conclusions and Future Work

Nowadays the usage of current mobile applications is guided by the visual access to on screen representation of targets in which users interact with. To cope with visually impaired users or eyes-free scenarios, mobile developers rely on platform specific APIs that provides special accessibility features.

This work evaluated the UI recognition accuracy rate on ten popular Android mobile applications by measuring how many UI elements are correctly identified by users when OS accessibility APIs are used. Our findings indicate that overall recognition rate is roughly 97 %, which include the recognition of the UI elements' location, size, type, and content along with the user interactions that triggered accessibility events.

Formal mobile accessibility API evaluations, especially on popular applications, are important to provide evidences that application are accessibly enough to be used by people with visual impairments or at eye-free situations. The results of the evaluation suggested in this work can influence mobile developers to review the accessibility of their applications and also provide basic support for other contexts, including (i) mobile accessibility services creation; (ii) automatic extraction of a task sequence; (iii) scripting of common actions; (iv) UI automation tests; and (v) support to collaboration frameworks.

Future work includes the evaluation and comparison of other Operating System mobile accessibility APIs and prospective validation of accessibility services (such as screen readers) that are based on the APIs. Another possible direction is the evaluation of the improvement that can be achieved on mobile applications when pixel-based techniques augment accessibility APIs.

References

1. Abou-Zahra, S., Brewer, J., Henry, S.L.: Essential components of mobile web accessibility. In: Proceedings of the 10th International Cross-Disciplinary Conference on Web Accessibility, article No. 5 (2013)
2. Accessibility | Android Developers (2015). http://developer.android.com/guide/topics/ui/accessibility/index.html
3. Dixon, M., Laput, G., Fogarty J.: Pixel-based methods for widget state and style in a runtime implementation of sliding widgets. In: Proceedings of the CHI 2014 Conference on Human Factors in Computing Systems, pp. 2231–2240 (2014)
4. Findlater, L., McGrenere, J.: A comparison of static, adaptive, and adaptable menus. In: Proceedings of the SIGCHI Conference on Human Factors in Computing Systems. ACM Press, pp. 89–96 (2004)
5. Hurst, A., Hudson, S.E., Mankoff, J.: Automatically identifying targets users interact with during real world tasks. In: Proceedings of the 15th International Conference on Intelligent User Interfaces, pp. 11–20 (2010)
6. Kaufman, D.R., Patel, V.L., Hilliman, C., Morin, P.C., Pevzner, J., Weinstock, R.S., Goland, R., Shea, S., Starren, J.: Usability in the real world: assessing medical information technologies in patient's homes. J. Biomed. Inform. 36(1/2), 45–60 (2003)
7. Keates, S., Hwang, F., Langdon, P., Clarkson, P.J., Robinson, P.: Cursor measures for motion impaired computer users. In: Proceedings of the ACM SIGACCESS Conference on Computers and Accessibility, pp. 135–142. ACM Press (2002)
8. MacKenzie, I.S., Kauppinen, T., Silfverberg, M.: Accuracy measures for evaluating computer pointing devices. In: Proceedings of the SIGCHI Conference on Human Factors in Computing Systems, pp. 9–16. ACM Press (2001)
9. StAmant, R., Lieberman, H., Potter, R., Zettlemoyer, L.: Programming by example: visual generalization in programming by example. Commun. ACM 43(3), 107–114 (2000)
10. Zhong, Y., Raman, T.V., Burkhardt, C., Biadsy, F., Bigham, J.P.: JustSpeak: enabling universal voice control on Android. In: Proceedings of the 11th Web for All Conference, p. 36 (2014)
11. Windows Automation API (2015). https://msdn.microsoft.com/en-us/library/windows/desktop/ff486375%28v=vs.85%29.aspx

Smartphones as User Interfaces in Public Events

Maximiliano Romero[1](✉), Marta Zambelli[1], Arturo Di Lecce[2], and Simone Pontiggia[2]

[1] PhyCo Lab, Design Department, Politecnico di Milano, Milano, Italy
maximiliano.romero@polimi.it, marta.zambelli@mail.polimi.it
[2] DEIB (Department of Electronics, Computer sciences and Bioengineering),
Politecnico di Milano, Milano, Italy
{arturo.dilecce,simone.pontiggia}@mail.polimi.it

Abstract. Nowadays, smartphone has become a diffused interface with digital world in daily life. The present paper describes an interactive installation based on smartphone appliance designed to control multimedia user experience. A survey of other case studies is presented. The entire system and function are described in detail. The user test and the results are presented as support of the conclusion. Is it possible to find an interactive presentation of the project at www.phycolab.it/pickchroma

Keywords: Smartphone · User Interface · Interaction design · Physical Computing

1 Introduction

Since the beginning of the mobile phone's diffusion, the use of the smartphone as an user interface for controlling the surrounding devices and environment, has been the topic of many research studies [1] and the possible interactions become particularly interesting when they involve a large amount of people at the same time. Since its large-scale adoption, the smartphone has become one of the favorite user interface for public events. [2–6]

A recent trend is to take advantage of the incredible popularity of the mobile devices, to provide the audience a way to take part at collaborative live events. The mass audience participation in live performances has led to the development of audience participation software frameworks like massMobile, a flexible clientserver system designed to be adapted to various performance needs (and performance venues) by allowing a wireless real time bidirectional communication between performers and audiences. [7]

Other studies concentrate on using the crowd smartphones as UI in the field of collaborative gaming. An example is Space Bugz!, a crowd game for large venues or cinemas that uses an Android app to transform the audience's smartphones in controllers for the game. [8]

© Springer International Publishing Switzerland 2015
M. Antona and C. Stephanidis (Eds.): UAHCI 2015, Part I, LNCS 9175, pp. 350–359, 2015.
DOI: 10.1007/978-3-319-20678-3_34

2   Proposal

The proposed system aims to involve users in an interactive multimedia experience. For a 360° involvement, participants must enter in a cylinder made by a tent of LEDs lights, 12mt diameter and 6mt high. Entering in the cylinder, people dive in a rich performance of sound and light stimulus. Participants have been grouped in 6 at time and one last generation smartphone has been given to each users. These users had to use a definite application of the smartphone in order to interact in real time with the exhibition, modifying colored lights and percussion sounds. Each phone sent information about its own ID and the user's actions. The smartphones and server has been connected using WiFi network. The server linked the incoming information with specific variables in the interactive firmware. Each device was correlated with a specific sound and light effect.

Finally, when people danced naturally inside the cylinder, shaking and touching the phone, the visual animation and music changed continuously.

3   Architecture of the System

Entire system was composed by 6 mobile phones Nokia Lumia 920, a WiFi antenna, a server Apple Mac G5, a sound system (NI Traktor Kontrol S4MK2 MiDi controller, mixer, amplifier and speaker) and a Barco MiSPHERE tent disposed in a 12mt diameter and 6mt high cylindrical shape (Fig. 1).

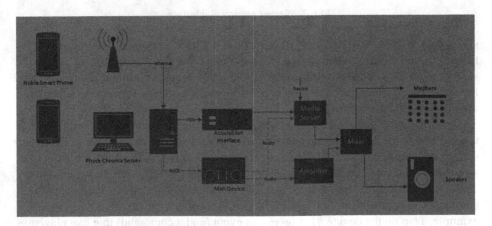

Fig. 1. Architecture of the system

3.1   Server Application

The server is the part of the system in charge to collect, filter and elaborate the data sent by the smartphones and reflect the appropriate changes to the video and to the audio of the performance.

It's coded in Java programming language and the GUI it's composed by two Java Applet windows. One of them is the control interface that allows to change the running

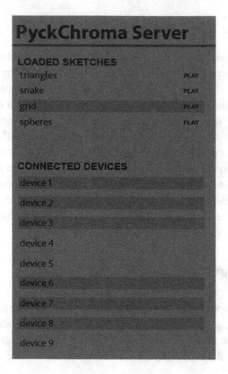

Fig. 2. Server graphical interface

sketch and to check the connected devices Fig. 3. The other Applet window is sent on the acquisition device and shows the video output of the running sketch.

The sketches (views) are implemented with Processing, a common Java class built for electronic arts, new media art, and visual design communities. Processing is available also with a standalone IDE [9].

To manage the video settings, the data received from the smartphones is filtered and used to update the opportune sketch parameters. For example, the number of times per second that the device #1 is shaked (integration of 3 axis acceleration), can affect the size of a related shape or its color gradient. To manage the audio, the server communicates via MidiBus to the midi device. When phone's data is received, opportune commands are sent to the midi device according to the type of event triggered. For example, a tap on the device #1, triggers an event (and a command) that can play/stop an audio sample, play/stop an audio track, edit the track's tempo or edit the parameters of the audio filter.

The communication with the phones, is described in detail later.

3.2   Mobile Application

The application builded on the smartphones is used as an interface for the server that generates sounds and visuals. The participants has to hold the device and do several sort of interaction, they can Jump, shake or touch the device.

In order to obtain a rich interaction with the system, mobile application, and mainly data collection and analysis, are a key factor. Many researches has been conducted in the field of gesture analysis in mobile phone [10–13].

What the app does is:

1. To collect the user's gestures and send the interactions data to the server
2. To give a feedback to the users, this functionality may seem trivial but has an important role since involve the people in a more intimate way. The whole experience is capable to collect the attention of the crowd, but the device interacts directly with each person and thus can generate a feedback directed to the individuals and not on the whole crowd.

In order to improve user interaction, some issues has been considered in the design process of the app:

- The movements used to control the whole system have to be simple: because people have to interact naturally with the system without the need of training. Too complex interactions are to avoid because the people gets frustrated rapidly and loses interest in interacting.
- The movements have to be powerful and expressive: we want to build a system with a deep interaction that can have many shades. So we try to avoid too simple movements that bring to a boring interaction.

These two principles could be in a conflict each others this demands to evaluate the trade of between having poor inexpressive movement and having movement too complex to understand by the user.

We came to a solution layering the interactions using both simple and more complex kind of interaction, dividing the interactions in such a way we could give to the crowd a straightforward way to interact with the ambient letting them discover a more deep interaction when they get bored with the simple one.

- Layer 1 (Simple): touch of the screen, this interaction is the simplest one but distract the people from the performance. As soon as the user touch the screen in every position a touch event is triggered.
- Layer 1 (Simple): shake, this interaction is aimed to detect particular kind of movement, the shakes occur when you drastically change the acceleration and velocity of the device. On each stationary point in the velocity function (inversion of movement) a shake is triggered.
- Layer 2 (Complex): touch, this interaction is more structured than the simple one. The screen is divided in different sensitive areas and a different command is sent when a user touch a different area of the screen.
- Layer 2 (Complex): tilt, this interaction is raised when you move the phone gently leaving the screen up. This interaction has two parameter: the tilt in both direction, x and y.
- Side Layer: Raw data, the phone is capable to send also Raw acceleration data, this mode can be disabled when you deploy the application, is main purpose is for debugging but could be also used for implementing new behavior coding on the server.

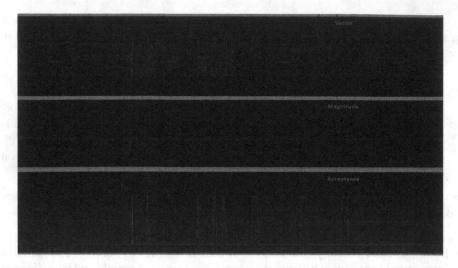

Fig. 3. Sample movement divided in three axes.

The application is continuously logging the data generated from the touch screen and the accelerometer analyzing the incoming data and triggering the message listed above. For the touch is simple to know where and when the user has interact with the screen using the phones api. But for distinguish between shake and tilt event we use boolean membership function that indicate if the data are in the set shake or in the set tlt.

Shake Membership Function. For identifying the shake movement we use the concept of Magnitude, the magnitude for a vector of dimension three is defined as:

$$M = \sqrt{z2+x2+y2}$$

We accept the movement if they have a magnitude superior of 5.5, the value has been calculated from observation and testing of a person shaking. Below we report a chart showing the function.

In the Fig. 3 are reported a sample movement divided on the three axes the computed magnitude and the corresponding acceptance output.

In the Fig. 4 it's possible to see the acceptance of the function respect to the derivative of x, y and z. The data are normalized to 1. We can clearly see the action of the identification, when a movement with a sufficient magnitude is recorded over the axes the membership function recognize the concentrated energy of the movement (Fig. 4).

Tilting Membership Function. For detecting the tilt action we use the derivative of Z, when the derivative is small enough and the vector Z is big enough in module: this two condition implies the user is holding the phone with the screen up and not shaking or doing other movements but tilting it.

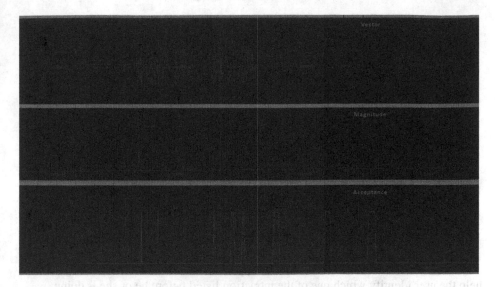

Fig. 4. Sample movement integrated

3.3 Communication and Interaction Types

Whenever a user gesture (all the interaction are gestures) takes place, the device sends a message to the server through an UDP datagram. The UDP protocol has been chosen due to the low communication overhead needed and helps to keep the communication latency low, key factor for a real-time application.

Different datagram structures were used depending on different interactions. Each message is composed by the device identification number, the type of the interaction and the data of the interaction.

The intercepted interactions are:

- touch: when the user presses or releases an area on the smartphone's screen. The message also specifies the number of the used fingers and the touched area's coordinates.
- tilt: when the user gently tilts the phone. The message also specifies the tilt direction.
- shake: when the user moving the phone in a direction, does a fast inversion of movement. The message also specifies the shake direction.

3.4 Graphical User Interface

We have choose to keep the UI very simple because the user hasn't to be distracted from the interaction with the phones. Below you can see a mockup of the final application.

We design the application with a big colorful area that identify the Smart Phones, plus ad identification number. In the middle of the screen is printed a cursor that helps the user interacting with the app. At the start up the screen is black and the cursor is static but when the connection with the server is established the cursor start to pulse, showing that the app is now live (Fig. 5).

Fig. 5. Graphical user interface in a range of colors

The graphics elements on this minimal app have a fundamental role: they guide and help the user identify which one of the intraction listed before he or she is doing.

- Touch: when the user touches the screen, the cursor is moved under the user finger, highlighting the touched area.
- Tilting: when the user starts a tilt gesture, the screen of the phone changes color, going from example from being black to a vivid green (depending on the color chosen for the device) and the pulsing cursor starts to move like a steel ball that is balancing on the screen with the purpose of indicating to the users the exact value they are sending to the server.
- Shaking: when the user starts a shake gesture, the screen makes a flash and vibrates. We chose to use an Haptic feedback because when the user shake the phone with an high probability he or she isn't looking at the screen.

3.5   User Experience

On the night of the performance, at the event entrance hostesses gave out the controller smartphones to visitors interested in interacting with the exhibition. Each device came preloaded with Pyck Chroma, the Windows Phone application developed to transform the stand' smartphones into an interface able to interact with the graphical and musical exhibition taking place at the location.

Up to six visitors at a time could control the way the light and music changed: by shaking and tilting the devices or by tapping on the screen of the stand' smartphones, the users produced a variation in the generative graphics displayed on the MiSPHERE screen and a particular recognizable sound was emitted and added to the playing music base (Fig. 6).

Each user interaction with the device was translated into a visual or audio output. Every smartphone had an assigned effect on the exhibition and affected the show in an unique and unambiguous way by emitting an univocally assigned percussion sound for

Fig. 6. Generative graphic examples

example, or by altering only the graphical elements of a specific color assigned to a specific phone and every user could thus easily recognize the way his action were controlling the light and sound exhibition. Different graphical themes were developed, each with it's own coordinated sound effects set, and each designed to work in a similar and intuitive way from the point of view of the user. The participators were left with the feeling of being a DJ at a collaborative interactive happening.

The exhibition took place as part of the Milano Design Week (the most relevant designrelated event in Milan beside the Salone Del Mobile) from 8 to 13 of April 2014. The location was in the festival zone designated as "Tortona Around Design", known as such from the name of the road it indicated, via Tortona.

A 12mt diameter and 6 mt hight cylinder made by a tent of lightbulbs (Barco MiSPHERE) was erected on a roundabout circulation. Every night, from sunset until 11.00 PM and for an entire week, people got a chance to interact with the system and try to control the atmosphere of the exhibition (Fig. 7).

Fig. 7. Users interacting with the system during user test and general set-up.

Since the event took place during a festival that as a whole is estimated to have attracted more than 300.000 people, there was a lot of affluence around the exhibit installation. A significant number of people thus participated to the collaborative happening, with an even greater audience watching their work.

To each participant was given a smartphone from a fair assistant, who quickly explained and demonstrated how to interact with the device to use it as a controller. "Teams" of participants interacted with the system for a couple of minute at a time.

Up to six different graphic and sound themes were used during the week. Some refinements to the themes were iteratively made with the purpose of achieving a better interaction quality.

4   Conclusion

In conclusion, smartphones can be regarded as an attractive and functional interface for designing engaging and interactive social experiences based on audience participation. Some consideration are however in order to acknowledge the different limitations and problematic we encountered in our experimentation.

We incurred in some technical difficulties with the design of the smartphones themselves: the lockdown buttons were located in a place that kept being bumped and hitten without purpose from the user, interrupting the signal from the devices to the server and severing the connection. Users were left feeling confused and this influenced their involvement and comprehension of the interaction.

Participants sometimes had a somewhat noticeable difficulty in identifying themselves and their action with the corresponding auditory and visual feedbacks of the system. This was due to a number of factors:

1. The screen was really big, for it had to be seen from the whole street, and it was meant to be seen from the outside, and from a considerate distance. The user instead found himself at the center of the circle and saw the lightbulb screen from the insideout. Both the shape of the screen and the excessive nearness to the screen left the user disoriented and unable to fully take in the effect of their action.
2. Even considering it's large dimension, the tent resolution was really low (at about 360 x 60 pixels/lightbulbs) and it didn't allow for the more elaborated shapes to be displayed. The graphics actually used had to be simple enough in nature to be displayed accurately by the tent while at the same time resulting recognizable and entertaining to the user.
3. On the audio front, since the communication isn't synchronous, the instant in which the gesture is made on the device is not the same as the one in which the server elaborates the command sent from the phone to output the sound from the mixer. The two instants result as not being near enough for there to be a perception of true synchronicity between the interaction and the emittance of sound, and the delay between the action of the user and the reaction of the system remains noticeable and distracting.

Even considering these limitations, the event was a success and people genuinely enjoyed interacting with the system and were left feeling like main actors of a collaborative interactive show. Both kids and adults from all ages enjoyed playing in such a novelty way with the smartphones and had little to no trouble understanding the way the interaction worked. All the participants were completely awed by the musical and visual effects produced by their actions.

References

1. Myers, B.A.: Mobile Devices for Control. In: Paternó, F. (ed.) Mobile HCI 2002. LNCS, vol. 2411, pp. 1–8. Springer, Heidelberg (2002)
2. Oh, J., Wang, G.: Audience participation techniques based on social mobile computing. In: Proceedings of the International Computer Music Conference. Huddersfield, UK (2011)
3. Turner, H., White, J. et al..: Engineering challenges of deploying crowdbased data collection tasks to enduser controlled smartphones. In: 3rd International Conference on Mobile Lightweight Wireless Systems (2011)
4. Roberts, C.: Control: software for enduser interface programming and interactive performance. In: Proceedings of the International Computer Music Conference. Huddersfield, UK, July 31–August 5 2011
5. Savage, S., Chavez, N.E., Toxtli, C., Medina, S. AlvarezLopez, D., Hollerer, T.: A social crowd controlled orchestra. In: Proceedings of the 2013 Conference on Computer Supported Cooperative Work Companion, pp. 267–272. ACM (2013)
6. Roberts, C., Hollerer, T.: Composition for conductor and audience: new uses for mobile devices in the concert hall. In: Proceedings of the 24th Annual ACM Symposium Adjunct on User Interface Software and Technology, UIST 2011 Adjunct, pp. 65–66. ACM, New York (2011)
7. Weitzner, N., Freeman, J., Garrett, S., Chen, Y.-L.: massMobile an audience participation framework. In: Proceedings of the International Conference on New Interfaces for Musical Expression (NIME). University of Michigan, Ann Arbor, 21–23 May 2012
8. Birke, A., Schoenau-Fog, H., Reng, L.: Space bugz!: a smartphone controlled crowd game. In: Lugmayr, A. (ed.) MindTrek, pp. 217–219. ACM, New York (2012)
9. Reas, C., Fry, B.: Processing: A Programming Handbook for Visual Designers and Artists, 2nd edn. The MIT Press, Cambridge (2014). ISBN 978-0262028288
10. Choe, B., Min, J.-K., Cho, S.-B.: Online gesture recognition for user interface on accelerometer built-in mobile phones. In: Wong, K.W., Mendis, B.U., Bouzerdoum, A. (eds.) ICONIP 2010, Part II. LNCS, vol. 6444, pp. 650–657. Springer, Heidelberg (2010)
11. Dachselt, R., Buchholz, R.: Natural throw and tilt interaction between mobile phones and distant displays. In: Proceedings of the 27th International Conference Extended Abstracts on Human Factors in Computing Systems, pp. 3253–3258 (2009)
12. Liu, J., Wang, Z., Zhong, L., Wickramasuriya, J., Vasudevan, V.: uWave: Accelerometer-based personalized gesture recognition and its applications. Pervasive Mob. Comput. 5(6), 657–675 (2009)
13. Pylvänäinen, T.: Accelerometer based gesture recognition using continuous HMMs. In: Marques, J.S., Pérez de la Blanca, N., Pina, P. (eds.) IbPRIA 2005. LNCS, vol. 3522, pp. 639–646. Springer, Heidelberg (2005)

A Model for the Use of Social Paradigms in Mobile Ubiquitous Interactions

Vitor Santos(⊠)

NOVA Information Management School, Universidade Nova de Lisboa,
Campus de Campolide, 1070-312 Lisboa, Portugal
vsantos@novaims.unl.pt

Abstract. The mobile devices and their use for Internet access, for georeferentiation and services consumption had a huge increase. Nowadays, these devices ability to establish cooperation networks and to interact intelligently and cooperatively with the surrounding environment has growing importance. In this work we present a model where a minimum set of features and information could be embedded in mobile devices to dynamically enable their integration into computer systems with pre-defined formal structure. It is argued that if a device is only partially competent to perform a particular role in a given context, may yet play this role in collaboration with other devices also partly responsible for the performance of this role in this context. This model is inspired by concepts originating in organization theory and sociology as they are typical, the notions of "social role", "ownership" and "responsibility."

Keywords: Mobile computing · Context-aware computing · Organization theory · Knowledge systems

1 Introduction

In a time where mobile devices usage is widespread and its usage for the internet, georeferenced (Global Positioning System- GPS) and for the use of services is expanding, the ability of these devices to establish cooperation networks and interacting in an intelligent and collaborative way in the surrounding environment is of growing interest. To Schmidt, the way people interact with devices is paramount for their success [6]. Mobile and ubiquitous computing may be characterized through the ubiquity of communications and devices with computational power, that become an integrating part of the physical space in which we live, as well as the various activities in our day-to-day lives [3].

Mobility of devices comes mainly from the mobility of its carriers, by so originating a constant change of the informatics environment that surrounds the device. More so the availability of public and private wireless network access, as well as ad hoc connections to other devices, provides integration opportunities for integrating devices in diversified contexts. To understand and capture the contexts automatically, in what is commonly named context sensible computing, to participate and cooperate with different context member elements, to supply and use services and information, seems relevant.

© Springer International Publishing Switzerland 2015
M. Antona and C. Stephanidis (Eds.): UAHCI 2015, Part I, LNCS 9175, pp. 360–371, 2015.
DOI: 10.1007/978-3-319-20678-3_35

The main objective of this article is to propose a model which is capable to effectively represent the formal structure of one or several computing system in a mobile device, thinking on what role the device may perform in each system and their relation with other devices, so as to make it possible to be dynamically integrated in those systems, and the cooperation with other elements belonging to the system. In order to do so, we propose a minimum of functions and information inspired in concepts from the theory of organizations and sociology, as the notions of "social role", "ownership" and "responsibility", to be incorporated in each device.

2 Mobile Computing, Ubiquitous Computing and Context Sensible Computing

We commonly call mobile computing the use of small dimension computer devices and laptops on wireless networks, connected to public and private servers, to the internet or other devices. Among these computing devices are laptops, notebooks, tablet PCs, palmtops and personal assistants (PDAs).

Ubiquitous computing is a way to improve computer usage, making many computers physically available and making them effectively invisible to the user [7]. Ubiquitous computing has as main objective to make person-machine interaction invisible, be it, to integrate in a whole informatics and people's natural actions and behaviors [8]. By invisibility we mean to be able to interact with computing systems without realizing they are machines, rather as if one were talking with another person. In ubiquitous computing we assume that surrounding computing systems are proactive, and are connected, or are permanently trying to connect. This characteristic is often called "omnipresence".

Context sensitive computing (Context-Aware Computing) appeared as an ubiquitous computing branch that studies the connection between environmental and informatics systems changes. Dey et al. [2]. It is a recent investigative area with difficult implementation techniques challenges, and one that has caught the attention of investigators everywhere in the world. In context sensible computing, the devices try to understand and capture automatically the surrounding contexts so as to provide a better interaction between the environment and the user, regarding hardware, software, and or communication [1].

3 A Proposal Model

In order to reach the dynamic integration of a device in a context sensitive computing system, with a pre-defined formal structure, it is necessary that the device has a minimal set of functionalities and a representation of different formal structures of the different context sensitive computing systems where it might fit. The representation of the system's formal structure we propose in this article is based on the concepts of Role, Ownership and Responsibility that are liable to be reused in different computing contexts [5]. We call Role the particular connection of a device to the cooperative structure of a system that establishes, in that system, that determines a certain number of obligations and responsibilities to the device; Ownership will be the association of a device to a role to perform in the system; we call Responsibility task association to roles that bind role holders as responsible for the full task fulfillment, regardless of that fulfillment being assured by themselves or any other device in which the task execution is delegated.

Ownership, (role/roles that are performed by the device and those it interacts with in a given context, can be represented as shown in Table 1. Ownership is a relation between a device and a role that can be expressed under the form: Owner (X,R1) where X is the device and R1 is the role performed by the device. A device can own more than one role as long as it implements per se all the required functionalities for the correct performance of all roles. On the other hand, there may be more than one device that owns the same role.

Table 1. Ownership chart

Ownership	
Role	Device
Device X	Role 1
Device Y	Role 2
Device Z	Role 3
Device X	Role 4

When a device owns a given role, a competency principle is admitted: the device implements per se all the functions that are required for the correct performance of the role(s). This means the device has the ability of executing all the necessary functions to fulfill the tasks it's responsible for in the role(s) it owns.

Competency to execute a task associated to a role can be defined in the following way:

1. Being Capac_Exec(X,F1) the ability to execute from X in order to execute the function F1
2. Being Execute(R1,T1) the Responsibility to Execute the task T1 attributed to role R1
3. Being Owner(X,R1) the relation of ownership of X to execute the function F1

So, if F1 is a function that pleases T1 we may conclude that the device X is competent to execute the task T1. The relation F1 pleases T1 can be expressed by: Pleases(F1,T1).

Formally, the competency to execute a task associated to a role is translated as: If Capac_Exec(X,F1) $\wedge$ Execute(R1,T1) $\wedge$ Pleases(F1,T1) => Competent_Exec_Task(X, T1). The competency to execute all the tasks associated to a role- Principle of competency for the performance of a role is translated as: $\forall i \in n$ (Execution(R1, Ti) => Competent_Exec_Task(X,Ti)) => Competent_Exec_Papel(X,R1). In the conception of the knowledge representation model there is the possibility of a device belonging simultaneously to more than one system, to be able to change roles and to perform more than one role within the same context. Therefore, in order for the model to support this possibility, we need to contextualize the ownership representation as illustrated in Table 2.

Table 2. Ownership chart

Extended ownership		
Role	Device	Context
Device X	Role 1	Work context
Device Y	Role 2	Work context
Device X	Role 4	Work context
Device Y	Role 1	Friends context
Device Z	Role 6	Friends context

Ownership is a relation between a device, a role and a context, expressed formally as: Owner(X,R1,Ca) where X is the device, R1 is the role performed by the device and Ca the context in which X owns the R1 role.

A device can own roles with the same name in more than one context. However, by considering a model that includes more than one context, the definition of the roles is contextualized, so the roles can have the same name in different contexts and have different aims, depending on its definition for each specific context. Different devices can be owners of the same role provides the model with the required hardiness to compensate performance flaws and to admit structural changes and role ownership.

In Fig. 1, we present, schematically a simplified model of the representation structure of knowledge relative to a given context.

The association between tasks and roles that exist in a given context, where Owners are responsible for their fulfillment, regardless of it being assured by themselves or others in which the task is delegated, is called Responsibility. The Responsibility is a relation between a role and a task, in a Ca context, and may be formally defined as:

Responsibility(R1,T3,Ca)

In Table 3, "Task 4" is of the responsibility of the device owner of "Role 1", but the latter may choose not to perform it directly.in order to do so, it delegates the task, which means it must obligatorily know which roles are responsible for "Task 4".

The way the device chooses between delegating or performing must be previously defined. In terms of model, any criteria may be implemented. A possible criteria is as follows:

"If the device knows any other device with the responsibility of Executing the task at hand, then delegate the task by producing a message with an order for executing the task for that device. Or, if you don't know who is responsible of executing and has the ability to perform the task, then execute it". To be responsible for a task, in a given context, admits that this may or not be a composite task. If the task is composite, then the device must be able to control and monitor the execution of subtasks, thus assuring these are successfully executed in the right sequence and appropriated timing.

So it is possible to coordinate the execution of composite tasks, to have control and monitor them, it is necessary that the communication language between the devices

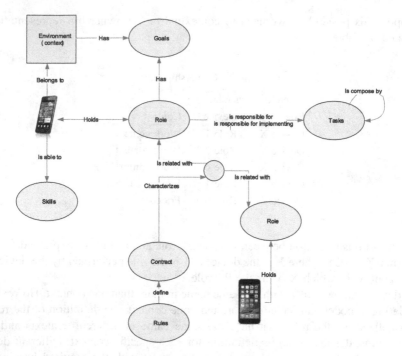

Fig. 1. Simplified model

Table 3. Responsibility chart

Responsibility		
Role	Task	Context
Role 1	Task 4	Work context
Role 3	Task 3	Work context

supports specific primitives destined to manage and coordinate tasks. The discussion of primitives destined to the coordination of tasks is complex, and is not included in this article.

Another designation is "Execution Responsibility"- Tasks associated to roles existing in Context, for which the Owners are responsible to ensure the fulfillment in terms of execution. In the presented model, being responsible for the execution by a task doesn't consider this task to be composite.

Responsibility of Execution is a relation between a role and a task, in a context Ca, and is normally defined as: Execute(R1,T1,Ca).

In Table 4, T2, T4 and T5 are atomic tasks, i.e. they have no defined Break Down: Execute(R1,T1,Ca), Execute(R1,T2,Ca).

"Task 2" may be executed by the Owner of "Role 2" or the Owner of "Role 3".

Table 4. Responsibility of execution chart

Responsibility of execution		
Role	Task	Context
Role 1	Task 1	Work context
Role 2	Task 4	Work context
Role 2	Task 2	Work context
Role 3	Task 3	Work context

A device is responsible for a given Task if it's responsible for its fulfillment, regardless that fulfillment is assured in terms of execution by itself or a "subcontract" of other devices.

A device is responsible for executing a given task if the task length is assured in terms of execution by the device. A particular aspect occurs when the same device performs a role where it is simultaneously responsible for the fulfillment and execution of a task. Responsibility(R1,T1,Ca) $\land$ Execute(R1,T1,Ca). In this case, we must define which of the two relations is stronger and overlaps the other. The definition of this criteria must be programmed.

In the case where the strongest relation is Execute(R1,T1,Ca) then the task is executed and the Responsibility(R1,T1,Ca) is overlooked.

In the case the strongest relation is Responsibility(R1,T1,Ca), depending on the criteria used by the device in order to choose between executing or delegating, the relation Execute(R1,T1,Ca) may or not be used. If the criteria is to delegate the task in a device that is responsible for the execution, then it is possible that the device will delegate the task onto another one or on itself, once it is also responsible for the execution. In this case the relation Execute(R1,Y1,Ca) may or not be used.

If the criteria is to check first whether the device is responsible for the execution and only delegate in case it isn't, then the relation Execute(R1,T1,Ca), if it exists, is used.

By trying to characterize the delegation, three important questions emerge [4]:

- What is the nature of the relations between which delegates and which accepts the relation;
- Through which types of communication can this delegation be made and how is it specified;
- Under which conditions is it possible to say the delegation was achieved successfully.

The answer to the first two questions comes from what is specified in the model itself. The answer to the third question is provided by using two mechanisms, used together or in separate. The first mechanism is based on message exchanges and between the device that delegates and the one the delegation is made onto.

When a device delegates a task it produces a message with an order to execute the task to the device it delegates the task onto. This one answers with a message like "Info", indicating it received the order and tries to execute the task. If it is able to execute it sends a message and informs the delegating device of its success, otherwise it sends a message pointing out the flaw. This mechanism assumes the device trusts who delegates.

A second, more complex and fallible mechanism, consists on the attempt observation by the device that delegates, of the fulfillment of the task it delegated, in order to come to conclusions about the success of the delegation. Some tasks can be broken down into elemental tasks, as shown in Table 5.

Table 5. Break down chart

Break down			
Task	Subtask	Order	Context
Task 1	Task 1.1	1	Work context
Task 1	Task 1.2	1	Work context
Task 3	Task 3.1	1	Work contex
Task 3	Task 3.2	2	Work context
Task 3	Task 3.3	2	Work contex
Task 3	Task 3.4	3	Work contex

In this example "Task 1" is made of 2 tasks. Since they have the same order to execute there is no specific sequence in its execution.

"Task 1" will only be finished when tasks 1.1 and 1.2 are both concluded.

"Task 2" isn't made of any other tasks.

"Task 3" is made of 4 tasks that must be executed the following way: Tasks 3.2 and 3.3 can only be executed after the task 3.1 is finished. There is no particular execution sequence between them. However, task 3.4 can only be executed after tasks 3.2 and 3.3 are both concluded. Breaking down tasks is the relation between a task and others that break it down. It may defined as follows:

Break down(T3,T3.1,1,Ca)
Break down(T3,T3.2,2,Ca)
....

To each relation between roles a certain Contract is determined (set of rules). A relation between two roles is always one-way (Ex: "Role1" to "Role 2"). The definition of bi-directional relations is achieved through two one-direction relations, in opposite ways.

A relation between roles is defined by the expression Relation(R1,P2,Contract,Ca) which means there is formally a relation in context Ca, between the roles R1 and R2, from R1 to R2. This formal relation is, in this model, called "Contract" (Table 7).

A contract is defined by a set of rules. Rules define the contract relative to the interactions between roles it is associated with, namely, in what concerns processing the various types of message. We will formally come up with:

Caract(ContractA,Rule1)
Caract(ContractA,Rule2)
Caract(ContractB,Rule1)

Table 6. Relation chart

Relation			
Role	Role	Contract	Context
Role 1	Role 2	Contract A	Work context
Role 2	Role 1	Contract C	Work cntext
Role 3	Role 2	Contract B	Work context
Role 4	Role 3	Contract C	Work context
Role 5	Role 3	Contract A	Work context

Table 7. Relation chart

Contracts	
Contract	Rule
Contract A	Rule 1-Contracting
Contract A	Rule 2
Contract B	Rule 1

For each message sent from an emitter to a receiver, the latter makes an applicability test to the kind of message in question, the rules associated between emitter-receiver. This check is achieved in two phases. In phase one, when check if the rule, according to the relation between the emitter and the receiver, is applicable in the given context. The messages between devices have the following format: Msg(D1,D2, Tm,C). Where D1 is the emitting device, D2 is the receiving device, T is the type of message and C is the contents. The general condition for applying a Rule r in treating a message, as "Tm", send from X to Y, in context Ca, can be expressed this way:

msg(X,Y, Tm,C) $\wedge$ Owner(X,R1) $\wedge$ Owner(Y,R2) $\wedge$ Relation (R1,R2,) $\wedge$ Caract (ContractA, r)

If this check fails, we go on to the second phase, where we execute a check to the condition for applicability of the rule in a given context. The general condition for the applicability of a Rule r in any given context that determines a given message treatment as "Tm" can be seen in the expression: msg(X,Y, Tm,C) $\wedge$ Owner(X,R1) $\wedge$ Owner(Y, R2) $\wedge$ Relation (R1,R2, ContractA) $\wedge$ Caract (ContractA, r)

4   Competencies for the an Acceptable Role Performance in Formal Organizations

When a device owns a given role, we assume a competency principle: the device implements per se all the required functions for the correct performance of the role(s). this means the device has the ability to execute all the necessary functions to fulfill the tasks it's responsible for in their execution in the role(s) it owns.

The competency for executing a task associated to a role can be defined in the following way:

Be it Capac_Exec(X,F1) the Capacity for executing X to perform the function F1
Be it Execution(R1,T1) the Responsibility for the Execution of task T1 attributed to Role R1
Be it Owner(X,R1) the ownership relation of X by the Role R1, then, if F1 is a function that pleases T1 we can conclude that the device X is competent to execute task T1. The relation F1 pleases T1 can be expressed by: Pleases(F1,T1) [5].

Formally, the competency to execute a task associated to a role can be translated as:
If Capac_Exec(X,F1) ∧ Execute(R1,T1) ∧ Pleases(F1,T1) => Competent_Exec_Task(X,T1). The competency to execute all tasks associated to a role, illustrated in Fig. 2- Principle of competency for the role performance- is translated as:

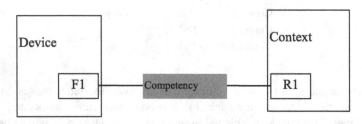

Fig. 2. Execution competency

$\forall_i \in n$, (Execução(R1, Ti) => Competente_Exec_Tarefa(X,Ti) => Competente_Exec_Papel(X,R1))

However, in the situation there is no device that implements per se all the functions required for the correct performance of a role R1, two hypothesis are to consider:

(A) The breaking down and recursive distribution of the tasks associated to Role R1 by new roles created for that effect until a set of Devices is identified that are able to fully satisfy the functional requisits of all the new roles, or until primary tasks are attained (impossible to break down as subtasks) as shown in Fig. 3, be it {T1.1, T1.2, ... T1,i} the set of subtasks of T1 and {Da, Db, ...Dn}the set of devices that perform the Roles {R1.1, R1.2,... R1.i} Then: $\forall_i \in n$, (Competent_Exec_Task(Xi,T1.i) => Competent_Exec_Role({Da, Db,..Dn},R1)).

In the example presented on Table 6, we can see that:

"Task 1" is composed of 2 other tasks (subtasks). Since they have the same order to execute, there is no particular sequence in its execution.

"Task 2" isn't composed by other tasks.

"Task 3" is composed by 4 tasks that have to be executed the following way: Tasks 3.2 and 3.3 can only be executed after Task 3.1 is complete. Between them there is no particular sequence of execution. However Task 3.4 may only be executed after Tasks 3.2 and 3.3 are both concluded (Table 8).

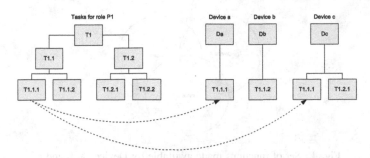

Fig. 3. Recursive breaking down of tasks (adapted from Cunha [9])

Table 8. Breaking down chart

Breaking Down			
Task	Subtask	Order	Context
Task 1	Task 1.1	1	Work context
Task 1	Task 1.2	1	Work context
Task 3	Task 3.1	1	Work context
Task 3	Task 3.2	2	Work context
Task 3	Task 3.3	2	Work context
Task 3	Task 3.4	3	Work context

Task breaking down is a relation between a task and others that break it down. It may be defined in this way:

Breakdown(T3,T3.1,1,Ca)
Breakdown(T3,T3.2,2,Ca)
....

(B) Attributing Ownership of R1 to several Devices where, although each one isn't competent per se to satisfy de performance of the role R1,•in their whole they satisfy in total the functional requisitions of R1, by complementing their functions. Be it {T1.1, T1.2, T1.3, ... T1.i} the set of subtasks of T1 and {Da, Db... Dn} the set of devices that would at the same time perform the role R1, then: Competent_Exec_Task(Da,{T1. k,...}) ∪ Competent_Exec_Task(Db,{T1.p,...}) ∪ ... ∪ Competent_Exec_Task(Dn, {T1.m,...}) => Competent_Exec_Role(Da + Db + ...Dn, R1)).

The first case, breaking down and distributing subtasks by different Devices presents as main disadvantage the difficulty in controlling the execution of the delegated tasks, mostly if it is recursive. In the second case, distributing of the same role through several Devices, that are not competent on their own to perform the role, but are together, recursive breaking down is not needed. This fact tends to simplify the control over task execution. Thus, having for basis the situation shown in Fig. 4, considering T1 as the set of tasks associated to Role R1 and Ta, Tb and Tc as being the set of tasks able to be satisfied respectively by devices a, b and c, it suffises that T1 ⊂ (Ta ∪ Tb ∪ Tc), as shown in Fig. 5.

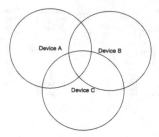

Fig. 4. Set of functions made available by Devices a, b and c

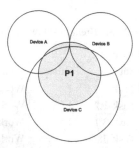

Fig. 5. Contribution of the Devices A, B and C for the performing of Role R1

The fact that different Devices owners of the same Role make available some same functions (intersection zones in Fig. 5) gives enough hardiness to the model so it is possible to compensate an eventual flaw of performance in those functions. In Table 9, we examplify the application of this strategy by illustrating saved information for a situation where the performance of role R1 is assured by two devices X and Z.

Table 9. Partial ownership chart

Partial Ownership			
Device	Role	Tasks	Context
Device X	Role 1	Task 1	Work context
Device X	Role 1	Task 2	Work context
Device Z	Role 1	Task 1	Work context
Device Z	Role 1	Task 5	Work context
Device X	Role 2	Task 1	Work context
Device Z	Role 2	Task 3	Work context

5   Conclusions

With the transcribed model in this article, we aim to contribute to the debate on mobile and context-sensible computation, by proposing a model that allows us to integrate dynam-ically devices in computerized systems distributed in a pre-defined formal structure.

The model, structured on concepts originated from organizations and sociology theories, brings with a minimal of functions and information to be incorporated in each device.

In this paradigm, when a device is owner of a given role, we admit that the device implements per se all the required functions for the correct performance of the role(s). Be it: the device has the ability to execute all the necessary functions to fulfill all the tasks for which it is responsible for, in the role(s) it's responsible for.

However, such a principle: $\forall i \in n$, (Execute(R1, Ti) => Competent_Exec_Task(X, Ti) => Competent_Exec_Role(X,R1)), may complicate the use and integration of devices in contents, once it forces availability functions of the devices to cover in full the roles' requirements. In this article we seek, without resourcing to the classical and always complex recursive breaking down of tasks, to point out a new way in order to minimize this problem, by proposing a set of minimal personal capabilities that a Device should have to be able to perform with success a role in a formal mobile and ubiquitous computing structure in which it is partially competent, considering the possibility of cooperation with other Devices totally or partially competent for this role.

As future work, we aim to adapt the model in the use of Service Oriented Model models, an effective development of a system that implements the suggested model and the building of a web site where it is possible, using this model, to register and obtain information on the valence of different devices and, to define and import formal structures on computing systems.

References

1. Dey, A.K., Abowd, G.D.: Towards a better understanding of context and context-awareness, College of Computing, Georgia Institute of Technology, Atlanta GA USA, Technical report GIT-GVU-99-22 (1999)
2. Dey, A.K.: Understanding and using context. Personal Ubiquit. Comput. 5(1), 4–7 (2001)
3. Greenfield, A.: Everyware: The Dawning Age of Ubiquitous Computing. New Riders Press, Berkeley (2006). http://www.amazon.ca/exec/obidos/redirect?tag=citeulike09-20&path=ASIN/0321384016
4. Norman, T.J., Preece, A., Chalmers, S., Jennings, N.R., Luck, M., Dang, V.D., Nguyen, T.D., Deora, V., Shao, J., Gray, W.A., Fiddian, N.J.: Agent-based formation of virtual organisations. Knowl.-Based Syst. 17, 103–111 (2004)
5. Santos, V.: Utilização de paradigmas sociais em computação móvel e computação sensível ao contexto. In: First Workshop on Information Systems for Interactive Spaces (WISIS 2011) inserido na 6ª Conferência Ibérica de Sistemas e Tecnologias de Informação (CISTI), Chaves 15 a 18 de Junho (2011)
6. Schmidt, A.: Implicit human computer interaction through context. Personal Technol. 4(2&3), 191–199 (2000)
7. Weiser, M.: Some computer science issues in ubiquitous computing. Commun. ACM 36(7), 75–84 (1993)
8. Wikipedia: "Computação ubíqua" Retirado em 15 de Janeiro de 2011 de (2011). http://pt.wikipedia.org/wiki/Computação_ubíqua
9. Cunha, M.M.: Organization of a market of resources for agile and virtual enterprises integration, Doctoral thesis, University of Minho, Guimarães (2003)

Universal Access to Information, Communication and Media

An Enriched ePub eBook for Screen Reader Users

Valentina Bartalesi and Barbara Leporini[✉]

CNR-ISTI, via Moruzzi 1, 56124 Pisa, Italy

{valentina.bartalesi,barbara.leporini}@isti.cnr.it

Abstract. Our study aims at obtaining ePub accessibility for all, including screen reader users. Since an ePub document is made up of several (X)HTML files, we analysed and worked with those (X)HTML tags that affect the blind user's experience in the reading. As a case study we developed an "enriched" ePub book which applies technical solutions (i.e. tags and attributes) with the purpose to overcome the accessibility and usability issues observed when interacting via screen reader. In this work we present the results collected through an online survey conducted with 25 users to evaluate the "enriched" ePub compared with the original PDF format in terms of accessibility and usability. Positive responses about the proposed solutions emerged from the survey: the easy access to the table of content, to the images, to the text and also the ease of navigation. In short, 88 % of the users preferred the ePub format instead of the PDF. This confirms that quite simple technical solutions can really improve the reading experience for not only visually impaired people. The results from the survey also showed accessibility issues and limitations of the screen readers and eBook reader software which still exist.

Keywords: eBook accessibility · eBook usability · ePub format · Blind users

1 Introduction

Nowadays electronic books (eBooks) are increasingly used by everyone, especially on mobile devices. This is particularly important and useful for people who are not able to access the print version, such as the visually-impaired, including for educational purposes [10]. Unfortunately, currently available eBooks don't allow the blind users to properly and satisfactorily read the content via screen reader [11]. The content is usually not well designed, because: (i) the images are not equipped with alternative descriptions; (ii) the table of contents is not available or well-structured; (iii) the organization of the eBook in chapters, sections and sub-sections is not well-designed for effective interaction via screen reader, especially on touchscreen devices.

In our study we took into account the ePub format since it is made up of several (X)HTML files. EPub is a free and open eBook modeled by the International Digital Publishing Forum (IDPF) and it is widely used by the eBook vendors. Several guidelines and criteria have been proposed to support the accessibility and usability for (X)HTML contents (e.g. ePub 3 Accessibility Guidelines, WCAG 2.0). Our aim is to investigate if such guidelines are likewise appropriate for an ePub when interacting via screen reader.

© Springer International Publishing Switzerland 2015

M. Antona and C. Stephanidis (Eds.): UAHCI 2015, Part I, LNCS 9175, pp. 375–386, 2015.

DOI: 10.1007/978-3-319-20678-3_36

A screen reader is software that allows the identification and interpretation of what is displayed on the User Interface (UI). In this study we focused specifically on the reading of eBooks using the screen reader VoiceOver, especially through mobile devices. Based on the observed issues [4], we worked with those (X)HTML tags that affect the blind user experience in the reading of an ePub book. Our proposed solution aims at enriching the ePub format for satisfactory screen reader interaction, not affecting the visual layout at the same time. Through the Book4All tool [6] – adequately extended with a specific module - we handled three existing books to apply our proposed solutions. Herein we present the results collected through an online survey conducted to evaluate the accessibility of one of our enriched ePub books compared with its PDF original version.

After a short introduction of other works in the field, the case study is presented. Next, we will report the evaluation results collected by the survey.

2   Related Works

Several solutions and tools have been proposed to provide valuable support to people who encounter serious difficulties in reading paper-books. The Daisy consortium, for example, develops, maintains and promotes open international DAISY (Digital Accessible Information System) Standards for documents. This form is designed to provide eBooks accessible in both audio and text format. On 11th Oct 2011, ePub3 (= DAISY 4 distribution format) which uses HTML 5 was approved as a final Recommended Specification by IDPF (International Digital Publishing Forum). Thus the publishers' standard and accessibility format has been integrated to achieve accessibility in the mainstream eBook industry.

Some studies have been investigated for how the reading can be improved. Adjouadi et al. [2] introduce an automatic book reader for blind people: a fully integrated system with a high reading accuracy. In particular, concerning the state of art reader devices actually available, [9] an evaluation in usability and accessibility perspective is presented. El-Glaly et al. [7] present a novel interaction for reading texts depending on situated touch. Using an iPad, the text of an eBook is rendered audible in response to the user's touch. Attarwala et al. [3] propose the tablet-based e-reading application ALLT which enhances the capabilities of older adults and visually impaired e-book readers through customizable and intelligent accessibility features. Bottoni et al. [5] propose a system to support the users' interactivity for editing, annotating, and indexing e-documents. On the other hand, various tools that aim at generating and adapting the eBook content have been proposed. The Starlight platform [8] allows the users to develop and interact with electronic textbooks. The Starlight platform is composed of two tools: (a) the "Reader", for interactive delivery of electronic textbooks combining visual, acoustic and haptic modalities; and (b) the "Writer", a tool for producing eBooks supporting editing facilities.

Henry [12] reports a study on text-customization needed by visually-impaired users for reading PDF documents. The results encourage better text customization functionalities in the reading tools. AbdelRazek and Modayan [1] describes the importance of the eBook content adaptation when compared to a simple digital version. The adaptive eBook resulted more accessible and usable in terms of content navigation. Our approach aims at exploring new opportunities to use the widespread ePub format via common reading tools.

3   Accessibility Issues

As discussed in [4], the main problems experienced by blind users when accessing the eBook contents may be especially due to:

1. Lack of context – i.e. accessing only small portions at any one time, losing the overall current content;
2. Information overload – unchanging portions (such as the page header, the page number, etc.) may overload the reading and slow down content exploration;
3. Excessive sequencing in reading the information – reading may force access of the (long) content sequentially if no specific mechanism is applied.

Based on these issues, the most important eBook requirements we considered for blind people can be summarised in:

- a logical order in the reading of eBook content (that is the same order of the sighted users);
- a correct linearization of tables and lists;
- an accurate detection of the images by reading their alternative descriptions, if any, and their captions;
- a suitable communication to the user about the type of the elements (e.g. titles, lists, etc.);
- a simple and quick navigation within the content.

Unfortunately these aspects are not well considered when generating ePub documents by means of automatic tools. The (X)HTML code of an ePub is often not standard or not well-formed. In the same way, the table of content, created by conversion tools, are often incomplete and with broken links. Consequently, the screen reader does not interact appropriately with the content. For example, VoiceOver when reading an ePub is not able to inform the user about the presence of images or titles: it just reads the caption and alternative descriptions, but it does not give any detail on the item type (i.e. if it is an image caption or a title). In addition, even though a heading level (i.e. <h1>, <h2>) is applied to titles, no gesture is available to skip from one title to another (for example, as is laid out in a Web page). Concerning images, other specific usability issues were observed in [4]:

1. When encountering more than one consecutive image, the content is not read appropriately: i.e. the alternative descriptions are read before all the captions (e.g. Image-ALT-text1, Image-ALT-text2, Caption 1, Caption 2).
2. No particular issue for images located in the same page and with text in the middle of them, but it is not easy to understand if the read text is a figure description, a caption, or textual content.

Other similar issues are related to tables and lists. The screen reader is not able to appropriately inform the user about the semantics of the 'list' and of the 'table' elements (e.g. it does not say "table" when a table is encountered).

To solve these kinds of problems we suggested adding a word before titles, tables and lists to describe the element. Such information can be added via a hidden label that can be detected by the screen reader but that is not visible to everyone. This solution lets us preserve the eBook layout while the screen reader is able to announce additional information to a blind user (e.g. semantic information).

4   The Case Study

4.1   Method

In order to evaluate our proposed solutions, aimed at overcoming the issues summarized in the previous section, we selected an eBook – the PDF book *Storia Illustrata di Firenze* (*Illustrated History of Florence*)[1]- as a case study. The eBook was chosen according to the following aspects:

1. the table of content as a book structure that has several chapters in order;
2. a number of images to be managed by assistive technologies and small screens;
3. ordered and unordered lists to evaluate how the screen reader is able to easily interact with them.

We especially focused on those aspects that affect the (X)HTML code by arranging the appropriate tags and attributes to have an accessible and enriched ePub output version.

In this work we present the results of a survey conducted to collect further suggestions and comments by end-users on the interaction with both ePub and PDF versions in order to compare their accessibility and usability. According to the requirements described in Sect. 3, the survey investigated the content perception and user interaction. We developed an accessible online survey via Google Docs. Thus we sent to the participants, via e-mail, the URL of the ePub and PDF versions to be evaluated plus the address of the on-line questionnaire. The potential blind users were found thanks to collaboration with the Italian Association for the Blind in Tuscany. To collect comments on the visual user interface, sighted people were involved in the evaluation. The users were asked to interact with the two eBooks by assigning them some tasks in order to focus on specific text portions or book elements. In particular, the users were asked to interact with the table of contents, chapters and sub-chapters, images and lists. Questions were asked based on the aspects considered in the tasks carried out by the users. The results of the evaluation are reported in Sect. 5.2.

Figure 1 shows two pages from the ePub *Illustrated History of Florence*.

---

[1] Cardini, F. *Storia illustrata di Firenze*. Pacini Editore, Pisa, Italy (2009).

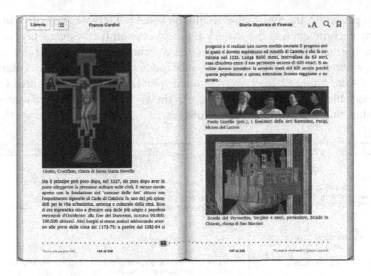

Fig. 1. Two pages of ePub with images, captions and text

4.2 A Tool to Support eBook Generation

To generate our case study eBook, we used the automatic procedure designed for the Book4All tool [4]. Book4All is a tool designed to support the adaptation of PDF documents into three accessible formats for blind users: XHTML 1.0, DAISY 3.0, and ePub 3.0. The tool extracts text and images from the PDF source. Later, an operator can manually manage images, tables, and content by (1) adding descriptions (i.e. 'ALT' attribute) for each image; (2) by managing the table code and structure; and (3) adding content. Once the content has been edited, the operator can export the result into the three supported formats. In particular, the tool supports the following operator's actions:

Table of Content. For the content structure we used Heading Levels. The H1 tags were considered as criterion to automatically create a navigable table of content.

Titles and Headings. Headings can be useful to structure the contents and move through the sections as well. As recommended by the ePub 3 Accessibility Guidelines, we included only a single heading in each chapter. Unfortunately some screen readers, like VoiceOver, are not currently able to detect them in an eBook. A possible solution to inform the reader about titles could be to add the hidden label "title 1" before each title (i.e. H1 tags). This solution has been applied to our case study eBook.

Images. Following the ePub 3 Accessibility Guidelines and WCAG 2.0, when the images were central to the understanding of the content we always included an alternative text in their alt attribute. However some screen readers for the mobile have some issues when reading consecutive images. To this end, the proposed procedure arranges the source code so that the screen reader reads correctly the contents also in presence of images. In particular, the tool applies a solution suitable for two consecutive images, by embedding each image (i.e. the <img> tag) and caption (i.e. <span> tag) in a single anchor tag (i.e. <a> tag). In addition, in order to announce to the reader that an item is an image, we applied the solution based on the hidden label: each image is marked with the hidden word "image". Such word is not displayed thanks to a specified CSS class but it is readable via screen reader. Figure 2 shows how VoiceOver can interpret the content when there are two consecutive images.

What VoiceOver reads	Related HTML code

Image:
Sandro Botticelli, Venus and Mars, particular with Mars sleeping, London, National Gallery
 	
Image:
Sandro Botticelli, Lamentation over the Dead Christ, with san Gerolamo, san Paolo e san Pietro, Monaco, Alte Pinakothek
	``<p>
	  <a>
	    <img
	    src="../images/page194/Venere.png"></img>
	
	    <span id="hidden">Image:</span>
	    <span>Sandro Botticelli, Venus and Mars,
	    particular with Mars sleeping, London, National
	    Gallery</span>
	  </a>
	</p>
	<p>
	  <a>
	    <img
	    src="../images/page194/Compianto.png"></img>
	
	    <span id="hidden">Image:</span>
	    <span> Lamentation over the Dead Christ, with san
	    Gerolamo, san Paolo e san Pietro, Monaco, Alte
	    Pinakothek </span>
	  </a>
	</p>```

...text content... Image: The painting is part of a cycle on the life of Saint Peter, and describes when Jesus directs Peter to find a coin in the mouth of a fish in order to pay the temple tax. The Tribute Money, fresco in the Brancacci Chapel, Santa Maria del Carmine, Florence ...text content...	```<p> <img src="../images/page16/Ghirlandaio.png" alt="The painting is part of a cycle on the life of Saint Peter, and describes a scene from the Gospel of Matthew, in which Jesus directs Peter to find a coin in the mouth of a fish in order to pay the temple tax"></img> <span id="hidden">Image:</span> <span>The Tribute Money, fresco in the Brancacci Chapel, Santa Maria del Carmine, Florence</span> </p>```

Fig. 2. How VoiceOver can read images

5 Evaluation

5.1 The Online Survey

The survey included 35 questions about the most accessible aspects. After a brief overview to identify the sample, we focused our attention on comparison of the following aspects of the ePub and PDF formats: assistive technology usage, eBook favorite formats (electronic versus audio books), eBook navigation usability, and access to the content using different eBook readers (both for desktop and mobile devices). A specific attention put was on accessibility/usability of images, section titles and table of contents. Questions were presented through multiple choice and text area. The same questions required a personal judgment on selected features. A Likert 5-scale values from 1 (totally positive) to 5 (totally negative) was used to express the opinion.

5.2 Participants

We collected suggestions and comments from 25 users; some of them did not answer all the questions. Our sample included 16 females and 9 males.

70 % of the participants were in the range of 21–59 years old, 20 % were people over 60, and 10 % were under 20. More details are reported in Fig. 3.

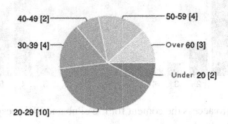

Fig. 3. Age distribution of the users

Regarding the type of disability, 14 users are blind, 4 low vision-impaired, and 7 sighted. 56 % of the participants used a screen reader as assistive technology, 4 % used the Easy Access to Windows, 4 % used a screen magnifier, and 4 % used the combination between a screen reader and a screen magnifier; the remaining 28 % didn't use any assistive technology.

Concerning technological skills, 47 % declared to regularly use iPhone 4 or higher, 19 % an iPod touch 4 or higher, 16 % an iPad, 16 % a smartphone with Android, and one person used a tablet with Android.

5.3 Results

The preference of the eBook usage is confirmed by the collected data from the books format: 64 % of the users usually read electronic books, 12 % listen to Audiobooks, while the remaining 24 % prefer the paper version. With regards the favorite eBook formats, the participants expressed: the ePub with 50 % of users, TXT with 21 %, PDF with 13 %, RTF with 8 %, and finally MSWord and Daisy with 4 % respectively (see Fig. 4).

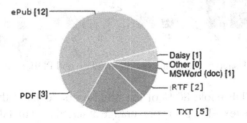

Fig. 4. Preferred eBook formats by the users

With reference to the ePub evaluation, as shown in Fig. 5, the users expressed a positive opinion. The overall score for the eBook usage was '1' (not difficult) according to the

17 users (68 %), '2' according to 5 users (20 %), '3' according to 2 users (8 %), and '4' according to 1 user (4 %). No one expressed a totally negative opinion (score '5').

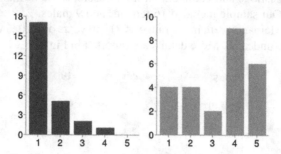

Fig. 5. Difficulty degree to access the content for the ePub and PDF, respectively (1-not difficult to 5-very difficult).

On the other hand, regarding the PDF navigation, 6 users (24 %) expressed a totally negative opinion choosing the value '5', 9 users (36 %) chose the value '4', 2 users (8 %) chose the value '3', 4 users (16 %) evaluated the navigation with the value'2', and only the remaining 4 users (16 %) assigned value '1'.

64 % of the users asserted that the ePub document structure is very easy to understand (score equal to 1). Only 9 % of the users expressed the same evaluation regarding the PDF file.

Regarding the navigation, 14 users (64 %) used the table of contents to navigate the ePub document without problems (score equal to 1). Only 2 users (9 %) chose the value '1' for the navigation using the index in the PDF file. More details are reported in Fig. 6.

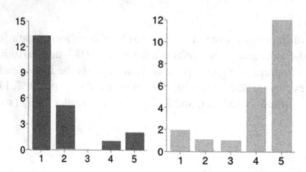

Fig. 6. Usage of the table of content (ePub and PDF, respectively)

Relating to the PDF book, 80 % of the blind users declared they were not able to identify images in the text. The same percentage asserted also that the screen reader was not able to read the images and their captions in the correct order.

On the contrary, as reported in Figs. 7 and 8, the users declared to perceive the images well (57 % expressed '1' that is no difficulties, 30 % '2', 9 % '3', and 4 % '4') and their descriptions (63 % expressed '1', that is no difficulties, 13 % '2', 17 % '3', 8 % '4') in the ePub book.

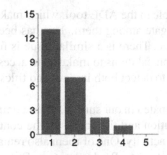

Fig. 7. Difficulty degree to detect the images in the ePub book

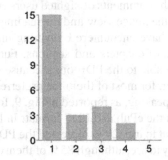

Fig. 8. Difficulty degree to detect the captions in the ePub book

Several users commented that long descriptions could be useful just for specific cases; for example when an image is a key element to understanding the text content. Other users suggested using a short description by default and a longer one available on demand. Some users also observed that a mechanism to "include" or "exclude" the images along with the content could be a useful functionality to simplify the reading.

Regarding the titles of the text sections, the blind users declared they were able to detect them well thanks to the (hidden) label "title" before each heading. Blind users also suggested considering the opportunity to skip from a heading to another one as it happens for the Web pages. Although the tags <h1> , <h2> , etc., have been applied to the eBook source code, the screen reader (for both desktop and mobile devices) is not able to detect them. In fact, concerning headings and titles, several issues were reported by the users when reading, also through the Adobe Digital Edition (ADE 4.0) tool.[2] The users were not able to correctly skip from one section to the next via the commonly preferred command "h" offered by the screen reader Jaws[3] or via any other reader command available in the ADE tool. Although the most recent version of ADE (i.e. 4.0) includes more accessibility features than the previous versions, the majority of them cannot yet be supported, like the use of headings as logical partitioning of the Web content. However, headings allow the users to get an overview of the contents through

---

[2] http://www.adobe.com/it/products/digital-editions.html
[3] http://www.freedomscientific.com/products/fs/jaws-product-page.asp

a hierarchical structure available in the ADE tool, which makes possible to get an overview of the contents and navigate among them. This has been observed for both ADE versions for Windows and Mac. There is a similar issue is for the images. There is no mechanism used to detect graphical items to make them accessible to the assistive technologies. The users were able to detect both images and titles only thanks to the hidden labels (i.e. 'image' and 'title').

Seven sighted users participated in our survey. Their comments were positive, especially about the eBook navigation and the access to the content. All users highlighted the friendliness of the reading activity. One of them also remarked the usefulness of the index to have a direct access to the eBook chapters. Even though we added hidden information to "enrich" the content (i.e. "image" before the < img > tag, or "title" before the chapter and sub-chapter), the comments of sighted users confirmed that our solution does not influence the layout, the image view and the reading of the content. In fact, no non-blind person reported to have encountered anything unusual or particular when showing the images and titles of chapters and sections. Furthermore, for the sighted users the ePub format is preferable to the PDF one, because the text size can be easily and better magnified. However, for most of them the preferred format to read a book is the paper version. Generally speaking, as reported in Fig. 9, for sighted users there is no significant difference between the ePub and PDF format. In fact, 43 % of them replied that "ePub" as the easier format to use, 29 % indicated the PDF to be easier and the rest stated that they are equally easy to use, although 85 % of them observed some differences between the two formats, such as image detection, availability of the content index, title announcement and document lightness as well.

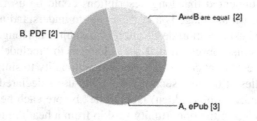

Fig. 9. Preferred formats by the sighted users (either PDF or ePub)

5.4   Discussion

We focused on evaluating those (X)HTML tags affecting the main interaction aspects, e.g. headings for structuring the content, alternative descriptions for the images, presence of a table of content. Even if the ePub format is complete with accessibility standards, several problems in detecting the semantic of text objects by the screen reader are still present in the ePub books. Thus, we proposed to apply simple tags and attributes to add useful semantic information (e.g. hidden labels) to make the content more understandable by blind users who use assistive technologies.

The users expressed positive comments on the evaluated eBook. However, the responses collected by the survey, revealed also some limitations by the assistive technologies and eBook reader applications in supporting a satisfactory reading. At the same time, the users suggested some aspects to improve the reading interaction. In brief, the suggestions are related to:

- applying short alternative descriptions for the images, and use more detailed explanations for crucial images;
- making available mechanisms for the assistive technology in order to (1) facilitate structure navigation (section by section), (2) include/exclude image visualization, (3) detect element type (i.e. image, table, title).
- providing functionalities for the eBook reader in order to (1) quickly and easily use the table of contents, (2) show/hide more complex objects like images and tables, and (3) easily read the notes. This requires that assistive technologies as well as reading applications must be able to support: (i) detection of elements type (e.g. recognition of semantic tags or attributes); (ii) more customizable image management (e.g. via specific mechanisms); and (iii) exploitation of content structure (e.g. via table of contents and heading navigation). On the other hand, developers should be able to use specific (X)HTML semantic tags and attributes, which are adequately supported by the applications.

6 Conclusions

In this work we presented a survey conducted on ePub eBook interaction via screen reader to collect suggestions and comments on a possible solution proposed to overcome the accessibility and usability issues observed when reading a book on a mobile touchscreen device via screen reader. We used the eBook Illustrated History of Florence as a case study to apply and evaluate some technical solutions to improve the blind user interaction.

We had a total of 25 users of which 18 visually-impaired and 7 sighted. Positive responses on the ePub emerged from the survey: 88 % of the users preferred such format. More than 60 % expressed a satisfactory opinion for the navigation (64 %) and for image descriptions and detection as well (63 %). On the other hand, the PDF format has not been appreciated in the same way. The comments of visually-impaired users were positive, especially about the access to the content, the reading of the images and the detection of the titles. All users highlighted the friendliness of the reading activity. We also included the answers given by the sighted users because they revealed some interesting usability aspects of our eBook when it is read without an assistive technology. The sighted user experience confirmed that the features added to improve screen reader interaction do not influence the visual layout, or the image rendering or the reading of the content. Some limitations by the screen reader should be considered by developers when updating the available versions.

Other features and functionalities should be further investigated in terms of accessibility, such as how to underline, highlight and read text with specific characteristics (e.g. text in bold, italic, highlighted, etc.). Novel gestures to carry out more specific actions need to be further investigated. We plan to extend our study in this perspective.

References

1. AbdelRazek, M., Modayan, A.: Adaptive eBook framework. In: Proceedings of IEEE-2012, pp. 324–329 (2012)
2. Adjouadi, M., Ruiz, E., Wang, L.: Automated book reader for persons with blindness. In: Proceedings of ICCHP, pp. 1094–1101 (2006)
3. Attarwala, A., Munteanu, C., Baecker, R.: An accessible, large-print, listening and talking e-book to support families reading together. In: Proceedings of MobileHCI 2013, pp. 440–443. ACM (2013)
4. Bartalesi Lenzi, V., Leporini, B.: Investigating an accessible and usable ePub book via VoiceOver: a case study. In: Holzinger, A., Ziefle, M., Hitz, M., Debevc, M. (eds.) SouthCHI 2013. LNCS, vol. 7946, pp. 272–283. Springer, Heidelberg (2013)
5. Bottoni, P., Ferri, F., Grifoni, P., Marcante, A., Mussio, P., Padula, M., Reggiori, A.: e-Document management in situated interactivity: the WIL approach. Univ. Access Inf. Soc. **8**(3), 137–153 (2009)
6. Calabrò, A., Contini, E., Leporini, B.: Book4All: a tool to make an e-Book more accessible to students with vision/visual-impairments. In: Holzinger, A., Miesenberger, K. (eds.) USAB 2009. LNCS, vol. 5889, pp. 236–248. Springer, Heidelberg (2009)
7. El-Glaly, Y., Quek, F., Smith-Jackson, T., Dhillon, G.: Audible rendering of text documents controlled by multi-touch interaction. In: Proceedings of ICMI 2012. ACM (2012)
8. Grammenos, D., Savidis, A., Georgalis, Y., Bourdenas, T., Stephanidis, C.: Dual educational electronic textbooks: the starlight platform. In: Proceedings of the 9th International ACM SIGACCESS Conference on Computers and Accessibility, pp. 107–114. ACM (2007)
9. Huthwaite, A., Cleary, C.E., Sinnamon, B., Sondergeld, P., McClintock, A.: Ebook readers: separating the hype from the reality. In: Proceedings of ALIA Information Online Conference & Exhibition (2011)
10. Patel, H., Morreale, P.: Education learning: electronic books or traditional printed books? J. Comput. Sci. Coll. **29**(3), 21–28 (2014)
11. Petrie, H., Weber, G., Völkel, T.: Universal access to multimedia documents. In: Stephanidis, C. (ed.) The Universal Access Handbook, pp. 46–51. CRC Press, Tokyo (2009)
12. Henry, S.L.: Developing text customisation functionality requirements of PDF reader and other user agents. In: Miesenberger, K., Karshmer, A., Penaz, P., Zagler, W. (eds.) ICCHP 2012, Part I. LNCS, vol. 7382, pp. 602–609. Springer, Heidelberg (2012)

On the Understandability of Public Domain Icons: Effects of Gender and Age

Gerd Berget[1] and Frode Eika Sandnes[2(✉)]

[1] Faculty of Technology, Art and Design, Institute of Information Technology,
Oslo and Akershus University, College of Applied Sciences, Oslo, Norway
Gerd.Berget@hioa.no
[2] Faculty of Technology, Westerdals School of Arts, Communication and Technology,
Oslo, Norway
Frode-Eika.Sandnes@hioa.no

Abstract. Icons and symbols are often deployed in graphical user interfaces. It is commonly believed that icons add to the user friendliness of products. Developers have great trust in icon libraries and they are likely to use icons they understand themselves without verifying users' understanding. Interfaces relying on icons that are misinterpreted can lead to erroneous operation. In this study a set of icons in the public domain was interpreted by 64 participants to assess how well general icons are understood. Of the 105 icons included only 67 were correctly identified by all the raters. The results confirm that some basic icons are universally known. However, nearly half of the icons where not identified by all. Recognition correlated with gender, as males were more likely to identify icons connected to masculine concepts and females were more likely to recognize icons connected to feminine concepts. Moreover, a positive correlation was found between the age of the participants and icons depicting ideas from the past versus timeless icons. The results thus support the practice of user testing of icons rather than relying on assumptions.

Keywords: Icons · Recognition · Gender · Age

1 Introduction

Icons are commonly used in graphical user interfaces. Attempts have even been made at making complete icon-only based interfaces [1], as icons are believed to consume less real-estate on mobile handsets with small displays. Icons have been applied in a vast range of domains including translation tasks where texts and icons are used in parallel to aid translation [2].

There is a general belief that icons improve user friendliness of user interfaces. However, unlike text which is read, icons are recognized. Consequently, icons must be learned in order to be correctly interpreted as it is impossible to recognize an icon of a concept unknown to the viewer. Many icons, however, rely on the users' general

© Springer International Publishing Switzerland 2015
M. Antona and C. Stephanidis (Eds.): UAHCI 2015, Part I, LNCS 9175, pp. 387–396, 2015.
DOI: 10.1007/978-3-319-20678-3_37

knowledge about the world and items and notions in the real world that can be considered universal – concepts and notions that most of us have learned, such as the Isotype diagrams for man and woman. These universal symbols are thus frequently used in both the physical and digital domain.

Humans decode simple symbols more rapidly than complex and detailed symbols. This is the reason why traffic signs are simple – many of which are impossible to understand without training. Driving licenses ensures that the driver has gone through sufficient training and has knowledge of all these traffic signs.

Icons are also known to be connected to the users' context and culture, as icons that are meaningful in one cultural setting may be difficult to understand in another cultural setting [3–5]. A study of Taiwanese students' understanding of icons showed that icon recognition was linked to the students' English proficiency, but mostly to their computer literacy [6]. The effect of culture and context is strong because icons are learned. To study how children perceive icons is therefore particularly relevant as they are less affected by the context and experience compared to older users [7].

The challenge of designing icons that users understand is well known. Several voices argue for the user testing of icons during development [8] and more detailed test methodologies have been proposed such as lexical analysis, semiotic analysis, long distance visibility testing [9], icon intuitiveness testing [10] and magnetic resonance imaging [11]. However, others argue for better icon design methodologies [12].

Attempts have also been made at improving icon recognition performance. In one study the researchers relied on the users' visual memory and ability to memorize locations and hence make associations between automatically generated landmark icons [13]. Research has also found that larger icon spacing leads to shorter icon recognition times [14]. Other approaches use multiple modalities such as visual icons and audio to improve recognition [15]. The issue of how many icons users can relate to before reducing recognition performance has also been addressed [16]. In a study of icons intended for a music application rules based on a model of emotions were used in the design [17]. Other studies of performance related to icons have addressed effects of physical constraints such as few or no colors, limited pixel resolution and size [18].

Despite the vast literature on icons and attempts at organizing icons into taxonomies [19], icons are still often employed on the basis of assumptions that users are familiar with universal shapes. Thus the motivation of this study was to shed light on the understandability of general icons.

2   Method

2.1   Participants

A total of 64 students participated as icon raters of which 76.6 % were female and 23.4 % were men. Their mean age was 27.8 years. All the participants were first year students in library and information science at Oslo and Akershus University College of Applied Sciences.

2.2 Stimuli

A total of 105 icons were selected from the Noun Project (http://thenounproject.com/) and are all released into the public domain under a Creative Commons license. The Noun collection is too large to be included in its entirety in this study for practical reasons. The icons investigated were thus prescreened and selected according to the principal investigators subjective impression of clarity and understandability. Unclear and obscure icons where discarded.

A paper based questionnaire was created with the icon on left and a line for writing the name of the icon on the right.

2.3 Procedure

The questionnaires were distributed in class. Students were asked to write down a word (noun) to describe what they thought the icons represented. The primary investigator personally administered the questionnaire session. The questionnaires were collected after 20 min when all of the students appeared to have completed the questionnaires.

2.4 Analysis

Four of the questionnaires were discarded as outliers as too many of the fields were not completed. The remaining 60 questionnaires were included in the analysis. Each reply was tallied if the response matched the intended meaning of the icon or using a description which was sufficiently similar.

3 Results

Most of the icons were identified by all the participants, that is, a total of 67 icons. These are shown in Fig. 1 and are not discussed any further herein. Next, 22 icons were recognized by between 97 % and 98 % of the subjects (see Fig. 2). This is close to a rater agreement of 100 % since only one or two individuals failed to recognize the icons.

Consequently, these icons are considered understandable as the error rate is less than 5 % and the misinterpretation is more likely to be caused by individual ad hoc factors.

The remaining items incurred error rates of 5 % of more and are considered significantly challenging to interpret. Of these a total of 10 icons where identified by 90–95 % of the participants (see Fig. 3) and are thus the easiest to recognize among the set of icons that were not successfully identified by all the participants. These were ghost, factory, hand, pot, calculator, scooter, cannon, ant, bathtub and spool of thread.

One possible explanation may be that the ghost was printed in black on a white background, while stereotypical ghosts usually are white on a dark background representing night. The calculator could be interpreted as a mobile phone. Two decades ago there were few mobile phones and calculators where common, while today mobile phones are more common and even used as calculators. The bathtub visualization includes a shower which perhaps is confusing. One may speculate whether the misidentification of the bathtub could

Fig. 1. Icons successfully identified by all the participants (100 % recognition rate)

be connected to the trend that more Norwegian homes are fitted with showers than bath-tubs compared to three decades ago.

Next, Fig. 4 shows four icons recognized by 69–81 % of the subjects, namely wind-surfing board, parking meter, hammer and floppy disk. Possible explanations could be that there was a windsurfing craze a few decades ago, while it is not as popular today. The parking meter icon depicts a coin operated mechanical device, while current day parking meters often are larger wall mounted self-service terminals offering credit card

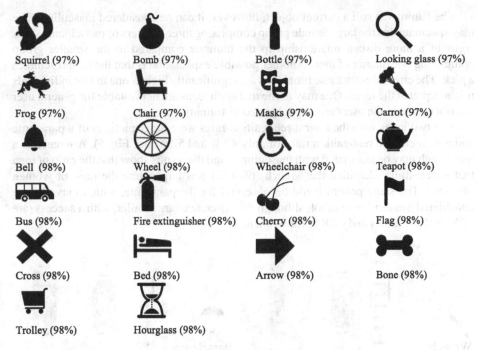

Squirrel (97%)   Bomb (97%)   Bottle (97%)   Looking glass (97%)

Frog (97%)   Chair (97%)   Masks (97%)   Carrot (97%)

Bell (98%)   Wheel (98%)   Wheelchair (98%)   Teapot (98%)

Bus (98%)   Fire extinguisher (98%)   Cherry (98%)   Flag (98%)

Cross (98%)   Bed (98%)   Arrow (98%)   Bone (98%)

Trolley (98%)   Hourglass (98%)

Fig. 2. Icons recognized by 97 % and 98 % of the participants

Ghost (91%)   Factory (92%)   Hand (92%)   Pot (92%)   Calculator (94%)

Scooter (95%)   Cannon (95%)   Ant (95%)   Bathtub (95%)   Spool of thread (95%)

Fig. 3. Icons recognized by 90–95 % of the participants

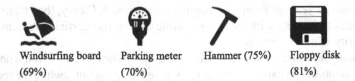

Windsurfing board (69%)   Parking meter (70%)   Hammer (75%)   Floppy disk (81%)

Fig. 4. Icons recognized by 69–81 % of the participants

or mobile payment via text messaging. Moreover, the floppy disk is obsolete and it is possible that younger individuals do not have the same relation to the floppy disk as older individuals.

The hammer is still a current object, however, it can be considered masculine. One may speculate that the large female group comprising three quarters of participants show signs of a more distant relationship to the hammer compared to the smaller group comprising one quarter of men. Another possible explanation is that the icon resembles a pick. The error rates for these four icons are significantly high as one in five individuals misinterpreted the icons. One may argue that such icons are not suitable for general user interfaces where the users are not subjected to training.

The two icons with the lowest recognition rates were the depictions of a parachute and a wrench with recognition rates of only 47 % and 52 % (see Fig. 5). A wrench is a tool which may be associated with masculinity and the results show that the ratio of men that successfully identified the wrench (66.9 %) was larger than the ratio of women (46.7 %). The same pattern could be observed for the parachute, which may also be considered a masculine symbol, although the differences are smaller, with a success rate of 53.3 % for males and 44.8 % for women.

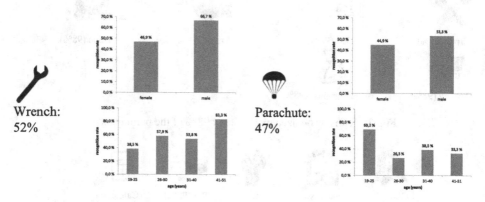

Fig. 5. The wrench and parachute icons recognized by only approximately half of the subjects with recognition rates according to gender and age

To further explore the effect of age the participants were organized into four age groups: participants 25 years old or younger, participants aged 26–30, participants aged 31–40 and those aged 41 or older. The results show that age has an effect in both cases as the participants 40 years or older had a recognition rate of 83.3 % while only 38.8 % the participants 25 years or younger recognized the wrench. Cleary, the mature subjects demonstrated a familiarity with the wrench while the younger participants demonstrated less familiarity with the wrench.

Surprisingly, this pattern was somewhat reversed for the parachute icon where 69.2 % of the participants of 25 years or younger recognized the parachute, while the recognition rates were less than 40 % for all the other age groups. If this is due to parachutes being part of younger individuals' lives or whether they have more imagination in interpreting the icons is only a speculation.

Next, to explore the hypothesis that icon recognition is related to gender the icons were subjectively classified as masculine, feminine and neutral (see Table 1).

Masculine icons were related to war such as bomb, parachute and cannon, and typical male dominated professions such as factory work, or work involving tools such as hammer and wrench.

Table 1. Gender icon categories

Gender	Icons
Masculine	Bomb, cannon, factory, floppy disk, hammer, parking meter, wind-surfing board, wrench, parachute
Feminine	Teapot, squirrel, spool of thread, pan, ghost
Neutral	Remaining icons

Feminine icons were related to household items such as teapot, pan and spool of thread, as well as cute animals such as squirrel – assuming squirrel décor is more common on girls' toys. The ghost was also categorized as feminine as the depicted ghost is cute and based on a weak assumption that females are generally more interested in spirituality than men.

Next the ratio of successfully recognized icons in each category according to males and females were counted and the results are shown in Fig. 6. The results confirm the hypothesis that icons can be connected to gender as more females (97.1 %) recognized feminine icons than males (86.7 %). Moreover, more males (84.4 %) successfully recognized masculine icons compared to females (72.6 %), while the recognition ratios where more even for the neutral icons with 96.9 % and 98.3 %, respectively. One may conclude that it is advisable to use gender neutral icons unless the user interface is specifically intended for a specific group of individuals.

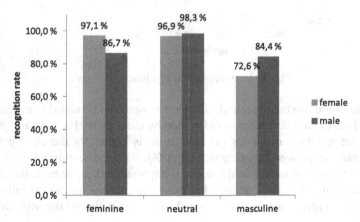

Fig. 6. Recognition of feminine, masculine and neutral icons as a function of gender

Finally, to explore the hypothesis that certain icons are outdated and thus more easily recognized by older and more experienced participants, the icons where subjectively classified into aged and timeless icons as shown in Table 2. Aged icons are those depicting items no longer in use such as the hour glass, floppy disk and coin operated parking meters. Factory was classified as aged as there are very few actual factories in Norway since most of the factory industry has moved overseas. The participants were divided into those 25 years or younger, participants in the range of 26–30, 31–40 and those older than 40. The ratio of aged and timeless icons recognized where counted and the results are shown in Fig. 7.

Table 2. Aged versus timeless icons

Category	Icons
Aged	Hour glass, spool of thread, bathtub, cannon, factory, floppy disk, parking meter, windsurfing board, wrench
Timeless	Remaining icons

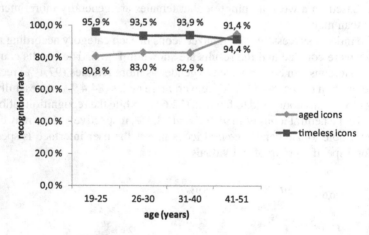

Fig. 7. Icon recognition as a function of age

The results confirm the hypothesis that icon recognition is related to experience and time periods as the timeless icons are identified by more than 91.4 % by all age groups. However, the recognition rate for the aged icons is higher for the older participants (94.4 %) than the youngest participants (80.8 %), with the remaining participants in between. One may conclude from this that it is important to keep in mind that the notion of universal symbols is not constant, but rather in continuous change reflecting our culture and the current objects we surround ourselves with and the activities we are involved in.

4   Conclusions

This study explored the understandability of a set of general icons in the public domain. The results revealed that general icons are not necessarily universally recognized.

The results further suggest that there are effects of gender and age, as the recognition of icons is related to the viewers' context, knowledge and experience and not only the result of the rendering of the icon. Consequences of these findings are that icons should be used with care by avoiding gender specific icons and icons representing outdated concepts. One way to ensure that the icons are understandable is to perform user testing of the icons. Since icons are commonly used in a wide range of products, commercial icon providers should be expected to extend their service beyond being graphical artists by conducting such recognition studies and bundle icon packages together with recognition rates or icon quality certificates. In this way, developers can focus on essence of application development and not superficial visual details.

Acknowledgments. This project has been financially supported by the Norwegian ExtraFoundation for Health and Rehabilitation through EXTRA funds grant 2011/12/0258. The authors are grateful to the participants for their helpful cooperation.

References

1. Schröder, S., Ziefle, M.: Making a completely icon-based menu in mobile devices to become true: a user-centered design approach for its development. In: Proceedings of the 10th International Conference on Human Computer Interaction with Mobile Devices and Services, pp. 137–146. ACM (2008)
2. Song, W., Finch, A., Tanaka-Ishii, K., Yasuda, K., Sumita, E.: picoTrans: an intelligent icon-driven interface for cross-lingual communication. ACM Trans. Interact. Intell. Syst. **3**(1), 1–31 (2013)
3. Heukelman, D., Obono, S.E.: Exploring the African Village metaphor for computer user interface icons. In: Proceedings of the 2009 Annual Research Conference of the South African Institute of Computer Scientists and Information Technologists, pp. 132–140. ACM (2009)
4. Kim, J.H., Lee, K.P.: Cultural difference and mobile phone interface design: icon recognition according to level of abstraction. In: Proceedings of the 7th International Conference on Human Computer Interaction with Mobile Devices & Services, pp. 307–310. ACM (2005)
5. McDougall, S., Forsythe, A., Stares, L.: Icon use by different language groups: changes in icon perception in accordance with cue utility. In: Proceedings of the 2005 IFIP TC13 International Conference on Human-Computer Interaction, pp. 1083–1086. ACM (2005)
6. Wang, H.F.: Are icons used in existing computer interfaces obstacles to Taiwanese computer users? In: Proceedings of the 14th European Conference on Cognitive Ergonomics: Invent! Explore! pp. 199–202. ACM (2007)
7. McKnight, L., Read, J.C.: Designing the 'record' button: using children's understanding of icons to inform the design of a musical interface. In: Proceedings of the 8th International Conference on Interaction Design and Children, pp. 258–261. ACM (2009)
8. Kascak, L., Rebola, C.B., Braunstein, R., Sanford, J.A.: Icon design to improve communication of health information to older adults. J. Commun. Des. Q. Rev. **2**(1), 6–32 (2013)

9. Bhutkar, G., Poovaiah, R., Katre, D., Karmarkar, S.: Semiotic analysis combined with usability and ergonomic testing for evaluation of icons in medical user interface. In: Proceedings of the 3rd International Conference on Human Computer Interaction, pp. 57–67. ACM (2011)
10. Ferreira, F., Noble, J., Biddle, R.: A case for iconic icons. In: Proceedings of the 7th Australasian User Interface Conference, vol. 50, pp. 97–100. ACM (2006)
11. Huang, S.C.: Icons: pictures or logograms? In: Proceedings of the 2011 iConference, pp. 819–820. ACM (2011)
12. Payne, P.R.O., Starren, J.: Presentation discovery: building a better icon. In: CHI 2006 Extended Abstracts on Human Factors in Computing Systems, pp. 1223–1228. ACM (2006)
13. Lewis, J.P., Rosenholtz, R., Fong, N., Neumann, U.: VisualIDs: automatic distinctive icons for desktop interfaces. ACM Trans. Graph. 23(3), 416–423 (2004)
14. Everett, S.P, Byrne, M.D.: Unintended effects: varying icon spacing changes users' visual search strategy. In: Proceedings of the SIGCHI Conference on Human Factors in Computing Systems, pp. 695–702. ACM (2004)
15. Hoggan, A.E.E., Brewster, S.A.: Crossmodal icons for information display. In: CHI 2006 Extended Abstracts on Human Factors in Computing Systems, pp. 857–862. ACM (2006)
16. Fan, M., Ko, K.: Managing icon abundance on eBay. In: CHI 2004 Extended Abstracts on Human Factors in Computing Systems, pp. 1555–1555. ACM (2004)
17. Kim, H.J., Yoo, M.J., Kwon, J.Y., Lee, I.-K.: Generating affective music icons in the emotion plane. In: CHI 2009 Extended Abstracts on Human Factors in Computing Systems, pp. 3389–3394. ACM (2009)
18. Stilan, E., Chen, A., Bezuayehu, L.: Accessible icon design in enterprise applications. In: Proceedings of the International Cross-Disciplinary Conference on Web Accessibility, pp. 1–4. ACM (2011)
19. Wang, H.F., Hung, S.H., Liao, C.C.: A survey of icon taxonomy used in the interface design. In: Proceedings of the 14th European Conference on Cognitive Ergonomics: Invent! Explore! pp. 203–206. ACM (2007)

Visual Communication of Lovely Characters in Digital Development Arena

Cheih-Ying Chen[1]([✉]) and Xu-Qin Zhunag[2]

[1] Department of Commercial Creativity Management,
National Taipei University of Business, Taipei City, Taiwan, R.O.C.
c.y.chen@ntub.edu.tw
[2] Corporate Synergy Development Center, Taipei City, Taiwan, R.O.C.

Abstract. The term character economy starts to emerge, when a particular image is authorized and transferred onto a variety of goods sold into retail channels and formed economic benefits, thus the creation of character economy, such as: Hello Kitty, Mickey Mouse, Angry Birds and other images. In addition, with the increase sales for tablets and smartphones, and the economic rise of APP, we can foresee that besides the basic content and function demands in digital development, the interface design of digital APP has included design elements and symbol values to attract consumers, which will create a more diverse human sensory experience and a luminous digital humanities civilization. Our plan is to look into these characters' simple designs, forthright colors, and cute images, and research the influence of these symbolic characters on consumers' willingness to spend, we explored the consumer preference related to these lovely characters in consumer goods industry and digital development arena.

Keywords: Lovely characters · Character economy · Digital APP

1 Introduction

Consumer choices are rapidly changing due to globalization; choices emphasizing on the cultural and economic aspect of digitization, the importance of creativity and the competitive advantage of a designed brand, and the advent of the knowledge and economy era in ideological and digital intangible assets. While market continued to tighten, consumer choices have become diversified, and gradually followed the trend of significant and symbolic purchases. Consumers no longer buy because of the need and consumption; instead, they turn to culture and consumption semiotics as the importance in a commodity in addition to "material value," which is symbolic consumption, i.e., "symbol value".

The term character economy starts to emerge, when a particular image is authorized and transferred onto a variety of goods sold into retail channels and formed economic benefits, thus the creation of character economy, such as: Hello Kitty, Mickey Mouse, Angry Birds and yellow ducklings and other images. The authorization of these symbolic roles originates this symbolic society consumption, wide-spreads into entire industry, stimulates endless business opportunities for all. In addition, with the

© Springer International Publishing Switzerland 2015
M. Antona and C. Stephanidis (Eds.): UAHCI 2015, Part I, LNCS 9175, pp. 397–405, 2015.
DOI: 10.1007/978-3-319-20678-3_38

increase sales for tablets and smartphones, and the economic rise of APP, we can foresee that besides the basic content and function demands in digital development, the interface design of digital APP has included design elements and symbol values to attract consumers, which will create a more diverse human sensory experience and a luminous digital humanities civilization.

Our plan is to look into these characters' simple designs, forthright colors, and cute images, and find out the secret of success to the principles of these lovely graphic designs, and impression on the consumers of the color and form image on these of symbolic characters, and research the influence of these symbolic characters on consumers' willingness to spend, we explore the consumer preference and industry developments related to these lovely characters in consumer goods industry and digital development arena.

2 Lovely Imagery Roles

All along, the lovely imagery roles, which originated in nature and exist in human society, are not related to specific cultural. Some traditional culture conducive to experience of lovely life, but culture is not the source of the lovely life, it is lovely experience results lovely culture. Lovely culture spread out popularly in different societies by it's cultural penetration and globalization. Lovely culture has been generally accepted for interest, fun, novelty and other positive traits, and often with a little bit of negative traits, such as: childish, immature, foolish and so on. Regardless of the positive or negative traits, designers use lovely traits to enhance consumer preference of character image. Lovely image of characters exist different countries and social. Lovely image of characters has a large head, wide forehead, full cheeks, rounded chin, small nose, large pupils, big eyes, stubby limbs and other lovely elements, and dolls and cartoon stars which have these elements can also be widely loved in different countries. Human proportion of infants and children generally have three to four headed figure to highlight the human body petite and cute. From the terms of the proportion, characteristics of infants and children contain a large head, short limbs, small palms, small soles, slender ankles and wrists, almost invisible neck, and so on (Shanghai cartoon culture Development Co., 2009). It can be seen that communication of lovely imagery is not be geographic, social, national and cultural restricted. Lovely imagery of characters includes head shape, eyes, mouth, limbs proportion and other elements changes, the role of image presenting brings people positive and negative characteristics. It can be used as the basic elements of design to enhance the consumer's preference of the characters.

3 Character and Illustration Design of Picture Book

Kiefer stated that in the best picture books, the illustrations are as much a part of the experience with the book as the written text [1]. Picture book used the illustrations to present the context of the article and emphasize the original of story, so picture book combines visual and verbal narratives in a book format with complete independence characters and styles. The characteristics of characters in stories have three aspects including contents, meaning and value, and to constitute the spirit of characters. It shows qualities of picture books and different stories characters symbolize different meanings and style.

A good picture book transfers the story and reveals the content, meaning and value with the protagonist, and character design can boost the overall meaning of the story, express emotions, so that readers can enter the story atmosphere and generate spiritual consolation by the character image.

British woman writer-cum-illustrator Helen Beatrix Potter published children's book "Peter Rabbit" in 1902, the protagonist Peter Rabbit has been 100 years old [2]. British children's literature writer Roger Hargreaves first published "Mr. Men Little Miss" in 1971, created a variety of lovely characters to represent each kind of distinct personality, like: good personality, bad temper; clever, confused; good example of bad habits … and other characteristics [3]. Though humorous way, let simple interesting characters perform the child's own story, so "Mr. Men Little Miss" was sold 100 million of the total sales volume in more than 30 countries around the world.

4 Character Design of Corporate Identity

Corporate Identity System, (referred to as CIS) mainly consists of Mind Identity (referred to as MI), Behavior Identity (referred to as BI) and Visual Identity (referred VI) three elements. Corporate visual identity plays a significant role in the way an organization presents its strategy, philosophy, culture [4]. Corporate visual identity expresses the values and ambitions of an organization with logos, colors, typeface, mascot and other elements.

Mascots or advertising characters are very common in the corporate world. The role of corporate identity, meaning a symbolic corporate identity, also referred to as the mascot. Design of corporate mascot by entity, cute, intends people of performance to attract more visual focus and strengthen the memory to convey corporate culture. The most famous and most well-known role of the corporate mascot is Mickey Mouse; it has been six decades as the mascot of the Walt Disney Company. Mascot can enhance the effect of corporate marketing, by the joyful character design, can quickly deepen memory of commodities activities and the company's image, and make a variety of changes in the advertising and marketing, either anthropomorphic of McDonald and Tatung Baby, or lovely imagery of Michelin, Sesame Street cartoon characters can give consumers the feeling of joy and happiness by their own attractive.

5 Role Design of Digital Develop Image

APP mobile software has a significant positive effect on perceived usefulness, perceived entertainment and perceived compatibility for system social presence In the graphical user interface, including Window, Icon, Menu, and Pointer four elements to convey the functional significance to the user, does not require additional supplementary text description for quick operation. App for mobile devices has shown flowers contend boom, and the roles of mobile devices App are very widespread and popular, such as Angry Birds, LINE texture images. Angry Birds was first released Apple's iOS platform in December 2009, the 2011 net profit of 48 million Euros on revenue of 75.4 million Euros, and has been downloaded over 10 million times in 2012. LINE has 17 million users in Taiwan, currently 2013 users around the world have rushed 300 million people. LINE's success lies in the lovely images better than words. Protagonists Brown, Cony, Moon and James scored everyday life, cute, exaggerated, adorable and funny facial expressions, and images can be used to convey situational prompting significant increase in utilization of the image.

6   Study Method

This study investigated lovely characters with graphic design and image word. Today consumer market lead consumers to attach importance to the meaning and value of consumption, then consumers focus on consumption semiotics for symbolic goods. Character images display different feelings, and the image is authorized and sold with goods popularly. In this study, Kansei Engineering as a basis method to integrate all of visual design, graphic composition, color theory and semiotics, etc. The analysis of lovely characters, which are classified to two categories of digital development and illustrator of picture books, are researched through focus groups interviews, cluster analysis, questionnaire, T-test and ANOVA analysis to examine lovely characters and consumer preference.

6.1   Focus Groups Interviews

In the January 8 and 18, 2014, In this study, we had two focus group interviews with two groups of four people to explore lovely image, consumers feel, visual communication. We selected homogeneous visual communication design and marketing management in the background as the interviewee.

Management group with 4 people was characterized by marketing background, and habitual purchase role authorized merchandise. Design groups with 4 people was characterized by visual communication design background, and for the role design-related awards, trainers and training coaches.

The collation and analysis of this study for cute characters selection criteria were maximum of four colors and simple shapes, personification form, and then according those criteria collected forty image of lovely characters from the picture book illustrator or digital development related samples, see Fig. 1. Through focus group discussion 8 interviewees selected the role of representative and visual communication image words.

A total of eight people with two focus groups discussed and select eight representative role lovely images, and respectively picture book illustrator 56 imagery words and 58 digital development imagery words, show as the following Table 1.

Through SPSS software, clustering analysis showed the 17 taxonomic clusters for 56 imagery words of picture book illustrator, and the 8 taxonomic clusters for

56 imagery words of digital development group. Finally, the images words of two lovely role groups interacted to get the same total of five taxonomic clusters were cute, childlike, funny, vitality and vigor. Those five visual communication design image words provided the reference imagery feel of lovely imagery role.

Fig. 1. Forty image of lovely characters

Table 1. Lovely image words

Categories	Quantity	Image word
Picture book illustrator	56	colorful, joyful, textured, soft, dreamy, calm, single, cheerful, sunny, generous, weird, humor, funny, energetic, festive, tender, vitality, sweet, feminine, classical, childhood, innocent, happy, lazy, unified, kind, playful, simple, realistic, friendly, relaxed, lyrical, blankly, interesting, weird, disgusting, casual, bright, honest, close to the heart, anthropomorphic, naive, energetic, convivial, gentle harmony, naivety, viridity, adora-ble, healing, childhood memories, happy, enjoyment, friendly, cute
Digital development	58	straightforward, cunning, angry, happy, flexible, arrogant, domineering, ugly, bright, nausea, naughty, novelty, funny, silly, stupid, boring, delight, retro, uniform, funny, effort heavy, stiff, special, mystical, humor, a sense of flow lines, strange, weird, cheerful, sunny, normal, lovable, single, hon-est, blankly, close to hearts, affinity, innocence, comfortable, anthropomorphic, simple, spanking, fun, vitality, innocent, happy, does not make sense, rounded, happy, relaxed, lively, playful, energetic, happy, funny, interesting, cute

Table 2. Eight cute imagery of lovely characters

No.	Characters	Imagery	Selection factor
1	Rilakkuma		To 2009, the cumulative turnover of all the goods and 100 billion yen, which is about 10,000 products, the total sales of books for 2.73 million.
2	Hello Kitty		2012 best-selling global retail products by a single cartoon character $ 70 billion.
3	Mr. Men and Little Miss		Has been translated in 15 languages in over 30 countries around the world, tired performance 100 million in total sales.
4	Gaspard et Lisa		Animations showed in 19 regions (countries) In Japan there are more than a hundred licensees.
5	LINE Moon		Players 4.2 rating, rating number of 1,386,259 or more. the most important sticker for line.
6	Funghi gardening kit		Players 4.5 rating, rating the number of 116,784 or more (a total of five series of games in the aggregate.)
7	Angry Birds		Players rating 4.6 points, rating more than the number of 1,817,996
8	Where's My Water		Players rating 4.6 points, more than 452,600 the number of ratings

Table 3. T test for gender

	1 Gaspard et Lisa		2 Mr. Men and Little Miss		3 Rilakkuma		4 Hello Kitty	
	mean	SD	mean	SD	mean	SD	mean	SD
Male	4.142	2.3042	4.210	2.6913	6.127	2.3065	5.470	2.6753
Female	4.986	2.4419	4.777	2.6425	6.423	2.5348	6.171	2.7800
p-value	0.947		0.773		0.282		0.574	

	5 LINE Moon		6 Funghi gardening kit		7 Angry Birds		8 Swampy crocodile	
	mean	SD	mean	SD	mean	SD	mean	SD
Male	6.341	2.4391	5.444	2.9756	4.973	2.6327	6.392	2.5823
Female	4.979	2.2535	4.736	2.5874	4.314	2.4272	6.159	2.5275
p-value	0.179		0.183		0.880		0.934	

Table 4. ANOVA analysis for age

1.Gaspard et Lisa p-value	After 1995	1990– 1994	1984– 1989	Before 1983	mean	SD
After 1995		0.486	0.388	0.188	4.174	2.4637
1990–1994			0.844	0.481	4.525	2.3078
1984–1989				0.616	4.615	2.3378
Before 1983					4.853	2.5616
2.Mr. Men and Little Miss p-value	After 1995	1990– 1994	1984– 1989	Before 1983	mean	SD
After 1995		0.010	0.001	0.024	5.695	2.6062
1990–1994	*		0.454	0.769	4.279	2.7703
1984–1989	*			0.310	3.904	2.5265
Before 1983	*				4.427	2.5577
3.Rilakkuma p-value	After 1995	1990– 1994	1984– 1989	Before 1983	mean	SD
After 1995		0.939	0.588	0.455	6.118	2.9460
1990–1994			0.495	0.364	6.079	2.6911
1984–1989				0.819	6.396	1.7793
Before 1983					6.506	2.2841
4.Hello Kitty	After 1995	1990– 1994	1984– 1989	Before 1983	mean	SD
After 1995		0.406	0.023	0.004	5.195	2.3566
1990–1994			0.001	0.000	4.742	2.9396
1984–1989	*	*		0.471	6.464	2.5261
Before 1983	*	*			6.835	2.5118
5.Line Moon	After 1995	1990– 1994	1984– 1989	Before 1983	mean	SD
After 1995		0.782	0.528	0.230	6.241	2.7494
1990–1994			0.691	0.105	6.095	2.6280
1984–1989				0.048	5.902	2.5672
Before 1983			*		6.892	2.2355
6.Funghi gardening kit	After 1995	1990– 1994	1984– 1989	Before 1983	mean	SD
After 1995		0.073	0.004	0.000	6.441	2.6118
1990–1994			0.199	0.007	5.432	2.8339
1984–1989	*			0.151	4.770	2.6869
Before 1983	*	*			4.008	2.5963
7.Angry Birds	After 1995	1990– 1994	1984– 1989	Before 1983	mean	SD
After 1995		0.811	0.686	0.412	5.641	2.6484
1990–1994			0.852	0.245	5.519	2.2133
1984–1989				0.186	5.432	2.6315
Before 1983					6.069	2.3285
8.Swampy crocodile	After 1995	1990– 1994	1984– 1989	Before 1983	mean	SD
After 1995		0.033	0.000	0.311	5.590	2.8176
1990–1994	*		0.105	0.236	4.488	2.4142
1984–1989	*			0.006	3.719	2.6071
Before 1983			*		5.055	2.0948

7 Consumers Difference for He Preference of Cute Role Imagery

Two categories of eight cute imagery: (1) picture book illustration class: Rilakkuma Lazy Bear, Hello. Kitty Kitty, Mr Mr Men Little Miss odd wonderful lady and Gaspard et Lisa Lisa and Casper; (2) the development of several categories: LINE Moon, Funghi gardening kit, Angry Birds and Where's My Water? Swampy crocodile. Selection principles are as follows:

- The role authorization of picture book illustration drive the output value of 100 million yuan a year, and circulation over the country more than 15 countries.
- Digital developed to exceed the rating on Google Play platform 4 points or more (5 points), rating of more than 100,000 more than the number of APP software for the selected principle (Table 2).

200 experimental subjects were expected, men and women of each 100, including age distribution was attending high school, attending the University or Research Institute, employed persons under the age of thirty years of age and more than three years old, a total of four groups. This study explored each gender and age groups feeling for cute characters.

Through 200 valid questionnaires, this study discussed consumer preference of 8 lovely character images with T test and ANOVA analysis of multiple comparisons, Understanding of gender and age, and consumers have a significant impact on the consumer's preference image. The results are as follows (Tables 3 and 4):

8 Conclusion

This Study shown consumer preference for Mr. Men Little Miss: People born after 1995 AD favorite Mr. Men Little Miss, followed by AD 1990–1994 and AD 1984–1989, last was AD 1983 before.

This Study shown consumer preference for Hello Kitty: People born AD 1984–1989 and before AD 1983 favorite Hello Kitty, next was after 1995, last was AD 1990–1994.

This Study shown consumer preference for LINE Moon: People born 1984–1989 tend to not like LINE Moon, the other people favorite LINE Moon.

This Study shown consumer preference for Swampy crocodile: People born after 1995 AD favorite Swampy crocodile, followed by AD 1983 before, last was and AD 1984–1989 and AD1990–1994.

This Study shown consumer preference for Funghi gardening kit: People born after 1995 AD and AD1990–1994 favorite Funghi gardening kit, the other people less like Funghi gardening kit.

About the rest the lovely imagery role, consumer preferences are not significant differences, including Gaspard et Lisa, Rilakkuma, Angry Birds.

This Study shown consumer preferences in gender are not significant differences. No significant difference whether male or female love cute characters.

References

1. Kiefer, B.Z.: Charlotte Huck's Children's Literature. McGraw-Hill, New York (2010). ISBN 978-0-07-337856-5
2. Squire, S.J.: Meanings, myths and memories: literary tourism as cultural discourse in Beatrix Potter's Lake District. Dissertation, University of London (1991)
3. Hasebe-Ludt, E.L.: In all the universe: placing the texts of culture and community in only one school. Dissertation, University of British Columbia (1995)
4. Gray, E.R., Balmer, J.M.T.: Managing corporate image and corporate reputation. Long Range Plan. 31(5), 695–702 (1998)

Universal Access to Alternate Media

Lars Ballieu Christensen[✉] and Tanja Stevns

Synscenter Refsnæs and Sensus ApS, Hillerød, Denmark
{lbc,tanja}@robobraille.org

Abstract. This paper discusses the need for automated alternate media solutions in a world of increasing mainstream inclusion. While society as a whole is shifting from educational, vocational and social segregation of people with disabilities towards inclusion and equal rights, the need to support the blind, partially sighted, dyslexic and other print impaired with textual material in alternate formats remains. Production of alternate media is non-trivial and subject to significant skills and technical proficiency. However, the shift towards mainstream inclusion also means distribution, dilution and erosion of competencies, practices and experience involved in producing alternate media. RoboBraille, an alternate media conversion service, has attempted to distil the competencies and experience of producing alternate media into a set of automated workflows. While emerging digital media and technical platforms should make it easier to obtain alternate versions of mainstream publications, a number of counterproductive measures work in the opposite direction.

Keywords: Alternate media · Inclusion · Braille · E-books · Audio books · Digital accessibility · Universal design · Copyright

1 Introduction

Many people with disabilities are unable to use printed material and therefore require alternate versions of the material in order to be able to complete an education, sustain a job or take part in society. The blind require material in Braille, either digital on Braille display or embossed on paper using a Braille embosser. The partially sighted require large-print material, preferably adapted in accordance with individual diagnoses and preferences in terms of enlargement, typeface, colors, contrasts and line spacing. The visually impaired also frequently use audio books. People with dyslexia, learning disorders, poor reading skills or poor language skills need audio books and printed material that has been adapted to individual preferences. People with physical disabilities may need digital editions that can be navigated on e-book readers using switch controls. And the list goes on.

Preparing, editing and converting a mainstream publication such as a textbook, scientific paper, work instruction or patient information leaflet into an alternate format that can be used by a person with sensory, physical or cognitive disabilities is usually a non-trivial task that requires significant knowledge, skills and technical proficiency.

Traditionally, many groups of people with disabilities have been segregated from the rest of society in special schools and, subsequently, in sheltered employment. In such

© Springer International Publishing Switzerland 2015
M. Antona and C. Stephanidis (Eds.): UAHCI 2015, Part I, LNCS 9175, pp. 406–414, 2015.
DOI: 10.1007/978-3-319-20678-3_39

specialized environments, it has rarely been a problem to maintain the knowledge, skills and technical proficiency required to convert material into alternate media. However, as societies move from educational, vocational and social segregation of people with disabilities towards inclusion and equal rights, it becomes difficult to maintain these competencies.

In Denmark, the move from segregation towards mainstream inclusion amongst the visually impaired commenced in the 1960 s, culminating in 1980 with the abandonment of legislation that had mandated segregated education in previous decades [1]. Similar changes were implemented for other disability groups, and today only a few individuals with multiple disabilities and complex needs do not enroll in mainstream education. For the blind and partially sighted in Denmark, the abandonment meant that rather than attending a special school, all blind and severely partially sighted children and youth were enrolled in their local, mainstream schools. To illustrate the challenge, Denmark has approx. 2.500 primary and lower secondary schools. The number of blind and severely partially sighted children and youth under the age of 18 is in the order of 500. Of these, less than 50 are blind.

Denmark may have been amongst the first countries to engage in this shift from segregation towards mainstream inclusion. Although it can be argued that education levels and employment rates amongst those affected have not improved, the changes have impacted not only primary and secondary education, but also paved the way for inclusion in further education and mainstream employment amongst those with special needs [2, 3]. On a universal scale, the shift from segregation towards mainstream inclusion is likely to be adapted as the norm, as upheld in numerous treaties and conventions, most notably the UN Convention the Rights of Persons with Disabilities and the UNESCO Salamanca Statement on Principles, Policy and Practice in Special Needs Education [4, 5].

2   The Problem at Hand

Integrating those with special needs into mainstream environments does not remove the need to be able to provide material in alternate formats such as Braille, simple and structured audio books, large-print and e-books. However, such integration does create a significant challenge in how to have material converted, properly as well as timely.

Conversion of material into alternate formats is non-trivial and subject to significant knowledge, skills and technical proficiency. Converting a text-only document into an MP3-audio file may be rather simple. Converting a math exercise into a structured audio book with spoken math equations is slightly more difficult. Converting an anatomy textbook with hundreds of illustrations into a usable Braille book is time consuming and complicated. Depending on the quality of the source material and the required target format, the conversion can be done automatically or it may require significant human value adding.

The core requirement in any alternate media production is the availability of a digital copy of source document. In case of published material, it may or may not be possible to obtain a digital copy of the material from the publisher. Similarly, it may or may not be possible to make use of an e-book version of a publication depending on local copyright legislation as well as any digital rights restrictions. Otherwise, the typical starting point will be to acquire the book, cut off the spine, run it through a high-speed scanner, convert the scanned file using Optical Character Recognition (OCR) software and edit the final result. Depending on how the document is going to be converted, it must be adapted with varying levels of detail.

Deciding on proper alternate formats may also be complicated. An MP3-file may be easy to create and highly portable as it plays on everything from dedicated MP3 players to smartphones, tablets and computers. Depending on the source material and the situation where the material is going to be used, the MP3-format may be more or less useful. Because of its linear nature and lack of navigational aids, material in MP3 may prove difficult to use in a classroom situation where students must be able to locate specific pages or chapter or section. On the other hand, the same material may be highly useful for students reading it during workouts or while they commute. Similar situational trade-offs can be made on material in a structured audio book format such as DAISY as well as e-book documents and Braille material. The end conclusion is often that multiple alternate formats must be provided.

3   Designing for Alternate Media

Converting a document from one format to another may be a straightforward process or it may require significant editing, modification or value adding. Figure 1 below illustrates the general, hierarchical principles of adapting a document based on best practices at the National Center for Visually Impaired Children and Youth in Denmark:

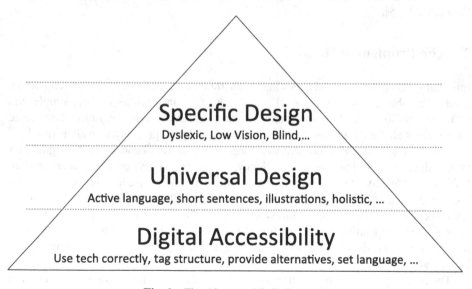

Fig. 1. The Alternate Media Pyramid

At the base of the hierarchy is the requirement that the document complies with the principle of digital accessibility. These principles are generally accepted and documented by various industry bodies, such as the International Standardization Organization (ISO) and the World Wide Web Consortium (W3C) [6, 7]. The purpose of the digital accessibility principles is to ensure that the document can be accessed by as many people as possible, from as many technological platforms as possible, and in as many different situations as possible.

The principles of digital accessibility require the document to be authored properly and in accordance with the specification of the particular document format, that features of the authoring tools not be abused for purposes that these were not intended for, that the semantic structure of the document such as headings, tables, lists and notes be marked up, that alternatives be provided for non-textual contents such as illustrations and graphs, that the natural language of the document as well as any changes to the natural language throughout the document be specified and that the reading order of the document be logical. By observing these design principles for digital accessibility, the document will – at least in theory – be accessible by people with disabilities with or without the use of assistive technology. It also means that the document can be converted and be presented in other modalities than print. However, it does not mean that the document is intelligible.

The middle layer in the hierarchy contains a set of universal design principles derived from general definition of universal design by Ronald L. Mace and others [7]. The purpose of applying universal design principles of document design to the document is to improve the general intelligibility of the document. These principles require the language of the document to be as direct as possible, not to use unnecessary complex language, to use short sentences, to keep accompanying illustrations and text together on the same page or on the same opening and to use a consistent design.

The top layer in the hierarchy is a set of specific adaptations that can be used to support specific users. If a document is being prepared specifically for a reader with low vision, it may make sense to provide it in a high-contrast, large-print format with an easy-to-read, sans-serif typeface. If the ultimate reader is dyslexic or have limited language skills, it may make sense to reduce the complexity of the language even further. If the reader has cognitive disabilities or is illiterate, it may make sense to alter the presentation and substitute contents for pictograms or use a cartoon format. This is also the layer where decisions on supporting material such as tactile graphics, 3D models, soundscapes and similar can be made. Altering the material in such ways, however, is likely to impact the reusability and ability to repurpose the material for other groups of readers.

The Alternate Media Pyramid is applied at different angles by different categories of publishers and material producers. Publishers and media producers with a general audience such as general publishers, mainstream educational institutions, mainstream teachers, public institutions and alternate media producers serving multiple groups of users are likely to start at the bottom and move upwards, frequently skipping the digital accessibility principles. In contrast, special schools, special education teachers, parents and alternate media producers servicing select user groups are likely to start at the top layer and move downwards.

4   Automating Knowledge and Competencies

In Denmark, the decision to include the blind and partially sighted in mainstream education sparked the development of a number of new technologies. As this happened prior to the personal computer, world wide web and e-books, a number of basic assistive technologies, reading platforms and distribution channels had to be developed. Furthermore, technologies that enabled teachers, students and relatives to produce material in alternate formats without any particular skills, had to be created. Throughout the 1980 s and 1990 s, a number of such technologies were developed and introduced with varying levels. The breakthrough in decentralized material production was the invention in 2004 of Robo-Braille, a self-service solution for alternate media. Automating the workflows from the former specialized schools and alternate media production facilities, RoboBraille guides the user through a few simple steps to have documents converted into digital Braille, MP3 audio files, DAISY structured audio books and various types e-books. As an added benefit, RoboBraille can also be used to convert otherwise inaccessible documents such as image-only PDF files or JPG pictures as well as tricky documents such as Microsoft PowerPoint presentations into more accessible, less tricky formats [9, 10]. Figure 2 below shows the main interface to the RoboBraille service:

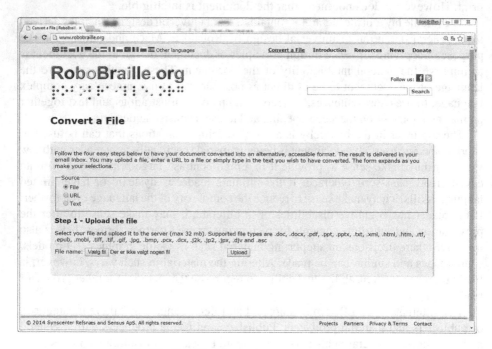

Fig. 2.   The RoboBraille service at www.robobraille.org

As an inclusion technology, RoboBraille addresses a number of challenges. Initially a Danish Braille service serving Danish users, it soon became clear that the service could be expanded with more languages and more functionality. By attracting users in other countries as well users beyond Braille readers, it was possible to establish a critical mass of users while at the same time being able to provide the Danish users with support for foreign languages. Several projects have explored how RoboBraille can be used as an assistive technology as well as a mainstream learning technology [11, 12]. Today, RoboBraille remains a free service for individual, non-profit use whilst academic institutions are subject to an annual subscription fee for usage of the SensusAccess interface amongst students, faculty, staff and alumni [13]. The language-specific parts of the service currently supports all main European languages, some smaller European languages as well as American English, Latin American Spanish, Russian and Arabic.

In 2012, RoboBraille was complemented by a digital library that allows alternate media producers to distribute material in alternate formats in a controlled manner, thus automating the former manual practices and workflows for material distribution. The Danish implementation of the digital library is called Biblus, and is available for all visually impaired children and youth in the Danish educational system as well as their teachers and relatives [14]. The digital library has since been implemented in several other countries and institutions as a resource-sharing platform, as an in-house repository of digital media and as member libraries.

In recent years, the introduction of digital books in EPUB and other formats has suggested that the time of cumbersome document conversions may soon be over. The rationale seems to be that once a commercial book is available as an e-book, it can be downloaded to an a-book reader, tablet or computer and read with or without assistive technology. While that may come true sometime in the future, inaccessible e-books, poor support beyond text and pictures, lacking assistive technology and restrictive copyright enforcement are still major hindrances.

However, around RoboBraille a number of technologies have been developed to explore the possibilities of e-books amongst people with print impairments. VI Reader, a free app for iOS and Android devices illustrated in Fig. 3 above, can be used to by people with low vision or dyslexia to read digital material in EPUB format. With VI Reader, readers can change the appearance of the contents in terms of scaling, background color, foreground color, contrasts, typefaces, line spacing and reading direction to fit personal preferences and diagnoses. Furthermore, RoboBraille is capable of producing e-books in the most popular formats (EPUB, EUB3 and MOBI) and can even increase the baseline of body text in the e-books to enable mainstream readers to display commercial e-books and other digital material in large print.

5 Key Challenges

Some of the challenges of producing material in alternate formats in a decentralized, mainstreamed environment have been overcome by automating the previous workflows of highly skilled specialists. However, a number of somewhat interrelated issues remain to be addressed.

Of all issues, the competing legislation between the rights to treatment on equal terms on the one side of and the stringent copyright legislation, tough enforcement and unwillingness to collaborate amongst many publishers on the other seems the most damaging.

Fig. 3. VI Reader – a free e-book reader for people with low vision or dyslexia

The Marrakesh Treaty to Facilitate Access to Published Works for Persons Who Are Blind, Visually Impaired, or Otherwise Print Disabled (MVT) [14] administered by the World Intellectual Property Organization (WIPO) may eventually help resolve some of the issues. However, ratification seems slow and primarily in countries with legislation similar to the proposals in the treaty.

A derived effect on the copyright legislation and enforcement is the increased use of streaming amongst the special libraries. Rather than making digital files available to readers with print impairments, many special libraries are moving towards streaming models where content can only be accessed through special readers or browser plugins. Obviously, this is a problem in a world of alternate media conversion that relies heavily on digital files. Furthermore, streaming services are rarely available for off-line consumption.

A third challenge is the lack of skills amongst those producing digital material. Whereas traditional skilled workers are typically taught how to use tools and materials, so-called knowledge workers are frequently expected to know how to use word processers, PDF converters and similar in a correct and accessible way. Furthermore, few are aware of the principles of digital accessibility and even fewer attempts to comply with these. The result is that the vast majority of all published material is inaccessible to readers with print disabilities. A unpublished survey (2014) by the Danish Ministry of Education of the practices at 13 educational institutions in Denmark revealed that almost all education material produced by the educational institutions failed accessibility criteria and that approx. 80 per cent of the errors were introduced by the authors themselves.

A forth challenge is the lack of skills amongst those converting material into alternate formats on behalf of others. While the requirements of the print impaired remain the same, alternate media producers often have few or no sources to turn to for training. As the general level of proficiency gradually erodes with the disbandment of the special schools and other sheltered environments, chances are that competence levels will continue to dwindle.

6 Conclusions

To some extend it has proved possible to extract key competencies and automate main workflows used to convert material into alternate formats to support those with print disabilities in mainstream environments of education, vocation and elsewhere. Services like RoboBraille can be used by people with very limited skills to automatically convert a significant proportion of material into alternate formats. Availability of material in digital formats, limited IT skills amongst knowledge workers and lack of awareness of the importance of digital accessibility in all types of digital publications, however, are likely to hinder a smooth transition as more countries adopt the route of inclusion. And once segregation with special schools and sheltered employment has been abandoned, the remaining knowledge and practical skills of teaching and supporting those with print impairments are likely to erode unless initiatives are launched to document and preserve knowledge and skills.

In conclusion, alignment of copyright legislation and the rights of equal access should be implemented on a universal scale. Combining technologies such as digital rights management, digital wallets, digital watermarking and digital identification, it should be possible to create systems that protects against proliferation of pirated copies of copyrighted digital material whilst ensuring efficient access to digital documents by those with a need to convert into alternate formats. Mandatory filing of digital copies in proper formats with national libraries of all publications with availability for the print disabled through the special libraries would be a natural development.

Secondly, proper use of authoring technology such as word processors, editors in content management systems and similar should be a mandatory part of any curriculum beyond primary education, ensuring that mainstream technology is used properly and that published documents comply with the basic principle of digital accessibility.

Thirdly, the skills and knowledge in countries that still operate special schools and sheltered vocation should be collected and documented in a way that can be used to train future generations of teachers, educators, careworkers and alternate media professionals on how printed material is adapted to alternative formats to meet the varying needs of readers with print impairments.

References

1. Danish Association of the Blind: Dansk Blindesamfunds historie årti for årti (2015). https://blind.dk/om-os/dansk-blindesamfunds-historie/dbs-historie
2. SFI: Blinde børn – Integration eller isolation? Blinde børns trivsel og vilkår I hjemmet, fritiden og skolen (2010)
3. SFI: Blinde og stærkt svagsynede. Barrierer for samfundsdeltagelse (2010)

4. United Nations: Convention on the Rights of Persons with Disabilities (2006). http://www.un.org/disabilities/convention
5. UNESCO: The Salamanca Statement on Principles, Policy and Practice in Special Needs Education (1994). http://www.unesco.org/education/pdf/SALAMA_E.PDF
6. ISO/W3C: Web Content Accessibility Guidelines (WCAG) 2.0. (2008). http://www.w3.org/TR/WCAG20/
7. W3C: Guidance on Applying WCAG 2.0. to Non-Web Information and Communications Technologies (WCAG2ICT) (2013). http://www.w3.org/TR/wcag2ict/
8. Mace, R.L., et al.: The principles of universal design (1997). http://www.ncsu.edu/ncsu/design/cud/about_ud/udprinciplestext.htm
9. Christensen, L.B.: RoboBraille – automated braille translation by means of an e-mail robot. In: Miesenberger, K., Klaus, J., Zagler, W.L., Karshmer, A.I. (eds.) ICCHP 2006. LNCS, vol. 4061, pp. 1102–1109. Springer, Heidelberg (2006)
10. Christensen, L.B.: RoboBraille – Braille unlimited. The Educator, ICEVI 2009 **XXI**(2), 32–37 (2009)
11. Goldrick, M., Stevns, T., Christensen, L.B.: The use of assistive technologies as learning technologies to facilitate flexible learning in higher education. In: Miesenberger, K., Fels, D., Archambault, D., Peňáz, P., Zagler, W. (eds.) ICCHP 2014, Part II. LNCS, vol. 8548, pp. 342–349. Springer, Heidelberg (2014)
12. Refsnæs, S., et al.: RoboBraille in education. Catalogue of good practice (2013). http://www.robobraille.org/sites/default/files/resourcefiles/The%20Robobraille%20Service%20in%20Education%20Catalogue%20Long%20Version%20August%202013%20FINAL.pdf
13. Christensen, L.B., Keegan, S.J., Stevns, T.: SCRIBE: a model for implementing Robobraille in a higher education institution. In: Miesenberger, K., Karshmer, A., Penaz, P., Zagler, W. (eds.) ICCHP 2012, Part I. LNCS, vol. 7382, pp. 77–83. Springer, Heidelberg (2012)
14. Christensen, L.B., Stevns, T.: Biblus – a digital library to support integration of visually impaired in mainstream education. In: Miesenberger, K., Karshmer, A., Penaz, P., Zagler, W. (eds.) ICCHP 2012, Part I. LNCS, vol. 7382, pp. 36–42. Springer, Heidelberg (2012)
15. WIPO: Marrakesh Treaty to Facilitate Access to Published Works for Persons Who Are Blind, Visually Impaired or Otherwise Print Disabled (2013). http://www.wipo.int/treaties/en/ip/marrakesh/

A Grounded Theory Approach for Designing Communication and Collaboration System for Visually Impaired Chess Players

Sujit Devkar[✉], Sylvan Lobo, and Pankaj Doke

TCS Innovation Labs Mumbai, Tata Consultancy Services Ltd., Mumbai, India
{sujit.devkar,sylvan.lobo,pankaj.doke}@tcs.com

Abstract. Social interactions for visually impaired take place in the traditional way, such as meeting and calling, digital platforms are largely not utilized by them. Empirical research for visually impaired has focused largely on accessibility, usability and is yet to understand the problems from CSCW aspect holistically. We carried out a qualitative study of communication and collaboration activities for 43 visually impaired chess players in India. Through semi-structured interviews, the participants' experiences in using existing collaboration and communication channels were noted. A Grounded Theory based analysis was performed using Atlas.ti and themes were identified. Research indicates that - social collaboration and 'staying in touch', searching and sharing new information, exploiting existing ways of mobile interactions, and having several interests help visually impaired in their daily lives for social collaboration and communication. This study provides insights concerning designing CSCW mediums for them.

Keywords: Grounded theory · Visually impaired · Human-computer interaction · Communication and collaboration mechanism · Computer Supported Collaborative Work

1 Introduction

Social networking and mobile technology have made social interactions easy. Users create content such as images, videos and text, and share them among different social groups on WhatsApp, Facebook and Twitter. These social platforms have rich interfaces and heavy content for the users. As technology progresses, older interfaces and interactions become obsolete, and new modes of interactions are introduced. Rapid changes in interfaces are daunting for everyone including visually impaired (VI). Assistive tools such as screen readers - JAWS and Talks exist, but the tools are yet to reach the masses [15]. These tools are expensive and support a few languages only. Besides, they are not compatible with many mobile devices and apps. Though visually impaired have started adapting themselves to the social networking sites [3], social interactions for them are still restricted to meetings and calling. Literature study shows accessibility and usability

© Springer International Publishing Switzerland 2015
M. Antona and C. Stephanidis (Eds.): UAHCI 2015, Part I, LNCS 9175, pp. 415–425, 2015.
DOI: 10.1007/978-3-319-20678-3_40

as a major research area for VI [2, 3, 10] and we are yet to understand problems from Computer Supported Collaborative Work (CSCW) perspective in totality.

As per global statistics, the estimated visually impaired population is 239 million [9]. A significant number of them reside in developing countries and about 5 million reside in India [7]. A large visually impaired population from developing countries belongs to low income group [14] who do not afford smartphones and Internet; they use basic mobile phones. Though mobile technology has integrated into their lives, communication and collaboration for the geographically dispersed visually impaired is yet to take place holistically. Effective design intervention is required while taking holistic perspective towards the users, context and problems. We need to design socio-technical systems that capture these factors and bridge the gap between users and the world.

This paper presents a qualitative study of phenomena - communication and collaboration for 43 geographically dispersed visually impaired chess players, who attended blind chess tournament in Hyderabad, India. We investigated the participants' existing ways of communicating and collaborating, and delved into the details of their exposure to Information and Communications Technology (ICT) tools. This qualitative research was embarked with data collection and subsequent data analysis using Atlas.ti. We audio recorded the interviews and identified quotations, codes, categories and core theme for data categorization. We developed a theoretical model for the phenomena. This work provides a holistic way for HCI designers to design socio-technical systems for the VI and does not focus on the specific cases of interface or interaction.

2   Background

There are a few researchers who investigated usability, accessibility, interface design aspects of collaboration and communication for the visually impaired. Studies in the developed countries have evaluated social apps such as Twitter [3] and Facebook [2], and usability evaluation of both the apps shows that many tasks cannot be performed by a visually impaired even with a screen reader. Even though W3C has developed web accessibility guidelines [18], many of them are not followed. Besides, screen reader restricts users to perform sequential content consumption. In addition, users feel that a lot of content is not relevant or interesting for them. To overcome this, users develop their own strategies for consuming the content from these sites [10]. As the studies were performed with a few participants only, further large scale research is required.

Geographical location of the participants seems to play an important role in effectiveness of communication and collaboration. A research shows that physical proximity of the participants helped to increase collaboration. 'Social awareness network' helped people to identify other visually impaired in the vicinity and to initiate interactions with them [8]. Researchers have investigated the use of handheld devices for remote collaboration [17]. Survey shows that 'distributed collaboration' has been in focus in both synchronous and asynchronous way. In fact, people do not get time for synchronous collaboration because of time and place constraints. An investigation of asynchronous collaboration among visually impaired is required, which has not been the focus of investigation.

A research on mobility explored various aspects of mobility in CSCW such as micro mobility, remote mobility, and remote and local mobility [12]. They emphasized on the fact that mobility can improve collaboration and reveal newer opportunities. Telephone, which has only sound as output and keys and sound as input, has a huge potential for different applications. Resnick [16] carried out a survey of telephone based applications and tools for applications development for cooperative work. The study identified factors such as expressiveness of voice, anonymity, needs to remember large chunks of information, cost, and benefits among users influenced the success and failure of any application. Though these studies are not related to the visually impaired, they provide insights which could be adopted into design for them.

Voice has been a well-known medium for interactions and interface design for visually impaired. A voice based social network exists, but it is not well-known and used. Klango.net [11] is a social network for visually impaired, which provides voice messaging, audio themes and voice forums. But, the social network is a Web site and people with no Internet cannot access it. Furthermore, Klango users are native English speakers, and low literate population in India is not comfortable with English. Thus, it poses barriers of communication among geographically dispersed users. Though, Klango is helping in communication for a user base, a significant population from other contexts is left out.

Researchers have identified 'awareness' as a key for collaboration and have performed empirical studies for collaborative tasks such as graphs reading by the visually impaired [13]. Audio and haptic tool were found to facilitate collaborative activities [13]. But, communication and collaboration challenges of the visually impaired from developing countries is yet to be discovered. As Activity Theory advocates understanding user activities, context and building theoretical foundations for the designers, we need to investigate the field from a holistic perspective. The present study is our first step towards designing a collaboration and communication platform for the visually impaired.

3   Methodology

The objective of the study was to investigate the ways in which geographically dispersed visually impaired communicate and collaborate among themselves. Further, our objective was to investigate different communication mediums used and challenges faced while using the mediums. Qualitative methods for data collection, analysis and modeling were used as it would reveal issues that experimental research may have overlooked.

As the visually impaired from various parts of India were supposed to gather for the chess competition in Hyderabad, India; we selected it as the venue for our data collection. The tournament was funded by Devnar School for the Blind and arranged by All India Chess Federation for the Blind.

3.1   Participants

43 visually impaired people, in the age group of 15–64 years (SD = 11.46), participated in the study. The participants were in various occupations - student, telephone operator,

retired lecturer, and so on. Largely, participants from Mumbai, Maharashtra had participated and remaining participants belonged to other parts of India. 25 participants were completely blind and 18 partially blind. Except school students, all the other participants had mobile phones. 20 participants had accounts either on Facebook or Twitter. About 28 users were using Internet either on personal computer or mobile phone. Participants with screen reader on their handset could use some of its features such as playing songs, using WhatsApp.

3.2 Procedure

After procuring necessary permissions and assuring no interference during the tournament, we started interacting with the participants. We collected data for four days of the tournament. We did not have a preplanned participant recruitment plan as we did not know who would be participating.

We randomly selected the participants for interview based on age. As a standard protocol, we informed participants about voice recording; obtained verbal consent and started recording. We told them the objective of our study and that the information shared with us would be used for the research only. We informed the participants that they could skip a question, if it felt inappropriate, or could stop us any time during the interview. As we selected participants who had completed their rounds of chess, we did not have any incident of a participant leaving the interview midway. We conducted one-on-one semi-structured interviews for 30–45 min each.

Initially, we tried to build rapport with the participants with questions related to chess. Later, we asked questions such as "Which different modes have you used for connecting with people and sharing information with them?", "Could you share your experience of playing chess over telephone?", "What kind of challenges did you face in playing over telephone?", and "What issues did you face using the social networks? How do you use them?" All the interviews were in Hindi and a few in Telugu; field notes were prepared and voice recordings were transcribed and then analyzed using Atlas.ti.

We followed Strauss's method for Grounded Theory based analysis [5]. Initially we used open coding for new codes and later we compared data and selected earlier codes, if they felt appropriate. In vivo coding was not used except for a few quotations, for instance, 'Voice has its own effect'. To keep a log of the thoughts, memos were used and memos were found useful for getting appropriate direction for the analysis. We followed Kathy Charmaz style of coding as 'code data as actions' [4].

We followed axial coding after open coding, to capture the relationship between codes and make connections. Finally, we used selective coding to come up with themes as a part of analysis. We refined themes and used appropriate names for the themes. Finally, we had 199 codes, which were categorized as follows: causal conditions, phenomena (causes), context, strategies and consequences.

4   Analysis

After rigorous coding, sorting, and code comparisons with interviews, we identified themes under Causal Conditions, Phenomena i.e. Causes, Strategies, Context and

Consequences as proposed by Strauss [5]. We restricted our themes to those that correlate with the core category - communication and collaboration among visually impaired. Following sub-categories were identified: Common Interests, Unawareness, No Friend in Vicinity, Feeling Helplessness, Feeling Technology Gap, Search for Information, Understanding Technology Limitations, Technology Exposure, Group Formation, Developing Interests, Consciousness, Visualization and Memorization, Social Networking, Information Sharing, Affordability Considerations, and Technology Adoption. The themes are described under sections as follows, but the intricate connections among the themes may seem overlapping in different sections (Fig. 1).

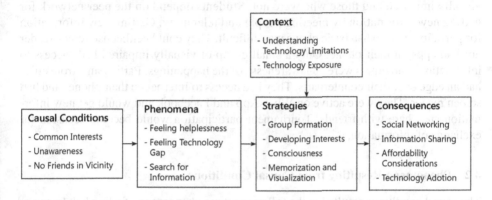

Fig. 1. Theoretical model for communication and collaboration among visually impaired chess players

4.1 Causal Conditions Related to Communication and Collaboration

We found three types of causal conditions that led to communication and collaboration - common interests, unawareness and no friend in vicinity. A significant number of participants shared that they do not have friends staying nearby their place. They could play with sighted people, but they are proficient in chess language, and many people do not know the chess language. For students who stay in hostel, playing chess is a regular activity. They do not 'find' friends near their home, thus, tournaments become a place to play. Tournaments give them access to the 'resources' and enable them to play their interested game. Local and national organizations do organize chess tournaments for them regularly, and they have 'groups' where they get this information.

> *"Only my friends who stay in hostel can play daily. I play very rarely as there is no one to play at home, but during tournaments, I play a lot. No one from my village knows chess language."*

Chess playing has been a common interest among visually impaired. Most of them start playing chess from a very young age. People who developed blindness after birth were not interested in chess initially; they developed it later as they attended tournaments or watched other visually impaired playing it. Most of them had chess ranks and they were proud of it. Participants who had a laptop or desktop play daily. But, many of them did not have access to a laptop or personal computer and hence, chess playing had become a tournament phenomenon. Parents were the motivating factor for them; participants who had lost vision after birth were inspired by friends. Observing peer play and enjoy chess make them learn and take interest in the play. This makes them a part of the "small" community and they are not left out of the community.

"My mother taught me chess. Whenever I get time, I start playing it. It is not the game I practice, I play it for enjoyment. I play chess every morning while having breakfast."

There were two types of the participants, those who were in connected with other visually impaired and those who were not. Students depend on the peer network for getting new information by meeting people and telephony. Getting new information for participants who had basic phone was difficult. They could neither use screen reader nor had apps on their phone. Only a small group of visually impaired had "access to information" and others were "unawareness" of the happenings. Participants from cities had an edge over their counterparts. They had access to Internet on their phones and had screen reader. They were active on WhatsApp and Facebook and would get new information and share with friends. Tournament participation would become occasion for exchange of information.

4.2 Phenomena Resulting from Causal Conditions

The causal conditions resulted in the following three phenomena - feeling helplessness, feeling technology gap and search for information. To use the mobile phone, they have to either use screen reader or depend upon others. Participants who had basic phone could not read the SMSs and had to request others to read to them. Hence, they preferred talking and requested people to call. They feel they do not have control over the actions they perform using mobile phone. "We cannot handle it.", "I used to send message from my Nokia phone, but this touch screen is very difficult to type. We can't type confidently."

"There is always a tension that no one should hear what you say. So, (SMS) is kind of unsecure at public places. I face difficulties many times because of SMSs. I have to depend on others even for storing contacts, but now I memorize them."

Some of the participants were using Facebook and Twitter using Talks from their phone, but many features are not accessible to them. Their friends would share photographs, which they cannot read. This resulted in low usage of the social networking sites. When they share something on Facebook, the post would go down the timeline (different people keep writing on the timeline). Hence, they would not get any response on what they share. They 'feel' their post should get response. If they are not frequent user, then they would build 'expectations' for a response. Thus, some of the participants wanted to 'pin' their post on Facebook groups.

To overcome these limitations and to get new information of interests, they would 'search' how to overcome the issues on websites. They would connect with friends, talk about the issues on social groups like Access India. Hence, they join NGO who regularly arrange gatherings, meeting, etc. Some of them follow people on Twitter, join Facebook and WhatsApp groups and have SMS subscription too.

"We follow certain people on Twitter so we come to know about tournaments. We have subscribed for SMSs, so we get SMSs. There is a site called chess-results.com where you can get all tournament related details."

4.3   Context in Which Strategies Are Developed

The strategies were developed considering the technology limitations and the limited technology exposure. The strategies were developed when situation was out of control or with limited control. Participants play chess over phone, but due to network issues, they prefer playing face to face. They feel they have better 'control' on the moves and they can use their abilities when they have control. Control has been an important factor in their decision making. It even decides whether they would like to talk about personal information to people at public places. *"We avoid talking about personal things at public places, if it happens, then we talk in soft voice."*

"When I am playing on telephone, if the other player does not know notations, I have to ask him repeatedly. Sometimes there is network issue and I cannot understand what the player is saying and we play wrong moves and we end up losing. But, when I play face to face, I can visualize what moves the player has played."

The strategies were developed as they realized limitations of tools available for them. Talks software is useful for reading messages, but they avoid using at public places. Besides, messages sent by their friends in native language in Devanagari script are not read by Talks. Some of the participants use earphone, but they 'fear' that earphone may get entangled in something and they would lose control.

4.4   Strategies for Communication and Collaboration

Participants developed a few strategies such as Consciousness, Developing Interest, Group Formation, and Visualization and Memorization. Privacy has been a concern for them which they could not 'control'. They know a number based language which they use for talking privately at public places, and they are quite proficient in it. For instance, if they wants to say 'H', they would use a number associated with it. This number is also known to other visually impaired. Hence, number language sometimes becomes lingua franca.

"I feel that talking privately should be done in more calm (secretive voice), otherwise someone might listen it. Whenever I am at public place, I try to postpone the talk. We also have number language which I use."

As they did not have 'friends in vicinity', they started playing chess over telephone, on computer and also joined chess classes. *"Yes, we play verbally!"* There were a few students who started playing chess recently. To understand and learn chess better, they started reading chess books. They started participating in chess tournaments.

For participants who lost vision by birth did not require chess board while playing over phone, they could memorize all the moves and play. Others keep chess board in front of them and played. They could visualize the chess board and pieces and would play.

"(In telephony) difference is that you need to visualize the board while playing orally, so this leads to increase in memory and concentration so that you can remember the whole board. So, it becomes easy when you play on actual board."

They formed and joined groups as Access India - email group for blind, SMS groups and WhatsApp groups. A few of them joined an international social network developed specially for blind - Klango.net. However, not many Indian blind people use this site and most of the conversations happen in local languages which is difficult for non-native.

"Yeah, I have joined some groups. There is a group for blind people in India called Access India. It is very good. I follow some people on twitter so we come to know and I have subscribed for SMSs."

To get new information, they started widening their friends circle. They enjoy while playing chess with people with similar needs. They play over phone by calling friends and keeping the chess board in front of them. Now every visually impaired owns a mobile phone. They prefer Nokia phone with keypad as it supports Talks and it has keypad. Typing with keypad is easier than using touch screen.

They were enthusiastic about the games and would dedicate four-five days for tournament. Participants come to "enjoy and meet people".

"I play before and during the competition period only. I practice (chess) on mobile with my friends. After the tournament I don't get time. I stay at my home, there is another blind person with me and that's my brother. When I come to play tournaments I got to make new friends; I have a lot of blind people around me."

4.5   Consequences of Strategies

The strategies developed by participants helped them stay motivated from other people in the group. They felt that technology is sometimes not affordable for them considering their occupation as the income is not much to afford expensive screen readers.

"I hear that there are software for the visually impaired which are too costly and there are many educated and working visually impaired people but they cannot use computers. So, even if technology is developed, it won't be used by the people. I have heard that there is software called Lekha for Hindi, but I don't have it as it costs a lot of money."

We observed technology adoption by many visually impaired. They started playing on Skype, on mobile and computer. They could share tournaments information and places to meet with the help of Facebook and Twitter. People who had screen reader in their mobile phone could change their phone wallpapers and use many features of the phone. We found that many visually impaired could change their wallpaper, profile and ringtones for others to see. SMSs enable them asynchronous communication, hence they prefer it over other mediums of communication. Thus, Access India is popular among them.

"All are busy, so meeting them is not possible, so in free time, everyone prefers to use phone, while travelling, etc. They use Facebook to connect with friends. You can be in touch with your best friends all the time."

The sharing trend was seen in visually impaired where they share many things with their friends on WhatsApp, Facebook and Twitter. These include interests, news, views, photos, opinions, interesting things, about chess, jobs and career guidance for visually impaired, difficulties, and so on. Many visually impaired don't have formal jobs; hence, sharing helps people to know jobs specifically for visually impaired. A significant number of people shared about chess games and the difficulties faced in their daily lives. It has led to increased communication and collaboration among visually impaired.

5   Discussion

We carried out a systematic study for investigating communication and collaboration among visually impaired chess players. Although there have been a few studies on a few aspects of communication and collaboration such as usability and usability evaluation of Facebook and Twitter for visually impaired, a systematic study to understand the phenomena was lacking. In this paper, we uncovered, practices followed by the visually impaired chess players for communication and collaboration. Further, we developed a theoretical model based upon the qualitative data analysis using grounded theory.

Visually impaired have adopted themselves to their mobile phone even when that doesn't support a screen reader. Using their memorability, they dial any number and # key to access contacts from their SIM card to dial a particular person, and it does not need screen reader. Use of chess language and playing chess over phone verbally, travelling to newer places by remembering the 'checkpoints' have convinced us to justify their choices. For privacy assurance, they disguise people by using 'codes' to talk to each other, whenever necessary, as well as using their handset such as to show people that they are partially impaired and not fully impaired. Constant search for new information useful to them and being part of the community, 'not to leave out', has resulted into collaboration. Mobile technology helped them to stay in touch with other chess players and to take part in social gathering, for instance, the chess tournaments. There are many social networking sites which provide both synchronous and asynchronous communication; it is interesting to understand that an email group keeps people updated and SMS subscriptions reach any time and at any place. Some of their sharing habits are coherent with the Facebook study [19]. It was found that slow response from friends, privacy and accessibility, etc. were major concerns. People use social networking sites such as Facebook and Twitter, but do not expect much from them. This is coherent with the study by Brady [1].

A strategy used by participants for playing chess over telephone – visualization and memorization - opens up new avenues for designing and developing solutions for the visually impaired. Audio interfaces especially Interactive Voice Response (IVR) Systems are being investigated in the domain on ICT4D. Considering the skills of visually impaired, audio and voice interfaces could be made richer, 'complex' audio interfaces could be designed which would be at par with the visual interfaces. Participants were quite fast with number processing for constructing digit strings for the text given to them, and text entry using numbers could be tested with the visually impaired on IVRS.

Presently, some of the participants follow people on Twitter for getting new information. They use SMS services and have email groups, but are restricted to people who have Internet connectivity. An IVR system could be designed to integrate Twitter content for the visually impaired people who do not have access to Internet. Besides, a collaboration system dedicated to the visually impaired could be designed where everyone creates content and shares with their friends in the form of audio clips. In addition, IVR games could be designed such as Chess, some of the number games played by the participants could be digitized and converted into asynchronous IVR games. Here, we would need to consider affordability in terms of monetary value and time value.

We evaluated the theory which emerged from the data. A primary validation is performed with the evaluation criteria by Strauss and Corbin [6]. During the analysis and comparison among the interview data, significant codes repeated which would ascertain a level of theory validation. Further research is required to validate the theory as a tool by its application in designing a communication and collaboration system.

6 Conclusion

This paper provides guidance for understanding collaboration and communication among visually impaired chess players. It suggests opportunities for designing applications and systems based on visualization, memorization, group formation, and constant search for information. It helps to understand technology adoption, which is required for successful ICTD research. In future, we need to investigate in detail the effect of chess playing on the cognitive abilities of visually impaired chess players. We need to further understand ways in the model could be evaluated, enhanced and abstracted to cater to large visually challenged population. It would help us to finalize approaches for designing cognitive interface for visually impaired at par with visual interfaces. We hope this paper encourages researchers in this field to take different aspects of CSCW research for the visually impaired.

Acknowledgement. We would like to thank the participants and organizers for their valuable time and support. This research was funded by Tata Consultancy Services Ltd., Mumbai.

References

1. Brady, E., Zhong, Y., Morris, M., Bigham, J.: Investigating the appropriateness of social network question asking as a resource for blind users. In: Proceedings of the 2013 Conference on Computer Supported Cooperative Work, San Antonio, Texas, pp. 1225–1236 (2013)
2. Buzzi, M., Buzzi, M., Leporini, B., Akhter, F.: Is Facebook really "open" to all? In: Proceedings of the 2010 IEEE International Symposium on Technology and Society (ISTAS), Wollongong, NSW, pp. 327–336 (2010)

3. Buzzi, M., Buzzi, M., Leporini, B.: Web 2.0: Twitter and the blind. In: Proceedings of the 9th ACM SIGCHI Italian Chapter International Conference on Computer-Human Interaction: Facing Complexity, Alghero, Italy, pp. 151–156 (2011)
4. Charmaz, K.: Constructing Grounded Theory, 2nd edn. Sage Publications Ltd., California (2014)
5. Corbin, J., Strauss, A.: Basics of Qualitative Research: Techniques and Procedures for Developing Grounded Theory, 2nd edn. Sage Publications, London (1998)
6. Corbin, J., Strauss, A.: Grounded theory research: procedures, canons, and evaluative criteria. Qual. Sociol. **13**, 3–21 (1990)
7. Data on Disability, Disabled Population by type of Disability, Age and Sex - C20 Table (India & States/UTs - District Level). http://www.censusindia.gov.in/2011census/Disability_Data/India/C_20-India.xls. Accessed Jan 2015
8. Gilfeather-Crowley, P., Smith, C., Youtsey, S.: Connecting visually-impaired people to friends through wireless sensor networks. In: Proceedings of the 2011 IEEE International Conference on Systems, Man, and Cybernetics (SMC), Anchorage, AK, pp. 3224–3229 (2011)
9. Global Data on Visual Impairments (2010). http://www.who.int/entity/blindness/GLOBALDATAFINALforweb.pdf. Accessed Jan 2015
10. Guerreiro, J., Gonçalves, D.: Blind people interacting with mobile social applications: open challenges. In: Proceedings of the CHI 2013 Mobile Accessibility Workshop, Paris, France (2013)
11. Klango.net: the social network you can listen to. http://klango.net/en/default/coolthings. Accessed Jan 2015
12. Luff, P., Heath, C.: Mobility in collaboration. In: Proceedings of the 1998 ACM Conference on Computer Supported Cooperative Work, pp. 305–314 (1998)
13. McGookin, D., Brewster, S.: An initial investigation into non-visual computer supported collaboration. In: Proceedings of the CHI 2007 Extended Abstracts on Human Factors in Computing Systems, San Jose, USA, pp. 2573–2578 (2007)
14. Organization, W.: Disability - a global picture. http://www.who.int/disabilities/world_report/2011/chapter2.pdf. Accessed Jan 2015
15. Pal, J., Pradhan, M., Shah, M., Babu, R.: Assistive technology for vision-impairments: an agenda for the ICTD community. In: Proceedings of the 20th International Conference Companion on World Wide Web, pp. 513–522 (2011)
16. Resnick, P.: HyperVoice: a phone-based CSCW platform. In: Proceedings of the 1992 ACM Conference on Computer-Supported Cooperative Work, Toronto, Canada, pp. 218–225 (1992)
17. Schmidt, A., Lauff, M., Beigl, M.: Handheld CSCW. http://www.teco.edu/conf/hcscw/sub/120.Schmidt/120.Schmidt.pdf. Accessed Jan 2015
18. Web content accessibility guidelines (WCAG) 2.0. http://www.w3.org/TR/2008/REC-WCAG20-20081211/. Accessed Jan 2015
19. Wu, S., Adamic, L.: Visually impaired users on an online social network. In: Proceedings of the 32nd Annual ACM Conference on Human Factors in Computing Systems, pp. 3133–3142 (2014)

Context-Aware Communicator for All

Paola García[1]([✉]), Eduardo Lleida[1], Diego Castán[1], José Manuel Marcos[2],
and David Romero[3]

[1] ViVoLab I3A, University of Zaragoza, Zaragoza, Spain
paolag@unizar.es
[2] CPEE Alborada, Zaragoza, Spain
[3] IES Damian Forment, Teruel, Alcorisa, Spain

Abstract. We describe the design of a communicator for people with speech impairments of several ages, but that can also be used by everybody. The design is based on the accurate definition of user models and profiles from which we extracted technical goals and requirements. The current design shows the factors to consider to provide a successful communication between users. The system is prepared to be used with children and elderly people with some kind of speech impairment. Moreover, the communicator is able to spontaneously adapt to each user profile and be aware of the situation, summarized in: location, time of the day and interlocutor. Therefore, the vocabulary to be used relates to a particular situation with the possibility to be broadened by the user if needed. This "vocabulary" is not restricted only to the word or syntactic domain but to pictograms and concepts. Several machine learning tools are employed for this purpose, such as word prediction, context-aware communication and non-syntactic modeling. We present a prototype scenario that includes examples of the usage of our target users.

Keywords: Communicator · Augmentative and alternative communication · Pictograms · Word prediction · Context-aware communication · Non-syntactic modeling · Speech impairment

1 Introduction

Communication is an essential part of the social and *Personal* development of an individual. It is a two way process in which individuals share their understanding of the world [9]. People with speech impairments may have limitations that affect this process. One of the main issues is the difficulty they experience to convey a successful communication with others. In this respect, the research community has shown great advances producing algorithms, applications and devices that facilitate their interaction [5,7,9,14].

One of the areas that has acquired popularity is the augmentative and alternative communication (AAC) mainly based on visual aids [5]. Its success relies on the real improvement of the *Quality of Life* of the users. However, there is still much to do to adequate applications and systems to support *Personalized*

© Springer International Publishing Switzerland 2015
M. Antona and C. Stephanidis (Eds.): UAHCI 2015, Part I, LNCS 9175, pp. 426–437, 2015.
DOI: 10.1007/978-3-319-20678-3_41

settings considering a particular context[1]. For example, the system must automatically adequate the vocabulary needed for a particular activity, at a specific time of the day, with the usual people interaction (for example, the children's vocabulary needed for breakfast, in the morning, with mom and dad).

We describe the design of a *Personal*ized communicator that covers the necessities of a wide range of people with impairments that go from a child with autism to an elderly lady that was diagnosed with dementia. We address the system characteristics as immersed in specific environments and contexts that give solution to the user needs. To accomplish the effective operation of the system, we create a model of use centered in the interaction between the user and the desired service in the system, according to the ETSI technical document ETSI EG 202 848 [4] and TR 108 849 [3].

In the next sections, we will give an overview of our communicator design that can lead the reader to a comprehensive summary of the system. Section 2 shows how the user was modeled and the characteristics that the communicator must accomplish. Section 3 details the context-aware adaptability of the system. Section 4 defines the functional communication specifications for the communicator. Section 5 shows the way the communicator will transform a message from one domain to another. Section 6 details a complete example of the usage. Section 7 opens discussion for further research. Finally, Sect. 8 gives the conclusion to this approach.

2   User Modeling

The user model gives an explicit representation of the abilities, intentions and attributes of an individual user who is interacting with the system. We used Persona *mechanism* [8] to obtain a clear idea of our target users. *Persona* modeling design suggests representing the users with as real characteristics as possible to extract their goals and requirements.

For the purpose of this research and to contextualize our research, we defined a six-member family. The Ramos-Castro family is composed of two children, the parents, a grandparent, an uncle and a dog. They are living in a neighborhood on the suburbs of a big city, with all kind of educational and health facilities. The house is fully connected with fixed and mobile telephones as well as high-speed Internet connection in all the rooms (so the communicator can easily connect to a server and perform updates). The two children are Luis and María. Luis is a 14 years old boy. He suffers from Autism Syndrome Disorder (ASD). He is one of the main actors (*Primary Persona*) of the scenario as his communication greatly depends on the technological tools. María (*secondary Persona*) is 12 years old girl with a normal development. She is interested in technology to communicate with family and friends. The parents are Inés and Manuel (*secondary Personas*). Inés, the mother, is 36 years old and she is a teacher in a special education school. She is learning how to use the ICT tools to help her students and Luis. Manuel,

---

[1] Most of the applications are fixed to general profiles that try to cover all possibilities for a specific group of people and impairment.

Table 1. User goals and requirements for people with impariments

	Child with autism	Elderly people	Hearing impaired
Technical key goal	– To communicate efficiently with people (express feelings, desires, pain, etc.)	– To communicate efficiently	– To communicate efficiently
	– To organize daily activities	– To organize activities	
		– To reinforce memory	
Requirement	– Pictogram application	– Pictogram application	– Sign language
	– Agenda	– Agenda	– Pictograms
	– Synthesized voice application	– Voice recognition and synthesis	– Synthesized voice
		– Memory reinforcement applications	

the father, is 37 years old and he is CEO of a medical electronic devices company. He would like to have a tool that can organize his activities and that can give flexibility to communicate with his family. The grandparent is Beatriz (*Primary Persona*). Beatriz is 70 years old and she has some memory and cognitive problems due to a stroke she suffered when she was 68 years old. She would like a tool that can facilitate the communication with others. The uncle is Jorge (*Primary Persona*) and he is Inés brother. Jorge is 30 years old and he was diagnosed with sensory-neural deafness at the age of 7. He is interested in technology for hearing impaired people.

From these context, we obtained relevant information of what the family might need in terms of a communicator.

2.1 Target User Model

The communicator can be used by all people, but it is mainly focused on people with speech impairments. From the *Persona* information, we extracted the target user goals and requirements, see Table 1. This information is a step for the final design and prototype. Although refinement may be needed, it shows a general view of the expected attributes that the system must fulfill.

To ensure that the system covers people with no-impairments, we included the secondary *Persona* characteristics. The secondary *Persona* for our communicator are: business man, professional, teacher and teenager. The secondary *Persona* information gives an extra degree of freedom to the final design: the system should include an easy way to switch between communication domains

Table 2. User goals and requirements for people with no impairments

	People with no impairment
Technical Key goal	– To communicate efficiently with people with impairment and no impairment.
	– To organize daily activities and help people with impairments to organize theirs
Requirement	– A translator: a two way system that allows communication from two different domains (for example: spoken speech to pictograms, pictograms to synthetic speech, spoken language to subtitles or pictograms, etc.).
	– Agenda

Table 3. User model design

User Model			
Personal information	Type of impairment	Level of communication	Computer skills
Experience level		Device type and familiarity	
Form of interaction (speech, pictogram, etc.)		Socioeconomic inferred characteristics	

(pictograms, speech, text, etc.). Although the secondary *Persona* interests are very broad, we selected the following (Table 2):

According to Table 1 and 2, the user model must include attributes that can ensure that the goals and requirements are covered. Table 3 summarizes these attributes.

Therefore, special care was given to these characteristics while deciding the methods to employ in the design and to ensure the adaptability to different type of people and impairment.

3   User and Context Adaptability

The communicator performance is strongly related to the context in which it is being used [15]. This information is contained in the profile and considers the age, level of speech impairments and the context in which the communicator is being used. Three context directives are then defined: time, space and person.

1. Person: The type of language that people use depends on who the interlocutor is. Then, the probability of a word to appear in a phrase is a function of the interlocutor.
2. Time: The time of the day is also a variable the system should be consider. It defines the topics to address. For example, if it is morning 7:00 AM, it is probable that the user might be having breakfast. Then, the language to be used is related to food.
3. Space: The location also defines the language to be used.

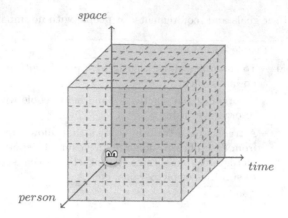

Fig. 1. Context-aware cube

The idea can be viewed in Fig. 1.

In principle it is hard to cover the wide range of characteristics that conform each cube. However, if we define a fine set of elements on the axis, it is possible to create a probabilistic model for each sub-region. For example, in our context, each sub-region will contain a language model adapted to that specific situation (for example, from 7 to 7:30, talking to Mom, at home).

In the next section, we can define how this notion of prediction takes place.

4   Functional Communication Specifications

To establish a functional communication between the system and the user, the communicator needs the information of the user skills to handle the applications. Therefore, the system must adapt for each user abilities to communicate: pre-communicative, communicative, linguistic and conversational. In this paper, we explored mainly from the communicative to the conversational levels, but an extension can be performed to the rest[2]. The user profile will be updated every time the user logs in the system to provide better responses.

The purpose of this research is to establish a functional communication, meaning that the user can clearly share his/her ideas with others via speech or some other aid device is the final goal of this research. In the next subsections, we will detail the methods explored to accomplish this goal considering the broad range of people and that in some cases the users cannot convey a pure functional communication.

4.1   Concept and Prediction

One of the first questions, we may ask is if it is possible to go from non-functional communication to functional communication. A considerable range of

---

[2] The user skills should cover, at least, to be able to respond to requests with words and be able to understand and focus on pictograms.

children with autism (around 50 %) have a functionally non-verbal communication [12,13]. From this set a huge number uses pictograms or signs.

We are used to establish a structured and linear communication, meaning that for example if we utter the group of words:

> I soup ate.

is meaningless. We have to put them in the correct order for others to understand what we really mean. However, for the wide range of impaired people it is difficult to produce a semantically and syntactically correct sentence of this type and even more difficult to organize complex sentences.

As exemplified by Avaz [1] it may be possible to start from every element from the desired phrase and then continue building up the complete sentence. This approach can be used with words, but also with pictograms. Our purpose is then that given any meaningful word, predict the possible words that are related to that word.

For a clear explanation and to exemplify (see Fig. 2), lets consider that the user points the verb "eat". The system suggests the category food with its options: "soup", "juice", "snack". The user selects soups. The missing element is the subject; then, the options might be: "mom", "dad","I".

The communicator outcome is:

> I ate soup.

The user finally gets a complete meaningful sentence that others can understand. Although this is a very simple example, the approach can be extended to complex phrases by just suggesting the most probable concept that follows.

To achieve this goal the system uses machine learning tools to train a concept network. The system trains a generic concept network with all the possibilities based on concept net database. The system adapts this model to each of the users, at first using the profile information and then, by adapting along the usage.

Although we are just referring to concepts in their word form, the method can be extended to the pictogram domain.

4.2 Word-Prediction

As in the concept prediction, the system will include a word predictor[3]. The word predictor suggests the most probable word following syntax rules. Although, this might be thought as a linear sequence of words derived from the *part of speech* POS, it is also possible to use the same approach as in concept prediction to give robustness to the system.

The success of this part of the system relies on the *Language Model* and the correct training and *Personalization* for each situation. We have to keep in mind

---

[3] Every word has a match or matches within a set of pictograms.

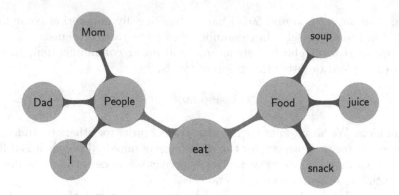

Fig. 2. Conceptual map

that although we can generate a general model that includes all possible situations, a special adaptation must be performed for the given context restrictions (time of the day, person with whom the user is talking to, location).

4.3   Pictogram Prediction

It is known that from the children with some degree of autism [10], more than 50 % are functionally non-verbal [12,13]. Depending on their ability level to communicate, a big set of them prefers pictograms. These children, among other groups, such as elderly people [6,11] with difficulty to understand spoken and written language, rely on *augmentative and alternative communication*, AAC. These methods frequently use pictograms, pictures, sketches, drawings, sign language and videos as their core part.

The system offers a big set of pictograms that covers mainly children necessities, and a combination of both, pictograms and pictures that are useful for elderly people. However, one of the main issues, is how to enhance the fluency of the communication. It is difficult and time consuming to be searching for a particular pictogram among thousand of pictograms. The system uses a prediction algorithm in three domains: the word, the concept domain and the word domain. The word prediction approach follow the POS rules (linear). In the pictogram approach, the initial condition is a random selection of an element of a phrase. Then, the next probable pictogram will also convey the rules of the concept prediction or word domain (time, space and location).

5   Translator

The translator converts the language from one domain to another as shown in Table 4.

The transformation from one domain to the other is not an easy task. The straightforward conversion is speech to written words and vice versa. There is

Table 4. Domain conversion

Input	Output
speech	pictograms
pictograms	synthetic speech
written words and phrases	pictograms
speech	written words and phrases

an exact correspondence between a spoken word and its written representation. However, one of the main challenges is that there is not a one to one match between words and pictograms. Pictograms tend to have several meanings, so the system selects the closest depending on the situation. In here, the system ensures that the words are context dependent and uses synonyms as part of the choices to ensure an efficient communication.

Moreover, to allow a functional communication, the most challenging part is how to deal with POS, verb tenses, conjugation and articles, without increasing the complexity of the system[4]. In this sense, the system flexibility and adaptation are the key points. The system models for each approach (pictograms, speech, concept) are context dependent and are updated and readapted continuously to give the user a set of expected answers. However, it must also give the possibility to select from a huge set of unexpected answers the desired pictogram or word.

6   A Full Example

Figures 3 and 4 include a full example of the capabilities and usage of the communicator.[5] The communicator architecture consists of mainly two parts: a main unit (server) and a mobile device (iPad, tablet, smartphone). All the intensive computation the acoustic, concept and language models are trained and updated in the server. Every profile and sensitive information is stored in the server as well and sends updates to the end users devices. The mobile devices employ a user friendly interface which updates the interface output at every system request.

The first part (Fig. 3) includes a usage scenario for a child with autism with medium level of communication. The system uses concept prediction. The profile is already downloaded in the device and the next step is to wait for a user request. The user, selects the communicator, although some other applications are possible (gallery, agenda, chat, etc.), see Fig. 3(a). The communicator shows a first screen with a set of preferred categories, see Fig. 3(b). Luis selects a

---

[4] Although there are languages with no gender articles, in Spanish every noun has its corresponding article. Moreover, in languages like English, the verb tenses include extra words or minimum changes, in Spanish the endings change for every tense but also for every person.

[5] The used symbols are work of Sergio Palao for CATEDU (http://catedu.es/arasaac/) that publishes under Creative Common's License [2].

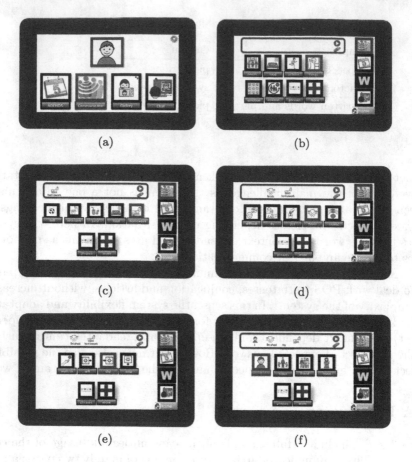

Fig. 3. Luis example of usage (concept prediction approach, the sequence is from left to right and from top to bottom). Luis shows "I finished my homework", starting from the element "homework" and selecting the suggested categories or pictograms until he terminates the phrase.

random pictogram. The system reconfigures the screen choices according to the first selection, see Fig. 3(c). For the concept prediction, the phrase can start at any element and the completion is performed according to the suggested categories. Luis chooses a second pictogram and the screen reconfigures again, see Fig. 3(d). The second selection is a verb which may need conjugation, see Fig. 3(e). The system is prepared to construct correct conjugations and missing words. Finally, the screen reconfigures again to add a subject to the sentence, see Fig. 3(f). The final output could be: pictograms, text or synthetic speech.

Figure 4 includes a usage scenario for an elderly person with a medium level of communication based on word and pictograms. The user employs correct syntactic phrases. The first screen shows the available options. Beatriz selects the communicator application, see Fig. 4(a). The categories are then located at

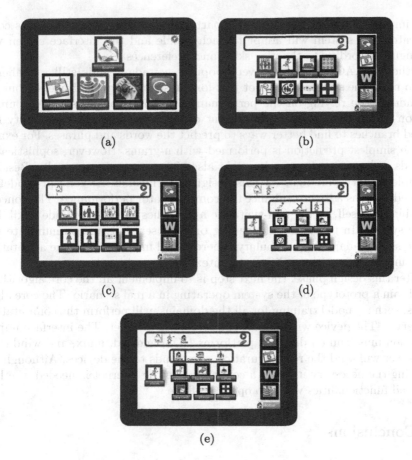

Fig. 4. Beatriz example of usage (word prediction approach, the sequence is from left to right and from top to bottom). In here, Beatriz employs word prediction with pictograms. She writes "I want to go home" with the correct syntax. Note that the categories also exist at word level.

certain positions depending on the most used categories, see Fig. 4(b). She is able to construct syntactically correct phrases. She selects the category: people. The communicator updates the screen choices with the words contained in the people category, see Fig. 4(c). She selects I and the screen reconfigures again with the most probable options. She chooses a verb, which is correctly conjugated by the system, see Fig. 4(d). Finally, she selects the complement of the phrase.

For both systems, the log files are sent to the server; the profiles and models are updated and send back to the device.

7   Discussion

We have detailed the design of a context-aware communicator that will be beneficial for people with impairments of different ages. The accurate definition of the models and the profiles together with the requirements that the system should fulfill impacts the design. Therefore, apart from providing the services as communicator, the system will adapt to each profile and the interface screen will reconfigure according to the user skills and preferences.

Although AAC systems are very popular nowadays, it is still a challenge how to make the systems work not just for a restricted group of people, but for a broader range relying on the performance of the system to specific communication levels. From the technical point of view, the research community has opened branches to find better ways to predict the words and phrases. For example, the simplest prediction is performed with n-grams. However, sophisticated methods such as neural networks might also give more accurate results. Besides, a complementary paradigm for this design is to include the concept modeling and prediction as a tool to enhance the communicator performance. The concept modeling, by itself, or the non-syntactic approaches can also provide flexibility to the system. In this sense, depending on the user skills to communicate the system should adapt the vocabulary. There is still much to do in the adaptation of our methods to work on different contexts.

After this design phase, the next step is to implement all the core algorithms and obtain a prototype of the system operating in a real scenario. The core algorithms, such as model training for all the domains, will perform the computation in a server. The device will connect the server via internet. The interface implementation must run on different platforms (IOS, android, linux, and windows). The server will send the reconfiguration commands to the devices. Although for acquiring the necessary updates a connection to the internet is needed, the last uploaded functionalities will also operate offline.

8   Conclusions

We have shown a design of a multiage system that also covers context-aware requirements. This research shows a communication system as an aid for people with communication impairments. We focused mainly on two target groups: children with autism, and elderly people. However, the system can be used by everybody as an agenda or communicator. It is, then, a context-aware system that offers *Personal*ized services depending on the time of the day, location and interlocutor. Apart from being context-dependent, the communicator transforms the vocabulary elements to different domains that go from simple pictogram structures to complete sentences. Moreover, to facilitate the communication it predicts the next element (word, pictogram or concept) to be selected. We showed examples of how the system would work in a real scenario and made special emphasis on personalized services for people with impairments.

Acknowlegments. – This research is supported by the Iris project that received funding from European Union's Seventh Framework Programme for research, technological development and demonstration under grant agreement no 610986.

– We would like to thank the people from Alborada Special School for all the information given for this research http://cpeealborada.blogspot.com.es/.

References

1. Avaz aac app. http://www.avazapp.com/
2. http://www.arasaac.org/
3. ETSI TR 102 849, Technical report Human Factors (HF); Inclusive eServices for all; background analysis of future interaction technologies and supporting information (2010–2011)
4. ETSI EG 202 848, Human factors; inclusive eServices for all: Optimizing the accessibility and the use of upcoming user interaction technologies (2011–2012)
5. Beukelman, D., Mirenda, P.: Augmentative and Alternative Communication. Brookes, Baltimore (2005)
6. Beukelman, D.R., Fager, S., Ball, L., Dietz, A.: Aac for adults with acquired neurological conditions: a review. Augmentative Altern. Commun. **23**(3), 230–242 (2007)
7. Cook, A.M., Polgar, J.M.: Assistive Technologies: Principles and Practice. Elsevier Health Sciences, UK (2014)
8. Cooper, A., Reimann, R., Cronin, D.: About Face 3: The Essentials of Interaction Design. Wiley, New York (2007)
9. Glennen, S., DeCoste, D.C.: The Handbook of Augmentative and Alternative Communication. Cengage Learning, New York (1997)
10. Hughes, V.: Researchers track down autism rates across the globe (2011). http://sfari.org/news-and-opinion/news/2011/researchers-track-down-autism-rates-across-the-globe
11. Light, J., McNaughton, D.: The changing face of augmentative and alternative communication: past, present, and future challenges. Augmentative Altern. Commun. **28**(4), 197–204 (2012)
12. Lord, C., Anthony, B.: Autism spectrum disorders. In: Rutter, M., Taylor, E. (eds.) Child and Adolescent Psychiatry: Modern Approach. Blackwell Publications, Oxford (2002)
13. Lord, C., Risi, S., Pickles, A.: Trajectory of language development in autistic spectrum disorders. In: RIce, M.L., Warren, S.F. (eds.) Developmental Language Disorders: From Phenotypes to Etiologies, pp. 7–29. Lawrence Erlbaum Associates, Mahwah (2004)
14. Mirenda, P.: Toward functional augmentative and alternative communication for students with autism, manual signs, graphic symbols, and voice output communication aids. Lang. Speech Hear. Serv. Schools **34**(3), 203–216 (2003)
15. Schilit, B.N., Hilbert, D.M., Trevor, J.: Context-aware communication. IEEE Wirel. Commun. **9**(5), 46–54 (2002)

Mediating Asymmetries in Family Communication: Supporting the eInclusion of Older Adults

Francisco J. Gutierrez[1(✉)], Sergio F. Ochoa[1], and Julita Vassileva[2]

[1] Computer Science Department, University of Chile, Beauchef 851,
3rd Floor, Santiago, Chile
{frgutier,sochoa}@dcc.uchile.cl
[2] Computer Science Department, University of Saskatchewan, 176 Thorvaldson Bldg.,
110 Science Place, Saskatoon, SK S7N 5C9, Canada
jiv@cs.usask.ca

Abstract. *Background:* The rise of mobile Web-based technologies has diversified the mechanisms used by people to socialize, which results in issues in family communication. Among these concerns, the reluctance of older adults to use digital media may cause them social isolation, leading to negative effects in their physical and mental health.

Objective: This paper aims to formalize a model to mediate asymmetries in cross-generational communication and support the eInclusion of older adults.

Methods: We conducted semi-structured interviews to the members of 20 cross-generational families. Following the grounded theory approach, we identified emerging themes regarding asymmetries in family communication practices when older adults are involved. We then derived and formalized computer-based mediation strategies using a model-driven engineering approach.

Results: We identified three main sources of asymmetries: (1) implicit family agreements in terms of social interaction, (2) capability and preferences for using particular media, and (3) unbalanced socio-affective coupling between the involved parties. The proposed model addresses these asymmetries and provides strategies to coordinate the communication effort of family members with their elders.

Conclusions: By using the proposed model, designers of software that supports family communities can conceive effective mechanisms to coordinate and mediate social communication among cross-generational family members through digital means. This allows the elderly to show a better reaction to digital media, thus facilitating their acceptance and appropriation of information technologies.

Keywords: Family communication · Older adults · Asymmetry · Model · Mediation · Social and digital inclusion

1 Introduction

As a society, we experience our lives as much more dynamic than ever, being mainly focused on reaching individual goals [11]. The downside is that time for socializing is

© Springer International Publishing Switzerland 2015
M. Antona and C. Stephanidis (Eds.): UAHCI 2015, Part I, LNCS 9175, pp. 438–448, 2015.
DOI: 10.1007/978-3-319-20678-3_42

reduced [22]. Therefore, people find in social media (e.g. email, social networking services and videoconference) an efficient way to interact with others, because these mechanisms provide ubiquity, flexibility and efficiency.

In the case of intergenerational families, this social interaction paradigm typically produces a communication gap between older adults and the rest of the families [20]. Some of the causes that explain this gap can be found in elders being reluctant to use technology, even for socializing [8]. Consequently, older adults become more and more socially isolated [14]. Although most elders are eager to address this technological shift, they usually fail due to their physical and cognitive limitations produced by the aging process [5, 12]. Therefore, they need support and guidance to face this complex scenario in a pleasant way [26]. Otherwise, technological adoption by older adults dramatically diminishes.

This paper proposes a model of computer-mediated communication strategies to facilitate the eInclusion of elderly people. In order to improve user acceptance, such mediation strategies need to consider the interaction preferences of each party.

Although promoting social interaction among family members is a commendable objective, such interaction must not overwhelm people having little time for socializing. Therefore, effective mediation strategies should intelligently coordinate all the members in a family community based on specific criteria, such as location, time of day, and the available communication media to support the interaction. This necessarily implies that such mediation process should be adapted to both, the individual's interests and those shared among groups of his/her community. Besides, a mediator system should not be too proactive, since people will eventually refuse to react when there is no urgency, and therefore would not respond in a really important situation. In this interaction scenario, understanding the social and technological context of the involved people is fundamental to ensure the success of the social mediation process.

As a first attempt to tackle the social personalization issues inherent to the proposed communication mediator, we conducted an interview study in cross-generational families. We had a particular interest in understanding communication practices from and toward the elderly, as well as identifying the perceived issues by the latter in a digital communication scenario. By acquiring such knowledge, we identified an initial set of variables that characterize communication asymmetry in cross-generational family communities. We synthesized these findings into a model, aiming to provide social personalization when mediating the communication process between two people. Then, we derived a set of computer-based mediation strategies aiming to connect family members and favoring the eInclusion of the elderly.

Our proposal suggests that the identified asymmetries can be covered by aligning preferences in different levels: communication media, socializing capability, availability for socializing, and routine flexibility. Besides, asymmetries in the social link between two people also shape how the mediation process needs to be modeled, especially in terms of who will be the initiator and how long the mediation will take. If the asymmetries between them turn to be too large to be resolved solely by both parties, the introduction of a third family member into the communication process, acting as a communication broker, would be necessary.

The rest of the article is structured as follows. Section 2 reviews recent literature on family connection from a HCI perspective, and discusses the role of technology as impeller of eInclusion in older adults as well as the issues that need to be overcome. Next section presents and formalizes the model proposed to address asymmetries in cross-generational family communication. Section 4 shows how computer-based mediation strategies can be derived from the proposed model. Finally, Sect. 5 concludes and provides future research directions.

2   Related Work

With the proliferation of social media and ubiquitous technology for communicating with family and friends, it is likely that older adults face increasing challenges when interacting with their younger relatives, who typically use those kinds of supporting technology to socialize [16, 17]. In fact, while most family members desire to enhance their communication with at least one relative, literature suggests that in practice this process is difficult to achieve due to social or technological concerns [28].

When looking deeper into family communication practices, some forms of interaction do not necessarily involve an explicit sharing of messages between older adults and their close family members, but rather an ongoing awareness of the other party's communication state [24]. In other words, people use both personal and environmental cues to help them understand what is happening to the other communication party. Furthermore, Lindley [18] found that elders usually prefer a prolonged contact, which is typically offered by synchronous media (e.g. through face-to-face or phone communication); in turn, asynchronous communication offers advantages to facilitate inter-generational exchanges, such as adapting communication time to a schedule, and providing control over how much effort is dedicated to this kind of interaction.

The eInclusion of older adults through social media or social networking services can effectively assist the integration of the elderly to their families [6]. In addition, it also empowers them with social engagement and self-expression tools [29]. There is also evidence that one of the main benefits of social media usage by older adults is the possibility to enhance their social linking with younger family members, which eventually tends to be appreciated by both parties [23]. Indeed, Bell et al. [3] found that older adults who actively use Facebook state that their main reason to use the platform is to stay connected with their families.

Unfortunately, most older adults do not feel capable of using digital media [13], and therefore are not able to benefit from them. Therefore, when designing software that support social interaction and social presence for families (particularly if they include older adults), there is an explicit need to consider face-to-face interaction, provide presence awareness mechanisms, assume heterogeneous preferences of social media, allow the mutual social interaction, and properly address usability and accessibility concerns [19].

Several efforts have been done in order to bridge this interaction gap. For instance, Cao et al. [4] identified design implications for facilitating family communication when its members are located in different time zones. Baecker et al. [2], Cornejo et al. [7],

Garattini et al. [10], Judge et al. [15], Lindley [18], Muñoz et al. [20], and Rodríguez et al. [25] have adopted a different approach to deal with that challenge. They designed specific domestic media spaces where remote family members, particularly older adults, can connect with each other using video-mediated communication and others kinds of messaging mechanisms. These social media spaces aim to integrate older adults into their families, and also reduce and prevent eventual negative effects of social isolation.

In summary, the literature indicates that these asymmetries can indeed jeopardize communication among members in a family community. Furthermore, since different generations have different preferences regarding what media they are able or willing to use under a particular social context, it is necessary to follow a personalized approach when facilitating and/or mediating communication between two family members. This is particularly relevant when communication is targeted to be performed with older adults, since further restrictions limit the ways in which the mediation process can be conducted. By actively considering the needs and concerns of older adults into the design of computer-based strategies that mediate asymmetries in family communication, software designers can conceive usable and accessible services that would naturally help enhance the technology appropriation by the elderly, thus favoring their eInclusion.

3   A Model to Mediate Asymmetries in Family Communication

In this section we first present the methodology followed to collect the information used to build the model. Then, we present and describe the formal model proposed to mediate asymmetries in family communication. This model intends to support social interaction among members of middle-class family communities living in urban areas, in Chile. The model particularly considers the interactions from/to older adults. Possible extensions to this model and its application to other social realities are part of the future work.

3.1   Data Collection Methodology

In order to identify not only asymmetries in cross-generational family communication practices, but also the features that characterize a family community, we used two main data sources: (1) a literature review of the most recent systems designed to enable and facilitate family communication, particularly when they involve older adults, and (2) a qualitative interview study.

We conducted semi-structured interviews with the members of 20 cross-generational middle-class families living in urban settlements. For convenience reasons, we focused our study in the metropolitan area of Santiago, Chile and we followed a snowball sampling strategy to recruit the participants. In each family we interviewed three members: an older adult, an adult, and a teenager. Out of the 60 participants, 25 were men (42 %) and 35 were women (58 %). The interviews were held at the participants' homes. Beforehand, we conducted a small-scale pilot study with three families in order to identify and resolve wording and ambiguous statements in the interview script.

In order to identify emerging themes on cross-generational asymmetries in family communication, we followed the grounded theory approach. Indeed, this resonates with current recommendations and research trends in human-computer interaction [1]. Each interview was tape-recorded with the explicit, free and informed consent of each participant. They were later transcribed, processed through open, axial and selective coding, and analyzed by the authors.

By contrasting the obtained findings with the existing literature, we built a model covering the main characteristics, issues, and social expectations of the stakeholders involved in a family community scenario. Next section presents and formalizes the proposal following the model-driven engineering approach.

3.2 Family Communication Metamodel

Communication in family communities can be represented as a metamodel, where each particular family is an instance of such abstract structure. This conception adheres to the model-driven engineering approach [27], and it can be easily implemented using existing tools, such as Eclipse Process Framework [9]. Figure 1 shows the UML class diagram that represents the metamodel.

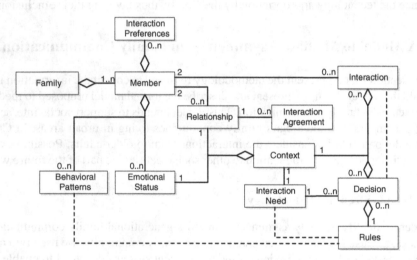

Fig. 1. Family communication metamodel

This representation considers a *family* as composed at least by a *member*. Each member has *interaction preferences* (e.g., preferred tools to conduct synchronous and asynchronous communication), *emotional status* (set of emotions detected during a certain time window) and eventually *behavioral patterns* that determine the way in which a person is going to behave under particular circumstances. Every pair of members in a family community has a *relationship*, which includes several variables that range from the affective attachment among them, to their formal relatedness. There could be an implicit and/or explicit *interaction agreement* between these pairs, which establishes the interaction frequency and also the time space and digital media involved in these interactions. Based on these agreements, and also in the emotion status of each member, it is possible to determine *interaction needs*, which represent people that are currently in need of emotional support.

Every interaction need has a *context* that determines who, how and when other family members could deal with such emotional support. Provided that various family members can potentially intervene in that situation, and trying to not overloading all of them, one or more *decisions* should be made concerning who will be encouraged to provide support to the member in need. The decision process can be repeated until getting a successful result or using up all the available alternatives.

Decisions are made using a set of rules that indicate how to intervene a relationship considering the social needs of the involved people and their behavioral patterns. The decision process also considers the historical record of interactions between these people. Each decision is translated into particular actions that are made by the system mediating the communication among family members; e.g., an invitation message can be received by a person for contacting other family member that is currently in need of external support. Such an action can be materialized in an interaction, or eventually it can fail. In the latter case, a new decision could be made. Next section describes the process that each particular family communication model uses in order to promote the social interaction from/to older adults.

3.3 Processing the Family Communication Model

This process involves four uncoupled stages: *data gathering, monitoring, decision-making*, and *intervention* (Fig. 2). Rectangles represent classes of the family model described in the previous section, while rounded rectangles represent processes. Next we explain each model component.

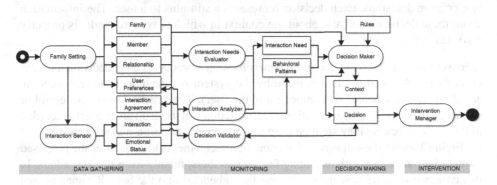

Fig. 2. Basic architecture of the model processing

Data Gathering. This stage is in charge of obtaining the basic data of the system; e.g. family composition, user preferences and their interaction agreement. This information is provided through a *family setting* process, which is performed when the community is created. There is also information that is not provided by the end-users (i.e. family members), but that is automatically captured by the system, and also used as input. Examples of this information are the current emotional status of a family member, or the interactions performed by the participants in a community. Various social media tools, like SocialConnector [21], can act as *interaction sensors* capturing and recording this information.

Monitoring. This stage adds meaning to the basic information captured in the previous stage. The system tries to determine if there are new interaction needs that should be addressed. Particularly, the *interaction needs evaluator* analyzes the basic information of family members as well as their emotional status to determine if there is a new need for social support. If it does, the process records such need in the system, and then other components are going to address it. Such need can also be identified by comparing the interaction agreement between each pair of members, and their effective interaction record. The analysis of interactions is also used to determine or adjust behavioral patterns of a user or his/her interaction preferences. The *interaction analyzer* is the process in charge of performing these activities. Finally, the *decision validator* process tries to determine if an effective interaction recorded by the system is the result of a stimulus triggered by the system to a user; i.e., a decision made by the system to promote the interaction between two people. If it does, the result is recorded and then used to make future decisions.

Decision-Making. This stage takes each interaction need recorded in the communication model, and based on the behavioral patterns and the basic information gathered in the first stage, determines a set of zero or more actions that could be taken to support the people in need. These actions can either be to trigger participation using persuasive strategies, or to raise an alarm and consequently provide awareness on the possible need to family members. The *decision maker* is the process that determines which decision will be made in each situation. Such process uses a set of rules as support, and makes one or more decisions. Each decision represents a stimulus to a user. The information about these decisions and also about the context in which they were made, is properly recorded in the system.

Intervention. In this stage, the *intervention manager* processes each decision and acts accordingly. A specific action is made by the system per each decision (e.g. send an email, or show an awareness component to the user). The actions can be successful or not. Regardless the results of an action, such an action and its result are properly recorded in the model, because they are then used to improve the decision-making process.

Figure 3 shows the software architecture of a social media tool that uses the proposed model to promote interactions among family members, mainly from/to older adults. In this case, we indicate how the model can be embedded into the SocialConnector tool [21] to reach such a goal. SocialConnector, as most social mediators, allows family members to interact using communication mechanisms like videoconferences (through Skype), emails and sharing contents (through Facebook). However, these tools do not identify when a person is in need of external support nor persuade other family members to help reduce or mitigate such situation. That role can be played by the proposed intervention model, which is complementary to the existing tools and can be added as an extension.

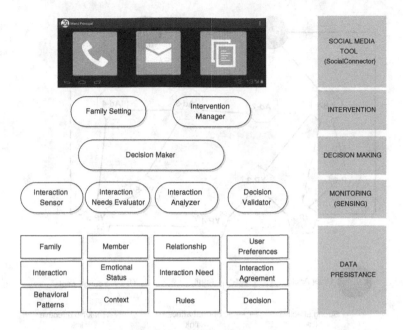

Fig. 3. Architecture of a social media tool that uses the proposed model

As most modern software tools, we propose to separate the design concerns using layers. In this case, the software extension should involve four layers: data persistence, monitoring, decision-making and intervention. This matches with the stages of the process used to compute the model (Fig. 2). The components and roles of each layer are also those mentioned for the model processing.

4   Using the Model

In order to illustrate the use of this model as a support for SocialConnector, let us consider a family community composed by twelve members: two older adults (OA), four adults (Ad) and six young people (YP). Considering the relationship existing between them (in terms of social interaction), we can build an interaction graph similar to the one shown in Fig. 4. The different types of links indicate how strong is the affective relationship between each pair of nodes (i.e., between two family members).

Let us suppose that the system detects that OA2 has been with a negative mood during the whole morning. Such detection is done by the *interaction needs evaluator* (Figs. 2 and 3), which creates and records a new need in the persistence layer (i.e., it creates a new instance of the class *interaction need*). Then, the *decision maker* component should determine, based on the set of available rules and the context describing that situation, how to support the person in need. By analyzing the graph, we can see that Ad-3 and OA-1 are the closest family members for OA-2. Probably, the first priority should be to try contacting Ad-3 because adult people usually have better capabilities to deal with problems than older adults. However, Ad-3 would be the first option only

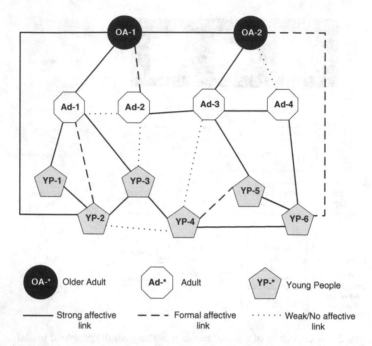

Fig. 4. Example of a simplified family community graph

if the *interaction agreement* between Ad-3 and OA-2, and also their *interaction preferences*, are aligned. In other case, other options must be analyzed.

Once the model determines the most suitable family member to help in this situation, it should make one or more decisions. The *decisions* are stored in the corresponding class of the model. Each decision triggers an action that the system must perform autonomously in order to persuade the chosen member (e.g., Ad-3) to help the person in need. These actions could be either sending an email or instant message to Ad-3 informing such a situation. The *intervention manager* component is in charge perform these actions. The result of each action should be verified or guessed (in the worst case) by the system, in order to determine if new decisions should be made because all of the stimuli to Ad-3 failed. Thus, the system uses the model to determine second options, and so on until exhaust all the available intervention alternatives, or eventually succeed.

5   Conclusion and Future Work

Asymmetries are inherent to family communication, particularly when they involve intergenerational members. While some people perceive their ability to adapt to other's preferences as natural in terms of communication media and flexibility, external mediation usually needs to be performed in order to increase the chances of effective communication.

After conducting a literature review and a qualitative interview study, we have identified asymmetry sources related to: media preference, socializing capability, the availability of both parties, and their flexibility for performing social interaction. The quality and strength of the affective tie between the involved parties is also relevant when studying family communication. In particular, if the asymmetries between two people appear to be quite strong, the inclusion of a third person acting as a broker in the mediation process is recommended, as it is already naturally considered in family settings.

By providing effective mechanisms to coordinate and mediate social communication among family members through digital means, the elderly appear to show a better reaction to digital media. This facilitates not only their social inclusion to their families, but also to their acceptance and appropriation of ICTs.

As future work we are embedding this model (and its processing) into the Social-Connector system [21]. Then, we will evaluate in the field the model performance through empirical studies that would allow us to determine its impact, as well as gathering feedback to improve it.

Acknowledgements. This work has been partially supported by the Fondecyt Project (Chile), grant: 1150252. The work of Francisco J. Gutierrez has been supported by the Ph.D. Scholarship Program of Conicyt Chile (CONICYT-PCHA/Doctorado Nacional/2013-21130075).

References

1. Adams, A., Lunt, P., Cairns, P.: A qualitative approach to HCI research. In: Cairns, P., Cox, A. (eds.) Research Methods for Human-Computer Interaction. Cambridge University Press, Cambridge (2008)
2. Baecker, R., Sellen, K., Crosskey, S., Boscart, V., Barbosa Neves, B.: Technology to reduce social isolation and loneliness. In: Proceedings of ASSETS 2014, Rochester, USA, pp. 27–34. ACM Press (2014)
3. Bell, C., Fausset, C., Farmer, S., Nguyen, J., Harley, L., Fain, W.B.: Examining social media use among older adults. In: Proceedings of HT 2013, Paris, France, pp. 158–163. ACM Press (2013)
4. Cao, X., Sellen, A., Bernheim Brush, A.J., Kirk, D., Edge, D., Ding, X.: Understanding family communication across time zones. In: Proceedings of CSCW 2010, Savannah, USA, pp. 155–158. ACM Press (2010)
5. Carmichael, A.: Style Guide for the Design of Interactive Television Services for the Elderly Viewers. Independent Television Commission, Winchester, UK (1999)
6. Cornejo, R., Tentori, M., Favela, J.: Ambient awareness to strengthen the family social network of older adults. Comput. Support. Coop. Work **22**, 309–344 (2013)
7. Cornejo, R., Tentori, M., Favela, J.: Enriching in-person encounters through social media: a study on family connectedness for the elderly. Int. J. Hum.-Comput. Stud. **71**(9), 889–899 (2013)
8. Czaja, S.J., Charness, N., Fisk, A.D., Hertzog, C., Nair, S.N., Rogers, W.A., Sharit, J.: Factors predicting the use of technology. Psychol. Aging **21**, 333–352 (2006)
9. The Eclipse Foundation. Eclipse Process Framework Project (EPF). http://eclipse.org/epf/. Accessed 29 Dec 2014
10. Garattini, C., Wherton, J., Prendergast, D.: Linking the lonely: an exploration of a communication technology designed to support social interaction among older adults. Univ. Access Inf. Soc. **11**(2), 211–222 (2012)

11. Giddens, A.: Conversations with Anthony Giddens: Making Sense of Modernity. Stanford University Press, Palo Alto (1998)
12. Hawthorn, D.: Possible implications of aging for interface designers. Interact. Comput. **12**, 151–156 (2000)
13. Hope, A., Schwaba, T., Piper, A.M.: Understanding digital and material social communications for older adults. In: Proceedings of CHI 2014, Toronto, Canada, pp. 3903–3912. ACM Press (2014)
14. House, J.S.: Social isolation kills, but how and why? Psychosom. Med. **63**, 273–274 (2001)
15. Judge, T.K., Neustaedter, C., Harrison, S.: Inter-family messaging with domestic media spaces. In: Neustaedter, C., Harrison, S., Sellen, A. (eds.) Connecting Families, pp. 141–157. Springer, London (2013)
16. Lindley, S.E., Harper, R., Sellen, A.: Designing for elders: exploring the complexity of relationships in later life. In: Proceedings of British-HCI 2008, Liverpool, UK, pp. 77–86. British Computer Society (2008)
17. Lindley, S.E., Harper, R., Sellen, A.: Desiring to be in touch in a changing communications landscape: attitudes of older adults. In: Proceedings of CHI 2009, Boston, USA, pp. 1693–1702. ACM Press (2009)
18. Lindley, S.E.: Shades of lightweight: supporting cross-generational communication through home messaging. Univ. Access Inf. Soc. **11**(1), 31–43 (2012)
19. Moser, C., Fuchsberger, V., Neureiter, K., Shellner, W., Tscheligi, M.: Elderly's social presence supported by ICTs: investigating user requirements for social presence. In: Proceedings of SocialCom 2011, Boston, USA, pp. 738–741. IEEE Press (2011)
20. Muñoz, D., Cornejo, R., Gutierrez, F.J., Favela, J., Ochoa, S.F., Tentori, M.: A social cloud-based tool to deal with time and media mismatch of intergenerational family communication. Future Gener. Comput. Syst. (2014). http://dx.doi.org/10.1016/j.future.2014.07.003
21. Muñoz, D., Gutierrez, F.J., Ochoa, S.F., Baloian, N.: SocialConnector: a ubiquitous system to ease the social interaction among family community members. Int. J. Comput. Syst. Sci. Eng. **30**, 57–68 (2014)
22. Neal, A.G., Collas, S.F.: Intimacy and Alienation: Forms of Estrangement in Female/Male Relationships. Garland Publishing, New York (2000)
23. Nef, T., Ganea, R.L., Müri, R.M., Mosinmann, U.P.: Social networking sites and older users – a systematic review. Int. Psychogeriatr. **25**(7), 1041–1053 (2013)
24. Riche, Y., Mackay, W.: PeerCare: supporting awareness of rhythms and routines for better aging in place. Comput. Support. Coop. Work **19**, 73–104 (2010)
25. Rodríguez, M.D., Gonzalez, V.M., Favela, J., Santana, P.C.: Home-based communication system for older adults and their remote family. Comput. Hum. Behav. **25**(3), 609–618 (2009)
26. Roupa, Z., Nikas, M., Gerasimou, E., Zafeiri, V., Giasyrani, L., Kazitori, E., Sotiropoulou, P.: The use of technology by the elderly. Health Sci. J. **4**(2), 118–126 (2010)
27. Schmidt, D.C.: Model-driven engineering. IEEE Comput. **39**(2), 25–31 (2006)
28. Tee, K., Brush, A.J.B., Inkpen, K.M.: Exploring communication and sharing between extended families. Int. J. Hum.-Comput. Stud. **67**, 128–138 (2008)
29. Waycott, J., Vetere, F., Pedell, S., Kulik, L., Ozanne, E., Gruner, A., Downs, J.: Older adults ad digital content producers. In: Proceedings of CHI 2013, Paris, France, pp. 39–48. ACM Press (2013)

Comparison of Age Groups on the Readability of an E-Reader with a Built-in Light

Yuki Ishii, Tatsuya Koizuka, Kohei Iwata, Takehito Kojima,
Paul Lege, and Masaru Miyao[✉]

Nagoya University, Furo-cho, Chikusa-ku, Nagoya, Aichi, 468-8603, Japan
callistemon.r.br@gmail.com, miyao@nagoya-u.jp

Abstract. We carried out experiments to evaluate the readability of e-paper devices using different systems. In the experiments, we conducted subjective evaluations under staged illuminance conditions. This study found that different age groups showed differences in reading e-paper devices with a built-in light under different conditions of illuminance.

Keywords: Evaluation of accessibility · Usability · User experience · E-books · E-paper · Kindle DX · Ipad · Readability · Illuminance

1 Introduction

As display technologies have advanced in recent years, there has been an increase in high quality content on mobile devices, such as smart phones, tablet devices or e-readers. In addition, the number of mobile devices has increased rapidly in recent years and such devices are used by both young and old. The spread of e-books has been helped by e-readers that specialize in the clarity of the text. Most e-readers have an e-paper display system, and people can read these as easily as reading a paper text even when outdoors. Our previous study showed that under conditions of low illuminance, the readability of the e-paper was poor [1]. However, a built-in light system could improve the readability of the e-paper under low illuminance conditions (e.g. Kindle Paperwhite [2]). Compared with the young, the elderly have lower visibility. In this study, we carried out reading experiments to evaluate the readability of e-paper with built-in light. We investigated the contributions of built-in light on the readability of e-paper devices by age groups.

2 Method

2.1 Subjects

The subjects for this study included 110 healthy males and females between the ages of 19 and 86 years (Table 1). The subjects who usually wore glasses or contact lenses used them for the experiments. We obtained informed consent from all subjects and approval for the study from Ethical Review Board in the Graduate School of Information Science at Nagoya University.

© Springer International Publishing Switzerland 2015
M. Antona and C. Stephanidis (Eds.): UAHCI 2015, Part I, LNCS 9175, pp. 449–454, 2015.
DOI: 10.1007/978-3-319-20678-3_43

Table 1. The age groups of the subjects

	Age groups	The number of people	Average	Standard deviation
Young	19–4	44	27.5	7.2
Middle	45–64	45	50.9	4.2
Elderly	65–86	21	72.8	5.0

2.2 Experimental Design

We carried out the reading experiments in a darkened room. In order to adjust to constant illumination, we used an original lighting system consisting of a fluorescent light and LED for reading. In the experiment, the illumination was adjusted to 14 levels. Table 2 shows both the target illuminance and measured illuminance values.

Table 2. Target illuminance and measured illuminance values (lx)

10	20	50	100	150	200	300	500	750	1,000	1,500	2,000	5,000	8,000
13.47	22.73	51.60	101.4	151.4	176.3	261.7	516.7	787.7	1,042	1,591	1,983	4,670	8,017

In the experiment, we used an e-reader with built-in light (Kindle Paperwhite released in 2012) and e-reader without built-in light (Kindle DX released in 2009). We also used backlit LCD (iPad released in 2012) and conventional paper text. We used the Kindle Paperwhite and iPad at a configuration of maximum brightness. We put the reading devices in small compartments placed on a desk (Figs. 1 and 2).

Fig. 1. Appearance of experiment

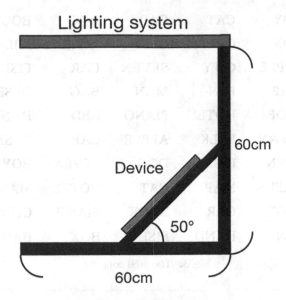

Fig. 2. Outline of the compartment

2.3 Task Design

The experimental task was for the subjects to read aloud a written text displayed on the devices. There were five words in English per line, and ten lines in each text passage (Fig. 3). The character font was 9 pt using a typeface of Times New Roman. The subjects began to read form the upper left in 15 s. We recorded the number of words that the subjects could read in 15 s as well as their viewing distance. After reading, the subjects evaluated the readability of the text. The subjects evaluated the readability of the devices using Analog Visual Scale, converted to between 0 and 100 points.

3 Results

We classified subjects as those who were 44 years old or younger as "Young", those who were 45–64 years old as "Middle aged", and those who were older than 65 years old as "Elderly".

Below, we will refer to the Kindle Paperwhite as PW, the Kindle DX as DX and the paper as Paper in Figs. 4, 5 and 6.

Figure 4 shows the subjective evaluations of each device by the young group. Under low illuminance conditions, the younger subjects rated the Kindle Paperwhite higher than that of the Kindle DX. For conditions of more than 750 lx, the ratings Kindle Paperwhite were lower than Kindle DX.

Figure 5 shows the subjective evaluation of each device by the middle aged group. In lower conditions of illuminace this group evaluated the Kindle Paperwhite higher

BOY	CAT	CAP	DOG	BOOK
BOX	GREEN	OPEN	JAPAN	MILK
APPLE	CITY	SEVEN	CAR	FISH
MAP	PEN	MAN	BAG	DESK
STOP	HOTEL	PIANO	RED	HAND
JAPAN	MILK	APPLE	CAP	DESK
OPEN	RED	DOG	SEVEN	BOY
GREEN	MAP	CAT	HOTEL	MAN
STOP	CAR	BOOK	PIANO	CITY
PEN	HAND	FISH	BOX	BAG

Fig. 3. The used contents

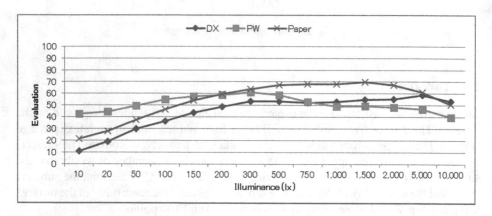

Fig. 4. Subjective evaluation of each device by young

than that of Kindle DX. Under the conditions of more than 750 lx, they rated theKindle Paperwhite lower than the Kindle DX.

Figure 6 shows the subjective evaluation of each device by the elderly group. This last group also rated theKindle Paperwhite higher than that of Kindle DX under low illuminance conditions. Under conditions of more than 500 lx, they ratings were almost the same.

4   Discussion

The younger group evaluate the Kindle Paperwhite higher in lower conditions of illumination. We found that there were no differences between the group evaluations of the Kindle Paperwhtie in lower conditions of illuminance All of the evaluations were consistent in rating the Kindle DX above 10,000 lx.

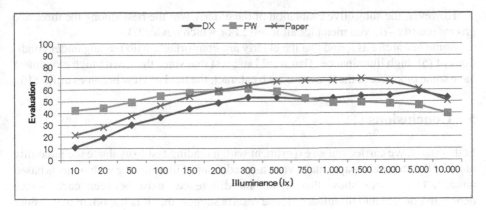

Fig. 5. Subjective evaluation of each device by middle aged

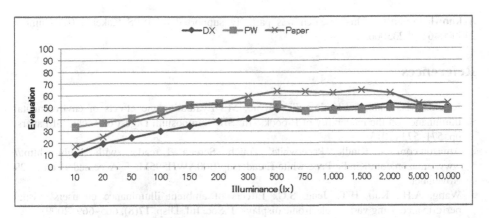

Fig. 6. Subjective evaluation of each device by elderly

The evaluations of Kindle Paperwhite was higher than that of the Kindle DX and paper text in the lower levels of illuminance.

One of the biggest advantages of the built-in light system is the sustained readability of e-paper under low conditions of illuminance. According to some previous studies, the use of the backlit LCD terminal is desired under low illuminance [3]. But according to our results, a built-in light system has a profound effect on readability under the low conditions of illuminance because the picture resolution and contrast ratio of the Kindle Paperwhite are superior. Since we used the Kindle Paperwhite at a configuration of maximum brightness, the subjects found the back light device much easier to read.

With an illuminance of more than 750 lx, the subjective evaluations of Kindle Paperwhite did decrease compared to the Kindle DX. The picture resolution and contrast ratio of the Kindle Paperwhite were superior, but Kindle Paperwhite has a light guide over the e-paper display. At higher levels of illuminace, the light guide appears to affect the evaluation of readability because it reflects light [4].

However, the subjective evaluation of the elderly was the best among the three age groups (clarify –do you mean for all levels? For which device??).

Some research has found that the elderly are comfortable with reading under conditions of [5], high illuminance. That would suggest that since those with high cloudiness have some blocking of the lenses for each cataract, the field of view becomes diffuse [6].

5 Conclusions

In this study, we carried out an experiment with a reading test to evaluate the redability of tablet devices and e-paper under various conditions of illuminance with subjects based on age. Our results show that significant differences exist between each device depending on age and illuminace. These results suggest that it is important to consider the age when developing such reading devices.

Acknowledgments. This research was partially supported by JSPS Kakenhi (B) Number 24300046 and 23300032.

References

1. Koizuka, T., Sano, S., Kojima, T., Miyao, M.: Evaluating the effects of environmental illuminance on the readability of E-books. In: SID Symposium Digest of Technical Papers, pp. 571–573 (2013)
2. Amazon.com - Kindle Paperwhite Touch Screen E-reader with Light. http://www.amazon.com/Kindle-Paperwhite-Ereader/dp/B00AWH595M. Accessed on 29 November
3. Wang, A.H., Kuo, H.T., Jeng, S.C.: Effects of ambient illuminance on users' visual performance using various electronic displays. J. Soc. Inf. Disp. **17**(8), 665–669 (2009)
4. NYTimes.com, How the Kindle Paperwhite works. http://www.nytimes.com/interactive/2012/12/26/technology/light-reading.html?_r=0
5. Wang, A.H., Hwang, S.L., Kuo, H.T., Jeng, S.C.: Effects of ambient illuminance and electronic displays on users' visual performance for young and elderly users. J. Soc. Inf. Disp. **18**(9), 629–634 (2010)
6. Ishii, Y., Koizuka, T., Lege, R.P., Kojima, T., Miyao, M.: Evaluation of Readability for Tablet Devices by the Severity of Cataract Cloudiness. In: SID Symposium Digest of Technical Papers, vol. 45, Issue 1, pp. 1089–1092, June 2014

Visualizing Database-Performance Through Shape, Reflecting the Development Opportunities of Radar Charts

Verena Lechner and Karl-Heinz Weidmann[(✉)]

User Centered Technologies Research Institute, University of Applied Sciences Vorarlberg,
Achstrasse 1, 6850 Dornbirn, Austria
uct@fhv.at

Abstract. At a time where databases contain millions of data records and their organization gets complex, the visualization especially of metadata gets a necessity to get an overview of the database performance. In this paper we'll provide an insight into a research project commissioned by Crate Technology GmbH, who developed an elastic SQL Data Store that is massively scalable [1]. The aim of our efforts in the UCT Research Institute is to find different ways to visualize the data state in such a cluster. In particular we investigated the development opportunities of radar charts in database metadata visualization and the visual appearance of the developing shapes. During the paper, the primary challenges of the project will be displayed and comparable products will be investigated. In the last part, we'll give a short insight to our work in progress, deal with the issue of form perception and also present further required efforts.

1 Introduction

When thinking of visualizing database-performance today, our thoughts are most likely with a large amount of meta data records, which are updated regularly. To keep track of these meta data seems to be difficult. Moreover, upcoming problems, which a bad condition of the database may trigger in future seem to be invisible. But especially for employees dealing with big data and being responsible for the optimal functional capability of databases, finding the sources of problems in advance in order to counteract could be absolutely helpful. Therefore providing an easily comprehensible overview about the real-time condition of databases could be a particularly forward-looking development. In this paper we will propose the use of radar charts and the resulting shapes as a possible solution and investigate the potential of these shapes.

2 Definition of Metadata

Before we can start with the description of the initial situation of the project, it's necessary to define the term "metadata" because there exist innumerable definitions [2] that could have a confusing effect.

Metadata can be used in different matters and targets, but mostly have the following functionalities: supporting data discovery, enabling the dealing of data by humans and

© Springer International Publishing Switzerland 2015
M. Antona and C. Stephanidis (Eds.): UAHCI 2015, Part I, LNCS 9175, pp. 455–463, 2015.
DOI: 10.1007/978-3-319-20678-3_44

facilitating the automated handling of data in the subdivisions of data discovery, ingestion, processing and analysis [3].

Moreover, in all metadata schemas semantics can be found as a characteristic. So they give data elements a meaning and help people working with metadata to understand the individual elements [4].

The term "metadata" comes from the field of computer science, where the prefix "meta" means "about", so the aim of metadata is to describe other data. Two main requirements that metadata have to fulfill can be defined: firstly the information has to be structured and therefore recorded according to a documented metadata approach. Secondly a resource of information has to be described by the metadata, where the question will arise what exactly could be an information resource, especially when we think of the numerous fields metadata play a key role [5].

Looking at database metadata in a more precise sense, it can be defined as "data about database data" as for example a list of all tables of a database, their sizes and their number of rows. So metadata (also seen more generally) has the task to describe data, but it isn't the data itself [6].

After having defined metadata in particular for our purpose of database-performance visualization, some general challenges in this field as well as some of the main challenges especially in the context of the research project for Crate will be described.

3   Challenges of Visualizing Database-Performance in a Big Data Environment

When working in a big data environment probably the most obvious fact may be that either the data collections or the data objects itself are big [7]. Regarding our research task, big data collections but as well the wide variability of users and therefore the variability of the size of their data collections represent a challenge for finding ways to visualize the data state. Moreover, the visualization needs to take into account the fact that some databases are under constant transformation, therefore the metadata change constantly as well, depending at which intervals the metadata are queried.

A Cluster running on Crate contains a certain amount of nodes, defined by the user, which according to the experience values of Crate Technology GmbH can be assumed with a number between 8 and 300 nodes. As a result, when starting with the visualization work, the capability of the visual sense has to be kept in mind and a presentation method has to be found which should communicate the content precisely and let it be perceptible in an intuitive level [8]. So in our specific task situation where the main goal is to give an overview over the condition of the whole amount of nodes (putting aside the second goal for the time being, which is to provide further information about selected individual nodes) we are talking not only about communicating the condition of up to approximately 300 nodes, but also about taking into account the simultaneous view of different points in time. So the number of objects to be detected can rise sharply. And as the user of the visualization should be able to make decisions about manual optimization measures, any incorrect representation and any resulting wrong interpretation may have far-reaching consequences.

Moreover, as the database-performance can be assessed according to many different criteria, there has to be found a way to group them to logical categories that answer upcoming questions of the employees being responsible for their databases. As a result, the number of necessary parameters for answering these questions can vary widely. So when trying to find a way to visualize them, a very flexible form concerning the representable parameters has to be found.

Summing up what has been said so far, the main challenges for projects working with the visualization of database-performance in a big data environment are:

- the enormous amount of data objects itself,
- the constant transformation of the database,
- the variety of the number of nodes that have to be presented and perceived intuitively,
- the variety of criteria that determine the performance and therefore the visualization of answers to upcoming questions that consist of a different amount of parameters.

As the baseline situation and the major challenges of such projects has been described, the following section takes a closer look on other tools and products that try to visualize database performance or other comparable data.

4   Analysis of Comparable Tools and Products

4.1   Planning of the Comparison Procedures

For the analysis of tools that visualize comparable issues as Crate does, eight products on the market have been chosen and investigated. The main challenges but also characteristics of these will be discussed and examples will be given in order to illustrate the development potential for our research project.

4.2   Limited Number of Parameters Shown per Visualization

As already mentioned previously, database performance depends on various parameters, therefore when trying to visualize the condition of a database cluster, many different criteria have to be taken into account. When examining for example the user interfaces of Zabbix [9], cacti [10], Ganglia [11], NuoDB [12] or Pivotal HD [13], it can be noted that in one single visualization they mostly use only two dimensions when producing bar charts or line charts. In order to be able to present more than these few dimensions, they add more charts or other visualization types, resulting in a dashboard-like collection of different views. As a result, the situation for the user could be confusing, because associated dimensions or criteria aren't displayed in the same visualization.

4.3   Necessary Prior Knowledge for the Usage of Modular Systems

Kibana, for instance, allows the user to adapt its queries and also the visualization types and attributes in order to offer a totally personalized visualization [14]. But this assumes that the user is able to combine different parameters in a way that the output makes sense and decisions can be made. As in our research project Crate Technology GmbH requests a solution, that not only offers an optimal integration into existing company processes but also a maximum of the ease of use, we decided to specify the research questions and therefore the shown parameters the user could be interested in when observing the cluster state.

4.4 Difficult Determinability of the Condition of the Elements Shown

Whenever producing a visualization of parameters that affect the condition of elements in order to make human decisions, in the end it lies in the hands of the observer to determine whether the viewed visualization contains negative or improvable content. With the help of human intuition, the viewer should get a contextual understanding of the data condition, so it is necessary to offer an intuitive human-machine interface to integrate intuition into the analysis process [15].

In the example of software diagnostics [16], a spatial model was found to present answers to different questions concerning software systems. Individual code units are represented as blocks ordered in a way that intuitively let the user think of a city view consisting of skyscrapers with different heights and base areas. The system detects bad code units, lets them appear in red and therefore give hints to possible improvement potential. In comparison to software diagnostics, MongoDB MMS [17] (a cloud service that can be used to support the usage of MongoDB) offers more possibilities to specify individual queries and shows the selected metadata of a database as a chart, but the system doesn't interpret the chart nor gives a hint to a dangerous state of data. So the user has to decide on his own whether the presented data could contain a problematic issue or not, and this could develop difficulties when thinking of visualizations of really large metadata sets. For that reason, what we have been looking for in our project is a visualization, that lets the user get a quick and intuitive impression of the database performance and highlight problematic issues in any way to facilitate the improvement work.

So with these three challenges the main potential of our visualization development has been formulated. This leads us to a detailed presentation of our approach using radar charts and the shapes developed through an intuitive handling of radar charts.

5 Using Radar Charts as a Form Generator and Intuitive Observation Tool

5.1 General Information to the Work with Shapes in this Project

As already described earlier, a Cluster running on Crate consists of a variable amount of single nodes, the state of which has to be monitored. Just as to mention a single example, overloaded servers could cause unintended waiting periods, so the parameters "average load", "used disk", "used heap" and "number of shards" could be interesting when observing all the nodes.

What we started to do in the beginning of the research project is to find a way to give an overview over all nodes that is flexible regarding the number of parameters that have to be taken into account, shows the user all the problematic information in an intuitive way and doesn't require much specialist knowledge to work with. For this reason we combined the flexible properties of radar charts with findings of form perception and developed an opportunity to show various values of different parameters and let them build a shape, that deviates more or less of an ideal circle (Fig. 1).

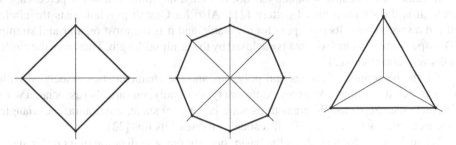

Fig. 1. Radar charts with a flexible number of axes or displayed parameters

In Fig. 2 the transformation from a radar chart to a shape, which could represent the state of one single node can be seen. Visible in the background of the shape on the right is the contour of the ideal circle. For the development of the shape in the foreground the four vertices of the ideal circle have been moved along the four axes to or away from the center of the circle, maintaining the rounding of the four vertices.

Fig. 2. Transformation of a radar chart with four axes to a shape that deviates from the ideal circle

When talking of a circle as the ideal form (the form where all the values on the axes are on the ideal position), the reason why we didn't use a regular polygon in this place has to be explained.

5.2 Form Perception of Primitives

Perception of Circles and Polygons. Considering how circles and polygons are perceived, the principle arises very quickly that round forms are perceived as soft, continuous, fluent and natural, whereas angular ones are perceived as unnatural and lifeless [18, 19]. The reason for the above named associated characteristics isn't only the fact that we associate them with other shapes known to us, but also with the visual process itself, where the shapes are patted down by the eyes [19].

In other words, forms are findings of the sense of movement. For instance when we view a circle, the eye tracks the whole form bit by bit, until we experience the completely enclosed circle [20].

Because of its centric symmetry it doesn't exist any direction when perceiving a circle, it is the simplest visual pattern [21]. Also for Gestalt psychologists the circle played a special role: Its percept is totally stable and it is the most regular and simple 2D shape because its surface area is enclosed by the minimal-length. Therefore the circle looks very compact. [22]

So, the perception of circles and polygons and the characteristics associated with them as well differ much. Moreover different types of polygons are also associated with different characteristics: Whereas the square has a very static, quiet aura, the triangle appears as very active, especially if it stands on one of its tips [23].

When deciding for a circle as the basic form for our visualization of a cluster state, we therefore solved the problem, that questions, which need a variable amount of parameters to be answered (and already in it's ideal form lead to polygons with a different amount of vertices) are associated with different characteristics. Using a circle and modify it according to the number of parameters (and therefore axes) leads to a much more constant perception, because in it's ideal state it always has a circle as a result (Fig. 3).

Fig. 3. Examples of the construction of shapes out of a circle with three, four and eight axes

The Circle and its Reason to Describe an Ideal State. As a unique exception of the basic geometric shapes, the circle doesn't consist of different directed lines, but of a uniform curvature [23]. It is completely directionless, has no beginning nor end and is a symbol of perfection, having already been described by Plato (in Timaeus), but also appears in other cultures like the Chinese or the Hindu culture [24].

When perceiving a shape, we start looking for a structural framework [19, 21]. Examples for elements of this framework include symmetry, angle or side length. Regular shapes in general include such a framework that puts in order the single parts of it. The brain is able to quickly complete the form, without determining it over a long time. By comparison, irregular forms don't have this framework but get associated with something already known [19].

So when using a regular shape (e.g. the circle) as the basic shape and modify it according to the angles of the axes allows the viewer of many of these shapes (in our purpose that represents the state of the whole amount of nodes of a database-cluster) to quickly identify the irregular shapes. This leads to a fast detection of nodes that are in a bad condition and need improvement measures, which only a human being is able to deduce.

5.3 Difficulties of the Concept

During the first tests of this concept with real data (with four parameters as described in Sect. 5.1) received from Crate Technology GmbH, we detected a few difficulties that need to be taken into account when thinking of adapting this concept to various questions that could interest the employees responsible for their databases. Some of the most important ones will be clarified below.

Firstly, the size of a single node presented as one piece of a big group of nodes has to decrease in order to give an overview about the whole cluster. This results in a large number of very small elements (nodes), the curvatures of which may be difficult to detect, depending on which end-device the database is observed. So in the further planning of the interface, a suitable order has to be found, a very contrasting coloration of the nodes and the background as well as enough space around each element has to be ensured.

Another fact we have to take into account is that the ways to define the ideal value of the different parameters may vary. For example when one considers the parameters "average load", "used disk", "used heap" and "number of shards" of each node, the arithmetical average of all nodes may be the ideal value for the used disk, used heap and number of shards as these values should be as balanced as possible. But for the average load it could be more interesting to see just the values that exceed a specific value (for example 1). As already described previously, the curvatures necessary to produce a circle when the values are ideal have to be taken with the vertices moving along the axes.

If the values of all axes are on the same level but not ideal (too high or too low values), this principle produces either too big or too small completely round circles. So if the variation of the size of the circle doesn't stand out regarding the whole cluster, another variation of the curvatures has to be developed in order to avoid misunderstandings.

6   Further Tasks and Conclusion

Our next steps will be to tackle the previously described difficulties, to perform tests with a broader range of participants selected from the expected customer group of Crate Technology GmbH and to revise the visualization according to the results. Subsequently we plan to extend the visualized answers to a broader range of answers to questions that may be valuable as well and to think of opportunities to integrate these visualizations into the user interface of Crate. In this process, the necessary functions of the visualization interface will reveal, such as a possibility to see and compare the cluster state at different points in time, or the zooming from the view of the whole cluster to a single node view with further details.

First budget usability tests of the visualization of single nodes with real-time data have already shown that the participants are able to deduce the state of the node via a shape developed through the merging of radar charts and circles. This suggests further research in the simplicity and intuitiveness of the perception and assessment of shapes, in particular when working in the environment of big data.

References

1. CRATE Technology GmbH: Crate. Your Elastic Data Store. https://crate.io/
2. Olson, J.E.: Database Archiving: How to Keep Lots of Data for a Very Long Time. Morgan Kaufmann, Burlington (2009)
3. Sicilia, M.-A., Lytras, M.D. (eds.): Metadata and Semantics. Springer Science & Business Media, New York (2009)
4. Taylor, A.G.: Much about metadata. The Whole Library Handbook 4: Current Data, Professional Advice, and Curiosa About Libraries and Library Services, pp. 303–313. American Library Association, Chicago (2006)
5. Caplan, P.: Metadata Fundamentals for all Librarians. American Library Association, USA (2003)
6. Parsian, M.: JDBC Metadata, MySQL, and Oracle Recipes: A Problem-Solution Approach. Apress, Berkeley (2006)
7. Cox, M., Ellsworth, D.: Managing Big Data for Scientific Visualization. Siggraph 97, Computer Graphics Annual Conference Series, Course 4, Exploring Gigabyte Datasets in Real-Time: Algorithms, Data Management, and Time-Critical Design. Assn for Computing Machinery, Los Angeles (1997)
8. Hahn, B., Zimmermann, C.: Visueller Atlas des Spitalalltags - Visualisierung organisatorischer und kommunikativer Abläufe im Patientenprozess. In: Mareis, C., Joost, G., and Kimpel, K. (eds.) entwerfen wissen produzieren. Designforschung im Anwendungskontext, pp. 271–291. Transcript, Bielefeld (2010)
9. Zabbix SIA: Zabbix. The Enterprise-class Monitoring Solution for Everyone. www.zabbix.com
10. The Cacti Group, Inc.: Cacti. the complete rrdtool-based graphing solution. http://www.cacti.net/
11. Ganglia Monitoring System. http://ganglia.info/
12. NuoDB, Inc.: NuoDB. http://www.nuodb.com/
13. Pivotal Software, Inc.: Pivotal HD. http://www.pivotal.io/big-data/pivotal-hd
14. Elasticsearch: Kibana. Visualize logs and time-stamped data. http://www.elasticsearch.org/overview/kibana/
15. Schulz, H.-J., Nocke, T.: Maschinelle Datananalyse im Informationszeitalter - Können oder müssen wir ihr vertrauen? Ordnungen des Denkens. Debatten um Wissenschaftstheorie und Erkenntniskritik, pp. 121–132. LIT Verlag, Berlin (2007)
16. Software Diagnostics Presents the Effectiveness Platform (2014)
17. MongoDB, Inc.: MongoDB MMS. Cloud Managed MongoDB. https://mms.mongodb.com/
18. Grillo, P.J.: Form, Function, and Design. Original Title: What Is Design? Paul Theobold and Company, Publisher, Chicago 1960. Dover Publications Inc., New York (1975)
19. Bernhard, T.: Wahrnehmung der Schönheit in der Architektur. epubli, Berlin (2012)
20. Naumann, A.: Raimer Jochims: FarbFormBeziehungen. Anschauliche Bedingungen seiner Identitätskonzeption. Königshausen & Neumann, Würzburg (2005)

21. Arnheim, R.: Art and visual perception: a psychology of the creative eye. 50th Anniversary Printing. Original edition: Art and Visual Perception: A Psychology of the Creative Eye. Universitiy of California Press, Berkeley and Los Angeles 1954. University of California Press (2004)
22. Pizlo, Z.: 3D Shape: Its Unique Place in Visual Perception. MIT Press, Massachusetts (2008)
23. Alexander, K.: Kompendium der visuellen Information und Kommunikation. Springer, Heidelberg (2013)
24. Neumann, E.: The Origins and History of Consciousness. Original Edition: Ursprungsgeschichte des Bewusstseins. Rascher Verlag Zurich 1949. Karnac Books, London (1989)

Rapid Model-Driven Annotation and Evaluation for Object Detection in Videos

Marc Ritter[1]([✉]), Michael Storz[2], Manuel Heinzig[1], and Maximilian Eibl[2]

[1] Junior Professorship Media Computing, Technische Universität Chemnitz,
09107 Chemnitz, Germany
{marc.ritter,manuel.heinzig}@informatik.tu-chemnitz.de
[2] Chair Media Informatics, Technische Universität Chemnitz,
09107 Chemnitz, Germany
{michael.storz,eibl}@informatik.tu-chemnitz.de

Abstract. Nowadays, the annotation of ground truth and the automated localisation and validation of objects in audiovisual media plays
an essential role to keep pace with the large data growth. A common
approach to train such classifiers is to integrate methods from machine
learning that often demand multiple thousands or millions of samples.
Therefore, we propose two components. The first constraints the annotation space by predefined models and allows the creation of ground truth
data while providing opportunities to annotate and interpolate objects in
keyframes or in-between by granting a user-friendly frame-wise access.
The graphical user-interface of the second component focuses on the
rapid validation of automatically pre-classified object instances in order
to alter the assignment of the class label or to remove false-positives to
clean-up the result list which has been successfully applied on the task
of Instance Search within the TRECVid evaluation campaign.

Keywords: Model-based annotation · Object detection · Instance
search · Rapid evaluation · Image and video processing · Big data

1 Introduction

One way to cope with the ever increasing amounts of audiovisual data recorded
day by day is the automatic detection and storage of object instances in databases in order to make large archives searchable. In the last decades, scientific
research has focused on the detection of specific object classes like faces and
pedestrians [1]. However, the creation of robust systems for such unconstrained
amounts of data still appears as a very challenging task even in the well-known
field of face detection [2]. Frequently, the mere complexity entails the need for
hundreds or thousands of intellectually selected positive training samples as well
as millions to billions of negative non-object samples while being utilized in
appearance-based machine learning algorithms.

Beyond that, the development of algorithms and systems for the automatic
detection of various object instances with a small sample size has been pur-
sued by the community of the *Text Retrieval Evaluation Campaign on Videos*

© Springer International Publishing Switzerland 2015
M. Antona and C. Stephanidis (Eds.): UAHCI 2015, Part I, LNCS 9175, pp. 464–474, 2015.
DOI: 10.1007/978-3-319-20678-3_45

(TRECVid) [3] for many years. Ordinarily, it is well-known that the intellectual annotation and localization of target objects [4] is a repetitive, time-consuming, demanding, but yet necessary and critical task when processing large data collections in order to determine the performance of automatic detection algorithms, draw assumptions over possible misfits, or identify areas of improvement.

The previous work of Ritter & Eibl [5] and Storz et al. [6] proposed a strategy to conduct image-based annotations of extracted keyframes after the application of shot boundary detection algorithms by using predefined models. While building on that work, this contribution introduces some handy methods to facilitate the creation of almost arbitrary ground-truth data while providing the means and opportunities for rapid model-driven annotations in videos by restricting the annotation space to specified properties of the underlying domain. Furthermore, a fast selection scheme is introduced to increase the speed in which the assessment and evaluation of object detection algorithms is performed.

The remainder of this paper is organized as follows: Sect. 2 gives an overview about other approaches from the literature concerning model-based annotation as a base methodology. Section 3 describes our approach for video annotation and the validation of outcomes yielded from automated detections of object classifiers in the context of a specified TRECVid use case scenario that is also evaluated shortly in Sect. 4. A brief summary and an outlook to future work in Sect. 5 concludes this contribution.

2   Related Work

In visual media we need algorithms to be able to classify a vast range of concepts. According to Forsyth et al. [7], we can differentiate visual concepts in *stuff* meaning materials (e.g. grass, road) and *things* meaning objects like cars or persons. The concepts can be content-independent (i.e. author name), content-dependent (e.g. texture, shape), and content-descriptive (semantics, shape is a car) [8]. These visual and theoretical differences between annotations open up a vast annotation space that lead to the development of a variety of different annotation tools. Tools and applications vary greatly from e.g. game based web applications like *ESP Game* [9] to fairly complex tools like the *LHI* annotation tool [10] that includes sophisticated methods for graph based segmentation, scene decomposition, and semantic annotation as well.

However, the usage of annotation models allows to cover a broad range of possible annotation types that are often directly related to different use cases. Specific use cases like video annotation or the verification and evaluation of object candidates that were detected and localized by a trained detector are described in the following paragraphs.

2.1   Model Based Annotation

Similarly to *ViPER-GT* [11] we apply annotation models to precisely define the amount and scope of information that needs to be annotated in visual media.

Models serve as a annotation template consisting of different geometric (e.g. bounding boxes or polygons) and semantic components like text called *model elements* [6].

The incorporation of such a model facilitates the workflow within the annotation process while reducing the necessary input of information to constraint properties. With regards to the annotation of objects and their position in an image this might comprise actions like adjusting marker points, determining the area of a bounding box or entering a textual caption. This procedure leads to a specific and dependable structure of the annotated results making them comparable even if the intellectual annotations are created collaboratively by multiple workers with differing experience.

2.2   Video Annotation

The annotation of video sequences can serve different purposes and the creation of a training or validation dataset for training object classifiers is only one of them. Tools like *Anvil* [12], *ELAN* [13], or *VCode* [14] focus on the annotation of speech or the coding of behaviour and interactions of actors. These most frequently used video analysis tools are applied to many different research domains like human-computer interaction, linguistics, and social sciences.

Another category comprises tools like *Advene* [15] and *VideoANT* [16] that facilitate the sharing, communication, and comprehension of video content by providing interfaces to comment, to discuss, and to link other media.

However, the most important category within the context of this contribution focuses on the aforementioned task of video annotation for the creation of training and validation datasets. The subsequent tools differ greatly in presentation style and in the range of functionality, but share the ability to create spatial annotations in videos.

VATIC [17] is a web annotation tool that can be used with *Mechanical Turk*[1] in order to outsource annotation tasks. In comparison to other tools, it offers a very reduced and easy to learn interface. After drawing a bounding box around an object, it offers a brief categorization of the object class (e.g. person or car) and allows to specify certain properties that for instance might be used to mark an object as occluded. Object annotation over time is accomplished by the intellectual masking of a small subset of frames and the automatic interpolation in-between. To the best of our knowledge, the tool does not differentiate between annotations that were created by hand or result from automated interpolations while lacking frame-wise access, whereas a modification of previous annotations may be challenging.

In contrast the *Semantic Video Annotation Suite (SVAS)* [18] offers a more complex interface with semi-automatic annotation capabilities. *SVAS* uses a automatic video preprocessing to detect shots, extract key frames and capture image features. In the keyframe based annotation process the video is divided into the detected shots. A *SIFT* based object and shot re-detection can be

---

[1] https://www.mturk.com, 19.02.2015.

applied to an intellectual object annotation in a keyframe to retrieve the specific object in other keyframes as well. An object tracking mechanism is used to track the object in between. The described process can effectively minimize the intellectual annotation effort assuming automatic annotation is accurate enough. According to the authors, accuracy decreases if object has low textural information, is small in size or moving, which is quite a common case in challenging object recognition tasks.

The video annotation tool *ViPER-GT* can either be used for intellectual annotation of video content or to view automatically generated markups. In a similar way to *VATIC*, annotation can be achieved via an interpolation approach that visualizes the intellectual annotations and interpolations likewise in a *timeline view* while allowing the definition of annotation models. Displayed in a spreadsheet view, it shows the current values of the selected frame like the location of a bounding box. Unfortunately the support for different video formats turns out to be minimalistic. Furthermore, interpolation proves to be slightly cumbersome since it requires the navigation of several context menus and the manual typing of frame numbers. Nevertheless, intellectually annotated frames are highlighted in the *timeline view* and can be adjusted easily.

All the aforementioned tools contain similar components since they are used to navigate in a video file, to display, or to employ some sort of annotation. A video player component is often composed of a control bar that allows to play, rewind and fast-forward the video and a graphical editor to create localized annotations like bounding boxes in a displayed frame. Most tools also visualize the occurrence of annotations over time in a *timeline view* by associating a row with an object or coded item. Usually, a colored section in the row of the timeline represents the time span of an occurrence. The linkage of *timeline view* and the video player allows for an annnotation-based video navigation.

Annotating objects on a frame by frame basis is prohibitively time consuming so that assisting mechanisms like linear interpolation, object tracking or even the application of computer vision algorithms for semi-automatic annotation are highly required. The mere availability of assisting mechanisms is not sufficient, they need to be easy to use. If large amounts of objects needs to be annotated, the tools must provide instruments to focus on the current work at hand and by enabling the user to hide annotations or their representations in the interface.

2.3   Evaluation of Detection Results

The aforementioned video annotation tools can be used to create ground truth data that is needed to automatically evaluate trained classifiers. But the creation of accurate ground truth data can be prohibitively time and resource consuming in large datasets on which evaluations are performed nowadays.

A convenient way to measure the quality of a trained classifier is to compare results with annotated ground truth. However, the creation of the ground truth is not always possible. With exemplary application to face labeling and in accordance to *Jain & Learned-Miller* [2, p. 4] it can be stated that "[f]or some image regions, deciding whether or not it presents a 'face' can be challenging.

Several factors such as low resolution, occlusion, and pose of the head may make this determination ambiguous." These findings are especially considered to be meaningful when dealing with large collections of video footage, where validation data might not be available. When considering the exemplary case of detecting frontal faces, the evaluation procedure boils down to a mere supervised reevaluation of all available face detections that were created with a certain classifier repeating the simple but yet not always distinct binary question: "Is a frontal face present in the shown image patch?"

This common situation demands different evaluation mechanisms that do not always require large amounts of ground truth data. Detections need to be scanned for false positives to assess the performance of a trained classifier and enable their improvement. Similarily photo management software like *iPhoto*[2] or *Picasa*[3] require the user to manually accept or decline the assignment of faces to specific persons which is proposed by an integrated face recognition algorithm.

For instance in *iPhoto*, users can select an already defined person whereupon the application retrieves and shows other similar faces from the dataset. Users then may accept or decline proposed faces by clicking on them once or twice respectively. This simple selection scheme allows a very fast evaluation of large amounts of faces. Moreover, this interaction concept can be easily applied to the evaluation of custom classifiers. It could also be regarded as a more concrete implementation of a more generalized scheme that assigns one of several predefined values (here accept or decline) to a specific object (in this case a detection). Hence, the concept can be used for the annotation of relevant position-independent object properties like occlusion or the color of objects. An application that incorporates this kind of functionality should focus on an easy to use interface in order to allow for rapid evaluation or annotation of potentially thousands of detections. Additionally, it should allow the user to customize the number and size of objects shown at the same time on the screen in order to find an adequate representation that is also simple to perceive to account for the large visual variations in classes and properties of different objects.

3   System Description

This section investigates the structures of our two main components: The *video annotation component* should enable the user to make use of predefined models in order to grant fast object annotations in videos whereas the main objective of the *evaluation component* consists in the validation of previously classified objects or properties that might be used to improve the performance of machine learning algorithms or to remove false-positives from data sets.

3.1   Video Annotation Component

In a first step we build a paper prototype of the *video annotation component* afterwards the prototype was refined in a usability tests with four students (two

---

[2] https://www.apple.com/de/mac/iphoto/, 19.02.2015.
[3] http://picasa.google.com/, 20.02.2015.

Fig. 1. The *video annotation component* consist of three parts. The *video player* (A) shows the annotations on the current frame. The *model instance list* (B) displays all available objects and their current values. The *timeline view* (C) visualizes all continuous annotations over time, differentiating manual from interpolated annotations.

domain experts). Although representing continuous media in interface mock-ups appears as rather difficult task, the handling of the static interface elements was effectively studied and led the omission of unused components. Most important functionality hidden in context menus was externalised into buttons to facilitate the usability.

Our proposed video annotation component (Fig. 1) consists of the three fundamental parts:

(A) The part of the *video player* shows annotations of the current frame. Colors correspond with object representations in the other parts. The player controls can be used to navigate within video. Besides the regular VCR like functionality (play, jump to start/end) the video can also be navigated frame wise or one can jump to the next intellectual annotation of a selected object.

(B) The *model instance list* on the righthand side represents objects in a row or block of a single color. The list shows all objects in the video file. While colored rows represent objects that are annotated in the current frame, grey rows represent the opposite. All rows can be expanded and collapsed to reveal or hide all model elements. Model element values always correspond to the current frame (like the position of a bounding box). Non changing properties can be marked as static.

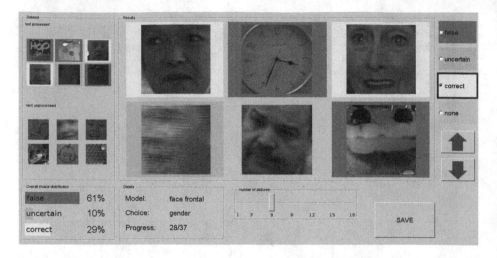

Fig. 2. The *evaluation component* allows the fast validation of detection results. A small subset of the detection results is shown in the center of the application including some statistics about the current state of the evaluation process (bottom left). Users can cycle through and assign the available classification labels to an image with a left mouse click. In uncertain situations, a right mouse click may be used to pop up the original image to display the surrounding context of the image patch.

(C) Similarly to the model instance list the rows in the *timeline view* correspond to the annotated objects. The timeline further indicates the time spans in which the object is annotated. A black line symbolizes an intellectual annotation. The colored space in-between denote linear interpolations between the reference points. The *timeline view* enables the user to switch between annotation modes like the intellectual annotation inside the player component and the interpolation inside the timeline between two or more manual annotations. Only continuous model elements are shown in the timeline. Timeline rows can be collapsed to view only the most relevant objects.

3.2 Evaluation Component

Similarly to the previous component, a paper prototype was developed prior to implementation. It was tested with the same four users from above. Major results showed that detections should be displayed separately and not solely as over-layed annotated rectangles in the original corresponding image. Furthermore, the assignment of the predefined options to the detections should apparently and intuitively made visible. Therefore, we decided to allow switching trough a given set of available options while continuously clicking on a detection result that appears to be slightly similar to interaction scheme within *iPhoto*.

The evaluation tools main workspace (see Fig. 2) is a section in the middle of the screen where the results are displayed in a rectangle. The number of pictures N displayed at a time can be changed by using the slider. The lefthand

Table 1. Results of our preliminary user study for the video annotation component in contrast to ViPER-GT on the task to annotate pedestrians in a video sequence of 500 frames.

Tool	Tester	Time (mm:ss)	Mean (Stddev)
Video annotation component	#1	10:58	12:33 (04:28)
	#2	08:05	
	#3	09:16	
	#4	16:02	
	#5	18:25	
ViPER-GT	#6	11:01	11:18 (01:53)
	#7	09:35	
	#8	13:19	

view contains thumbnails of the previous and next group of N image patches. In order to start the evaluation process, a user has to select a classification group that is derived from the the currently selected model. Consequently, the first N images are shown for annotation within the main window. A simple left click assigns the chosen label to the image patch. A right-mouse click can be used to pop-up the original image yielding the highlighted detection inside. The up and down arrows on the right side allow a group-wise navigation through the data collection. Besides, we decided to add a statistical overview about the distribution of the choices that have already been made on the bottom left side, indicated by the length of horizontal color bars and the numbers shown, respectively. Summarized information depict the selected model, the choice and the progress as well.

4   Preliminary Evaluation

A small preliminary user study with eight participants (three female, five male) was conducted for a performance comparison between our *video annotation component* (five testers) and ViPER-GT (three testers). Participants were given a brief introduction into the application and could familiarize themselves with the interaction by applying several manual annotations and linear interpolations in between, before starting the actual scenario, where they had to annotate three walking persons in a 500 frame video clip that is provided by ViPER-GT.

The mean annotation time of *video annotation component* exceeded that of ViPER-GT and therefore performed slightly weaker, but had the best completion time. However, annotation strategy and annotator motivation influenced the annotation time greatly and are mainly responsible for the diverging completion times (see Table 1). Especially motion turning points of objects or video segments of no, less or irregular motion patterns usually compromise linear interpolations and therefore reduce the accuracy and usability of straight interpolating techniques.

Ritter et al. [19] conducted a study that uses the principles of the second component in the interactive part of last years evaluation of *TRECVid Instance Search*[4] [3], whereas an instance can be roughly denoted as the occurrence of a specific object in a shot in the video footage. This main task consists in retrieving up to 1.000 shots of given instance within the large archive of 464 hours of the British soap opera *BBC East Enders*. This comprises 24 different categories each resembling up to four instances that were given by sample pictures together with a segmented binary image, a short text description and a sample clip file. The automated detectors from the authors retrieved 1.000 classified instance candidates for each category. Eight human annotators were given a period with a maximum of 15 min to validate the specific object instances in each category and eliminate false-positives. This work was achieved by using the proposed approach yielding to an average completion time of 11 min per category.

5   Summary and Future Work

We presented two components to speed up the process of object annotation in videos and the validation of large data collections with multiple thousands of previously classified object candidates. Our preliminary evaluations showed the potential usefulness of these approaches. However, larger evaluations with more participants could be helpful to draw more reliable conclusions for the video annotation component. Moreover, the presented framework could benefit from the integration of semi-automated methods for object tracking like block-matching within automatically detected shots. A combination with any well-known object recognition descriptors like SIFT operators within a bag-of-word approach [20] should prove effective in order to retrieve the object from other shots of the video footage. Both components improve the ground truth or the availability of object training samples that could at least be integrated as feedback components into the machine learning workflow from Storz et al. [6] in order to consecutively optimize already trained classifiers.

Acknowledgments. This work was partially accomplished within the projects *ValidAX – Validation of the AMOPA and XTRIEVAL* framework (VIP0044), and *localizeIT* (03IPT608X) funded by the *Federal Ministry of Education and Research* (BMBF, Germany) in the program of *InnoProfile Entrepreneurial Regions*, and the *Research Training Group CrossWorlds - Connecting Virtual and Real Social Worlds* (GRK1780), funded by the DFG (Deutsche Forschungsgesellschaft), Germany. We would like to thank Gerald Meier and Markus Keller for their contributions.

References

1. Dollár, P., Wojek, C., Schiele, D., Perona, P.: Pedestrian detection: an evaluation of the state of the art. IEEE Trans. Pattern Anal. Mach. Intell. **34**(4), 743–761 (2012)

[4] http://www-nlpir.nist.gov/projects/tv2014/tv2014.html#ins, 20.02.2015.

2. Jain, V., Learned-Miller, E.: FDDB: a benchmark for face detection in uncon-strained settings/University of Massachusetts, Amherst, Technical report (UM-CS-2010-009), 19 February 2015, pp. 11 (2010). http://vis-www.cs.umass.edu/fddb/fddb.pdf

3. Smeaton, A.F., Over, P., Kraaij, W.: Evaluation campaigns and TRECVid. In: Proceedings of the 8th ACM International Workshop on Multimedia Information Retrieval, pp. 321–330. ACM, New York (2006)

4. Dasiopoulou, S., Giannakidou, E., Litos, G., Malasioti, P., Kompatsiaris, Y.: A survey of semantic image and video annotation tools. In: Paliouras, G., Spyropoulos, C.D., Tsatsaronis, G. (eds.) Multimedia Information Extraction. LNCS, vol. 6050, pp. 196–239. Springer, Heidelberg (2011)

5. Ritter, M., Eibl, M.: An extensible tool for the annotation of videos using seg-mentation and tracking. In: Marcus, A. (ed.) HCII 2011 and DUXU 2011, Part I. LNCS, vol. 6769, pp. 295–304. Springer, Heidelberg (2011)

6. Storz, M., Ritter, M., Manthey, R., Lietz, H., Eibl, M.: Annotate. Train. Evaluate. A unified tool for the analysis and visualization of workflows in machine learning applied to object detection. In: Kurosu, M. (ed.) HCII/HCI 2013, Part V. LNCS, vol. 8008, pp. 196–205. Springer, Heidelberg (2013)

7. Forsyth, D.A., Malik, J., Fleck, M.M., Greenspan, H., Leung, T., Belongie, S., Carson, C., Bregler, C.: Finding pictures of objects in large collections of images. In: Ponce, J., Hebert, M., Zisserman, A. (eds.) ECCV-WS 1996. LNCS, vol. 1144, pp. 335–360. Springer, Heidelberg (1996)

8. Hanbury, A.: A survey of methods for image annotation. J. Vis. Lang. Comput. **19**(5), 617–627 (2006)

9. Ahn, L., von Dabbish, L.: Labeling images with a computer game. In: Proceedings of the 2004 Conference on Human Factors in Computing Systems, pp. 319–326 (2004)

10. Yao, B., Yang, X., Zhu, S.-C.: Introduction to a large-scale general purpose ground truth database: methodology, annotation tool and benchmarks. In: Yuille, A.L., Zhu, S.-C., Cremers, D., Wang, Y. (eds.) EMMCVPR 2007. LNCS, vol. 4679, pp. 169–183. Springer, Heidelberg (2007)

11. Doermann, D., Mihalcik, D.: Tools and techniques for video performance evalua-tion. In: Proceedings of the 15th International Conference on Pattern Recognition, vol. 4, pp. 167–170 (2000)

12. Kipp, M.: Spatiotemporal coding in ANVIL. In: Proceedings of the 6th Interna-tional Conference on Language Resources and Evaluation (2008)

13. Brugman, H., Russel, A.: Annotating multimedia/multi-modal resources with ELAN. In: Proceedings of the 4th International Conference on Language Resources and Evaluation (2004)

14. Hagedorn, J., Hailpern, J., Karahalios, K. G.: VCode and VData: illustrating a new framework for supporting the video annotation workflow. In: Proceedings of the Working Conference on Advanced Visual Interfaces, pp. 317–321. ACM (2008)

15. Aubert, O., Pri, Y.: Advene: active reading through hypervideo. In: Proceedings of the 16th ACM Conference on Hypertext and Hypermedia, pp. 235–244. ACM (2005)

16. Hosack, B.: VideoANT: extending online video annotation beyond content delivery. TechTrends **54**(3), 45–49 (2010)

17. Vondrick, C., Patterson, D., Ramanan, D.: Efficiently scaling up crowdsourced video annotation. Int. J. Comput. Vis. **101**(1), 184–204 (2013)

18. Schallauer, P., Ober, S., Neuschmied, H.: Efficient semantic video annotation by object and shot re-detection. In: Posters and Demos Session, 2nd International Conference on Semantic and Digital Media Technologies, Koblenz (2008)
19. Ritter, M., Heinzig, M., Herms, R., Kahl, S., Richter, D., Manthey, R., Eibl, M.: Technische Universitt Chemnitz at TRECVid Instane Search 2014. In: TRECVid Workshop 2014, 10–12 November 2014, Orlando, Florida, pp. 8 (2014). http:// www-nlpir.nist.gov/projects/tvpubs/tv14.papers/tuc_mi.pdf. 01 March 2015
20. Jiang, W., Zhao, Z., Chen, Q., Zhao, J., Huang, Y., Zhao, X., Li, L., Zhao, Y., Su, F., Cai, A.: BUPT-MCPRL at TRECVid 2014 Instance Search Task. In: TRECVid Workshop 2014, 10–12 November 2014, Orlando, Florida, pp. 22 (2014). http://www-nlpir.nist.gov/projects/tvpubs/tv14.slides/bupt-mcprl.tv14. ins.slides.pdf. 01 March 2015

SweetBuildingGreeter: A Demonstration of Persuasive Technology for Public Space

Ted Selker[1(✉)], Shih-Yuan Yu[2], Che-Wei Liang[2], and Jane Hsu[2]

[1] University of California, Berkeley, CA, USA
Ted.Selker@gmail.com
[2] National Taiwanese University, Taipei, Taiwan
{louis29418401, a50119729}@gmail.com,
yjhsu@csie.ntu.edu.tw

Abstract. This paper shows how a persuasive interactive system can impact community behavior. SweetBuildingGreeter includes an interactive display and a gumball dispenser with environmental sensors. It provides media and tangible rewards. It has been located in buildings' public entry areas to encourage people to be conscious of and to empower saving energy. What makes the system ignored or engaging? The first experiment attracted participants to fill out a questionnaire to dispense candy and display problems which could be fixed in the building. Newcomers to the building filled out the questionnaire, but few returned to do it again. The second experiment provided images of energy savings and was effective at making people aware of energy issues, but it did not change their likelihood of using the system. Soliciting people with sound was more effective. This was especially true in a case where people had earlier negative experiences.

Keywords: Persuasive computing · Green technology ACM H.5.2 information interfaces and presentation · UI styles · Input devices and strategies

1 Introduction

While incentives can cause behavior modifications [19] automated systems report successfully changing behavior or beliefs [4, 7]. Human energy usage is substantial and is implicated in global warming [12]. Indeed, 30 % of energy used by a building is caused by people's actions that could easily be modified or reduced in the building [20].

Can persuasion technology change people's behavior and affect energy usage in a community? We tested this with the SweetFeedback Reward System, a computer-controlled gumball delivery system and environmental sensing platform [10]. It was designed to be easily deployed on people's desks throughout a building to create an incrementally expandable sensor and feedback network. This paper uses the Sweet-Feedback platform in public instead of the personal space use it was designed for.

Behavior change requires, among other things, a recognition that it matters. The Fogg Behavior Model [6] predicts that the requirements for a person to perform an identified behavior include (1) enough motivation, (2) the user's ability to perform the behavior, and (3) the need for a trigger in order to guarantee that people will achieve the target behavior. All three factors should be present for targeted behavior to be performed and learned by a person.

© Springer International Publishing Switzerland 2015
M. Antona and C. Stephanidis (Eds.): UAHCI 2015, Part I, LNCS 9175, pp. 475–486, 2015.
DOI: 10.1007/978-3-319-20678-3_46

1.1 Related Work

A number of research projects aim to perform persuasion technology with tangible feedback. BinCam installed a camera underneath a garbage bin lid and uploaded the photos taken onto Facebook whenever a user threw garbage into BinCam [22]. The system worked to persuade users to engage in self-reflection of their waste management and recycling habits through social media. The Chocolate Machine applied Ego Depletion theory to show that people can be trained to resist eating by dispensing the chocolate at scheduled intervals [13]. Utmi engaged students on campus to help with exam grading tasks to successfully use a special public vending machine to give tangible non-monetary feedback [9]. Utami attracted many students to resolve expert tasks, and they performed better than a single student expert. Our work focuses on also using tangible feedback, but also uses auditory and visional techniques to attract participants.

Many previous studies have revealed the major challenges: how to entice passers-by to approach the display, how to make them aware of the interactive features, and finally how to motivate them to actively interact with it. The "first click" enticement problem must be solved to achieve any of the other goals [3, 11, 14, 15]. To begin addressing this problem requires understanding the nature of public engagement interactives. A public display must work with a first-time user and a user that has seen it before [11]. Passers-by are typically carrying out other activities [3]. Simply providing attractive appearance, utility, usability, and likability may not be enough to draw people to engage with it. Unlike other computing technologies, interaction with public displays does not start with the interaction itself [15].

To get a person to engage, (1), they must notice the interactive, (2), they must see the interactive as interesting to them, and (3), they must decide that they can interact with it without fear of public embarrassment, intimidation, disrupting their intended activity, or offending someone they are with [14]. They must then understand how to interact and commit to interacting. Finally, they must follow though to get the value of the interaction. Similar to this, Brignull & Rogers [3] defined three activity spaces in respect to the flow of interaction within a crowd: peripheral awareness, where people notice the display; focal awareness, where people engage in social activities associated with the display, such as talking or gesturing, or in other words performing indirect interaction; and direct interaction, where people actively interact with the display.

Several studies about how to improve making a public display noticeable and enticing [14] showed text more effective than icons, color more effective than grey-scale, and static imagery more effective than animation. Ju et al. [11] found that physical gestures significantly attract more looks and use of an information kiosk than verbal gestures alone. Oftentimes, the audience doesn't seek the public displays actively, but discovers it incidentally, which Dix [5] called "incidental interaction". Spatial configuration indeed matters; a public display is better put near traffic flow in order to ensure a steady stream of people [15] and may trigger more incidental interactions.

Peripheral awareness, regardless of how it is gained, has a significant impact on people's initial understanding of a public display. Interactive displays often fail to deal appropriately with the social inhibition associated with interaction in public [15].

"Display blindness" is a phenomenon related to audience expectation: if the audience expects that the display shows uninteresting content, they tend to ignore it [8]. Another phenomenon discovered by Kukka et al. [14] is "display avoidance," when people intentionally avoid looking at the display to avoid a deprioritized engagement.

Those phenomena are highly related to the social context. Akpan et al. [2] explored the role of social context in the success of an interactive public display. The idea is based on the notions of "space" and "place" [8]. A *space* is a physical, spatial structure which affects humans' activity and behavior. A *place*, on the other hand, attaches social meanings, which may include understanding, experience, cultural expectations and norms, and patterns of behavior. SweetFeedback first focused on the desk *place*. The SweetBuildingGreeter tests it in a vestibule *space*. Past studies show how individual's interpretation of "place" instead of "space" to a large degree determined whether they would actively engage with a display [8]. The most successful places to engage passers-by were those where the social context supports "comfort space" or "license to play" with the interactive. This is a challenge that SweetBuildingGreeter must face.

Previous studies have also explored various technical and social aspects regarding engagement. The contribution of social context within space and place has shown interactivity often relies on incidental interactions; however, "forcing" passers-by to notice may fail to move people from being spectators to being active users [2]. This limits the explorations as it may disturb the nature of interactivity in the place. Our approach is to extend the goal of interaction in a space to appropriately engage one or a few people [3]. Our work moves beyond screen color or/and content, attempting to entice a passerby to view a display in a space. Can persuasive words and physical feedback entice people to perform important altruistic community service?

How to engage passers-by in a public area, with the goal of helping save energy? Our first model required a user to log in with a QR code on their phone, then close a window to receive a candy reward [10]. It added steps and time to the simple act of closing a window. An alternative might be a simple flag that flies into the hall attracting attention to the open window more concretely. Could SweetFeedback be as concrete and more rewarding?

2 The SweetBuildingGreeter Scenario and System

SweetBuildingGreeter system is divided into several components in Fig. 1. The system utilizes the SweetFeedback reward system [10, 21], which is a gumball dispenser device with an Arduino board. It runs a program to sense and react to the environment. A client on a PC communicates between SweetFeedback and the supervisor server. A server program makes decisions from a user's behavior, environmental data, and interaction. A web graphical interface presents information to the user (Fig. 2).

A PC complements the Arduino to add an interactive display, voiced comments, a people-recognizing camera, and Bluetooth network communication. Processing.org is used to write a Java program to manage the communication between the gumball machine and the PC [18]. For example, when the server sends a capital B to the gumball machine, the gumball machine sends calibrated sensor data to the server's database repository. This program reads sensors and manages the timing to give audio

Fig. 1. The SweetFeedback reward framework.

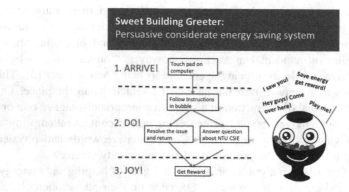

Fig. 2. The small poster describes how to play with the system in just three steps.

Fig. 3. Screensaver comics to make people aware of energy

or tangible feedback to users. When a user wins a reward, the program sends a capital A to the serial port to control the dispensing motor. The server display might also show rewards by an animation.

As well as the SweetFeedback sensors, the PC scans nearby Bluetooth-based devices for identifying users and integrating a transportation app. OpenCV [16] is used to interpret webcam data to detect the presence of a person or people. The camera program was further developed to differentiate when to attempt to engage people by applying blob detection. If it notices that there are more than two people, it does not try to intrude or distract them. Without a model of peer pressure, our theory is that people in groups are less likely to be interested or able to take their attention away from the other people to be able or willing to actually focus on a building problem, especially one that is trying to change their behavior.

SweetBuildingGreeter stores user and building models and behavior in a server. The server is implemented in a Python Flask framework, and it provides several restful API to client applications. A MySQL database stores user behavioral data. The feed-back mechanism, environment problem detection, and verification is evaluated by this server. Whenever a user fixes an environment problem, such as turning off the light, the server knows it by acquiring the sensor data from the sensor data repository to check if the problem still exists. Once the problem is solved, the server waits for the person to go back to the gumball machine and rewards him or her with visual imagery, sound, or candies. This application server also provides a webpage as a user interface (Figs. 4 and 5). Several iterations made a simpler and clearer interface, with user messages that are easier to understand. The main view of the interface is comprised of a map diagram of the building and a caricatured drawing of a gumball machine. The map diagram shows the location of a problem with a blinking red spot, to let the user identify where to go to solve the problem. Also, it visualizes the sensor data by showing people and light bulbs on the map. The drawing of the gumball machine has speaking bubbles over it, asking the person to do things or answer questions.

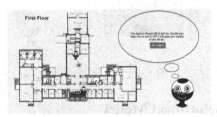

Fig. 4. The problem map

The sensor data from the gumball machine is stored in a local database, including light data, temperature, sound level data and window open/close data. Furthermore, we started with a third-party sensor repository from another research group to get all the environmental information for the campus. They provided several kinds of restful APIs for a variety of sensor data queries, especially for the real-time light sensor and motion sensor data. Whenever the server needs to check for environmental problems, the server checks the third-party sensor data repository and gets real-time data.

2.1 Persuasive Application Design

"Turn off the light" was our example scenario to test our persuasive system. The server program checks the status of local sensor repository and third-party sensor network repository periodically and performs simple environmental diagnosis to verify if a light is in correct state. If a motion sensor detects that there is no one in a room but the light is on, the server program will show the problem on the map. We want passers-by to notice the problems on the screen, use it to guide them to solve them, and get a reward. When a user chooses a target problem and clicks the button, "Yes, I will take it", our server program begins to monitor the target light. When it detects the problem has been solved, the server program sends a reward message. The server program will estimate how long it takes for the problem to be solved (walking to the room to turn off the light and walking back to the machine) after the button "Yes, I will take it" is pressed. It senses with Bluetooth or time that the person is back and deliver the reward when appropriate.

2.2 Questionnaire Application

When there is no pressing environmental issue in the building, the system teaches users about their building, campus environment and energy use. The drawing on the side of graphical user interface shows a question for passers-by (Fig. 5), with four possible answers. If the user does not select the correct answer, we enable them to retry until they get the right one. They then get rewarded with candy.

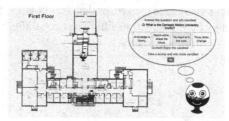

Fig. 5. The questionnaire

3   A Persuasive Behavioral Model

Initially, the SweetFeedback reward system was designed to be a personal persuasion process. For use in a public space, it was deployed with a secured laptop, a cloth draped stand, and a sign. OpenKiosk was installed in the laptop [17], which simplified the way users interact with SweetBuildingGreeter's web interface.

After several days of short experiments, we found that only a few people would use the system. We thought maybe it was because they didn't know they could use it or how to use it, so we made a small poster describing the flow of the process (Fig. 3). It attempted to attract people and show them that they are welcome to use the machine.

The process was: (1) *Arrive* - touch the pad to dismiss the energy slideshow screen saver; (2) *Do* - solve the environmental problem or answer the questionnaire; (3) *Joy* - if 1 and 2 are done correctly, get the reward.

We then wondered if changing the content of the poster to tell people to try the new system would make people curious about the new system and come to try it out. So we waited for a few days and changed the previous poster to a new poster with a cute gumball machine saying, "Try out the new experiment."

The system provides motivations for users based on a behavioral model to persuade energy-efficient behaviors; the gumball dispenser device will give candies as the major reward if users follow the interaction flow for SweetBuildingGreeter. The biggest changes in moving from a personal to a public persuasive system were motivation for engagement, enough trigger and higher simplicity for the performance of persuasive behavior. There was also a camera with an OpenCV program that can distinguish between one person approaching or several people approaching. The gumball machine tries to be noticed, to engage a person by triggering the voice on the laptop when it detects them approaching.

In idle time, the kiosk display also showed motivational comics found from 9GAG [1], Google, with the message of energy-saving and green technology, to motivate users to think about their energy behaviors. These comics were more attractive to passers-by than the screen saver that only displayed a simple message like, "Save energy and get reward." To better attract people, the screen saver was turned into a comic slide show with images about energy saving and candy, and with words inviting them to try it out by touching the trackpad (Fig. 3).

When the camera detects a passerby, the system would attempt to beckon them with two different audio probes tested: "Help me!" or "Try out the new experiment and save energy!" We added a voice to attract the person.

4 Experiments

The effectiveness of SweetBuildingGreeter in engaging people and persuading energy-saving behavior was first tested at a small campus with about 300 people including MS students, PhD students, staff, and visitors. A participant sees a visualization of the building's environmental condition (Fig. 4); a bubble states how to solve a problem. The supervising server monitors changes depending on the environmental condition, and makes decisions about giving rewards. After the interaction, the participant could fill out a survey to get more candy. The survey asked how participants felt about the system, the least useful feature in the system, what got their attention to interact, the rating of each feature, etc. We also spent a few mornings observing how different interventions (slide show or voice) affected how many passers-by would approach it. Finally, we conducted a user study and interviewed people about their experiences with the system.

5 Results

The system was deployed for 6 weeks. The data shows that in the beginning many people were attracted to our system (Fig. 6). Engagement decreased as people were repeatedly exposed to it, presumably because the novelty had worn off. The rate of correctly answered questions improved over time, shown in Fig. 6. This indicates that people did learn about their campus and building environment.

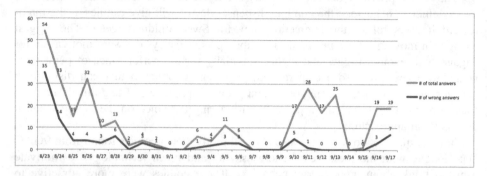

Fig. 6. New student first tried the system on 8/23. The number of wrong answers decreased because people learned and shared the information. Usage also decreased.

As the results show (see Table 1), version 1 and 3 did not attract anyone to the system with a poster. Voice worked better in triggering the behavior, as we see in versions 2 and 4; we succeeded in beckoning 2 out of 15 and 5 out of 20 passers-by respectively to look at our system. Version 4 was the most successful at beckoning, perhaps because it also said that there was a new experiment. Version 4 also had 3 out of 20 passers-by not only look at, but actually interact with our system and complete the process to save energy. These results show that the voice, a broadcast medium, is a more powerful feature to beckon people than the poster.

Table 1. Attracting people U.S. Version 1: a poster only. Version 2: "Help me." Version 3: New poster without the voice. Version 4: "Try the experiment and save energy."

Version	Ignored	Stared & walked	Use	Total
Ver. 1	16	0	0	16
Ver. 2	15	2	0	17
Ver. 3	20	0	0	20
Ver. 4	12	5	3	20

All participants were asked to help us fill out a survey to provide their feelings and suggestions about SweetBuildingGreeter; 16 were collected. Participants rated the poster as the least useful feature. The blue bar charts show what did get their attention (see Fig. 7). Surprisingly, most of the participants did not state that the voice had attracted them. They stated that the slide show or the promise of candies had attracted them, when our data shows that it was the voice promising something new that brought them to the system.

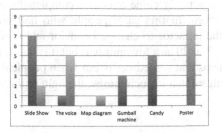

Fig. 7. Blue bars: "What got their attention." Red bars: "The least useful feature." (Color figure online)

Our final set of experiments were performed with students in Taiwan. It included versions 1, 2, and 4 (Table 2). All Taiwan students encountered a building problem (a window that needed to be closed). 7 out of 23 passers-by took a look at our system in version 1. More than half the passers-by looked at our system in versions 2 and 4. 4 out of 20 passers-by in version 2 and 2 out of 30 in version 4 used the system to close the window (Fig. 8).

Table 2. Attracting people Taiwan. Version 1: a poster only. Version 2: "Help me." Version 4: "Try the experiment and save energy."

Version	Ignored	Stared	Checked	Total
1	15	7	1	23
2	2	13	5	20
4	8	15	7	30

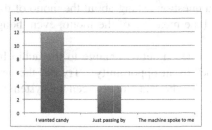

Fig. 8. "Why did you use the Sweet Building Greeter today?" People said they wanted candy but the beckoning sound making a request got them to come.

Still, because they had previously not associated any opportunity they could do for the building with the previous system, they may have thought they had already used the gumball machine and didn't imagine they would get anything new by taking time with it again.

We then tried a new auditory message, "Try out the new experiment and save energy." Of 20 people, 3 actually came over and completed the process of turning off the light in the other room. In this case, people who had not responded to earlier systems responded to the attractor to change behavior and used it to solve a building problem. One might see 3 of 20 as a low number, but it is not, for the goal of the system is to solve simple problems that sometimes occur when people don't take responsibility for the building. We realized that in such things, the light or thermostat only needs to be dealt with episodically.

6   Discussion

We have described a platform for increasing awareness of energy use and promoting behavior to save energy in a public space. The system could use audio feedback that sounds like candy being dispensed... or some other sound or stated affirmation instead of candy, so as not to overwhelm users with too much candy in their experience.

Adding a camera that made something happen when someone arrived made a huge improvement in people's willingness to attend to the kiosk. The system evolved to include a continually animating attractor that shows where the problems are in the building graphically.

The addition of a quiz about energy use in the building and on campus succeeded in attracting people.

Adding a slide-show of comics that would run between interactions made the system more noticeable, but an audio attractor was the most effective beckoner to get them to interact.

Our camera is designed to welcome people that are alone, but not people that are together. We anticipate that such groups don't want to wait around for one member to go turn off the lights for others.

The system did make people consider the environment and learn about their campus. A student saw a question asking about the motto of the campus. He turned to his friends and discussed the meaning of the motto, even though he already knew the motto.

The last experiment tested a subtle change to the audio beckon, from a request, "Come over and help me" to an opportunity, "Try out the new experiment and save energy." This caused people who had already seen the system to stop and work with it.

7   Conclusion

The overall purpose of SweetBuildingGreeter is solving building problems, not attracting every user. If the system is working correctly, the lights might be turned off a few times a day by the system's intervention. Statements of opportunity instead of requests were crucial. The gumball machine was shown to be useful in many ways; the installation was a community focus that people used to learn about their campus and become more aware of energy saving.

As we contemplate the many persuasive applications that have been built and tested, we come to important questions of place and space. Which interactivities are useful for a private desk experience and which are useful for a public experience? For the desk environment, SweetFeedback includes a number of personal performance monitoring and feedback applications. If the feedback occurs too often or requires a person to engage too often it will be distracting. The public interface would most naturally present different and social experiences. The SweetBuilding interface may succeed by making everyone aware of its ability to remind them of group commitments and a culture of energy savings. This experiment showed that audio beckoning was a necessary part of this peripheral computing system's mode of communication to attract participants to interact with the system to save energy. Public interfaces for green interaction can succeed at episodically engage while staying a focus of interest and energy savings. We further show that even when tangible rewards are present, active graphics and motivational sound are helpful at attracting users.

Acknowledgements. This paper is a tribute to the generosity of the Japanese government for paying for Chihiro Suga to come work at CMU Silicon Valley for a summer to create the first Sweetfeedback system and software. Equally valuable was Jane Hsu, chairperson of National Taiwan University, supporting Ken 梁哲瑋, and Yu Louis' trip to CMU Silicon Valley to work on SweetFeedback and SweetBuilding.

References

1. 9GAG. http://9gag.com/
2. Akpan, I., Marshall, P., Bird, J., Harrison, D.: Exploring the effects of space and place on engagement with an interactive installation. In: Proceedings of the SIGCHI Conference on Human Factors in Computing Systems, pp. 2213–2222. ACM (2013)
3. Brignull, H., Rogers, Y.: Enticing people to interact with large public displays in public spaces. In: Proceedings of INTERACT, vol. 3, pp. 17–24 (2003)
4. Chiu, M.-C., Chang, S.-P., Chang, Y.-C., Chu, H.-H., Chen, C.C.-H., Hsiao, F.-H., Ko, J.-C.: Playful bottle: a mobile social persuasion system to motivate healthy water intake. In: Proceedings of the 11th International Conference on Ubiquitous Computing, pp. 185–194. ACM, New York (2009)
5. Dix, A.: Beyond intention-pushing boundaries with incidental interaction. In: Proceedings of Building Bridges: Interdisciplinary Context-Sensitive Computing, Glasgow University, vol. 9 (2002)
6. Fogg, B.J.: A behavior model for persuasive design. In: Proceedings of the 4th International Conference on Persuasive Technology, p. 40. ACM, New York (2009)
7. Fogg, B.J.: Persuasive technology: using computers to change what we think and do. Ubiquity **2002** (2002). Article No. 5, doi:10.1145/764008.763957
8. Harrison, S., Dourish, P.: Re-Place-ing space: the roles of place and space in collaborative systems. In: Proceedings of the 1996 ACM Conference on Computer Supported Cooperative Work, pp. 67–76. ACM (1996)

9. Heimerl, K., Gawalt, B., Chen, K., Parikh, T., Hartmann, B.: Community sourcing: engaging local crowds to perform expert work via physical kiosks. In: Proceedings of the SIGCHI Conference on Human Factors in Computing Systems, pp. 1539–1548. ACM (2012)

10. Huang, Y.-C., Tsai, B.-L., Wang, C.-I., Yu, S.-Y., Liang, C.-W., Hsu, J.Y., Selker, T.: Leveraging persuasive feedback mechanism for problem solving. In: 2013 AAAI Spring Symposium Series (2013)

11. Ju, W., Sirkin, D.: Animate objects: how physical motion encourages public interaction. In: Ploug, T., Hasle, P., Oinas-Kukkonen, H. (eds.) Persuasive 2010. LNCS, vol. 6137, pp. 40–51. Springer, Heidelberg (2010)

12. Karl, T.R., Trenberth, K.E.: Modern global climate change. Science **302**(5651), 1719–1723 (2003)

13. Kehr, F., Hassenzahl, M., Laschke, M., Diefenbach, S.: A transformational product to improve self-control strength: the chocolate machine. In: Proceedings of the SIGCHI Conference on Human Factors in Computing Systems, pp. 689–694. ACM (2012)

14. Kukka, H., Oja, H., Kostakos, V., Gonçalves, J., Ojala, T.: What makes you click: exploring visual signals to entice interaction on public displays. In: Proceedings of the SIGCHI Conference on Human Factors in Computing Systems, pp. 1699–1708. ACM (2013)

15. Muller, J., Alt, F., Michelis, D., Schmidt, A.: Requirements and design space for interactive public displays. In: Proceedings of the International Conference on Multimedia, pp. 1285–1294. ACM (2010)

16. OpenCV. http://opencv.org/

17. OpenKiosk. https://www.mozdevgroup.com/products/openkioskdistro.html/

18. Processing. http://processing.org/

19. Fill, J.H., Brown, B.S.: Letters on B. F. Skinner's "Beyond Freedom and Dignity". J. Contemp. Psychother. **4**(2), 126–130 (1972)

20. ENERGY STAR: Commercial real estate: an overview of energy use and energy efficiency opportunities

21. Sweetfeedback. http://www.sweetfeedback.com/

22. Thieme, A., Comber, R., Miebach, J., Weeden, J., Kramer, N., Lawson, S., Olivier, P.: We've bin watching you: designing for reflection and social persuasion to promote sustainable lifestyles. In: Proceedings of the SIGCHI Conference on Human Factors in Computing Systems, pp. 2337–2346. ACM (2012)

Speech Enabled Ontology Graph Navigation and Editing

Dimitris Spiliotopoulos[1(✉)], Athanasios Dalianis[2],
and Dimitris Koryzis[3]

[1] Distributed Computing Systems, Institute of Computer Science Foundation
for Research and Technology – Hellas, Heraklion, Greece
dspiliot@ics.forth.gr
[2] Innovation Lab, Athens Technology Centre, Athens, Greece
t.dalianis@atc.gr
[3] Hellenic Parliament, Athens, Greece
dkoryzis@parliament.gr

Abstract. Graphs are commonly used to represent multiple relations between many items. Ontology graphs implement the connections and constraints between levels of interdependence between nodes; the nodes themselves being the members of the data types. As part of a design-for-all approach, this paper reports on the use of speech for ontology graph navigation and editing. The graphs can be fully created by using voice commands only, essentially creating large and complex ontologies by speech. The formative usability evaluation and user involvement experimentation results revealed that the introduction of speech, greatly enhanced specific parts of the navigation and improved the speed of editing, especially for the trivial, yet time consuming tasks of editing large and complex graphs.

Keywords: Speech · Ontologies · Graph editing · User interface design

1 Introduction

Graphical representation of complex relations between items has been used in abundance in the recent years. Social graphs, in particular, may result in very large structures that deploy techniques such as zoom and pan and instant search for users to be able to browse effectively [1, 2]. Ontology graph is one of several ways of authoring and browsing ontologies, from a range that spans from list, trees and tables to 3D representations [3]. To ensure the visibility of the relations between the entities and the visual recognition of clusters, graphs are opted as an optimal means to visualise for almost all (small to very large) representations.

Recently, graphs have been used as part of advanced web interfaces that were designed for authoring complex ontology applications such as policy modelling [4]. As the graphs become large, problem arise for users that need to view specific entities or clusters. Depending on the size and complexity, ontology graphs may become too hard to follow, especially during the authoring of the ontology itself. Taking a few steps back, the new problem becomes proportionally larger as the size of the graph grows. In

© Springer International Publishing Switzerland 2015
M. Antona and C. Stephanidis (Eds.): UAHCI 2015, Part I, LNCS 9175, pp. 487–494, 2015.
DOI: 10.1007/978-3-319-20678-3_47

application-specific approaches like the one mentioned before, nodes have names that can be as large as sentences. Adding new nodes and relations becomes cumbersome even when the graphs are medium sized, as in Fig. 1.

This work implements and evaluates a speech-enabled navigation and editing approach to enhance the user experience of authors of complex ontology graphs. The following sections present the design rationale and requirements, the set of speech commands that were implemented and the evaluation of the speech based interface compared as part of a new two-modal solution from the initial traditional web interface.

2   Design Considerations

For our design, an existing web interface that was designed to author ontology graphs was used [4]. The aim of the web authoring interface was to enable non-technically proficient authors from diverse work environments (parliamentary assistants, policy makers, crowdsourcing private sector, students) to create domains and policy models with the data that will drive the collection of documents from news pages and social media (Facebook, Tweeter), the sentiment analysis of the collected data sets and the argument extraction. That information is then fed back to the authoring environment for the fine-tuning and later extension of the models [5].

Figure 1 depicts a typical policy model authored and viewed on the aforementioned web interface.

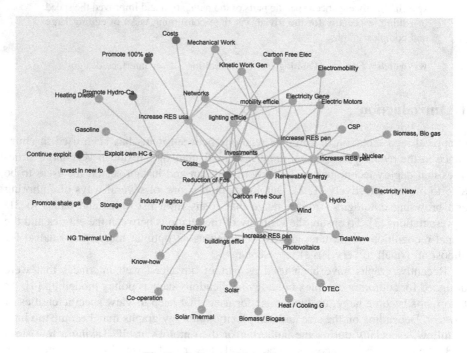

Fig. 1. Policy model ontology graph

The authoring of a policy domain or model is through the same generic concept. The author specifies the ontology domains by adding and editing instances of entities, norms and arguments. These can be connected as to describe the relations between them, essentially forming a graph. The simplest form for a vary small domain or model is a tree. The aim of the web interface was to provide a seamless user experience to the end users, yet enable them to create the envisioned ontology models. The high-level requirements were selected from groups of users from crowdsourcing service provision organizations and political bodies. The contextual framework for the interface speci-fications has been identified and described by a list of policy model domain specific items. The items include entities, sentiment and opinions, social and demographic information, sentence level arguments from a range of traditional web and social media-related sources, such as Blogs, Wikis, and Social Networks, namely Twitter and Facebook.

The described web interface and authoring approach work very well, utilizing the freedom of relation visualization of graphs to represent ontological structures like policy models and domains. Specific techniques for graph visualization were deployed in order to aide the users, such as zooming in/out and fast centering, panning, high-lighting neighbouring nodes on node selection (Fig. 2). Additional non-graph related issues such as the large node names were addressed by displaying the first 16 characters of each node name.

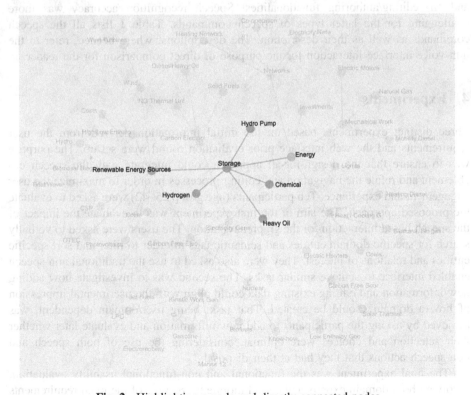

Fig. 2. Highlighting a node and directly connected nodes

However, as the authors progressed and created very large graphs, they reported increasing difficulty finding the node they wanted to edit and clicking to it. Focus group discussion of issues during the next round of design revealed usability issues that directly relate to accessibility. This was evident also from previous studies that explored usability and accessibility as part of the design-for-all methodology for designing voice user interfaces [6].

3 Speech Interface for Graph Editing and Browsing

To address the usability issues above, the second round of the iterative design included the decision to utilize state-of-the-art web speech synthesis and recognition [7, 8] in order to improve the user experience with the ultimate aim to be able to provide a fully speech-driven interface by the end of the lifecycle.

A set of voice commands was implemented over the functionalities of the web interface in order to allow multimodal input to the system. All possible actions that the policy model/domain ontology authors may perform were matched by the voice interface. Two types of input were designed, the commands that initiate content-free interaction with the interface and the ones that include actual content of the model/domain, such as the title text of nodes. A slightly different look into the type of interaction would be to categorize the input as (i) browsing/navigation functionalities and (ii) editing/authoring functionalities. Speech recognition accuracy was more challenging for the latter types of speech commands. Table 1 lists all the speech commands as well as their description. The descriptions, where needed, refer to the non-voice interface interaction for the purpose of direct comparison for the reader.

4 Experiments

Three distinct experiments based on the initial information derived from the user requirements and the web interface prior evaluation round were set up. The purpose was to ensure that the design-for-all approach could integrate with the speech en-ablement and refine the navigation and editing processes in order to maximize the user engagement and experience. Ten participants (age group 25–42) were asked to evaluate the proposed approach. The aim of the first experiment was to evaluate the impact of the speech based interaction for the graph navigation. The users were asked to verbally search for specific domain entities and semantic tags in order to filter and sort specific entities and relations of interest. They were also asked to use the traditional non-speech enabled interface to achieve similar tasks. The second was to investigate how adding new information and editing existing data could align with the user mental impression of how a domain should be created. That task, being user/domain dependent, was achieved by asking the participants to add new information and evaluate later whether their selection and choices were optimal, considering the use of both speech and non-speech actions that they had at their disposal.

The final experiment was the functional and non-functional usability evaluation, involving both domain experts and casual mobile users. One of the main requirements

Table 1. List of voice commands for graph editing

Command	Description
Open domain	Presents the user's domains. Equivalent to the selection of the action "Open Domain" in the model actions menu
Open policy	Presents the user's policies. Equivalent to the selection of the action "Open Policy" in the model actions menu
New domain	Presents to the user the new domain dialog. Equivalent to the selection of the action "New Domain" in the model actions menu
New policy	Presents to the user the new policy dialog. Equivalent to the selection of the action "New Policy" in the model actions menu
Use model	Presents to the user the reusable models window. Equivalent to the selection of the action "Use models" in the model actions menu
Preview *modelName	Presents the graph of the model (domain or policy) matching the "modelName". If there is no model matching the provided name a message is presented, if there is only one the graph of the model is presented and if there are more than one models matched an options dialog is presented The modelName can be a word or a phrase. It is the same as the mouse over the 'bubble' of the model action
Select node *nodeName	Selects a node from the current model graph matched the "nodeName" provided. If there is no node matching the provided name a message is presented, if there is only one match the node is selected and if there are more than one node matches, an options dialog is presented to the user. Same as clicking the node on the graph for the single result
Select option *option	It selects the option number (integer) from an options dialog presented to the user
Close options	It closes the options dialog
New node	Presents a new node dialog. The new node will be connected to the selected node of the graph. Same as double clicking on the canvas after a node is selected
Create	Completes the creation of the new node and closes the add node dialog
Edit node *nodeName	Presents the edit dialog for the node matching the nodeName. If multiple results the options dialog appears. Same as double clicking a graph node for the single result
Update	Completes the update of the node's data and closes the edit dialog.
English *text	It changes the English text of an add or edit dialog
Access level *level	Changes the access level of a domain or policy when the new model or update dialog is open. Values can be 'private' or 'public'

(Continued)

Table 1. (*Continued*)

Command	Description
Argument type *type	Changes the argument type of an argument when the new argument or update dialog is open.
Delete node	Presents the deletion confirmation dialog for the selected node
Delete	Completes the deletion of the node and closes the confirmation dialog
Cancel	Cancels current dialog or action
Connect to node *nodeName	Adds a new link between the node selected and the node matching the nodeName. For the single result case, it is the same as clicking a node after another node is selected
Disconnect node *node1 from node *node2	Deletes the link between two nodes matching the node1 name and node2 name. In case of multiple nodes matching the user is presented an options dialog, holding the combinations found. For the single result case it is the same as double clicking on the link
Deactivate voice commands	The system stops accepting voice commands

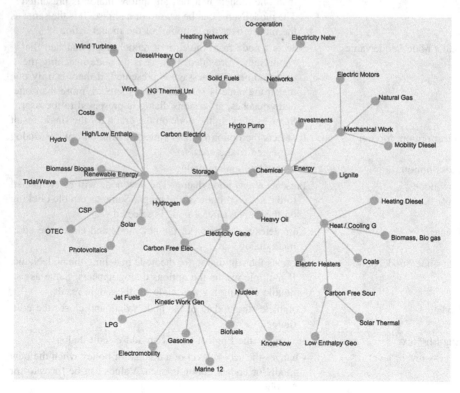

Fig. 3. The test policy domain graph for evaluation

was to measure the impact of the speech driven authoring in terms of time, clarity and acceptance. Figure 3 depicts the test policy domain that the participants were asked to navigate and edit.

5   Evaluation

The participants evaluated the interaction between the traditional non-speech interface and the speech-enabled (Fig. 4). Almost all opted to use speech for the search-related actions expecting to locate the node of interest much faster than by navigating the graph. The overall satisfaction feedback was overwhelmingly favorable for the speech modality, especially for the *find* and *select nodes* actions. The reason was that the voice interface enabled the users to search quickly and center the graph in on their selection. This was particularly apparent for the nodes that had long title text. Editing functions such as the *add* and *delete node/relation* were marginally easier through the use of both modalities, since the users were able to use speech whenever they deemed as an easier path to their goal.

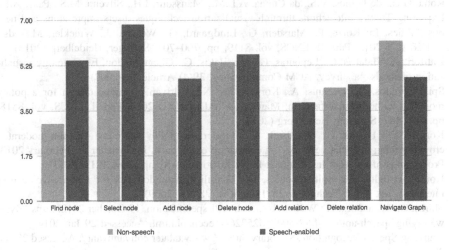

Fig. 4. Evaluation results for non-speech versus speech-enabled interaction

Lastly, the navigation of the graph itself, as a casual browsing task, revealed the shortcomings of the absence of speech commands for the specific generic functionality. No specific commands existed for zooming in/out or panning the graph, hence the users reported that they would have preferred an innovative way to browse, hinting at further research into this method.

6   Discussion

Based on the results of the experimenting with the speech recognition and synthesis tasks, the design of the user interface has been extended to the speech modality that has led to less complexity, as reported by the users. The visual modality was also polished to a more inviting and clear overview of the ontology domain graphs and special features, such as highlighting of the nodes that contain text identified via spoken search, were added. Further work is currently underway for the backend extension of the services that are needed to fully implement the speech web API for the generic graph view functionalities. Additionally, other functionalities that are commonly used in graphs such as dynamic insets [9] may also be implemented into the speech API, essentially allowing the user to preview the insets over the larger graph, while editing. The results of this work are expected to enhance the design of the user interface to support and sustain a multimodal approach to ontology graph authoring.

References

1. Moscovich, T., Chevalier, F., Henry, N., Pietriga, E., Fekete, J.D.: Topology-aware navigation in large networks. In: CHI 2009: Proceedings of the SIGCHI Conference on Human Factors in Computing Systems, pp. 2319–2328. ACM Press, Boston (2009)
2. Rotta, G.C., de Lemos, V.S., da Cunha, A.L.M., Manssour, I.H., Silveira, M.S., Pase, A.F.: Exploring Twitter interactions through visualization techniques: users impressions and new possibilities. In: Kotzé, P., Marsden, G., Lindgaard, G., Wesson, J., Winckler, M. (eds.) INTERACT 2013, Part III. LNCS, vol. 8119, pp. 700–707. Springer, Heidelberg (2013)
3. Katifori, A., Halatsis, C., Lepouras, G., Vassilakis, C., Giannopoulou, E.: Ontology visualization methods—a survey. ACM Comput. Surv. **39**(4) Article 10 (2007)
4. Spiliotopoulos, D., Dalianis, A., Koryzis, D.: Need driven prototype design for a policy modeling authoring interface. In: Marcus, A. (ed.) DUXU 2014, Part II. LNCS, vol. 8518, pp. 481–487. Springer, Heidelberg (2014)
5. Koryzis, D., Fitsilis, F., Schefbeck, G.: Moderated policy discourse vs. non-moderated crowdsourcing in social networks – a comparative approach. In: Jusletter IT, February 2013, Proceedings of the 16th International Legal Informatics Symposium, IRIS (2013)
6. Kouroupetroglou, G., Spiliotopoulos, D.: Usability methodologies for real-life voice user interfaces. Int. J. Inf. Technol. Web. Eng. **4**(4), 78–94 (2009)
7. Shires, G., Wennborg, H.: W3C web speech API specification, 19 October 2012. https://dvcs.w3.org/hg/speech-api/raw-file/9a0075d25326/speechapi.html. Accessed 29 Jan 2014
8. Annyang Speech Recognition JS Library. https://www.talater.com/annyang/. Accessed 29 Jan 2014
9. Ghani, S., Riche, N.H., Elmqvist, N.: Dynamic insets for context-aware graph navigation. Comput. Graph. Forum **30**(3), 861–870 (2011)

Promoting Better Deaf/Hearing Communication Through an Improved Interaction Design for Fingerspelling Practice

Rosalee Wolfe[1]([☒]), John McDonald[1], Jorge Toro[2], Souad Baowidan[1], Robyn Moncrief[1], and Jerry Schnepp[3]

[1] DePaul University, Chicago, USA
{wolfe,jmcdonald}@cs.depaul.edu
{sbaowida,rmoncrie}@mail.depaul.edu
[2] Worchester Polytechnic Institute, Worchester, USA
jatoro@wpi.edu
[3] Bowling Green State University, Bowling Green, USA
schnepp@bgsu.edu

Abstract. Fingerspelling is a manual system used by many signers for producing letters of a written alphabet to spell words from a spoken language. It can function as a link between signed and spoken languages. Fingerspelling is a vital skill for ASL/English interpreters, parents and teachers of deaf children as well as providers of deaf social services. Unfortunately fingerspelling reception can be a particularly difficult skill for hearing adults to acquire. One of the contributing factors to this situation is a lack of adequate technology to facilitate self-study. This paper describes new efforts to create a practice tool that more realistically simulates the use of fingerspelling in the real world.

Keywords: Deaf · Deaf accessibility · American sign language · Fingerspelling · Voice input

1 Introduction

Fingerspelling is a manual system used by many signers for producing letters of a written alphabet to spell words from a spoken language [1]. Members of the Deaf[1] community in the United States use fingerspelling for proper nouns such as person and place names, and for spelling loan words from other languages. An additional use of fingerspelling is to convey technical terminology for which there is no generally accepted sign [2].

---

[1] The term Deaf ("capital-D Deaf") refers to the community that uses American Sign Language (ASL) as their preferred language and share a history, cultural norms, beliefs and values in common.

© Springer International Publishing Switzerland 2015
M. Antona and C. Stephanidis (Eds.): UAHCI 2015, Part I, LNCS 9175, pp. 495–505, 2015.
DOI: 10.1007/978-3-319-20678-3_48

1.1   Need for Fingerspelling Skill

Fingerspelling skill is important not just for members of the Deaf community, but is essential for interpreters of signed language, parents of deaf children [3], teachers of deaf children [4], and providers of deaf social services. Ninety percent of deaf children have hearing parents [5], but when these children experience increased contact with finger-spelling, the result is a significant positive impact on their reading ability [6]. Further, in a university setting, fingerspelling is useful for linking the instructor's lecture with the readings in the assigned text [7]. Additionally, it has long been considered a highly desirable skill for vocational rehabilitation counselors working with Deaf clients [8].

1.2   Difficulty of Fingerspelling

Unfortunately fingerspelling reception (recognizing fingerspelled words) is particularly difficult for hearing learners [9]. Due to this fact, many teachers of deaf children are not skilled in fingerspelling [10], and rely on interpreters for this critical skill [11]. This is often not possible due to the scarcity of educational interpreters [12], many of whom are underqualified in fingerspelling [13]. Hearing interpreter training students regularly mention fingerspelling reception as a difficult, if not the most difficult, skill to master [14, 15]. Fingerspelling receptive skills are much harder to acquire than fingerspelling production [16]. Even interpreters, who have already graduated from interpreter training programs and have been hired at interpreter agencies, list fingerspelling as one of their top training needs [17].

Why is fingerspelling so hard? The reasons are myriad but can be grouped into two major categories. The first barrier has to do with the nature of fingerspelling itself. It is not formed as a sequence of static letters, but as a smoothly changing movement where the fingers never stop in their transitions from letter to letter [18]. As a result, the letters in a fingerspelled word are rarely, if ever, perfectly produced. Coarticulation plays a major role since letter handshapes are heavily influenced by preceding and succeeding letters. Simply studying the static positions of the manual letters does not facilitate recognition of a word from the smooth flow of the motion envelope [9].

The second barrier to fingerspelling fluency is the paucity of practice opportunities. Textbooks recommend pair practice [19], but a practice partner will most likely be another classmate. Unfortunately, a fellow student will not be able to produce finger-spelling smoothly or at fluent speeds [20]. Further, due to demanding schedules, it is not always possible to schedule face-to-face practice sessions. These barriers can motivate the typical student to seek options for self-study.

2   Options for Practice

Although technology has provided alternatives to paper-based fingerspelling texts [21], each alternative has drawbacks. VHS video recordings of fingerspelling appeared in the 1980s, and the 1990s witnessed the appearance of DVDs designed for fingerspelling practice [22]. For these media, the fingerspelled words were recorded and thus fixed. It was not possible to create new words without incurring the costs of producing a new recording. Because the videos were recorded at low frame rates, motion blur was also a problem, as was the lack of variation in the presentation order. As students studied the same recording over and over again, it was not clear if they were improving their skills or memorizing the recording.

In the early 2000s, an alternative to fixed, prerecorded media appeared on web sites such as [23]. On these sites, students can use software to view a word as a succession of snapshots, each displaying a single manual letter. The advantage of these sites is extensibility. The site software can rearrange the snapshots in any order and thus produce new words without incurring any additional cost. However, the static nature of the snapshots is a problem. There is no connective movement between the letters. This limits its utility as a practice tool since most of fingerspelling is comprised of the motion between the letters, not the letters themselves [9].

A third alternative is 3D animation technology, which promises the extensibility for new word formation while producing smoothly flowing motion, but it poses some challenges as well. The lack of physicality in 3D animation complicates the situation. Unless prevented, the thumb and fingers will pass through each other when transitioning between closed handshapes such as M, N, T, S and A in ASL, as demonstrated in Fig. 1. This requires a system to prevent finger collisions. Additionally, 3D animation requires simulating the flexible webbing between the thumb and index finger and mimicking the complex behavior of the base of the thumb [24].

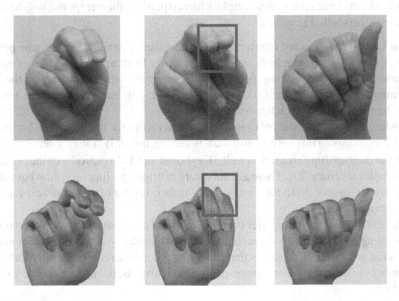

Fig. 1. Comparing physical motion with a naive animation for the transition from N to A

These complexities entail large computational requirements, and require significant resources to render fingerspelling in real time. For this reason, some previous efforts sacrificed realism to gain real-time speeds by using a simplified 3D model that did not accurately portray a human hand and/or did not prevent collisions [25, 26]. Others sacrificed real-time responsiveness to maintain the realism of the model [27]. To address this, researchers have developed a method to pre-render and organize the transitions in such a way that the software can form new words that display natural motion while maintaining real time responsiveness [28].

However, accurate and realistic fingerspelling movement is only the first step. Practice software needs to offer appropriate user interaction to enhance the learning process. When practicing, students need to be able to respond to questions and receive feedback on their answers.

3   Previous Interaction Designs

In all of the previously-discussed technologies that offer interactive feedback, students view a fingerspelled word and supply their answer by either selecting from a list of choices or by typing. Neither of these interaction options accurately simulates real-life situations where fingerspelling reception skills are needed. Consider the following scenarios:

- When an interpreter is facilitating a conversation between a Deaf and hearing person, the interpreter will be voicing the signing produced by the Deaf conversant. The voicing, of course, will require that the interpreter recognize any fingerspelled words.
- When parents or teachers view a child's fingerspelling, their response will be signed and/or fingerspelled in return.

While it is true that a skilled interpreter will make use of context to eliminate possible choices, this is very different from choosing an answer from a pre-created list of options. Interpreters and other hearing people who converse with members of the Deaf community need to recognize a word in order to voice it, but rarely is there a need to vocally reproduce the word letter-for-letter.

Insisting on text input not only requires users to recognize the word, but forces them to spell it correctly. Thus current software is testing not only a user's receptive capabilities, but their spelling abilities as well.[2] Keyboard input also introduces the possibility of typographical errors [29]. These are not errors in fingerspelling reception but conventional software cannot make this distinction. Further, typing can be slow, especially on mobile devices [30].

Teachers of ASL and interpreter trainers are aware of the shortcomings of evaluating fingerspelling receptive skills through English orthography. An examination of national certification procedures [31] shows that no testing procedure requires applicants to write out words but instead assesses fingerspelling receptive skills through voicing or sign production.

---

[2] It is true that interpreters will need skills in English orthography to *produce* fingerspelled words when signing the voiced discourse of a hearing person, but the skill we are focusing on here is not fingerspelling *production*, but fingerspelling *reception*, which is the area of greater need.

4 Exploring Alternatives for a More Natural Interaction Style

Most modern digital devices provide for speech input, permitting users to voice an answer rather than type it. Researchers [32] have noted that speech is preferable for typing character strings requiring more than a few keystrokes. Further, speech has the potential for generating text more quickly than keyboard typing [33]. Speech input has even more potential benefit when using hand-held devices where keyboards are small [34]. A voice alternative for fingerspelling practice has several potential benefits:

- *More focus on fingerspelling.* The necessity of typing an answer after viewing a fingerspelled word requires a user to shift visual attention away from fingerspelling. The user's mental effort is divided between typing a correct answer and attempting to recognize fingerspelling. Voice input utilizes a separate channel, and the shift of mental modes is much shorter.
- A *shorter distance between user and answer.* In the Keystroke-Level Model used to model complexity of human/machine interactions [35], a vocal operator of *speak* is modeled at 150 ms/syllable, but a manual operator of *Type_in* is modeled at 280 ms/character. Given that each English syllable contains at least one and typically more letters, there should be a shorter distance between a user and the answer when a response is spoken.
- *Closer modeling of real-world usage.* Using speech more closely resembles the real-life scenarios where fingerspelling receptive skills are required. Further, the interaction would more closely match the testing procedure of the national certification agency and could potentially provide better preparation for the examination.

4.1 Design Considerations for Speech Input

Despite the potential benefits, the feasibility of using voice input hinges on the accuracy of the automatic speech recognition engine. In addition to environment [36], major factors affecting accuracy include

- Single speaker/multiple speakers. Speech from a single speaker is easier to recognize because most parametric representations of speech are sensitive to the characteristics of a particular speaker.
- Isolated words/continuous speech. Speech containing isolated words is much easier to recognize than continuous speech because word boundaries can be hard to identify.
- Vocabulary size. Large vocabularies are more likely to contain multiple entries that are difficult to disambiguate.

Because the majority of people will be practicing fingerspelling on a personal device such as a phone, tablet or laptop, they will likely have established a user profile for speech recognition. This facilitates the use of single-speaker recognition strategies. Additionally, a response will consist of a single word, thus the recognition engine will not be forced to identify word boundaries. Finally, the vocabulary size is a single word which means that there will be no ambiguous entries in the vocabulary. Thus we have what appears to be the perfect confluence of single speaker, isolated word input and highly constrained vocabulary.

However we found that spoken words which are similar to the fingerspelled word were also being recognized as correct. For example, words such as "rendition" and "perdition" were sometimes accepted as matching the fingerspelled word "condition". A vocabulary of a single word opened the door to an unacceptably large number of false positives.

4.2 Evaluating Vocabulary Configurations

To determine the optimal vocabulary size, we set up a software test bed that could simulate errors on the part of the user. The test bed exercised a commercial speech recognition engine via a simple program that displayed a word, and prompted a user to say it. After the user said the word, the program displayed a new word to pronounce. No other feedback was given.

Unbeknownst to the user, sometimes the word displayed was not the word that the speech recognition engine was expecting but was instead a similar word. Two words were deemed similar when they had the same length and matched in initial and final letters. We chose this definition based on coarticulation studies of fingerspelling [9, 18, 37], which indicate that the initial and final letters of a fingerspelled word are the most distinct and most easily recognized. These studies imply that words deemed similar by this definition can be easily confused when reading fingerspelling. This definition was use to simulate the type of false positive discussed in the last section.

Five testers (three male, two female) used the test bed for two sessions each. Each session consisted of 40 trials. Each trial involved viewing and speaking a single word, for a total of 400 trials from the five testers. Half of the trials contained a simulated error. Since the trials were randomized and no feedback given, the testers did not know which words were considered errors.

The outcome is summarized as a confusion matrix [38] in Table 1. There was an unacceptably high number of Type I errors, which corresponds to the test bed accepting a simulated error as being correct. Thus the strategy of using a single-word vocabulary, which is appropriate in a conventional interactive voice response (IVR) system or voice menu, will not be satisfactory for this application, which requires greater specificity. The approach of configuring the recognition engine to accept only one word would not be satisfactory.

Table 1. Confusion matrix for a vocabulary size of one

	Correct word	Simulated error
Accepted as correct	192 (hit)	83 (Type I error)
Rejected as error	8 (Type II error)	117 (correct rejection)

Given the assumption that users will have already trained their device for voice input, a second alternative would be to use the entire dictation vocabulary of the device's speech recognition engine. The test bed was modified to use the large dictation vocabulary instead of the single-word vocabulary, and the same testers used the new version for a total of 400 trials. The confusion matrix for this second alternative is shown in Table 2. For this configuration, the number of Type I errors has dropped to zero, but the number of Type II errors, which correspond to rejecting a correctly-spoken word, has risen to the point where this configuration is also not an acceptable alternative.

Table 2. Confusion matrix for a large vocabulary

	Correct word	Simulated error
Accepted as correct	56 (hit)	0 (Type I error)
Rejected as error	144 (Type II error)	200 (correct rejection)

The third alternative would be to find a vocabulary size that is somewhere between the two extremes. To evaluate this approach, the test bed was again reconfigured to use progressively larger vocabularies of sizes {1, 6, 11, 21, 41, 81}. Words picked for the vocabularies were again matched with the target word for length, initial letter and final letter. Figures 2 and 3 contain graphs of the summary statistics for each of the six vocabulary sizes. Figure 2 is a plot of the sensitivity (hit rate), and specificity (correct rejection rate) of the confusion matrices and shows the inverse relationship between sensitivity and specificity. The two curves cross near a vocabulary size of 11. The accuracy curve in Fig. 3 clearly exhibits peak accuracy around a vocabulary size of 11 (the target word and 10 distractors).

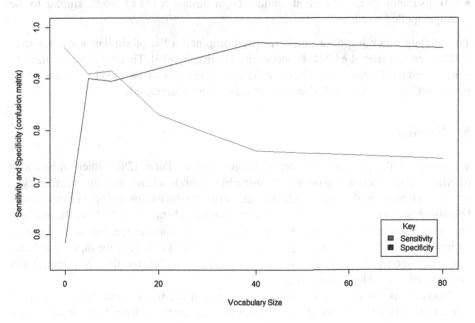

Fig. 2. Sensitivity and specificity plots

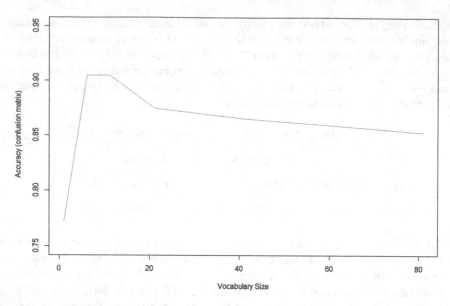

Fig. 3. Accuracy plot

These results informed our design decisions for configuring the speech engine vocabulary. The vocabulary for each fingerspelling trial contains:

- The fingerspelled word
- 10 distractor words chosen at random from among a list of words similar to the fingerspelled word.

To maintain quick response times, we pre-computed a list of similar words for over 100,000 entries from the CMU Pronouncing Dictionary [39]. This did increase the software's memory footprint, but since the dictionary size is still dwarfed by the size of the fingerspelling video, overall size was not significantly impacted.

5 Results

We modified the previous version of Fingerspelling Tutor [28], which only had a multiple choice interface, to offer a fill-in-the blank mode where students can either type or speak an answer. We did not add a voice option to the extant multiple choice mode, because its input is already very direct, being only a single tap or click. Also, the multiple choice mode is not one that accurately simulates real-world usage, but instead acts as an intermediate step for acquiring receptive skills [40]. Further, voice input could also introduce speech recognition errors into a response format that is intentionally constrained to help beginners avoid errors.

Speech input is more appropriate for the fill-in-the-blank mode because it more closely resembles real-life usage. However, there are situations when typed input is more appropriate such as:

- in environments with high ambient noise,
- in situations where there is no acoustical privacy,
- or when user decides that keyboard input is preferable.

Thus the modified interface includes both the option to type or to speak the response. Since Fingerspelling Tutor supports both physical and on-screen keyboards, we chose to follow an interaction style that has the microphone attached to the textbox as demonstrated in Fig. 4. This both reduces the distance that a user has to move the mouse in order to activate the microphone and makes it more visible in the interface.

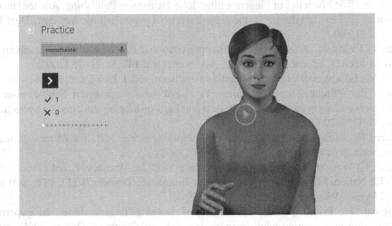

Fig. 4. Screen shot of voice interface

6   Future Work

We are in the process of conducting usability tests to compare user performance and preference of the newly-configured voice interface with the conventional keyboard interface. In addition, we are looking to expand Fingerspelling Tutor for use in signed languages other than ASL.

References

1. Battison, R.: Lexical Borrowing in American Sign Language. Linstok Press, Silver Spring (1978)
2. Padden, C.: The acquisition of fingerspelling by deaf children. In: Siple, P., Fischer, S. (eds.) Theoretical Issues in Sign Language Research, pp. 191–210. University of Chicago, Chicago (1991)
3. Caulderon, R.: Parental involvement in deaf children's education programs as a predictor of child's language, early reading, and social-emotional development. J. Deaf Stud. Deaf Educ. 5(2), 140–155 (2000)

4. Strong, M., Prinz, P.: A study of the relationship between American sign language and English literacy. J. Deaf Stud. Deaf Educ. **2**(1), 37–46 (1997)
5. Meyers, J., Bartee, J.: Improvements in the signing skills of hearing parents of deaf children. Am. Ann. Deaf **137**(3), 257–260 (1992)
6. Ramsey, C., Padden, C.: Natives and newcomers: gaining access to literacy in a classroom for deaf children. Anthropol. Educ. Q. **29**(1), 5–24 (1998)
7. Napier, J.: University interpreting: linguistic issues for consideration. J. Deaf Stud. Deaf Educ. **7**(4), 281–301 (2002)
8. Quigley, S.: The vocational rehabilitation of deaf people. SRS-72-25037, Washington, DC (1972)
9. Wilcox, S.: The Phonetics of Fingerspelling. John Benjamins Publishing, Amsterdam (1992)
10. Grushkin, D.: Lexidactylophobia: the irrational fear of fingerspelling. Am. Ann. Deaf **143**(5), 404–415 (1998)
11. Jones, T., Ewing, K.: An analysis of teacher preparation in deaf education: programs approved by the council on education of the deaf. Am. Ann. Deaf **147**(5), 71–78 (2002)
12. Hitch, M.: Educational interpreters: certified or uncertified. J. Law Educ. **34**, 161–165 (2005)
13. Schick, B., Williams, K., Kupermintz, H.: Look who's being left behind: educational interpreters and access to education for deaf and hard-of-hearing students. J. Deaf Stud. Deaf Educ. **11**(1), 3–20 (2006)
14. McKee, R., McKee, D.: What's so hard about learning ASL?: students' & teachers' perceptions. Sign Lang. Stud. **75**(1), 129–157 (1992)
15. Shaffer, L., Watson, W.: Peer mentoring: what is that? In: Maroney, E. (ed.) Proceedings of the 15th National Convention Conference of Interpreter Trainers (CIT), CIT, Still shining after 25 years, Washington, DC, pp. 77–92 (2004)
16. Shipgood, L., Pring, T.: The difficulties of learning fingerspelling: an experimental investigation with hearing adult learners. Int. J. Lang. Commun. Disord. **30**(4), 401–416 (1995)
17. Hernandez, R.A.: New ideas of teaching and learning fingerspelling. In: McIntire, M. (ed.) New Dimensions in Interpreter Education: Curriculum and Instruction, pp. 121–124. Registry of Interpreters for the Deaf, Silver Spring (1987)
18. Jerde, T., Soechting, J., Flanders, M.: Coarticulation in fluent fingerspelling. J. Neurosci. **23**(6), 2383–2393 (2003)
19. Smith, C., Lentz, E.M., Mikos, K.: Signing Naturally Student Workbook Level 1. Dawn Sign Press, San Diego (1988)
20. Reed, C., Delhorne, L., Durlach, N., Fischer, S.: A study of the tactual and visual reception of fingerspelling. J. Speech Lang. Hear. Res. **33**, 786–797 (1990)
21. Guillory, L.: Expressive and Receptive Fingerspelling for Hearing Adults. Claitors Publishing Division, Baton Rouge (1966)
22. Jaklic, A., Vodopivec, D., Komac, V.: Learning sign language through multimedia. In: International Conference on Multimedia Computing and Systems, Washington, DC, pp. 282–285 (1995)
23. Vicars, B.: Dr. Bill Vicars' American sign language (ASL) fingerspelling practice site. http://asl.ms. Accessed 2005
24. McDonald, J., Alkoby, K., Carter, R., Christopher, J., Davidson, M.J., Ethridge, D., Furst, J., Hinkle, D., Lancaster, G., Smallwood, L., Ougouag-Tiouririne, N., Toro, J., Xu, S., Wolfe, R.: An improved articulated model of the human hand. Vis. Comput. **17**(3), 158–166 (2001)
25. Su, A.: VRML-based representations of ASL fingerspelling on the world-wide web. In: The Third International ACM SIGCAPH Conference on Assistive Technologies, Marina del Rey, CA (1998)

26. Dickson, S.: Advanced animation in mathematica. Math. J. **15**(2) (2013)
27. Adamo-Villani, N., Beni, G.: Automated finger spelling by highly realistic 3D animation. Br. J. Educ. Technol. **35**(3), 345–362 (2004)
28. Toro, J.A., McDonald, J.C., Wolfe, R.: Fostering better deaf/hearing communication through a novel mobile app for fingerspelling. In: Miesenberger, K., Fels, D., Archambault, D., Peňáz, P., Zagler, W. (eds.) ICCHP 2014, Part II. LNCS, vol. 8548, pp. 559–564. Springer, Heidelberg (2014)
29. Kukich, K.: Techniques for automatically correcting words in text. ACM Comput. Surv. **24**(4), 377–439 (1992)
30. Parhi, P., Karlson, A., Bederson, B.: Target size study for one-handed thumb use on small touchscreen devices. In: Proceedings of the 8th Conference on Human-Computer Interaction with Mobile Devices and Services, pp. 203–210 (2006)
31. Registry of interpreters for the deaf: NAD-RID National Interpreter Certification. http://rid.org/userfiles/File/NIC2CandidateHBFFeb2014_1.pdf. Accessed 2014
32. Hauptmann, A., Rudnicky, A.: A comparison of speech and typed input. In: Proceedings of the Speech and Natural Language Workshop, Stroudsburg, PA, pp. 219–224 (1990)
33. Rebman Jr., C., Aiken, M., Cegielski, C.: Speech recognition in the human-computer interface. Inf. Manag. **40**(6), 509–519 (2003)
34. Cherubini, M., Anguera, X., Oliver, N., De Oliveira, R.: Text versus speech: a comparison of tagging input modalities for camera phones. In: Proceedings of the 11th International Conference on Human-Computer Interaction (MobileHCI 2009), Bonn, Germany, pp. 1–10 (2009)
35. Kieras, D.: A guide to GOMS model usability evaluation using COMSL and GLEAN3, Ann Arbor (1999)
36. Peacocke, R., Graf, D.: An introduction to speech and speaker recognition. Computer **23**(8), 26–33 (1990)
37. Geer, L., Keane, J.: Exploring factors that contribute to successful fingerspelling comprehension. In: Language Resources and Evaluation Conference (LREC), Reykjavik, Iceland, pp. 68–69 (2014)
38. Fawcett, T.: An introduction to ROC analysis. Pattern Recogn. Lett. **27**(8), 861–874 (2006)
39. Carnegie Mellon University: The CMU pronouncing dictionary. http://www.speech.cs.cmu.edu/cgi-bin/cmudict
40. Jamrozik, D., Davidson, M., McDonald, J., Wolfe, R.: Teaching students to decipher fingerspelling through context: a new pedagogical approach. In: Proceedings of the 17th National Convention Conference of Interpreter Trainers, San Antonio, TX, pp. 35–47 (2010)

Author Index

Printed in the United States
By Bookmasters